THE MORMON HISTORY ASSOCIATION'S TANNER LECTURES

The Mormon History Association's Tanner Lectures

The First Twenty Years

EDITED BY

Dean L. May and Reid L. Neilson

with Richard Lyman Bushman, Jan Shipps,
and Thomas G. Alexander

UNIVERSITY OF ILLINOIS PRESS

URBANA AND CHICAGO

Library of Congress Cataloging-in-Publication Data

The Mormon history association's Tanner Lectures : the first twenty
years / edited by Dean L. May and Reid L. Neilson ; with Richard
Lyman Bushman, Jan Shipps, and Thomas G. Alexander.
p.   cm.
Includes index.
ISBN-13: 978-0-252-03052-9 (cloth : alk. paper)
ISBN-10: 0-252-03052-4 (cloth : alk. paper)
ISBN-13: 978-0-252-07288-8 (pbk. : alk. paper)
ISBN-10: 0-252-07288-X (pbk. : alk. paper)
1. Church of Jesus Christ of Latter-day Saints—History.   2. Mormon
Church—History.
I. May, Dean L.   II. Neilson, Reid Larkin.
BX8611.M665   2006
289.309—dc22   2005034479

CONTENTS

INTRODUCTION

In his 1991 Tanner Lecture, Martin Ridge praised the Mormon History Association Tanner Lectures, seeing their institution in 1980 as "a mark of maturity and sophistication" uncommon among learned societies. But, as he worked on his lecture he "came to feel this was essentially a shrewd Mormon plot to take a good, self-respecting gentile academic, and make him . . . think far more deeply about Mormonism than he had in the past."[1]

As usual, Professor Ridge was on target, and on both counts. It happens that three of us were part of discussions in 1979 as to what could be done to make the 1980 annual meeting, marking the 150th anniversary since the founding of the Church of Jesus Christ of Latter-day Saints, extraordinary. Jan Shipps was president that year. Claudia and Richard Bushman were chairs of the program committee. Other members of the program committee were Alfred Bush, Sharon Pugsley, and Dean and Cheryll May. Sometime during our discussions, Richard proposed the idea of seeking funding for a lectureship that would invite an eminent scholar, whose work has paralleled the Mormon history but has never addressed it directly, to expand a facet of his or her ongoing research to include a Mormon dimension. The president would have the privilege of choosing the lecturer, the lecture would be given each year in a plenary session of the annual meeting of the association, and the lecturer would be invited to spend as much time as possible at the meeting, getting acquainted with the members and they with him or her.

As soon as the idea was broached, we all recognized its potential. Yes, it would be a mark of maturity and sophistication. We were quite willing, even eager, to give the membership an opportunity to learn from and be challenged by whatever perspectives and insights the lecturer might offer. And we welcomed the chance to raise the awareness of the lecturer, to entice eminent scholars into thinking more deeply about the Mormon past.

It was a great idea, but we all suspected that it would take a bit of doing to divert world-renowned intellectuals from the trajectory of their well-filled research agendas into our particular byway. That thought led quickly to the idea of approaching Obert C. and Grace Adams Tanner, generous endowers of water fountains and lectureships, to consider helping our cause. On a warm spring day, we visited Sterling McMurrin, a professor of history at the University of Utah, in his office on the second floor of Carlson Hall. Sterling was a close friend of Obert Tanner and an astute and much-honored student of Mormonism. He immediately caught the vision and agreed to take the matter to the Tanners. Within a day or two he contacted us with the good news that the Tanners would like to fund the lectureship, on a year-by-year basis at first, and perhaps eventually with an endowment (which they later did).

We immediately made plans to inaugurate the series with panache, inviting not one but two eminent scholars, to prepare lectures for the 1980 meeting: Gordon Wood, professor of history at Brown University, and Timothy L. Smith, professor of history at Johns Hopkins. It was an auspicious beginning.

The Tanner Lectures have since become a rich and rewarding staple of the Mormon History Association annual meeting. Nearly always the scholar invited to prepare the lecture has accepted the invitation warmly and without hesitation. The Tanner lecturers have been genuinely impressed with the vitality of the organization and of Mormon historical studies. They always speak to overflow audiences. They provide stimulating and important insights, all the more valuable because, in looking in on Mormon studies, they frequently bring greater breadth and offer perspectives that insiders have difficulty accessing. And the lectureship over the years has indeed brought an impressive body of renowned scholars to "think far more deeply about Mormonism than [they have] in the past."

It was against this background that the officers of the association invited us to edit a volume that would make the first twenty years of this distinguished body of scholarship more accessible to interested readers. It seemed sensible to arrange the lectures in thematic and roughly chronological order according to content rather than year of presentation. Since our particular interests complement one another, we have each helped to prepare for publication and written a brief introduction to the set that falls most clearly within our areas of expertise. Richard Bushman thus has taken on the "Beginnings," those lectures that deal principally with the founding of Mormonism; Thomas Alexander has worked on "Establishing Zion," essays considering especially the last half of the nineteenth century; and Jan Shipps has dealt with "Mormonism Considered from Different Perspectives," essays treating twentieth-century Mormonism or drawing especially from the insights of academic religious studies.

Larry and Alene King, executive directors of the Mormon History Association, have provided invaluable service in scanning the original essays. The redoubtable Lavina Fielding Anderson has provided editorial insight and service. And we thank the Tanner lecturers who took the time to add to their usual academic interests a consideration of issues relating to Mormon history. They have generously given permission for the publication of their lectures in this volume. Finally, we thank our editor at the University of Illinois Press, Elizabeth G. Dulany. She truly is the midwife of Mormon studies publishing.

Dean L. May
Richard Lyman Bushman
Jan Shipps
Thomas G. Alexander
Reid L. Neilson

Note

1. Martin Ridge, "Mormon 'Deliverance' and the Closing of the Frontier," *Journal of Mormon History* 18 (Spring 1992): 137.

PART 1

Beginnings

Richard Lyman Bushman

One may ask why an association made up of experts in Mormon history would invite "outsiders" with only a general knowledge of the Latter-day Saints to lecture on Mormon history. If anyone can interpret Mormon history, one would think, it is the historians of the Mormon History Association (MHA). Interlopers, we would assume, can hardly tell MHA members anything they don't know already. The fallacy of this assumption was well stated by one of the Tanner lecturers, Nathan Hatch, who pointed out that historians writing from within their religious communities—description that fits the bulk of MHA historians—commonly make one mistake. Denominational historians write with a preference for "that which is similar to, or that which anticipates, the present."[1] Try as they will, historians whose lives are invested in Mormonism now can scarcely avoid focusing on aspects of their history that foreshadow the future. They want to know how the past became the present, and anomalies and contradictions are left out. That is why we need help from the outside. By bringing fresh eyes to Mormonism, historians with less personal attachment identify the oversights.

The distinguished scholars who have lectured the MHA on the beginnings of Mormonism adopted a common strategy for identifying new aspects of the founding years. They matched Mormonism with some other strand of American culture and made comparisons. All the essays, save the opening article by Gordon Wood, have a crucial conjunction in their titles. They all speak of Mormonism *and* something else: the Churches of Christ, Methodism, the church-state question, and so on. Wood's essay, though lacking the "and" in the title, followed the same methodology by putting Mormonism in the context of early American evangelism and general social disruption. The historians began with something they knew well and approached Mormonism along that avenue. The historical comparisons highlight elements of Latter-day Saint history that could not be seen as well from any other perspective.

Taken together, the essays drive home a simple lesson that is easily forgotten by historians looking for the significance of Mormonism, namely that it is a complex phenomenon. When writing about the place of Mormonism in American culture, one can easily make the mistake of thinking that the key to the subject has been discovered. Entire books have been written about Mormonism and republicanism, Mormonism and the magic worldview, Mormonism and hermeticism—and seeker religion, and millenarianism, and restorationism. In the enthusiasm of writing and reading these works, one comes to believe that the central impulse, the main source, and the chief attraction of Mormonism have been found. Individually each study is persuasive and exciting. Each one opens new vistas. Only when we view them together do we realize that while each study tells us something, no single study tells us everything about the subject.

The difficulty of capturing the movement in its entirety extends to the methods of analysis. Every attempt to propose a set of causes or to break down the key doctrines has limitations. Something is left out of the picture. This applies to an analysis as sophisticated as Gordon Wood's in his much-cited essay "Evangelical America and Early Mormonism." No one understands better than Wood the complex currents swirling about Mormonism when it first emerged. No one is better qualified than he to offer the judgment that Mormonism "was born at a peculiar moment in the history of the United States, and it bears the marks of that birth."[2] In fact, he is of the opinion that "it appeared at precisely the right moment in American history; much earlier or later and the Church might not have taken hold."[3] He bases that claim on his sense of the particular nature of American culture in the early decades of the nineteenth century. That was a time when long-suppressed streams of folk culture burst to the surface and flowed freely for a time. No entrenched rational culture was in place to discipline the wild and flamboyant ideas that found expression. In the aftermath of the American Revolution, when all kinds of hierarchical structures had toppled, the authority of the learned fell too. Buoyed by an ebullient democracy, people felt competent to decide the truth for themselves without the approval of authority. No body of educated men could stand against the democratic masses. In that atmosphere, Mormonism's angels and golden plates won a hearing. In another few decades, the rise of science to cultural ascendancy would have tested the Book of Mormon by standards it could never have met. But in that unbridled moment in the first half of the nineteenth century, Mormonism had a chance of survival.

What catches Wood's eye when he looks at Mormonism is the amalgam of strange contradictions bound in the movement like a "steel spring."[4] Instead of consisting solely of extravagant folk superstitions, Mormonism embodies elements of the Enlightenment in its witnesses to the Book of Mormon and its emphasis on scriptural texts. Rather than an undisciplined fellowship of ecstatic spirituality, it erected a complex, hierarchical organization. Wood goes on for pages listing the contradictions: communitarian and individualistic, authoritarian and democratic, anticlerical and priestly, revelatory and empirical.

This analysis, revealing as it is, ignores the experience of Mormons themselves. They did not seem to feel that their religion was a combination of contradictory impulses. One would think that living "a religion in tension" would tear members apart.[5] Were they rationalists or spiritualists, democrats or hierarchs, for priesthood or against it? But their journals and diaries give little evidence of suffering from divided minds. The tensions noted by the modern analyst did not seem to bother the participants. We easily forget that every cultural system is riven with contradictions that fail to break down actual lives. For the most part, Mormons seemed satisfied with their religion, even though analytically it was a tangled mess. The dichotomies that Wood finds in Mormonism had little effect on Mormons themselves.

This disjuncture makes the absence of an active agent in the forming of Mormonism all the more noteworthy. In Wood's story, no person makes Mormonism, either by artistry or inspiration. The religion seems to form spontaneously in the stew that was bubbling away in the United States in these decades. Wood identifies the ingredients of the stew and, finding them in Mormonism, seemingly provides an explanation for the movement's formation. But there is no cook; only history is the chef. A set of forces and social circumstances made Mormonism, not the individual who wrote the Book of Mormon or organized the church or planned Zion. If Mormonism is such a puzzling combination of contradictions, we want to know all the more how human minds contrived this peculiar concoction. Did not it require some kind of ingenuity, perhaps even genius or inspiration, to put it all together? The creator of Mormonism is left out, not because Wood refuses to give credit where it is due but because his mode of historical analysis leaves no place for a maker.

Richard Hughes's illuminating and tightly logical comparison of two restorationist churches, the Mormons and the Disciples of Christ, presents a more intellectual analysis than Wood's but with many of the same qualities. Hughes compares two churches bound together by the word "restoration," which he defines as the impulse to leap over the history intervening between the present and Bible times to that earlier era when a more authentic Christianity was believed to prevail. Alexander Campbell and Joseph Smith both believed that they were restoring the ancient order of things found in the Bible. Under that rubric, however, cultural influences led the two restorers along divergent paths. Campbell was a rationalist, a child of the Enlightenment, who thought of the New Testament as a guidebook to right doctrine and true practice. He parsed its meaning with disciplined rationality, while Smith, a romantic, wished to commune with the heavens and bring God into the lives of humans, in the mode of Ralph Waldo Emerson. Having broken down restoration traditions into Enlightened and Romantic, Hughes then looks at millenarianism, finds pessimistic and optimistic strains, and sees how they played out in the thinking of Smith and Campbell.

These components are so clearly defined and work so well together that a reader is mesmerized by Hughes's artistry and appealing logic. But as with Wood, no agents have a part in the interaction of the isms. Traditions shape and mold religion as if they were the active agents. The various strands of thought wind about one another without people being allowed to interrupt their stately ballet. Religion consists of a series of cultural systems with their own purposes and messages combining with one another to form theologies and churches. One does not need a prophet or a preacher to make them perform. No one struggles to believe or resist these ideas. They carry on without human intervention. History is unpeopled.

Timothy Smith is less interested in distinguishing religious currents in the nineteenth century than in conceiving of Christians as swimming in one vast sea of biblical faith. His aim is not to distinguish Mormonism from other churches but, in a generous ecumenical spirit, to include Mormons with all the other swimmers. Smith makes the startling but reasonable suggestion that Mormonism would never have gotten off the ground if its unique teachings had constituted its major attraction. The appeal of the early missionaries lay in "their confident testimony to beliefs that were central to the biblical culture of the evangelical Protestant sects."[6] Mormons not only preached doctrines that Methodists also promoted, such as the call to ethical righteousness and the presence of the Holy Spirit, but saw the Book of Mormon as supporting biblical belief. They did not set their new scriptures off against the old but understood them as mutually sustaining one another. The aim was to revitalize biblical belief, not to undermine it. Smith even considers Joseph Smith's revision of the Bible a testimonial to its importance in Mormon doctrine.

Timothy Smith blazes a new methodological path for Mormon historians. His essay suggests that historians' inclination to distinguish Mormon doctrines from conventional religious beliefs of the time should be reined in. Believing historians are so eager to prove the originality of Joseph Smith's teachings that they lose sight of the vast overlap with standard Christianity in this biblical age. The message of the missionaries was a simple program of faith, repentance, baptism, and the Holy Ghost, right out of the New Testament. Missionaries were even discouraged from teaching doctrines such as the three degrees of glory. People accepted Mormonism because they wanted a more vital and authentic Christianity, not a bizarre offshoot of biblical religion. Smith's critique of conventional methodology forcefully reminds us of a simple fact about Mormonism that has been too often overlooked. It was fundamentally biblical and Christian.

Nathan Hatch continues Smith's Methodist comparison and begins again with similarities between the two. Both Mormonism and Methodism carried the gospel to the scattered population of the nation, the Methodists with their itinerants and the Mormons with their lay missionaries. In a sense they both knew how to market religion, and both had immense success in increasing membership—especially the Methodists, who constituted 34 percent of all church members in the United States by 1850.

But once in the faith, converts found themselves in quite different worlds. Methodists moved away from religious enthusiasm toward middle-class respectability. Methodism had begun as a vibrant, supernaturalist religion that enjoyed dreams and visions and emotional religious experiences. As the early lower-class converts moved toward the middle class, this older faith was sloughed off. Methodism became orderly and circumspect. Later Methodist historians, under the influence of their newfound gentility, downplayed the early extravagances and claimed that Methodism had always been a civilizing influence. The first stages of the movement were lost in the haze.

Converts to Mormonism did not ascend into respectability like the Methodists. Instead they found themselves in a maelstrom of religious furies. "Early Mormonism remained radical, apocalyptic, absolutist, extreme, combustible, and militant," Hatch claims. Mormons pronounced judgment on corrupt society and eventually announced that "they would rule America and the entire world." Their neighbors were terrified when Mormons "trained, marched, and on a few occasions waged pitched battle, as a military unit." Mormons, moreover, infuriated other citizens by the "denial of the most basic liberty imaginable, freedom of thought." Joseph Smith, after consolidating power into his own hands, would brook no resistance. Such extremes can only be accounted for, Hatch believes, by the failure of the free-market economy to care for "the lonely and forlorn" who subscribed to Mormonism out of sheer desperation.[7]

All that is left out of the denominational histories, Hatch tells us. Hungry for intellectual respectability, modern Mormons have passed over this side of their history, obscuring the real character of primitive Mormonism. I wish I had been present when Hatch delivered these stinging words to the MHA. Who would have gone to the podium to congratulate him after he delivered this rebuke? Was most of the audience frozen in horror, while those less sympathetic to modern Mormonism exulted?

Hatch certainly made his point about Mormon historians diminishing parts of their history. The violent religious zealots in Hatch's retelling do not figure in histories by denominational historians. On the other hand, does Hatch himself distort the past in his eagerness to right the balance? Do the diaries and reminiscences of the Mormons who lived through the early decades reflect fanaticism and a lust for domination? Are militance and judgments on the wicked the prevailing message of the revelations? One cannot deny the presence of those themes in early Mormonism; plenty of passages in the revelations threaten the wicked world with destruction. But do they predominate?

Hatch's observations require historians to acknowledge the violent streak in Mormon culture, but his method of piling up all the passages, all the events, and all the doctrines that sustained extremism necessarily distorts the picture. This is not the primitive Mormonism you find by reading the entire record. Hatch has fallen into the virulent anti-Mormon view of early Mormonism, the view that led to the Missouri extermination proclamation and the slaughter at Haun's Mill. He plays upon Americans' deeply embedded fear of religious fanaticism. He does not get the facts wrong, but by distilling them into a poisonous concentration, Hatch gives us the Mormonism that its enemies loved to hate.

It is a relief to move from Hatch to the more diplomatic and statesmanlike tone of John Wilson's essay on church-state relations viewed through Mormon history. Wilson points out the reluctance of U.S. courts to base decisions on the definition of religion. The boundaries are so indefinite that it is difficult for judges to get a firm purchase on the exact limits. Most church-state decisions were based on other issues to avoid the quagmire of an exact definition. Paradoxically, nearly everyone, including the Mormons, agreed on the basic principles. Religion and government exist in separate spheres. Government is secular but supported by God for its role in keeping order. The two spheres should not interfere with one another. Those principles have always been clear, but the application to particular cases has been contentious from the beginning, and one of Mormonism's roles was to force the issue on the government. Considering that Mormons did not receive much protection from the state or federal governments, Wilson finds it remarkable that Joseph Smith never lost confidence in the principles of the U.S. Constitution. He instituted freedom of religion in Nauvoo, Illinois, and made support of the government one of the Church's articles of faith.

Near the close of his essay, Wilson offers an intriguing insight that surely deserves further development. He notes that in the 1840s Smith recognized that the Constitution was a platform for action as much as a set of fixed principles. The virtue of constitutional government was the opportunity it afforded for enacting beneficial laws. This recognition pointed toward further engagement with government. Rather than withdrawing from society—the natural impulse of sectarians such as the Mormons with their commanding religious goals—citizens had to take part in making the laws. Wilson suggests that Smith's recognition of the need for involvement may account for his seemingly quixotic presidential candidacy. He had come to understand that to enjoy good government, citizens had to participate. This change in attitude, Wilson points out, signified a narrowing of the gap between Mormons and American government. They were taking the first steps toward the peace negotiations that would eventually conclude at the end of the nineteenth century, when Mormonism entered into the mainstream of American society.

Until that time, Mormons were still out of step with the rest of American religious culture in one peculiar way, according to Laurence Moore. They believed
in having fun. Moore puzzles over Brigham Young's endorsement of theaters
and dances at a time when most Protestants thought that amusements were a
threat to morality and the social order. Suffering from the social disorientation
of the early nineteenth century, and especially the breakdown of small, face-to-
face communities, the clergy tried to shore up the restraints on bad conduct.
With so much else falling down around them, these clergymen had to discourage activities such as dancing that seemed to hasten the collapse.

Brigham Young, Moore suggests in an appealing hypothesis, could take more
chances because Mormons had constructed coherent communities in the Great
Basin. They were less worried about the dangers of fun because conduct was
monitored in their tightly knit congregations and villages. It was safe to go to
balls and plays with so many communal restraints in place.

Though they may not have learned the lesson from the Mormons, Protestants
after midcentury emulated the Saints by forming artificial communities that
would serve the same function as Mormon villages. At Chautauqua and the
YMCA, young people could engage in sports and dance because the organizers
controlled the overall environment. The artificial vacation communities—
formed at the shore for both preaching and good fun—helped Protestants gradually lose their fear of amusements too. In time the tail wagged the dog, as
recreation squeezed out religion and the various formed communities accepted
recreation as their primary purpose. Ironically, Mormons who had led other
religions in the nineteenth century fell behind in the twentieth when Mormons'
straitlaced amusements seemed puritanical to a nation now dedicated to fun.
Moore enjoys the irony of the trick that history played on the Mormons, putting
them behind when once they were ahead in advocacy of recreation.

What Moore might have added if his investigation had gone forward in time
is that Mormons too had to create artificial communities. In the twentieth century, as the population flowed out of the Great Basin to the Pacific and the East
Coasts, Mormon congregations tried to reproduce village life in big cities by
organizing wards that made dances, athletics, drama, and music a lure for young
people. Now those cultural arts and athletic programs have been severely
reduced, and Mormons have retreated from the amusement front almost
entirely. A historian with Moore's interest in popular culture could offer useful
judgments on what this retreat means for the Mormon sense of community.

From their various viewpoints, this potpourri of historical studies brightly
illuminates the Mormon past. At the same time, the essays illustrate the inescapable pitfalls that historical methodologies inevitably encounter. A commitment to one approach inevitably involves the individual in its limitations.
This is one reason that no historian alone can tell the story perfectly. We need
many historians, approaching from many directions, with ever new perspectives

and comparisons. Viewed together, this collection of Tanner Lectures explains why, for more than twenty years now, experts on Mormon history have happily listened to views from the outside.

Notes

1. Nathan O. Hatch, "Mormon and Methodist: Popular Religion in the Crucible of the Free Market," *Journal of Mormon History* 20 (Spring 1994): 35.

2. Gordon S. Wood, "Evangelical America and Early Mormonism," *New York History* 61 (October 1980): 386.

3. Ibid., 381.

4. Ibid., 380.

5. Ibid.

6. Timothy L. Smith, "The Book of Mormon in a Biblical Culture," *Journal of Mormon History* 7 (1980): 8.

7. Hatch, "Mormon and Methodist," 38, 41, 42, 43, 44.

CHAPTER 1

Evangelical America and Early Mormonism

Gordon S. Wood

It is one of the striking facts of U.S. history that the American Revolution was led by men who were not very religious. At best the Founding Fathers only passively believed in organized Christianity, and at worst they scorned and ridiculed it. Although few were outright deists, most, such as David Ramsay, described the Christian church as "the best temple of reason." Washington was a frequent churchgoer, but he scarcely referred to God as anything but "the Great Disposer of events." Like the principal sources of their Whig liberalism—whether John Locke or the Commonwealth publicist "Cato"—they viewed religious enthusiasm as a kind of madness, the conceit "of a warmed or overweening brain."[1] Jefferson's hatred of the clergy knew no bounds, and he repeatedly denounced the "priest-craft" for converting Christianity into "an engine for enslaving mankind . . . into a mere contrivance to filch wealth and power to themselves." For Jefferson and his liberal colleagues, sectarian Christianity was the enemy of most of what they valued—the free and dispassionate inquiry of reason into the workings of nature. As enlightened men they abhorred "that gloomy superstition disseminated by ignorant illiberal preachers" and looked forward to the day when "the phantom of darkness will be dispelled by the rays of science, and the bright charms of rising civilization." When Hamilton was asked why the members of the Philadelphia Convention had not mentioned God in the Constitution, he allegedly replied, speaking for many of this remarkable generation of American leaders, "We forgot."[2]

By 1830, less than a half century later, it was no longer so easy to forget God. The American's world had been radically transformed. The Enlightenment seemed to be over, and evangelical Protestantism had seized control of much of the culture. The United States, said de Tocqueville, had become the most thoroughly Christian nation in the world.[3]

The year 1830 was, in fact, a particularly notable one in the history of American religion. In that year, the great preacher Charles G. Finney came to Rochester,

New York, the fastest-growing community in the United States, and launched a revival that eventually shook the nation. In that same year, the Shakers had more members than at any other time of their history. In 1830 the religious fanatic Robert Matthews experienced the revelation that turned him into a wandering Jewish prophet predicting the imminent end of the world. At the same time, Alexander Campbell broke from the Baptists and began publication of the *Millennial Harbinger* in preparation for his momentous alliance with Barton Stone and the creation of the Disciples of Christ. And in that same crucial year, Joseph Smith published the Book of Mormon.[4]

These remarkable religious events of 1830 were only some of the most obvious manifestations of a firestorm of evangelical enthusiasm that had been sweeping through American society for at least a generation. This movement—generally called the Second Great Awakening—was itself the expression of something bigger and more powerful than even religion. Evangelical revivalism, utopian communitarianism, millennial thinking, multitudes of dreams and visions by seekers, and the birth of new religions were in fact all responses to the great democratic changes taking place in America between the Revolution and the Age of Jackson. The remains of older eighteenth-century hierarchies fell away, and hundreds of thousands of common people were cut loose from all sorts of traditional bonds and found themselves freer, more independent, more unconstrained than ever before in their history.

It is not surprising that 1830—the same year in which so many spectacular religious events occurred—was also the year in which the American's drinking of alcoholic spirits reached its peak: in 1830 Americans consumed nearly four gallons of alcohol per person, the highest rate of consumption in any year in all of American history.[5] The drinking of spirits and the search for spiritualism were but different reactions to a common democratic revolution and the chaos it had created. By 1830 Americans had experienced a social and cultural upheaval scarcely matched in their history.

The national outpouring of religious feeling during the early decades of the nineteenth century was very much a part of this upheaval. This Second Great Awakening brought religion to the remotest areas of America, popularized religion as never before, and created a religious world unlike anything in Christendom. It was not just a continuation of the first Awakening of the mid-eighteenth century. It was more popular, more evangelical, more ecstatic, more personal, more secular, and more optimistic. It combined the past and present, communalism and individualism, and folkways and enlightenment in odd and confusing ways. The sovereignty of Christ was reaffirmed, but people were given personal responsibility for their salvation as never before. Nearly everyone yearned for Christian unity, but never before or since was American Christendom so divided. For many the world was coming to an end, but at the same time everything in the here and now seemed possible. It was the time of greatest religious chaos and originality in American history. During this unique moment in the annals of American religion, Mormonism was born.

At the time of the Revolution, no one foresaw what would happen to American religion. Many of America's religious leaders, including the Calvinist clergy, endorsed the Revolution and its enlightened liberal impulses wholeheartedly. For most Protestant groups, the great threat to religion came from the Church of England, and enlightened rationalists such as Jefferson and Madison had little trouble in mobilizing Protestant dissenters against the established Anglican church. The Enlightenment's faith in liberty of conscience that justified this disestablishment of the Anglican church scarcely seemed dangerous to American religion. Even in Connecticut and Massachusetts, where religious establishments existed but were Puritan, not Anglican, Presbyterian and Congregational clergy invoked enlightened religious liberty against the dark twin forces of British civic and ecclesiastical tyranny without fear of subverting their own peculiar alliances between church and state. The Revolution and enlightened republicanism blended with evangelical Protestantism to promise all Americans, secular and religious-minded alike, the moral regeneration that the country needed.

Yet the Revolution was scarcely over before many clergymen began having second thoughts about what separation of church and state and religious freedom really meant. Few could share Jefferson's enlightened belief, expressed in his 1786 Virginia Act for Establishing Religious Freedom, that religion was only a matter of opinion having no more relation to government than our "opinions in physics or geometry." Since religion was the principal promoter of morality and virtue, without which no republic could long exist, it now seemed increasingly dangerous "To carry the idea of religious liberty so far, as . . . to rob civil government of one of its main supports."[6] The enlightened liberalism of the Revolutionary leaders appeared to be having more devastating effects on religion than many clergy had expected.

By the 1790s organized religion was in disarray. The Revolution had destroyed churches, interrupted ministerial training, and politicized people's thinking. The older established churches, now either dismantled or under attack, were unequipped to handle a rapidly growing and moving population. The proportion of college graduates entering the ministry fell off, and the number of church members declined drastically, with, it is estimated, scarcely one in twenty Americans being members of a church.[7] At the same time the influence of enlightened liberalism was growing. It underlay the First Amendment and infected the thinking of gentlemen everywhere. It ate away the premises of Calvinism, indeed, of all orthodox Christian beliefs. It told people they were not sinful but naturally good, possessed of a moral sense or instinct, and that evil lay in the corrupt institutions of both church and state. For some enlightened gentlemen, Christianity became simply the butt of dinner party jokes. Everywhere orthodox clergymen tried to reconcile their traditional beliefs with liberal rationalism and to make sense of what Jefferson called "the incomprehensible jargon of the Trinitarian arithmetic, that three are one, and one is three."[8] This rational deism could not be confined to the drawing rooms of the gentry but even spilled into the streets. The antireligious writings of Ethan Allen, Thomas Paine, Comte de Volney, and Elihu Palmer, reached out to new popular audiences and gave many ordinary people the sense that reason and nature were as important (and mysterious) as revelation and the supernatural. By the early nineteenth century, enlightened leaders such as Jefferson and young John C. Calhoun were enthusiastically predicting that the whole country was rapidly on its way to becoming Unitarian.[9]

All this accumulated evidence of religious apathy and growing rationalism has convinced many historians that the decade and a half following the Revolution was "the most irreligious period in American history, . . . the period of the lowest ebbtide of vitality in the history of American Christianity." The early republic has even been called "a heathen nation—one of the most needy mission fields in the world."[10]

We are now only beginning to realize how misleading these common historical interpretations of popular infidelity and religious indifference in post-Revolutionary America are.[11] The mass of American people had not lost their religiosity during the Enlightenment. Certainly the low proportion of church membership is no indication of popular religious apathy, not in America, where church membership had long been a matter of an individual's conversion experience and not, as in the Old World, where membership was a matter of birth. To be sure, there were fierce expressions of popular hostility to the genteel clergy with their DDs and other aristocratic pretensions. It was this egalitarian anticlericalism rather than any widespread rejection of Christianity that lay behind the popular deism of these years. For most common people, Christianity remained the dominant means for explaining the world; all they wanted was for it to be adapted to their newly aroused and newly legitimated needs.

During the last quarter of the eighteenth century, powerful currents of popular evangelical feeling flowed beneath the refined and aristocratic surface of public life, awaiting only the developing democratic revolution to break through the rationalistic crust of the Enlightenment and to sweep over and transform the landscape of the country. Once ordinary people found that they could change traditional religion as completely as they were changing traditional politics, they had no need for deism or infidelity. By 1800 there was as little chance of all Americans becoming rational Unitarians as there was of their all becoming high-toned Federalists. Evangelical Christianity and the democracy of these years, the very democracy with which Jefferson rode to power and destroyed Federalism, emerged together and were interrelated.

This democracy and the popular evangelicism of the early nineteenth century were both products of a social disintegration unequaled in American history. All the old eighteenth-century aristocratic hierarchies, enfeebled and brittle to begin with, now collapsed under the impact of long-developing demographic and economic forces. The population grew at phenomenal rates and spread itself over half a continent at speeds that astonished everyone. Between 1790 and 1820, New York's population quadrupled, and Kentucky's multiplied nearly eight times. People were on the move as never before, individuals sometimes uprooting themselves four or five or more times in a lifetime. Joseph Smith's father moved his family seven times in fourteen years.[12] Ohio in a single decade grew from a virtual wilderness to become larger than most of the colonies had been at the time of the Revolution. This growth and movement of people combined with the spread of market economies to shatter all sorts of paternalistic social relationships and to excite the acquisitive impulses of countless individuals. Young people left their parents, women found new roles for themselves, servants stopped living in households, apprentices and journeymen grew apart from their masters and became employees, and numerous patrons and clients switched roles. In thousands of different ways, connections that had held people together for centuries were strained and severed, and people were set loose in unprecedented numbers.

The effects and symptoms of this social disintegration appeared everywhere in the early republic. Urban rioting became more prevalent, more destructive, and more class-conscious. Major strikes of employees against employers occurred for the first time in American history. Poverty in both the countryside and the cities increased dramatically. Everything seemed to be coming apart, and murder, suicide, theft, and the phenomenal drinking of Americans became increasingly common responses to the burdens that the new individualism and the expectation of gain were placing on people.

The ideology of the Revolution aggravated this social disintegration but at the same time helped make it meaningful. The egalitarianism of the Revolution explained and justified for common people their new independence and distance from one another. The change and disruptions were offset by the Revolutionary promises for the future of the country. Improvement became an everyday fact of life for unprecedented numbers of people. Traditional structures of authority crumbled under the momentum of the Revolution, and common people increasingly discovered that they no longer had to accept the old distinctions that had separated them from the upper ranks of the gentry. Ordinary farmers, tradesmen, and artisans began to think that they were as good as any gentleman and that they actually counted for something in the movement of events. Were not the people being equated with God, with every last humble one of them being celebrated for possessing a spark of divinity? Were not half-literate plowmen being told that they had as much moral sense and insight into God as professors and doctors of divinity?[13]

As the traditional connections of people fell away, many Americans found themselves in a marginal (or what anthropologists call a liminal) state of transition and were driven to find or fabricate new ways of relating to one another. Fraternity became as important to Revolutionary Americans as liberty and equality. Never in Western history did so much intellectual effort go into exploring the bonds that tie individuals together. From Lord Shaftesbury to Francis Hutcheson to Adam Smith, eighteenth-century philosophers were drawn upon to explain and reinforce what seemed to be the natural affections and moral sympathy that even unrelated individuals had for each other. People were urged to transcend their parochial folk and kin loyalties and to reach out to embrace even distant strangers. The Enlightenment's stress on modern civility came together with the traditional message of Christian charity to make the entire period from the Revolution to the Age of Jackson a great era of benevolence and communitarianism. Figures as diverse as Jefferson, Samuel Hopkins, and Thomas Campbell told people that all they had to do in the world was to believe in one God and to love other people as themselves.[14]

By the early nineteenth century, a radical and momentous transformation had taken place. Countless numbers of people involved in a simultaneous search for individual autonomy and for new forms of community experienced immense psychological shifts. While educated gentry formed new cosmopolitan connections, increasing numbers of common people found solace in the creation of new egalitarian and affective communities. From the Revolution on, all sorts of associations—from mutual aid societies to Freemasonry—arose to meet the needs of newly detached individuals, but most important for ordinary folk was the creation of unprecedented numbers of religious communities. The disintegration of older structures of authority released torrents of popular religiosity into public life. Visions, dreams, prophesyings, and new emotion-soaked religious seekings acquired a validity they had not earlier possessed. The evangelical pietism of ordinary people, sanctioned by the democratic revolution of these years, had come to affect the character of American culture in ways it had not at the time of the Revolution. It now became increasingly difficult for enlightened gentlemen to publicly dismiss religious enthusiasm as simply the superstitious fanaticism of the illiterate and lowborn.

Yet this transformation was not simple and stark. The world did not simply turn upside down and replace the skeptical Founding Fathers with new evangelical-minded popular leaders. The reason of the Enlightenment was not suddenly supplanted by the revelations of Protestant Christianity. To be sure, some of the leading Revolutionary figures, including John Jay, Benjamin Rush, and Noah Webster, did experience a religious rebirth in the early nineteenth century and abandoned enlightened rationalism in favor of traditional Christianity.[15] But more than such dramatic changes of mind were involved. What came after contained much of what had existed before.

The Enlightenment was not repudiated but popularized. The great democratic revolution of the period forged a new popular amalgam out of traditional folk beliefs and the literary culture of the gentry. Through newspapers, almanacs, chapbooks, lectures, and other media, ordinary people increasingly acquired smatterings of knowledge about things that hitherto had been the preserve of educated elites. And at the same time they were told that their newly acquired knowledge was just as good as that possessed by those with college degrees. "Hitherto," said Dr. Daniel Drake in 1821 to a group of Ohio medical students, "the philosophers have formed a distinct *caste* from the people; and like kings have been supposed to possess a divine right of superiority. But this delusion should be dispelled, is indeed fast disappearing, and the distinction between scientific and the unscientific, dissolved. . . . All men to a certain extent may become philosophers."[16] Under such egalitarian circumstances, truth itself became democratized, and the borders that the eighteenth century had painstakingly worked out between science and superstition, naturalism and supernaturalism, were now blurred. Animal magnetism seemed as legitimate as gravity. Dowsing for hidden metals appeared as rational as the workings of electricity. Scholarly studies of the origins of the Indians and the mounds of the Northwest seemed no more plausible than popular speculations about the lost tribes of Israel. And crude folk remedies were even thought to be as scientific as the bleeding cures of enlightened medicine.[17]

The result was an odd mixture of credulity and skepticism among people. Where everything was believable, everything could be doubted. All claims to expert knowledge were suspect, and people tended to mistrust, as George Tucker complained in 1827, anything outside of "the narrow limits of their own observation." Yet because people prided themselves on their shrewdness and believed that they now understood so much, they could be easily impressed by what they did not understand. A few strange words such as "hieroglyphics" spoken by a preacher or a documentary patent displayed by a medicine seller could carry great credibility. In such an atmosphere, hoaxes of various kinds and quackery in all fields flourished.[18]

Like the culture as a whole, religion was powerfully affected by these popularizing developments. Subterranean folk beliefs and fetishes emerged into the open and blended with traditional Christian practices to create a wildly spreading evangelical enthusiasm. Ordinary people cut off from traditional social relationships were freer than ever before to express publicly hitherto repressed or vulgar emotions. Thousands upon thousands became seekers looking for signs and prophets and for new explanations for the bewildering experiences of their lives. These marginal people came together without gentry leadership anywhere they could—in fields, barns, or homes—to lay hands on one another, to offer each other kisses of charity, to form new bonds of fellowship, to set loose their feelings both physically and vocally, and to Christianize a variety of folk rites. From the "love feasts" of the Methodists to the dancing ceremonies of the Shakers, isolated individuals found in the variety of evangelical "bodily exercises" ungenteel and sometimes bizarre but emotionally satisfying ways of relating to God and to each other. When there were no trained clergy to minister to the yearnings of these lost men and women, they recruited leaders from among themselves. New half-educated, enterprising preachers emerged to mingle exhibitions of book-learning with plain talk and appeals to every kind of emotionalism. They developed and expanded revivalistic techniques because such dynamic folklike processes were better able to meet the needs of rootless egalitarian-minded men and women than were the static churchly institutions based on eighteenth-century standards of deference and elite monopolies of orthodoxy.[19] These common people wanted a religion they could personally and bodily feel. They wanted sermons free from "literary quibbles and philosophical speculations." Each person wanted, as one spiritual song put it, to literally and physically "see bright angels stand / . . . waiting to receive me."[20]

We are now only beginning to appreciate the power and immensity of this Second Great Awakening. There was nothing like it on this popular scale since the religious turbulence of seventeenth-century England or perhaps the Reformation. It was very much a movement from below, fed by the passions of very ordinary people. To describe it, therefore, as some historians have done, as a conservative antidemocratic movement is to miss its popular force and significance.[21] To be sure, some Congregational clergy in New England saw in evangelical Christianity a means by which Federalists might better control the social disorder resulting from the Revolution. But these Federalist clergy such as Timothy Dwight scarcely comprehended, let alone were able to manage, this popular religious upheaval.[22] In New England, the clergy scrambled to keep up with the surging emotional needs of people—by creating new colleges and academies to train ministers, by restructuring the churches, and by founding missionary societies—but elsewhere, especially in the fluid western areas, the religious yearnings of people simply overwhelmed the traditional religious institutions.[23] Between 1803 and 1809, for example, more than half the Presbyterian clergy and church membership of Kentucky were swept away by the torrents of revivalism.[24]

This genuine folk movement spawned hundreds and thousands of camp meetings and religious communities throughout the early republic. By focusing on the most bizarre behavior of the revivals, such as the "jerks" and "laughing jags," or on the most exotic expressions of the communalism, such as the Shakers, we have sometimes missed its popular strength and scope. It is obvious that this religious enthusiasm tapped long-existing veins of folk culture, and many evangelical leaders had to struggle to keep the suddenly released popular passions under control. Some enthusiasts drew on folk yearnings that went back centuries and in the new free atmosphere of republican America saw the opportunity to establish long-desired utopian worlds in which all social distinctions were abolished, diet was restricted, and women and goods were shared.[25] But for every such ascetic or licentious utopian community, there were hundreds of other evangelical communities that clung, however tenuously, to one or another of the Old World religions. Presbyterian, Methodist, and Baptist evangelicals all participated in the Awakening and constituted its main force. Yet in the end, perhaps, our fascination with the unusual sects and prophets is not mistaken, for the radical enthusiasts and visionaries represented the advanced guard of this popular evangelical movement, with which they shared a common hostility to orthodox authority.

All of the evangelicals—from the Shakers to the Baptists—rejected in one degree or another the ways in which traditional society organized itself and assigned prestige. Thousands of ordinary people—farmers, bricklayers, millers, carpenters, petty businessmen of every sort, and their mothers, wives, and sisters—found in evangelicalism a counterculture that condemned the conventional society and offered them alternative measures of social esteem.[26] Being called by polite society "the scum of the earth, the filth of creation," these evangelicals made their fellowship, their conversion experiences, and their peculiar folk rites their badges of respectability.[27] They denounced the dissolute behavior they saw about them—the profanity, drinking, gambling, dancing, horse racing, and other amusements shared by both the luxurious aristocracy at the top of the society and the unproductive rabble at the bottom. By condemning the vices of those above and below them, evangelicals struck out in both social directions at once and thereby began to acquire a nineteenth-century "middle-class" distinctiveness.

The American Revolution itself was invoked by this evangelical challenge to existing authority, and Christianity for some radicals became republicanized. As in government so in religion: the people were their own theologians and could no longer rely on others to tell them what to believe. We must, declared the renegade Baptist Elias Smith in 1809, be "wholly free to examine for ourselves, what is truth, without being bound to a catechism, creed, confession of faith, discipline or any rule excepting the scriptures."[28] From northern New England to southern Kentucky, Christian fundamentalists called for an end to priests, presbyters, associations, doctrines, confessions—anything and everything that stood between the people and Christ. The people were told that they were quite capable of running their own churches, and even clerical leaders of the conservative denominations such as the Presbyterian Samuel Miller were forced to concede greater and greater lay control.[29] Those who tried to resist this democratic religious thrust had to contend with the Enlightenment itself; for there was little essential difference between Jefferson's desire to knock down "the artificial scaffolding, reared to mask from the view the simple structure of Jesus," and the primitive restorationist message preached by the most radical evangelicists.[30]

Everywhere the people were "awakened from the sleep of ages" and saw "for the first time that they were responsible beings" who might even be capable of their own salvation.[31] Although Calvinists and others still stressed the grace and sovereignty of God, conversion more and more seemed to be within the grasp of all who desired it. The new groups of Universalists who promised salvation for everyone were widely condemned, but they were only starkly drawing out the logic implied by others. Sin was no longer conceived as something inherent in the depravity of man but as a kind of failure of man's will and therefore fully capable of being eliminated by individual exertion. Thus, the immediate and personal awareness of God bred by revivalism led not to a quiet and introverted mysticism but to stirring and engaging activism.

Because the criteria of religious affiliation were now so personal, so emotional, so subjective, individuals moved easily from one religious group to another in a continual search for signs, prophets, or millennial promises that would make sense of their disrupted lives. With no group sure of holding its communicants, competition among the sects was fierce. Each claimed to be right, called each other names, argued endlessly over points of doctrine, mobbed and stoned each other, and destroyed each other's meetinghouses.[32] Nowhere else in Christendom was religion so broken apart. Not only were the traditional Old World churches fragmented, but the new fragments themselves shattered in what seemed at times to be an endless process of fission. There were not just Presbyterians, but Old and New School Presbyterians, Cumberland Presbyterians, Springfield Presbyterians, Reformed Presbyterians, and Associated Presbyterians; not just Baptists, but General Baptists, Regular Baptists, Free Will Baptists, Separate Baptists, Dutch River Baptists, Permanent Baptists, and even Two-Seed-in-the-Spirit Baptists. Some groups cut their ties completely with the Old World churches and gathered themselves around a dynamic leader such as Barton Stone or Thomas Campbell. Other seekers formed only single congregations, and isolated clergymen—freelance revivalists with folk names such as "Crazy Dow" or "Father Havens"—roamed the countryside in search of lost souls.[33]

In some areas, churches as such scarcely seemed to exist, and the traditional identification between religion and society, never very strong in America to begin with, now finally dissolved. The church became for many little more than the building in which religious services were conducted. Religion that made each person alone responsible for his theology and salvation, as Lyman Beecher and other evangelicals acutely came to see, left nothing holding "society, against depravity within and temptation without," except the force of God's law "written upon the heart" of each individual. Only the self-restraint of individuals—their "character"—now remained to keep this new society together.[34] By concentrating on the saving of individual souls, the contending denominations abandoned their traditional institutional and churchly responsibilities for organizing the world along godly lines.

From the disruptions and bewilderments of their lives many people could readily conclude that the world was on the verge of some great transformation—nothing less than the Second Coming of Christ and the Day of Judgment predicted in the Bible. Millennialism of various kinds, both scholarly and popular, flourished in the turbulent decades following the Revolution and became the means by which many explained and justified the great social changes of the period. Although old and new millennial ideas mingled confusedly, some of the Adventist beliefs in the early nineteenth century now assumed a character appropriate to the realities of a new, improving American society. Older popular Christian beliefs in the millennium had usually assumed that Christ's coming would precede the establishment of a new Kingdom of God. Christ's advent would be forewarned by signs and troubles, culminating in a horrible conflagration in which everything would be destroyed. Christ would then rule over the faithful in a New Jerusalem for a thousand years until the final Day of Judgment. Those who held such millennial beliefs generally saw the world as so corrupt and evil that only the sudden and catastrophic intervention of Christ could create the new world. But in the America of the early nineteenth century, such older cataclysmic interpretations of the millennium began to be replaced by newer ideas that pictured the Second Coming of Christ as following, rather than preceding, the thousand years of glory and bliss. And such an approaching age of perfection seemed to be beginning in America itself.[35]

This new millennialism of many post-Revolutionary Americans represented both a rationalizing of revelation and a Christianizing of the Enlightenment belief in secular progress. It was optimistic and even worldly; it promised not the sudden divine destruction of a corrupt world but a step-by-step, human-dominated progression toward perfection in this world. Since the United States was itself leading humankind toward the earth's final thousand years of bliss, millennial hopes came to focus on contemporary events occurring in America as signs of the approaching age of perfection—a perfection that would be brought about, some said, "not by miracles, but by means," indeed, "BY HUMAN EXERTIONS."[36] Every advance in America's material progress—even new inventions and canal-building—was now interpreted in millennial terms. Such millennial beliefs identified the history of redemption with the history of the new republic. They reconciled Christianity with American democracy, and they explained and justified the troubled lives and the awakened aspirations of countless numbers of ordinary Americans for whom the world had hitherto never offered any promise of improvement. Such popular millennial thinking not only reinforced nineteenth-century Americans' sense of their peculiar mission in history but kept alive an older folk world in which prophets and prophesying were still conceivable and important.

"In the midst of this war of words and tumult of opinions"—rivaling the early days of the Reformation—it is no wonder that troubled seekers such as young Joseph Smith were asking "What is to be done? Who of all these parties are right; or, are they all wrong together? If any one of them be right, which is it, and how shall I know it?"[37]

The inevitable reactions to this extreme sectarianism and religious individualism were diverse, and they came from both the left and the right. Some radical evangelicals thought they could end the religious chaos by appealing to the
Bible as the lowest common denominator of Christian belief. The Scriptures
were to be to democratic religion what the Constitution was to democratic politics—the fundamental document that would bind all American Christians
together in one national community. The biblical literalism of these years
became, in fact, popular religion's ultimate concession to the Enlightenment—
the recognition that religious truth now needed documentary "proof." In that
democratic age where all traditional authority was suspect, some concluded
that individuals possessed only their own reason and the Scriptures—the "two
witnesses," said Joseph Smith's grandfather, "that stand by the God of the whole
earth."[38] The only difficulty, of course, as Joseph Smith himself came to perceive, was that "the different sects understood the same passages of scripture so
differently as to destroy all confidence in settling the question by an appeal to
the Bible" (JS–H 1:12). Only some final interpreter, some supreme court of
Christianity, could end the confusion. But, as radical evangelicals such as the
maverick Methodist James O'Kelley realized, if such an ultimate authoritative
interpreter existed here on earth, "he must be a Prophet or Apostle."[39] Although
young Smith was told "that there were no such things as visions or revelations in
these days" (JS–H 1:21), the time was obviously ripe for the emergence of the
greatest of America's prophets.

The reaction from the right to the excesses of revivalism was also concerned
with reestablishing religious authority. It began during the second decade of the
nineteenth century among conservative churches, particularly High Church
Episcopalians and Old School Presbyterians, but did not become important
until the second quarter of the century. These conservative groups wanted to
offset the personal and emotional character of revivalism by restoring the corporate rituals and doctrines of the historic churches. They reemphasized the
sacerdotal authority of the clergy and called for a strengthening of bishops,
presbyters, and general ecclesiastical leadership and organization. They reaffirmed the organic nature of church society and traced the historic roots of their
churches as far back as they could, even to apostolic times. And, as much as the
Christian fundamentalists, they rejected the sectarianism of the day. They thought
that American "denominationalism"—the division of the visible church into
different contending denominations—violated the traditional ideal of a single,
catholic, and apostolic church.[40] Although these High Church Episcopalians
and Old School Presbyterians had little in common, either socially or intellectually, with the primitive "Christians" who eventually made up the Disciples of
Christ, they were alike in their desire to re-create a single, visible church that
would encompass all Christians. While conservative churchmen sought to realize this goal by strengthening the institutions and creeds of the churches, the

Disciples thought that only the tearing away of the various trappings of the different churches could expose the scriptural foundations common to all Christians. It would be the Mormons' peculiar contribution to this aim of regaining the one apostolic Christian church to do both—to combine the radical and conservative efforts to end sectarianism.

This, then, was the evangelical world out of which Mormonism arose. The Church of Jesus Christ of Latter-day Saints, for all its uniqueness, was very much a product of its time, but not in any simple or obvious way. Mormonism was undeniably the most original and persecuted religion of this period or of any period of American history. It defied as no other religion did both the orthodox culture and evangelical counterculture. Yet at the same time it drew heavily on both these cultures. It combined within itself different tendencies of thought. From the outset it was a religion in tension, poised like a steel spring by the contradictory forces pulling within it.

Mormonism was both mystical and secular, restorationist and progressive, communitarian and individualistic, hierarchical and congregational, authoritarian and democratic, antinomian and Arminian, anticlerical and priestly, revelatory and empirical, utopian and practical, ecumenical and nationalist. Alexander Campbell was not exaggerating by much when he charged in 1831 that "this prophet Smith" had brought together in the Book of Mormon "every error and almost every truth discussed in New York for the last ten years." Mormonism set out to meet a wide variety of popular needs. It spoke, said John Greenleaf Whittier, "a language of hope and promise to weak, weary hearts, tossed and troubled, who have wandered from sect to sect, seeking in vain for the primal manifestations of the divine power."[41]

Mormonism was a new religion, but it was not to be simply another denomination among the many others of America. The Church did not see itself as just another stage in the ongoing Protestant Reformation. It marked a new beginning in the Christian faith. Like the Disciples of Christ, with which it had much in common, Mormonism was to be "the only true and living church upon the face of the whole earth."[42] But unlike the primitive gospelers, Mormonism did not seek to strip Christianity of its complexities and to ground itself in the literalism of the Bible in order to have the broadest common basis of appeal. Instead, it added new complexities and institutions to Christianity, new rituals and beliefs, and new revelations and miracles. Most importantly, it added an extraordinary complement to the Scriptures. The Book of Mormon published in 1830 was undoubtedly the most distinctive and important force in establishing the new faith.

The Book of Mormon together with Joseph Smith's revelations gave to Mormonism a popular authoritative appeal that none of the other religions could match. Even the primitive gospelers' return to the simplicity of the New Testament had not ended their quarreling over interpreting the Scriptures. The Book of Mormon cut through these controversies and brought the Bible up to date. It was written in plain biblical style for plain people. It answered perplexing questions of theology, clarified obscure passages of the Bible, and carried its story into the New World. And it did all this with the assurance of divine authority. The Book of Mormon brought to the surface underlying currents of American folk thought that cannot be found in the learned pamphlets or public orations of the day. It reveals in fact just how limited and elitist our understanding of early-nineteenth-century popular culture really is.[43] The Book of Mormon is an extraordinary work of popular imagination and one of the greatest documents in American cultural history.

Its timing in 1830 was providential. It appeared at precisely the right moment in American history—much earlier or later and the Church might not have taken hold. The Book of Mormon would probably not have been published in the eighteenth century, in that still largely oral world of folk beliefs prior to the great democratic revolution that underlay the religious tumult of the early republic. In the eighteenth century, Mormonism might have been too easily stifled and dismissed by the dominant enlightened gentry culture as just another enthusiastic folk superstition. Yet if Mormonism had emerged later, after the consolidation of authority and the spread of science in the middle decades of the nineteenth century, it might have had problems verifying its texts and revelations. But during the early decades of the nineteenth century, the time was ideally suited for the establishment of the new faith. The democratic revolution was at its height, all traditional authorities were in disarray, and visions and prophesying still had a powerful appeal for large numbers of people. A generation or so later, it might have been necessary for Smith and his followers to get some university professors to authenticate the characters on the golden plates. But Martin Harris's failure to get such "professional" and "scientific" verification in the 1820s did not matter. After all, ordinary plowmen had as much insight into such things as did college professors.[44]

Yet the American plowmen of the 1820s were no longer the simple folk of the eighteenth century. They had been touched by the literary culture and rationality of the Enlightenment, and despite their lingering superstitions they had their own small shrewdness and their own literal-minded standards of proof. The odd tales of "Joe Smith," this "ignorant plough-boy of our land" who had a local reputation as a "fortune teller," staggered the wits of many in that credulous but skeptical age.[45] To think that "angels appear to men in this enlightened age! Damn him," critics said, "he ought to be tarred and feathered for telling such a damned lie!"[46] In that enlightened age even ordinary farmers no longer dared to invoke "apparitions, or ghosts," in religion, wrote Emily Austin, an early but temporary convert to Mormonism, "for the very reason that we see no just grounds on which to build our faith." For many, the Book of Mormon provided those "just grounds" of faith, though not in the end for Emily Austin. When she eventually concluded that the Book of Mormon lacked "the spirit of conviction," her faith fell away. But for hundreds and thousands of other seekers, "Joe's Gold Bible" offered what one of Smith's early revelations called "the surety that these things are true" for "this unbelieving and stiff-necked generation" (D&C 5:12, 8). One Methodist preacher who converted to Mormonism reputedly even reasoned that "the New Bible" was four times better substantiated than the New Testament because "the disciples of Joseph Smith had four living witnesses to sustain the Book of Mormon."[47]

It is not surprising that opponents of the new faith spent so much energy trying to discredit the origins of the new scripture, for it was precisely this kind of "surety," this concrete material evidence, that gave Joseph Smith's prophesying a legitimacy that the visions and predictions of the many other prophets of the day could not equal. The Book of Mormon nicely answered the warnings of the rational genteel world against "running into extremes, and making ourselves wise above what is written."[48] It had a particular appeal for people emerging from a twilight folk world of dreams and superstitions and anxious to demonstrate their literacy and their enlightenment. Such a tangible document fit the popular belief that what was written was somehow truer and more authentic than what was spoken.

In other ways, too, Mormonism brought the folk past and enlightened modernity together. It sought to reconcile the ecstatic antinomian visions of people with the discipline of a hierarchical church. It drew upon the subjective emotionalism and individualism of revivalism and institutionalized them. Mormonism, in fact, can be understood as a popular version of the elitist churchly reaction to revivalism that began in the second and third decades of the nineteenth century. Just as High Church Episcopalians were looking back to the earliest days of their church for new apostolic authority, so too did Mormons appeal to ancient, pre-Reformation history as set forth in the Book of Mormon. Mormonism offered people the best of both the popular world of millenarian evangelicism and the respectable world of priestly churches. Almost overnight, Mormonism created an elaborate hierarchy, mysterious rituals, and a rich churchly tradition that reached back to apostolic times.[49]

In dozens of different ways Mormonism blended the folk inclinations and religiosity of common people with the hardened churchly traditions and enlightened gentility of modern times. Like many other religious groups, the Mormons built a separate community of gathered saints, but at the same time they rejected the idea that they were just another sect representing a particular social fragment. They reversed America's separation of church and state and tried to reestablish the kind of well-knit commonwealth that John Winthrop had envisioned two hundred years earlier. Mormonism readily responded to the ancient popular yearnings for ascetic communal living and sharing, but at the same time, unlike Shakerism, it recognized modern Americans' individualistic desires for property-owning. Since in the eyes of the gentry the Mormons were "the miserable Mormons," drawn from "the lowest and most ignorant walks of life," they, like other evangelicals, sought to establish among themselves new standards of respectability and prided themselves on what would become "middle-class" decorum and moral behavior.[50] Mormonism answered the powerful anticlerical, egalitarian feelings of people by erecting a church without a professional clergy and by making every man a priest.

Its theology, too, mingled supernatural folk wisdom with modern rationalism. It allied the deep-lying popular emotionalism of the period with Enlightenment's faith in useful knowledge and education. By drawing on the folk habit of identifying the physical and spiritual worlds, Mormonism gave God a more corporeal human character and at the same time made man more divine. Its beliefs fit the needs of lost, lonely people unsure of who they were and where they were going. It sought to counter the disruptive mobility of the times by strengthening the extended family. The baptism of the dead even reached across generations and recaptured for people the sense of ancestral continuity that modern rootlessness had destroyed. This practice, in fact, did for ordinary people what the formation of genealogical societies in the 1840s did for anxious elites. Mormonism recognized the uneasiness, the guilt, and the sinful feelings of people created by their social and geographical displacements, but at the same time it promised these people redemption through their own efforts. However much Mormonism harked back to ancient folkways, it was a religion designed for the future.

Like many other popular faiths of the period on both sides of the Atlantic, Mormonism was thoroughly millennialist. "We believe," wrote Smith, "in the literal gathering of Israel and in the restoration of the Ten Tribes. That Zion will be built upon this continent. That Christ will reign personally upon the earth, and that the earth will be renewed and receive its paradisiac glory."[51] Again in its millennial ideas, as in so many other ways, early Mormonism combined disparate traditions. As scholars have noted, its belief in the Second Coming cannot be easily fitted into any single pattern of millennialism.[52] Early Mormons followed the traditional belief in the corruption of the world and the imminence of Christ's arrival, and they searched the times for signs and omens of the cataclysmic event. At the same time, however, they shared in the more modern millennialist idea that the Kingdom of God could be built in this world and that the everyday material benefits of progress were but the working out of God's purpose. Although other millenarians on both sides of the Atlantic emphasized the special role of their respective nations in the coming age of perfection, no American believers in Christ's Second Coming ever identified the New Jerusalem so particularly and so concretely with America as did the Mormons. Zion was literally to arise within the borders of the United States.[53]

The identification between Mormonism and America was there at the beginning. No doubt it was and is a unique faith, but it is also uniquely American. It was born at a peculiar moment in the history of the United States, and it bears the marks of that birth. Only the culture of early-nineteenth-century evangelical America could have produced it. And through it we can begin to understand the complicated nature of that culture.

Notes

1. Henry F. May, *The Enlightenment in America* (New York: Oxford University Press, 1976), 73; [John Trenchard and Thomas Gordon], *Cato's Letters* (London, 1748), IV, No. 123; John Locke, *An Essay Concerning Human Understanding* (London, 1695), Bk. IV, chap. 19.

2. George Harmon Knoles, "The Religious Ideas of Thomas Jefferson," *Mississippi Valley Historical Review* 30 (September 1943): 194; Nicholas Collin, "An Essay on Those Inquiries in Natural Philosophy, Which at Present Are Most Beneficial to the United States of North America," *Transactions of the American Philosophical Society* 3 (1793), vii; Douglass Adair, *Fame and the Founding Fathers* (New York: Norton, 1974), 147n.

3. Alexis de Tocqueville, *Democracy in America,* trans. and ed. Phillips Bradley, 2 vols. (New York: Vintage, 1956), 1:303.

4. Paul E. Johnson, *A Shopkeeper's Millennium: Society and Revivals in Rochester, New York, 1815–1837* (New York: Hill and Wang, 1978); Henri Desroche, *The American Shakers: From Neo-Christianity to Presocialism* (Amherst: University of Massachusetts Press, 1971), 132; William L. Stone, *Matthias and His Impostures: Or, the Progress of Fanaticism* (New York: Harper & Brothers, 1835); Winfred Ernest Garrison and Alfred T. DeGroot, *The Disciples of Christ: A History* (St. Louis, Mo.: Bethany Press, 1958), 180–230.

5. W. J. Rorabaugh, *The Alcoholic Republic: An American Tradition* (New York: Oxford University Press, 1979), 10.

6. Gordon S. Wood, *The Creation of the American Republic, 1776–1787* (Chapel Hill: University of North Carolina Press, 1969), 427; Henry Cumings, *A Sermon Preached before His Honor Thomas Cushing, Esq., May 28, 1783* (Boston: T. & J. Fleet, 1783), 47.

7. Russel Blaine Nye, *The Cultural Life of the New Nation, 1776–1830* (New York: Harper & Brothers, 1960), 230; Franklin Hamlin Littell, *From State Church to Pluralism: A Protestant Interpretation of Religion in American History* (Chicago: Aldine, 1962), 32.

8. G. Adolph Koch, *Religion of the American Enlightenment* (New York: Crowell, 1968), 83; Thomas Jefferson, Letter to Timothy Pickering, 27 February 1821, in *The Writings of Thomas Jefferson,* ed. Andrew A. Lipscomb and Albert Ellery Bergh (Washington, D.C.: The Thomas Jefferson Memorial Association, 1903–4), 15:323.

9. Thomas Jefferson to Benjamin Waterhouse, 26 June 1822, ibid., 15:385; Clarence Gohdes, "Some Notes on the Unitarian Church in the Ante-Bellum South," in *American Studies in Honor of William Kenneth Boyd,* ed. David Kelly Jackson (Durham, N.C.: Duke University Press, 1940), 327.

10. John W. Chandler, "The Communitarian Quest for Perfection," in *A Miscellany of American Christianity: Essays in Honor of H. Shelton Smith,* ed. Stuart C. Henry (Durham, N.C.: Duke University Press, 1963), 58; William Warren Sweet, *The Story of Religions in America* (New York: Harper & Brothers, 1930), 322; Littell, *From State Church,* 29.

11. Douglas H. Sweet, "Church Vitality and the American Revolution: Historiographic Consensus and Thoughts towards a New Perspective," *Church History* 45 (September 1976): 341–57.

12. My thanks to Richard L. Bushman for this information.

13. Koch, *Religion of the American Enlightenment*, 181; Thomas Jefferson, Letter to Peter Carr, 10 August 1787, in *Writings of Jefferson*, 6:257–58.

14. Conrad E. Wright, "Christian Compassion and Corporate Beneficence: The Institutionalization of Charity in New England, 1770–1810" (PhD diss., Brown University, 1980). On the similarity of the messages of Jefferson, Hopkins, and Campbell, see H. Shelton Smith, Robert T. Handy, and Lefferts A. Loetscher, *American Christianity: An Historical Interpretation with Representative Documents* (New York: Charles Scribner's Sons, 1960), 1:516, 543–44, 579–86. For a recent interpretation stressing the communitarian aspects of Jefferson's thought, see Garry Wills, *Inventing America: Jefferson's Declaration of Independence* (Garden City, N.Y.: Doubleday, 1978). The anthropologist most responsible for the concept of "liminality" is Victor W. Turner, *The Ritual Process: Structure and Anti-Structure* (Chicago: Aldine, 1969).

15. Frank Monaghan, *John Jay* (New York: Bobbs-Merrill, 1935), 427–36; Benjamin Rush, Letter to Granville Sharp, 8 October 1801, in John A. Woods, ed., "The Correspondence of Benjamin Rush and Granville Sharp 1773–1809," *Journal of American Studies* 1 (April 1967): 35–36; Richard M. Rollins, *The Long Journey of Noah Webster* (Philadelphia: University of Pennsylvania Press, 1980).

16. Daniel Drake, "Introductory Lecture for the Second Session of the Medical College of Ohio" (1821), in *Physician to the West: Selected Writings of Daniel Drake on Science and Society*, ed. Henry D. Shapiro and Zane L. Miller (Lexington: University Press of Kentucky, 1970), 171.

17. Stone, *Matthias and His Impostures*, 298; Herbert Leventhal, *In the Shadow of the Enlightenment: Occultism and Renaissance Science in Eighteenth-Century America* (New York: New York University Press, 1976), 114–15; Robert Silverberg, *Mound Builders of Ancient America: The Archaeology of a Myth* (Greenwich, Conn.: New York Graphic Society, 1968); Curtis Dahl, "Mound Builders, Mormons, and William Cullen Bryant," *New England Quarterly* 34 (June 1961): 178–90; Marion Barber Stowell, *Early American Almanacs: The Colonial Weekday Bible* (New York: Burt Franklin, 1977), 183–89.

18. Joseph Atterley [George Tucker], *A Voyage to the Moon* (New York: Elam Bliss, 1827), 11; Charles Coleman Sellers, *Lorenzo Dow: The Bearer of the Word* (New York: Milton, Balch, 1928), 245; Daniel Drake, "The People's Doctors" (1830), in *Physician to the West*, 197–99; Neil Harris, *Humbug: The Art of P. T. Barnum* (Boston: Little, Brown, 1973), 67–89.

19. See especially Rhys Isaac, "Evangelical Revolt: The Nature of the Baptists' Challenge to the Traditional Order in Virginia, 1765 to 1775," *William and Mary Quarterly*, 3rd Ser., 31 (July 1974): 345–68; Donald G. Mathews, *Religion in the Old South* (Chicago: University of Chicago Press, 1977). On the folk aspects of Methodist preachers, see Donald E. Byrne Jr., *No Foot of Land: Folklore of American Methodist Itinerants* (Metuchen, N.J.: Scarecrow, 1975).

20. Gordon Esley Finnie, "Some Aspects of Religion on the American Frontier," in *Miscellany*, 92 n; Ralph H. Gabriel, "Evangelical Religion and Popular Romanticism in Early Nineteenth-Century America," *Church History* 19 (1950): 39. On the literal personification of God and saints in folk sermons, see Bruce A. Rosenberg, *The Art of the American Folk Preacher* (New York: Oxford University Press, 1970), 17.

21. Dixon Ryan Fox, "The Protestant Counter-Reformation in America," *New York History* 16 (January 1935): 19–35; Clifford S. Griffin, "Religious Benevolence as Social Control, 1815–1860," *Mississippi Valley Historical Review* 44 (December 1957): 423–44;

Charles I. Foster, *An Errand of Mercy: The Evangelical United Front, 1790–1837* (Chapel Hill: University of North Carolina Press, 1960).

22. See Stephen E. Berk, *Calvinism versus Democracy: Timothy Dwight and the Origins of American Evangelical Orthodoxy* (Hamden, Conn.: Archan, 1974).

23. Donald M. Scott, *From Office to Profession: The New England Ministry, 1750–1850* (Philadelphia: University of Pennsylvania Press, 1978), 52.

24. Ralph E. Morrow, "The Great Revival, the West, and the Crisis of the Church," in *The Frontier Re-Examined*, ed. John Francis McDermott (Urbana: University of Illinois Press, 1967), 78.

25. For a remarkable revelation of some of these deep-rooted folk yearnings in a six-teenth-century Italian village, see Carlo Ginzburg, "Cheese and Worms: The Cosmos of a Sixteenth-Century Miller," in *Religion and the People, 800–1700*, ed. James Obelkevich (Chapel Hill: University of North Carolina Press, 1979), 87–167.

26. Mathews, *Religion in the Old South*, 34–38.

27. William Gribbin, *The Churches Militant: The War of 1812 and American Religion* (New Haven, Conn.: Yale University Press, 1973), 102.

28. Elias Smith, *The Loving Kindness of God Displayed in the Triumph of Republicanism in America* (Massachusetts: n.p., 1809), 27. On republican radicalism among evangelicals, see Nathan O. Hatch's insightful study "The Christian Movement and the Demand for a Theology of the People," *Journal of American History* 67 (December 1980): 545–67.

29. Belden C. Lane, "Presbyterian Republicanism: Miller and the Eldership as an Answer to Lay-Clerical Tensions," *Journal of Presbyterian History* 56 (Winter 1978): 311–14.

30. Jefferson, Letter to Pickering, 27 February 1821, in *Writings of Jefferson*, 15:323.

31. John Rogers, *The Biography of Eld. Barton Warren Stone, Written by Himself; with Additions and Reflections by Elder John Rogers* (Cincinnati, Ohio: J. A. & U. P. James, 1847), 45.

32. For examples of religious conflict, see Beverley W. Bond Jr., *The Civilization of the Old Northwest: A Study of Political, Social, and Economic Development, 1788–1812* (New York: Macmillan, 1934), 486; Finnie, "Religion on the American Frontier," in *Miscellany*, 90–91.

33. Sellers, *Lorenzo Dow*, 23. See Whitney R. Cross, *The Burned-Over District: The Social and Intellectual History of Enthusiastic Religion in Western New York, 1800–1850* (Ithaca, N.Y.: Cornell University Press, 1965); T. Scott Miyakawa, *Protestants and Pioneers: Individualism and Conformity on the American Frontier* (Chicago: University of Chicago Press, 1964); John B. Boles, *The Great Revival, 1787–1805: The Origins of the Southern Evangelical Mind* (Lexington: University of Kentucky Press, 1972); Richard Carwardine, *Transatlantic Revivalism: Popular Evangelicalism in Britain and America, 1790–1865* (Westport, Conn.: Greenwood, 1978).

34. [Lyman Beecher], "The Necessity of Revivals of Religion to the Perpetuity of Our Civil and Religious Institutions," *Spirit of the Pilgrims* 4 (September 1831): 471.

35. See J. F. Maclear, "The Republic and the Millennium," in *The Religion of the Republic*, ed. Elwyn A. Smith (Philadelphia: Fortress Press, 1971), 183–216; David E. Smith, "Millenarian Scholarship in America," *American Quarterly* 17 (Autumn 1965): 535–49; Ernest Lee Tuveson, *Redeemer Nation: The Idea of America's Millennial Role* (Chicago: University of Chicago Press, 1968); James West Davidson, *The Logic of Millennial Thought: Eighteenth-Century New England* (New Haven, Conn.: Yale University Press, 1977); J. F. C. Harrison, *The Second Coming: Popular Millenarianism, 1780–1850* (New Brunswick, N.J.: Rutgers University Press, 1979); Sacvan Bercovitch, *The American Jeremiad* (Madison: University of Wisconsin Press, 1978).

36. Timothy Dwight (1813) and Elephalet Nott (1806) cited in Davidson, *Millennial Thought*, 275–76.

37. "Joseph Smith—History," *Pearl of Great Price* (Salt Lake City: Church of Jesus Christ of Latter-day Saints, 1974 printing), 47; hereafter cited as JS–H by chapter and verse.

38. Asael Smith (1799), in *Among the Mormons: Historic Accounts by Contemporary Observers*, ed. William Mulder and A. Russell Mortensen (Lincoln: University of Nebraska Press, 1958), 24.

39. James O'Kelley, *A Vindication of the Author's Apology* (Raleigh, N.C.: Joseph Gales, 1801), 49; Smith, *Pearl of Great Price*, 49.

40. Smith, Handy, and Loetscher, *American Christianity*, 11, 66–74.

41. Harrison, *Second Coming*, 184, 191–92. The best single-volume history of Mormonism is Leonard J. Arrington and Davis Bitton, *The Mormon Experience: A History of the Latter-day Saints* (New York: Alfred A. Knopf, 1979).

42. *The Doctrine and Covenants of the Church of Jesus Christ of Latter-Day Saints, Containing Revelations Given to Joseph Smith, the Prophet* (Salt Lake City: Church of Jesus Christ of Latter-day Saints, 1974 printing), 1:30; hereafter cited as D&C by section and verse.

43. Richard L. Bushman, "The Book of Mormon and the American Revolution," *BYU Studies* 17 (Autumn 1976): 3–20, shows how little the Book of Mormon reflected the elitist public literature of the day.

44. Donna Hill, *Joseph Smith: The First Mormon* (New York: Doubleday, 1977), 75–78. For Joseph Smith, Columbia Professor Charles Anthon's inability to read the language on the plates only fulfilled the prophecy of Isaiah 29:11 that the book was "sealed . . . to one that is learned."

45. Emily M. Austin, *Mormonism or, Life among the Mormons* (Madison, Wis.: M. J. Cantwell, 1882), 31–32. See also Nancy Towle, "Vicissitudes Illustrated" (1833), in *Among the Mormons*, 61.

46. Martin Harris, in *Among the Mormons*, 30; Austin, *Mormonism*, 53, 62.

47. Robert Frederick West, *Alexander Campbell and Natural Religion* (New Haven, Conn.: Yale University Press, 1948), 183–84.

48. Stone, *Matthias and His Impostures*, 313.

49. Parley P. Pratt in the late 1820s heard the restorationist message of the Christian Campbellites and was amazed. "But still one great link was wanting to complete the chain of the ancient order of things; and that was, the *authority* to minister in holy things—the apostleship, the power which should accompany the form." Mormonism gave him that link. Parley Parker Pratt, *Autobiography of Parley P. Pratt*, edited by his son Parley P. Pratt (1874; Salt Lake City: Deseret Book, 1985 printing), 32, 39, 43.

50. Stone, *Matthias and His Impostures*, 39. For a non-Mormon's sympathetic interpretation of Mormon culture, see Thomas F. O'Dea, *The Mormons* (Chicago: University of Chicago Press, 1957).

51. Joseph Smith, "The Wentworth Letter," in *Among the Mormons*, 16–17.

52. Tuveson, *Redeemer Nation*, 175; Klaus J. Hansen, *Quest for Empire: The Political Kingdom of God and the Council of Fifty in Mormon History* (Lincoln: University of Nebraska Press, 1974), 13–14; Harrison, *Second Coming*, 181.

53. Robert Flanders, "To Transform History: Early Mormon Culture and the Concept of Time and Space," *Church History* 40 (March 1971), 108–17.

Two Restoration Traditions: Mormons and Churches of Christ in the Nineteenth Century

Richard T. Hughes

In the spring of 1841, only eleven years after Joseph Smith and his colleagues had organized the Church of Jesus Christ of Latter-day Saints, four men met for debate at the Ridge Meetinghouse in the foothills of the Smoky Mountains, just east of Nashville in Smith County, Tennessee. Those four were John D. Lee and Alfonso Young, representing the Mormons, and Abraham Sallee and Samuel Dewhitt, representing the Churches of Christ. The second proposition for debate defined the critical difference between these two traditions. That proposition read: *Are the gifts and offices of the ancient Apostolic Church of Christ, necessary in this age, in order to constitute a perfect church or body?*[1] The Mormon preachers affirmed; the Church of Christ preachers denied.

In spite of their very fundamental differences, one finds in this debate two upstart Christian movements that, in many ways, shared far more in common with each other than they shared with any of the older denominations. Indeed, Mormons and Churches of Christ alike rejected the surrounding denominations that they viewed as "man-made churches" and based their authority instead on their respective understandings of the ancient church of the primitive era.

Historiographic Presuppositions

To come to terms with these two traditions in the nineteenth century, we first must assess the intellectual heart and soul of each, namely, their restorationist orientation. In this task, however, we will find little help from most historians who write of Mormons and/or Churches of Christ from the perspective of social history. While several social historians have produced some of the finest work in recent years dealing with these traditions, most of these same historians typically have not taken the restoration ideal seriously as a powerful, defining theme in its own right. Often, if they acknowledge this ideal at all, they implicitly—and sometimes explicitly—explain it chiefly as a function of various social factors without which, one presumes, the restoration sentiment would collapse and disappear.

Thus, Rhys Isaac, speaking of the profoundly restorationist Separate Baptists of Virginia, altogether missed the power of the restoration ideal and interpreted Separate Baptists simply "as a popular response to a mounting sense of social disorder." Likewise, Gordon Wood ascribed the popularity of several restorationist traditions in the new republic, including Baptists, "Christians," and Mormons, to "a social disintegration unequaled in American history."[2]

Again, Nathan O. Hatch explained the genius of both the "Christian" movement and the Latter-day Saints in terms of a populist, democratic revolt against their social betters. He viewed the "Christians" or Churches of Christ especially in terms of a "pervasive collapse of certainty within popular culture."[3] And Mormons he understood chiefly in terms of poverty and social estrangement. Thus, he wrote that "the *Book of Mormon* is a document of profound social protest, an impassioned manifesto by a hostile outsider against the smug complacency of those in power and the reality of social distinction based on wealth, class, and education. . . . The single most striking theme in the *Book of Mormon* is that it is the rich, the proud, and the learned who find themselves in the hands of an angry God."[4]

David Edwin Harrell, who has written eloquently and perceptively of the restoration theme within the history of Churches of Christ, has nonetheless explained that theme and its peculiar directions within this fellowship largely in terms of social forces. Thus, in attempting to explain the theological genius of Churches of Christ, he focused especially on the Civil War and argued that "Social force, class prejudice, sectional bitterness, and theologies shot through with economic presuppositions were the base upon which doctrinal debates were built." He therefore judged that the sectarian theology of the largely southern Churches of Christ in the years following the Civil War often amounted to little more than "a thinly veiled appeal for backing to the supporters of the lost cause."[5]

Such judgments, I suspect, may often reveal more about the materialistic and scientific biases of those of us who inhabit the modern academy than they do about the spiritual struggles and insights of ordinary Americans some two hundred years ago. To the modern mind, steeped in the conviction that material reality is the only reality there is and convinced that spiritual concerns are but reflections of more fundamental material issues, the nineteenth-century search for the Kingdom of God almost inevitably becomes a search for social and economic standing.

I would be the last to deny the substantial merit of these historians' arguments, so long as one does not imagine that they take us to the center of these traditions. Likewise, I would be the last to suggest that social and economic factors play no role in shaping religious perspectives, for they clearly do. Further, it is obvious that the methods and presuppositions of social history are especially productive when one studies movements that clearly are driven by social rather than by intellectual or spiritual concerns. But it may well be that the presuppositions and methods of social and economic history are ill-equipped to uncover in a meaningful way the driving power behind such religious movements as Mormonism and Churches of Christ.[6]

Indeed, the historian who instinctively places social and economic issues front and center will almost inevitably miss the genius of restorationist movements in America, for most restorationist movements in antebellum America struggled with a profoundly spiritual crisis that simply cannot be explained by social, economic, and military pressures. That spiritual crisis typically revolved around the quest for the true church, for the Kingdom of God, or for the sacred in the midst of a profane and fallen world. And that is a quest historians should take seriously in its own right.

One begins to grasp the immense dimensions of that spiritual crisis when one recalls how central had been the concern for the "true, apostolic church" among Puritans on both sides of the Atlantic.[7] Further, as Dan Vogel recently pointed out, this concern bedeviled a host of British and American Seekers from the seventeenth through the nineteenth centuries, including Lucy Smith, the mother of Joseph.[8] Moreover, this concern stood at the very center of American restorationist traditions such as Mormonism and Churches of Christ.

Religious pluralism in the United States, however, compounded the problem beyond measure for those who began with this concern. Joseph Smith tells us that he found himself "in darkness and confusion" over this very issue. Accordingly, the crisis that stood at the very heart and soul of the Mormon experience in the early nineteenth century was neither economic nor social but spiritual, captured in the question Joseph put to the Lord in the spring of 1820: "which of all the sects was right—and which I should join."[9] John D. Lee echoed this same concern in his debate with the Church of Christ preachers at the Ridge Meetinghouse in 1841. "We now see six hundred and sixty sects," he lamented, "all professing to be the Church of Christ. Each sect contending for its own infallibility—and each contending that every other one is wrong." Then Lee asked that simple but penetrating question that lay at the heart of the spiritual crisis that ultimately defined both Mormons and Churches of Christ in the nineteenth century: "Why is this?"[10]

This question, however, seems both quaint and irrelevant to most Americans in the waning years of the twentieth century when tolerance and pluralism have become an accepted way of life. Accordingly, historians, with little sense of the spiritual urgency of that question and schooled in the scientific methods and materialistic presuppositions of modern social history, often find lurking beneath such a question overtones of social and economic deprivation. Such presuppositions not only miss the spiritual core of many restorationist traditions but also tend toward a variety of conclusions unsupported by the evidence. Thus, several recent studies have simply overturned, in many instances, the conventional wisdom that Mormon primitivism reflects social and economic deprivation. These studies have pointed out that the Kirtland Saints in the mid-1830s stood far closer to the economic mainstream of their neighbors than generally has been supposed.[11] After exploring the evidence, Grant Underwood finally concluded that if Mormon millenarians wished to see the world destroyed, it was because "it had deprived them of spiritual, not economic, opportunity."[12]

All of this suggests that intellectual history, not social history, may be the path that will lead us into the center and core of most of the restorationist movements of the antebellum United States.

The Spiritual Core of the Restoration Vision

If we choose to follow that path, we quickly make several important and highly relevant discoveries. First, we learn that the restoration vision was in no way peculiar to antebellum America, much less to the process of democratization or to social marginality in the new republic. Instead, this vision in the modern world grew from the bias toward pure beginnings generated by the Christian Humanists in the Renaissance who despaired of the moral and intellectual corruption of their age. Through the influence of the universities, this theme quickly dominated the sixteenth-century Protestant Reformation, especially in Zurich. Reformed leaders like Heinrich Bullinger and Martin Bucer exerted powerful influences on the English to find the center and core of the Christian faith in the restoration theme. It is little wonder, then, that during the Marian Exile, the commitment to primitive Christianity became a defining characteristic of the Puritan party.[13]

From there, the restoration vision took two routes in its journey to America. The first route, important for Mormons, took the Puritans across the Atlantic to the New World, where the restoration vision became fundamental to their task. In New England, then, one finds the intellectual tradition that finally shaped a young seeker by the name of Joseph Smith. Indeed, the ways in which both Puritans and Mormons virtually reenacted the sacred dramas from both the Old and New Testaments were strikingly similar—and that was not coincidental.

The second route, important for Churches of Christ, was far more circuitous and involved an extensive layover in Scotland. John Knox carried the restoration vision from England to his native land, where it became central to Scottish and later to Scotch-Irish Presbyterianism. Thousands of those Presbyterians later settled in the middle colonies, in the American South, and in northern Appalachia.

Among them were the earliest leaders of Churches of Christ—Thomas and Alexander Campbell in northern Virginia and Barton W. Stone in Kentucky and Tennessee. Especially in the South, Baptists and Methodists also shared the vision of the primitive Christian faith. It is little wonder, then, that Churches of Christ found there an especially fertile soil for their appeal to "the ancient order of things."

Clearly, then, by the time of the American Revolution, restorationist thinking had become an important fixture in American intellectual life from New England to Georgia. Further, it proliferated and thrived, especially between the Revolution and the Civil War. There are several social and cultural factors that prompted this proliferation, and indeed, it is precisely in this context that the work of the social historians is particularly valuable.

First, there can be no doubt that the radically democratic and populist qualities of American life in the early nineteenth century rendered the restoration vision especially urgent. Here, the work of Nathan Hatch is particularly helpful. Indeed, if Americans had abolished the tyrannies of princes and kings in the political realm, Christian primitivists now sought to do the same in the religious realm by declaring the jurisdiction of Christian history null and void.

Second, the American political system seemed radically new, altogether discontinuous with any political system that had ever gone before. The Great Seal of the United States captured this perception with the phrase *novus ordo seclorum* (a "new order of the ages"). But if the American political system was new, it was also ancient, even primeval, descending, as Thomas Paine insisted, from God himself, at the beginning of the world.[14] In short, this new democratic order stood outside human history, derived from the primordium and now restored in the American millennial dawn. Such a powerful cultural myth would inevitably quicken and heighten the centuries-old restoration vision that a variety of English dissenters had brought to these shores.

But of all the social and cultural factors that facilitated the restoration vision, none was more important than the bewildering array of churches that competed on the American frontier. This was the problem that prompted Alexander Campbell to seek to unify American churches by pointing them to the apostolic faith. And this was the problem that prompted Joseph Smith to ask the Lord which of all the churches was His own. Indeed, this was the source of the spiritual crisis that demanded an answer. The solution came, both to Mormons and to Churches of Christ, in the venerable form of the restoration heritage, now quickened and heightened by democratic expectations and by the radical newness of the American experience.

Thus, Walter Scott, one of the early leaders of the Churches of Christ, was simply mistaken when he ascribed the success of the early Mormons to principles he thought the Mormons had learned from the Campbellites. Indeed, he charged that Sidney Rigdon "filched from us" the concept of immersion for the forgiveness of sins, thus accounting "for the success of the ministers of Mormonism."[15] This myth has been a powerful theme among Churches of Christ from the 1830s until the present day. Nothing, in fact, could have been further from the truth. Mormons succeeded for the same reason that Churches of Christ succeeded: each inherited a restoration vision, which spoke in powerful and urgent ways in the cultural climate of antebellum America.

Differences between Mormonism and Churches of Christ

Yet for all their similarities, Mormonism and Churches of Christ were radically different. The most striking difference obviously involved Mormonism's new scripture, the Book of Mormon, and its latter-day prophet, developments that Churches of Christ rejected. Indeed, those two developments have dominated anti-Mormon rhetoric on the part of Churches of Christ for more than a century and a half. Yet to focus on the Book of Mormon and the prophet obscures both the fundamental similarity and the fundamental differences between these two traditions.

The fundamental similarity that must be recognized is the profoundly restorationist quality of both churches. Churches of Christ, however, find it difficult to discern in Mormonism any restorationist dimension whatsoever. A restorationist, according to most in Churches of Christ, is one whose restorationist efforts concentrate exclusively on the New Testament. Thus, one of several who took me to task for involving Latter-day Saints in a "Christian Primitivism and Modernization" conference[16] complained, "I am asking you to explain what rationale was used in including the Mormons in a conference such as this. Is it your view . . . that the Mormon church is seeking to restore primitive Christianity?" That, of course, is precisely my view; but to understand the crucial difference between Churches of Christ and Latter-day Saints in this regard, we must resort once again to intellectual history.

Our beginning point is the recognition that the restoration vision is, in a fundamental sense, a vacuous vision. It is finally nothing more than a method, a perspective that looks backward to what one discerns as the first and therefore normative time. In this context, to say that one focuses on the Bible is hardly adequate, for there are many ways of reading and interpreting the Bible, each shaped and informed by one's intellectual presuppositions. This means that to understand Mormonism and Churches of Christ, we must first understand the intellectual traditions that shaped and molded these two movements. What we find, however, is not at all straightforward or simple to unravel, for both Mormonism and Churches of Christ drew on intellectual traditions that in many ways competed with one another and that pointed in very different directions.

Churches of Christ

In the case of Churches of Christ, the two competing traditions were apocalyptic revivalism and Enlightenment progressivism. The apocalyptic revivalistic perspective belonged to the earliest leader of the Churches of Christ, Barton W. Stone, who performed the bulk of his ministry in Kentucky and Tennessee. Stone's thought bore the indelible imprint of Calvinism on the one hand and revivalism on the other. Indeed, by virtue of his teachers, Stone stood squarely in the heritage of the Great Awakening and then, in 1801, emerged as a pivotal leader of the Great Kentucky Revival at Cane Ridge.

Revivalism and Calvinism together bred in Stone an apocalyptic outlook, which became the cornerstone of his life, often expressing itself in an explicitly premillennial eschatology and virtually defining his restoration vision.[17] Convinced that the Kingdom of God would finally triumph over all human governments and institutions, Stone and his considerable band of followers remained fundamentally pessimistic about human progress.

Further, they exhibited far less interest in the formal structures of the church than in the rule of God over human affairs. They therefore conceived of primitive Christianity chiefly in terms of biblical ethics and refused to serve in the military or vote, since all human governments, they imagined, stood squarely under the judgment of God. Time and again, they summoned one another to abandon themselves in the interest of the poor, to free their slaves, and to reject both fashion and wealth.

This apocalyptic/ethical emphasis, with its negative assessment of human progress and human culture, comprised the earliest understanding of primitive Christianity among Churches of Christ. Indeed, long before Churches of Christ in Kentucky and Tennessee had even heard of Alexander Campbell, Stone had mobilized some two hundred preachers and a membership of perhaps twenty thousand.[18] It is little wonder, then, that his pessimistic, apocalyptic orientation prevailed among many Churches of Christ—especially in their Middle Tennessee heartland—until World War I, when those churches embarked on the process of modernization and acculturation.[19]

In the meantime, however, the second intellectual tradition—that of the Enlightenment—increasingly came to dominate Churches of Christ, especially through the leadership of Alexander Campbell, whose restoration vision I choose to call *rational, progressive primitivism*. A Scotch-Irish immigrant who settled in Bethany, Virginia (later West Virginia), Campbell arguably became the most influential first-generation leader among Churches of Christ over the long term. Steeped in Lockean empiricism and the "Baconian" perspective of the Scottish "Common Sense" Realists, Campbell rejected Stone's apocalyptic outlook and embraced a robust, postmillennial optimism about the world in which he lived. Indeed, Campbell imagined that through a rational and scientific reconstruction of primitive Christianity, he and his movement would unify a fragmented Christendom and, as a consequence, raise the curtain on the millennial dawn.

In keeping with his rational vision, Campbell concerned himself not so much with biblical ethics as with the forms and structures of the ancient church. He viewed the New Testament almost as a divinely inspired, scientific text that supplied precise directions for admission into the church, for church organization, for proper worship, and for a variety of other details pertaining to church life. Further, just as a scientific experiment carried out in the same way under the same conditions would yield the same results time and again, in the same way, Campbell imagined, faithful attention to biblical directions would produce the same church today that it produced in the days of the apostles.

With such a scientific perspective and in the political climate of antebellum America, it was inevitable that Campbell's followers would increasingly view the New Testament as a veritable constitution for the church. Indeed, this was the central metaphor that the Church of Christ preachers used against their Mormon opponents in the Tennessee debate of 1841. Accordingly, Samuel Dewhitt argued that the New Testament "is *perfect,* and . . . all which is necessary to constitute a perfect church or body is obedience to that law. The Apostles were lawgivers acting by divine authority. The Elders were only executive officers whose business it was to see these laws enforced. If the laws, given by the Apostles, were sufficient to constitute churches in *their* day—we having the same laws, need nothing more."[20]

He continued: "When the framers of the Constitution of the United States of America had formed that instrument their work was accomplished, and that duty ceased and can never be resumed until the Constitution is abolished and it becomes necessary to make another. Now Jesus Christ and his Apostles made the laws for his government on earth, and the overseers of the Church now have nothing to do but to see those laws executed."[21] Here, in these statements, we find the very heart of the restorationist perspective, conformed to the contours of Enlightenment thought that dominated Churches of Christ under the influence of Alexander Campbell.

It is important to recognize, however, that both Abraham Sallee and Samuel Dewhitt began their careers as Stoneite preachers, only later embracing the more rational and more progressive primitivism of Alexander Campbell. This point is instructive, since Campbell's Enlightenment optimism eventually buried Stone's apocalyptic influence in virtually all quarters of the movement[22] and, in so doing, paved the way for extensive modernization and acculturation among Churches of Christ in the twentieth century.

Latter-day Saints

When one turns from Churches of Christ to the Latter-day Saints, one enters a radically different though no less restorationist world. The restoration vision among Latter-day Saints drew from both apocalypticism and the Enlightenment, and in this they shared with Churches of Christ. But Romanticism quickly emerged as the defining intellectual influence on Latter-day Saints, and this was the difference that made *all* the difference.

Though he never spelled it out, Harold Bloom hinted at this point when he praised the imaginative genius of Joseph Smith and consistently placed Smith in the company of Ralph Waldo Emerson. Indeed, Bloom confessed, "I myself can think of not another American, except for Emerson and Whitman, who so moves and alters my own imagination."[23]

While American Romanticism shared with the Enlightenment a profound celebration of human potential, it stood starkly opposed to the scientific constrictions and materialistic biases of Enlightenment ideology. Indeed, romantics of practically every stripe—including both spiritualists and transcendentalists—sought to shed their earthy constraints, to enlarge the boundaries of the human spirit, and to touch in some meaningful way that spiritual realm that transcended the merely rational structures of the here and now.

When we understand the genius of American Romanticism, we draw near to the genius of the restoration vision as articulated by Latter-day Saints. They cared little for the forms and structures of primitive Christianity, rationally perceived and reconstructed as ends in themselves. Instead, they hungered for communion with the divine, valuing forms and structures only insofar as they facilitated that communion. They longed for the heavens to open and for God himself to descend once again to humankind, just as he had done in the days of Adam, Moses, David, John, and Paul. Moreover, they were convinced that no restoration could occur apart from immediate, divine authority, which would come as contemporary and continuous revelation. Further, Romanticism served Mormons as the eclectic umbrella under which they drew from Judaism, Christianity, Masonry, and the American experience, fusing their selections into a grand perspective that pointed beyond itself and beyond all its singular components to the infinite that embraced them all.

Mormons, from their distinctly romantic perspective, occasionally lampooned and scorned the rationalist and materialist biases of their own age as grossly inferior to their own romantic vision. Perhaps no one in all of early Mormon literature more effectively captured this contrast than Parley P. Pratt:

> Witness the ancients conversing with the Great Jehovah, learning lessons from the angels, and receiving instructions by the Holy Ghost, . . . until at length the veil is taken off and they are permitted to gaze with wonder and admiration upon all things past and future; yea, even to soar aloft amid unnumbered worlds. . . . Compare this intelligence with the low smatterings of education and worldly wisdom that seem to satisfy the narrow mind of man in our generation; yea, behold the narrow minded, calculating, trading, overreaching penurious sycophant of the nineteenth century who dreams of nothing here

but how to increase his goods, or take advantage of his neighbor, and whose only religious exercises or duties consist of going to meeting, paying the priest his hire, or praying to his God, without expecting to be heard or answered, supposing that God has been deaf and dumb for many centuries, or altogether stupid and indifferent like himself.[24]

Indeed, for Latter-day Saints, the fall of the church from its perfect original occurred not in the loss of material forms and structures, which might now be rationally perceived and restored, but rather in the loss of divine revelation and the wonder-working power of the Holy Spirit. In the absence of immediate revelation, human beings had taken it upon themselves to interpret the Bible through human wisdom and human rationality, and to erect a myriad of denominations, which were miserable substitutes for the true church of Christ, founded on the wonder-working power of God. Even Campbell, Mormons claimed, for all his restorationist rhetoric, had acted without immediate, divine authority and therefore had founded yet another man-made sect.[25]

This was precisely the point, which the Mormons made in their debate with Abraham Sallee and Samuel Dewhitt in 1841. Thus, when John D. Lee inquired into the reasons for religious pluralism in the United States, he quickly answered his own question. "We answer," he affirmed, "because they have lost the spirit which was possessed by the primitive Christians, and they lack the gifts which were originally and still are necessary to create a perfect church or body." Alfonso Young concurred. "The Church was once perfect and united," he declared, "and why is it not so now? I answer, because the professed Christians of the present day deny spiritual influences. In short, because they neither possess nor seek the *gifts* which the apostles and primitive Christians possessed."[26]

In short, the debate at the Ridge Meetinghouse in 1841 featured two religious movements that shared a common restoration heritage but had conformed that heritage to radically different intellectual molds: the Enlightenment and Romanticism. Perhaps in no single exchange was the difference between these two molds more effectively illumined than in the exchange over the relation of faith to miracles. The Church of Christ preachers, following John Locke and Alexander Campbell, claimed that miracles functioned as empirical evidence, which in turn produced faith. John D. Lee, however, turned this conception virtually upside down. "I will not only contend that miracles do not produce faith," he argued, "but that faith is necessary for the production of miracles." Later in the debate, he elaborated on this very point: "if Christians of the present day would exercise the same measure of faith and obedience as did the primitive Christians, they would receive the same blessings which were enjoyed by the first disciples of Christianity. *They* spake with tongues and wrought miracles. And so would Christians of the present day if they possessed the same faith and exercised the same degree of obedience and holiness."[27]

When one discerns the power of the romantic vision in antebellum America, one is hardly surprised to learn that disillusioned members of the Church of Christ in Mentor, Ohio, abandoned Alexander Campbell for Joseph Smith and thereby comprised the first corps of converts to the Latter-day Saints. At one level, those conversions are easily understood, for the converts simply moved from one restoration tradition to another. Yet, at another level, the conversions are puzzling. Why the disillusionment with Campbell, and why the attraction to Joseph Smith? And even more puzzling, why would these converts begin with a church rooted in the Enlightenment, then abandon that church for one more in tune with the romantic mood of the time?

In effect, to ask that question is to answer it. Elizabeth Ann Whitney in many ways spoke for all the converts: "My husband, Newel K. Whitney, and myself were Campbellites. We had been baptized for the remission of our sins, and believed in the laying on of hands and the gifts of the spirit. But there was no one with authority to confer the Holy Ghost upon us." Or as John Murdock, an 1830 convert from Churches of Christ to the Latter-day Saints, reported, "Finding their principal leader, Alex Campbell, with many others, denying the gift and power of the Holy Ghost, I began to think of looking me a new home."[28] Indeed, Whitney and Murdock were essentially romantics whom Campbell initially attracted by virtue of his restoration vision. But the Enlightenment dimensions of Campbell's vision chilled them.

This romantic thirst for a direct encounter with the Spirit of God turned the restoration vision among Mormons in several directions, which the rationalistic Churches of Christ would find incomprehensible. First, it meant that Latter-day Saints viewed as normative the entire Bible, not the New Testament alone, for the entire Bible contained the records of a God who routinely broke into the orbit of human affairs to commune with humankind. For this reason, Latter-day Saints found no compelling reason to distinguish between Old and New Testaments, as did Alexander Campbell. For his part, on the other hand, Campbell thought simply absurd the Book of Mormon idea that "the Nephites, . . . were good christians, . . . preaching baptism and other christian usages hundreds of years before Jesus Christ was born!"[29]

Second, Latter-day Saints had little interest in mere obedience to biblical commands and replication of biblical data. Indeed, they never viewed the Bible as data at all. Instead, they viewed the Bible as story, as drama in which they themselves were participants along with Adam and Eve, Enoch, Abraham and Sarah, the patriarchs and their plural wives, Moses and Miriam, Paul and Dorcas. As Philip Barlow recently observed, Joseph Smith "placed himself *inside* the Bible story" and put "endings . . . on stories that had their beginnings in the scriptural text." Or, as Jan Shipps has pointed out, Mormon restorationism involved far more than mere replication of events of the biblical long ago. It involved instead a "recapitulation" or a virtual living out of those events in the here and now.[30] To the rational mind of an Alexander Campbell, such an agenda seemed sheer nonsense. But to one who approached the restoration task from the perspective of Romanticism, as many did in antebellum America, such an agenda was irresistibly compelling.

Third, the romantic dimensions of the Mormon restoration led Latter-day Saints to place enormously more importance on the experience of God than on the Bible itself. Indeed, for Mormons, the Bible simply pointed beyond itself to divine power and authority that not only manifested itself in the first age but continued to manifest itself in the here and now. This attitude clearly accounts for the fact that Joseph Smith felt comfortable revising the Bible—an act that would have horrified Alexander Campbell. The act of revision itself abundantly proclaims the romantic dimensions of the Mormon faith. As Barlow points out, Smith never sought to determine "the intent of the ancient authors." Instead, he "used the Bible less as a scholar than as a poet," or as Barlow finally concludes, as "a prophet."[31]

Fourth, if the heart of Churches of Christ was their appeal to a fixed and permanent first-century norm that would never change, the principle of continuing revelation meant that the heart of Latter-day Saints was change and adaptation, guided by a latter-day prophet. This difference had enormous implications for the way in which these two restoration traditions would adapt themselves to the modern age.

Finally, if Romanticism provided the intellectual underpinnings for the restoration vision of Latter-day Saints and thereby dramatically separated Mormonism from Churches of Christ, there is a sense in which the inner dynamics of Mormonism and Churches of Christ in the early nineteenth century were fundamentally similar. For if early Churches of Christ split on their assessment of human progress, so did the Latter-day Saints. Indeed, like the followers of Barton W. Stone, Latter-day Saints were profoundly apocalyptic and even premillennial and, therefore, deeply suspicious of human potential apart from the divine initiative.[32] This theme dovetailed nicely with their peculiar brand of Romanticism, for the Saints looked not to human reason but to the Spirit of God to open the heavens and speak to humankind, to establish God's people in Zion, to defeat their enemies, and to renew the earth.

Simultaneously, Latter-day Saints shared profoundly in the spirit of optimism that characterized Alexander Campbell—but with a difference. If Campbell exuded optimism over human progress and the larger culture, the optimism of the Saints pertained not so much to the larger culture as to the Saints themselves. We find this optimistic strand especially in Mormon soteriology, perhaps classically expressed in Joseph's King Follett Discourse of 1844: "God himself was once as we are now, and is an exalted man, and sits enthroned in yonder heavens!" Lorenzo Snow later summarized the point: "As man now is,

God once was; as God now is, man may become." Whatever one makes of this passage, it clearly expressed enormous confidence in human potential. Further, as the nineteenth century wound on, that confidence became more and more central to Mormon thought.[33]

There is no reason to ascribe this optimism to the Enlightenment, for it squares well with the exuberance over human potential that characterized many romantics. At the same time, however, Mormon optimism inevitably absorbed Enlightenment characteristics. Thus, an 1833 revelation proclaims: "The glory of God is intelligence" (D&C 93:36). By 1889, Orson F. Whitney combined that theme with the notion of eternal progression: "So says Joseph Smith. Intelligence is the glory of God. It is his superior intelligence that makes him God. The Gospel . . . is nothing more or less than a ladder of light, of intelligence, or principle, by which man, the child of god, may mount step by step to become eventually like his Father." Little wonder, then, he continued, that Brigham Young could praise education "in every useful branch of learning" and urge his people "to excel the nations of the earth in religion, science, and philosophy."[34]

The fundamental question regarding Latter-day Saints, therefore, has to do with the relation between the pessimistic, regressive strands of Mormon thought on the one hand and the optimistic, progressive strands of Mormon thought on the other. In the case of Churches of Christ, Enlightenment optimism finally triumphed over apocalyptic pessimism and thereby paved the way for full-scale modernization. My sense is that precisely the same pattern has prevailed among Latter-day Saints.

Conclusion

Finally, we conclude where we began, with a consideration of the scholars. Klaus Hansen's work is relevant here in a backhanded kind of way since his reading of Mormonism stands precisely opposite to my own. Indeed, Hansen found Mormonism essentially a reflection of Enlightenment optimism and order, radically opposed to Romanticism. He drew this conclusion because he interpreted the restoration vision as an Enlightenment phenomenon, virtually antagonistic to the romantic mind, and because he imagined that few in antebellum America had much interest in such a peculiar, restorationist worldview. Joseph had asked, "Which of all the sects was right?" However, "Most American Protestants had been sufficiently influenced by the romantic mood so that the question simply never occurred to them. Conversion was an individual experience that could happen to a Baptist as well as a Methodist or a Presbyterian. All of them had a pathway to heaven; as long as they got there, it did not matter very much how. In the literal mind of Joseph, however, there had to be one church that was objectively true."[35]

It is manifestly the case that Joseph searched for a church that was objectively true. But objectivity for Joseph—and for Latter-day Saints in antebellum America—was not a matter of rational and scientific precision, as it was for Alexander Campbell and the Churches of Christ and as it is for the modern mind today. It rather was a matter of the immediate power of God that carried for Latter-day Saints fully as much objective truth as the Bible carried for Alexander Campbell.

When all is said and done, that was the critical difference between Mormons and Churches of Christ in nineteenth-century America.

Notes

1. "Debate between [the] Mormons and Church of Christ," *Crihfield's Christian Family Library and Journal of Biblical Science* 1 (18 July 1842): 210. This debate appears in four issues: 18 and 25 July and 1 and 15 August 1842. Hereafter cited as "Debate" by page. I am grateful to Verne R. Lee of Loomis, California, for a typescript of John D. Lee, Diary, 28 and 29 May 1841. In the published debate, Lee's name appears as John DeLee.

2. Rhys Isaac, *The Transformation of Virginia, 1740–1790* (Chapel Hill: University of North Carolina Press, 1982), 168; Gordon S. Wood, "Evangelical America and Early Mormonism," *New York History* 61 (October 1980): 365.

3. Nathan O. Hatch, "The Christian Movement and the Demand for a Theology of the People," *Journal of American History* 67 (December 1980): 561, 546. See also Hatch, *The Democratization of American Christianity* (New Haven, Conn.: Yale University Press, 1989), 68–81.

4. Hatch, *Democratization of American Christianity,* 116–17.

5. David Edwin Harrell, *The Social Sources of Division in the Disciples of Christ, 1865–1900* (Athens, Ga.: Publishing Systems, 1973), ix; Harrell, "The Sectional Origins of the Churches of Christ," *Journal of Southern History* 30 (August 1964): 270.

6. Furthermore, some restorationist movements were virtually driven by social and economic considerations, for example, Elias Smith's "Christian" movement in New England in the early nineteenth century, as Nathan Hatch accurately points out. Hatch, however, is on far less solid ground in identifying the same social and economic motives as central to Alexander Campbell and Barton Stone, also leaders of nineteenth-century "Christian" movements. Hatch, *Democratization of American Christianity,* 68–81.

7. Theodore Dwight Bozeman, *To Live Ancient Lives: The Primitivist Dimension in Puritanism* (Chapel Hill: University of North Carolina/Institute of Early American History and Culture, 1988).

8. Dan Vogel, *Religious Seekers and the Advent of Mormonism* (Salt Lake City: Signature Books, 1988), 25–28.

9. Joseph Smith's "First Vision," in Joseph Smith Jr. et al., *History of the Church of Jesus Christ of Latter-day Saints,* ed. B. H. Roberts (Salt Lake City: Deseret News Press, 6 vols. published 1902–12, vol. 7 published 1932; reprinted by Deseret Book, 1976, paperback issue, 1978): 1:4–6.

10. "Debate," 238.

11. Mark R. Grandstaff and Milton V. Backman Jr., "The Social Origins of the Kirtland Mormons," *BYU Studies* 30 (Spring 1990): 47–66; Marvin S. Hill, C. Keith Rooker, and

Larry T. Wimmer, "The Kirtland Economy Revisited: A Market Critique of Sectarian Economics," *BYU Studies* 17 (Summer 1977): 391–472.

12. Grant Underwood, *The Millenarian World of Early Mormonism* (Urbana: University of Illinois Press, 1993), 3.

13. This history is spelled out in more detail in Richard T. Hughes, "Christian Primitivism as Perfectionism: From Anabaptists to Pentecostals," in *Reaching Beyond: Chapters in the History of Perfectionism*, ed. Stanley M. Burgess (Peabody, Mass.: Hendrickson Publishers, 1986), 213–23. The Marian Exiles were English Protestants who accepted self-imposed exile to the Continent to avoid persecution by Queen Mary, a zealous Catholic.

14. Philip S. Foner, ed., *The Complete Writings of Thomas Paine* (New York: Citadel Press, 1945), 1:376, 1:273–75.

15. W. Scott, "The Mormon Bible," *The Evangelist* 7 (1 July 1839): 160.

16. "Christian Primitivism and Modernization: Coming to Terms with Our Age" conference, Pepperdine University, Malibu, California, 6–9 June 1991.

17. By *apocalyptic* I do not mean *premillennial*. The apocalyptic view is the conviction that one belongs not to the kingdoms *of* this world but to the Kingdom *of* God, which finally will triumph over all human institutions. Premillennialism, on the other hand, points to how God's Kingdom will come, namely, through the premillennial Second Coming of Jesus Christ. As it turns out, Stone was both apocalyptic and premillennial in his outlook, but his apocalyptic perspective was the fundamental term in his thought.

18. R. I. Roberts, "Early Tennessee and Kentucky Preachers," photocopy of typescript in my possession.

19. Richard T. Hughes, "The Apocalyptic Origins of Churches of Christ and the Triumph of Modernism," *Religion and American Culture: A Journal of Interpretation* 2 (Summer 1992): 181–214.

20. "Debate," 236–37.

21. Ibid., 237.

22. Anthony L. Dunnavant, ed., *Cane Ridge in Context: Perspectives on Barton W. Stone and the Revival* (Nashville, Tenn.: Disciples of Christ Historical Society, 1992).

23. Harold Bloom, *The American Religion: The Emergence of the Post-Christian Nation* (New York: Simon and Schuster, 1992), 102, 127.

24. Parley P. Pratt, *A Voice of Warning* (1837; reprint, Salt Lake City: Deseret Book, 1978), 88.

25. Parley P. Pratt, "Grapes from Thorns, and Figs from Thistles," reprinted from *Millennial Star* in *Writings of Parley Parker Pratt*, ed. Parker Pratt Robison (Salt Lake City: Parker Pratt Robison, 1952), 303.

26. "Debate," 238, 236.

27. Ibid., 217, 236.

28. Edward W. Tullidge, *The Women of Mormondom* (New York: Tullidge and Crandall, 1877), 41–42; John Murdock, "Abridged Record of the Life of John Murdock, Taken from His Journals by Himself," 4–10, typescript copy courtesy of Milton V. Backman.

29. Alexander Campbell, "Delusions," *Millennial Harbinger* 2 (7 February 1831): 87.

30. Philip L. Barlow, *Mormons and the Bible: The Place of the Latter-day Saints in American Religion* (New York: Oxford University Press, 1991), 21; Jan Shipps, *Mormonism: The Story of a New Religious Tradition* (Urbana: University of Illinois Press, 1985), 53–65.

31. Barlow, *Mormons and the Bible,* 73; see also p. 70.

32. Underwood, *The Millenarian World of Early Mormonism.*

33. See, for example, O. Kendall White Jr., *Mormon Neo-Orthodoxy: A Crisis Theology* (Salt Lake City: Signature Books, 1987), esp. chap. 3.

34. Quoted in ibid., 83, 79.

35. Klaus J. Hansen, *Mormonism and the American Experience* (Chicago: University of Chicago Press, 1981), 70–71.

CHAPTER 3

The Book of Mormon
in a Biblical Culture

Timothy L. Smith

The study of the religion of the earliest Latter-day Saints is only now being freed, I think, from the distortions that Alice Felt Tyler and Whitney R. Cross imposed on it nearly forty years ago. Tyler, perhaps remembering the lectures of Arthur M. Schlesinger Sr. on new American religious movements, set Mormons alongside Shakers, Adventists, and Spiritualists and stressed the peculiarly American dimensions of all four movements. Professor Cross, following geographical clues that, with Mario S. De Pillis, I believe are the wrong ones, spotted Wesleyan Methodists also in the weed patch of "ultraist" movements, which he thought grew on the ash heaps of burnt-out Puritanism in central New York.[1] David Brion Davis and others, however, have argued that Joseph Smith's religion stemmed from the persistence rather than the decay of Puritanism. With Klaus Hansen, these more recent students of the subject perceive millennialism to have been a dominant strain in the New England heritage, and they attributed to the sense of chosenness and destiny that it nurtured the Protestant and Anglo-Saxon Calvinism that they thought were characteristic of both Mormonism and mid-nineteenth-century nationalism.[2]

Linking Mormon history thus to normative rather than offbeat Protestantism was a step forward, certainly. But I have a quite different view of what was normative in the regions where the movement took root—Vermont, the New York lake country, the Western Reserve of Ohio, southeastern Pennsylvania, and the West Midlands of England. In all these places, the faith of the Latter-day Saints won converts who cared very little for Yankee Puritanism whether in the style of John Cotton, Jonathan Edwards, or Samuel Hopkins. Rather, in both America and England, the biblical culture of remarkably diverse free-church Protestantism nourished them.[3]

The religious dialogues that shaped Joseph Smith's youthful perceptions and dominated the imaginations of those first converted to his beliefs took place

among what were to become the most numerous American denominations—
Methodists, Baptists, Disciples of Christ, and Presbyterians. All of these, and not
simply the fringe sects, were deeply engaged in revivals aimed at securing the
conversion of the unawakened who were the majority in every locality. All participated in the spreading debates over free will, universal redemption, original
sin, moral perfection, the nature and nearness of the millennium, and the
recovery in the last days of primitive Christianity through the outpouring of the
Holy Spirit.

In those debates, each group appealed directly to the authority of the Bible.
Usually they did so in such a manner as not to deny the long tradition of scriptural interpretation each had inherited. But continuous argument nurtured the
conviction among both preachers and hearers that the plain teachings of the
New Testament offered sufficient guidance for all aspects of Christian faith and
doctrine. Moreover, all sects were caught in the tendency of religious debate to
focus the attention of each one on what seemed unique to itself, rather than
what it shared with others.

These governing preoccupations and tendencies toward biblicism and sectarianism characterized the first Latter-day Saints as well, though the appearance
of an additional set of Scriptures, whose publication is being celebrated this
year, kept both contemporaries and modern students from realizing that was
the case.

While still residing in Vermont, the parents and kinsfolk of Joseph Smith
were deeply affected by the appeals that various sects made on behalf of their
special interpretations of Scripture. Donna Hill has carefully summarized the
available information in her recent biography.[4] The consistent or inconsistent
Calvinism of the Congregationalist churches and their established membership
in the larger villages held little interest for socially marginal families such as the
Smiths. Whenever such families did turn to religion, they were more likely to
respond to Methodist affirmations of free grace, free will, and Christian perfection; to the Universalist insistence that a God of justice and love must save all
human beings from eternal punishment; or to the Baptist declaration that none
would experience the remission of sins unless faith and repentance were joined
in baptism by immersion. All these shared the speculations about the ancient
and the future history of Indians and Jews that were springing up in Vermont,
as throughout the Christian world, during these years.[5]

Joseph Smith Sr., during a period of deep religious concern, rejected the suggestion of his wife, Lucy, that he become a Methodist, awaiting, he said, some resolution of the disagreements over the meanings of Scripture advanced to sustain
contradictory doctrines.[6] After grueling misfortune removed the family to the
Lake Canandaigua country, both the parents and the teenaged children experienced in Methodist and Presbyterian revival meetings the same tensions. The
chief question then was whether and how fully to follow the Presbyterians, who

were the social and religious elite of the community, in the face of Methodist moral and spiritual fervor. Whatever the attractions of each sect, both seemed to leave important issues of conscience and Scripture unresolved.[7]

Crucial among these issues was the extent and nature of the authority of the Bible. This was especially important in America, where both civil and ecclesiastical government had broken with the forms of the past and declared allegiance to constitutions of the people's composition. Equally crucial to individuals, however, was the validity and assurance of their hope of salvation, in this life and in the world to come. I believe the latter concern chiefly explains the willingness of so many to commit themselves to religious movements that called for a radical restructuring of church and society on models they thought were drawn from the one New Testament church of primitive Christianity.[8]

The two most notable of such movements were the Disciples of Christ, whose frame of government affirmed the independence of congregations and pastors but bound both to Alexander Campbell's understanding of Scripture,[9] and the Church of Jesus Christ of Latter-day Saints, whose government subjected its followers to awesome discipline and understood even groups of congregations to comprise only a stake for the tabernacle of God. The two movements drew together in differing patterns the central religious ideas that permeated the preaching of Methodists, Baptists, and Presbyterians and of the gadflies to all of them, the Universalists.

One does not need, therefore, to look beyond the established revivalistic sects to discover why the first Mormon elders won an immediate hearing for their sacred book. Its firm call for personal righteousness, for obedience to the moral demands of the Old Covenant through faith in the New, was by 1830 a dominant motif in all denominations. The experience of the remission of sins and an assurance of salvation, sustained by communal ritual as well as by an inward "witness of the Spirit," as the Methodists called it, were coveted goals in all evangelical witness.[10] And its doctrine of the promise of the Holy Spirit to all believers had long been central to the preaching of John Wesley and his successors.[11] Moreover, Mormons and Disciples added to such widely shared beliefs strong convictions about the destiny of Christians and Jews in the last days. In the antithetical moods of either apocalyptic or millennial expectation, these convictions seem to have swept through both English and American revivalistic culture in, astonishingly, the same five years—from 1825 to 1830. Mormon converts, therefore, like the Millerites a few years later, found in the eschatology they embraced answers to questions that not only they but many other Protestants had begun insistently to ask about the Second Coming.[12]

This was as true in Preston and its surrounding towns in the English West Midlands as in central New York. Heber C. Kimball's *Journal* reveals the flowering of biblical study and speculation, which had in similar fashion prepared the soil for the early Mormon witness there. He found at Preston and the surrounding towns Baptist, Methodist, and Independent (presumably "Congregationalist") ministers and an Anglican pastor or two who had combined their long-standing emphasis on a life-transforming experience of the Holy Spirit with a more recent interest in the miraculous gifts of the Spirit that British millenarians thought would accompany the end of the age. The most forbidding barrier to these ministers was the demand that they accept the Baptist belief, now fortified by the Book of Mormon, that the remission of sins required submission to the rite of immersion. Several clergymen who were not able to cross that threshold nevertheless testified to their congregations that the teachings of the Saints "were the same principles as taught by the apostles in ancient days" and urged their people to receive them.[13]

For Joseph Smith and his early followers, then, the Book of Mormon not only resolved doubts about the general authority of Scripture but also gave clear direction on issues that, in sectarian argument, had been decreed crucial to faith and salvation. These included baptism by immersion;[14] the promise that all modern believers and not simply those of the apostolic age may be "filled with the Holy Ghost" and made pure in heart;[15] universal redemption, that is, salvation by a free response to free grace, in opposition to the Calvinist belief in decrees of predestination;[16] and the necessity of righteousness, of obedience and good works, as both the moral responsibility of human beings and the fruit of the experience of remission of sins.[17]

The book also affirmed the historical veracity of the Hebrew and Christian Scriptures by accounts of the Jewish ancestors of the American Indians that plausibly supplemented biblical history. It recapitulated long sections of the prophecies of Isaiah and Ezekiel, the four Gospels, and the Acts of the Apostles.[18] It defined the membership and described in detail the priesthood and the hierarchy of offices of the true church of Jesus Christ, to be reconstituted in the last days.[19] And it renewed the biblical image of a God who, in apocalyptic judgment, would reward the righteousness of the Saints and destroy their opposers at the Second Coming of Christ. These teachings about the apocalypse identified as separate entities the two Jerusalems of prophecy, the old and the new, one to which Jews and the other to which believing Gentiles should gather. Each would enthrone the returning Jesus as Messiah and King, after which he would launch his millennial reign on earth.[20] Finally, the volume both exhibited and promised the raising up in the latter days of a prophet who would infallibly interpret both old and new Scriptures, give divine direction to the restored church, and confer the baptism and the gifts of the Holy Spirit upon the Saints.[21]

Several scholars have noted that many doctrines peculiar to the Latter-day Saints, particularly in the years since their settlement in Utah, rest not upon the Book of Mormon but upon the revelations to Joseph Smith that took place after the publication of that volume. Accounts by believers, apostates, and outsiders during the first decade or so of the Church's witness in America and England convince me that the movement would never have gotten off the ground if these unique teachings had constituted its major appeal. The persuasive power of both the new Scriptures and of the missionaries who proclaimed and expounded them lay in their confident testimony to beliefs that were central to the biblical culture of the evangelical Protestant sects in both Jacksonian America and early Victorian England.[22] These beliefs seem in the early years, at least, to have also dominated the thought and devotion of the Saints themselves, even when debates with outsiders revolved around their special doctrines of continuing revelation, the gathering of Jews and Saints in the two Jerusalems, and the material nature of all reality, whether human or divine.

Viewed in this light, the Book of Mormon was not, as Parley Pratt pointed out to his English readers, "calculated to displace or do away with the Bible."[23] The uncertainties about the Bible that had prompted the various sects "to contend with one another from age to age, respecting the meaning of its contents," Pratt wrote, stemmed from two errors: the widespread beliefs that "direct inspiration by the Holy Ghost was not intended for all ages of the Church," and that, in the absence of such inspiration, the various sects had no choice but "to institute their own opinions, traditions, and commandments." Concerning the "gathering" of the Jews promised in Jeremiah 16, he noted that "*uninspired* men were not to send *uninspired* missionaries to teach Israel several hundred different doctrines and opinions of men, and to tell them they suppose the time has about arrived for them to gather; but the God of heaven is to call men by actual revelation, direct from heaven, and to tell them who Israel is; who the Indians of America are, if they should be of Israel; and also where the ten tribes are, and all the scattered remnant of that long lost people. He it is who is to give them their errand and mission, and to clothe them with power from on high to execute the great work." Appealing thus to the Bible, Pratt laid the basis for his later apology for the revelations of Joseph Smith, scorning "the whole train of modern divines" who profess "no revelation, later than the Bible, and no direct inspiration, or supernatural gift of the Spirit."[24] The first impact of the Book of Mormon upon readers thus seems in many cases, as in those of Pratt and Newel Knight, to have been to confirm or authenticate their belief in the old Scriptures.[25]

And why not? The idea of making the Bible alone the foundation of Christian faith had become an obsession on the strength of a larger affirmation, stemming from the Protestant Reformation but reaching the popular level only in the previous century, that Scripture contained all truth necessary to salvation and constituted, therefore, "a sufficient rule of faith and practice." In America such a declaration had special force, given the newness of social, political, and ecclesiastical structures and a culture in which the future loomed larger than the past.[26]

To declare in the nineteenth century that the Bible was the sole ground of religious authority, however, raised profound questions. Fifteen hundred years had passed since the Council of Nicaea had defined the canon, choosing its contents from among a wider cluster of writings, most of which were even then of very ancient origin. The world of Jews and Egyptians, of Jerubbaal and Babylon, and of chariots and evening sacrifices was far removed indeed from frontiersmen and Indians, parliaments and political parties, and canals and camp meetings. Many a village skeptic found it difficult to accept a book about such a world as the sole foundation of faith. Some of these, while less sophisticated than Thomas Jefferson, opted for only the ethical authority of the teachings of Jesus—partly, I think, because they seemed less distant in both time and cultural space. Meanwhile, deacons, elders, and some evangelical pastors, unable thus to dismember the Scriptures, struggled with grave temptations to doubt the truth and relevance of large portions of the book upon which they as well as the Christians around them must stake all of life.[27] Such a Bible needed all the help it could get.

Even the rumors that preceded the publication of the Book of Mormon anticipated that it would affirm the truth of biblical history. "It is written on a kind of gold leaf," a farmer from Covert, New York, had heard. "It is the same that ours is" except that "It speaks of the Millenniam day and tells when it is a going to take place and it tells that the man that is to find this bible his name is Joseph and his father's name is Joseph."[28] When such persons read the volume it unfolded, in the cadences and metaphors of the King James Bible as well as in narratives reminiscent of that book's ancient stories, nearly a thousand years of the history of a family of Jews and their vast progeny in America. The details of the histories were radically different, but they fit together wondrously. And the theology, the moral strictures, the story of Jesus, the promise of salvation, and the descriptions of the last days were remarkably similar. In the mouth of two witnesses, the Bible and the Book of Mormon, many found the truth confirmed, just as the prophecy of Nephi had predicted (1 Ne. 13:35–42, esp. 40–41; 2 Ne. 29:3–14, esp. 8).

They also found that the new Scriptures leaned heavily toward Methodist and Disciples theology, at the expense of the Calvinist system long dominant in America. This fact reminds us of Joseph Smith's prior experiences in Methodist revivals and of the significant impact of early Mormon witnesses upon Methodists, not only in western New York and Ohio but in England as well. Early leaders with Methodist backgrounds included the Prophet's wife, Emma Hale Smith; Joseph Young, brother of Brigham Young; Hosea Stout; and, during the period of his apostasy in the 1840s, Oliver Cowdery.[29] The conversions and key roles of the brothers Parley and Orson Pratt, who had passed from Baptist to Disciples affiliation, and of Sidney Rigdon, pastor of a radical Disciples community in Kirtland, demonstrate the appeal of the Book of Mormon to the followers of Alexander Campbell as well. Its union of moralism with universal redemption and its insistence on the linkage between the Baptist rite of immersion and remission of sins resembled Campbell's. And its emphasis on the immediate availability of the baptism of the Holy Spirit promised divine power to make that linkage an ethical and permanent one.[30]

In five important ways, the Book of Mormon strengthened the authority of Scripture in the minds of all who listened seriously to the elders who expounded it, whether or not they accepted the new faith.

First in importance, I think, was the volume's powerful affirmation that the Christian religion was grounded upon both the Old and New Testaments—this in an age when evangelical Protestants and particularly Campbell's Disciples of Christ were tending to take seriously only the New Testament. Non-Mormon millenarian doctrine linked Daniel and the book of Revelation, thus contributing to the same end. But the witness of the Saints affirmed what recent biblical scholarship is now making plain—the continuity also of the theology, ethics, and spirituality that the Hebrew and Christian Scriptures proclaimed. The Book of Mormon accomplishes this by the repeated appearance in passages of the Nephite and Lamanite prophets (who stood in the tradition of Old Testament religion) of concepts and terminology long familiar to nineteenth-century readers in the key salvation promises of the New Testament.[31]

In Joseph Smith's text, the prophet Nephi recited the words of ancient Isaiah in a way that left unquestionable the identity of the Messiah; he was Jesus of Nazareth, the suffering servant (2 Ne. 10:1–16, 25:7–30, 26:1–3, 12; cf. Mosiah 13:11–15:11). The third book of Nephi revealed that after his resurrection Jesus had appeared to those in the New World who had been loyal to the Hebrew covenant that their prophets had renewed after they settled in North America. In that appearance, the risen Lord had delivered exactly the same messages of redemption, faith, and a new life of righteousness through the Holy Spirit that the New Testament had attributed to him during his earthly ministry in Palestine. And he had proclaimed a new Kingdom, whose government, ethic, and source of authority was at once prophetic and pentecostal, thoroughly Hebraic and, therefore, fully Christian (3 Ne. 11–26).

If radical Protestantism in America has tended toward historylessness[32] (a point I gravely question), Joseph Smith's recovery and reaffirmation of the unity of the religion of the Old and the New Testaments—in separate patterns molded to fit an Old World and a New—ran dramatically in the opposite direction. He and his missionary elders linked prophecy to history, memory to hope, in a narrative of the past whose every incident pointed to the unfolding of an earthly future hallowed by the presence of the Lord.[33]

The Book of Mormon also reinforced the ecumenical vision of biblical religion, grounded in the conviction of a common humanity that the stories of the creation and of Noah declare and in God's promise to Abraham that in his seed all peoples of the earth should be blessed (Gen. 17:1–8, 22:17–18; 1 Ne. 15:18, 17:35; 2 Ne. 29:1–14). In a century when romantic nationalism, in America as elsewhere, rushed toward racism, the testimony of the Latter-day Saints and of their sacred book declared that the American Indians had always been included among God's chosen people and that the Jews always would be. In the last days the Jews would be gathered by God's providence to Old Jerusalem and, after being miraculously rescued from otherwise certain destruction in the wars of Gog and Magog, would both acclaim their savior as Messiah and discover that he was in fact Jesus of Nazareth.[34] Meanwhile, the descendants of the lost tribes of Israel, wherever they might be, would find their way back to God's favor and blessing, and those Gentiles who embraced the Mormon proclamation of universal redemption would gather with the Saints of Zion to await their equal inheritance of the glorious promises made to God's chosen (3 Ne. 20:12–46, 21:22–29; Ether 18:8–12).

Insofar as puritan millennialism may have inspired a chauvinistic view of America's Anglo-Saxon destiny (a point I also gravely doubt),[35] the image of the future in the Book of Mormon was a wholly opposite one. Its teachings, and the early revelations of Joseph Smith as well, sustained the ecumenical vision that had flowered among eighteenth-century British evangelicals, both in and outside the established church, and in Pietism, Puritanism, and the peace churches on both sides of the Atlantic. That vision had in fact awakened the modern missionary movement.[36] The Mormon prophet's understanding of a worldwide recruitment of the faithful, looking always to Zion and gathering there, took off where John Wesley's "world parish" had left off.

True, the Saints expected only a peculiarly obedient fraction of the Gentiles to heed the call. Their faith was on that account quintessentially countercultural. Neither in its outer orbit of universalism, therefore, nor in its inner circle of sectarianism could the Mormon scenario of the future fit the chauvinistic Americanism that recent commentators have assigned to mid-nineteenth-century millennialism. But no matter. The broad visions of the Methodist bishops, of the American Board of Commissioners for Foreign Missions, and of the offspring of that other Zion in Missouri—the German Lutheran one—will not fit the assigned role very well either.[37] Indeed, the Old Testament's picture of the tragedy of ancient Israel makes it difficult for any biblical ideology to exalt a nation at the expense of justice, mercy, and walking humbly before God. And the Saints had been given, in the account of the destruction of the Nephites that explained the existence of the golden plates, a second tragic story to underline the point (Morm. 6:1–22, 8:1–16). God's advocacy of the cause of any people requires and depends upon their advocacy of the cause of all. Chauvinism, whether ethnic or national, was not for them an option.

The Mormon Scriptures, and early Mormon preaching, also sustained the call to ethical righteousness that seemed to a widening circle of evangelicals the central theme of the Old and New Testaments.[38] The biblical bond linking holiness to hope for both individual and social salvation inspired revivalist preaching in America from the early 1820s until the Civil War. Certainly Methodists had no corner on that insight. The Unitarian challenge to the Congregationalist establishment had been from the outset a firmly ethical one. So was the challenge to the Old Calvinism that Lyman Beecher mounted by his revivals in Connecticut and that Charles G. Finney began in 1828 in central New York, eventually bringing it, with Beecher's reluctant consent, to Boston.[39] William Ellery Channing is reported to have told a parishioner, after Finney's revival in Boston in 1841, that if he were an evangelical he would preach exactly as the evangelist did because the doctrine of sanctification is what the Bible teaches.[40] By that time, Alexander Campbell's moralism had for two decades reflected his generation's perception of the New Testament emphasis upon holy living.[41]

The ethical teachings of the Book of Mormon, identical to those in the Bible, and the reiteration of the moral law in an early revelation at Kirtland[42] reinforced this growing evangelical emphasis on righteousness by faith. The buried plates had yielded a lengthy replication of many of the most ethical passages of Isaiah's prophecy (2 Ne. 15:7–30; 2 Ne. 16:1–13 replicates Isa. 6). Ancient Nephites who heeded the word of the prophets looked forward to Christ, the "Son of righteousness" who, when he appeared, called them to obey all the teachings of the Sermon on the Mount (2 Ne. 26:8–9, 31:9–10; 3 Ne. 12:3–14:27). The golden age of the Nephite-Lamanite theocracy that followed knew neither poverty nor slavery, thievery nor murder (4 Ne. 1:16–17). By moral standards common to both the old and new Scriptures the Latter-day Saints must live in purity of heart; Zion would be glorious because of holiness (Jacob 3:2–3; Moro. 10:31–33). Moreover, as in the Old and New Testaments but with more frequent and explicit use of pentecostal imagery, the Book of Mormon declared such righteousness to depend upon the power of God's active grace, conferred in "the baptism of fire and of the Holy Ghost" (2 Ne. 31:13–14; cf. 2 Ne. 12:1–2; Alma 13:10–13; 3 Ne. 19:9–14).

The evidence that the elders and early apostles made these calls to holiness a central part of their witness is overwhelming.[43] And the earliest informed critics of the Kirtland community acknowledged it. "I saw nothing indecorous," feminine evangelist Nancy Towle wrote of her visit there in September 1831, "nor had I an apprehension of anything of the kind."[44] Ezra Booth, a Methodist both before and after what he called his months of "delusion" as a Mormon convert, criticized at length Joseph Smith's materialism, his autocratic rule and his claims to miraculous gifts, and noted what he thought was the failure of some of the prophet's revelations to fit the subsequent facts. But Booth had no complaint at all of Smith's doctrine of radical obedience to biblical commandments.[45] A Presbyterian observer from Portage County wryly accredited to the emphasis on holiness the conversions of so many Disciples, Universalists, and Methodists, as well as some Baptists and Presbyterians. "They have been down through the ice in the mill-pond and their sins are all washed away," he wrote, "and they are clothed with self-righteousness as with a garment."[46] What critics did complain about was the economic radicalism implicit in the explicitly biblical "Law of Consecration," proclaimed on 9 February 1831, and the extent to which the Prophet's "Word of Wisdom," published in February 1833, outdistanced the evangelicals who had recently adopted total abstinence from alcoholic beverages by requiring Saints to forgo tobacco, coffee, and tea as well.[47]

Instructed in such a tradition, Heber C. Kimball presented the Word of Wisdom to several hundred new converts in England on his first Christmas there, having taught it during the previous months, as he wrote a bit later, "more by example than precept."[48] The subsequent friendliness of numerous local temperance societies and the willingness of so many English Methodists to embrace Mormon millenarianism would not have been possible in the absence of this rigorous call to righteousness.[49]

A bit later Orson Pratt demanded that the Saints in England exercise "Strictness of discipline in plucking off dead branches . . . laying the axe at the very root of every species of wickedness." Not only elders but members of the Twelve and if necessary the president of the Church in Britain must be "dealt with strictly by the law of God," if found to "teach or practice any iniquity," particularly that of adultery. Such strictness, he thought, had the tendency to build up the weak and enlighten the honest investigator.[50] The outrageous Gentile perception of Mormons as polygamous libertines, implanted deeply in popular consciousness later by the debates over the admission of Utah to the Union, grossly belies the prim moralism of the early Saints.

The crisis that the revelation concerning plural marriage brought on for Joseph Smith in Nauvoo stemmed not only from his perception that it contradicted the painfully explicit teachings of the Book of Mormon and earlier revelations on the subject recorded in his Doctrine and Covenants (Jacob 2:23–33, 3:5; D&C 19:25, 63:14–18). It also contradicted the recent actions that he and the other Mormon leaders had taken, in the name of those precepts and out of respect for the biblical sensibilities of all the Saints, to discipline elders who had taught or practiced the contrary.[51] The biblical sensibilities in the long run prevailed. This was due partly, I suppose, to the sturdy moralism that shines through the last paragraph of the prophet's February 1842 letter to John Wentworth, which in the twentieth century has passed for the creed of the Latter-day Saints. Its second and third articles read: "We believe that men will be punished for their own sins and not for Adam's transgression. We believe that through the atonement of Christ all mankind may be saved by obedience to the laws and ordinances of the Gospel."[52]

Turning now to another facet of the question, the Book of Mormon also helped bring to fruition the movement, rooted in Puritan, Pietist, Quaker, and Wesleyan experience, to restore to prominence the doctrine of the presence of the Holy Spirit in the lives of God's people and in the testimony of his witnesses. That the prophecy of Isaiah and Acts were so central in the Book of Mormon encouraged this result. And the surge of interest in the promise of the outpouring of the Spirit in the last days that had recently permeated Protestant culture, serving as a rationale for both revivalism and millennialism, sustained it.[53]

In Charles G. Finney's case, as I have recently tried to show more clearly, the promise of the Holy Spirit provided crucial resolution of the inadequacies he saw in the lives of his converts. He had preached the law of radical love in the unfounded hope that if sinners truly repented and believed, they would be able to love God supremely and keep that law. Converts who proved unable to overcome temptation forced him to reconsider the doctrine of sanctification. In the winter and spring of 1839, Finney worked his way through the Bible, pursuing the links between the promise of the New Covenant, made through Jeremiah and Ezekiel, and the fulfillment of that "promise of the Father," as Jesus had called it, in the pouring out of the Holy Spirit at Pentecost.[54]

To be sure, the interpretation of the events of Pentecost and the development of charismatic doctrine among Latter-day Saints proceeded in a different direction. Nevertheless, the testimony of both inside and outside observers indicates that in the early years, something akin to modern pentecostal phenomena took place among at least the inner circle of the Saints, despite its confinement in most instances to the ceremony in which elders by the "laying on of hands" formally conferred the gift of the Holy Spirit upon baptized believers.[55]

I wish to stress here, however, the impact upon the use of Scripture by other Christians of the constant appeal by Mormon apologists to the presence of the Holy Spirit in their community. After 1830, evangelicals in several traditions greatly expanded their use of the language of Pentecost to declare the power of God to be at work in the present world. John Wesley, of course, had carefully distinguished for his followers what he called the "extraordinary" gifts of the Spirit—languages and their interpretation, healing and other miracles—from the "ordinary" one of hallowing, or sanctifying, grace. The latter, he proclaimed, was available to all Christians in all ages.[56] But until the mid-1830s, at the earliest, American and English Methodists active in the promotion of Christian perfection used only occasionally, and with some reluctance, John Fletcher's language calling for a pentecostal baptism of the Spirit. After Finney's lectures of 1839 appeared, that reluctance seems to have vanished.[57] Charles Simeon, Cambridge pastor and chief inspiration to the evangelicals in the Church of England, had visited John Fletcher in his youth but seems to have first preached earnestly on the doctrine of the Holy Spirit in the early 1830s. The widespread use of pentecostal rhetoric did not take place in England, therefore, until the decade of the 1840s.[58] When Charles G. Finney and Phoebe Palmer arrived in the 1850s, however, they found that rhetoric quite acceptable there.[59] In America, meanwhile, Protestant preachers of all sorts had long since fulfilled Ralph Waldo Emerson's hope that they might be bards of the Holy Ghost.[60] In 1857 Henry Clay Fish, Baptist pastor in Newark, won a well-advertised national prize for his essay, "Primitive Piety Revived," calling for a rebirth of pentecostal power in the American evangelical churches.[61] The Latter-day Saints thus helped to revitalize a literal expectation of the fulfillment of biblical promises that had long been explained away.

In similar but even grander fashion, the Book of Mormon shared as well in what believers thought was the restoration of Christian expectations of the literal fulfillment of prophecies of the last days. It offered supporting testimony on behalf of the apocalyptic prophecies of Daniel and Revelation and defined more precisely than the Bible did what their mysterious passages might mean. To be sure, during the succeeding years of Adventist excitement, Smith and the Mormon evangelists in England and America resisted the detailed speculations about the date of Christ's return that obsessed the Millerites. The reason was not a preference for place over time, I think, but the undeniably biblical doctrine that the Jews must return to Jerusalem in the last days. No wonder Parley Pratt, when he got to England, read with such keen interest the works of the "celebrated Jewish missionary" Joseph Wolff.[62]

The Book of Mormon added the parallel promise that those who by faith and baptism became Latter-day Saints were God's people also, chosen in "the eleventh hour." They, too, should gather in Zion—the New Jerusalem—before Christ should return. This latter promise set Mormons to work. Though premillennialists, they must prepare the way of the Lord by uniting under his kingship now and accepting all the commands that came from the mouth of his prophet. They thus laid upon themselves the responsibility to hasten the millennium, much as the main body of American and English evangelicals, called postmillennialists, had accepted responsibility to prepare a Kingdom for the King.[63]

The doctrine of gathering, applied thus to both Jews and Latter-day Saints and sustained by appeals to both the Bible and the Book of Mormon, gave powerful support not only to millenarian doctrines but to the preference for a literal interpretation of Scripture that they sustained.[64] The outcome was to provide Protestants with another set of handles by which to bind together the Old and the New Testaments and a motivation grounded in awe about the future by which to recover reverence for the ancient past.

Viewed in this light, the Saints perceived themselves to have caught hold of the little end of the biggest thing in the universe—a cornucopia of unimaginable blessings promising "the riches of eternity," the elders said in 1831, to "those who are willing to live by every word that proceedeth out of the mouth of God."[65] These riches they could share with the whole world, and with every ancestor whose name they could learn. One did not have to feel marginal to the existing social and economic order to opt for such an inheritance. Yeomen and craftsmen, captains and queens could recognize the infinite value of this "pearl of great price."[66]

Turning now more briefly to the other side of the complex relationship between Mormonism and biblical culture, it seems evident also that Joseph Smith and the early apostles relied upon the Bible to establish the credibility of both the Book of Mormon and the revelations recorded in his Doctrine and Covenants. A large portion of their preaching and teaching consisted of appeals to biblical arguments. Perhaps nowhere is this clearer or more crucial than in the tracts that the brothers Parley and Orson Pratt published in the early years of their witness in Great Britain.

Parley Pratt's *A Voice of Warning and Instruction to All People* was intended, as the subtitle put it, to be "an introduction to the faith and doctrine of the . . . Latter-day Saints." The first three chapters rested the doctrine on the tradition of prophecy in the Old and New Testaments. And they displayed a literalism in the exposition of that tradition, which rivals that of John N. Darby, founder and lifelong leader of the most important English millenarian movement, the Plymouth Brethren. These chapters, comprising half the book, did not appeal at all to the Book of Mormon, though they displayed on every page its passion for certainty, clarity, and immediately understandable authority in religion. The literal fulfillment of Old Testament prophecies recorded in later passages of the Bible or in secular history were proof that Christians should expect an equally literal fulfillment of prophecies in the New Testament concerning the Second Coming, the establishment of the Kingdom of God on earth, and a renewed outpouring of the Holy Spirit in the last days.[67] Scorning the long tradition of spiritualizing the meanings of such prophecies, Pratt commented that it was fortunate that Noah, Abraham, Lot, and Joseph were not "well versed in the spiritualizing systems of modern divinity." Such spiritualizing denied what to Mormons seemed the literal fulfillment of Daniel's prophecy of the appearance of the Kingdom of God among the Latter-day Saints.[68] Even worse, it had impoverished Christianity by destroying hope for the continued inspiration of the Holy Spirit in the Church.

The event of Pentecost, Pratt went on to explain, was not simply history but prophecy. It declared both what individual Christian experience involved—faith and baptism by water and then, as he put it here, remission of sins through the baptism of the Holy Spirit—*and* what God's latter-day Kingdom would be like. It required a king, Jesus Christ (Pratt did not at this point mention the prophet); apostles commissioned by Christ and empowered with the miraculous gifts promised in Mark 16:15–18; and the presence of the Holy Ghost "to guide into all truth, bring all things to remembrance . . . [and] show them things to come and enable them to speak with other tongues."[69] If Scripture intended to teach that these signs were limited to the apostolic age, he wrote, then Christ must also have intended to confine to that era his command to go into all the world and preach the gospel[70]—an interpretation that he knew nineteenth-century evangelicals would find unthinkable.

Even Pratt's later chapter on the last days grounded the truth of the Book of Mormon on Scripture. He argued that the new revelation supplemented the Bible chiefly by clarifying it. Isaiah's prophecy of a forerunner testified not only to John the Baptist but to Joseph Smith, a latter-day voice in the wilderness preparing the way of the Lord.[71] From many other passages of Isaiah, as well as from Ezekiel's vision of the "dry bones" and from the 102nd Psalm, Pratt continued, we learn that "there is a set time to build up Zion, or the city of which Isaiah wrote"; that "when this city shall be built, the Lord will appear in his glory, and not before"; and that "the people and kingdoms are to be gathered together to serve the Lord, both in Zion and in Jerusalem."[72]

A few years later Orson Pratt buttressed his argument in the *Divine Authenticity of the Book of Mormon* with even more literal interpretations of the Bible. Daniel's description of God smiting the great beast with a stone "cut out of the mountain without hands" seemed to him, as to many Saints before and since, a clear reference to the Kingdom being hewn out in the mountains of Utah. Isaiah's prophecy of a nation "brought down" and speaking "out of the ground" was an equally clear prediction of the disclosure to Joseph Smith of the golden plates on which a nation brought low by God's judgment had left behind the words of its prophets.[73] Pratt also laid out what was by then the conventional Mormon argument that the description in Ezekiel 37, of two scrolls, one for Judah and the other for Joseph, clearly predicted a second Scripture for the descendants of the tribe of Ephraim after they had migrated to America.[74]

Those whom such arguments convinced were also told, however, that the same passage, literally interpreted, freed the theology of the Saints from bondage to biblical literalism. In Mormon understanding, both the Hebrew and the Nephite Scriptures promised a renewal of prophecy in the last days that would provide an infallible interpretation of their teachings and, by inspiration of the Spirit, such revisions of their contents as the sovereign God should will. English cleric Charles Mackay saw at once the challenge of these views of inspiration to the Protestant tendency "to substitute for the idolatry of the priest the idolatry of the book" and to neglect the Bible's own word that "where there is no vision the people perish." Ralph Waldo Emerson, Mackay remembered, "felt the burden of the Protestant yoke in this particular" and, in one of his lectures, had declared "that its teaching is equivalent to an admission that 'God is dead.'"[75]

I cite the brothers Pratt at length only because of the unusual clarity and thoroughness of their treatments; they wrote within what was by then a well-established apologetic tradition that Joseph Smith himself had begun in his Doctrine and Covenants, which then included seven Lectures on Faith delivered before the elders at Kirtland, Ohio. The first lecture, Charles Mackay pointed out later, rejected, as John Wesley had, the notion that saving faith consisted only of speculative belief. Rather, such faith involved the experience of a "principle of power," both human and divine. By that principle "the worlds were framed" and believers' lives were transformed. Experiencing such faith depended on the inspiration of the Holy Spirit.[76] Although the Book of Mormon contained many passages that would have sustained this view, the lectures appealed extensively to such favorite Wesleyan texts as Hebrews 11, Romans 8, Matthew 5:2–12, 48, John 17, Ephesians 3:19, and 2 Corinthians 3:18. By faith, Christians were to be changed into the image of Christ, "even as by the Spirit of the Lord." They were to be "filled with all the fulness of God" and become "perfect even as their Father in heaven is perfect," whether they were Jews or Gentiles.[77]

Indeed, the prophet's revelations published in the Doctrine and Covenants expounded and appealed to the Hebrew and Christian Scriptures on almost every page. They make clear, as the important revelation concerning the sacraments and the structure of the restored church declares, that ministering angels had by the Book of Mormon "declared unto the world" that "the Holy Scriptures are true, and that God does inspire men and call them to his holy work in this age and generation . . . thereby showing that he is the same God yesterday, today, and forever" (D&C 20:11–12). Smith's statement in the Wentworth letter of 1842 seems precisely accurate: The Scriptures he declared had been buried for so long in the Hill Cumorah were destined to "come forth and be united with the Bible for the accomplishment of the purposes of God in the last days."[78]

It is little wonder that in his first months at Kirtland, the Prophet gave so much of his time and energy, under what he declared was the inspiration of the Holy Spirit, to a new "translation" of the New Testament, beginning with the Gospel according to St. Matthew.[79] The alterations of the King James Version were few indeed. What the effort demonstrated was not the distance but the close parallels that the early Saints and their first converts saw between the Bible and the Book of Mormon.

Notes

1. Alice Felt Tyler, *Freedom's Ferment: Phases of American Social History to 1860* (Minneapolis: University of Minnesota Press, 1944), 86–107; Whitney R. Cross, *The Burned-over District: The Social and Intellectual History of Enthusiastic Religion in Western New York, 1800–1850* (Ithaca, N.Y.: Cornell University Press, 1950), 138–50, 264–67. Cf. Mario S. De Pillis, "The Social Sources of Mormonism," *Church History* 37 (March 1968): 350–79; and Thomas F. O'Dea, *The Mormons* (Chicago: University of Chicago Press, 1957), following Cross's lead, *The Burned-over District*, 11–13, 15.

2. David Brion Davis, "The New England Origins of Mormonism," *New England Quarterly* 26 (June 1953): 147–68. Cf. Klaus J. Hansen, *Quest for Empire: The Political Kingdom of God and the Council of Fifty in Mormon History* (East Lansing: Michigan State University Press, 1967), 6–10.

3. Alexander Campbell, *Delusions, An Analysis of the Book of Mormon; with an Examination of the Internal and External Evidences* (Boston: Benjamin H. Greene, 1832), 7, suggests that the Disciples of Christ leader sensed this possibility as early as February 1831; for the Book of Mormon, he wrote, recorded the prophet Nephi as teaching "every thing which is now preached in the state of New York." The broad inclusiveness of state-church Lutheranism in Scandinavia obscured beneath its umbrella a similar root system for Mormon faith in popular piety there; see William Mulder, *Homeward to Zion: The Mormon Migration from Scandinavia* (Minneapolis: University of Minnesota Press, 1957), 34–53; and Einar Molland, *Church Life in Norway, 1800–1950,* translated by Harris Kaasa

(Minneapolis: Augsburg Publishing House, 1957), 2–3, 10–19, 35–41, 48–52. On the English situation, the clearest summary is P. A. M. Taylor, *Expectations Westward: The Mormons and the Emigration of Their British Converts in the Nineteenth Century* (Edinburgh: Oliver & Boyde, 1965), 35–38.

4. Donna Hill, *Joseph Smith, the First Mormon* (Garden City, N.Y.: Doubleday, 1977), 32–38.

5. Hill, *Joseph Smith*, 104; Lucy Mack Smith, *Biographical Sketches of Joseph Smith, the Prophet, and His Progenitors for Many Generations* (1853; reprint, New York: Arno, 1969), 34, 44, 46–48, 56–58. Cf. David M. Ludlum, *Social Ferment in Vermont, 1791–1850* (New York: Columbia University Press, 1939), 20–24, 32–37.

6. Hill, *Joseph Smith*, 48; Smith, *Biographical Sketches*, 56–57.

7. Hill, *Joseph Smith*, 47–50; Smith, *Biographical Sketches*, 74–75; William Smith, selection from William Smith on Mormonism in *Among the Mormons: Historic Accounts by Contemporary Observers*, ed. William Mulder and A. Russell Mortensen (New York: Knopf, 1958), 24–25.

8. Gordon Irving, "The Mormons and the Bible in the 1830s," *BYU Studies* 13 (Summer 1973): 473–88, an article I read only after the first draft of this essay was completed, anticipated this point with close reference to early Mormon periodicals inaccessible to me. See also Mario S. De Pillis, "The Quest for Religious Authority and the Rise of Mormonism," *Dialogue: A Journal of Mormon Thought* 1 (Spring 1966): 68–88, reprinted without documentation in *Mormonism and American Culture*, ed. Marvin S. Hill and James B. Allen (New York: Harper & Row, 1972), 29–34; Leonard J. Arrington and Davis Bitton, *The Mormon Experience: A History of the Latter-day Saints* (London: Allen & Unwin, 1979), 26–29.

9. Alexander Campbell, *The Christian System*, 4th ed. (1866; reprint, New York: Arno Press and The New York Times, 1969), 6–12, 15, 72–77, 80–81, 106–9. The best brief account is in Sydney E. Ahlstrom, *A Religious History of the American People* (New Haven, Conn.: Yale University Press, 1972), 445–52.

10. Campbell, *The Christian System*, 32, 54, 60, 64, 194–95; George M. Marsden, *The Evangelical Mind and the New School Presbyterian Experience: A Case Study of Thought and Theology in Nineteenth-Century America* (New Haven, Conn.: Yale University Press, 1970), 17–23, 34–39, 49–53; Timothy L. Smith, *Revivalism and Social Reform in Mid-Nineteenth-Century America* (New York: Abingdon, 1957), 85–88, 103–34. I believe that Cross, *The Burned-over District*, 238–51, 263–66, errs in associating the doctrine of Christian perfection principally with John Humphrey Noyes and the Oneida community and minimizing its relationship to either Methodist or Oberlin abolitionism.

11. I have summarized the widespread interest in the doctrine of the Holy Spirit and its relationship to both ethics and eschatology in Timothy L. Smith, "Righteousness and Hope: Christian Holiness and the Millennial Vision in America, 1800–1900," *American Quarterly* 31 (Spring 1979): 21–45. See also Campbell, *The Christian System*, 64–65, 80; John Wesley, "Scriptural Christianity" and "Salvation by Faith," in *Works*, 14 vols. (1872; reprint, Kansas City, Mo.: Nazarene, 1978), 5:11–12, 37–52; Timothy L. Smith, "How John Fletcher Became the Theologian of Wesleyan Perfectionism, 1770–1776," *Wesleyan Theological Journal* 15 (Spring 1980): 68–87.

12. Ernest R. Sandeen, *The Roots of Fundamentalism: British and American Millenarianism, 1800–1930* (Chicago: Fortress Press, 1970), 13–27; David T. Arthur, "Millerism," in *The Rise of Adventism: Religion and Society in Mid-Nineteenth-Century America*, ed.

Edwin S. Gaustad (New York: Harper & Row, 1974), 154–61; Ludlum, *Social Ferment in Vermont,* 37–39.

13. Heber C. Kimball, *Journal of Heber C. Kimball* (Nauvoo, Ill.: Robinson & Smith, 1840), 24; see also 26, 30–33, 56.

14. Most explicitly in 3 Ne. 11:22–28. Cf. Mosiah 18:10–17; Moro. 8:5–22, rejecting infant baptism; and 2 Ne. 31:7–15, describing the baptism of Jesus, with special emphasis on the baptism of the Holy Spirit. See O[rson] Pratt, *An Interesting Account of Several Remarkable Visions, and of the Late Discovery of Ancient American Records* (Edinburgh: Ballantyne & Hughes, 1840), 4–5, 23.

15. The account in 3 Ne. 19:9, 13, 21, 23, 28–29 parallels, though with different chronology, John 17 and Acts 2. Cf. 2 Ne. 31:8, 12–14, 17; Mosiah 18:10, 12–13; 3 Ne. 11:35–36, 12:2; Alma 31:36.

16. For examples, see 2 Ne. 2:21–29, 9:20–26, 45–49; Alma 41:8. Cf. Pratt, *Several Remarkable Visions,* 25–28.

17. The theme is continuous: Mosiah 16:1–15; 2 Ne. 4:17, 21, 31–32; 3 Ne. 6:17–21, 12:17–20, 46–48, 21:22–25, and 27:19–29; Moro. 6:4, 16, and 10:32–33. The Sermon on the Mount opens in 3 Ne. 12:1–2, as it does in Joseph Smith, *The Holy Scriptures, Translated and Corrected by the Spirit of Revelation* (Plano, Ill.: [Reorganized] Church of Jesus Christ of Latter Day Saints, 1867), Matthew 5:1–2, with a passage on saving faith, baptism, and the grace of the Holy Spirit that does not appear in the generally received Greek text of Matthew's gospel. The revision implies clearly that good works flow from the experience of saving faith. The translation was done at Kirtland, Ohio, in 1831.

18. See generally 1 Nephi, Jacob, and Mosiah and, for long Isaiah recapitulations, 2 Ne. 12–24.

19. Mosiah 18:17–18 seems out of harmony with Alma 13:2–18.

20. Alma 41:2–13; 2 Nephi 6:8–18, 25:2–20, 30:3–18; 3 Nephi 16:1–17, 21:22–25; and Mormon 8:27–41. Cf. Orson Pratt, *New Jerusalem; or, The Fulfillment of Modern Prophecy* (Liverpool: R. James, 1849), 4–5, 18.

21. 2 Nephi 3:5–24 and 26:6–33.

22. De Pillis, "Social Sources of Mormonism," 62–63, 78–79. Cf. Donna Hill, *Joseph Smith,* 98–101, 105.

23. Parley P. Pratt, *A Voice of Warning, and Instruction to All People; or, An Introduction to the Faith and Doctrine of the Church of Jesus Christ of Latter Day Saints,* 2nd ed. (1841; reprint, Lamoni, Iowa: n.p., 1885), 68.

24. Parley Pratt, *A Voice of Warning,* 10, 33–34. Cf. Pratt, *Several Remarkable Visions,* 30–31.

25. Hill, *Joseph Smith,* 101–2. Cf. Parley P. Pratt, *Autobiography of . . . One of the Twelve Apostles of the Church of Jesus Christ of Latter-day Saints* (New York: Russell Bros., 1874), selection in *Among the Mormons,* 54–55.

26. Jerry Wayne Brown, *The Rise of Biblical Criticism in America, 1800–1870: The New England Scholars* (Middletown, Conn.: Wesleyan University Press, 1969), 5–6, 96–108.

27. Martin E. Marty, *The Infidel: Free Thought and American Religion* (Cleveland: Meridian, 1961); Ludlum, *Social Ferment in Vermont,* 25–31.

28. Lucius Fenn, Covert, N.Y., 12 February 1830, Letter to Birdseye Bronson, in *Among the Mormons,* 28–29.

29. Cf. 2 Ne. 33:1–5 with John Wesley's sermon, "Scriptural Christianity," *Works,* 5:37–52. In my opinion, Klaus J. Hansen, "Mormonism and American Culture: Some

Tentative Hypotheses," in *The Restoration Movement: Essays on Mormon History*, ed. F. Mark McKierman et al. (Lawrence, Kans.: Coronado Press, 1973), 10–11, underestimated the parallels of the attack on Calvinism in 2 Nephi 2:15–30 with Methodist and Disciples doctrine and overestimates the "liberal" implications of the singular treatment of free will in the passage. Hill, *Joseph Smith*, 47–50, 62, 94, 101, 152, recounts the Prophet's early contacts with Methodists and the Methodist backgrounds of other early leaders.

30. Hill, *Joseph Smith*, 119–20.

31. See, among many examples, 2 Ne. 9:15–51, esp. 41–43; cf. Melodie Moench, "Nineteenth-Century Mormons: The New Israel," *Dialogue: A Journal of Mormon Thought* 12 (Spring 1979): 42–45, 54. See also E. P. Sanders, *Paul and Palestinian Judaism: A Comparison of Patterns of Religion* (Philadelphia: Fortress, 1977), 1–12, 442–97; Nils A. Dahl, Review, *Religious Studies Review* 4 (July 1978): 153–60. See also the "anathema" against the errors of the Disciples, including their deprecation of the Old Testament, pronounced by the Beaver, Pennsylvania, Association of Baptists in 1829, summarized in Ahlstrom, *Religious History*, 451; and Campbell, *Delusions*, 11, 13.

32. Sidney E. Mead, *The Lively Experiment: The Shaping of Christianity in America* (New York: Harper & Row, 1963), 108–9.

33. See, among many examples, 2 Ne. 6:8–18 and Orson Pratt, *Divine Authenticity of the Book of Mormon* (Liverpool: S. W. Richards, 1850–51).

34. Jacob 3:5–9; Morm. 7:1–10. Cf. 2 Ne. 25:12–18, 29:3–7, 33:8; Pratt, *A Voice of Warning*, 41–43.

35. Contrast Martin E. Marty, *Righteous Empire: The Protestant Experience in America* (New York: Dial, 1970), 16, 49, 93–99, with Stephen J. Stein, "Introduction," in Jonathan Edwards, *Works*, Vol. 5, *Apocalyptic Writings*, ed. Stein (New Haven, Conn.: Yale University Press, 1977), 19–20, 24, 26–27, and Edwards, *Humble Attempt*, 309–436.

36. John Wesley, "Catholic Spirit" (1749) and "The General Spread of the Gospel" (1783), in *Works*, 5:492–504, 6:277–88; F. Ernest Stoeffler, *German Pietism during the Eighteenth Century* (Leiden: E. J. Brill, 1973), 45–55; Oliver Wendell Elsbree, *The Rise of the Missionary Spirit in America, 1790–1815* (Williamsport, Pa.: Williamsport Printing & Binding, 1928), 43–49, 102–9, 122–45.

37. Elsbree, *Missionary Spirit*, 109–14; William Gravely, *Gilbert Haven, Methodist Abolitionist: A Study in Race, Religion, and Reform, 1850–1880* (Nashville, Tenn.: Abingdon, 1973), 114–18, 126–27; Walter O. Forster, *Zion on the Mississippi: The Settlement of the Saxon Lutherans in Missouri, 1839–1841* (St. Louis, Mo.: Concordia, 1953), 86–89, 322–23, 520–27.

38. Smith, *Revivalism and Social Reform*, 103–34, 225–26.

39. Smith, "Righteousness and Hope," 21–24, 27; Daniel Walker Howe, *The Unitarian Conscience: Harvard Moral Philosophy, 1805–1861* (Cambridge: Harvard University Press, 1970), chaps. 5–7; Charles G. Finney, *Lectures to Professing Christians* (New York: Revell, 1878), 352–59.

40. Charles G. Finney, "Memoirs," Mss., Oberlin College Library, in the closing pages of chap. 25, identified Channing as the "Dr. C." in Finney, *Memoirs* (New York: A. S. Barnes, 1876), 356–57. Cf. William Ellery Channing, *The Perfect Life, in Twelve Discourses*, ed. William Henry Channing (Boston: Roberts Brothers, 1873), 52–54, 74–75, 113–14, 117–19, 244–45. These sermons date from the 1830s and are the only volume of Channing's published sermons.

41. Campbell, *Christian System,* 32, 54, 60, 64, 80.

42. Mosiah 12:34–36, 13:11–24; Joseph Smith, *The Book of Doctrine & Covenants of the Church of Jesus Christ of Latter-Day Saints, Selected from the Revelations of God* (Liverpool: Wilford Woodruff, 1845), 42:18–29. Quotations, hereafter cited as D&C by section and verse, are from the 1845 edition, the earliest available to me.

43. Pratt, *Several Remarkable Visions,* 28–29, 31; Kimball, *Journal,* 29–30; Pratt, *A Voice of Warning.*

44. Nancy Towle, *Vicissitudes, Illustrated,* 2nd ed. (1833), in *Among the Mormons,* 61.

45. Ezra Booth, Nelson, Portage County, Ohio, September 1831, Letter to Ira Eddy (presiding elder, Methodist Episcopal Church), in E. D. Howe, *Mormonism Unvailed* (Painesville, Ohio: E. D. Howe, 1834), 177–80, 187–90, 201–3.

46. Quoted in Mulder and Mortensen, *Among the Mormons,* 63.

47. Hill, *Joseph Smith,* 153–54; D&C 89:5, 8–9.

48. Kimball, *Journal,* 29–30.

49. Robert Bruce Flanders, *Nauvoo: Kingdom on the Mississippi* (Urbana: University of Illinois Press, 1965), 63, citing Willard Richards.

50. Orson Pratt, *Epistle to the Saints throughout Britain,* quoted in [Charles Mackay,] *The Mormons, or Latter-Day Saints; with Memoirs of the Life and Death of Joseph Smith, the "American Mahomet"* (London: Office of the National Illustrated Library, 1851), 321.

51. Notice of Hiram Brown's excommunication, *Times and Seasons* 5 (1 February 1844): 423. Cf. Hill, *Joseph Smith,* 335–43; Charlotte Haven, Nauvoo, 8 September 1843, Letter to relatives, Portsmouth, New Hampshire, in *Among the Mormons,* 126–27.

52. Joseph Smith, "Wentworth Letter," in *Among the Mormons,* 16.

53. Timothy Smith, "Righteousness and Hope," 34–37, 40–44. Cf. Lycurgus M. Starkey Jr., *The Work of the Holy Spirit: A Study in Wesleyan Theology* (New York: Abingdon, 1962), 15–22, 53–62.

54. Timothy L. Smith, "Introduction," Charles G. Finney, *The Promise of the Spirit,* ed. Smith (Minneapolis, Minn.: Bethany House, 1980), 18–19, 21, 23, 184–90, 260–65.

55. Booth, Letter to Eddy, Fall 1831, in *Mormonism Unvailed,* 180, 183–85. Cf. 2 Ne. 32:2; Moro. 10:16–17.

56. John Wesley, "Scriptural Christianity," *Works,* 5:37–38; John Wesley, *A Farther Appeal to Men of Reason and Religion* (London: W. Strahan, 1745), part I, sec. V; *Works,* 8:76–111.

57. Smith, "Righteousness and Hope," 35–37.

58. "The Spirit's Work in Believers," in *Let Wisdom Judge: University Addresses and Sermon Outlines by Charles Simeon,* ed. Arthur Pollard (London: Inter-Varsity Fellowship, 1959), 140–52. This sermon was the last of a series he preached before the University of Cambridge in 1831 on "The Offices of the Holy Spirit."

59. Phoebe Palmer, *Four Years in the Old World,* 3rd ed. (New York: Foster & Palmer, 1866), 113–20; Finney, *Memoirs,* 395, 453, 459–61, 468–69.

60. Ralph Waldo Emerson, "The Divinity School Address," in his *Nature* (Boston: J. Munroe, 1849), 138–39.

61. Smith, *Revivalism and Social Reform,* 135, 145.

62. Pratt, *A Voice of Warning,* 12–13, 16–17, 21, 23, 26, 34–35, 39–45, 96–99; Pratt, *New Jerusalem,* 18.

63. Pratt, *A Voice of Warning,* 106–8.

64. They thus anticipated several decades of the merging of these two tendencies, which Sandeen describes in *Roots of Fundamentalism,* 103–31.

65. Quoted in Hill, *Joseph Smith,* 141.

66. Flanders, *Nauvoo,* 62–67, presents evidence that denies the working-class interpretation of the origins of evangelical dissent so dear to English scholars; cf. Towle, "Vicissitudes," in *Among the Mormons,* 60.

67. Pratt, *A Voice of Warning,* 9–49.

68. Ibid., 12, 13, 16–17.

69. Ibid., 56–57.

70. Ibid., 53–54.

71. Ibid., 96–99.

72. Ibid., 96–99, 104–6.

73. Orson Pratt, "Prophetic Evidence in Favour of the Book of Mormon," *Divine Authenticity,* 85–87, 95; 2 Ne. 26:15–17. He alludes to Psalm 85, "truth shall spring out of the earth."

74. Pratt, *Divine Authenticity,* 94–95.

75. Ibid., 26–28, 31–32; Mackay, *Mormons,* 293.

76. Lectures on Faith 1:13–24, 2:24–25, in D&C (1845). Cf. Starkey, *Work of the Holy Spirit,* 47–51; and for easily accessible excerpts from a number of John Wesley's writings, see Robert W. Burtner and Robert E. Chiles, eds., *A Compend of Wesley's Theology* (Nashville, Tenn.: Abingdon, 1954), 156–62.

77. Lectures on Faith 1:13; 5:2; 7:7, 10–12.

78. Joseph Smith, "The Wentworth Letter," in *Among the Mormons,* 13.

79. Hill, *Joseph Smith,* 131, 153.

CHAPTER 4

Mormon and Methodist: Popular Religion in the Crucible of the Free Market

Nathan O. Hatch

One of the great ironies of American religious history is the parallel origins of the Methodist and Mormon movements, the most revered and the most despised of American churches on the eve of the Civil War. Both came to the fore in the crucible of the early republic, a time of revolutionary change in a polity that turned its back on state-sponsored religion and embraced, for good or ill, the realities of a market economy, the individual pursuit of self-interest, and the legitimation of competing factions. Both movements broke decisively with the kinds of churches that had dominated the American colonies. Both witnessed explosive growth that would have been unthinkable without the collapse of the monopolistic relationship between religion and the state and between religion and the local community—a social disintegration possibly unequaled in American history.[1] Both succeeded because they were willing to market religion beyond ecclesiastical space and to cater to the interests of specific market segments—a proliferation that Adam Smith had predicted would result upon government deregulation of religion.[2]

Both empowered ordinary people by taking their deepest spiritual impulses at face value, by shattering formal distinctions between lay and clergy, by releasing the entrepreneurial instincts of religious upstarts, and by incarnating the gospel message in the vernacular—in preaching, print, and song. When referring to the gospel and its proclamation, both groups relished the word "plain."

At the same time, the Methodist Episcopal Church and the Latter-day Saints, embracing divergent conceptions of Christian reality, developed in strikingly different ways. Between 1776 and 1850, the Methodists in America achieved a virtual miracle of growth, rising from less than 3 percent of all church members in 1776 to more than 34 percent by 1850, making them far and away the largest religious body in the nation. Methodist growth terrified other more established denominations. By the middle of the nineteenth century, Methodists boasted four thousand itinerants, almost eight thousand local preachers, and more than a million members. The Methodist Episcopal Church was nearly one and a half times larger than any other Protestant body and could muster more than ten times the preaching force of the Congregationalists, who in 1776 had double the number of clergy of any other church. By 1840 one in twenty Americans was a member of a Methodist church. By 1850 almost one in fifteen Americans belonged to a Methodist church—1.5 million Methodists out of 23 million people.[3]

Methodism in its message and structure embodied a liberal conception of reality that broke decisively with the pre-Revolutionary pursuit of homogeneous community. As a movement of self-conscious outsiders, Methodism embraced the virtue of pluralism, of competition, and of marketing religion in every sphere of life—far behind the narrow confines of ecclesiastical space,[4] Methodism also appealed to the petty bourgeoisie, people on the make. As a movement, Methodism became a powerful symbol of social mobility, a beacon of aspiring respectability. Methodists who railed at luxury and refinement at the turn of the century had wedded the gospel to refined civility by the 1850s, as Richard Bushman has documented.[5] American Methodism resonated with the logic of the market. Successful as a counterculture in England, the Methodists succeeded in America in defining the core of a democratic culture: "Arminian evangelical Protestantism," points out David Martin, "provided the *differentia specifica* of the American religious and cultural ethos."[6]

In sharp contrast, the Latter-day Saints as a religious movement sprang from an abiding conviction that America had forfeited its promise as a land of opportunity and spiritual renewal. I find the most striking theme in the Book of Mormon to be the apocalyptic judgment that hangs like an ominous cloud over the rich and successful businessmen of Jacksonian America and those who blessed their ventures, the learned and orthodox clergymen.[7] In his influential defense of Mormonism, *A Voice of Warning,* Parley P. Pratt likewise castigated "the narrow-minded calculating, trading, overreaching, penurious sycophant of the nineteenth century, who dreams of nothing here but how to increase his goods, or take advantage of his neighbor." Likewise, he indicted the "modern invention and moneyed plans" of respectable churches who expected to bring about the millennium but were ripening instead "for the fire as fast as possible"—for "behold the sword of vengeance hangs over you."[8] Marvin Hill's interpretation—that Mormonism sprang from an overt repudiation of pluralism, entrepreneurial ambition, religious competition, and freedom of individual thought—seems entirely convincing.[9]

The goal of this essay is to view the origins and early years of the Mormon experience against the backdrop of the Methodists, movements that seem to grow out of the market revolution but that relate to it in fundamentally different ways. In reviewing recent literature of these movements and, more broadly, of the early republic, I hope to bring into clearer focus some of the central themes that characterize the experience of the Mormons in the movement's first fifteen years and to note certain limitations in historical perspectives on the Mormons, despite the avalanche of studies that have recently appeared.

Supernatural Faith, Methodical Organization

Recent historical studies, colored by the dramatic Christianizing of the American people in the early republic, have placed greater importance on the significance of "upstart sects" such as the Mormons and Methodists.[10] These studies underscore the success of groups that uncoupled religion from social authority and high culture and welcomed its incarnation into popular modes of thought and behavior. They also point to how limited and elitist our understandings of the Second Great Awakening have been. Scholars are now beginning to understand the torrents of folk religion that washed through popular culture, beyond established ecclesiastical control. Studies of the New England frontier and hill country by social historian Alan Taylor have noted the striking incidence of radical religious seers, visionaries, prophets, mystics, and fortune tellers and how easily traditions of folk magic and mystical insight become intermingled with Christian beliefs for religious seekers, many of whom were self-consciously unchurched.[11]

In two striking ways Methodists and Mormons were alike in drawing strength from these folk religious impulses: in relishing the reality of the supernatural in everyday life and in recruiting and organizing disciplined bands of young followers, hungry for achievement, sacrificial in their zeal, and driven by a sense of providential mission. In the first two decades of the nineteenth century, Methodist experience was brimming with overt enthusiasm, supernatural impressions, and reliance on prophetic dreams and visions. Methodist journals and autobiographies were replete with this kind of supernaturalism. Freeborn Garrettson took seriously the veracity of supernatural impressions, prophetic dreams, and divine healing. In addition to stories of dreams, shouting, and divine healing, Billy Hibbard's memoir included an account of a woman apparently raised from the dead. Methodism dignified religious ecstasy, unrestrained emotional release, and preaching by blacks, by women, by anyone who felt the call. Two African American women who became successful Methodist exhorters, Jarena Lee and Zilpha Elaw, were dramatically converted through direct revelation and found guidance in prophetic dreams.[12]

The most celebrated and notorious Methodist itinerant of his day was "Crazy" Lorenzo Dow, after whom three early Mormon leaders were named: Lorenzo Dow Young, Lorenzo Dow Hickey, and Lorenzo Dow Watson. Dow, celebrated as a holy man with unusual powers, embodied the continuing presence of the supernatural in everyday affairs. Nicholas Snethen warned British

Methodists in 1805 of Dow's presumed prophetic powers: "He has affected a recognizance of the secrets of men's hearts and lives, and even assumed the awful prerogative of prescience, and this not occasionally, but as it were habitually, pretending to foretell, in a great number of instances, the deaths or calamities of persons, &c."[13] Even Nathan Bangs, who eventually set his face to rid Methodism of the stigma of enthusiasm, began his itinerant career as a white-hot enthusiast who, at the Hay Bay Camp Meeting in Upper Canada in 1805, was so overtaken by the power of God as he preached and shouted that friends had to support his outstretched arms. Afterward, he had to be "carried out of the camp into a tent where he lay speechless being overwhelmed for a considerable time with the mighty Power of God." Assessing this kind of evidence, John Wigger argues that the defining characteristic of American Methodism under Francis Asbury was not a theological abstraction like Arminianism but a quest for the supernatural in everyday life.[14]

By the time Joseph Smith announced his prophetic mission, enthusiasm was being pushed to the margins of the Methodist Episcopal Church, but still central was the popular yearning for divine action in day-to-day existence. In fact, the clarion call of Joseph Smith and his followers was to a militant supernaturalism: a demonstrable revelation from heaven, the reality of miracles and apostolic gifts, and a sure and ongoing channel of prophecy. Arguing that modern churches had a form of godliness but without its power, Pratt announced that "the most miraculous displays of the power and majesty of Jehovah" were being revealed in the latter days and that believers could expect "miracles, signs and wonders, revelations, and manifestations of the power of God, even beyond anything that any former generation has witnessed."[15] "I am a God of miracles," the Lord proclaimed in the Book of Mormon, and Latter-day Saints insisted on taking that claim literally.[16] Many, such as Sidney Rigdon, found the prophetic claims of Joseph Smith compelling; others found compelling the reported incidents of divine healing or the overt enthusiasm that reached a fever pitch in Kirtland, Ohio.[17]

Mormons and Methodists shared a common yearning for the miraculous power of the biblical world—in sharp contrast to the starkly rational biblicism of Alexander Campbell. They also embodied a common organizational style that distanced them from the Disciples and Churches of Christ: a genius for organizing and consolidating the expansion of the faith. Methodists and Mormons were, at their core, youth movements with an extraordinary capacity to mobilize people for a cause and to build an organization sustained by obedience and discipline rather than ties of parish, family, and patronage. In both movements a battery of young leaders without elite pedigrees constructed fresh religious ideologies around which the movement coalesced. Marvin S. Hill has estimated that 92 percent of those converted before 1846 whose birth and conversion dates are given (211 of 229) were under forty years of age at the time of baptism. The median age was between twenty and twenty-five; more than 80 percent (182) were thirty or under.[18] W. R. Ward has noted that Francis Asbury was an entrepreneur in religion, a man who perceived a market to be exploited. The itinerant-based machine he set in motion was less a church in any traditional sense than a military mission of short-term agents who were not pastorally related to the flock in the traditional European sense.[19] Abel Stevens estimated that nearly half of the first 650 preachers died before they were thirty years old, almost 200 of them in the first five years of service.

Mormons and Methodists were driven by a consuming passion to convert the unconverted. They emphasized an urgent missionary purpose as the principal reason for their existence and tailored their preaching to warn people of the wrath to come and to "draw in the net." More importantly, they yoked their drive to proselytize to relentless and systematic efforts to deluge the country with preaching. Unlike the young itinerants of the Great Awakening, whose efforts were largely uncoordinated and short-lived, these movements developed regimented and ongoing schemes for sending out gospel preaching to even the most remote pockets of American civilization. Two Baptist clergymen overlooked partisanship in 1816 to praise the Methodists' "complete system of missions, which is by far the best for domestic missions ever yet adopted. They send their laborers into every corner of the country."[20]

Equally committed to sending forth a cadre of lay preachers, the Mormons had enlisted a preaching force of nineteen hundred young men by 1845. The earliest men sent forth on missions included flatters, carpenters, cobblers, glaziers, potters, farmers, schoolteachers, and former preachers from other denominations. As outlined in Joseph Smith's 1835 compilation of revelations, the Doctrine and Covenants, Mormonism, like Methodism, resisted the Puritan tradition of painstaking study, advising preachers against using careful forethought, written notes, and detailed plans. The overriding theme was convincing the unconvinced of the new restoration. According to an ex-Mormon preacher, the approach was to employ "the most plausible means" available "to get people to unite with them."[21]

What is particularly striking about Methodists and Mormons was their relentless drive to broadcast their message, what the Methodist Discipline called "the continual extension of that circumference on every hand."[22] Both movements did this by a threefold strategy of transforming earnest converts into preachers with unprecedented speed, urging them to sustain a relentless pace of engagements, and confronting people with preaching everywhere, at any hour of the day or night. The Methodist commitment to leave no circuit unattended forced their leadership to channel young converts into preaching assignments in record time. Education for eager young Methodist recruits was a hands-on experience. They moved into exhorting and preaching while they served apprenticeships as class leaders, and they moved into circuits as understudies to more experienced preachers. The early Mormons were even less concerned about ministerial training. On several occasions, a man heard a discourse, submitted to baptism and confirmation, received a call to priesthood, and was sent on a mission—all on the same day. Canadian Samuel Hall, for instance, found a Latter-day Saint tract on a Montreal street and traveled to Nauvoo to hear the teachings of Joseph Smith himself. On the day of his arrival, he heard a sermon by Smith, requested baptism, received ordination, and started on a mission—without even pausing to change his wet clothes.[23]

Methodists and Mormons also multiplied the number of hearers by making preaching a daily occurrence. They moved house to house, if necessary, to gain an audience and purposely sought out people who would not ordinarily be reached. The New England circuit-rider Dan Young described this approach: "My practice was to commence on Monday morning as soon as I had taken breakfast, make my first call at the first house, say to them, 'I am the preacher sent to this charge; I have called to make you a religious visit; will you please to call your family together; I wish to talk with them, and to pray with and for you.' I left no house unvisited in my way, but took them of all sects and no sect."[24] The result was that preaching assumed an almost omnipresent quality, extending from the intimacy of the house to the mass audience of the camp meeting. It was this pervasive presence of Methodism that confounded a Roman Catholic priest attempting to minister in Maryland in 1821: "How can one priest attend so many different places at such great distances from each other? There are Swarms of false teachers all through the Country—at every Crossroad, in every School house, in every private house—you hear nothing but night meetings, Class meetings, love feasts &c &c."[25]

The early mission efforts of the Mormons were characterized by the same mass proclamation of the word: a relentless pace, the manifest intent to allow no one to escape the sound of the gospel, and the unending quest to convince hearers to join the new fold. Like the Methodist movement, the Mormon movement was a communications crusade springing from the deepest commitments of young missionaries such as Brigham Young: "I wanted to thunder and roar out the Gospel to the nations. It burned in my bones like fire pent up. . . . Nothing would satisfy me but to cry abroad in the world, what the Lord was doing in the latter-days."[26]

The organizational genius of Methodists and Mormons was to embrace and empower common people in a system that was centrally directed in a fixed, even authoritarian, system. In their early years, both movements were volatile and unstable, as a variety of fledgling and self-ordained leaders vied for influence, tested the limits of the prescribed authority, and in numerous cases hived off to form their own versions of the gospel.[27] Yet Mormons and Methodists, unlike Disciples and Baptists, swore by institutional coherence. In the face of clamoring dissent, sometimes fueled by democratic impulses, sometimes by visionary ones, Methodists and Mormons were willing to exercise discipline, even ruth-lessly, to preserve a movement in the name of God.

Mormonism and Methodism: Denominational History

The Mormons and the Methodists also share certain resemblances in the way that they have been studied. In the traditional canon of American religious his-tory—which is oriented to intellectual history and to Puritanism, Calvinism, and their heirs—Methodists and Mormons do not quite measure up. Both have borne the stigma of their origins in religious enthusiasm and among people without social standing. If intellectual profundity or political influence remains a prime measure of importance, then the Wesleyans and the Latter-day Saints in their early years can be safely avoided. Despite the considerable work done in the last generation and with a few noteworthy exceptions, the story of both tra-ditions remains surprisingly insular, undertaken principally by denominational historians who write from within these religious communities.[28] Revering their past, both traditions have brought to life the story of their own faith community with great affection and exacting detail. In recent years, a veritable army of young Mormon historians has ransacked the story of Mormon origins from every imaginable perspective. If this trend continues, early Mormonism may soon rival the Puritans as the most studied of American religious phenomena.

Yet this intense cultivation has born limited interpretive fruit. The besetting sin of believers as historians is the fallacy of Whig history, to survey the histori-cal landscape with a preference for that which is similar to, or that which antic-ipates, the present. Thus, the ecumenist, when coming to history, finds its direction and movement in ecumenical successes, the high church devotee in the church's organic development, the pacifist in peace movements, the funda-mentalist in militant defense of the truth, the social activist in examples of reform. Once we begin with our own commitments, the selection of the facts to fit them is all too easy, the more so since selectivity is usually unconscious. The parts of the story that we underline are very often merely just the ones that seem important because they bear out our own convictions.

In this vein, Methodist and Mormon historians have shared a tendency to sanitize their history, albeit in different ways. For at least a century, Methodist historians have focused on those aspects of their own heritage linked to cultural enrichment, institutional cohesion, and intellectual respectability. They have underemphasized or ignored the crudely enthusiastic side of Methodist life that seems an embarrassment.[29] William Warren Sweet has done more than any other single scholar in the twentieth century to promote the serious study of Meth-odists on the frontier. He was committed, however, to a vision of Methodists as bearers of civilization to the uncouth, unrestrained society of the frontier. Emphasizing the disastrous effects of migration upon civilization and culture,

Sweet depicted the Wesleyan impulse as bringing moral order and the first seeds of culture to a rampantly individualistic society. He emphasized how the churches brought order, education, and moral discipline to the frontier. In his hands, even the camp meeting became a well-regulated institution. Sweet had little interest in evidence that hinted at radical shaking within the walls of Zion— that churches served as agents of liberation as well as of control.[30] Modern church historians, in short, have had difficulty identifying with dimensions of their own ecclesiastical heritage that are diametrically opposed to the modern embrace of intellectual, liturgical, and ecumenical respectability. In doing so, the Methodists have overlooked the very engine that propelled their religious movement into national prominence.

Historians of Mormonism who themselves are Latter-day Saints have also constructed their history in ways that are theologically faithful. In Mormon discourse about their own history, the most powerful magnet arranging the iron filings of the historical evidence is the conviction that Joseph Smith was a divine prophet. Through him and the restoration that he proclaimed, the light of truth pierced the spiritual darkness that had enveloped the Christian world since the age of the apostles. Given this presupposition, it is clear why many Mormons, including a fair number of Church authorities, find historical research both alluring and terribly threatening.[31]

In an effort to be faithful to the historical evidence and to the truth, Mormon historians, like conservative scholars of biblical texts, have often employed the strategy of reconstructing the story from the perspective of how Joseph Smith and his followers viewed the world. This approach typically forgoes the kind of interpretive methodologies used to explain other religious movements or to explain the behavior of those who opposed the Mormons. The net effect is one-dimensional scholarship that isolates much of Mormon history from the currents of contemporary scholarship on the early republic, one of the most dynamic fields in American history over the last decade.[32]

Accepting the theological claims of Joseph Smith does color the work of Mormon historians, to be sure. But there is an even more subtle reason that Mormon historians are likely to sanitize their own history: So many of the attitudes and impulses of early Mormonism have little resonance with contemporary Mormon belief and practice. Mormon life today is a bastion of respectability, of staid family values, and of rock-ribbed Republican conservatism. Unlike most Protestant denominations and the Roman Catholic Church, in which culture wars divide and polarize their ranks, the Latter-day Saints line up squarely on the side of order and traditional values. As a people, Latter-day Saints are overwhelmingly patriotic and hard-working, the very embodiment of middle-class values, the Protestant work ethic, and the American way of life. No religious group in America today seems more in harmony with the spirit of free-enterprise capitalism.

Mormon religious life is stable and predictable. Few Latter-day Saints today expect divine fire imminently to consume their unbelieving neighbors, expect the miraculous to become a daily occurrence, or await a revelation that would radically alter their lifestyle. Mormonism today seems more attuned to the upscale image of Marriott hotels and to the melodious strains of the Mormon Tabernacle Choir.

Mormon intellectuals may express more diversity in social and political outlook. Yet they also continue to make peace with the modern world. Latter-day Saints are hungry for intellectual respectability and increasingly aspire to attend the best graduate programs and publish their research with the finest journals and university presses. In short, Mormons still think of themselves as a distinct people, but that identity has shifted and reflects more an aspiring church establishment than a movement of fiery sectarian origins. The danger, of course, is that a quest for respectability leads to a veneer of refinement over Joseph Smith that thus distorts the real character of primitive Mormonism.

Whatever Mormonism became, and whatever one thinks about the hand of providence guiding its unfolding, the fact remains that early Mormonism remained radical, apocalyptic, absolutist, extreme, combustible, and militant. Taking early Mormon self-descriptions at face value makes it difficult not to conclude that primitive Mormonism was a radical, apocalyptic sect that invoked and anticipated divine wrath upon the core institutions and values of Jacksonian America —its pluralism, enlightened rationality, religious optimism and reform and its successful entrepreneurs and managers. In *Quest for Refuge,* Marvin Hill has brilliantly captured this fundamental alienation from a society that boasted of its liberty and opportunity. If Mormonism brimmed with an overwhelming sense of certainty, it was because, despairing of conventional answers, they gathered a faithful remnant from among those whose aspirations, materially and spiritually, a market society had dashed to pieces.

Historians of Mormonism, both outside the Church and within, have continued to gentrify the movement. They follow the tradition of treating the Book of Mormon as intellectual history, as if Joseph Smith were sipping tea in a drawing room, engaged in polite theological debate with Nathaniel William Taylor and William Ellery Channing. Recent interpretations of the Book of Mormon have emphasized its rationality in contrast to the religious enthusiasm of American revivalism, its calm millennial hope in contrast to Millerite enthusiasm, its progressive optimism in contrast to Calvinist determinism, and its quest for order in contrast to romanticism.[33] In this vein, R. Laurence Moore has suggested that Mormonism was generally in line with other liberalizing theological trends in Victorian America and that Mormon distinctives were but a deliberate and contrived invention in order to gain attention: "'Theologically, in fact, Mormonism was in its beginnings a dull affair."[34] Similarly, in the Tanner Lecture of 1992, Richard Hughes suggests that Mormon distinctives can be grasped by focusing on intellectual rather than social history. His framework for the Mormon restorationist vision includes Christian humanism of the Renaissance, New England Puritanism, and above all Romanticism. Joseph Smith becomes best understood in the company of Ralph Waldo Emerson.[35]

In a similar move, Kenneth Winn's noteworthy study, *Exiles in a Land of Liberty*, attempts to frame discussions of Mormon origins in terms of ideological debates about republican ideology. Winn, who wrote his doctoral dissertation at Washington University where the shadow of J. G. A. Pocock lingers, attempts to place Latter-day Saints "shoulder to shoulder with Thomas Jefferson," finds that the Mormons sought to create a variation of the society of the New England Puritans and the founding fathers, and concludes, "Yet in reality, the Mormons unconsciously patterned themselves on no people more closely than their New England grandfathers." "They breathed new life into the New England heritage of communal republicanism."[36]

These studies miss the mark, not by analyzing the wrong kind of evidence, but by locating it in the wrong comparative framework, one that reflects our own values rather than the animating spirit of primitive Mormonism. Our studies are simply too elitist; we are scandalized by the reality that most popular religion is vulgar religion. Mormonism was a deeply spiritual movement, as Richard Bushman has continued to remind us, but more than any other religious movement in American history, it also reflected what Edith Wharton referred to as "the underside of the social tapestry where the threads are knotted and the loose ends hang."[37]

The reading of early Mormon texts and the tracing of their troubled and violent experience with their neighbors underscore three themes about primitive Mormonism: its apocalyptic and supernatural literalism, its expansionist rhetoric and appeal to arms, and its absolute control over its members. Whatever Mormonism would become as a distinct society in Utah and, in the twentieth century, as a faith reflecting mainstream American values, its first fifteen years were breathtaking in their radical claims and accomplishments.

In the first place, the Mormons distinguished themselves from other churches by claiming that mundane life was alive with angels, visions, healings, foreign tongues, fulfilled prophecies, and, through Joseph Smith, immediate access to the godhead—on any matter ranging from whom one should marry, how economic life should be structured, where missionaries should travel, what kind of temple should be built, or upon whom divine wrath was soon to fall. In an age when American denominations came to acknowledge the benefits of religious pluralism, the Mormons pronounced that all clergy were blind leaders of the blind and that swift and sudden judgment would fall upon everyone who did not seek refuge in the gospel announced by Joseph Smith.

Mormon revelations and pamphlets make plain that they are not speaking of judgement in some figurative sense; they were announcing literal judgment:

destruction, famine, pestilence, earthquakes, tempests, melting elements, and flames of devouring fire. That is the burden of the compelling and widely circulated tract by Parley Pratt, *A Voice of Warning*. He provides a litany of biblical prophecies literally fulfilled, from God saving Noah in an ark, to Israel's deliverance from Egypt, to the walls of Jericho falling down, to the Babylonians destroying Jerusalem. To rational skeptics, Pratt countered: "I reply, it was the power of God made manifest by prophecy and its fulfillment; not in a spiritualized sense, not in some obscure, uncertain, or dark, mysterious way, which was difficult to be understood; but in a positive, literal, plain demonstration, which none could gainsay or resist." Pratt pleaded with people far and wide to seek the one and only refuge from the impending conflagration: "But this destruction is to come by fire, as literally as the flood in the days of Noah, and it will consume both priests and people from the earth, and that, too, for having broken the covenant of the Gospel, with its laws and its ordinances; or else we must get a new edition of the Bible, leaving out the 24th [chapter] of Isaiah."[38] Through Joseph Smith's day-to-day revelations, the Mormons were confident that they possessed a divine blueprint for the unfolding affairs of everyday life. According to Pratt, "The predictions of the prophets can be clearly understood as much as the Almanac."[39]

Living out this sense of divine immediacy meant building a literal kingdom on earth. The successive experiments—at Kirtland, Ohio; Jackson County and Far West, Missouri; and Nauvoo, Illinois—all were understood as beachheads for the very Kingdom of God, soon literally to be constructed. From these centers, the Saints, dismissed by Gentiles as fanatics and extremists, announced that they would rule America and the entire world. Kings and princes, whom Americans could remember as mere farmhands, carpenters, and cobblers, were moving to take charge of all earthly and heavenly affairs.

As thousands of people flocked to Mormon settlements, evidence mounted that these expansionist claims and prophecies were being fulfilled. Bolstered by defiant rhetoric about the fate of surrounding Gentiles, Mormon community-building came to terrify Mormon neighbors, particularly when it became clear that Mormons did not want to retreat from the world of politics and be left alone. Instead, their dream of a theocratic empire encouraged them to influence and, if possible, dominate local politics—an attainable goal in Missouri and Illinois given their considerable numbers and their willingness to exercise bloc voting at the behest of Joseph Smith. Americans perceived the Oneida community and the Shakers as odd and quirky; they pitied Adventists as hopelessly deluded. But the presence of the Mormons struck fear and dread into the bravest American heart.

A main reason was that, when provoked, Mormons were willing to revert to violence and overt military action in the name of God. There is little question that Mormon military endeavors were initiated in self-defense. But the significant point is that for the only time in American history, religious zealots trained, marched, and on a few occasions waged pitched battle, as a military unit. Apocalyptic conviction, expansionist claims, and guns in their hands—a more explosive combination had not existed since the interregnum when Diggers, Ranters, and Fifth-Monarchists struggled to define what they depicted as the end of history.

By the time Nauvoo mushroomed into one of the largest towns in Illinois in the early 1840s, the Latter-day Saints had a significant reputation as warrior-saints. The paramilitary expedition from Kirtland, Zion's Camp, in 1834; the creation of a secret military fraternity, the Danites, employed to purge dissent; the belligerent Independence Day address by Sidney Rigdon in 1838; and the ensuing skirmishes and raids—all combined to create a military ambiance about Mormonism that deeply troubled dissenting apostles Thomas Marsh and Orson Hyde.[40]

Joseph Smith himself was certainly not exempt from this military spirit. In Missouri he had covenanted with three hundred of his men—like the New Model Army—never to accept peace at the sacrifice of truth. He thundered, "I have drawn my sword from its sheath and I swear by the living God that it never shall return again till I can go and come and be treated by others as they wish to be treated by me." The troops sounded three rounds from a cannon and shouted, "Hosanna to God and the lamb!" Before the Battle of Crooked River, an outraged Joseph Smith admonished his troops, "Go and kill every devil of them."[41] Led into battle by their white-cloaked captain, Apostle David W. Patten, known as "Captain Fearnought," Mormon troops shouted their watchword, "God and liberty!" By 1841, when Joseph Smith became lieutenant general of the Nauvoo Legion, fourteen hundred strong, it is no wonder that their neighbors worried that "they now come with the Bible in their hand but ere long they will come with a sword also by their side."[42]

The primitive Mormons were an apocalyptic sect, intent on expansion and willing to unsheathe the sword in retaliation for the persecution of their own. What also infuriated their neighbors and makes it difficult to think of them in any sense as classical republicans was their denial of the most basic liberty imaginable: freedom of thought. At its inception, Mormonism throbbed with diversity, multiple revelations, and an array of spiritual gifts. After the failure at Kirtland because of internal dissent, Smith determined to adopt more drastic measures to assure the unity of the Saints.[43] As external threats to the movement increased, the Saints closed ranks, demanded the strictest loyalty to the commands of Joseph Smith, and moved toward greater intellectual isolation. In the most startling revelation of all, in 1843 Joseph Smith announced that all earthly commitments were null and void save the ones sealed by himself, all "covenants, contracts, bonds, obligations, oaths, vows, performances, connections, associations, or expectations."[44] No human obligation—even the solemn vow of marriage—had any meaning unless it flowed from sealings that only Joseph Smith had the power to administer for earth and heaven. Smith explained the redemptive power of "celestial marriage" in this way and demanded that his followers submit to it or be damned. As divine prophet, military general, political boss, and even candidate for the presidency of the United States, Smith consolidated power into the hands of a single man and equated compliance to the divine will with loyalty and strict obedience.[45] This demand for absolute control was accompanied by a flurry of striking revelations—the plurality of gods, the tangibility of the divine, and the human potential of becoming a god. In submitting to their prophet and revelator on these matters, Mormon followers were willing to dismiss the architecture of classic Christian theology.[46]

The Mormons represent a striking symbol of the failings of a free-market economy, of its disorienting instability, its crisis of authority, its failure to integrate meaning, to care for the lonely and forlorn. Methodism, on the other hand, used all the resources of the market, first to discomfit more respectable denominations and next to play catch-up in a quest for respectability. Methodists were quintessentially American: they represent the petty bourgeois, rising groups, average people on the make.

To depict primitive Mormonism as a radical, apocalyptic sect that terrified its neighbors with expansionist intent and absolutist ideology leaves open the question of divine origins. If, as Joseph Smith claimed, the sweep of Church history constituted nothing but a whited sepulcher, would it not require a radical protest to wake up a slumbering world? If Jacksonian America had become corrupted by the oppressions of the rich, should not the gift return "as in former times, to illiterate fishermen"?[47] And if freedom of thought and a free market of religion were corrupting the truth, would not a ruthless enforcing of the truth serve as the appropriate antidote? More than once in biblical history the Lord has raised up prophets to himself who wandered as outcasts and pilgrims, proclaimed fire and brimstone, and performed miraculous signs. A real question for Mormon historians on the eve of the twenty-first century is whether they would recognize or welcome the kind of scandalous effort that Joseph Smith and his followers thought necessary to turn the world upside down.

Notes

1. David Martin, *Tongues of Fire: The Explosion of Protestantism in Latin America* (Oxford, UK: Blackwell, 1990), 21. On social dislocation, see Gordon S. Wood, "Evangelical America and Early Mormonism," *New York History* 61(4) (1980): 365.

2. Adam Smith, *The Wealth of Nations* (1776; reprint, New York: Modern Library, 1933), 746. See Roger Finke and Rodney Stark, *The Churching of America, 1776–1990: Winners and Losers in Our Religious Economy* (New Brunswick, N.J.: Rutgers University Press), 51–52.

3. Roger Finke and Rodney Stark, "How the Upstart Sects Won America: 1776–1850," *Journal for the Scientific Study of Religion* 28 (1989): 27–44.

4. Methodist itinerant Peter Cartwright recounted how a Presbyterian minister objected to his starting another church within the "bounds of his congregation." *Autobiography of Peter Cartwright, the Backwoods Preacher* (New York: Hunt and Eaton, 1856), 123.

5. Richard L. Bushman, *The Refinement of America: Cities, Houses, People* (New York: Knopf, 1992).

6. Martin, *Tongues of Fire*, 21, 43. See also Mark Chaves and David E. Cann, "Regulation, Pluralism, and Religious Market Structure: Explaining Religion's Vitality," *Rationality and Society* 4 (1992): 272–90; and R. Stephen Warner, "Work in Progress toward a New Paradigm for the Sociological Study of Religion in the United States," *American Journal of Sociology* 98 (March 1993): 1044–93.

7. For an extensive discussion of this theme, see Nathan O. Hatch, *The Democratization of American Christianity* (New Haven, Conn.: Yale University Press, 1989), 113–22.

8. Parley P. Pratt, *A Voice of Warning and Instruction to All People* (Manchester, UK: W. Shackleton & Son, 1841), 92, 45.

9. Marvin S. Hill, *Quest for Refuge: The Mormon Flight from American Pluralism* (Salt Lake City: Signature Books, 1989).

10. Jon Butler, *Awash in a Sea of Faith: Christianizing the American People* (Cambridge: Harvard University Press, 1990); Hatch, *The Democratization of American Christianity;* and Finke and Starke, *The Churching of America.*

11. Alan Taylor, *Liberty Men and Great Proprietors: The Revolutionary Settlement on the Maine Frontier, 1760–1820* (Chapel Hill: University of North Carolina Press, 1990), 123–53; D. Michael Quinn, *Early Mormonism and the Magic World View* (Salt Lake City: Signature Books, 1987).

12. John H. Wigger, "Taking Heaven by Storm: Enthusiasm and Early American Methodism, 1770–1820," *Journal of the Early Republic* 14 (1994): 167–94; and Dee E. Andrews, *The Methodists and Revolutionary America, 1760–1800* (Princeton, N.J.: Princeton University Press, 2000).

13. Lorenzo Dow quotes Snethen's letter in *History of the Cosmopolite* (New York: John C. Totten, 1814), 353–55. See also Charles Coleman Sellers, *Lorenzo Dow: The Bearer of the Word* (New York: Minton, Balch, 1928), 148–51.

14. Reports of enthusiasm and ecstacy in Nathan Bangs's manuscript journal were deleted in the printed version. See George Rawlyk's extensive discussion of Bangs at this camp meeting in his forthcoming book on evangelical conversion in early-nineteenth-century Canada. See also Wigger, "Taking Heaven by Storm."

15. Pratt, *A Voice of Warning*, 29–30.

16. 2 Ne. 27:23; see also 2 Ne. 28:6 and Morm. 9:10–19.

17. Hill, *Quest for Refuge*, 33.

18. Hill, "The Rise of Mormonism in the Burned-over District: Another View," *New York History* 61 (1980): 411–30. Hill derives these figures from analysis of Davis Bitton, *Guide to Mormon Diaries and Autobiographies* (Provo, Utah: Brigham Young University Press, 1977).

19. W. R. Ward, "The Legacy of John Wesley: The Pastoral Office in Britain and America," in *Statesmen, Scholars and Merchants: Essays in Eighteenth-Century History Presented to Dame Lucy Sutherland,* ed. Anne Whiteman, J. S. Bromley, and P. G. M. Dickson (Oxford, UK: Clarendon, 1973), 347.

20. John F. Schermerhorn and Samuel J. Mills, *A Correct View of That Part of the United States Which Lies West of the Allegheny Mountains, with Regard to Religion and Morals* (Hartford, Conn.: Peter B. Gleason and Co., 1814), 41.

21. Oliver H. Olney, *The Absurdities of Mormonism Portrayed* (Hancock County, Ill.: n.p., 1843), 28, quoted in Barbara McFarlane Higdon, "The Role of Preaching in the Early Latter Day Saint Church, 1830–1846" (PhD diss., University of Missouri, 1961), 35, 56–57, 72–73.

22. Thomas Coke and Francis Asbury, *The Doctrine and Discipline of the Methodist Episcopal Church in America* (Philadelphia: Henry Tuckniss, 1798), 42.

23. Higdon, "Role of Preaching in the Early Latter Day Saint Church," 59.

24. *Autobiography of Dan Young, a New England Preacher of Olden Time*, ed. W. P. Strickland (New York: Carlton & Porter, 1860), 90.

25. James Redmond, Letter to Archbishop Maréchal of Baltimore, 22 May 1821, quoted in John Ronin Murtha, "The Life of the Most Reverend Ambrose Maréchal" (PhD diss., Catholic University of America, 1965), 107.

26. *Journal of Discourses*, 27 vols. (London and Liverpool: LDS Booksellers Depot, 1855–86), 1:313.

27. Steven L. Shields, *Divergent Paths of the Restoration: A History of the Latter Day Movement* (Bountiful, Utah: Restoration Research, 1982).

28. See Martin E. Marty, "Two Integrities: An Address to the Crisis in Mormon Historiography," *Journal of Mormon History* 10 (1983): 3–19; Davis Bitton and Leonard J. Arrington, *Mormons and Their Historians* (Salt Lake City: University of Utah Press, 1988).

29. R. Laurence Moore, *Religious Outsiders and the Making of Americans* (New York: Oxford University Press, 1986), 3–21; Richard Carwardine, *Transatlantic Revivalism: Popular Evangelicalism in Britain and America, 1790–1865* (Westport, Conn.: Greenwood, 1978), xiv.

30. William Warren Sweet, *Religion in the Development of American Culture, 1765–1840* (New York: Scribner, 1952), 129–59. Sweet begins his major collection of source materials on the Methodists with the assertion: "No single force had more to do with bringing order out of frontier chaos than the Methodist circuit-rider." *Religion on the American Frontier, 1783–1840*, Vol. 4, *The Methodists* (Chicago: University of Chicago Press, 1946), v. He defined the central theme of *Religion in the Development of American Culture* as the part played by groups such as the Methodists in the transit of civilization westward—hence his chapter title, "Barbarism vs. Revivalism." According to James L. Ash Jr., "American Religion and the Academy in the Early Twentieth Century: The Chicago Years of William Warren Sweet," *Church History* 50 (1981): 461, Sweet "patronized the multitude of sectarian groups in America as little more than institutional and theological anomalies which attracted the mentally unstable."

31. On the dynamic and often embattled state of Mormon historical scholarship, see David Brion Davis, "Secrets of the Mormons," *New York Review of Books*, 15 August 1985, 15–19.

32. One unfortunate feature is a tendency among Mormon historians to color the discussion by the very nomenclature employed—for example, references to Joseph Smith as "the Prophet," his followers as "Saints," and his opponents as "Gentiles."

33. The first two interpretations are made by Thomas F. O'Dea, *The Mormons* (Chicago: University of Chicago, 1957), 31, 25; the second two are made by Klaus J.

Hansen, *Mormonism and the American Experience* (Chicago: University of Chicago, 1981), 68–83.

34. Moore, *Religious Outsiders and the Making of Americans*, 30.

35. Richard T. Hughes, "Two Restoration Traditions: Mormons and Churches of Christ in the Nineteenth Century," *Journal of Mormon History* 19 (Spring 1993): 34–51.

36. Kenneth H. Winn, *Exiles in a Land of Liberty: Mormons in America, 1830–1846* (Chapel Hill: University of North Carolina Press, 1989), 52, 62.

37. Richard L. Bushman, *Joseph Smith and the Beginnings of Mormonism* (Urbana: University of Illinois Press, 1984). Edith Wharton quoted in *New York Review of Books* 40 (1993): 20.

38. Pratt, *A Voice of Warning*, 23, 38.

39. Quoted in Hill, *Quest for Refuge*, xxi.

40. Stephen C. LeSueur, *The 1838 Mormon War in Missouri* (Columbia: University of Missouri Press, 1987), 135.

41. Quoted in ibid., 236, 138.

42. John Nevius, quoted in Hill, *Quest for Refuge*, 112.

43. Ibid., 63, 113.

44. Doctrine and Covenants 132:7.

45. For a helpful discussion on Joseph Smith's increasing emphasis on unquestioning loyalty, see Lawrence Foster, *Religion and Sexuality: Three American Communal Experiments of the Nineteenth Century* (New York: Oxford University Press, 1981), 140–43.

46. Hill, *Quest for Refuge*, 143.

47. Joseph Smith, quoted by Nancy Towle in *Among the Mormons: Historic Accounts by Contemporary Observers*, ed. William Mulder and A. Russell Mortensen (New York: Knopf, 1958), 61–62.

CHAPTER 5

Some Comparative Perspectives on the Early Mormon Movement and the Church-State Question, 1830–45

John F. Wilson

> Thus were we persecuted on account of our religious faith—in a country the Constitution of which guarantees to every man the indefeasible right to worship God according to the dictates of his own conscience—and by men, too, who were professors of religion, and who were not backward to maintain the right of religious liberty for themselves, though they could thus wantonly deny it to us.
>
> —Joseph Smith Jr., 1830

In this poignant passage in the *History of the Church*, Joseph Smith Jr. indicates that religious liberty, or more generally the relationship between religious convictions and political rights, was a burning issue for the Church of Jesus Christ of Latter-day Saints from its earliest years. In this particular passage, the Prophet was reflecting on the "molestations" he experienced at Colesville in 1830; his frustration was with treatment he and friends received at the hands of Presbyterians. Other incidents make it plain that members of numerous other denominations as well were involved in what Mormons perceived as denial of rights to members of the church—precisely because they were members of that church. The range of occasions on which persecutions took place in time, location, and circumstance indicates that this broad issue was enormously significant in the first years of the church.

Of course, it is conventional to identify the Mormons with the church-state problem in American society. The locus classicus is considered to be the issue as it arose because of the practice of plural marriage, an issue posed directly by the possible entrance of Utah into the Union as a state. Thus *Reynolds v. United States* (1879) is ordinarily taken to be the first clear interpretation of the church-state question involving the Church of Jesus Christ of Latter-day Saints. No doubt that case, and other subsequent ones, were of great significance in beginning both the accommodation of the Church to American society and the formal exploration of what the religion clauses of the First Amendment to the U.S. Constitution might actually mean as applied to specific issues.

We tend to forget that aside from this foray into the church-state conundrum in the late nineteenth century, the Supreme Court generally managed to avoid interpretation and application of the relevant clauses until a first tentative venture with the "religious liberty clause" in the 1930s and 1940s and then an initially bolder address to the "establishment clause" that came in the 1940s, 1950s, and 1960s. One of my chief points is that the confused and confusing welter of issues that comprises the church-state problem was actually very much a part of the collective life of the new nation from the outset, although formal attention to it came only later. The experiences of the Prophet Joseph and his followers provide us with a lens through which to view the early national period in an especially intense light. That is the perspective in which we shall explore the first period of Mormonism, that is, the years until the death of the Prophet, as a means of reflecting upon the church-state problem in American culture. Thus I hope we may gain insight into both the early Mormon movement and church-state aspects of American society.

In order to avoid confusion, let me make one other point at the outset. My title proposes comparative perspectives upon our subject, and it is important to be clear about what I mean by that. Specifically, I will try to interpret relevant characteristics of early Mormonism in relationship to those of religious movements more generally. While doubtless it would be interesting (and desirable) to compare Mormon experiences with respect to religious liberty and church-state issues in the United States with Mormon experiences in other societies and cultures, as well as with other American movements, that was not part of my original intent and in any case was beyond the scope of what has proved to be possible. By means of this comment, let me signal that it would be desirable to explore these further dimensions of comparison while making it clear that the primary framework in which we shall here undertake comparison concerns the movement itself.

Ideally it would be useful to trace these considerations beyond the period of the Prophet's life. But this terminus is at least defensible on the objective grounds that in the existence of the movement, circumstances changed significantly in the resolve to undertake the trek to and the building up of the Mormon empire in the West. There is an additional subjective or attitudinal reason for treating this initial period as separate and subject to analysis in its own right: A fundamental recasting of Mormon collective self-understanding in relationship to the United States seems to have occurred as a result of the Prophet's death.

At least through April 1844, shortly before his fateful submission to arrest and jailing in Carthage, the Prophet continued to believe that in some sense "Zion" would embrace (or at least arise throughout) America, perhaps at many points. And although by August 1843 exploration of the possibilities and prospects for removal farther west had become important within the movement, at that very time Orson Pratt in a meeting of the Twelve in New York City still held that the Book of Mormon revealed the "final fate and destiny" of the United States. "By reading [it], you can clearly see what will befall this nation, and what will be its final end."[1] Of course, the point of view I am advancing would not be challenged by consideration of subsequent periods of the movement. On the contrary. But the frame of reference becomes so very different both objectively and subjectively that confinement of this discussion to the early period is a proper limitation.

A selective discussion of points at which the early Mormons experienced frustration in relationship to governmental authorities, and the religious interpretations of the claims they made, initially requires us to ask some questions about the characteristics of the movement in this period. More especially it poses a question: What kind of movement was it in its early years, and what were its characteristics as a religious movement?

Here we encounter a problem that all historians learn to live with but never take for granted. Between 1830 and 1845, shall we say, the Church of Jesus Christ of Latter-day Saints was "coming to be." Often in the perspective of 1900—or 1950, or 1980—it seems inevitable that the movement should have gone through building up the isolated basin kingdom in the West and then a subsequent development out into American society, not to say the world. But of course that outcome might not have materialized. We have already remarked upon the assertions made by the Prophet that the whole of America was to be "Zion," even while tentative steps were being taken to explore western migration. As historians, we must resist the natural inclination to view the past, which we know to have taken place, as if it had been the foreordained outcome of yet earlier eras. So rather than assume that what did happen was inevitable—inappropriate within the framework of conditionality espoused by the Church in any case—we should attempt a fresh look at salient features of the Mormon movement in the context of that era.

Nathan Hatch of Notre Dame explicitly traces the development of the "Christian movement" in the early years of the nineteenth century—a topic directly relevant to interpretation of the context of Mormon origins.[2] The broader significance of Hatch's argument concerns the cultural conditions at large. In this essay he takes a position on the era very close to that advanced by Gordon Wood in his Tanner Lecture.[3] Hatch argues against the view that the Second Great Awakening was a conservative response to social change. Rather, he believes that attention should be called to "the intensity of religious ferment at work in a period of chaos and originality unmatched, perhaps, since the religious turbulence of seventeenth-century England." This was "a religious environment that brought into question traditional authorities and exalted the right of the people to think for themselves."[4] Thus Hatch would have us look at the context of popular culture as the matrix to assessing the emergence of Joseph Smith Jr. as prophet as well as the coalescence of the movement that responded to him.

If we posit this kind of open, even seething, democratic culture as background and context—a setting in which all authorities were uncertain—the critical years 1830–45 may come into somewhat different focus. Simply put, the culture at the popular level ought to be seen as protean and capable of yielding to direction. In a broader perspective, that is what new religions do: they propose the organization or the reorganization of existing and unsatisfying cultural experience.

From such a point of view, and in a comparative religious framework as opposed to a theological one, certain basic characteristics of the early Mormon movement stand out very clearly. Let us direct our attention to four elementary characteristics common to comparable periods of religious generation that would mark Mormonism as effective in this kind of cultural context. This set is not complete or exhaustive but does indicate some primary issues: first, the figuralist cast to the symbolism of the movement; second, its strong millenarian component; third, its ecstatic aspects; and fourth, its improvising or inventive organizational thrust. These sum to describe a nascent and potentially strong (and durable) religion in its early stages, but they do not characterize a developed church in a technical sociological sense.

First, the figuralism. We owe current use of this term to Erich Auerbach, who thus described the characteristics of the literature of ancient Israel in contrast to that of classical Greece.[5] But he went on to identify it as a strand or thread in Western literature generally, certainly of tremendous significance in the interpretation of the Bible until the Enlightenment introduced a critical approach, which recast our understanding of it. Hans Frei has recently picked up this insight in his phrase "the eclipse of biblical narrative," under which he traces the loss of the figural mode in understanding Scripture as the enterprise of technical criticism developed in the eighteenth century.[6] Auerbach most succinctly describes this tradition in terms of the action of biblical figures taking place in two realms—in both their own times as literal events and simultaneously shadowing forth more fundamental realities of a deeper realm in relationship to both the current period and future generations. Figuralism thus stood behind not only the complex, many-leveled interpretations of Scripture in the Middle Ages but also the Protestant, and especially the English Puritan, reduction of interpretation to a single literal level that yet permitted typological readings.

This insight has recently been developed with respect to American Puritans and their literary successors by Sacvan Bercovitch and his collaborators.[7] This school has helped us recognize how marvelously plastic and constructive interpretation of Scripture could be—even while interpreters were fundamentally limiting themselves to an ostensibly literal or historical sense. In the hands of someone such as Jonathan Edwards, the types rise out of extrabiblical sources, indeed even from nature. Thus the connection on to Emerson at the level of high culture is very clear. In this sense, we have recently come to a renewed scholarly appreciation for the formative role of Scripture in the shaping of the culture at large. At its most basic, this was a deep understanding of history that gave to those standing in the tradition a direct warrant for action and thus utmost confidence in their undertakings.

These brief introductory comments to a complex and highly significant development in understanding the role of the Bible in American culture provide a bridge over into the topic at hand. As we read the materials of the early Mormon years, it seems absolutely clear that Joseph Smith Jr. and his collaborators, associates, and of course his family members were grounded and rooted in the soil of this broadly figural understanding of Scripture. Their "world" was patterned and structured in terms of outsized biblical figures and events in the life of Israel. These provided not so much reference points or literary allusions as fundamental warrants, indeed compelling and urgent models, for their own lives. Their actions all took place with reference to that "other world" as well as this one—Auerbach's characterization of the figural mode. This is so un-self-conscious on their part that it pervades their consciousness, setting the terms in which their thought occurred. Occasionally it comes to direct expression, as in a passage that identifies an early vision of the Prophet's as a "transcript from the records of the eternal world."[8]

We could readily set illustration upon illustration to make this point secure. Under the limitation of time I hope that one will suffice—although the perspective applies to virtually all the direct autobiographical reflections upon early Mormon activity, and it certainly identifies the framework in which the collective decisions were taken and official explanations of the movement given. One superb example is provided by Lucy Mack Smith as she recounts the removal to Kirtland. She describes her role in these words: "I then called the brethren and sisters together, and reminded them that we were traveling by the commandment of the Lord, as much as father Lehi was, when he left Jerusalem; and, if faithful, we had the same reason to expect the blessings of God."[9] Those of us affected by modernity tend to read this as a nice figure of speech, an apt metaphor, a powerful image, a stirring allusion. I suggest it was much more than that. The actions of Joseph and his associates were a living out on the American stage of roles identified in and sanctioned by God's disclosure of the eternal world through ancient Israel. The fundamental *figura* for the Mormons was first set forth in the Old Testament and secondarily replicated with special reference to America in the supplementary Scriptures vouchsafed to the new Church. Of course, it is this latter point and only this latter point (the secondary replication of types and the assumptions that went with it) that sets the early Mormons apart from their contemporaries in the period of origin of the movement.

A second characteristic of the early movement has also received a great deal of attention in recent scholarship on the era. This is the millenarianism that has come to be invoked as explanation for so much that is otherwise inexplicable about the period. So pervasive was it in the cultural medium in which Joseph Smith and his associates came to consciousness that we would have to explain its absence if it were not present. My point is not simply its presence, however, but the special characteristics it takes within the movement.

We are deeply indebted to Klaus Hansen's identification of the "political Kingdom of God" as an emerging objective that continued to play an important if covert role in the movement for many years. No doubt he is correct in pointing out that by the second decade, that of the 1840s, a special development has taken place in Mormon millenarianism.[10] In the development of the concept of a political Kingdom of God, emphasis shifted to the role of human agency in preparing the way for the emerging millennium. This is, of course, a particular form of postmillennialism in which the gradual development of the Kingdom, without dramatic divine intervention, usually postpones a specific return of Christ to the end of the millennium when the last judgment occurs.[11] In light of the Hansen study and the more general recent attention to millenarianism in nineteenth-century American culture, I will not dwell upon this characteristic of the movement except for two points—one concerning its interpretation and the other regarding the data available to us.

First, if figural elements are a part of the movement's self-understanding, the degree of dependence upon human initiative required to secure the Kingdom should not be overinterpreted. This is to say, if the Prophet and his associates viewed themselves as, so to speak, acting out revelatory roles in this world, written in another and transmitted through Scripture, the degree of the "initiative" they were required to take would seem to be less striking than it is ordinarily held to be. I think that insofar as their activities were authorized and rendered coherent by convictions they held about the millennium, their actions were not only their own but understood to be divinely inspired and directed throughout.

The second point concerns certain developments of the period in question. In reading the materials of the 1830s and early 1840s, I think that the millenarian convictions were protean in that they were being formed and were not yet exclusively focused in what we might term the political Kingdom of God mode. For example, references to the Indians suggest this. The Zion's Camp expedition to Missouri also appears fully in line with such a perspective. At the point of termination of the expedition in early July 1834, the high council is organized as a vehicle for receiving disclosure of divine will—implying that confusion in determining the latter may have plagued that exercise. Shortly thereafter, it inadvertently comes out that 11 September 1836 is projected as "the appointed time for the redemption of Zion"; its location is to be Jackson County, Missouri. More than a year later that hope is still very much explicitly espoused, at least within the inner circle, although the "land of promise" is not so specifically located at that point. In the months preceding the date in question, the historical report becomes extremely thin—although it may be significant that, apparently in anticipation of that event, Joseph undertook a mission to the Boston region, specifically Salem. The mission terminated only at an unspecified "time in the month of September." The silence about the eschatological disappointment may say as much or more than extensive records would, for it is clear that the Prophet's energies immediately turned to the building up of Kirtland.[12]

In July 1839 Joseph addressed the Twelve and prophesied·imminent wars and the necessity of fleeing to Zion. To this end, no effort ought to be spared in building Zion up as a refuge. His dark and somber visions of destruction suggest that a new interpretation has been placed upon this rich symbol. Evidence for further reflection about and transformation of the Kingdom symbol may be found in the synopsis of a sermon the Prophet delivered in January 1843. At the same time there is evidence that the Twelve experienced confusion about its interpretation, as suggested by the minutes of a meeting set in New York City in August of the same year. Finally, as late as 1 April 1844, a general conference pronounced explicitly that "the whole of America" is Zion, requiring the building up of stakes "in the great cities, as Boston, New York, &c."[13]

I am certainly arguing for the centrality of millenarian convictions to early Mormonism in line with Klaus Hansen's interpretation. But I am also suggesting that the specific content of, and references to, Zion as the master symbol probably shift and metamorphose in the course of this period. This is in line with the extraordinary direction and redirection of energies throughout these years. Probably all the particulars of these changes of reference are beyond recovery, for they are veiled and in some respects even intentionally obscured. But especially in periods of severe stress and rapid change, religious symbols do permit this multiplicity of meanings. That is why they are so valuable. They enable a community to cope with the uncertainties of life while retaining what is of most value to it—namely its continuing existence as a community. We would find the same features in seventeenth-century England or during the struggles of the Reformation era on the Continent—or within the data on early Christianity. So from the point of view of analyzing early Mormonism as a religious movement in comparative perspectives, the elusiveness of its millenarianism is a typical characteristic and not unexpected.

Two other salient features of this subject are significant for our purposes. The early Mormon movement exhibits pronounced ecstatic displays. It is important to stress this point, because current stereotypes of Mormons emphasize industry, business acumen, etc.—and no doubt these can be traced back into the community-building impulses of the early years. Of course, ecstasy has not been emphasized as a general aspect of religious movements in the American culture. A case could be made that this oversight and neglect have led to significant misperceptions of Puritans and Shakers, of Awakeners and Revivalists, of Pentecostalists and Charismatics. I think that there is evidence that the early Mormon movement should be seen in this light.

One locus classicus for discussion of this phenomenon occurred at the dedication of the Kirtland Temple on 27 March 1836. In an evening meeting with the quorums after the main event, Joseph Smith Jr. positively encouraged "spiritual manifestations." At this point, he reports, the whole congregation "simultaneously arose, being moved by an invisible power; many began to speak in tongues and prophesy; others saw glorious visions; and I beheld the Temple was filled with angels." Later that week a veritable pentecost occurred when an eight-hour service of exhortation, prophesying, and speaking in tongues finally ended at 5:00 A.M.[14] In one perspective the increase in spirit manifestations, and glossolalia in particular, is surely linked to the belief in the impending coming of Zion, then anticipated in September of that year. With respect to glossolalia, it seems clear that it was continued within the corporate life of the group—and especially adapted to mission ventures where its use was explained on the model of Pentecost in early Christianity—as an answer to the problem of the many human languages spoken by the converts. Of course in this case an institutionalization of the spirit impulse is occurring within the religious community.

I think we should also see these spiritual manifestations as underlying more individual phenomena. This may be a promising perspective on the emphasis given to the marriage covenant and its eternity, which comes out explicitly in the revelation of 12 July 1843.[15]

This particular point is less important, however, than the more general one that spirit infusion is a central ingredient in religious movements and that the latter must simultaneously foster and yet contain it. Prophecy, glossolalia, and espousal of sexuality are all classical expressions of ecstasy in religious movements. But unless brought to serve the purposes of the group, they will unleash forces that will surely destroy it.

This leads directly to the fourth characteristic to which I wish to call attention, the invention of organizational structures. From the perspective of our time, Mormonism developed a marvelously complex set of structures for its inner life as a community and a church. At once simple—in the universality (at least for men) of the priesthood—but complex in its hierarchy and procedures, the Church of Jesus Christ of Latter-day Saints is a fine exhibit of what the sociologists with some admiration call a "church-type" organization. In the perspective of the early period of the movement itself, however, this modern outcome seems to have been less foreordained. In many respects, one marvels at the inventive or improvisational skill of the Prophet. He was gifted with an ability to make use of the diverse talents of others to the fullest while never relinquishing his final authority. At the same time, he created what appear to have been redundancies—should we call them competing structures of author-ity?—that probably evolved in unforeseen ways.

My point is to focus our attention on the fluidity and flux of this early period. With the Prophet's death and the emergence of Brigham Young, a task orienta-tion focused the objectives of the movement and directed all energies to its one overriding goal, the removal to and building up of the great western kingdom. But to my reading, the prior period is much more confused and confusing. Not in a disrespectful way, we could say that the Prophet repeatedly started some-thing that seemed always on the verge of getting out of control and that the improvising of structures contained but did not control the movement.

In directing attention to these four characteristics of early Mormonism, we confront characteristics that dominate the period of origin of most vital reli-gious movements, at least in western societies. And religious movements in their early years literally envision and advocate a new world—that is, conditions of life and a culture very different from what prevail. The conventional differ-entiations that characterize normal life do not exist within such a movement. What is "religious," as opposed to "worldly," when a mission is involved? What is "political," as opposed to "religious," when Zion's Camp is to be organized? In short, early Mormonism, like early Christianity and a host of other vital reli-gious movements in their years of origin, did not rest content with the conven-tional lines of distinction it might establish between itself and the whole society and the culture. In the urgency and compellingness of a new movement, con-ventional distinctions are unimportant and thus disregarded. The categories of the Old World are literally rendered anachronistic—and that is precisely why the church-state or religious liberty–governmental authority formulations of the society have little claim in the experience of the members.

This discussion of the early Mormon movement in terms of some particular features of religious movements generally, and those in antebellum American society in particular, directs attention to its dynamic and changing aspects, and it suggests the power of the movement to enlist believers and behavers in new patterns of life. Of course, it also suggests that at the same time a power exists sufficient to stimulate opposition. In a larger perspective, I can think of no such vital religious movement—at least in Western culture—that has failed to arouse hostility in just these terms. And the reason is clear. For claims are being made that, so to speak, the world is divided into realms of good and evil, and, further-more, that some persons possess knowledge of this division of the world and have benefits as a result of it, while others are to bear the consequences of either their fate or their obstinacy.

Religiously based claims such as these are incendiary. No matter that compara-ble claims, though often softened by time or hidden under familiar symbols, are made by others, and that some version of such claims may be linked to political power, perhaps even through informal religious establishments that may tacitly encourage persecution of dissenters. This ancient dialectic in American history is nowhere more strikingly exhibited than in seventeenth-century New England, where those who had been persecuted in old England readily adopted the role of persecutors in the new world. I am not defending the persecutions in seventeenth-century old England or New England, or in nineteenth-century Missouri or Illinois. I am insisting that the early Mormon movement willy-nilly found itself necessarily having to come to terms with what in shorthand fashion we term the church-state problem: how does religious authority, especially when so preroutinized and still essentially charismatic, relate to political authority structures—in this case also relatively protean?

Perhaps it is worth offering a brief digression to comment on why I pose the problem in this way—how the religious authority relates to the political, rather than vice versa. In general, it seems to me (at least with respect to the federal government, but I also think to the state jurisdictions as well) that the category "religion" has been problematical before the law from the outset. The clauses of the First Amendment, while explicitly only a limitation on legislative power, are framed in such a way as to suggest the deeper problem. The American solution has been to pretend that no problem existed. "Congress shall make no law as respecting an establishment of religion, or prohibiting the free exercise thereof." (Article 6, the only point at which the Constitution proper mentions religion, is in no sense a positive construction of the category: "No religious test shall ever be required as a qualification to any office.") Even in form, this provision is not strictly parallel to the other more substantial "rights" conferred less equivocally and interpreted more fully within the Bill of Rights. Certainly at the federal level, and very largely at the level of the states, there has been a prevailing inclination to avoid religion as an operative social category. Of course, when the Supreme Court has interpreted the religion clauses in the mid-twentieth century, it has with remarkable frequency sought to locate other grounds than religion—rights of property, speech, assembly, etc.—on which to adjudicate cases.

In short, while the interests of religious groups and the rights of religious individuals have been thoroughly a part of politics in the United States from the outset, the federal government has not, in spite of Jefferson's misleading phrase about the "wall of separation," conceived of an alternative authority structure—the church or even churches—to which to relate as a rival or subordinate. Nor has it undertaken to dominate such bodies where they might exist. In this sense our national history would have benefited from an appropriation of Madison's image—tracing a line between the rights of religion and the civil authority with sufficient distinctions to avoid collisions and doubts in unessential points—in preference to Jefferson's.

But if from the side of government the church-state issue in terms of competing authority structures has not existed, from the side of vigorous and vital religious movements it certainly has. For to take the case of early Mormonism, while the government authorities refused to admit that the conflict generated might raise church-state issues for those suffering appropriation of property and denial of personal rights, the only "cause" the subjects admitted was their religion. For this reason, I think it was inevitable that within the early Mormon movement there should have been direct concern about the church-state problem—the issue of how religious authority related to political authority. Indeed we find explicit reflection on this issue by Joseph Smith Jr. as early as 1834. For the next decade, in varying specific contexts, different formulations of the issue appear. While to my knowledge they do not appear systematically formulated in any one place, the separate positions taken—chiefly by Joseph Smith Jr.—do in general cohere. I will try to analyze the general position on that basis. Given the manifest claims of authority on the part of the Mormon movement, then, how was its relationship to the American government understood?

First, the most basic assumption is directly appropriated from the traditional Christian position that there is a fundamental division between this world and the next. Of course, in sayings attributed to Jesus such as "My kingdom is not of this world," "Render unto Caesar," etc., there is identified the foundation for development of the whole church-state tradition in the West. A particularly explicit discussion of this premise occurs in a communication sent early in 1834 to the Mormons displaced from their homes in Jackson County, Missouri. In this long epistle written at Kirtland, the Prophet explored the nature of the law and, more particularly, the relation of human law to the law of heaven, a subject of intense relevance under the circumstances. The general framework advanced is that obedience is owed to both sets of law; although the law of heaven is coherent, existing in one version, human laws are diverse and the governments of men dissimilar. In effect, Joseph Smith Jr. argues that while the realm of divine law is unitary and that of human law plural and dissimilar, God authorizes both sets of law. God's law is established directly and unequivocally, human law indirectly and for instrumental purposes: "God is the source from whence proceeds all good: and if man is benefited by law, then certainly, law is good; and if law is good, then law, or the principle of it emanated from God; for God is the source of all good; consequently, then, he was the first Author of law, or the principle of it, to mankind."[16]

This is the classical Christian position that, religiously speaking, human law serves an end that is good in God's eyes—ordering human community—but does not itself serve a positive function in relationship to salvation. The Prophet stops short of explicitly addressing the difficult issue of what should happen if human law contradicts divine law. He does refer to the trials and tribulations experienced by Saints "keeping the commandments of the Lord" and walking "in His statutes" and the glorious Kingdom promised those who are faithful. Indeed, in the day of judgment, just deserts will be awarded all. This significant declaration occasioned by the first Missouri persecution indicates how thoroughly the early movement was committed to a framework in which there were two orders of obligation—the one eternal and divine, mediated through the Church, the other temporary only, pending the completion of the great plan of salvation, an instrumental authority granted to the government of society.[17]

It is interesting to set beside this document from the hand of the Prophet, occasioned by the troubles in Missouri, an article written by Oliver Cowdery titled "Of Government and Laws in General." This document was composed to be incorporated into the Doctrine and Covenants in August 1835.[18] In any case, it is a more systematic statement and did not arise out of such immediately difficult circumstances as the elders' statement to the scattered Saints in Missouri. This declaration unequivocally asserts that governments—as well as laws— were instituted by God for the benefit of human society. Of course, however, religion was also thought to be "instituted of God." Men are responsible to God through conscience for the exercise of religion—"unless their religious opinions prompt them to infringe upon the rights and liberties of others." In a nicely balanced statement Cowdery declared, "We believe that rulers, states, and governments have a right, and are bound to enact laws for the protection of all citizens in the free exercise of their religious belief; but we do not believe that they have a right, in justice, to deprive citizens of this privilege, or proscribe them in their opinions, so long as a regard and reverence are shown to the laws, and such religious opinions do not justify sedition or conspiracy."[19]

Furthermore, explicit counsel was given against the mingling of religious influence with civil government. In sum, the declaration traced a line of separation between religious institutions and civil governments that echoed precisely the cultural assumptions of the early national period. In passing, we might note with Mark De Wolfe Howe that this particular set of assumptions was biased directly toward the broadly "congregational polity" characteristic of Protestant movements in the early nineteenth century.[20]

A further clause is worthy of note: the claim to a right of defense of "themselves, their friends and property, and the government from unlawful assaults and encroachments" when immediate appeal cannot be made to the law courts and relief afforded.[21] The immediate relevance of this claim is clear to those familiar with the early years of the movement.

One question arising in the determination of the relation between religious and political claims is the means of authority presumed by the Church in the discipline of its members. Since the Church of Jesus Christ of Latter-day Saints was committed to religious liberty as a principle, it could not logically look to civil means for the enforcement of ecclesiastical discipline, an ancient pattern still thought appropriate in Puritan New England. Explicitly in the 1835 declaration, and implicitly elsewhere, the sanctions appropriate to the Church were identified as those of disfellowshipment or excommunication. The more interesting question, of course, concerns the attitude toward, and expectation placed upon, the civil government.

The general position espoused by the early movement echoed St. Paul's words, "the powers that be are ordained of God" (Rom. 13:1). In many subtraditions within Christianity, this text and the attitude it expressed led to an indifference toward the form of government under which the faithful lived. In extreme cases, of course, there has been an assumption that the more severely hostile the regime, the more likely that believers would be harrowed and therefore true in their convictions.

The early Mormon movement, however, in spite of its international thrust through missions abroad, including that to Palestine, was not indifferent to its American location. Indeed, its deep allegiance to the U.S. government, *in spite of* the latter's failure to provide relief from suffering and restitution for losses, is noteworthy. A striking exhibition of this attitude occurs in the letter that the Prophet and his fellow prisoners wrote from Liberty Jail in Clay County, Missouri, in March 1839. Toward the close of a long document, freedom of religion for groups as well as individuals is explicitly espoused. Because Smith believed this principle was enshrined in the Constitution, he termed it "a glorious standard . . . founded in the wisdom of God." Indeed, it is elevated into select company: "We say that God is true; that the Constitution of the United States is true; that the Bible is true; that the Book of Mormon is true; the Book of Covenants is true; that Christ is true; that the ministering angels sent forth from God are true."[22] Clearly their experience of the inadequacy of the American polity in protecting their interests did not diminish apparent Mormon loyalty to the higher standard it was thought to embody.

This idealistic attitude was at least an element in the Prophet's journey to Washington, beginning in November 1839 and continuing well into the early months of 1840, in an attempt to appeal against the outrages the Saints experienced in Missouri and their failure to obtain redress under local and state jurisdictions. Of course, the report of the Senate Judiciary Committee illustrates precisely the larger point I have argued: that certainly the federal government (and also the states) had been extremely reluctant to use religion as a category from which rights derive or obligations flow. Indeed, the Prophet's high estimate of the Constitution was contradicted by his experience in seeking redress for the Saints. It is at least a matter of historic interest that the Nauvoo City Council did adopt an ordinance on religious liberty approximately one year later that gave a positive grant of religious liberty to all citizens. The initial issue of the *Nauvoo Neighbor* explicitly reiterated support for this position.[23]

In the report of a sermon that Joseph Smith Jr. preached on 15 October 1843, it is clear that the shortcomings of government under the Constitution had rankled the Prophet. He identified very precisely what he termed the Constitution's defect, its failure to provide for what might be termed positive religious liberty. His own recommendation was: "The Constitution should contain a provision that every officer of the Government who should neglect or refuse to extend the protection guaranteed in the Constitution should be subject to capital punishment."[24]

In some ways Joseph Smith's view of the Constitution seems to change in these years. In the position we reviewed at the outset, the movement seemed committed to a broadly Pauline view that human law is indeed of God, even if particular laws may not be, and that the provision for laws in the United States is unparalleled. By 1843, a significant development appears to have taken place in the Mormon self-understanding. We might call this a shift to an enabling view of the Constitution: "The Constitution is not a law, but it empowers the people to make laws." And again "the Constitution is not law to us, but it makes provision for us whereby we can make laws." Is it too much to see in this shift to an emphasis upon the people making laws for themselves under the Constitution at least one key to the Prophet's active interest in politics that developed soon afterward?[25]

By early February 1844, Joseph Smith Jr. had issued his "Views of the Powers and Policy of the Government of the United States," which can only have been a declaration of his own readiness for a political career.[26] It should be seen as an indication of his willingness to accept the authority of the governmental realm to use the Constitution to make more adequate laws. We could propose that the evolution of the Prophet's attitude toward government represented a diminished emphasis on the transcendence of the religious kingdom over and beyond earthly regimes—in short that the millennium was nigh. I do not think there is sufficient evidence to make that a sure case. It does seem clear, however, that given the fluidity of the early Mormon movement, such shifts of emphasis and objectives are entirely plausible—indeed, to be expected. In any case, in April 1844 at a conference of the Church, the Prophet gave a ringing endorsement of religious freedom, evidence that he remained committed to these principles whatever other changes were taking place in his thinking.[27] Of course, within a very short period of time, the phase of the movement we have been discussing was brought to an end by the murder of the Prophet.

My objective has been to explore the characteristics of the Mormon movement in its early years. Let me summarize briefly the chief points.

First, certain basic characteristics of Mormonism in its period of origin are very much like those of other religions at comparable points in their development. Especially prominent in the Mormon case are strong figuralism, significant millenarian convictions, pronounced ecstatic elements, and inventive or improvised organizational forms. We should properly interpret Mormonism as a new culture-in-the-making. A new social world was in the process of being defined, and thus the Old World was outmoded for those who became committed to it.

Second, under persecution, the Mormon movement wrestled with and developed a general position on the relationship between religion and government.

The starting point was the two kingdoms or two realms pattern that is so deeply embedded in the Christian tradition.

Third, adoption of this twofold pattern as a means of defining church-state issues often means devaluation of this world in comparison with the next, or de-emphasis of the realm of governmental affairs in relationship to the religious realm. This devaluation does not take place in the early Mormon movement. Indeed, loyalty to the United States remains strong, and religious liberty is emphasized at Nauvoo.

Fourth, in the early 1840s, even after the Mormons experienced frustration with the government, their emphasis began to turn to the possibilities of using the government and directing it toward the realization of religious ends through a new interpretation of the Constitution.

I think that a review such as this helps us to see more clearly the characteristics of the particular movement on the one hand and the whole society and its culture on the other. No doubt Mormonism as a religious movement was securely a part of that environment. Indeed, the elements of figuralism, millenarianism, ecstasy, and inventive organizational structures were all characteristics shared to a lesser degree with other groups seeking salvation and pressing for a more satisfactory culture. Certainly no other movement of the period, however, combined them in such a way that a self-sufficient and vigorous separate culture and secure church were the outcome. Of course, the dramatic martyrdom of the Prophet served as a catalyst in this case.

It is also clear that the religious reality of the Mormon movement inevitably raised those classical church-state or religion-government issues that we Americans like to think were effectively separated and resolved at the outset of the national life. The Mormon case makes clear that they were scarcely separated and resolved by the 1830s and 1840s. I do not think they have been in the intervening decades either, and they certainly are not in our own time. Because these issues can be brought to some degree of focus through reviewing the period of Mormon origins, that case ought to help all of us Americans better understand our common present as well as the past we share.

Notes

The epigraph is from Joseph Smith Jr. et al., *History of the Church of Jesus Christ of Latter-day Saints*, ed. B. H. Roberts, 7 vols. (Salt Lake City: Deseret News Press, published 1902–12, 1932; reprint, Deseret Book, 1976, paperback issue, 1978), 1:97.

1. Ibid., 5:552. Editorial comment in the *History of the Church* observes that this statement of the elder's views is "doubtless faulty." More likely, the views of the Church leaders were subject to change within the early movement. The concern expressed by the editor is that the salvation of America, in line with the conditional framework espoused by Mormonism, depended upon its repentance, so that such a forthright prophecy as

Pratt seemed to find in the book would be out of the question. The most telling point to me is the pattern of dispersed meetings of the Twelve, which indicates deep belief in the redemption of the whole nation.

2. Nathan O. Hatch, "The Christian Movement and the Demand for a Theology of the People," *Journal of American History* 67 (December 1980): 545–67.

3. Gordon S. Wood, "Evangelical America and Early Mormonism," *New York History* 61 (October 1980): 359–86.

4. Hatch, "The Christian Movement," 565–66.

5. See Erich Auerbach, *Mimesis: The Representation of Reality in Western Literature,* trans. Willard R. Trask (Garden City, N.Y.: Doubleday, 1953); and Auerbach's essay "Figura" in his *Scenes from the Drama of European Literature: Six Essays* (New York: Meridian, 1959).

6. Hans W. Frei, *The Eclipse of Biblical Narrative: A Study in Eighteenth and Nineteenth Century Hermeneutics* (New Haven, Conn.: Yale University Press, 1974).

7. See especially Sacvan Bercovitch, *The American Jeremiad* (Madison: University of Wisconsin Press, 1978), and Sacvan Bercovitch, comp., *Typology and Early American Literature* (Amherst: University of Massachusetts Press, 1972).

8. Smith et al., *History of the Church,* 1:252.

9. Lucy Mack Smith, *Biographical Sketches of Joseph Smith, the Prophet, and his Progenitors for Many Generations* (1853; New York: Arno Press, 1969), 173. See also, for example, *Autobiography of Parley P. Pratt,* ed. Parley P. Pratt Jr. (1874; Salt Lake City: Deseret Book, 1970).

10. Klaus J. Hansen, *Quest for Empire: The Political Kingdom of God and the Council of Fifty in Mormon History* (East Lansing: Michigan State University Press, 1967), 18.

11. See Smith et al., *History of the Church,* 1:337, for an indication of the centrality of millennial beliefs.

12. Ibid., 2:145, 2:294, 2:466.

13. Ibid., 3:383, 3:390, 5:256, 5:550, 6:318.

14. Ibid., 2:428, 2:432.

15. Ibid., 5:501.

16. Ibid., 2:8–9, 2:13.

17. Ibid., 2:19.

18. Ibid., 2:246–50. Note that section 134 has the status of "a declaration of belief," not a revelation. In addition, it was accepted by the general assembly when the Prophet was not present.

19. Ibid., 2:248.

20. Mark De Wolfe Howe, *The Garden and the Wilderness: Religion and Government in American Constitutional History* (Chicago: University of Chicago Press, 1965), chap. 2.

21. Smith et al., *History of the Church,* 2:249.

22. Ibid., 3:289, 3:304.

23. Ibid., 4:90, 4:306.

24. Ibid., 6:57.

25. Ibid., 5:289.

26. Ibid., 6:197.

27. Ibid., 6:304–5.

CHAPTER 6

Learning to Play: The Mormon Way
and the Way of Other Americans

R. Laurence Moore

"My son," says the Christian father, "you should not attend a theatre,
for there the wicked assemble; nor a ball room, for there the wicked
assemble; you should not be found playing a ball, for the sinner does
that."
—Brigham Young, in commencing a defense of theater,
   6 March 1862

Americans, like people in any time and place, have always found ways to amuse
themselves. Social historians have virtually demolished the notion that a universal internalization of the Protestant work ethic explains the rise of the American
nation. Colonial Virginians were too lazy to work even when their lives literally
depended on more rigorously disciplined labor. Eighteenth- and nineteenth-
century artisans, apparently everywhere, came to work as much to drink and to
socialize as to get anything done. The fabled sobriety of New England Puritans
controlled but did not obliterate their interest in sensual pleasures and in games.[1]
The Protestant ethic, as Max Weber demonstrated with such brilliance, represented an effort to establish steady labor habits in people who had none. The
strategies developed by its proponents were intentionally repressive, and, given
what had to be done, they were enormously effective. Nonetheless, we should not
imagine that very many Americans ever regarded work as everything. Even Benjamin Franklin managed to prepare himself for Paris.

However, while recognizing that the demand for recreation is a historical
constant, we must still acknowledge that play had a tough time turning itself
into something fully legitimate in the United States. I want to focus on certain
components of that struggle for legitimacy in the middle part of the nineteenth
century. And I will begin by pointing to two seemingly antithetical religious
attitudes toward the subject of play. The first is a dour message that was printed
in 1851 in a Congregationalist publication, *The New Englander:* "Let our readers,

one and all, remember that we are sent into the world, not for sport and amusement, but for labor; not to enjoy and please ourselves, but to serve and glorify
God, and be useful to our fellow men. That is the great object and end of life."[2]
The second is from the records of a Mormon mother recalling a Utah Christmas
in 1850: "On this day I went to Brigham's mill to a Christmas party. Stayed all
night. We had a first rate supper at midnight. I helped to get it on the table. They
danced all night until five o'clock in the morning the party broke up."[3]

I assume that the contrast needs no extended comment. But there is an irony
that ought to be noted. Mormons are not highly regarded for their fun-loving
qualities, at least among the Gentiles whom I know. Skiers who journey to Utah
from the East Coast learn to identify Mormons by what they shun: alcohol,
tobacco, caffeine, and sex outside of marriage. These contemporaries identify
Mormonism with the sort of Puritanism parodied by H. L. Mencken—the haunting fear that someone, somewhere may be happy. Lest we attribute this judgment
solely to ignorance, we ought to remember that David Brion Davis, in one of the
most important articles ever written about the nineteenth-century Mormon
experience, saw the ghosts of John Winthrop and Cotton Mather pushing handcarts to the Great Salt Basin. "Mormonism," he wrote, "was a link in the Puritan
tradition, asserting a close and personal God, providential history, predestination, and ideal theocracy, the importance of a Christian calling, and a Church of
Saints."[4]

How did Mormons, these latter-day Puritans, manage to legitimate ideas of
pleasurable entertainment in the first half of the nineteenth century, an era when
many—perhaps most—other Christian ministers viewed fiction suspiciously,
identified the theater with the brothel, and looked with horror at evening parties
that included dancing? Why has this Mormon pioneering in the realm of popular culture been largely forgotten, even with the contemporary contributions of
the Mormon Tabernacle Choir, the Osmond family singers, and J. Willard Marriott? Elsewhere, I have risked writing in an interpretative way about the Mormon experience.[5] I do not plan to do much more of that. To add anything would
probably only confuse whatever I got right and repeat with embellishment whatever I got wrong. On the other hand, with respect to my current research on the
interplay between religion and commercial popular culture, the Mormon experience has once again opened up a lot of questions for me.

Let me remind you of some things that are, in a comparative sense, quite remarkable. While the Mormons were gathered in Nauvoo, Joseph Smith regarded theater as a medium of instruction and organized a dramatic company.
Brigham Young, one of the original Mormon thespians, went further. Already by
1850, he had mobilized the Salt Lake City Saints to build an amusement resort
north of the city near some warm springs. Also, a social hall, dedicated on the
first day of 1853, housed theatrical performances, musical programs, and social
dances. Most wondrously, Young ordered the construction of the famous Salt

Lake Theater, which was completed in 1862. It seated fifteen hundred people, was as well equipped as any theater in the United States, and mounted a set of serious and comic plays that was probably unmatched by any company west of the Mississippi. This was eight years before the railroad reached Utah and several months before the temple was finished or the Tabernacle started.[6]

What's more, revelers and theatergoers in Salt Lake City did things that Brigham Young did not wholly endorse. Sponsors of parties occasionally permitted a set or two of "round dances," polkas and waltzes that brought young bodies into dangerously close proximity.[7] Young's original troupe of amateur "actors," a company that included one of his daughters, successfully wrested professional status from their reluctant leader. They also ignored, within reason, Young's dislike of tragedies, and they found ways around his ban against the depiction of violence onstage. I do not mean to suggest that Mormon entertainments were permissive. Quite the contrary. But they were advanced, as judged by the standards of most other churchgoing Protestants in mid-nineteenth-century America. Brigham Young developed what we might call an "ideology" of play at a time when most other American clerics still thought of play as the devil's invention.

Young did grow sensitive to his reputation as a man who liked to dance. In a reply to critics who noted that Utah Mormons amused and enjoyed themselves a great deal, and who further suggested that entertainment must be part of their religion, Young issued a disclaimer: "dancing and theatrical performances were no part of our religion." The Social Hall in Salt Lake City existed as a "fun hall," not as a place where it was appropriate to administer the sacrament. However, in one vital sense the disclaimer was wrong, or at least governed by another one of Young's favorite refrains: "Our work, our every-day labor, our whole lives are within the scope of our religion."[8]

Recreation was not temple ritual, but like everything else that the Lord permitted as essential to human happiness, Mormon play was not a thing apart from Mormon service to God. Mormons could safely go to the theater because the stage, in Young's words, "can be made to aid the pulpit in impressing upon the minds of the community an enlightened sense of a virtuous life, also a proper horror of the enormity of sin and a just dread of its consequences."[9] The confidence that lay behind that statement, the fact that not only the theater but a full range of entertainments had been incorporated into daily routines sponsored and encouraged by the Mormon hierarchy, remained in the 1860s one of the most distinctive things about the Mormon Church.

To be sure, many other Protestant ministers were, by the middle of the nineteenth century, working their way toward a justification of play. Yet prior to 1850, their progress had not been rapid. It is worth trying to understand why. To say that they had moral objections to most commercial forms of popular entertainment is true, but it is not a sufficient explanation of their often-strident condemnation. If it were, then clerics could have developed an appreciation for leisured pleasures, as they finally did, only by becoming men of looser morals than their forebears. Doubtlessly some did just that. However, most of them justified play only when they were able to construe it as rigorously moral. To do that required some rethinking and a reconstruction of strategies of how best to impress religious values upon people who no longer found the church, as a simple spatial matter, at the center of their everyday activities. They faced problems that Mormons, in the gathered community, were able to solve with more confidence.

Every student of antebellum American culture has been impressed with the tremendous amount of prescriptive literature that was aimed at regulating and restraining behavior. The many advice books, written in particular for young men and young women, covered habits of diet, sex, sleep, reading, and work. The substantive part of what was good and proper to do could have been conveyed in a short list, even though it usually wasn't: serve God, avoid passion and excess, be disciplined and temperate, and stay busy in useful pursuits. The fulfillment of these primary duties entailed more and more a trained capacity to resist and avoid newly invented temptations. Almost everything that we associate with the emergence of popular commercial culture in the first half of the nineteenth century was either to be shunned altogether or approached with the utmost caution.

The Reverend Henry Ward Beecher, in the days before his own tastes for leisured pleasures were fully developed, rendered a typical list of proscribed amusements. No shooting matches; no taverns; no reading of novels, newspapers, and almanacs; no drinking, gambling, smoking, or swearing; no theatergoing; no card-playing or dancing; no attendance at balls, race tracks, or circuses. As for anything suggesting the life of a sexual libertine, Beecher wrote severely that had he a son of such tendencies, he would wish him in his grave. "The plague is mercy, the cholera is love, the deadliest fever is refreshment to man's body, in comparison with this epitome and essence of moral disease." Beecher counseled the "common duties" rather than the habits of "reverie and mental romancing." The imagination itself was a "wild pleasure."[10] The safe exercise of those common duties was restricted to the havens of church, work, and family.

Both Charles Dickens and Frances Trollope fled from the United States as a joyless society, and insofar as very many young men heeded all of Beecher's advice, it most certainly was.[11] As one champion of common laborers, Mike Walsh, complained at midcentury: "The gloomy, churlish, money-worshiping, all-pervading spirit of the age has swept all the poetry of life out of the poor man's sphere. . . . Ballad-singing, street dancing, tumbling, public games, all are either prohibited or discountenanced, so that Fourth of July and election sports alone remain."[12] Even the rowdy fun associated with those latter activities was contested.

The moral norms for behavior that we find in prescriptive literature written by Protestant clerics, by medical doctors, and by other champions of ordered domesticity are scarcely novel to the first part of the nineteenth century. Horse racing, drinking, gambling, and theatergoing had never at any point in the American past been regarded as activities that sustained Christian virtue. On the other hand, what deserves notice in the antebellum period are the vigorous efforts to tighten the norms, to render them more stringent. We are talking about an era when temperance came to mean not a moderate use of spirits, as had once befitted even religious meetings, but total avoidance; when the biblical commandment against adultery was interpreted to mean not a fidelity to one's spouse but virtual celibacy within the married state; when a religious people who had long practiced "bundling" as a way of staying warm on a cold night were told that dancing was a dangerously lascivious activity; and when the habit of reading, so long encouraged by Protestants, seemed suddenly to encounter Protestant objections that before would have suggested a Papist plot to keep books out of the hands of the people.

To say that antebellum American Protestants were suffering from a crisis of confidence is a safe and uncontroversial way to begin our analysis. But the observation has become so conventional that we often forget just how much they had to worry about. The American nation had been explicitly founded on principles of novelty. That bit of self-understanding was in part mythic, for no group of socially organized people exists without some foundation in collective experience that has spawned customs and traditions. Nonetheless, the very act of writing a Constitution signified that the American framework of government had no precedents among European governments. The uncertainties about whether it could work explain why virtually all Americans in public life agreed, by the end of the 1790s, that the future of their nation depended upon order and unity, that these societal requirements were in turn tied to public morality and virtue, and that the health of these depended on preserving and promoting the religious sentiments of American citizens. Some of the founders may have been Deists in private, but in the foxholes that they dug to fight the first political battles of the young nation, they became commonplace Christians.

The potential problems were formidable. The United States, although heavily agrarian in the first decades of the nineteenth century, was undergoing the first stages of industrialization and urbanization that had already transformed some parts of Europe. People poured into the country from abroad, and even more people moved around the country—from areas of older settlement to new communities on the frontier and, in a sort of reverse frontierism, from farms into cities. Between 1820 and 1850, those parts of the United States with the densest concentrations of population witnessed a revolution in the organization of workplaces and of the household, spatial changes that destroyed older forms of social cohesion and of social control. By midcentury, one could speak of distinct social classes in the United States: the very rich; the middle classes who had organized themselves explicitly on rules of conduct that linked work, virtue, and religion; and a large class of laborers who worked for wages, some of them as steadily as economic conditions permitted, others with as little effort as was necessary to meet their need for food and shelter. African American slaves were an additional affront to egalitarian ideals.

From a detached perspective, the whole enterprise of maintaining order was tenuous indeed. The urgent moral imperatives stressed in middle-class prescriptive literature addressed individuals because no one else, it seemed, had adequate power to enforce norms. The nation had disestablished religion and placed the churches on a voluntary basis. The hope that the absence of a state church would put an end to the destructive tendencies of religious bickerings went unfulfilled. Despite important examples of interdenominational cooperation, the trend was toward religious division, even angry division. Well before the Civil War so decisively demonstrated how many things Americans would never resolve peacefully, Latter-day Saints and Catholics had tested with their blood the limits of free religious practice in the United States.

The religious fragmentation of the nation prompted fears about another phenomenon—the lessened public authority of the clergy. By 1850, their power to conduct church trials as a way of controlling families and communities had disappeared. Ministers had become the hired hands of their congregations, and their tenure in office by the middle of the nineteenth century was less certain than it had been a hundred years earlier. Most Protestants were still prepared to let their ministers say anything they wanted on Sundays, but clerical authority over congregations ended with the last word of the sermons. After the 1820s, ministers themselves lamented their ineffectiveness in enforcing Sabbatarian legislation, in regulating the moral conditions of their communities, and to specify the conditions of work and play.

This background shaped their resistance to new commercialized forms of leisure. The problem faced by Protestant clerics was really no different from that faced by other officials and professionals who aspired to maintain the cultural hegemony of their values. The world was becoming more impersonal. In the cities of New York, Boston, and Philadelphia, even in the smaller towns of New England and of upstate New York, men and women who had once known one another, perhaps not intimately but by reputation, merged into nameless crowds. People lived in relatively close proximity, but their numbers created a density that altered the consequences of that nearness. Even people who had the forums to address crowds and congregations directly, who could try to impart to them in old-fashioned ways a sense of common civic responsibilities, often did not know the people in their audiences. Antebellum Americans attended lectures to be informed, instructed, and entertained. But their relation to those who instructed them or made them laugh was usually one of anonymity. The problem of how to impose order and morality on anonymous masses was daunting, and one can appreciate why the first reflex, and one that was long sustained, was a search for ways to tighten the standards of correct behavior. That move prejudiced almost all forms of diversion.

It won't do to call the reaction blind conservatism. The social progressives of the antebellum period worried the most about declining morality. As historical situations go, the rate of social change was unprecedented and seemed to spring from powerful technologies that were immune to moral control. For example, cheaper ways to manufacture paper, stereotype printing, and the steam-powered press were revolutionizing habits of reading, a development with important implications for the use of leisure time. The apparently insatiable demand for relatively new kinds of reading material (the novel, especially the serialized novel; the penny newspaper; the jumbo story newspaper; the illustrated periodical such as Godey's *Ladies Book*) signified not merely that more people were reading regularly but also that people were reading more randomly and with less reverence than before. The choice of what they read was exclusively in their hands. Reading became a private activity rather than one mediated by oral discourse in public places.

For moralists, the problem occasioned by the availability of cheap reading material, which in this context needs to be viewed as an invitation to play, was not simply one of ensuring proper didactic content. Most of the print material sold in the United States in the first half of the nineteenth century had little in it that was morally objectionable. Even sensational tales that graphically described the seamy underside of urban life stretched but did not destroy the boundaries of conventional moral discourse.[13] What was bothersome was the uncertainty of what people, especially women, made of reading material, even wholesome reading material, in the privacy of their boudoirs. The Protestant encouragement given to the private study of the Bible had formerly applied in a world where Protestants heard the Bible authoritatively interpreted weekly or even daily. But there were no fully enforceable authoritative guides to diverse reading material in the nineteenth century. In this situation, the danger of reading increased in direct proportion to its power to provoke or stimulate the imagination.

The Protestant response to cultural change was in many instances bold enough. However, in the period before the Civil War, Protestant ministers found it extremely difficult to mention the word "amusement" or "entertainment" or "leisure" in a favorable way if they could not specify a connection to what was "rational" and "useful" and "serviceable to God." To suggest that one could do something "light" and "diverting" because one was tired and wanted to give one's mind a rest from "serious" subjects represented to them an impossible confusion of concepts. Understandably, accommodation to the times was often managed by allowing the right hand to ignore what the left hand was doing. Ministers continued to proscribe in their public statements some forms of play that they were clearly allowing in their own homes. This is not as hypocritical as it might sound. A novel read by a minister's daughter in the living room of the rectory was much healthier than the same novel read elsewhere in secret. Censorship was concerned as much with the context of reading as with content.

This last point suggests why so many Protestant sermons and denominational tracts stubbornly opposed attendance at the theater and at balls. Unlike the saloon, or the racetrack, or any place where gambling was common, theatrical performances and balls began to gain moral-minded defenders in the first part of the nineteenth century. Their point of view was seductive. They noted that the plots of nineteenth-century melodramas regularly punished vice and rewarded virtue. They argued that the literary genius of William Shakespeare, who was the most popular playwright among all social classes in antebellum America, was tied to his moral genius.[14] Likewise, they reasoned, the artistically patterned forms of dance that dominated social behavior at fancy balls posed no problems to conventional morality. Balls did not have to be, nor were they always, gaudy displays of extravagant taste. Men and women managed to dance and socialize without any observable immodesty or lustfulness.

I would suggest that clerical opposition to balls and the theater persisted, despite the defenders, and perhaps grew stronger between 1820 and 1850 because ministers feared a deception that could not easily be detected in the changed environment of a rapidly expanding and urbanizing America. To notice only what was ostensibly going on in places of amusement was to miss the danger. It was the atmosphere of the theater, not the play itself (however much stage acting itself was an example of deception), that corrupted. It was the unspoken understandings of the ballroom, not the formal elegance of the dance, that perverted. In both theater and ballroom, the formal rules of propriety concealed the sexual excitement. In such situations, order was precariously balanced. In the theater, in fact, it constantly broke down when expressions of disapproval broke into fights, even riots. In the ballroom, the polite decorum that governed the manifest interaction between the sexes was more covertly subverted. The fundamental moral objection grew from the fear that in most public urban spaces, behavior could not reliably be controlled. That was because public surveillance no longer carried the authority of a morally unified community.

Significantly, when many theaters proved they could effectively regulate the actions of their patrons, when they at least got rid of the prostitutes in the "third tier" and could boast of audiences composed of husbands and wives and sometimes children, clerical hostility lessened. True, the process of "censuring" theatrical audiences drove many patrons out of the "opera house" toward pleasures that clerics had reason to regard as far worse. Nonetheless, various other experiments in urban planning helped ease the fears clerics had of urban spaces that drew crowds together for purposes other than work.

Perhaps no single thing was more important in this respect than the design and construction of Central Park in New York City. It in turn encouraged the landscaping of countless green acres in cities across the nation. The grand vision of Calvert Vaux and Frederick Law Olmstead, which was accepted by the government of New York City in 1858, institutionalized the display of leisure and pleasure. Central Park was a place for all social classes to mingle and to escape the hectic pace of the city that would one day enclose it. At the same time, the ideal of the park was "rational" recreation, the passive enjoyment of a quiet, natural setting that, according to Reverend H. W. Bellows, induced orderly and contemplative habits. "It has been observed," he noted, "that rude, noisy fellows, after entering . . . the park become hushed, moderate, and careful."[15]

For a long time, and for obvious reasons, team sports were banned from American parks. The idea of using architecture to control public pastimes, as a way of sacralizing leisure for some purpose higher than mere enjoyment, was through the rest of the nineteenth century a standard way to judge the success or failure of the design of any large project. The same criteria that were used to sponsor the park movement (in the words of Andrew Jackson Downing, to "soften and humanize the rude, educate and enlighten the ignorant") were applied to the great Chicago Columbian Exposition of 1893. This project, brought together under the genius of Daniel Burnham, was finally, over many objections, opened to the public on Sundays, in large part so that "our mind-hungry, beauty-starved, ignorant, but eagerly ambitious masses could best make use of its civilizing and uplifting ministrations."[16] We are, however, getting ahead of ourselves.

Possibly Protestant clerical accommodation to the proliferation of leisure or play opportunities, following the argument that leisure could be made effectively Christian, might have happened sooner and with less anxiety had it not been for the accelerating arrival of German and Irish Catholics into northeastern cities beginning in the 1840s. The German newcomers, with the evident pleasure that they took in beer gardens, their relish of sports, and their enthusiasm for street festivals, posed the lesser problem. The easy conscience that accompanied these pleasures struck many American-born Protestants as un-Christian, but since Germans usually pursued leisure as a family enterprise, it was hard to make out a clear case of unwholesomeness.

Fortunately for the Protestant conscience, the pleasures of the Irish were easier to condemn. Everything the Irish did smacked of the unsavory. Their leisure activities seemed to revolve around rituals of drinking, especially dangerous in the Irish case because it was feared that drinking was an end in itself rather than a way of refreshing the body for a renewed round of disciplined work. Protestant clergy, who blamed Catholics for introducing permissiveness into American society, redoubled their vigilance in the 1850s and their opposition to most forms of urban entertainment. Catholics represented the full range of threats that they associated with industrializing society. There might be safe ways to play, as some parts of their experience were persuasively demonstrating. However, there were new things to fear, new reasons to suspect popular pastimes that defied their effective control.

At this point, we can recognize the clear advantage that Joseph Smith and Brigham Young had over most other American Christians. They had much less to fear in the matter of leisure because they retained effective control over what happened when Mormons socialized with other Mormons. In a gathered community, where the line between public and private was indistinctly drawn, public behavior was not protected by anonymity. It was not that the rationale used by Young to justify dancing and theatergoing in Salt Lake City was unknown to other American Protestants. Frederic Sawyer, for example, in a book he published in 1847, *A Plea for Amusements,* urged it upon them: "Our amusements can never be made as healthy, and as useful, as they are capable of being made, until the religious portion of the community assumes their true position toward them. . . . If libraries, and reading rooms, and gymnasiums, and galleries of art, and halls of science, and parties, and dancing, and museums and theatres, are to be made useful, it must be through the agency, and under the fostering care, and regulating hand, of the wise, the prudent, and the good. Religion must enter into the common life and cease to be gloomy."[17] However, from the standpoint of many ministers, Sawyer and others who shared his opinion were simply underestimating the difficulties of achieving the supervision.

The fact that most American Protestants did not live in gathered communities seemed to limit severely what the churches could in fact sponsor and control. Arguably, the Catholic Church worried less about the moral behavior of urban immigrants, not because the Church was indulgent toward immorality, but because American urban Catholics lived in closely bonded, ethnic neighborhoods. Proximity had traditionally been the best form of social control. But for Protestants who no longer lived in the neighborhood of their churches, the impersonality that resulted from urbanization was a potential disaster and a cause for constant worry. They too had shown little concern over drinking when church trials still intervened in the family life of communities and when masters and artisans had lived together under the same roof. Leisure became a different sort of problem when privacy turned legislative prohibition into the only possible sort of control. At least many thought so.

As it happened, American Protestants had more experience with sponsored entertainments and with the control of anonymous crowd behavior than might be imagined from reading their lamentations. As sponsors of the revivals that had so successfully brought antebellum Americans under the sway of churches, they were in fact cultural innovators. Antebellum revivalist ministers have been given credit for many things, not all of them positive. However, two achievements are frequently overlooked. They were our first, and perhaps in their present-day successors our best, crowd psychologists, at least in the practical sense of knowing how to stir a crowd while at the same time controlling their behavior. And they engineered the first successful experiments in showing that a religious meeting could be both a devotional worship of God and a pleasure-filled social event.

At the beginning of the nineteenth century, of course, no one justified revivals as social events. People might gather for religious meetings in the wilderness for as long as a week. They might camp out in tents, stay up all night, and give license to their emotions in ways that were unthinkable in other situations. The people who came merely to watch and to scoff might have regarded the "riotous" behavior as entertainment. But for the pious, revivalism was serious business. And for those who organized the revivals, the emphasis was upon control and order. A revival meeting became as rule-bound as a regular church service.

Critics, of course, viewed the measures taken to ensure order as insufficient. The problem of regulation caused many denominational leaders, especially Presbyterians, to restrain their enthusiasm for revivals, and most revivals after 1820, in response to criticism, were conducted in urban areas under the strict sponsorship of organized churches. Only the Methodists continued to emphasize camp meetings in the wilderness or in rural locations. But those Methodist camp meetings, which go a long way to explain the rising popularity of Methodism in antebellum America, managed in the same process of development to regularize religious enthusiasm and to sponsor religious renewal under conditions that seemed very much like those we now associate with vacations.

Ellen Weiss, in a splendid book on a Methodist camp meeting that was founded on Martha's Vineyard in 1835, has suggested how it happened.[18] Her example, known as Wesleyan Grove, grew from a campground laid out for the temporary erection of tents into a thirty-four-acre compound of five hundred permanent cottages, many of them architectural gems. Since the site happened to command a magnificent ocean view, it inevitably tied those who came to worship there into activities of recreation. By 1867, Wesleyan Grove was closely linked to a neighboring community that was developed quite explicitly as a summer resort. Ocean Bluff had a boardwalk and, until it burned to the ground in 1892, one of the best-equipped resort hotels in the country.

Such a frank combining of religious revivalism with sea bathing, bands, and commercialism would not have been countenanced by any Protestant denomination in the antebellum period. But the Reverend B. W. Gorham, who had written a manual for organizing a camp meeting in 1854, was reaching toward a religious justification of leisure. The camp meetings, he said, were successful because they called "God's people away from their worldly business and cares for several successive days, thereby securing time for the mind to disentangle itself of worldly care, and rise to an undistracted contemplation of spiritual realities."[19] That is not yet copy for a travel agent's brochure, but it is an important step in that direction. Gorham found the divine justification he needed in the Jewish feasts of Passover and Tabernacles—great festivals, he said, that proved "there is an element in man which demands occasional excitement," a break from routine and above all a rest from labor.[20]

Not every Protestant observer saw in the Methodist innovations either proper religion or, alternatively, much that invited pure pleasure. Andrew Dickson White, the first president of Cornell University and a man with strict standards of propriety, was not taken by scenes at Oak Bluff. He was repulsed by the sight of young people roller-skating with arms around each other to a waltz version of "Nearer, My God, to Thee." Charles Dudley Warner, an American writer who coauthored with Mark Twain *The Gilded Age,* judged what he saw of the bathing frolics of Wesleyan Grove residents as "the staid dissipation of a serious minded people. . . . Most of the faces are of a grave, severe type, plain and good, of the sort of people ready to die for a notion."[21] Yet for Protestants who did not live in gathered communities, the institution of a summer retreat that temporarily joined religion and leisure was a significant innovation. Methodists built another famous vacation retreat at Ocean Grove on the Jersey shore. Its annual reports covered all the concerns of a settled community—transportation, sewage disposal, parks, street repair, police and fire departments, and bathing houses.[22] It was a Protestant genius of sorts that discovered so close a parallel between the enhancement of property values and the enhancement of religious values.

If it was not feasible to gather saints for the entire year, perhaps two weeks at the beach might restore Christians in their normal enthusiasm for work and moral discipline and leave them immune for the rest of the year to the siren call of "wicked assemblies." Christian camps at least provided a context where Protestant moralists imagined for the first time in industrializing America that it was all right to do absolutely nothing. This was indeed a pathbreaking thought. As we have seen, Protestants in their tentative efforts to embrace leisure moved forward most boldly when they could assign leisure a productive or useful purpose that made it the moral equivalent of work. Reading history or biography, helping a neighbor put up jam, writing instructive letters to one's children—these had always been unproblematic Protestant pleasures. But to lie on the beach and let the mind go blank and forget responsibilities? Once it had seemed that only Satan would encourage such behavior.

The Chautauqua Association, which was organized in the 1870s, stayed more carefully within the boundaries of utility. At least at the outset, its purpose was to combine recreation with a fixed program of mental training for Sunday School teachers of all denominations. Chautauqua also began under the sponsorship of Methodists—John Vincent, who was later to become a bishop in the church, and Lewis Miller, a wealthy Methodist layperson. Vincent wanted to carve from a splendid natural setting a human space where people would feel no break between the sacred and the secular, would sense no tension between the religious and the world. "Every day," he said, "should be sacred. . . . There should be no break between sabbaths. The cable of divine motion should stretch through seven days. . . . Kitchen work, farm work, shop work, as well as school work, are divine."[23]

One might say that this notion was what had always stood at the heart of the Protestant Reformation. It held that the Catholic Church had corrupted the practices of the first Christians by ritualizing an unscriptural separation between the sacred and the profane. In doing so, the Church had forced men and women to depend on its institutionalized power to dispense God's grace. Catholics had obligations to partake of the sacraments, their regular but interrupted connection to the sacred, and spent the rest of their time becoming corrupted by the worldly. Protestants imagined that they had rejected this sort of cyclical movement between the secular and the sacred and had insisted on linear moral progression through a world where Christians recognized God's steady judgment in everything they did. Certainly New England's first Protestants had to an extraordinary degree treated space and time as uniform. However, a changed society in the nineteenth century forced the re-creation of that ideal, not in the everyday lives of Protestant Christians, where sacred and secular too often seemed distinct, but in a retreat that gave them the leisure to remember a world of more harmonious meanings.

The original Chautauqua Sunday School Institutes lasted for two weeks and were organized around lessons, sermons, devotional meetings, and such recreations as concerts, fireworks, bonfires, humorous lectures, and music in all forms. The "Department of Entertainment" was not peripheral to the enterprise but essential. Vincent insisted: "Away with the heresy that man is stepping aside from his legitimate work as a Christian minister when he is trying to turn all secular nature into an altar for the glory of God!"[24] Once this was said by way of justification, the possible range of material to nurture the skills of Sunday School teachers expanded enormously. The Chautauqua Literary and Scientific Circle, which was launched in 1878, aimed to promote valuable reading of all sorts. Every year, people who had in their homes stuck with a correspondence course in reading journeyed to the now-famous lake in western New York for "Recognition Day," "the great day of the annual gathering."[25] The ceremony to honor them took place in the "Hall in the Grove," an open-sided structure that permitted the participants to look beyond the busts of Plato, Socrates, Homer, Virgil, Goethe, and Shakespeare, which lined the space, to the splendor of their wooded setting.

By the turn of the century, those who visited Chautauqua to hear lectures by distinguished preachers, college presidents, authors and editors, leaders in social reform, political leaders, and distinguished foreigners (as well as to play golf and tennis) were no longer primarily Sunday School teachers. One can argue that what had begun as an attempt to reunite the secular under the sponsorship of the religious had become merely secular, thus confirming what some Protestant clergy still feared as the corrupting allure of play. Perhaps that was so, but there is a counterargument. The growth of Chautauqua's popularity, which was evidenced in part by the spread of imitative institutions around the country, served the original vision of its founders quite well. It was one of the ways Protestant piety transcribed itself into other cultural forms and maintained religion as an important element in American public life.

The trouble with Chautauqua from the standpoint of its founders was not that it surrendered to the secular world but that it could reach, affect, and change the habits of only those people who were already safely and securely Protestant. It succeeded to the degree that it could establish a temporary community of face-to-face relations among people who did not initially know one another. On the other hand, through a process of self-selection, they were already very much alike when they arrived at Lake Chautauqua. Establishing friendly accords when nothing was demanded of the relationship was easy. The experience served to reassure middle-class Protestants that back home they could use environmental planning to adjust to new patterns of life. They could engineer playtime as part of their lives without endangering their souls. Chautauqua, however, was not a spiritual answer to the impersonal social distance that diverse Americans in urban areas normally set among themselves in their everyday affairs.

Another institution, in the long run perhaps more important than Chautauqua, helped legitimate the idea of the Protestant-sponsored play among urban populations. This was the Young Men's Christian Association (YMCA), a movement that began in England and organized its first American branches in Boston and New York City in the early 1850s.[26] The controlling or voting members of YMCA chapters formed in the nineteenth century were men who belonged to evangelical Protestant churches. That excluded Unitarians, Universalists, and, of course, Mormons. However, the YMCA movement sought to serve all young men, including those who were not church members or regular attenders of any religious meeting. Once again, the question was how.

By the end of the nineteenth century, local "Y" chapters had tried any number of means, most of them more successful among young men of the middle class than among factory workers or common laborers. In Chicago, the "Y" was dominated by one of its first members, Dwight Moody. As the most famous revival preacher of his time, Moody tended to stick with the old notions that the best way to deal with sinners was to preach to them and to organize Bible study programs. In other cities, the original emphasis upon religious meetings grew less pronounced. Almost always led by laypersons rather than clergy, many YMCA locals sought more indirect ways to exert influence, ways that paid less attention to dramatic conversion experiences and more attention to the unconscious influences that Horace Bushnell had said were essential to successful "Christian Nurture." The goal was to attract young men into a Christian environment, an association that promoted affective ties among its members through Christian patterns of work and play.

More and more, the lure was sports that were, at first cautiously and then enthusiastically, promoted under the rubric of Muscular Christianity. What most YMCAs learned to promote was the idea "that physical exercise in all forms can become a mighty factor in the development of the highest type of Christian character."[27] Insofar as athletics instilled obedience, self-discipline, self-sacrifice, honor, and truth, they were a useful surrogate for church attendance until the latter habit could be developed. The cause of Christian sports, of course, benefited from plausible associations made between them and work. Both encouraged the same virtues and left the body too exhausted to cause trouble for the soul.

The first YMCA gymnasiums were constructed in 1869 in New York City (the home base of the moral crusader, Anthony Comstock) and in San Francisco. Gymnastic training had already established itself as necessary to the proper formation of young men and women in the city. The German turnverein had done much to popularize the idea, but it independently established itself in colleges and elite boarding schools. Harvard, Yale, Dartmouth, and Williams were among the many American colleges to have constructed gymnasiums by the end of the 1850s. In 1861, Dio Lewis in Boston opened the first normal school to train teachers of physical education.[28]

The gymnasiums associated with the YMCA movement were part of a general trend, but they greatly expanded the number of gymnastic and sports facilities that were available to the young men who comprised the general public. By 1900, there were approximately fifteen hundred local YMCA chapters in the United States. The association counted 507 gymnasiums and 294 paid directors. To train those directors, the YMCA had in 1894 founded a college in Springfield, Massachusetts, with an innovative Physical Education Department. The president of Springfield College, Laurence Doggett, likened physical education directors to "medical missionaries in foreign lands . . . [to extend] Christ's Kingdom among young men."[29] How many souls were eventually won by these missionaries is uncertain. But they did invent two sports that we might liken to the "new" measures introduced by revival preachers in the first part of the nineteenth century—basketball in 1891 and volleyball in 1894.

"New" measures always have their critics, and the innovations sponsored by the YMCA movement were no exception. Even more strongly than with the Chautauqua movement, the ministers of many Protestant churches wondered whether they should cooperate with a movement that they feared was compromising with forces that, if not directly inimical to religion, arguably diluted interest in church attendance. If sports were so good for the soul, then it followed that

Protestant churches should look favorably on sporting events held on Sunday. And that, for a long time, they were not prepared to do.

It was, of course, predictable that the sponsors of the YMCA would have their troubles with many leaders of Protestant denominations. To play was one thing. Letting play crowd out everything that resembled religious devotion was another. Moreover, it seemed fair to ask how local YMCA chapters could guarantee a Christian environment when their facilities were open to virtually anyone and when people passed in and out of their doors without hearing so much as a prayer. The national YMCA convention was able as late as 1913 to reaffirm that its supreme aim was to lead boys and men to become disciples of Christ, pointing them toward church membership. It also (and this provision did not change until the 1930s) continued to limit voting rights to members who belonged to evangelical churches.

However, there was no getting around the fact that the YMCA sponsored gymnasiums as a substitute for formal religious services. The fate of the YMCA bureaucracy in the twentieth century was to develop a professional paid staff who were less noted for their Christian commitment than for their talents in providing well-run facilities to people who paid a fee. In the 1920s, the national YMCA found itself caught in a debate about whether to participate in the newly formed Community Chest. At stake was an issue of identification. To join was arguably to remove the YMCA from the Protestant church network and move it into the world of more general charitable and social services.[30]

The cultural meaning of these developments, and many others like them, reflect important changes. By the first decade of the twentieth century, most Protestants had learned to play, but not simply because their religious values had proved a poor defense against the pleasures of commercialized popular culture. We treat Protestant churchgoers with too little respect if we imagine that they approached formerly forbidden pleasures with a clear conscience because they no longer cared about virtue. Rather, they had learned to think of play as virtuous. The connection between play and virtue had not been a natural one to make or one that was possible with all forms of play. Many things simply got out of hand. Thomas Edison, the inventor of both the phonograph and important processes that made the movies possible, hated the thought that what he created might become mere amusements rather than means to promote education in the schools and business efficiency.[31] He was disappointed. Nonetheless, most Protestant clerics, however much they kicked and screamed, learned, or convinced themselves, that most forms of mass media could effectively carry a moral message. They also learned that organized leisure did not necessarily create unwholesome environments. Wholesome environments in fact created wholesome leisure.

Standards varied, of course. To this day, the strictest Protestant denominations deplore many forms of popular entertainments—dancing, the theater, the movies—and discipline members who defy religious censorship. All Protestant denominations, with varying degrees of rigor, discourage drinking. Moreover, even the most indulgent and liberal clerics on the subject of commercial entertainments have not stopped worrying. They have pledged themselves to work for moral wholesomeness in all public activities associated with recreation. Until very recently, the various censorship boards that have been formed in this country to combat immorality in books, in theatrical productions, in movies, and in television programming have had the strong support of Protestant clergy.

This brings us back to the Mormons and their largely forgotten pioneering efforts to legitimate many forms of entertainment once banned as inappropriate for a Christian people. Without recognizing their debt, American Protestants worked initially toward a more liberal position with respect to play by trying to follow the Mormon example. That is, they sponsored leisure in places specially designed to create a Christian atmosphere, thus trying to bring new forms of recreation within the boundaries of religious life. These experiments worked after a fashion, and they have been continued. No sizable church in the country is without its recreation facilities and its sponsored social activities.

What changed over time was not the Mormons or the significance of what they had done. It was the context for judging their success in maintaining play as something inextricably connected to religious life. Most Protestant denominations have long since abandoned the hope of duplicating the interconnected environment that Mormons maintain at least in the basin of the Salt Lake. In the twentieth century, if not before, it was clear that they could not, despite feverish and often effective activity, fully control what they had begun to permit. This failure, as well as the impossibility of recovering a credible voice to condemn, was reinterpreted as a great liberation by many twentieth-century Americans who had now learned to legitimate both work and play in ways that no longer concerned themselves with religious controversy. To those Americans, the gathered community of the Latter-day Saints, which had once sheltered what other Protestants regarded as dangerously permissive activities, began to look restrictive, even repressive. In this way, as in so many others, the rebellious, oppositional force of nineteenth-century Mormon culture has been transformed, by a trick that only passing time can perform, into something very like its opposite. Whether this means that the rest of the country has caught up with the Latter-day Saints and gone beyond, or is still lagging behind, is a dispute that prudent historians don't try to settle.

Notes

1. Edmund S. Morgan, *American Slavery, American Freedom: The Ordeal of Colonial Virginia* (New York: Norton, 1975), esp. chaps. 3–4; W. J. Rorabaugh, *The Alcoholic Republic: An American Tradition* (New York: Oxford University Press, 1979).

2. Quoted in Elliott J. Gorn, *The Manly Art: Bare-Knuckle Prize Fighting in America* (Ithaca, N.Y.: Cornell University Press, 1986), 102.

3. Quoted in Rex A. Skidmore, "Mormon Recreation in Theory and Practice: A Study of Social Change" (PhD diss., University of Pennsylvania, 1941), 33.

4. David Brion Davis, "The New England Origins of Mormonism," *New England Quarterly* 26 (June 1953): 147–68.

5. R. Laurence Moore, *Religious Outsiders and the Making of Americans* (New York: Oxford University Press, 1986), chap. 1.

6. In addition to Skidmore, see Leonard J. Arrington, *Brigham Young: American Moses* (New York: Knopf, 1985); George Dollinger Pyper, *The Romance of an Old Playhouse* (Salt Lake City: Seagull Press, 1928); Myrtle E. Henderson, "A History of the Theatre in Salt Lake City from 1850 to 1870" (MA thesis, Northwestern University, 1935); John S. Lindsay, *The Mormons and the Theatre; or, The History of Theatricals in Utah; with Reminiscences and Comments, Humorous and Critical* (Salt Lake City: Century Printing, 1905).

7. Leona Holbrook, "Dancing as an Aspect of Early Mormon and Utah Culture," *BYU Studies* 16 (Autumn 1975): 117–38; Davis Bitton, "'These Licentious Days': Dancing among the Mormons," *Sunstone* 2 (Spring 1977): 19.

8. Brigham Young, 9 February 1862, *Journal of Discourses*, 26 vols. (London and Liverpool: LDS Booksellers Depot, 1855–86), 9:194, and his remarks 18 July 1869, ibid., 13:60.

9. Brigham Young, 6 March 1862, ibid., 9:243.

10. Henry Ward Beecher, *Lectures to Young Men, on Various Important Subjects* (Salem, Mass.: John P. Jewett & Co., 1846), 122, 149.

11. Charles Dickens, *American Notes for General Circulation* (London, UK: Chapman and Hall, 1842); Frances Trollope, *Domestic Manners of the Americans* (London, UK: Whittaker Treacher, 1832), esp. chaps. 8, 11, 15.

12. Quoted in Roy Rosenzweig, *Eight Hours for What We Will: Workers and Leisure in an Industrial City, 1870–1920* (Cambridge: Cambridge University Press, 1983), 70.

13. R. Laurence Moore, "Religion, Secularization, and the Shaping of the Culture Industry in Antebellum America," *American Quarterly* 41 (June 1989): 216–42.

14. Lawrence W. Levine, *Highbrow/Lowbrow: The Emergence of Cultural Hierarchy in America* (Cambridge: Harvard University Press, 1988).

15. Ian R. Stewart, *Central Park, 1851–71: Urbanization and Environmental Planning in New York City* (Ithaca, N.Y.: Cornell University Press, 1973).

16. Reid Badger, *The Great American Fair: The World's Columbian Exposition & American Culture* (Chicago: Nelson Hall, 1979), 97.

17. Frederic W. Sawyer, *A Plea for Amusements* (New York: D. Appleton, 1847), 179–80.

18. Ellen Weiss, *City in the Woods: The Life and Design of an American Camp Meeting on Martha's Vineyard* (New York: Oxford University Press, 1987).

19. Rev. B. W. Gorham, *Camp Meeting Manual: A Practical Book for the Camp Ground* (Boston: H. V. Degen, 1854), 17.

20. Ibid., 32.

21. Quoted in Weiss, *City in the Woods,* 117.

22. Rev. E. H. Stokes, comp., *Ocean Grove: Its Origin and Progress, as Shown in the Annual Reports of the President* (Ocean Grove, N.J.: The Association, 1874–87).

23. John H. Vincent, *The Chautauqua Movement* (Boston: Chautauqua Press, 1886), 4–5. See also Theodore Morrison, *Chautauqua: A Center for Education, Religion, and the*

Arts in America (Chicago: University of Chicago Press, 1974); Jesse Lyman Hurlbut, *The Story of Chautauqua* (New York: Putnam, 1921).

24. Vincent, *The Chautauqua Movement*, 89.

25. Ibid., 79.

26. Sherwood Eddy, *A Century with Youth: A History of the Y.M.C.A. from 1844 to 1944* (New York: Association Press, 1944); C. Howard Hopkins, *History of the Y.M.C.A. in North America* (New York: Association Press, 1951); Paul Boyer, *Urban Masses and Moral Order in America, 1820–1920* (Cambridge: Harvard University Press, 1978).

27. William H. Ball, "The Administration of Athletics in the Young Men's Christian Association," *American Physical Education Review* 16 (January 1911): 21.

28. Fred Eugene Leonard, *A Guide to the History of Physical Education* (Philadelphia: Lea & Febiger, 1947); C. W. Hackensmith, *History of Physical Education* (New York: Harper & Row, 1966); Aileene S. Lockhart and Betty Spears, eds., *Chronicle of American Physical Education: Selected Readings, 1855–1930* (Dubuque, Iowa: W. C. Brown, 1972).

29. Laurence Locke Doggett, *Man and a School: Pioneering in Higher Education at Springfield College* (New York: Association Press, 1943), 122.

30. Samuel Wirt Wiley, *History of YMCA-Church Relations in the United States* (New York: Association Press, 1944); Mayer N. Zald, *Organizational Change: The Political Economy of the YMCA* (Chicago: University of Chicago Press, 1970).

31. See discussion in Lary May, *Screening Out the Past: The Birth of Mass Culture and the Motion Picture Industry* (New York: Oxford University Press, 1980), 25.

PART 2

Establishing Zion

Thomas G. Alexander

For the past quarter century, historians have tended to focus on social history more frequently than political or economic history. In Western and Frontier History, the trend has been somewhat different because with a few exceptions, such as Howard Lamar's work on Dakota and the Southwest, in the past historians often have given short shrift to the political history of the West. In the Old Western History, especially as practiced by Turnerians, historians generally studied the social and economic aspects of relations between various groups of Euro-Americans, the conquest of "unoccupied" (actually Native American) lands, economic development, and exploitation of resources. By contrast, the New Western History has tended to emphasize the social aspects of gender, race, and class.

After Patricia Limerick's *Legacy of Conquest* (1987) included a treatment of the Mormons, many of us had expected that other historians might add religion to the big three. Instead, with the exception of a few scholars such as Jan Shipps, Robert Hine, Ferenc Szasz, Charles Peterson, and Anne Butler, most historians have tended to ignore the role of religion in the lives of people in the West. Moreover, many of those historians who do include information on religion fail to consider its experiential—that is, spiritual—aspects. Instead, they choose to focus on conflict or on various social, economic, or political matters in which religious people have involved themselves.

Ignoring religion seems odd for historians who study a region in which matters of the spirit have played such a significant role. I suspect that the principal reason is that many historians are of a secular persuasion themselves, and as such they often see religion as of minor relevance. Another reason, though I think a minor one, may be that some social data and data on economics and politics are readily available, and we have only very sketchy data on religion. For instance, statisticians have yet to reconstruct the percentage of believers, as contrasted with church members, in the West, or in the United States for that matter, during the nineteenth century. Fortunately, we have somewhat better data on church membership. The best statistical information shows that church membership in the United States grew from about 25 percent of the population at the end of the Civil War to about 40 percent in 1900.[1]

Because of the failure to include non-churchgoing believers, the data are misleading. In an age of pervasive religiosity, which the nineteenth century arguably was, many people who belonged to no church considered themselves believers and seekers.

After the turn of the twentieth century, Census Bureau reports charted the percentage of people belonging to religious bodies. These reports reveal that church membership continued to climb until it plateaued at about 60 percent in 1950.[2] Most significantly, Utah, where the population is about 70 percent Latter-day Saint, has consistently ranked above the national average in church membership. In the nineteenth century, church membership in Utah ranged above 60 percent, and in the twentieth century it has ranged over 70 percent. In 1990, with a churched population of 79.6 percent, Utah had the largest percentage of church members of any state in the union.[3]

Perhaps because of the pervasiveness of religion in the lives of Latter-day Saints and the reluctance of many historians to address the subject, especially as an aspect of personal faith, many historians have failed to integrate the story of Utah's people into the larger story of the American West. Recognizing this phenomenon, Jan Shipps has remarked that the Mormon region has seemed like a hole in a donut. Historians of the West have tended to nibble around the edges but have often failed to include Utah and the Mormons as an aspect of western history.

In part, the Tanner Lectures have sought to remedy this deficiency. In establishing the lectureship, the Mormon History Association set out to invite scholars with national and international reputations in history, religious studies, and allied fields to spend a year studying the Mormons. The resulting lectures have helped historians to see how we might integrate the story of the Latter-day Saints and by extension other religions into the stories of life of the United States and of other nations as well.

For instance, in his essay on the Mormon nation and the American empire, Donald Meinig offers a comparative geographical perspective on Mormon nationalism and American imperialism. As an empire, the United States treated indigenous peoples in extremely harsh ways. The United States removed American Indians from their land and forced them onto reservations. The nation flooded French-speaking Louisiana with English-speaking immigrants. Americans tried to suppress Hispanic culture in New Mexico.

Comparing and contrasting the treatment of the Mormons with that of other Americans, Meinig argues that the concept of a special homeland—Zion— fueled the conflict between Mormon nation-builders and American imperialists. Although the Mormons intended to establish a nation on the American continent, imperial America had a competing vision, and the federal government used tactics to suppress Mormon identity similar to those it used with Indians, Mexicans, and the French. These included a military invasion of Utah, encouraging Gentiles to migrate to the Mormon homeland and enforcing draconian legislation. All of these actions had the effect of reeducating the Mormons. Although the Mormons capitulated to American imperialism and began during the 1880s, if not before, to integrate their nation into the American empire, like the Cajuns of Louisiana and the Mexicans of New Mexico they left their imprint on the land. Moreover, they exported their culture through various means including proselytizing, outmigration, and standard-plan religious architecture. Still, as Meinig shows, although tension has persisted, Mormons today tend to exemplify middle-class American and Christian values, which contrast quite markedly with their nineteenth-century nonconformity.

Reaching beyond the Mormon culture region, John Harrison researched and commented on the lives of working-class British who joined the LDS Church. These people worked in such occupations as domestic servant, tailor, shoemaker, brick maker, agricultural laborer, blacksmith, carpet maker, and button maker. Although most had little education, Harrison finds their simple and direct narratives more enlightening than those of similarly situated people affected by literary pretensions. In their narratives, the English people tend to locate themselves by parentage and education, but they tend to avoid much social detail. As converts, most focus on their religious lives.

Significantly, most of Harrison's subjects did not concern themselves with those political and economic problems that historians generally think of as the burning issues of the day. Harrison found in the personal narratives virtually nothing about Chartism, the Great Reform Bill, or the Corn Laws. Rather, in writing about those things they believed most important, the English converts tended to locate themselves in society through their professions, their families, and the influence of Mormonism on their lives.

Glenda Riley compares and contrasts the lives of Mormon and gentile women on the overland trail. Not surprisingly, Riley finds that both groups of women migrated to find a better life in the West. Moreover, both sorts contributed to the well-being of the migrating parties. Both groups of women developed close relationships with each other. In addition, though they began their journeys by dreading the danger posed by Indians, most changed those views, and many engaged in trade and domestic relations with native peoples.

Differences existed as well. Gentile women tended to shun and even abuse Mormons. Mormon women often traveled with the burden of split families, as their relatives had ostracized them for joining the Saints. Many, both gentile and Mormon women, felt alienated from the system of plural marriage. Utah's laws made divorce easy, but many Mormon women preferred to endure the burdens incumbent upon the practice of polygamy. In general, as Riley shows, the differences generally outweighed the similarities between the two groups of women.

As the late Martin Ridge noted, although many people are ignorant of Mormon history, the story of the Latter-day Saint people is a significant aspect of national history. In this essay, Ridge links the announced closing of the Turnerian frontier in 1890 with the co-option of the Mormon kingdom into the United States. During the nineteenth century, the Mormons had sought escape from an increasingly pluralistic American body politic in order to build the Kingdom of God on earth. Ridge recounts the well-known story of how the application of inexorable pressure from the federal government and from Utah Gentiles forced the Mormon kingdom to change and to integrate into the American nation. In a sense, he tells the same story that Meinig told, but in a different way.

In her usually colorful and insightful way, Patricia Nelson Limerick unpacks catch phrases such as "ethnic," "lifestyle," and "culture" in a peace initiative. She points out, quite rightly I believe, that most people construct their own ethnic identity by—in words she borrows from Carl Becker—acting as their "Own Historian." Americans, she points out, often carry a diverse genetic heritage. Instead of creating confusion, however, this diversity allows them to select from among various identities to characterize themselves.

She points out, however, that in many instances some people insist on the right to characterize the ethnicity of others. Many people will characterize as black anyone who has a scintilla of African American heritage. I have noticed this with some Euro-Americans as well. For instance, people frequently want to characterize me as "Anglo" when my principal heritage is Celtic. I descended from peoples whom Anglos frequently abused. Anyone who has seen the Mel Gibson film *Braveheart* will recognize that experience.

In treating Mormonism as religion and ethnicity, Limerick argues that historians can write both with honesty and sensitivity, showing respect for the tradition but at the same time offering "a full reckoning with their past."[4]

As Anne Firor Scott points out, both nineteenth-century Mormon and American society were patriarchal. Living in a patriarchal society, Mormon and other American women organized voluntary associations to accomplish a wide range of benevolent, social, and political purposes. With an accuracy of perception that many who have studied Mormonism have missed, Scott recognizes that in establishing policy and practice for women, nineteenth-century Mormonism "was at once more stringent in ideology [because of priesthood authority] and less stringent in everyday life [because of the wide range of activities women engaged in and in which priesthood authorities encouraged them to engage] than elsewhere."[5] Brigham Young and other church leaders encouraged women to remain active in their homes but also to pursue professions such as the law, medicine, and bookkeeping.

She also argues that in the period after 1896, the church leadership began to preach that Mormon women ought to occupy more traditional homemaking roles. She suggests several reasons for the change, including the increased emphasis on priesthood authority.

In extending Scott's argument, I would suggest that twentieth-century Mormon women have tended to act more like general American women than either pulpit sermons or comments by those critical of the church would suggest. For instance, statistical and sociological studies of twentieth-century Mormon women show that they tend to work out of the home at a rate similar to or even slightly higher than non-Mormon women. In practice, while Mormons generally treat priesthood leaders with respect, they nevertheless enter into pursuits they find personally fulfilling rather than remaining fully within the home.

Other evidences of the activities of twentieth-century women abound. Women share certain priesthood functions and blessings with men, especially in the temple. They exercise considerable independence in the governance and operation of the auxiliaries for which they bear responsibility, such as the Relief Society, the Primary, and the Young Women. Most importantly, priesthood leaders have with increasing frequency deferred to women in such things as organizing general women's conferences and including women as speakers at general conference.[6]

Moving the Mormon story down under, Peter Lineham offers a reflective counterpoint to Harrison's study of working-class members in England. In Lineham's case, the subjects are the Maori who governed the islands and owned New Zealand's lands until the Treaty of Waitangi in 1840 ceded authority to the British. After indifferent results during the initial efforts, Mormon missionaries enjoyed considerable success beginning in 1883 with the conversion of some three hundred Maoris in the Hawke's Bay area. By 1890 perhaps eight percent of the Maori population had joined the LDS Church.

Lineham discusses a number of reasons for relative success of the missionaries. Missionaries tended to succeed when they immersed themselves in the Maori culture, ate local foods, learned the language, and deferred to local customs and leadership (especially the rangatira, or chiefs). Though Mormon missionaries were often ignorant of the fact, many Maoris resented Anglican support for the expropriation of native lands. A number of these disgruntled Maoris studied Mormonism and converted. The emphasis that Mormon missionaries placed on the Israelite lineage of the Maori people helped in conversions as well.

The degree of success should not mask the difficulties that Mormon missionaries faced in founding and spreading the church. Conflicts over Maori culture, disputes with rangatira, and American ethnocentrism all created barriers. In some cases the missionaries overcame these; in other cases, they failed. The relative degree of success seems, however, remarkable.

Howard Lamar offers us a discussion of the reception of Utah statehood in various parts of the nation. Surveying newspapers from New York City, Washington, New Orleans, Chicago, San Francisco, and Los Angeles, Lamar finds virtually universal willingness by 1894 to release Utahns from the burden of past indiscretions and abuses and to accept Utah into the sisterhood of states. Negative comments from eastern newspapers generally emphasized that Utahns would favor the free coinage of silver. This was, however, a political condition unrelated to offensive Mormon beliefs or practices. Moreover, the general approval of free coinage in Utah delighted the western newspapers. Significantly, Frank J. Cannon, one of Utah's first senators, joined the leadership of a group of legislators, including Henry M. Teller and William Jennings Bryan, as a key figure in the fight for free coinage of silver.

Some observers lamented Utah's small population. To those, supporters pointed out that the beehive state already had a population larger than many other states. Some negative comments emanated from a few representative Evangelical churches in Utah, but these were largely muted and seem not to have represented a particularly widespread opinion. Most significant, as Lamar points out, admission was a matter of national interest and national consequence. The Utah enabling act had garnered the support of a range of politicians from both political parties and from the North, South, Midwest, and Far West.

Now, what can one say in general about these essays? By relying on analysis by historians whose specialties are other than Mormon history, these essays open a means of filling the hole in Jan Shipps's donut. Moreover, the Latter-day Saints provide a readily available case study of the importance of religion in the lives of Americans and others. Beyond this, the essays show that the history of the LDS past is an aspect not only of American history but of the history of Great Britain and the Pacific Islands as well.

Most importantly, the essays emphasize the need for historians to recognize the importance of religion in the lives of Americans and other peoples. Given the increase in church membership from the mid-nineteenth century to the mid-twentieth, it seems particularly important to include religious persuasion along with race, gender, and class in analyzing American society. Howard Lamar's observation that the major opposition to Utah's admission into the Union surfaced among Evangelical Protestants says something about the importance of religion in the lives of people during the late nineteenth century. Most significantly, a recent study indicates that the single most important factor in dividing Republicans and Democrats is the relative importance of religion in the lives of the people who make particular political choices. People who attend church regularly are more likely to be Republicans.[7] If they accomplish nothing else, perhaps these essays will spur historians to consider religion more seriously when studying the history of Americans and others.

Notes

1. Edwin Scott Gaustad and Philip L. Barlow, *New Historical Atlas of Religion in America* (New York: Oxford University Press, 2001), 352.

2. Ibid., 349.

3. Richard D. Poll, David J. Miller, Eugene E. Campbell, and Thomas G. Alexander, *Utah's History* (Logan: Utah State University Press, 1989), 692–93; U.S. Census Bureau, *Statistical Abstract of the United States, 2000*, http://www.census.gov/prod/www/statistical-abstract-us.html.

4. Patricia Nelson Limerick, "Peace Initiative: Using the Mormons to Rethink Ethnicity in American Life," *Journal of Mormon History* 21 (Fall 1995): 28.

5. Ann Firor Scott, "Mormon Women, Other Women: Paradoxes and Challenges," *Journal of Mormon History* 13 (1986/87): 6.

6. Marie Cornwall, "The Institutional Role of Mormon Women," in *Contemporary Mormonism: Social Science Perspectives*, ed. Marie Cornwall, Tim B. Heaton, and Lawrence A. Young (Urbana: University of Illinois Press, 2001), 239–64; Laurence R. Innaccone and Carrie A. Miles, "Dealing with Social Change: The Mormon Church's Response to Change in Women's Roles," *Contemporary Mormonism*, 265–86; Survey of Employment Outside the Home of Women in the East Sharon Stake, ca. 1971 (n.p., n.d.).

7. Geoffrey Layman, *The Great Divide: Religious and Cultural Conflict in American Party Politics* (New York: Columbia University Press, 2001); John Green and Mark Silk, "The New Religion Gap," http://www.trincoll.edu/depts/csrpl/RINVol6No3/2004%20Election/religion%20gap.htm (accessed 10 October 2005).

CHAPTER 7

The Mormon Nation and the American Empire

D. W. Meinig

I remember Obert Tanner from my years in Utah, and it is gratifying to partake of one of his many philanthropies. Despite the obvious honor conferred, however, I responded to the invitation to give the Tanner Lecture with considerable hesitation. I can hardly presume to inform this expert audience much about Mormons and Mormonism. Thirty years ago, as a historical geographer specializing in the American West and drawing upon my years of experience in Utah, I set forth my view of the creation and the character of a very prominent and distinctive Mormon Culture Region.[1] I think I may fairly claim that my essay did fix that region upon the map of American human geography, but I have little to add directly to that topic—being content to leave emendations and updatings to such meticulous scholars as my good friend Lowell "Ben" Bennion.[2]

For the last fifteen years I have been attempting to apply a geographical perspective to the whole course of Euro-American history, from Columbus onward to our own times.[3] No one, of course, can be comprehensive in such a task, and I have explicitly limited my range of topics. A central theme of that work is that the United States has been, always and at once, an empire, a nation, a federation, and a set of regional societies. Such terms refer to elusive formations and conceptions continually under construction and alteration; none of these are fixed entities, and they are interlocked in countless ways. I hope that by looking at the Mormon experience within that kind of framework I can perhaps offer something useful to your well-informed views of Mormon history. You will recognize how dependent I am on the good work of Mormon scholars.

American Imperialism

When I speak of the United States as an empire—an imperial power—I am not engaging in a polemic or an attack. I use *empire* and *imperialism* in a generic geopolitical sense to refer to the aggressive encroachment of one people and power upon the territory of another and the subjugation of that territory and people to some degree of control by the stronger power. Imperialism in that sense is as old as history; it has been a basic activity of all strong powers; it is one of the great processes that has formed our world.[4] In such terms the United States has been a huge, expansive imperial power since its formation. Half the territory then claimed as its sovereign realm was unconquered Indian country that it clearly intended to subdue and incorporate into the body of the republic, and it wasted no time in getting under way with that task. As many of you know, this view is becoming more common, an overdue corrective to the long-standing interpretation that an imperial America emerged only at the end of the nineteenth century with the annexation of the Philippines and Puerto Rico—*overseas* colonies—as if the subjugation of "other" peoples and their territories was something new to the American experience. By that date, however, we already had a great array of conquered, captive peoples within our national bounds.

Native American groups were at first legally defined as "resident foreign nations." Shoved aside from areas most desired by the whites, their early reserves were types of protectorates, a simple form of imperial relationship wherein the subordination of the weaker people is formalized by treaty, but they are left largely to themselves so long as they pose no threat to the interests of the empire. The term refers to the promise of protection from external enemies in return for recognition of the exclusive supremacy of the imperial power. But relentless American expansionism brought changes in status and relationships. By the 1830s, Native Americans were redefined as "domestic dependent nations" and found themselves increasingly marginalized and manipulated. A policy of reduction and dependence increasingly transformed reservations into areas of confinement administered by federal agents, with tribal members sustained by rations of goods from an imperial bureaucracy. The Cherokees of the southern Appalachians made a bold attempt to escape such pressures, undertaking their own systematic program of cultural change so as to qualify for statehood. Such an entity would have been a type of indigenous state, that is, a formal territory under "native" rulers, living under some degree of customary law and limited oversight by imperial authority.

As we know, no such "ethnic" state was created, and the hapless Cherokees were forced to take part in a new radical imperial program conceived on a grand scale: the removal of virtually all Native Americans from the eastern states to a large new Indian Territory on the margins of the Great Plains. Therein each tribe was assigned a reserve, with a federal agent and a set of specialists for technical assistance (farmers, millers, blacksmiths, etc.) and cultural change (teachers and missionaries). The geopolitical future of this large entity was controversial. Initial congressional proposals included a capital town, a general Indian council, delegates to Congress, and eventual statehood, the tribal areas becoming mere counties. The removal was carried out quite ruthlessly during the 1830s and 1840s, affecting some one hundred thousand Native Americans and with much loss of life. But the rest of the program was compromised, and American settler expansion soon overwhelmed the reserved area, reducing it to a remnant in what is now eastern Oklahoma. An attempt to create a predominantly Native American state out of that remainder (State of Sequoyah) was rejected in 1906.

The American intolerance of ethnic identity in territorial terms reached a peak in 1887 (a date Mormons well know) with the Dawes Act, which forced Native Americans to accept individual parcels of private property, allow the remainder of their lands to be taken by whites, and submit to a comprehensive program of cultural change involving the removal of children from their parents to federal boarding schools and systematic suppression of Native American languages, religious ceremonies, and marriage practices. For nearly fifty years thereafter, Native American reservations were regarded as "schools for civilization" aiming to destroy "tribalism" and convert Native Americans into individual American citizens conforming to the national norm.

It is still uncommon for historians to give much attention to the fact that with the acquisition of Louisiana, we not only doubled our sovereign territory but we also purchased a large set of peoples. Typical of imperial powers, no one in Paris or Washington gave much thought to the feelings of the French, who occupied the key area Jefferson had set out to acquire by whatever means. Typically, they were subjected immediately to direct rule—that is, placed under an American governor—with the imposition of language, laws, courts, and other U.S. institutions. The confident expectation was that this new French American minority would be easily assimilated into the encompassing Anglo American nation. But these French had other ideas. They naturally resented a governor who could neither speak nor read French, rejected American laws so at variance with their own esteemed code, and resisted interference with the patterns of their social relations (such as the status of slaves and of black Creoles). Moreover, French refugees from Cuba and Haiti soon enhanced their numbers and leadership.

Jefferson's geopolitical response was minoration, a favored technique of imperial management. It involved flooding the annexed area with Anglo Americans to reduce the captive French to a minority in their own homeland without direct diminution or deportations. Thus, he defined a Territory of Orleans with ample room for Anglo colonizations and this, together with the annexation of parishes from West Florida, soon made Louisiana a more balanced bicultural territory. When admitted as a state, the French civil code, the use of the French language in certain proceedings, and the need for Anglo French cooperation in government had been recognized. New Orleans, with new, quite sharply distinct ethnic districts, became a typical "colonial city," a common imperial type.

New Mexico was a clear case of a captive territory and several peoples under direct military rule, with garrisons in the main towns. The first civilian Anglo governor was assassinated by rebellious Taoseños. The treaty of annexation of 1848 declared that New Mexico would be admitted as a state "at the proper time"—that is, when Congress might agree to do so; an 1850 New Mexican initiative toward statehood failed. Unlike Louisiana, New Mexico was a long way from the Anglo American settlement frontier and had no discernible resources at the time to lure large numbers of American colonists. The Pueblo Indians, a settled, reclusive agricultural population, were quickly confirmed in their village lands, following Mexican practice—a simple kind of protectorate (and they were later excused from the Dawes Plan). It was immediately clear, however, that Americans did not regard the much larger captive Hispanic population as fit to become full-fledged citizens. In the vivid newspaper language of the day, New Mexicans were a "mongrel population . . . unfit for statehood" until they had been "Americanized." Imperial agents periodically reported on such progress. As a territorial attorney (and later acting governor) reported in 1857: "There is a decided improvement in the style of dress and mode of living; they wear a greater quantity of American goods, and tea, coffee, and sugar are becoming more common in use among the peasantry. Many are dispensing with the *serape* (blanket) as an every-day garment, . . . buckskin is giving way to woolen and cotton goods, and moccasins to leather shoes. There is also an improvement in the mode of building."[5]

This last sentence referred to the diminished use of adobe. In a parting shot to the New Mexicans in 1880, General William Tecumseh Sherman said: "I hope ten years hence there won't be an adobe house in the Territory. I want to see you learn to make them of brick, with slanting roofs. Yankees don't like flat roofs, nor roofs of dirt." Such were the relentless pressures of American imperialists. Captive peoples must be made over into proper progressive Americans, not just in allegiance, laws, and language but in dress and diet, in tools and trade ("You must get rid of your burros and goats," said Sherman), and in habits and habitations, if they were ever to become "respectable citizens."[6] It would take sixty-four years, the influx of many Americans following the arrival of the railroad (which created a whole string of classic imperial bicultural old town–new town, Hispano-Anglo pairs as at Albuquerque), and Anglo control of most of the resources before statehood was achieved. Even then, the imperial power was forced to recognize the basic integrity of this Hispanic population with specified safeguards of language, religion, and schools; a working relationship between Hispano and Anglo has characterized local politics ever since. New Mexico, therefore, began as a kind of quasi-indigenous state.

I trust I have demonstrated this view of the United States as an empire. I have noted half a dozen classic types of imperial territories and policies for the geopolitical management of captive peoples: protectorates, indigenous states, direct rule, minoration, reduction and dependency, relocation and programmed acculturation. It would take too long to trace further responses to imperial pressures.

Suffice it to say that all of these peoples have resisted assimilation and have made various adaptations to survive today as distinct ethnic groups. The greatest policy change was that affecting the Native Americans, whereby the formal program for cultural conformity and assimilation was ended in the 1930s and increases in tribal autonomy granted. Clinging tenaciously to their bit of tribal ground and to their status as peoples with treaty relations with the United States, Native Americans have won much greater recognition and respect. Reservations are no longer regarded as anomalies on the geopolitical map of America. Some of them, such as the Navajo reservation, which is the homeland of two hundred thousand people, have become virtually "indigenous states," with their own local governments, police forces, law courts, school systems, and much more.

Nation-Building

Before considering how the imperial power dealt with the Mormon nation, we may consider the pertinence of and some processes associated with the term *nation*. I define a nation to be a body of persons who see themselves as a distinct people, bound together by a common heritage, set apart by their own special character, and laying claim to a particular homeland. Nationalism can, of course, be contrived out of whatever characteristics and experiences lie at hand; that sense of common heritage need not be deep rooted or anchored firmly on the facts of history. And, of course, the strength of national feelings may wax and wane under changing circumstances. In many cases, however, we can see the emergence of nationalism as a more or less common process involving the role of leaders fostering an emotive self-awareness, a collective sense of grievance, a struggle for greater independence, and phases of organization, purification, and contention with internal and external "others."

Nation-building is necessarily a geographic phenomenon; it arises out of particular localities, generates fields of activity that tend to focus and crystallize in some area of special advantage, and forms the basic nucleus of the nation from which expansion extends outward toward the aspired bounds of the idealized homeland.[7] Within the national area, spatial systems of communication are elaborated, serving ever more effectively as the means of integrating various regional parts with the nuclear area and the capital city.

As a religious movement, Mormonism offered a clear identity and distinction to its followers, and its combination of centralized leadership and lay priesthood provided strong cohesion. But the really unusual and critical feature of Mormonism—from the perspective employed here—is its basic concern for place, for a homeland; its declaration of the special role and favor of North America in its essential heritage; and its search for a specific geographic nucleus for the Kingdom of God on earth. Mormonism was more than a Holy Scripture and a set of beliefs; it was work to be done *together,* as a society gathered to a special place. Thus we can see Kirtland, Independence, Far West, and Nauvoo as successive attempts to bring vigorous fields of activity into focus on a particular ground, to form the nucleus of a Mormon homeland.

And it was the special Mormon concept of that homeland—of Zion—that generated conflict with other peoples. The fundamental issue was geopolitical: the control of territory and of the character of society therein. Although Missourians disparaged Mormons as a "singular set of pretended Christians," their aggressive response to the Mormons was not simply an expression of endemic religious bigotry.[8] If for the Mormons the concept of Zion resonated with the heady prospect of building the Kingdom of God on earth, for others in the area it seemed to sound the death knell of American society as they knew it. As Mormons arrived in rapidly increasing numbers and not only bought all the land they could but proclaimed themselves a chosen people who were destined to "possess the country" for their New Jerusalem, the Missourians countered with the declaration that "every consideration of self-preservation, good society, public morals, and the fair prospects, that . . . await this young and beautiful country" required their expulsion.

Add to this vital contest over turf some of the well-known social tendencies of these particular contestants, the moralistic, self-righteous Yankee fervent for his uncompromising views and the fiercely independent upland Southern frontiersman ready to run roughshod over anyone who stood in his way; add, further, the militant response of beleaguered Mormon "warrior-saints,"[9] quite as willing as their opponents to take the law into their own hands to protect family and property; and still further, add on the larger state, regional, and national politics of this collision—the politics and emotions of slavery and of party and sectional interests—and the bitterness and fervor of this civil strife become understandable. But, again, the fundamental issue was geopolitical. The assertion of a divine right to all Palestine by militant Zionist settlers on the West Bank today is more than just an apt modern analogy; it is the modern expression of the original concept that the Mormons had adopted, transferring it from the Old World to the New.

We have already noted that despite the reality of an American empire, there was always resolute opposition to the creation or formal recognition of any kind of ethnic territorial unit. It is hardly a surprise that ordinary Americans demonstrated that they would not tolerate a militant, gathered, expansionist subnation claiming absolute control over its members and proclaiming itself as the nucleus and vanguard of a theocratic empire.

For the Mormons, there followed from this encounter the very kinds of experiences and reactions best calculated to form a cohesive nation: defeat, displacement, martyrdom, and alienation; a testing, a winnowing, and an emergence of new charismatic leadership; a shared history, a sense of grievance, a people apart, and a determination to transform exile into nationhood.

Creating the Mormon Nation

I need not review with this audience these well-known lamentations, exodus, and eventual triumph in a Promised Land except to summarize the peculiar conditions, principles, and processes of this geographic creation. In broadest terms, this implantation in the Far West was peculiar in that the Mormons gained access to a huge area without competition from other American settlers and with little hindrance from local Native Americans. They were thus able to apply an orderly system of colonization under centralized Church authority essentially unrestrained by U.S. laws and, in a word, initiate a nation-state essentially on their own terms.

The first task was to establish the nucleus along the Wasatch Front, overlooking the New World version of the Galilee–River Jordan–Dead Sea. Brigham Young placed this New Jerusalem within the frame of a vast, American Israel. His Deseret encompassed the Great Basin, the Colorado River Basin, and a corridor to the Pacific, and he sought to control the key portals and passageways: Fort Bridger, San Bernardino, and Mormon Station in Carson Valley. Assiduous attention to the practicalities of the gathering, bringing in thousands of members every year, sustained a program of contiguous expansion outward from the Wasatch oasis, filling in every habitable, irrigable spot to create an ever-enlarging, thoroughly Mormon region. Within that region, specialized projects were initiated to supply the Mormon nation with such essential goods as iron, coal, lead, cotton, and sugar. In addition, the Church sponsored or approved the development of basic facilities and services, such as a bank, newspaper, the ZCMI (Zion's Cooperative Mercantile Institution) system, roads, railroads, and telegraph lines. Furthermore, the life of the Church generated great periodic pulsations of messages and movements of persons throbbing through a hierarchical network of places anchored on Temple Square. President Young's great seasonal processions through the northern settlements and then through the southern were only the most famous of these; the routine movements of many lesser agents were equally important in binding this motley lot of mountain Saints together as a united people—the very essence of nation-building.

Over a span of forty years, the Mormons had created a distinctive region, a landscape imprinted with their own designs, a society knit together by their own spatial systems, which stretched more than six hundred miles from the lower Virgin Valley on the south to the upper Snake River on the north and which contained some 170,000 Mormons. There were, as well, Mormon settlements beyond these bounds, especially southward, a thin sprinkling in northern, central, and southern Arizona. But this proved to be a sector of Deseret that could not be dominated, at least for the time being, and it resulted in tiny enclaves within gentile ranching, farming, and mining country: outposts in Babylon rather than frontiers of Zion.

Whereas most Americans sat lightly upon the land, ready to sell out and move on at the slightest opportunity or disappointment—as the many streams of migrants filling up all the other regions of the West well displayed—the Mormons had taken firm root. For them it was the end of a search, a culmination, and the date of their entry into the Promised Land became their principal holiday and commemorative celebration. Thus, the Mormon region took on a human geographic duality unlike anything in surrounding areas. It was a homeland in a much more profound sense, with a homogeneity, unity, order, and self-consciousness unequaled in any other North American region and rivaled only by that other peculiar self-conscious captive nation of North America along the lower St. Lawrence.

Imperial Pressures

From initial colonization through every annual intake from eastern America and northwestern Europe, the creation of this great refugee commonwealth represented a continuous process of withdrawal from an outer world. But of course that withdrawal was never actually complete, and the Mormon nation was never actually independent, however much it may have aspired or prepared to be. The great geographical irony of Mormon history was the fact that hardly had the Mormons begun the creation of their new homeland in the remote wilderness when they found themselves astride the transcontinental thoroughfare, thronged with the very people they had fled, and enclosed within the imperial bounds of the republic that had failed to accommodate and protect them.

With the rejection of Deseret and the formation in its place of the Territory of Utah, the Mormons were a captive people and province. Imperial pressures were soon asserted. Even though Brigham Young was the first governor (and Deseret did in fact function for two years), federal officials sent out from Washington, seeing themselves up against a monolithic Mormonism, soon generated a stream of accusations. You are more familiar than I am with much of the subsequent history, but a review of a sequence of imperial attempts to force subservience and conformity upon a recalcitrant people might prove helpful.

The dispatch of an army to put down a reported rebellion elicited in response a remarkable display of cohesion of the threatened people in their open harassment of that invading force and, more astounding, in their massive evacuation of their capital and richest settlement area, and in the threat of scorched-earth tactics, the extreme nationalism of the rhetoric of that crisis making the modern reader think of an impending Mormon Masada![10] In the compromise that followed, the imperial power imposed its governor and its garrison, but the former could assert little power over the people, and the latter was marginalized, fifty miles from the capital.

A few years later came the reassertion of imperial coercion under Colonel Patrick E. Connor: the establishment of Fort Douglas overlooking the "native" capital and the colonel's assiduous fostering of opposition to this stubborn people in various forms, most effectively in his encouragement of prospectors to comb the area for gold and silver. His favored solution to this problem of imperial management was exactly the same as Jefferson's for Louisiana: "to invite a large Gentile and loyal population sufficient by peaceful means and through the ballot-box to overwhelm the Mormons by mere force of numbers, and thus wrest from the Church—disloyal and traitorous to the core—the absolute and tyrannical control of temporal and civic affairs, or at least a population numerous enough to put a check on Mormon affairs."[11]

But such a policy of minoration could not easily be applied, as the Mormons were rapidly taking possession of all the suitable lands. Whereas Jefferson had created an enlarged territory in Louisiana to accommodate a large Anglo American influx, Congress, responding to pleas of non-Mormon residents in bordering areas, repeatedly reduced the broad bounds of Utah Territory. Such excisions did not impinge seriously upon the body of contiguous Mormon settlements, but there were attempts to do so. In 1861 a bill in Congress proposed an extinction of Utah, splitting it in half and giving the pieces to Nevada and a proposed Jeffersonia (later Colorado). In 1869 the chairman of the Committee on Territories stated his wish "to blot out the [Utah] Territory" as a step toward disposing of the Mormon question, and his committee produced a bill drastically reducing Utah so "that they shall not have territorial area enough left to make a state."[12] These further reductions were not enacted, but they display the kind of territorial punishment that imperial powers are prepared to inflict.

More effective and fundamental, of course, was the influx of Gentiles, not just as imperial agents but as residents, workers, and businessmen, with their families. They created their own settlements with the railroad towns and mining camps scattered over the Mormon region, most heavily in the mountainous fringes of the Mormon core area. These smoking, volatile, ramshackle camps injected into the bucolic Mormon scene an unprecedented and inassimilable variety of creeds, tongues, and ethnic backgrounds.

Furthermore, this influx transformed the two largest Mormon settlements, Salt Lake City and Ogden, into bicultural cities, for they became the primary commercial centers for the entire Intermountain West. Aside from Mormon temples or an occasional Lion House palace, there was little difference in architectures. The result, therefore, was not so vivid in the landscape as in the old town–new town pairs in New Mexico, but a Mormon-Gentile duality was apparent to residents and visitors alike. "The railroad traveller gets a very wrong impression of Ogden," noted one reporter. "He sees nothing but the Gentile part of town, the stations of the U.P. and C.P. Railroads, their offices and engine houses, and a dozen or two shanties occupied as restaurants, grog shops, and gambling houses."[13] Actually more important were the banks, mercantile buildings, wholesaling houses, hospitals, churches, and residences, all discernibly clustered in some degree. The continuing growth of the gentile population and facilities during the railroad era meant a continuing erosion of Mormon homogeneity and dominance in the very core of their homeland. Ogden was the first Utah city to elect a gentile mayor.

The culmination of imperial pressures, of course, came with the Edmunds-Tucker Act of 1887, characterized by historian Howard Lamar as "one of the most far-reaching pieces of federal legislation ever passed in peacetime history."[14] (In view of our general imperial context, a Native American historian might well refer to the Dawes Act of that fateful, dreadful year in the same terms.) Setting federal marshals in pursuit of the polygamous Mormon leadership and dissolving the LDS Church as a corporate entity, the act was a display of imperial legislative power against members of the Union equaled only by some of the proposals and laws applied to the South twenty years earlier. Reconstruction applied to the South was, of course, an imperial process, and, not surprisingly, Southern congressmen tended to strongly oppose this coercion of the Mormons.

The long-standing refusal to admit Utah to statehood, the assault upon social nonconformity and theocratic political power, reconfirmed the basic U.S. refusal to accept geopolitical territories defined essentially in ethnic or religious terms. Throughout this period Native American reservations were regarded as a necessary anomaly, a temporary measure grudgingly sustained until tribal cultures could be dissolved and Native Americans transformed into individual citizens. To many Americans, Mormonism's centralized authority and bloc voting represented a species of "tribal culture" that similarly had to be broken up.

From "Peculiar" to "Mainstream"

With the Church's capitulation in 1890 to this imperial assault began the process of calculated adaptation to the encompassing geopolitical reality. The Mormon nation could be no more than a subnation, and even that status posed difficult adjustments. This great crisis coincided with essentially an end to expansion, for the Mormons were running out of land as well as time. Hemmed in by vigorous colonizations by other peoples on all sides, they simply found no more lands suitable for settlement, nor would there be any until federal irrigation projects began to make big deserts "blossom as the rose" during the twentieth century. Although Mormons continued to have large families and missionary efforts went on unabated, the number of converts lessened significantly, and the summons to Zion, heretofore virtually a command, was much subdued.[15] "Respect-

ing the gathering," commented a *Millennial Star* editorial in 1891, "the elders
should explain the principle when occasion arises; but acting upon it should be
left entirely to the individual." As Bill Mulder notes, this statement marked "a
startling transition from the days when the clarion call was to redeem the faithful and bring them singing to Zion."[16]

On the other hand, the Utah economy was expanding in other ways under the
initiatives of both peoples. In the early 1880s the Church had abandoned its boy-
cott of gentile merchants, and the formation in 1887 of a Chamber of Commerce
and Board of Trade that included both Mormons and Gentiles marked an
"important indication of change in the character of the leadership in Salt Lake
City."[17] Mormon entrepreneurs and workers fanned out over the West to compete for jobs in construction, mining, forestry, and transport; the Church itself
fostered new businesses.

Mormonism remained militant about its own strength and cohesion, giving
special attention to training and teaching the faithful, founding Church academies to counter increasingly secularized state school systems. Eventually, of
course, came the alternative to the gathering, with Church resources organized
to serve the faithful wherever they might reside. Of special interest to a geographer is the belated decision in midcentury to imprint the landscape—not just in
their mountain homeland but wherever a cluster of Mormons resided—with
distinctive, standardized meetinghouse architecture. As Jan Shipps notes in the
final entry in the new *Historical Atlas of Mormonism,* this was "a brilliant decision" with respect to Mormon identity in the world and for themselves: "The
very fact that these clearly identifiable LDS structures could be found in town
after town, and suburb after suburb cultivated among the Saints what might be
called a Zionic sense, making the very LDS meetinghouses themselves agents of
assimilation and signals that wherever the Saints gather, there Zion is."[18]

But as we all know, the really remarkable response was the gradual but unre-
lenting shift in image with respect to the larger society. Mormons changed themselves from a peculiar people into model Americans with resounding success. As
Nathan O. Hatch said in his own Tanner Lecture, "Mormon life today is a bastion
of respectability, of staid family values, and of rock-ribbed Republican conservatism." He was, as you know, emphasizing the stark contrast with early Mormonism. "As a people, Latter-day Saints are overwhelmingly patriotic and
hardworking, the very embodiment of middle-class values, the Protestant work
ethic, and the American way of life. No religious group in America today seems
more in harmony with the spirit of free-enterprise capitalism."[19] For a geographer's confirmation of this assessment, I recommend John B. Wright's book-
length comparison of Utah and Colorado in his prize-winning *Rocky Mountain
Divide.*[20] It is not quite as simple as that, of course, and the tensions between "the
angel and the beehive" are never quite stable, but that is beyond my explorations.[21]

Conclusion

Thus Mormon nationalism has passed through several phases. For years it was openly separatist, seeking isolation and cultural integrity with the least possible affiliation with the United States and welcoming independence should that fragile federal union fail, as Brigham Young's annual convening of the so-called ghost legislature of Deseret, initiated in 1862 and terminating in 1870, attested.[22] When that possibility ended, Mormon petitions for statehood were regarded, as before, as a means of maximizing local autonomy: Mormons desired "to join the United States in order to be free from it," as Leonard Arrington put it, referring to Brigham Young's forthright statement shortly before his death: "All we care about is for them to let us alone, to keep away their trash and officers so far as possible, to give us our admission into the Union just as we are, just as we have applied for it as near as may be to let us take care of ourselves, and they may keep their money, their lands and in fact everything which they can."[23]

In our imperial terms, the Mormons sought to be an indigenous state, and early on, under Young as governor, they were essentially that: a "native state" left largely to govern itself. But such a nation state so at variance with the national norms in its marriage practices and its theocratic operations was increasingly regarded as dangerous to the larger society, and so the empire insisted on direct rule and eventually on a coerced conformity.

The twentieth-century response of the Church shows that it has not only extracted itself from the American empire with Utah becoming a common member of the American federation, but it has also remade and repositioned itself to be an exemplary regional society of national significance. The geopolitical way for them to do so was opened long ago when, after being driven from Missouri, Joseph Smith had proclaimed "the whole of America is Zion itself."[24]

Notes

1. Donald W. Meinig, "The Mormon Culture Region: Strategies and Patterns in the Geography of the American West, 1847–1964," *Annals of the Association of American Geographers* 55 (June 1965): 191–220.

2. Lowell C. Bennion, "Meinig's 'Mormon Culture Region' Revisited," *Historical Geography* 24(1 & 2) (1995): 22–33.

3. D. W. Meinig, *The Shaping of America: A Geographical Perspective on 500 Years of History*, Vol. 1, *Atlantic America, 1492–1800* (New Haven, Conn.: Yale University Press, 1986); idem, Vol. 2, *Continental America, 1800–1867* (New Haven, Conn.: Yale University Press, 1993).

4. The following remarks on the nature of geography and imperialism are amplified in D. W. Meinig, "Geographical Analysis of Imperial Expansion," in *Period and Place: Research Methods in Historical Geography*, ed. Alan R. H. Baker and Mark Billinge (Cambridge: Cambridge University Press, 1982), 71–78; and D. W. Meinig, "Territorial Strategies Applied to Captive Peoples," in *Ideology and Landscape in Historical Perspective:*

Essays on the Meanings of Places in the Past, ed. Alan R. H. Baker and Gideon Biger(Cambridge: Cambridge University Press, 1992), 125–36 .

5. W. W. H. David, *El Gringo; or, New Mexico and Her People* (New York: Harper & Brothers, 1857), 255, 431–32.

6. Quoted in Thomas E. Chavez, *An Illustrated History of New Mexico* (Niwot: University Press of Colorado, 1992), 125.

7. See, for example, Meinig, "Generalizations: Nation-Building," in *The Shaping of America*, 1:395–407.

8. This quotation and those below are taken from 1833 accounts reprinted in William Mulder and A. Russell Mortensen, eds., *Among the Mormons: Historic Accounts by Contemporary Observers* (New York: Knopf, 1958), 82, 79–80.

9. Nathan O. Hatch, "Mormon and Methodist: Popular Religion in the Crucible of the Free Market," *Journal of Mormon History* 20 (Spring 1994): 42.

10. See, for example, Richard D. Poll and William P. MacKinnon, "Causes of the Utah War Reconsidered," *Journal of Mormon History* 20 (Fall 1994): 42.

11. Quoted in Howard Roberts Lamar, *The Far Southwest, 1846–1912: A Territorial History* (New York: Norton, 1970), 361.

12. Committee on Territories, *Congressional Globe*, 40th Congress, 3rd Session, 14 January 1869, 364.

13. An 1874 traveler quoted in Richard C. Roberts, "Railroad Depots in Ogden: Microcosms of a Community," *Utah Historical Quarterly* 53 (Winter 1985): 76.

14. Lamar, *The Far Southwest*, 398.

15. J. Matthew Shumway, "Membership Growth by States and Countries," in *Historical Atlas of Mormonism*, ed. S. Kent Brown, Donald Q. Cannon, and Richard H. Jackson (New York: Simon & Schuster, 1994), 122, observes that the annual growth rate between 1901 and 1950 was "2.2 percent, approximately one-half of the 4 percent growth rate during the previous half century."

16. Quoted in William Mulder, *Homeward to Zion: The Mormon Migration from Scandinavia* (Minneapolis: University of Minnesota Press, 1937), 30.

17. Thomas G. Alexander and James B. Allen, *Mormons & Gentiles: A History of Salt Lake City* (Boulder, Colo.: Pruett Publishing, 1984), 105.

18. Jan Shipps, "Emergence of Mormonism on the American Landscape," in *Historical Atlas of Mormonism*, 152.

19. Hatch, "Mormon and Methodist," 37.

20. John B. Wright, *Rocky Mountain Divide: Selling and Saving the West* (Austin: University of Texas Press, 1993).

21. Armand L. Mauss, *The Angel and the Beehive: The Mormon Struggle with Assimilation* (Urbana: University of Illinois Press, 1994).

22. Klaus J. Hansen, *Quest for Empire: The Political Kingdom of God and the Council of Fifty in Mormon History* (East Lansing: Michigan State University Press, 1967), 167.

23. Leonard J. Arrington, *Brigham Young: American Moses* (New York: Knopf, 1985), 238.

24. Quoted in Robert Bruce Flanders, *Nauvoo: Kingdom on the Mississippi* (Urbana: University of Illinois Press, 1965), 298.

CHAPTER 8

The Popular History of Early Victorian Britain: A Mormon Contribution

John F. C. Harrison

It is a daunting prospect for a non-Mormon to address a gathering of the Mormon History Association, where virtually everyone in the room knows more about Mormon history than the speaker. I shall not have the impertinence to lecture you on that subject. Rather, I would like to speak about my own recent enthusiasms and my discovery in Mormon archives of some (for me) very exciting material.

For some time now, I have been interested in exploring the history of the common people of Britain. This is a type of history that presents peculiar problems, among them the difficulty of sources. Imagine therefore my delight when I came upon the rich collection of Mormon journals and autobiographies and found that they contained a great deal of material relevant to my purposes. Here is a source, scarcely known outside Mormon circles, just waiting to be exploited by historians of nineteenth-century Britain. I would like to suggest some ways in which these sources might be used for purposes wider than strictly Mormon history. I hope that this will be in the spirit of the Tanner Lectures, to whose trustees I am greatly indebted for making possible this lecture today.

The writing of histories of the common people is not new.[1] Indeed, the tradition stretches from J. R. Green and Thorold Rogers in the later nineteenth century; through G. D. H. Cole, Raymond Postgate, R. J. Mitchell, and M. D. Leys; to the present.[2] Most of this work, however, has been either primarily economic history or social history of the "men and manners" variety. My concern is somewhat different. It is to write history from below, as it were, to start from the perceptions of the people themselves rather than accept the views of what others, whether contemporary reformers and sympathizers or later historians, thought about working people. These are the people who have usually been left out of history, and to write their history is to encounter formidable problems of chronology, theme, and sources.[3]

We cannot, for instance, ignore the historian's basic requirement of chronology, for history is essentially the study of change over time. But the chronology of popular history will not necessarily be the same as is appropriate for other types of history. Probably the traditional chronology and periodization of English history, being based on the political and economic decisions of the ruling classes, distorts or confuses the history of the common people, whose lives were largely determined by other considerations. We need an alternative periodization based on changes in popular experience and perceptions. Unfortunately, the danger of forcing popular history into a procrustean bed of traditional historiography cannot be entirely avoided. Until we have much more evidence to work on, we have to take some of the accepted historians' categories and periods, even though they may not be truly relevant. Moreover, although the history of the common people should not be submerged in general history, the two are obviously interrelated. The common people have always been faced with the problem of living in a world they did not create.

History of the common people is also different in its selection of themes. All history is a pattern made by interweaving chronological and thematic evidence from the records of the past, and for the common people, the themes will be those that seem to show most closely how they lived and what they made of their lives. This means (at least ideally) that the history of the common people will not be simply traditional history with highlights on the contributions of ordinary men and women but a completely different pattern, starting from different assumptions and ideas of what is important and what is not. Historians will never be able to re-create, no matter how sympathetic or imaginative they are, anything more than a tiny fragment of the experiences and sentiments of that infinite host of men and women that "have no memorial, who are perished as though they had never been born" (Eccles. 44:9). But if we start by asking the right questions and looking for answers in new directions, we may at least stand a chance of uncovering more than has been discovered about the common people in the past. The starting point must be those things that were central in the life of laboring people.

Here we come up against one of the greatest problems in writing the history of the common people: the scarcity of sources. We are dealing with that part of the community that was largely inarticulate. They did not, for the most part, leave written records in which they described their thoughts and feelings and the events in which they were involved. The literary sources upon which historians rely so heavily do not at present exist in the same form and quantity for the common people as for their social superiors. This, more than any other, has been the argument advanced by professional historians against the possibility of writing a history of the common people. Historians are bound by their evidence, and if it is not there, they can make no headway. This, of course, is correct, but it is not the whole story. Known sources can be reworked. Oral testimony, folklore, the work of human hands, and the comparative researches of archaeologists and anthropologists can be used to escape the tyranny of literary evidence. Most relevant here, many hitherto unknown autobiographies of working men and women have come to light in the past fifteen years, when scholars have deliberately gone out to look for them.[4] No truth is greater for the historian than that he who seeketh, findeth.

Mormon historians have been aware for some time of the great wealth of autobiographical material that exists among LDS records. Ten years ago Malcolm Thorp, James B. Allen, Thomas G. Alexander, and others made good use of it.[5] And we are all immensely indebted to Davis Bitton for his magnificent *Guide to Mormon Diaries and Autobiographies,* published in 1977 and surely a model of its kind.[6] Naturally, these historians were interested in using the material to explore aspects of Mormon history. My purpose is somewhat different. It is to suggest that we should examine the autobiographies, diaries, and journals as products of the common people of early Victorian England, as part of a popular culture, the evidence of which is still all too scarce. It is not primarily as a record of events but as a statement by and about the author that the autobiography is to be evaluated. Fascinating (often compelling) as are the accounts of missionary endeavor in the 1840s or the hardships endured in the handcart companies of the 1850s, it is the type of perception and quality of the testimony that is of primary concern here. The autobiography is to be used as a key, or way, into the mental world of laboring men and women. As an offshoot, it is possible that some aspects of early Mormon history may appear in a slightly new context—though that is hardly within my competence to determine.

The writing of autobiography, however, is an extremely complex activity, and its use as historical evidence is by no means straightforward. At the risk of getting embroiled in current literary debates about the nature of autobiography, the historian cannot avoid certain problems. If it is used simply as a record, we have to make allowances for the fallibility of memory, especially since autobiographies were often written many years after the events they purport to describe. Even greater are the difficulties when we try to squeeze out more complex matter. Autobiography, even of the simplest and most naive kind, is in fact an art form, closely akin to fiction. The selection of memories is made in the light of the author's present conception of himself or herself. A coherence and pattern have been imposed as the author looks back; a process of smoothing out and tying up has gone on; some things have been deliberately left out and others overemphasized; self-justification and explanation have been added. The result is a curious tangle with which the historian has to wrestle. Yet this is the challenge. Documents, as Marc Bloch reminded us, are witnesses, and our task is to force them to speak, even against their will.[7] To probe into the motives of the autobiographer, to examine the use of language and concepts of time, to try to disentangle the sense of self, opens up new vistas for the social historian. And nowhere are such opportunities greater than in a sample of early Mormon auto-biographies.

Patience Loader, born in 1827, was a domestic servant from an Oxfordshire village where her father was "head gardener to an English Nobler Man for twenty-three years."[8] There were thirteen children in the family, and at the age of seventeen she went into service, first in a neighboring village and afterwards in London. Following her parents' conversion to Mormonism, she too was baptized, although at first she had been uninterested. She immigrated to Utah in 1856, and in 1858 she married John Rozsa, a sergeant in the 10th Infantry, U.S. Army. Her autobiography, titled "Recollections of Past Days," is a marvelously vivid document. Through her oral speech style, phonetic spelling, and unpunctuated sentences, there shines the personality of a laboring woman. Unlike most such journal writers, she includes a great deal of how she felt about events and people. Now this is the very stuff of social history; for, as a great social historian once wrote, "The real, central theme of History is not what happened, but what people felt about it when it was happening."[9]

Patience's thoughts on leaving home for the first time, her observations on life in London in the late 1840s, the realities of life as a hotel housemaid—all make her so much more than the usual cardboard figure describing external events. Her natural powers of narration are perhaps shown at their best in her description of the journey by handcart to Utah in 1856. Terrified by hostile Indians, she writes an emotional and moving account of her sister giving birth in a tent and of her father's sufferings and death on the Plains. In this remarkable tour de force, told so simply and with such deep feeling, we are reminded of some of the qualities to be found in the common people. This is not to say that Patience Loader's autobiography is all on this level. At times she gives way to sentimentality. Looking back on her early days, she describes a romantic mist arising around "the old home" in England, where she had, she writes, "sweet recollections of childhood and girlhood when I think of the old home where I was born and raised it fills my heart with joy and pleasure the dear old house with thatched roof and old fashion casements windows with dimant cut glass and verada in front with woodbines roses and honeysuckles twing up to the upstairs windows a beautiful flower garden on each side of the walk from the street."[10]

The reality of a gardener's cottage in the 1830s was, alas, somewhat different. The oral tones of the popular culture also come through in other autobiographies. Edwin Smout, born in 1825, was a foreman tailor from Dudley, and his Black Country speech can be heard when the following passage from his unpunctuated and phonetically spelled journal is read aloud:

> I was rease and Brought up in the Town of Dudley Worcestershire England in my fourteen (14) year I was Bownd Apprentice to William Stokes in Said Town of Dudley I severed 18 mounth and then I when to the Taylors Cuting Bord for to

learn to be a foreman in a Taylors Shop which traide I like in my 17 years I became
acquainted with Leah Oakley She was born May 5th 1826 in Dudley Worcestershire England She was the Daughter of Samuel Oakley and Mary Adlington in
my 17 year I got made a odd Fellow in the love and Unity Lodge I was then
Choosen Secretary of the Lodge which office I held for 18 mounths when I was
elected Vice Grand of the Lodge After keeping Company with Leah Oakley for
upwards of four years we got Married. . . . we Spent 2 months at Mothers and
then we when to house Keeping I did at my trade firstrate I furnish a house good
I Rented a pew in the Methodist Church from them and other Churchs I got my
trade we appeared in the world firstrate and in good order On the 3 day of October 1847 my wife Brought my first Son Felix She had a Bad time with her first
Child it was a Seven months Child We had hard work to keep life in him for two
months then he did very well in December I Recevied invitation from John
Wever a Master Shoe Maker to go and hear the Later Day Saints Preach.[11]

He was baptized in 1848 and resigned from the Oddfellows: "I went to my Lodge
as I was Vicegrand of the Same and give up my office and gave them address I
tould them I had nothing against the Order of odd Fellows I love the Order But
I was a Latter day Saint I was in a member of a Church that was truth I Sould
hold to that and give up the odd Fellows."[12] This autobiography is significant for
its priorities: occupation, marriage and family, respectability, friendly society,
and religion; but it tells us little about the author's thoughts and feelings.

An autobiography of a different type is that of John Freeman. Born in 1807,
probably illegitimate and soon orphaned, Freeman spent his childhood in the
parish school of St. James, Westminster. Twelve months after being apprenticed
by the parish as a shoemaker, he ran away "owing to ill usage" and worked in a
brickyard at Hammersmith for ten years. In 1832 (the year of the Great Reform
Bill), he became a farmworker in Bedfordshire, Warwickshire, and the Midland
counties, and in between reaping times, he sang reform songs, with a companion, in marketplaces and at fairs. This arrangement, however, soon came to an
end, and the two singers parted after "having a few words."[13] Freeman was then

followed by a young woman of the name of Hannah Whiting, who had followed me for some months, but I not wanting to have anything to do with her,
evaded her as much as possible, until at last she found me out where I was reaping, and then I could not get rid of her, so we two went together, to Birmingham, then back to Alcester, Evesham, Cheltenham and Banbury, where we took
lodgings and I commenced to make cloth slippers and she sold them, I singing
in the markets and fairs at intervals. We next took a furnished house, and after
a bit we bought some goods of our own and took a house to ourselves where we
continued until December 18, 1834, when her temper being so bad and so quar-
relsome I at length resolved to leave her, which I did on the above day, leaving
her and goods altogether and travelled on to Stratford on Avon where I arrived
the same evening and took lodgings at Thomas Heritage's and went on with my
shoe making, having to bind them myself and likewise sell them.[14]

Then in February 1835 he got a young woman, Esther Smith, to bind shoes for him. After her father died, and she was being pressured by her family to leave home and go into service, he decided to marry her. "After some equivocations" she agreed, and they were married in Stratford parish church in April 1835. Their first child was born in November 1836 and died the following March. Freeman seems to have been very unsettled during the next few years and constantly moved back and forth between Stratford and Birmingham, living first in the one place and then in the other. He joined the Independents and attended their chapels but was soon attracted to the Chartists after hearing them speak in the Bull Ring, Birmingham, in 1839. He joined the Christian Chartists, their discourses being "as nigh the Truth as most of them inasmuch as they advocated the Golden Rule of our Saviour and the Rights of their fellow creatures—so I joined with them and we opened a new place of worship, thus starting another [of] the numerous sects already upon the earth." This last phrase has a distinctly LDS ring about it, and indeed, in 1844 Freeman was converted to Mormonism, convinced that it was what he was looking for: "on the evening of the 6th March I was so foolish as to follow Christ through the water of regeneration and thus became a Son of God by being born of the Water."[15]

Freeman's autobiography is one of those that is important not only for what it says but also for what it does not say. We sense something that is not wholly revealed. Why, for instance, does he tell us so little about his childhood and those ten years when he was working in the brickyard? We learn nothing about his schooling or level of educational attainment, though the journal is competently written and full of lively domestic detail. Nor does he fully explain his radical sympathies, although he was ready to sing songs supporting reform in 1832 and to join the Chartists in 1841. His views on marriage and the relation between the sexes, if deduced from his actions, are interesting, to say the least. He did not marry until he was twenty-eight, and then only because he feared he was about to lose the girl's services as a helpmate in his trade. Previously he had set up house with her predecessor, although (he would have us believe) only reluctantly. The contrast with the respectability and concern for worldly success manifested by the previous autobiographer, Edwin Smout, is marked.

Nevertheless, it is pointless for the historian to regret what he sees as the inadequacies and limitations of such evidence. Rather, we have to accept the autobiographies of common people as statements of how things appeared to them. Otherwise we fall into that "enormous condescension of posterity" against which we have been warned.[16] The things left out or treated only perfunctorily, the priorities accorded to different themes, and the foreshortened chronology are themselves the evidence for which we are looking. They are part of the consciousness of the common people. George Morris, a farm laborer, explained how it was: "This scrapbook is an index to my life and caracter as the scraps are arranged in it so it has been with me. If I got anything I had to take it as I could catch it running, standing up, sitting or laying down. I was born in Hanley, Cheshire, England—of poore parents in a poor country—in August 1816."[17]

And there in pencil, in large, unformed handwriting, written as he spoke, is his testimony of what it was like to work on the land. As soon as he could walk, he was employed in bird scaring, armed with a set of clappers and "hollering" to scare off the rooks from early morning to late at night. His account of how he learned all the jobs required of a farm laborer is reminiscent of William Cobbett, though without any touch of romanticism. The detailed descriptions of what plowing was really like when the plowman was coated with mud, of how his mother worked for the farmers in the fields digging potatoes, and of how he picked blackberries to sell in the market are memorable for their unaffected authenticity. Hardly surprisingly, he remarks ruefully that there was "no time for me to go to school to get any education," although he did occasionally attend a dame school for a few weeks "now and then."[18]

In due course Morris married: "After a while I thought that I must do as a great many other young men have done—get married. So I picked out a girl and married her—we were married at the parish church at Ashton under Lyne on the 6th of June 1840. She was an orphan girl, by the name of Jane Higinbotham." She was delivered of a baby girl "about a year after" and died in April 1841, "aged 20 years and 3 months."[19]

This laconic account contrasts with the detail provided for other aspects of his life. Whether it truly represented Morris's view of marriage, or whether for some reason he was reluctant to say more, we do not know. In later life (1863), he entered polygamous marriage, and afterwards he was arrested and tried.

When the writer of an autobiography was a person of superior education or aspired to literary fame, the result was usually less satisfying than more humble efforts in the vernacular. George Harris, the son of a Devonshire cabinetmaker, begins his autobiography thus: "Begoten and born in the usual manner, Gentle reader; I shal not tire U with particulars. Altho it may not be amiss to mention Dec. the 7th 1830 as the time; James and Eliza as the Parents; and the aforementioned lovely Ilfracombe as the location."[20]

He next tells an amusing story that his parents could not agree about his name, with the result that he was christened George Henry, his father always calling him George and his mother calling him Henry. The affectation of a humorous literary style reaches its extreme in his account of learning to walk: "It would be more difficult than interesting to tel of the number of fals that happened while tutering my pedal extremities to resist the effects of 'Atraction of Gravitation.'"[21]

Harris had a strongly Methodist upbringing and was apprenticed aboard a coaster in 1846. He was educated to high school standard and studied navigation. However, his spelling is highly erratic, and one shudders to learn that he actually taught school in Utah for a short time in 1854 before taking up farming.

The autobiography is full of amusing anecdotes and short poems, both humorous and sentimental, and the author's self-conscious attempt to write for an audience and to project himself as a very entertaining fellow suggests a fairly sophisticated personality.

Individual personality, indeed, is perhaps the dominant characteristic that emerges from the autobiographies so far cited. Loader, Smout, Freeman, Morris, and Harris all wrote as interesting people in their own right. Yet our purpose in examining these and other testimonies is to see what, if anything, they have in common—to try to discern common assumptions, perceptions, and degrees of consciousness. Virtually all the writers begin by seeking to establish their identity. This they do by reference to time, place, and parentage. By telling the reader the date and sometimes the hour of their birth in a certain town or village and their father's occupation, they feel that they have located themselves socially. Explanation, apology, or justification follows from this. The location is not usually very extensive. Few autobiographers give details of their grandparents or uncles and aunts unless they were sent to live with them, and siblings appear only as numbers. The family as a center of childhood seems to be taken for granted, of little interest to the reader, or perhaps as irrelevant to the main purpose of the writer, which was to present himself. Virtually none of the autobiographers spend much time on their childhood. They sometimes mention particular hardships connected with child labor but seldom give much detail or speculate about their childish thoughts at the time.[22] It is as if the years before the age of puberty were considered of no account or, at most, as preparation for earning a living later.

One thing the autobiographers virtually always mention is their schooling or, more usually, their lack of it. All of them had managed at some stage to become literate, and the writing of their autobiographies reminded them in many cases of the inadequacies that remained after their attendance at Sunday School, dame school, or common day school.[23] Andrew Sproul, a Scottish weaver born in 1816, in a journal that devotes only one paragraph to the whole of his life prior to the arrival of Mormon elders in 1840, nevertheless finds space to comment as follows: "My father Francis Sprowl and my mother Ann Nicol that being his fathers name were poor but honest and I being set to work at an early age, viz. weaving, I had no oppertunity of getting an education before I was set to work, three months previous to being put to labour and that was between the sixth and seventh years of my age I was put to school and that time was taken up in lerning the alphabet and to read a little this was all the time that was set apart for me in the way of being educated at school."[24]

The children of artisans and tradesmen were usually sent to school to learn at least the three Rs, but it is clear that they regarded schooling primarily as a utilitarian pursuit. It was not education in a broad sense that was expected but simply the acquisition of a skill, similar to any other craft. The consequent level of attainment was not, by today's standards, high. For example, Robert Hazen, born in 1832 and a molder by trade, says that he "learned to be a good writer, speller, arithmetician, geographer and was naturally quick at learning, perhaps not so quick as others."[25] But a typical entry in his journal runs thus:

1853

Tuesdy 12. long to be remembered. 21 years to day i was ushered into this state of existance. where shall i be 21 years hence. at work this day. went to see my intended. found her ill. administered to her in the name of Jesus. she partook of a good supper after and felt well. the Glory be to God.[26]

For common people, making a living was the central experience of their lives. The lifelong waking hours of all but a small minority of the population were dominated by work of some kind, and this comes through very clearly in the autobiographies. Two aspects stand out: first, the great variety of types of occupation, from many kinds of laboring to skilled crafts and trades, and second, the many different jobs at which an individual worker tried his hand. Thomas Day, born in 1814 near Wolverhampton, is a good example. First he worked as a blacksmith with his father, who was a machine blacksmith. After his father's death, he left the machine company and worked in a carpet factory at Kidderminster. He records a sixteen-week strike against reduction of wages, accompanied by riots in which, he assures us, he took no part. Nevertheless, he left Kidderminster and went to Worcester, where he worked with his stepfather in a rope yard. Next he got a job in a button factory in Bromsgrove but gave it up in favor of work in a foundry in Birmingham. Thence he returned to Bromsgrove and the button factory, and his last occupation was in a needle factory in Redditch. Despite, or perhaps because of, his peregrinations around the West Midlands, he apparently made a decent living. He was proud of the respectability he ultimately attained, and it was a sore trial that he forfeited this status when he became a Mormon: "My wife and I had been very respectable in society, but we now found that our friends became persecutors for the gospel's sake."[27]

Even when a boy was apprenticed to a skilled trade, he not infrequently ran away before completing his term, and if he finished his apprenticeship he often had to go "on tramp" in search of work. The autobiographies contain many examples of such cases. In fact, the general impression from them is of a good deal of mobility between job and job and from place to place. One senses a certain mood of restlessness, of searching for something that eludes the writer, whether security, respectability, or good health. It implies familiarity with, if not acceptance of, some form of change to an extent not common in traditional, preindustrial society. It is a form of seeking, paralleled by the often-mentioned movement from one religious sect to another before the acceptance of the Mormon message. Joseph Smith's rejection of existing churches and sects because of their competing and contradictory claims is echoed in most of these Mormon autobiographies. This may have been no more than an expected pattern, similar to the conversion experience repeated in countless Methodist autobiographies. But equally it may relate to something more fundamental in the culture of the common people. Some of them were already religious seekers when the Mormon mission arrived in England. Perhaps it was not only their religious quest that made numbers of them receptive to Mormonism but also the social and cultural context of their worldly experiences.

As with other working-class autobiographies, there is a paucity of emotional and intimate detail. References to marriage and courtship are usually purely factual. "On August the 10, 1842 I began to Pay my address to maryann Case eldes Daughter of Robert and ann Case who was born at Chipenham in the county of wilts in the year of our Lord 1822," wrote George Halliday, a plasterer from Trowbridge, "and we continued to pay our addresses to each other untill the 1 of April 1844 when we was married at the old Church, troubridge."[28] Two weeks later his wife was taken ill with "consumption," and after thirteen months she died. George Spilsbury, a Worcestershire bricklayer, notes baldly that "on Sept 5th I married Fanny Smith of Cradly [Cradley] parish, Herefordshire, England."[29] Only rarely do we find even as much feeling as Thomas Day allowed himself when he described his first wife, Ann Andrus Danks, as "a young widow of quiet, loving and lovable ways."[30] Children too are mentioned only to record the date of their birth and, sometimes, early death.

We would like to learn more about family affairs, the role of women, and the relation between spouses, but our sources are meager indeed. How to force these documents to yield more escapes us at present. The autobiographers are eager to tell us many things about themselves, particularly their religious experiences, but it is their public, not their private, selves that they are anxious to reveal. The historian of the common people perversely is not content with what the text of the autobiography says but looks for what was never intended to be heard. Sexual mores, for instance, are seldom mentioned directly, but John Freeman's account of his relationship with Hannah Whiting implies much. It is unlikely that prudery was a cause of reticence. Ralph Ramsay, a cabinetmaker born in 1824, described his visits to delinquent and apostate LDS members in the Newcastle-upon-Tyne area and did not mince his words. In 1854 he visited Elder Joshua Cutts, "who had been charged with having the venereal." Cutts's explanation was that his penis, which had been injured by a fall of stones while he was working in the pit, had become infected by his piles, from which he also suffered. The visiting elders told him that the evidence suggested he was guilty and that he should confess frankly. He protested his innocence and said that "he had not had any connection with any woman but his own wife since he entered the Church, that being about five years—what took place before that no one had any business with."[31] Frankness of this order lets in a little light upon the subject of popular sexuality and suggests that the conventions of middle-class Victorian morality were by no means universal in the 1850s.

In contrast to the scarcity of references to sexuality, all the writers have something to say about religion. This, of course, is to be expected, given the nature of the exercise that to the writer was essentially a spiritual autobiography. In the classic form of this genre, the early events lead up to a crisis out of which is born a new self. The search for personal salvation, the failure to find "rest" in any of the religious modes of institutions tried, and the final conversion experience are familiar from puritan models dating back to the seventeenth century. Methodism revitalized and strengthened this tradition and made it available to thousands of working people in the late eighteenth and early nineteenth centuries. As Malcolm Thorp has shown, Methodism was a very fruitful source of converts to Mormonism in the early Victorian years.[32]

Our Mormon autobiographies conform closely to the classic pattern of conversion narratives, albeit in a somewhat attenuated form. Little is said, for instance, about the inner spiritual strivings, more about going from sect to sect. The reasons given for the acceptance of Mormonism bear out the conclusions reached by Leonard Arrington and Davis Bitton, Richard Bushman, Jan Shipps, and others.[33] But always the climax of the first part of the autobiography is baptism in the LDS Church, usually after hearing a Mormon preacher. George Halliday was finally converted by his brother, John Halliday, who had come from Nauvoo on a mission: "I then heard the docktrine that he taught and I examined it with the Bible and after some examination I found that I had done the Best that I know how in serving the Lord But I found that there ware greater light come into the world and I was then willing to embraice it and on Sunday the tenth of November 1844 I was Baptised."[34]

Looking back over their lives, the Mormon autobiographers were unanimous that their baptism was the most important thing that had happened to them. It was a watershed, the reference point in their lives against which all else was to be assessed. The break with the past, the great discontinuity, was further emphasized by emigration, with its often traumatic journey and the building of a new life in a strange new environment. Time was to be measured as before or after the great event. The effect was to introduce a sense of chronology that previously had been absent. Working-class autobiographies tend to be fragmentary, anecdotal, chronologically vague, and reliant on traditional (sometimes generational) concepts of time. Mormonism introduced a greater degree of structure and a more disciplined ordering of events. Dates, notably the exact date of baptism, are more plentifully supplied.

Few of the Mormon autobiographers mentioned external events, although they were living through one of the periods of greatest political, economic, and social change in English history. Instead of relating the episodes in their lives to

happenings on the national scene, their reminiscences are, with very few exceptions, essentially local and familial. The things that stick in the memory are personal and even trivial. George Spilsbury, the Worcestershire bricklayer who
dismissed his marriage in one short sentence, described in considerable detail
how he caught an infectious disease while on his missionary labors in Herefordshire in the early 1840s:

> Having to sleep in so many different places and sometimes with very undesir-
> able bedfellows, I caught the itch which nearly cost me my life. An Elder that
> travelled with me on one occasion advised me to get some mercury, dissolve
> [it] in water and wash wherever I was broken out with this rash, which I did in
> a cold room which caused it to strike inwardly. O, I was very sick . . . [and he
> had to travel sixteen or seventeen miles]. The spirit of the Lord suggested to
> me to get some burdock roots and make some tea and drink it freely, which I
> did and it killed the effects of the mercury and I recovered.[35]

It may be that this anecdote was included as an example of divine help, but it
also reveals an order of priorities and a predilection for herbal remedies common to laboring people at this time. There is, of course, a simple explanation of
why the common people did not write about national events. It was because
they were not, for the most part, consciously involved in them. Their world was
not that of their rulers, and the daily concerns of laboring people, as these autobiographies make clear, lay elsewhere.

A crucial question in assessing the evidence of the autobiographies is the
nature of the sample. Davis Bitton lists perhaps 150 entries relating to England
in the 1830s and 1840s, and of these I have been able to examine some 35. This is
but a tiny fraction of the 17,849 Mormon baptisms and 4,700 emigrants from
Britain in 1837–46 and makes anything like generalization extremely hazardous.
The most that can be said is that the experiences and sentiments recorded in
the Mormon autobiographies examined are, by and large, very similar to non-
Mormon autobiographies of the same type and period. The sample is biased
geographically toward the West Midlands and Lancashire and also toward religion. But the language of blessings and gifts, the use of greetings such as *brother*
and *sister,* and the literalness of biblical references are very close to the culture
of Methodism and popular evangelical religion generally. Women, as ever, are
underrepresented among the autobiographers, and what we hear most clearly
are masculine voices.

With these provisos, a few tentative conclusions may nevertheless be drawn
from the witness of these autobiographers. First, they were nearly all poor people in the sense that they did not have much of this world's goods, and some of
them were at times in want. The pursuit of material well-being and escape from
the anxieties and stresses that poverty entails preoccupied most of them for
much of their time. A constant theme was the struggle to attain respectability,

with its implicit recognition of the division in working-class life between the "roughs" and the "respectables." Second, the common people did not exercise power. They did not, for the most part, make the decisions that affected their lives but were, in effect, controlled by others. A working man, even a skilled artisan with traditional notions of independence, could do little about external conditions that affected his work. Perhaps the biggest step toward emancipation that he could take was emigration, which seemed to offer a new dimension of freedom.

Despite, or perhaps because of, their poverty and exclusion from power, the common people developed their own consciousness and aspirations that were different from their rulers'. Deeper even than the laboring man's expectation of material sufficiency for himself and his family, there emerges from the autobiographies the elemental desire in all human beings to feel that they are wanted and that their efforts are recognized and rewarded. When this is denied, there is a loss in human dignity and sense of worth. The denial of some of the basic needs of ordinary people and the constant belittling of their opinions by the educated classes perpetuated a gulf between "them" and "us." There was a natural retreat into a working-class or popular religious world, where there were other values that recognized men and women for what they were worth, despite the contrary view of the dominant society. The "sons of want" knew that they had only themselves to turn to for help. Experience taught self-help through reliance on the family, the local community, the chapel, the friendly society, or the trade union. It was into this world of the common people that the Mormon missionaries penetrated in 1837 and from which they reaped such a rich harvest.

Notes

1. *Common people* is the term by which the great majority of ordinary people who had to work for their living were known in Britain. I have used the words *common* and *popular* throughout this chapter despite their slightly different usage in British and American English.

2. See J. R. Green, *A Short History of the English People* (London: Macmillan, 1875); James E. Thorold Rogers, *Six Centuries of Work and Wages: The History of English Labour*, 2 vols. (London: Swan Sonnenschein, 1884); G. D. H. Cole and Raymond Postgate, *The Common People, 1746–1938* (London: Methuen, 1938); R. J. Mitchell and M. D. Leys, *A History of the English People* (London: Longmans, Green, 1950).

3. These problems are discussed at greater length in the introduction to J. F. C. Harrison, *The Common People of Great Britain* (Bloomington: Indiana University Press, 1985), also published in the United Kingdom as *The Common People* (London: Fontana, 1984).

4. Notably in John Burnett, David Vincent, and David Mayall, *The Autobiography of the Working Class: An Annotated, Critical Bibliography*, Vol. 1, *1790–1900* (Brighton, UK: Harvester, 1984). See also David Vincent, *Bread, Knowledge and Freedom: A Study of Nineteenth-Century Working Class Autobiography* (London: Europa, 1981); and the intro-

duction to *Robert Lowery: Radical and Chartist*, ed. Brian Harrison and Patricia Hollis (London: Europa, 1979). A valuable recent study is Regenia Gagnier, "Social Atoms: Working-Class Autobiography, Subjectivity, and Gender," *Victorian Studies* 30(3) (Spring 1987): 355–63.

5. See Malcolm R. Thorp, "The Religious Backgrounds of Mormon Converts in Britain, 1837–52," *Journal of Mormon History* 4 (1977): 51–66, to which I am much indebted. See also James B. Allen and Malcolm R. Thorp, "The Mission of the Twelve to England, 1840–41: Mormon Apostles and the Working Classes," *BYU Studies* 15(4) (Summer 1975): 499–526; Thomas G. Alexander, "Wilford Woodruff and the Changing Nature of Mormon Religious Experience," *Church History* 45(1) (March 1976): 56–69.

6. Davis Bitton, *Guide to Mormon Diaries and Autobiographies* (Provo, Utah: Brigham Young University Press, 1977), on which I have relied heavily.

7. Marc Bloch, *The Historian's Craft* (Manchester, UK: Manchester University Press, 1954), 62–64; also quoted in Alan Macfarlane, *The Origins of English Individualism* (Oxford: Basil Blackwell, 1978), 190.

8. Patience Loader Rozsa Archer (1827–1921), "Recollections of Past Days," L. Tom Perry Special Collections, Harold B. Lee Library, Brigham Young University, Provo, Utah (hereafter Perry Special Collections).

9. G. M. Young, *Victorian England: Portrait of an Age* (Oxford: Oxford University Press, 1936).

10. Patience Loader Rozsa Archer, "Recollections of Past Days," Perry Special Collections.

11. Edwin Ward Smout (1823–1900), Journal, Perry Special Collections.

12. Ibid.

13. John Freeman (1807–?), Reminiscences and Diary, Church Archives, Church of Jesus Christ of Latter-day Saints, Salt Lake City (hereafter LDS Church Archives).

14. Ibid.

15. Ibid.

16. E. P. Thompson, *The Making of the English Working Class* (London: Gollancz, 1963), 12.

17. George Morris (1816–97), Reminiscences, LDS Church Archives.

18. Ibid.

19. Ibid.

20. George Henry Abbott Harris (1830–?), Autobiography, Perry Special Collections.

21. Ibid.

22. For example, Thomas Wright Kirby (1831–1908), Autobiography, LDS Church Archives. Kirby describes the working conditions in a Suffolk silk factory to which he was sent at the age of seven.

23. There is a considerable literature on literacy and schooling in the nineteenth century. See, for example, W. B. Stephens, *Education, Literacy and Society, 1830–70: The Geography of Diversity in Provincial England* (Manchester, UK: Manchester University Press, 1987).

24. Andrew Sproul (1816–?), Diary, Perry Special Collections.

25. Robert Hazen (1832–?), Diary, Perry Special Collections.

26. Ibid.

27. Thomas Day (1814–93), Autobiography, LDS Church Archives.

28. George Halliday (1823–1900), Journal, Perry Special Collections.

29. George Spilsbury (1823–?), Autobiography, Perry Special Collections.

30. Thomas Day (1814–93), Autobiography, LDS Church Archives.

31. Ralph Ramsay (1824–?), Journal, LDS Church Archives.

32. Thorp, "The Religious Backgrounds of Mormon Converts," 60.

33. See Leonard J. Arrington and Davis Bitton, *The Mormon Experience: A History of the Latter-day Saints* (London: Allen and Unwin, 1979); Richard L. Bushman, *Joseph Smith and the Beginnings of Mormonism* (Urbana: University of Illinois Press, 1984); Jan Shipps, *Mormonism: The Story of a New Religious Tradition* (Urbana: University of Illinois Press, 1985).

34. George Halliday, Journal, Perry Special Collections.

35. George Spilsbury, Autobiography, Perry Special Collections.

CHAPTER 9

Sesquicentennial Reflections: A Comparative View of Mormon and Gentile Women on the Westward Trail

Glenda Riley

The mid-1840s proved to be heart-wrenching and life-alerting for women who turned their faces toward the American West. During the 1840s as well as the succeeding decade, thousands of women undertook westward migration, some with certainty, others with misgiving. Whether hopeful or hesitant, illiterate or educated, single or married, native-born or from Canada or a European nation, women experienced many comparable—as well as some vastly diverse—circumstances on the westward trek.

The similarities and differences between early Mormon and gentile trail women will be explored here, including how Mormon women on the trail coped with their additional burdens. This essay maintains that these two groups of women experienced the westward migration in strikingly dissimilar ways.

Similarities on the Trail

Mormon and gentile women's trail diaries and other accounts, which constitute an important genre of historical documents, reveal many similarities.[1] For instance, virtually all women, except the most hardened, yearned for a better life ahead. A variety of media had done their job well. From rumors to newspaper accounts, from touring lecturers to guidebooks, from letters "back home" to railroad company and other "boomer" literature came the image of the American West as a promised land.

Myriad illustrations exist. As early as 1837, for example, the Dubuque *Iowa News* declared, "It is seldom that a person who has resided for some years here, can ever content himself to return and live in the east." Less than two decades later the *Eddyville Free Press,* also in Iowa, promised rewards that exceeded even the most hopeful fantasies of potential migrants. People had only to bring "strong minds and willing hands to work" to be "abundantly blessed and rewarded."[2]

Not surprisingly then, women often traveled on hope and dreams. In 1846, Eliza Roxcy Snow, a plural wife of both Joseph Smith and his successor Brigham Young who immigrated to the Salt Lake Valley, lauded in verse the opportunities the West offered:

> Let us go—let us go to a country whose soil
> Can be made to produce wine, milk, honey & oil—
> Where beneath our own vines we may sit & enjoy
> The rich fruit of our labors with none to annoy.[3]

In 1853, Hannah Tapfield King, another Mormon woman, similarly looked forward to entering "that renowned place, 'The Valley'" of the Great Salt Lake.[4]

In addition, Latter-day Saint wives often shared their husbands' visions. According to Mary Ann Hafen, a young handcart pioneer in 1860, her mother survived the trip by concentrating on her husband's assurances that Zion lay ahead, "that the Lord would take care of us, and that better times were coming."[5]

Gentile women also perceived the West as a paradise of sorts. In 1849, Catherine Haun, an Iowa woman married for just four months, undertook a demanding journey across the Great Plains in pursuit of improved health in California. Other women hoped to leave behind worn-out land, high taxes, the system of black slavery, or various kinds of prejudice in favor of richer soil and a more open society. And like Hafen's mother, some sustained themselves by listening to their spouses' promises. In 1860, Lavinia Porter of Hannibal, Missouri, turned her back on her family and followed her husband toward what he described as the "land of golden promise."[6]

Women of color also looked to the West as a haven from discrimination and the opportunity for a fresh start. Shortly after the Civil War, African American Jenny Proctor recalled how she, her husband, and their son climbed aboard their covered wagon with their "little mules hitched to it" and left Alabama for what they hoped would be a better life in Texas.[7]

Trail work constituted yet another similarity between Mormon and gentile women. With a few exceptions of all-male parties, women routinely participated in westward migrations and made a crucial contribution to a party's well-being and even survival. Among Mormons, women even took part in the 1846–47 march of the famed Mormon Battalion. One of these young women was on a honeymoon journey. Other women crossed the Plains without the assistance of husbands and sons who served in the battalion or who had undertaken religious missions.[8] On the trail, women provided such essential services as cooking regular, substantial meals whenever possible. Although men occasionally took over culinary tasks, it was not the norm. Gentile Francis Sawyer noted in 1852 that "the men do all the cooking in bad weather" but that she cooked otherwise.[9]

Even though food may sound commonplace, it played a critical role. Food sustained migrants as they crossed the trail, not only by giving them physical nourishment but frequently by supplying emotional sustenance as well. After a chilling dousing during a river crossing, for example, Mormon Patience Loader's mother gave her daughters tiny pieces of carefully hoarded bread and molasses. According to Patience, "This was a great treat to us. . . . It seemed to give us new strength to travle [*sic*] on."[10]

Through other dismaying times, food also provided tender memories of former homes and maintained "proper ways" despite wagon and tent living. The ritual of taking tea seemed nearly universal. In 1853, a Mormon migrant from England wrote: "Set the wagon & tent—washed & had tea," and again, "I went to tea." Other women, both Mormon and Gentile, also found comfort in drinking tea. American-born gentile Celina Hines frequently referred to "taking" tea while on the trail, a ceremony that helped her and other family members maintain a sense of continuity with their past. Similarly, Sarah J. Cummins and a friend used boiling water from a hot spring to prepare tea, which they sipped as they reminisced about former friends and happy occasions.[11]

Women also provided child care and medical treatment and acted as apothecaries. All three services, often in combination, were much in demand on the trail. In Winter Quarters, midwife Patty Sessions not only delivered babies but regularly doctored the sick, including many children. Among non-Mormon travelers, illness was also rampant, especially attacking children. In 1853, Clarissa Taylor began her journey with a feverish baby, while Amelia Knight's two children came down with mumps. In that same year, Charlotte Pengra treated her daughter for a swollen ear, fever, and dysentery.[12]

A different type of women's trail work fell in the psychological and spiritual realms. More specifically, women served as transitional forces on the westward journey. The trip provided a time for people to adjust from the known to the new, to learn fresh skills, and to develop ways of managing unexpected circumstances.[13]

In addition, many trail women bolstered other migrants through hard times by force of resilient personalities. Even several female Saints who had nothing to eat but "bone soup" were able to sing for their brethren and "enjoy" themselves for a few hours one evening in 1856. When they rose to breakfast on broth and one biscuit among them, they ate "with thankfull hearts."[14] Other women could glory in a sunrise, laugh at a mishap, and appreciate the beauties of the landscape. For instance, along the Platte River, gentile Tamsen Donner wrote, "The prairie between the Blue and Platte rivers is abundant beyond description. . . . Everything was new and pleasing." Teenager Elizabeth Keegan, who found the overland journey to Sacramento in 1852 "tedious in the extreme," waxed lyrical about "rolling praries [*sic*] . . . covered with verdure."[15]

Generally trail women drew upon the tenets of women's culture to direct them in this time of upheaval. Women's customary roles and domestic ideologies gave them guidelines to follow in chaotic circumstances. As wives and mothers, trail women especially played a crucial role by providing moral guidance in situations that often involved drinking, swearing, loose sexual practices, a state of near undress on the part of some natives, and omitting Sabbath observances. As Mormon Hannah Tapfield King complained, "I have no Sunday feelings while travelling on Sunday."[16]

Women especially worried about "civilizing" their children despite crude trail conditions. On an 1846 journey, one young Mormon woman recalled that her mother tried to further her social education by allowing her to attend dances but forbidding her to swim. Similarly, in 1852 gentile Mary Ellen Todd insisted that her daughters remain ladylike by avoiding running, jumping, and climbing, while the following year Amelia Knight spent a good deal of time "washing and scrubbing" each of her offspring.[17]

Another part of nineteenth-century women's culture involved the formation of reciprocal relationships with other women. Encouraged by the women's guidebooks of the day to practice cooperation, trail women often joined with their counterparts to get a job done, whether it be laundry, cooking, or child care. West of the Des Moines River, Eliza R. Snow and two other women went to "the Creek about a half mile distant, to wash, while Sis. Y. & Catherine stay to attend to the cooking department."[18]

Childbirth provided yet another opportunity for women to help one another. When women were "confined" or "in a poor fix to travel," midwives or other women usually delivered babies and even cared for mother and child afterward. During an 1848 trek led by Brigham Young, Mary Wickersham Wooley bore a robust baby with the help of her twelve-year-old daughter Rachel and a midwife. In another case, when non-Mormon Arvazona Cooper's breast milk stopped flowing, a female traveler even served as a wet nurse so the infant could survive to see the West.[19]

Of course, women's efforts to cope with the hazards of the Overland Trail demanded great physical energy, stamina, and fortitude. Traversing the trail to California was a twenty-four-hour, every-day-of-the-week undertaking often fraught with danger. Consequently, Mormon and gentile trail women also experienced corresponding tragedies and disappointments. Such notations as those by a Mormon woman on her way to Salt Lake City in 1853, "baby died" and "Sister How's baby died," were common. Moreover, members of the Willie and Martin handcart companies fell victim to intense cold and lack of provisions. During an 1856 crossing, both parents of the Holiton family died from overexposure, leaving behind four or five children. An eleven-year-old girl's father and mother died of hunger, and she later had to have her frostbitten feet amputated above the ankle. Mary Goble Pay's description of her family's arrival in Salt Lake City, also in 1856, is even more upsetting: "Three out of four that were living were frozen. My mother was dead in the wagon."[20]

Gentile women also confronted threats of varying natures. In 1852, Iowan Lucy Cooke crossed the plains to California with her husband, a new baby, and her in-laws. Along the way, she confronted outbreaks of cholera, her mother-in-law's unceasing lamentations, her husband's depression, and her baby's illness. Like Cooke, Eliza Ann McAuley Egbert journeyed to California in 1852. She recorded accidents, death, "impudent" Indians, and loss of stock.[21]

For many women, however, the worst menace was that posed by Indians, widely reported as "hostile" and "ferocious." Still, even though many women expressed fear of Indians, reports of attacks were relatively rare. Mormon hand-cart women, for example, reported a cow killed by Indians or an offer of marriage and ponies, but few recorded any serious trouble.[22]

Frequently, women gradually rejected the stories they had heard about Indians before leaving home and began to trade with them. Trail women bartered needles, thread, calico and flannel shirts, children's rag dolls, flour, and bread in return for potatoes, corn, pumpkins, melons, strawberries, blackberries, meat, fresh fish, dried salmon, baskets, moccasins, and tanned hides. On one occasion, gentile Lucia Williams, traveling to Oregon in 1851, traded two pancakes for a salmon and, on another, gave a native woman an apron, a needle, and some thread for enough salmon to provide several meals. Williams remarked that she had "never tasted any fowl or fish half so delicious."[23]

Moreover, trail women also began to visit with Indian women. A young gentile woman who migrated to Salem, Oregon, in 1851 recalled that "if there were Indians we would go visiting their lodges and go around among them." Some years later, Gentile Arvazona Cooper commented that when a Cherokee woman invited her for a visit, she found that Indian woman "well fixed with household affairs and very kind and sociable."[24]

Interchanges between female travelers and native women often led to warm feelings. Gentile Lucia Williams noted that her daughter and an Indian woman started to "jabber" and "laugh" so that "they got into quite a spree." Such friendly episodes not only eased female migrants' minds regarding Indians but often led to an exchange of important information. Especially during the 1840s and 1850s, before trails become overcrowded and mistrust between groups ran high, trail women showed native women how to use needles and bake yeast bread, while native women demonstrated how to prepare and preserve foods, find and use roots, brew herbal medicines, and create a baby jumper suspended between two bedposts.[25]

Clearly, crossing the overland trail acted as a great leveler, bringing women of many social classes and national backgrounds into contact over such basic concerns as nutrition, health, and physical safety. Yet differences existed as well. This pattern proved especially true for Mormon women, whose religious beliefs and practices often set them apart from other westbound women.

Differences on the Trail

The dissimilarities between Mormons and Gentiles proved crucial, especially to LDS women. For one thing, emotional trauma regularly characterized their departures. For another, the growing avoidance of Mormons and Gentiles along the trail isolated the Saints from the main body of westward migrants. This separation marginalized Mormon women and put them outside an easy reach of information, companionship, and assistance from other parties, trains, and even settlements along the way. Moreover, poverty was rife among the Saints. Although the 1847 Donner Party tragedy topped the list of overland trail disasters, Mormon women of this era routinely confronted hardship and hunger.[26]

For Mormon women, special problems occurred before they even set foot on the trail. Although both Mormon and gentile women wrestled with grief over leaving their homes, relatives, friends, and neighbors behind, many Mormon women bore the additional shock of split families caused by members who opposed conversion, migration, or both. Patience Loader was only one of many who left a split family behind. Patience's sister Eliza was so bitter about Patience's conversion to Mormonism that she refused even to bid her sister goodbye.[26]

In addition, unlike non-Mormons, violence and riots often propelled Saints westward, whether they desired to move or not. Although Church leaders had prophesied the exodus and believed that they must eventually lead their people to the West, the average Saint knew little of the forecast or plans for its implementation.[27]

Women especially became convinced of the move's necessity when their children and other family members suffered from bigotry against which they were powerless to protect them. As a case in point, Sarah Studevant Leavitt, who lived near Kirtland, Ohio, during the early 1840s, remembered that her children would come "from school with their nose bleeding and crying, saying that they had been pounded most unmercifully." Although Sarah visited her children's teacher and extracted a promise to stop such abuse, community censure against the family continued. The Leavitts relocated in Nauvoo, only to discover that they again had to leave a thriving farm, this time with just the things they could hastily load into a wagon.[28]

Other women of the early 1840s had, spurring them on, memories of mobs who drove women and children from their homes and set fire to the houses behind them, imprisonments, hangings, tarrings and featherings, and outright battles. One young woman left Nauvoo, Illinois, with her mother and siblings after a mob killed her father.[29]

It was at Nauvoo of course that such traumatic pressures eventually reached a peak and made it imperative that Church leaders activate their migration plan. It was there that Joseph Smith began to practice in secret the revelation commanding plural marriage—meaning that the husband wed several wives. He instructed his closest associates in this revival of Old Testament patriarchs. In 1843, for example, Smith was sealed to sisters Eliza and Emily Partridge. Smith also publicly preached about what would eventually be called celestial marriage, but he kept the details of his vision to himself. One woman remembered that, when asked, Smith simply replied, "If I were to tell you, the best friends I have, apparently, would shed my blood."[30]

The need to avoid open discussion of plural marriage led to rumors and resistance. Like others, Sarah Leavitt first heard about plural marriage when a friend "whispered" in her ear "that the authorities were getting more wives than one," a practice that dated back to at least 1841 and perhaps to the 1830s. Although Sarah at first resisted the idea, she demonstrated the strength of spirit and independence of thought characteristic of many Mormon women by consulting God rather than simply accepting or rejecting the word of the Church hierarchy. Sarah embraced plural marriage when God revealed the truth in a "heavenly vision." Similarly, after "considerable deliberation," including devout meditation, Mary Phelps embraced the principle of plural marriage and became the third wife of Charles C. Rich in January 1845.[31]

Jane Snyder Richards also fought plural marriage but eventually accepted her husband's need to take a second wife for religious reasons. Although the second wife died on the trek to Utah, Jane had discovered that plural marriage "was not such a trial as she had feared, when she was tested." She added that plural marriage proved the least of her troubles in a long lifetime.[32]

In subsequent years, many other Mormon women adopted plural marriage because they believed it was the will of God, necessary to their salvation and spiritual growth.[33] Still, plural marriage failed to convince all Mormon women. Sarah Hall Scott wrote in 1844 that "The people of the state will not suffer such things any longer. . . . Any one needs a throat like an open sepulchre to *swallow down* all that is taught here."[34]

As Joseph Smith foresaw, plural marriage also drew enormous enmity from some insiders as well as many outsiders. In 1844 an anti-Mormon mob murdered Joseph Smith and his brother Hyrum in the jail at Carthage, the county seat. After this calamity, thousands of Mormons mobilized to their leaders' growing certainty that the Saints would have to abandon Nauvoo and move west once again.[35] They trekked to the desert of the Great Salt Lake in Utah, which lay outside the boundaries of the United States.

Under the leadership of Brigham Young, who migrated with his wives from Nauvoo in 1846, Mormons established Salt Lake City in 1847 and the state of Deseret in 1849.[36] Although they hoped to live in peace, free from persecution and regulation by laws stipulating that marriages be monogamous, in 1850 the U.S. Congress recognized Deseret as the Territory of Utah, which brought Mormons back within the jurisdiction of the United States.

As Latter-day Saints flocked toward their new promised land, they traveled as outcasts from their homeland. Although they left a prosperous community and their temples behind, they had to develop a "don't-look-back" mentality. As Joseph Smith had suggested as early as 1840, their Zion and all it promised lay ahead.[37] They fastened their thoughts and hopes on the future and, wary from their recent traumatic experiences, held themselves apart as much as possible.

Yet distress followed the Mormons along the trail. In particular, plural marriage, now openly practiced, continued to bedevil untold numbers of Mormon women. The 1840s letters of Mary Haskin Parker Richards disclose one woman's emotional conflicts while in Winter Quarters, where the issue was frequently discussed. Richards herself begged her husband to wait before taking another wife, declaring that "there is no such a thing as happiness known here where a man has more than one [wife]." Near Fort Laramie, Hannah Tapfield King similarly noted that she could not reconcile herself to "the new doctrine" coming in such a form. And in 1852, when Iowan Sarah A. Cooke converted to Mormonism, she refused to accept plural marriage for herself or any other member of her family.[38]

In addition, the Saints quickly learned that most non-Mormon travelers had absorbed widespread prejudice against them. A storm of anti-Mormon cartoons, caricatures, newspaper articles, novels, sermons, speeches, and tracts had convinced numerous Gentiles that, as the New York Times reported, most Latter-day Saints were "intense and zealous religionists" who shared a "delusion."[39]

Several gentile women traveling westward included Mormons among their fears, for "the tales told of the Mormons . . . were worse than those of the Indians." Another said she had heard "so many vile things of these Mormons that I expected to see them with cloven feet."[40] Given such mistrust, members of the two groups often hurled accusations back and forth on the trail. During the 1850s, some Saints claimed that non-Mormon immigrants played "foul tricks," for which they blamed Mormons. In another instance Helena Rosbery, who converted in Sweden and traveled to Utah with a handcart company in 1859, also laid the suffering of the Latter-day Saints on Gentiles: "The gentiles have made laws that come in conflict with the laws of God and when that is so we will obey the laws of the Lord and let that of man go."[41] For their part, Gentiles indicted Mormons, saying they were "vile," immoral, and a source of constant trouble along the trail. Others agreed that the Latter-day Saints either perpetrated heinous deeds or incited Native Americans to do so.[42]

Despite such sentiments, some Gentiles appeared favorable toward Mormons. One woman noted that Mormon merchants at Council Bluffs charged reasonable prices and acted fairly in their dealings with travelers. Another, Margaret Hecox, who migrated to California in 1846, deplored the "abject poverty" suffered by the Saints and judged them not quite "as black as they were painted."[43]

Still, the two groups generally kept their distance as much as possible, particularly as the numbers of westward parties grew. Competition for scarce resources along the trail increased, and Gentile travelers became even more vit-riolic in their criticisms of Mormons. The Saints sensibly avoided contact with Gentiles when possible, intensifying the isolation they already imposed on themselves as an exiled religious community.

Clearly, the Saints' practice of plural marriage provided a major reason for Gentile mistrust. During the 1840s and 1850s, many Americans feared plural marriage as a threat to long-held and widely cherished conceptions of monog-amous marriage. Actually, about three-quarters of Latter-day Saints were monog-amous. Those who practiced plural marriage were in the minority. Moreover, Church leaders hedged the practice around, for the most part, with careful reg-ulations. But after the Latter-day Saints publicly announced plural marriage in 1852, few non-Mormons could be convinced of these facts.[44]

Meanwhile, an expanding number of Mormon women defended the idea of plural marriage. Eliza R. Snow maintained that she was learning to "love" the "principle and design of Plural Marriage." Snow deeply resented it when the inhabitants of Des Moines "manifested as much curiosity as though viewing a menagerie of wild beasts." She concluded that "their levity and apparent heart-lessness" demonstrated their "profound ignorance."[45]

Another 1840s migrant accepted plural marriage as a "sacred revelation." She explained that her religious beliefs led her to consent to her husband's second marriage and that the extended family lived in peace and happiness. Like Snow, she expressed hostility against those who held Mormon women "up to scorn" and caused them no end of trouble. Yet another traveler of the 1840s agreed. As one of two wives, she declared that she enjoyed a "poor but happy" life. And, unlike non-Mormon groups, she lived in a community free of vice and prostitution.[46]

Not unexpectedly, most Americans saw Mormon practices negatively. In 1850, John W. Gunnison, an army officer stationed in Salt Lake City, wrote to his wife that "some things happen in this polygamy loving community which would astonish the people in the States." He added that it was easy to see "the influence of polygamy in degrading the female sex."[47]

As Gunnison suggested, plural marriage could be perceived as a special peril to women. This factor may help explain why Gentile trail women reacted with such venom to the idea and to those who practiced it. In 1853, Gentile migrant Harriet Sherrill Ward judged the Saints "a miserable lot of extortioners upon whom the wrath of God will yet be poured out." Later, while crossing the plains in 1860, Mary Fish derided handcart women as "sadly in want of husbands to level themselves to brutes & after all their trouble to obtain one 4th or perhaps one 20th part of a man."[48]

As if the Latter-day Saints traveling westward did not already have enough negative aspects to their image, many Americans, troubled by a rising divorce rate, further condemned the Mormon kingdom as little more than a divorce mill. In 1847, Mormon leaders began granting divorces or cancellations of sealings.

Because Church officials lacked the legal power to terminate civil marriages, they limited themselves to divorcing polygamous couples whose marriages fell within the jurisdiction of the Church. They intended that Saints leave conflicted relationships in favor of ones that would foster their Christian qualities. Brigham Young reportedly granted more than sixteen hundred divorces during his presidency of the Church between 1847 and 1877. Although Young theoretically opposed divorce because it contradicted the Mormon belief in eternal marriage, he was willing to terminate contentious and other troubled marriages.[49]

On one day, Brigham Young freed George D. Grant of three wives and a few weeks later relieved him of a fourth. Apparently, Young personally lacked sympathy for men such as Grant. He stated in 1858: "It is not right for men to divorce their wives the way they do." He had slightly more compassion for women. Although he often counseled a distraught wife to stay with her husband as long "as she could bear with him," he instructed her to seek a divorce if life became "too burdensome." In 1861, Young instructed husbands to release discontented wives.[50]

As news of Mormon divorces reached the gentile world, public outrage against Mormons flared, at home and on the trail. The situation worsened in 1852 when the first Utah territorial legislature adopted a statute permitting probate courts to grant divorces. The 1852 Utah Territory statute was objectionable because, in addition to listing the usual grounds of impotence, adultery, willful desertion for one year, habitual drunkenness, conviction for a felony, and abusive treatment, it included an omnibus clause: judges could grant divorces "when it shall be made to appear to the satisfaction and conviction of the court that the parties cannot live in peace and union together and that their welfare requires a separation." Moreover, contrary to the customary one-year residency requirement, a Utah court need only be satisfied that a petitioner was "a resident of the Territory, or wishes to become one."[51]

As a result of the 1852 legislation, civil divorces were so easy to obtain in Utah Territory that a couple could receive a divorce on the same day they applied for it. On 12 February 1856, John and Sarah Wardall petitioned for divorce and requested equal division of their children and property. The judge agreed: John received custody of the two oldest boys, and Sarah got custody of their daughter and youngest boy.[52]

Rumors regarding such "easy" divorces further separated Mormons from Gentiles along the trail during the 1850s. Given the expanding animosity toward the Latter-day Saints, it is not surprising that gentile trail women disparaged Mormon women. Although Mormon women were often of similar ethnic background, race, and social class and shared a widespread belief in God, gentile women treated them as a minority group within trail society. One gentile woman, not content with disagreeing with religious practices, dismissed Mormon women as "very plain looking, many of them absolutely ugly." Another added that Mormon women were "not always inclined to be friendly"—perhaps understandably.[53]

Numerous gentile women also reveled in cases of Mormon failure and disappointment. Although relatively few Mormons regretted their commitment to Mormonism and left Salt Lake City, gentile women discoursed at length regarding parties of Saints heading back to the "States" and assumed that these people had their fill of Mormonism and now fled Zion. In 1857, Helen Carpenter described a contingent of returning Mormons as wearing "rags and tatters." In her view, they constituted "the very worst lot" she had seen but were only a few of many who "would be glad to leave Salt Lake if they could only get away."[54]

In 1860, Mary Fish concurred. She met two Mormon women "fleeing" Salt Lake because of their antipathy toward their plural marriages. According to Fish, one woman returned to her parents with "four little responsibilities," while her companion had "consoled herself for the loss of a small portion of a man by taking a whole one as she has married a trader."[55]

In addition, more often than not Mormon indigence inspired disgust rather than sympathy among gentile women. One remarked in 1852 that the Saints were not only "poor" but that their ranks included numerous "foreigners." In a sense, she was correct; poverty was endemic among the Mormons, and growing numbers of migrants to Salt Lake did originate in Canada and Europe, including uneducated people from the lower classes.[56]

In fact, poverty, which in turn led to a high death rate, was perhaps the worst single feature of the Mormon diaspora. In part because of mob violence, Mormon parties often departed without adequate preparation. Martha Pane Jones Thomas recalled that in 1846 her family of two adults and eight children "started for the Mountains without purse or scrip, wagon or team." As a result, people were famished. More than one pregnant woman bore a child under the worst of situations, afraid that she and her infant would starve to death. One woman summed up the misery: "hard times and much sickness and suffering prevailed, especially at Winter Quarters."[57]

Handcart companies, though few in number, probably experienced the worst privation, however, and the suffering of the Willie and Martin companies in the early winter of 1856 has become a symbol for unswerving devotion under unbelievable hardship. Although supply wagons attended these intrepid pioneers, provisions frequently ran short or were insufficient. As a result, handcart pioneer Patience Loader repeatedly noted "deplorable" conditions, death, and physical inability to pull handcarts any longer. She also underwent emotionally scarring events: "When we was in the middle of the river I saw a poor brother carreying his child on his back. He fell down in the water. I never knew if he was drowned or not. I fealt sorry that we could not hellp him but we had all we could do to save our ownselvs from drownding." In several places in her journal, Loader characterized the trip as a "hard" or "terrible" journey, which finally ended with her family's arrival in Salt Lake in November 1856.[58]

Surviving the Mormon Trek

The discussion of the special tribulations of Mormon women is not intended to diminish the courage, inventiveness, and determination of gentile trail women who likewise confronted and surmounted the hardships of the westward journey. It is meant, however, to raise a question: if Mormon trail women faced such additional burdens as trauma, isolation, and poverty, where did they find the added resources to endure?

In part, many Mormon trail women were able to persist because their entire family or community headed toward Salt Lake. Rather than being splintered as a result of their faith, these fortunate women migrated with relatives, friends, and neighbors who believed as they did. From Nauvoo, for example, people routinely left in parties who traveled together and gave each other support.[59]

Mormon trail companies also found themselves bound in a sacred undertaking. For courage and endurance, Mormon women drew on their loyalty to the Church and its basic unit, the family. Women derived further strength from their religious beliefs, their conviction that a promised land lay ahead, and their faith in the Second Coming of Christ.[60]

At the same time, Mormon travelers in general bred a sense of unity. As virtual outcasts, Mormon travelers developed a group identity. They generated vigor from the conviction that they participated in a special mission. In her poem "The Camp of Israel: A Song for the Pioneers," Eliza R. Snow especially demonstrated this spirit:

> We better live in tents and smoke
> Than wear the cursed gentile yoke—
> We better from our country fly
> Than by mobocracy to die.
> Chorus
> Tho' we fly from vile aggression
> We'll maintain our pure profession—
> Seek a peaceable possession
> *Far from Gentiles and oppression.*[61]

At the same time, as they faced various ordeals, Mormon women constructed an active sisterhood. From the beginning, Church doctrine encouraged women to develop their individual abilities, to exercise their personal wills, and to join together in a variety of endeavors. Church teachings also provided a strong work ethic. Thus, although Victorian precepts advised them against arduous labor, Mormon women realized its necessity and chose to work together, building strength in the face of adversity. Of the handcart companies, for example, Howard Christy has written, "Of particular note is the superb performance of the women."[62]

Mormon women joined together in other ways as well. An outstanding example was the Relief Society, which enacted Church teachings that "Charity Never Faileth." According to Mormon pioneer Nancy Naomi Alexander Tracy, the purpose of the first Relief Society, organized in Nauvoo in March 1842, was to assist "the poor and for every noble purpose that came within woman's sphere of action." Women's relief activities also gave women a measure of responsibility and authority, even within the formal Church structure.[63]

In dealing with the vagaries of plural marriage, many Mormon women also gained autonomy and vigor. In their diaries and journals, Mormon women often portrayed husbands as shadowy figures, sometimes not even giving their full names or other identifying features. Such spouses failed to appear as forces in daily family life and decision making. Frequently, however, Mormon women found such a husband's absences freeing. According to Mary Isabella Horne, plural marriage offered her an opportunity "to work out her individual character as separate from her husband."[64]

Women also argue that plural marriage created a work partnership of several women, including plural wives and their daughters. According to one daughter of a plural marriage, "Everyone worked united together and so were able to accomplish much."[65] Certainly, such organization of chores went far beyond the customary cooperative style practiced by most nineteenth-century women and must have proved a boon on the trail.

Mormon migrants also obtained aid from the Church, which provided strong leaders as well as financial help and supplies. Following the tradition established by Joseph Smith, who sold land and found other ways to help fund migrations of Latter-day Saints to Nauvoo, Church leaders in Utah instituted the Perpetual Emigrating Fund. This program allowed Utah settlers to donate money and supplies to aid other Mormons coming to Salt Lake. Emigrants later repaid their debts by working on Church projects or donating produce or cash. By 1870, the Perpetual Emigrating Fund had assisted more than thirteen thousand Saints from Scandinavia and Europe and more than thirty-eight thousand from Britain.[66]

In addition, through the auspices of the Church, women, acting as informal groups and later as ward Relief Society units, collected food, made clothing, and provided other supplies to assist needy migrants. On numerous occasions, men filled wagons with goods and headed toward the travelers, although sometimes the mounds of supplies proved more than the men and wagons could transport. Women cheerfully opened their homes to immigrants after they arrived in the Salt Lake Valley, providing medical care and provisions when needed.[67]

Mormon travelers also received assistance from outsiders. Because not every Gentile spurned every Mormon, women noted instances of help from gentile travelers. During an 1853 migration, for example, Mormon Hannah King recorded that in crossing a treacherous stream "The Californians came to our assistance, & we got the horses landed without a buckle being broken!"[68]

As a result of these factors, Mormon women did not face trail adversities without help. They could, and did, utilize every additional resource available to them, sometimes even turning liabilities into assets.

Conclusion

What, then, carried more weight, similarities or differences? Which had the most impact along the overland trails during the 1840s and 1850s? This brief survey indicates that in the case of Mormon and gentile women, similarities proved incapable of overcoming differences. Women's trail journals increasingly noted that Mormon and gentile trains simply passed by or avoided overtaking each other.[69] Further, Mormon women confronted factors ranging from mob brutality to plural marriage that never touched their gentile counterparts.

Consequently, although Mormon and gentile women often shared such personal characteristics as ethnicity, race, class, and an abiding belief in God, they found little common ground. Instead, they typically experienced the westward trail in parallel yet disparate ways.

Notes

1. Mormon women's diaries as a genre are discussed in Maureen Ursenbach Beecher, "'Tryed and Purified as Gold': Mormon Women's 'Lives,'" *BYU Studies* 34(4) (1994–95): 16–34. See also Judy Nolte Lensink, "Expanding the Boundaries of Criticism: The Diary as Female Autobiography," *Women's Studies* 14 (1998): 39–53.

2. *Iowa News* (Dubuque), 5 August 1837, and *Eddyville Free Press* (Iowa), 16 April 1855.

3. Quoted in "Elizabeth Roxcy Snow," in *Women's Voices: An Untold History of the Latter-day Saints, 1830–1900*, ed. Kenneth W. Godfrey, Audrey M. Godfrey, and Jill Mulvay Derr (Salt Lake City: Deseret Book, 1982), 163. See also Maureen Ursenbach Beecher, "The Eliza Enigma: The Life and Legend of Eliza R. Snow," in *Essays on the American West*, ed. Thomas G. Alexander (Provo, Utah: Brigham Young University Press, 1976), 29–46.

4. Hannah Tapfield King, "My Journal," in *Covered Wagon Women: Diaries & Letters from the Western Trails, 1840–1890*, ed. Kenneth L. Holmes, 11 vols. (Glendale, Calif.: Arthur H. Clark, 1986), 6:198.

5. Mary Ann Hafen, *Recollections of a Handcart Pioneer of 1860: A Woman's Life on the Mormon Frontier* (Lincoln: University of Nebraska Press, 1983), 24.

6. Catherine Margaret Haun, "Woman's Trip across the Plains," 25 April to 4 November 1849, Huntington Library, San Marino, California; and Lavinia Honeyman Porter, *By Ox Team to California: A Narrative of Crossing the Plains in 1860* (Oakland, Calif.: Oakland Enquirer Publishing, 1910), 7.

7. Jenny Proctor, interviewed in *The American Slave*, ed. George P. Rawick, 17 vols. (Westport, Conn.: Greenwood, 1972), 7:209.

8. Carl V. Larson and Shirley N. Mayne, eds., *Women of the Mormon Battalion* (Providence, Utah: Watkins Printing, 1995); Norma B. Ricketts, *Melissa's Journey with the Mormon Battalion: The Western Odyssey of Melissa Burton Coray, 1846–1848* (Salt Lake City: Utah Printing, 1994); Leonard J. Arrington and Susan Arrington Madsen, "Drusilla Dorris Hendricks: 'Mother's Little Christian,'" in their *Sunbonnet Sisters: True Stories of Mormon Women and Frontier Life* (Salt Lake City: Bookcraft, 1984); and [no author], Mr. and Mrs. James Casto, n.d., WPA Manuscripts Collection, Wyoming State Archives and Historical Department, Cheyenne.

9. "Francis Sawyer," in *Covered Wagon Women*, 4:88–89. Also helpful is N. Jill Howard and Glenda Riley, "Thus You See I Have Not Much Rest," *Idaho Yesterdays* 37 (Fall 1993): 27–25.

10. "Patience Loader," in *Women's Voices*, 225.

11. King, "My Journal," in *Covered Wagon Women*, 6:200–201; Celinda E. Hines, "Diary of Celinda E. Hines," *Transactions of the Forty-Sixth Annual Reunion of the Oregon Pioneer Association* (1918): 100; and Sarah J. Cummins, Autobiography and Reminiscences, 1815, Oregon Historical Society, Portland.

12. "Patty Bartlett Sessions," in *Women's Voices*, 184–97; Elizabeth Willis, "Voice in the Wilderness: The Diaries of Patty Sessions," *Journal of American Folklore* 101 (January–March 1988): 37–47; Clarissa E. Taylor, "Clarissa E. Taylor, July 6, 1853, Letter from Fort Laramie in 'Oregon Bound,'" *Oregon Historical Quarterly* (1922): 136; Amelia Stewart Knight, "Diary of Mrs. Amelia Stewart Knight" (1853) in *Transactions of the Fifty-Sixth Annual Reunion of the Oregon Pioneer Association* (1928): 40. Charlotte Stearns Pengra, Diary of Mrs. Byron J. Pengra, 1853, Lane County Historical Society, Portland, Oregon.

13. Glenda Riley, "The Frontier in Process: Iowa's Trail Women as a Paradigm," *Annals of Iowa* 46(3) (Winter 1982): 167–97; reprinted in *Iowa History Reader*, ed. Marvin Bergman (Ames: State Historical Society of Iowa in Association with Iowa State University Press, 1996), 37–60.

14. "Patience Loader," in *Women's Voices*, 237–38. See also Levi Edgar Young, "Pioneer-Day Musicians," in Beatrice B. Malouf, *Chronicles of Courage*, 8 vols. (Salt Lake City: Daughters of Utah Pioneers, 1993), 4:282–84.

15. Tamsen Donner, "Letter II," in *Covered Wagon Women*, 1:71; and Elizabeth Keegan, "Letters," ibid., 4:23–24.

16. King, "My Journal," in *Covered Wagon Women*, 6:208.

17. Rachel Emma Woolley Simmons, "Journal of Rachel Emma Woolley Simmons," in *Heart Throbs of the West*, 12 vols. (Salt Lake City: Daughters of Utah Pioneers, 1950), 11:159–63; Adrietta Adamson Hixon, *On to Oregon: A True Story of a Young Girl's Journey in the West* (Weiser, Idaho: Signal Printers, 1947), 2; and Knight, "Diary," 39.

18. "Elizabeth Roxcy Snow," in *Women's Voices*, 162.

19. "Rachel Emma Woolley Simmons: Twelve-year-old Teamster Who Crossed the Plains," in Arrington and Madsen, *Sunbonnet Sisters*, 43; and Arvazona Cooper, "Our Journey," 1863, Oregon Historical Society, Portland.

20. King, "My Journal," in *Covered Wagon Women*, 6:194–95; "Patience Loader," in *Women's Voices*, 233–34; and Mary Goble Pay, quoted in *A Believing People: Literature of the Latter-day Saints*, ed. Richard H. Cracroft and Neal E. Lambert (Provo, Utah: Brigham Young University Press, 1974), 145.

21. Lucy Rutledge Cooke, *Covered Wagon Days: Crossing the Plains in 1852* (Modesto, Calif.: Privately published, 1923); and Eliza Ann McAuley Egbert, Diary, 1852, California Historical Society, San Francisco.

22. Rebecca Bartholomew, *Audacious Women: Early British Mormon Immigrants* (Salt Lake City: Signature Books, 1995), 182–83.

23. Lucia Williams, "Diary," in *Covered Wagon Women*, 3:142–43. See also Sarah J. Cummins, Autobiography and Reminiscences; Catherine A. Washburn, "Journal, 1853, from Iowa to Oregon Territory," Huntington Library, San Marino, California; and Glenda Riley, *Women and Indians on the Frontier, 1825–1915* (Albuquerque: University of New Mexico Press, 1984), 165–72.

24. Mrs. H. T. Clarke, "A Young Woman's Sights on the Emigrant's Trail," 1878, Bancroft Library, Berkeley, California; and Cooper, "Our Journey across the Plains."

25. Williams, "Diary," in *Covered Wagon Women*, 3:132; and Cooper, "Our Journey across the Plains."

26. Arrington and Madsen, *Sunbonnet Sisters*, 21–22, 33–34, 54–55.

27. Reed C. Durham Jr., "Westward Migration, Planning and Prophecy," *Encyclopedia of Mormonism*, ed. Daniel H. Ludlow, 4 vols. (New York: Macmillan, 1991), 4:1563–64.

28. "Sarah Studevant Leavitt," in *Autobiographies of Mormon Pioneer Women*, Vol. 1, *Sarah Studevant Leavitt, Mary Brown Pulsipher, Mary Adeline Beman Noble, Martha Pane Jones Thomas, Eliza Dana Gibbs*, comp. Ogden Kraut (Salt Lake City: Pioneer Press, 1994), 1:15–38.

29. "Martha P. Jones Thomas," 81, 84, and "Eliza Dana Gibbs," in *Autobiographies of Mormon Pioneer Women*, vol. 1; "Emily Partridge Smith Young," in *Autobiographies of Mormon Pioneer Women*, Vol. 2, *Nancy Alexander Tracy, Eliza Partridge Smith Lyman, Emily Partridge Smith Young, Mary A. Phelps Rich*, comp. Ogden Kraut (Salt Lake City: Pioneer Press, 1994), 2:80; Nancy N. Alexander Tracy, Narrative, 1880, Bancroft Library; and Mrs. Martha Brown, Letter to Mr. H. H. Bancroft, 7 August 1880, Bancroft Library.

30. Richard Neitzel Holzapfel and Jeni Broberg Holzapfel, *Women of Nauvoo* (Salt Lake City: Bookcraft, 1992), 86–103; "Eliza Partridge Smith Lyman," in *Autobiographies of Mormon Pioneer Women*, 2:57; and "Martha P. Jones Thomas," in ibid., 1:93.

31. Holzapfel and Holzapfel, *Women of Nauvoo*, 97; "Sarah Studevant Leavitt," in *Autobiographies of Mormon Pioneer Women*, 1:31–32; "Mary A. Phelps Rich," in ibid., 2:119. See also M. Guy Bishop, "Eternal Marriage in Early Mormon Marital Beliefs," *The Historian* 53 (Autumn 1990): 76–88; George D. Smith, "Mormon Plural Marriage," *Free Inquiry* 12 (Summer 1992): 32–37, 60; and Danel W. Bachman and Ronald K. Esplin, "Plural Marriage," *Encyclopedia of Mormonism*, 3:1091–95.

32. Mrs. F. D. (Jane) Richards, Reminiscences, 1880, Bancroft Library.

33. See, for example, Phebe W. Woodruff, Autobiographic [*sic*] Sketch, 1880; Mrs. Mary J. Tanner, Letters to Mrs. H. H. Bancroft, 29 October 1880; and Mrs. F. D. (Jane) Richards, Reminiscences, 1880, all at the Bancroft Library.

34. Quoted in Holzapfel and Holzapfel, *Women of Nauvoo*, 103.

35. "Mary A. Phelps Rich," in *Autobiographies of Mormon Pioneer Women*, 2:117.

36. Described in Mrs. Clara Decker Young, "A Woman's Experiences with the Pioneer Band," 1884, Bancroft Library.

37. Durham, "Westward Migration, Planning and Prophecy," 4:1563.

38. Maurine Carr Ward, ed., *Winter Quarters: The 1846–1848 Life Writings of Mary Haskin Parker Richards* (Logan: Utah State Press, 1996), 30–31; King, "My Journal," in *Covered Wagon Women*, 6:190–222; and Mrs. Sarah A. Cooke, "Theatrical and Social Affairs in Utah," 1884, Bancroft Library.

39. *New York Times*, 26 May 1859. For discussions of anti-Mormon images, see Karen Lynn, "Sensational Virtue: Nineteenth-Century Mormon Fiction and American Popular

Taste," *Dialogue: A Journal of Mormon Thought* 14 (Autumn 1981): 101–12; and Gary L. Bunker and Davis Bitton, *The Mormon Graphic Images, 1834–1914: Cartoons, Caricatures, and Illustrations* (Salt Lake City: University of Utah Press, 1983). A typical attack was Mrs. T. B. H. Stenhouse, *A Lady's Life among the Mormons: A Record of Personal Experience as One of the Wives of a Mormon Elder* (New York: J. C. Derby, 1855).

40. Pauline Wonderly, *Reminiscences of a Pioneer* (Placerville, Calif.: El Dorado County Historical Society, 1965), 7; and Helen Carpenter, Diary, 1856, California State Library, Sacramento.

41. Tracy, "Narrative"; and Helena Erickson Rosbery, "History of Helena Rosbery," 1883, Huntington Library.

42. Elisha Brooks, *A Pioneer Mother of California* (San Francisco: Harr Wagner Publishing, 1922), 29; Ruth Peterson, "Across the Plains in '57," compiled by Nancy Campbell Lowell, 1931, California State Library; Emily McCowen Horton, *My Scrapbook* (Seattle: n.p., 1927), 27; and Carpenter, Diary.

43. Wonderly, *Reminiscences of a Pioneer*, 7; and Margaret H. Hecox, *California Caravan: The 1846 Overland Travel Memoir of Margaret M. Hecox* (San Jose, Calif.: Harlan-Young Press, 1966), 21–24.

44. Bartholomew, *Audacious Women*, 188; Bachman and Esplin, "Plural Marriage," 1094–95; and David J. Whittaker, "The Bone in the Throat: Orson Pratt and the Public Announcement of Plural Marriage," *Western Historical Quarterly* 18 (July 1987): 293–314.

45. Eliza Roxcy Snow, "Sketch of My Life," 1885, Bancroft Library.

46. Jane Snyder Richards, "Reminiscences," 1880, and Margaret S. Smoot, "Experience of a Mormon Wife," 1880, both at the Bancroft Library.

47. John Gunnison, Letter to "My Dear Martha," 1 March 1850, Huntington Library. For a fuller discussion of the reaction to Mormon polygamy, see Carol Weisbrod and Pamela Sheingorn, "*Reynolds v. United States:* Nineteenth-Century Forms of Marriage and the Status of Women," *Connecticut Law Review* 10 (Summer 1978): 828–58; Charles A. Cannon, "The Awesome Power of Sex: The Polemical Campaign against Mormon Polygamy," in *Procreation or Pleasure? Sexual Attitudes in American History*, ed. Thomas L. Altherr (Malabar, Fla.: Robert E. Krieger, 1983), 99–113. An attack on polygamy's effect on women is Jennie Anderson Froiseth, ed., *The Women of Mormonism; or, The Story of Polygamy as Told by the Victims Themselves* (Detroit: C. G. G. Paine, 1882). More recent scholarly accounts of Mormon women's views of polygamy are Julie Dunfey, "'Living the Principle' of Plural Marriage: Mormon Women, Utopia, and Female Sexuality in the Nineteenth Century," *Feminist Studies* 10 (Fall 1984): 523–36; Joan Smith Iversen, "Feminist Implications of Mormon Polygyny," *Feminist Studies* 10 (Fall 1984): 505–22; Kahlile Mehr, "Women's Response to Plural Marriage," *Dialogue: A Journal of Mormon Thought* 18 (Fall 1985): 84–97; and Jessie L. Embry and Martha Sonntag Bradley, "Mothers and Daughters in Polygamy," *Dialogue: A Journal of Mormon Thought* 18 (Fall 1985): 98–107.

48. Ward G. DeWitt and Florence Stark DeWitt, *Prairie Schooner Lady: The Journal of Harriet Sherrill Ward, 1853* (Los Angeles: Westernlore, 1959), 120; and Mary C. Fish, "Across the Plaines in 1860," Bancroft Library.

49. Eugene E. Campbell and Bruce L. Campbell, "Divorce among Mormon Polygamists: Extent and Explanations," *Utah Historical Quarterly* 46 (Winter 1978): 4–23; and Kristen L. Goodman, "Divorce," *Encyclopedia of Mormonism*, 1:391–93. See also Kimball Young, *Isn't One Wife Enough?* (New York: Henry Holt, 1954).

50. Quoted in Lawrence Foster, "Polygamy and the Frontier: Mormon Women in Early Utah," *Utah Historical Quarterly* 50 (Summer 1982): 285.

51. *Laws of the Territory of Utah* (Salt Lake City: n.p., 1852), 82–84.

52. Probate Court Records Book, 12 February 1856, Washington County, Utah, Huntington Library.

53. Ellen Tompkins Adams, "Diary of Ellen Tompkins Adams, Wife of John Smalley Adams, M.D.," 1863, Bancroft Library; and Haun, "A Woman's Trip."

54. Carpenter, Diary. For similar remarks see Ada Millington, "Journal Kept While Crossing the Plains," 1862, Bancroft Library; Horton, *My Scrapbook*, 27; and Agnes Stewart Warner, Diary, 1853, 1, Huntington Library. For a discussion of several disillusioned women who left Salt Lake, see Bartholomew, *Audacious Women*, 188–96.

55. Fish, "Across the Plains."

56. Mary Stuart Bailey, "Journal, Ohio to California," 1852, Huntington Library. For persecution of Canadian immigrants, see Martha Wilcox, "Autobiography of Martha Anna Wilcox Westwood Foy," copy in my possession. For British immigrants, see Bartholomew, *Audacious Women*. For foreign-born women in general, see Arrington and Madsen, *Sunbonnet Sisters*.

57. "Martha Pane Jones Thomas, in Kraut, *Autobiographies*, 1:73; and Tracy, "Narrative." See also Carol Lynn Pearson, "'Nine Children Were Born': A Historical Problem from the Sugar Creek Episode," *BYU Studies* 21 (Fall 1981): 441–44.

58. "Patience Loader," in *Women's Voices*, 225, 229, 232.

59. See, for example, Carol Cornwall Madsen, *In Their Own Words: Women and the Story of Nauvoo* (Salt Lake City: Deseret Book, 1994).

60. Kraut, *Autobiographies*, 24; and Reed H. Bradford, "Family, Teachings about the Family," *Encyclopedia of Mormonism*, 2:486–88.

61. Quoted in "Snow," in *Women's Voices*, 152–53. See also Patricia Nelson Limerick, "Peace Initiative: Using the Mormons to Rethink Culture and Ethnicity in American History," *Journal of Mormon History* 21 (Fall 1995): 1–29.

62. Howard A. Christy, "Handcart Companies," *Encyclopedia of Mormonism*, 2:573; see also Holzapfel and Holzapfel, *Women of Nauvoo*, 170–71.

63. Tracy, Narrative; and Janath Russell Cannon and Jill Mulvay Derr, "Relief Society," *Encyclopedia of Mormonism*, 3:1199–1206. For bonding activities of early Mormon women, see Maureen Ursenbach Beecher, "Women's Work on the Mormon Frontier," *Utah Historical Quarterly* 49 (Summer 1981): 276–90; Anne Firor Scott, "Mormon Women, Other Women: Paradoxes and Challenges," *Journal of Mormon History* 13 (1986–87): 3–19; and Karen W. Peterson, "Cottage Industries of LDS Women during the Early Period of the Church, 1836–1890" (MS thesis, Utah State University, 1988). Also useful are Marilyn Warenski, *Patriarchs and Politics: The Plight of the Mormon Woman* (New York: McGraw-Hill, 1978); and Donald G. Godfrey, "Zina Young Williams Card: 'No Ordinary Frontier Woman,'" Paper presented at the Mormon History Association annual meeting, Park City, Utah, 1994, photocopy in my possession, a revised version of which appeared under the title of "Zina Presendia Young Williams Card: Brigham's Daughter, Cardston's First Lady," *Journal of Mormon History* 23(2) (Fall 1997): 107–27.

64. Beecher, "'Tryed and Purified as Gold,'" 22; and Mrs. Joseph (Mary Isabella) Horne, "Migration and Settlement of the Latter Day Saints," 1884, Bancroft Library. For an analysis of the effect of husbands' frequent absences, see Carol Cornwall Madsen, "'Feme Covert': Journey of a Metaphor," *Journal of Mormon History* 17 (1991): 43–61. See

also Martha Nibley Beck, "Women, Roles of: Historical and Sociological Development," *Encyclopedia of Mormonism*, 4:1574–75.

65. Mary Elizabeth Cox Lee, "An Inspired Principle and a Remarkable Lady," Huntington Library. Also useful are Embry and Bradley, "Mothers and Daughters in Polygamy"; and Kathryn M. Daynes, "Plural Wives and the Nineteenth-Century Mormon Marriage System: Manti, Utah, 1849–1910" (PhD diss., Indiana University, Bloomington, 1991).

66. Smith's generosity is described in Tracy, "Narrative." For the PEF, see Arrington and Madsen, *Sunbonnet Sisters*, 70–71.

67. "Patience Loader," 240, and "Lucy Meserve Smith," in *Women's Voices*, 268.

68. King, "My Journal," in *Covered Wagon Women*, 6:204.

69. Maria J. Norton, "Diary of a Trip across the Plains in '59," Bancroft Library; Mary Jane Guill, "Overland Diary," 1860, California State Library; and Adams, "Diary." Carol Cornwall Madsen, "Decade of Detente: The Mormon-Gentile Female Relationship in Nineteenth-Century Utah," *Utah Historical Quarterly* 63 (Fall 1995): 298–319, suggests that rapprochement did not occur until the 1890s.

CHAPTER 10

Mormon "Deliverance" and the Closing of the Frontier

Martin Ridge

I feel highly honored to be invited to present the Tanner Lecture this year. When the Tanner Lectureship was established, I was genuinely impressed. The basic idea of this lectureship—to bring annually to the Mormon History Association an outsider—seemed to me both a mark of maturity and sophistication. No other learned society that I know of has the courage to do this. But when I began to think about what I would say today, I must confess that I came to feel this was essentially a shrewd Mormon plot to take a good, self-respecting Gentile academic and make him reread his old notes, look at new sources, and think far more deeply about Mormonism than he had in the past.

I also want to say a few things that do not fit into my formal presentation, although they may be annoying or perhaps even offensive to some of you. First, I remain completely astonished at how few historical landmarks exist in Utah that relate to some of the most significant and intimate aspects of Mormon history. For example, I could not find the site of the prison camp for cohabs in Salt Lake City without the help of a local historian, and he assured me that there were a score of other significant sites that remain equally hidden. What a pity! What a shame! Should not this organization make a case to the city of Salt Lake or to the state of Utah to act in this matter?

Second, in the clash of competing cultures that took place between Mormon and Gentile societies, the fact that Mormonism, as it existed prior to 1890, lost out is no sign of dishonor. That cultural conflict itself is an important part of the history of our evolving plural society. The sites and events of that struggle warrant as much recognition as Southern states give to the Confederate memorials of the Civil War.

Third, the record of what occurred during the first half century of Mormonism is not exclusively an LDS story; it belongs to our national history. In fact, from the point of view of civil liberties, it is one of our nation's darkest hours. If

Jews throughout the world can point to the Holocaust and say, "Never again," surely American students of Mormonism should, if history has any meaning, be the strongest advocates of the First and Fifth Amendments to the Constitution.

Fourth, half a decade ago, on commenting in recent books dealing with the Mormon experience, I wrote:

> Mormon historiography may not be a "dark and bloody ground" for most American historians but it is virtually terra incognita for many of them. . . . Non-Mormons who have been willing to approach the field objectively have rarely had access to sources. At the same time, a past generation of Mormon historians were either entirely defensive or even more questioning of the Church than some outsiders. Contemporary non-Mormon historians who have wanted to understand how the Mormons fit into both the American experience and a subset of American historiography, whether it be the American West or the history of religion in America, have come to rely on the new generation of Mormon scholars who demonstrate unusual sensitivity, tact, and honesty in dealing with their own past.[1]

As a non-Mormon who teaches the history of the Latter-day Saints, I have trusted to the validity of their work, even as they contend with one another about both the facts and the proper interpretations of Mormonism.

I must, however, take exception with Melvin T. Smith's view that non-Mormon scholars "rarely, if ever, reveal and explicate those special and immediate qualities that made believing Mormons and Latter-day Saints what they were and what they still are today."[2] To agree with Smith would be to create a privileged history—something that I must emphatically reject. I do not believe that the history of any race, class, gender, or religion is privileged. I must also reject Mario S. De Pillis's assertion that "All non-Mormon historians are anti-Mormons in so far as they reject that truth."[3] There are many historical and anthropological methodologies that can resolve the problem of dealing with acts of faith in religions other than that of the scholar.

Now, let me turn to my essay.

In Hubert Howe Bancroft's *The Book of the Fair*, published in 1893 to commemorate the Chicago World's Columbian Exposition, he points out that the Territory of Utah was represented by a fine pavilion with white pillars. It also boasted an Eagle Gate, a replica of that in Salt Lake City, and a statue of Brigham Young. Bancroft notes that the funds for the Utah exhibition came from Mormon sources, stating that they did not come from the territorial government.[4] Although he does not mention it, the Mormon Tabernacle Choir also performed splendidly at the fair.

The Chicago Fair was also the site of the World's Congress of Historians and Historical Students, a rather immodest title for a small meeting of professional and amateur historians who presented scholarly papers, most of which are fortunately now forgotten. I do not know if any Saints attended these historical meetings, but if they did, they were probably shocked at a paper given by a young historian from the University of Wisconsin named Frederick Jackson Turner.[5] The primary thrust and theme of his essay—that American democracy was born on the frontier—would have brought a taste of gall and wormwood to the palate of any Mormon during the 1890s.

Moreover, if any older Saints were in the audience that evening, Turner must have caught their attention when he paraded a litany of circumstances and behavioral characteristics of the Americans as a frontier people. On Turner's frontier, men and women were few, and arable land was abundant; pragmatism was the dominant philosophy of life; innovation and experimentation were common practices; attachment to place was unimportant if not insignificant; wasting natural resources was an acceptable credo; culture and tradition were abandoned in the process of making a living; materialism was the prevailing creed; hard work was a persistent habit; and skill rather than anything else was the critical factor in defining an individual's status. The frontier, too, was a powerful force for assimilation. Turner's Mormon audience would surely have seen how thoroughly the Saints were Turner's true American frontier people and yet how different was their overall experience.

Turner's paper, "The Life of an Idea: The Significance of the Frontier in American History," is a landmark in American scholarship,[6] but it should have a special relationship to Mormon history, because Turner predicated his essay on what he saw as a major disjunction in the history of the United States. He quoted from the superintendent of the census for 1890 who observed in a bulletin "that there can hardly be said to be a frontier line." "This brief official statement," Turner added, "marks the closing of a great historic movement."[7]

The closing date of the frontier has a unique meaning to Latter-day Saints, because by 1890 eastern America had steadily closed in around them and compelled such drastic changes in Mormon thought and action that the Church would never be the same again. Without a new frontier to which to retreat, Mormons had no place to move. They found themselves defenseless. The only deliverance seemed to be statehood, in the hope that it would give them enough self-government to protect their institutions.

There is a strange irony in this because the Saints, who lived an indigenous American religion, had previously escaped persecution by living outside the mainstream of American life. Protestant America had dictated that they do this, but by 1890, isolation was neither possible nor acceptable; the government now demanded a virtual revolution in Mormonism before it could be incorporated within the nation state. How did this come to pass?

As a Mormon missionary would say, "It all began in the year 1820, when a young man named Joseph Smith, Jr., went into a wooded grove to pray."[8] What followed during the next quarter century is a story of the founding, growth, and persecution of the Church and its members. The Saints found little support in New York, where the Smith family lived, but after they started their celebrated move westward into Ohio, the Church grew rapidly. Neither upstate New York nor Ohio may have been frontier regions, depending on your definition of a frontier, but they were certainly primitive, underdeveloped rural areas marked by social disorientation, where the rapidly changing social status of many fortunate individuals created a fluid society.[9] Traditional religious and social organizations suffered in this environment, as they did everywhere on the frontier. This was a fertile field for seers, evangelical revivalists, mystical gold hunters, visionary seekers, and founders of religions, new sects, and new communities. As Gordon Wood has observed, "The remains of older eighteenth-century hierarchies fell away, and hundreds of thousands of common people were cut loose from all sorts of traditional bonds."[10] Many people sought something that would bring meaning and order to their lives. This was a setting well suited to the Mormon style as well as the Mormon message. Discipline, emotion, reason, self-interest, and a unique egalitarianism were some of the weapons in the arsenal of conversion.[11] Mormonism successfully gathered followers not only in the agrarian West and South but also among the disenchanted of the urban East.

From the inception of Mormonism, Joseph Smith propounded the idea of "continuous revelation," an element that proved essential to the Church's vitality and success because its doctrines could be dynamic.[12] Therefore, during the years of migration from upstate New York to Kirtland, Ohio, to Far West, Missouri, and back to Nauvoo, Illinois, the Church gradually came to embrace a body of essential doctrines that ultimately defined its identity: stewardship, polygamy, millennialism, and the "gathering." It also accepted the idea of a unique political entity—the Kingdom of God—which, although quasi independent, was empowered to exercise control over the temporal Mormon world.

Whether the concept of plural marriage had its origin in Ohio is not so important as what it meant to the Church. No doctrine was more controversial, even to our day, unless it is the Book of Mormon itself.[13] The fact that plural marriage was only one aspect of Joseph Smith's concern for the family, for extended kinship ties, and for social solidarity—after all, he wanted to establish a tribe in the Old Testament sense—was not lost on both his contemporaries and later generations.[14] Plural marriage created a deep moral chasm between Mormons and non-Mormons that could not be bridged and that led to repeated episodes of persecution.

The idea of the Kingdom of God, a theocratic structure intimately tied to millennialism, was not a heavy hand within the Mormon community, but it was significant to Mormon thought and subject to easy misunderstanding in the Gentile world.[15] Joseph Smith sought to establish a cohesive new order in which the Mormon spiritual and temporal worlds were united. If it had a democratic dimension, it could only be described as a "guided democracy." Thus, although

Mormonism seemed in many ways quintessentially American, it stood "in radical opposition to the prevailing American religious and social pluralism."[16] It rejected the American ideal of the separation of church and state.

Moreover, it stood in opposition to the emerging spirit of manifest destiny that dominated mid-nineteenth-century America. Mormons never recognized the gentile concept of a great political democracy extending from pole to pole in the Western Hemisphere. Theirs was a different Zion. The Saints never expected more than a small fraction of Gentiles to heed their millennial call. "The gathering" would be for those who could accept and live in the truth. Almost by definition, then, Mormons perceived all non-Mormons as anti-Mormon. As the United States struggled toward a variety of pluralism, the Mormon community increasingly moved in the opposite direction toward homogeneity. It was a countercultural force.[17] Those who were not with them were against them, and those who were against them constituted Babylon, even if they spoke for an enlarged and tolerant American republic.

In Mormonism the ordinary American saw custom, kinship, and law replaced in their entirety. Americans not only saw the Saints as cult followers with a different view of the future, they also recognized the Saints as a people with a new revelation, scripture, and priesthood who rejected orthodox capitalism and federal authority. Little wonder then that even without Mormon economic success or increased political influence, the Church drew the wrath of the Protestant evangelical community, which viewed the Church as a serious threat.[18] Unable at the outset to manipulate effectively the tools of government to attack Mormonism, this community resorted to mob violence. This came as no surprise to the Saints, who believed that the greater their effectiveness, the harder Satan would fight against them. In this context, the martyrdom of the Prophet and other leaders seems to have been inevitable.

The Mormon trek from Nauvoo to the Salt Lake Valley came to symbolize both a religious and a temporal triumph in Mormon history and mythology. This flight to the Great Basin frontier proved a trial of faith. It may not have proven so arduous as has been sometimes stated, but for the participants, it was as much deliverance under God's hand as was depicted in the book of Exodus. It also led to the development of a spirit of identity and territoriality that differentiates Mormons from other religious groups.[19] It reinforced the significance of the West as the place of "the gathering." Moreover, it was a continuing and revitalizing process, as each year another group of Saints entered Zion, having shared with their brethren and sisters the cross-plains journey. Richard Jensen captured the spirit of joy associated with the overland trail's end and the integrating of the old and the new settlers when he wrote, "The wagons coming out to meet the immigrants with fruit and baked goods, and the throngs that met them as they arrived in Salt Lake City . . . [were] a welcome part of the process of assimilation."[20] They had arrived at the "place prepared."[21]

There is little reason to doubt Mormon assertions that for more than a decade prior to their departure from Nauvoo, the LDS leadership already held a deep religious conviction that the Saints were destined to find a refuge and sanctuary outside of the United States in the Rocky Mountains.[22] Since Brigham Young, like Moses, believed that God would guide him in his quest for the prepared place, his decisions were based as much on spiritual as practical detailed information. Even after reaching the Salt Lake Valley, despite what cynics might argue, Young waited for a divine confirmation that this was indeed the place.

The Mormons had leapfrogged the frontier line in 1847, and they were for the first time free from the restraints of gentile society. They had entered Zion and were now virtually responsible for their own actions. Therefore, Brigham Young and the Mormon host had no pangs of conscience in taking Indian land, because the Church believed that it was "both God's will and a positive virtue" to do so.[23] The leadership, under Brigham Young, instituted a theo-democratic legal system of ecclesiastical courts and a scheme of government that combined the temporal and the spiritual to create an orderly community where polygamy, the Kingdom of God, the communal goal, and "the gathering" could be emphasized.

The Mormons struggled to implement communal goals that had been established in Nauvoo. For example, they based their use of the region's natural resources on stewardship and mutual benefit instead of on individual gain; they planned their economy around cooperation and sought to achieve self-sufficiency.[24] They confronted an entirely new physical environment, however, in which Mormonism could not survive without adaptation and innovation. Indicative of innovation and the commingling of spiritual and temporal power, the Mormons laid out their irrigation system by linking it to religious directives. In any less cohesive community, this would have diluted the sacred, but in early-impoverished Utah, where no one knew how to farm successfully in the desert, spiritual control of temporal power made sound economic sense.[25]

There were other changes. The Latter-day Saints' strongly patriarchal system was restructured under frontier conditions. The pressing need for labor in an underdeveloped economy overcame quickly Mormonism's fundamental belief that women were primarily the guardians of the home and the family. This meant more than merely sharing the family farm workload. Despite the fact that the priesthood remained entirely in male hands, women were ultimately encouraged to enter professions and even assume large responsibilities of leadership within the female sphere. They were also among the first women to be enfranchised in the United States.

Even LDS doctrine regarding redeeming the Indians had to yield in the face of frontier reality. The Indians refused to be what Mormon theology said they were. Despite their brightest hopes, Mormon missionaries found Indians living in conditions loathsome yet difficult to change. When efforts to convert them resulted in open and protracted resistance, Brigham Young conceded that it was almost pointless to send missionaries among them, because that generation of Indians would never be converted. He remained optimistic, but he found his policy of "food not fight" taxing.[26]

Jan Shipps, drawing an analogy between the Israelites and the Mormons on the Utah frontier, has posited that for a brief period in their history, Mormons had escaped secular time.[27] This may be correct in a spiritual sense, but in a physical sense, the gentile world intruded early and harshly into Zion. Gold-seeking adventurers on their way to California were soon followed by pioneers from the very Mississippi Valley states from which the Mormons had been driven. The U.S. Army was not far behind, nor were a string of journalists, curious about Mormonism's "peculiar institution."

There is no need to catalog all the hostility and recrimination that the encounters between Saints and Gentiles produced during this time. One incident is so graphic and so problematic as to suffice. Even stripped of questionable evidence and disputed interpretations, the Mountain Meadows massacre is a monstrous example of frontier violence and retribution. Levi Peterson, who feels that it represents a Mormon loss of innocence, and Maureen Beecher, who disagrees with him, may debate over this dark and bloody ground on how the Saints want to explain themselves to themselves and perhaps to others, but in terms of the frontier experience, no one has ever believed that the frontier was a peaceable kingdom.[28] The English, the French, and the Spanish all used Indians as allies when they waged war against each other. White men killed each other throughout the history of the frontier when cultures clashed. Only a naive romantic can deny that brutality was commonplace on the frontier.

The Utah War of 1857–58 should have served as a timely warning to the Mormons that the U.S. government had the power to reach deep into the frontier, especially after the Mexican War and the annexation of the Oregon country. It demonstrated that Utah's isolation was more a matter of convenience than reality. The United States government could at any time exercise full authority and impose its national institutions and customs. But as long as transportation and communication remained difficult and as long as other parts of the frontier offered greater opportunity, expediency prevailed and the Mormon kingdom was left basically to its own devices.

The Utah War demonstrated the internal cohesion and discipline of the Saints, but it also disclosed critical economic weaknesses. Although official Church policy called for almost total economic self-sufficiency, Brigham Young and other Church leaders realized that it was impossible. Thus, they sought, as far as possible, to limit Mormon commercial ties to the outside world to prevent endangering the essentially communal character of their economy and to prevent making it dependent on the outside world by tying it marginally to the emerging capitalist society of the East. They remained, however, under steadily increasing pressures during the decade of the 1860s. The U.S. Army post at Camp

Floyd provided a market for Mormon products, and the opening of the mining frontier in Colorado, Nevada, and Idaho gradually turned Salt Lake City into a frontier commercial and business entrepôt. Furthermore, individual enterprise, even if Mormon-controlled, was on the rise.

The arrival of the railroad at Ogden in 1869 was the final blow to Mormon frontier isolation. The railroad's operations meant the introduction of a society of non-Mormon working-class males, and it also resulted in the arrival of business leaders who advocated competitive capitalism, sought to gain access to the territory's economy, and intended to develop the region's resources. The railroad encouraged Methodists and Episcopalians to settle in Ogden and opened its depots for denominational services.[29] When Gentiles opened schools to attract Mormon children, they set the stage for a controversy over control of the public schools.[30] For those Saints who still hoped to preserve Utah, or at least Ogden and Salt Lake City, as Mormon bastions or parts of the Kingdom of God, the railroad locomotive engine's bell sounded a warning—perhaps even a death knell—to Mormon culture as it had existed. For along with the railroad came a slow but steady end to the self-sufficient, homogeneous, and relatively egalitarian Mormon economy. Shrewdly aware of the implications of the coming of the railroad, Church leaders sought to profit as much as possible from it, and they did their best to stave off its direst portents through collective action.

The completion of the railroad also revolutionized the emigration patterns of Mormon converts. As Mormons spread over the valleys of Utah in search of more arable land, Saints proselytized vigorously abroad. An all-steam company was organized in 1869 that brought converts from Liverpool to Ogden in twenty-four days, a far cry from the era of the three- to five-month trip. The story of the Mormon immigrant changed from that of the overland covered wagon to that of the modern voyager.[31]

Mormon converts differed from other immigrants in that during the process of conversion, they had turned their backs not only on their former churches but also on their past cultures. In Utah, the Church's process of integration meant the creation of a whole new English-speaking American way of life. A new Saint's mother tongue was rejected along with other vestiges of Babylon.[32] It was the avowed aim of the LDS Church to assimilate immigrants and resettle them as rapidly as possible.[33]

Persistently high migration rates to Utah led to the progressive undermining of the Mormon social structure. By the 1880s, the Church had virtually given up trying to establish cooperative communities. Utah was filling up. Young Mormon men were being forced to move elsewhere if they wanted to farm for a living. There was an increase in individual or sibling-based migrations, and after 1875 the emphasis in migration was on economic advantages rather than building the Mormon kingdom. Although the Church still attempted to supervise and assist new communities, its aid came after rather than prior to the establishment of a town.[34] By 1890 the growth of the Church came primarily from within existing areas of settlement as colonization, both domestic and foreign, slowed.[35]

Equally indicative of the change in the Mormon community was a shift in attitude when John Taylor succeeded Brigham Young to the presidency of the LDS Church in 1877. Young was a firm adherent of self-sufficient communitarianism as the best form of human association. Taylor favored individualism and looked to legal incorporation and personal liberty. Under Taylor, the Church did not turn to unrestrained laissez-faire, but it did encourage greater individual enterprise among the faithful.[36] The ease of this transition from staunch communitarianism to modified individualism suggests that the frontier had begun to break down romanticized communalism, at least in Mormon cities.

As Gentiles joined Mormons in Salt Lake City, as the shift from cooperation to individualism persisted, and as attacks on polygamy increased in the 1880s, two types of Mormon community emerged. Charles Peterson put it aptly: "As Salt Lake City Mormons resisted the federal government they entered into a variety of interactions with their 'foes,' adopting many of the enemy's ways as they, in effect, fought fire with fire. . . . Like it or not, the City of the Saints had become a 'city of two peoples,' its history more the story of an American conflict than an escape from society."[37] Traditional LDS ideals were preserved in the outlying Mormon villages, where the ward and the village were one unit and where temporal and ecclesiastical affairs were intermingled.[38]

Leonard Arrington is doubtless in some measure correct in asserting that by 1884 the Church's well-directed program of protecting the Mormon way against the changes wrought by the railroad achieved a good deal of success. A great deal of economic autonomy and spiritual integrity was preserved. The boycotting of Gentiles, severe financial retrenchment, social investment in domestic capital programs such as railroads, and Church cooperative efforts did, after all, produce results. "The joining of efforts through the United Orders, temple construction, and Zion's Central Board of Trade," Arrington wisely observes, "left the Mormons . . . nearer the realization of their ancient goals than when the ox-cart was outmoded in 1869."[39] Even more important, the Mormons had managed to retain the quasi-religious nature of large-scale private enterprise by keeping decision-making power in the hands of the Church's official family. The year 1884, however, may have been some kind of watershed, as Arrington notes.[40] By 1890 there had been significant change. Private enterprise was profit-seeking and not necessarily concerned with the religious community's goals.

Modern Mormons like to think that where they live is not so important as how they live, but this was scarcely true in the earliest days and is strictly the result of the closing of the frontier. Zion was a specific place more than a style of life.[41] Then the cry was, "Let all who can procure a loaf of bread, and one garment on their back, be assured there is water and pure by the way, and doubt no longer, but come next year to the place of the gathering, even in flocks, as doves fly to their windows before a storm."[42] Mass immigration, however, had made that impossible. In 1887 the Perpetual Emigrating Company was disincorporated. The elders were now told to explain that migration was an individual calling. Zion now meant the pure in heart and where the people and condition of the pure in heart live—a far cry from "redeem the faithful and bring them singing to Zion."[43] By the 1890s, the original Mormon meaning of "the gathering" was no longer being preached.

By 1890, also, the failure of the Council of Fifty—the temporal-religious arm of the community—to restrain the federal government's attack on the LDS Church and its members because of plural marriage led to the ultimate weakening of the idea of the Kingdom of God.[44] In 1890 the First Presidency of the Church could truthfully state that it did not claim that it controlled a temporal Kingdom of God, and it reaffirmed that the Church and civil governments were distinct and separate bodies. An inevitable corollary of the decline of the idea of the temporal Kingdom of God was a decline in millennial enthusiasm. It meant that the Saints were in transition from believers in the immediacy of divine deliverance to adherents of a creed not unlike those of other American religious groups.

The great struggle in the 1880s to defend polygamy was in a sense the Armageddon of frontier Mormonism. Only the salvation of the ideal of plural marriage offered hope for retaining the Mormons' special view of a temporal and spiritual Kingdom of God on earth. In the balance, too, probably hung that powerful millennial drive that had nurtured the Church from its inception. Hope of "the gathering" at a "place prepared" had already been virtually abandoned. The communal order was, in increasing measure, giving way to a more individualistic society, except perhaps in the Mormon villages where near-frontier conditions still prevailed. But even in villages, in many instances tithes were being paid in cash.

Plural marriage was the linchpin of what remained of the old order, except for the vestiges of the cooperative spirit and civic virtue. It was the most controversial aspect of the Church as well as the source of continuing persecution of all the Saints, even those who were monogamous. For both Mormons and non-Mormons, it came to identify what the Church was. The defense of plural marriage, therefore, was critical. The desperate hope that Saints could escape the power of the federal government, if the Utah Territory could become a state and retain polygamy, prompted the Church leadership to engage in political lobbying activities on an unprecedented scale. Although many Eastern politicians seemed receptive to the idea, neither the Republican nor Democratic Party when in power was willing to award the Saints statehood despite the Church's promises of future support.[45]

Instead, beginning in the early 1880s, the full might of the federal government was gradually unleashed against both the LDS Church and its members. The Edmunds Act and the Edmunds-Tucker Act plus the Supreme Court's decision in *Davis v. Beason* (which, appropriately enough, was decided in 1890) were disastrous assaults on the First Amendment as well as the Fifth. The results were catastrophic. The federal government was empowered to seize the assets and property of the Church. The Morrill Act of 1862 had already made polygamy illegal in the territories. Now, the Saints were disfranchised and forbidden to hold office or serve on juries, unless they took an oath to repudiate polygamy. Polygamous Saints fled into exile, suffered imprisonment, and accepted fugitive status rather than give up a sacred principle.

Never was the leadership more troubled or divided or in need of guidance. On 25 September 1890, President Wilford Woodruff issued a Manifesto that advised Latter-day Saints to refrain from contracting any marriage forbidden by the laws of the land. On 6 October 1890, the Manifesto was sustained by the Church's general conference. For the many Saints who refused to yield on the question of polygamy, the Manifesto of 1890 was and is "deliverance unto Babylon."

The Manifesto no more marked the end of polygamy than did the superintendent of the census's statement mark an end to available free land, to economic opportunity, and to the growth of the democratic spirit in America. The Manifesto served its purpose in paving the way for statehood and political deliverance. This was yet another yielding to governmental power, since the Church leadership had earlier expressly stated that Saints were free to join the political party of their choice. It also called for the disbanding of the old People's Party, which had been the Mormon party in the territory.

These actions were to have serious broader and perhaps unanticipated consequences for the Church. Without "the gathering," without a compelling millennialism, without an overly intrusive temporal kingdom, and especially without polygamy, the Church stood at a threshold of a new century without much that it had developed during its frontier era. Of course, much remained—the tradition of the exodus of the overland trek, the repudiation of Babylon in individual conversion, the martyrdom of Joseph and Hyrum Smith, the Book of Mormon, the village—but it was not the Mormonism of the people of the "peculiar institution" who had arrived in the Salt Lake Valley under the guidance of Brigham Young and who had felt that they were carrying out the divine mandate of their prophet Joseph Smith. The Church, like the nation itself, would confront an urban plural society on a new footing after 1890. But that is another story.

If there were Mormons sitting in the audience when Frederick Jackson Turner remarked that 1890 witnessed the "closing of a great historic movement," they could certainly appreciate his words in more ways than one. They could wonder how their church would now endure. It had, after the immediate migration to the Salt Lake Valley, enjoyed the benefits of frontier isolation. The time had been used well and the kingdom well established. But by 1890, that was over; the members of the Church were now not only in the world but also of the world. Mormons who had found in the frontier a means to escape secular time and the secular world had been recaptured by both.

In the frontier context, the secular historian must ask what Mormon "deliverance" actually meant after the closing of the frontier in 1890. The answer must first and in some way come from Mormons themselves before a historical assessment can be made. Perhaps, for the time being, it would be enough if Mormon historians were to recognize the inextricability of the Mormon "deliverance" and the closing of the American frontier.

Notes

1. Martin Ridge, "Joseph Smith, Brigham Young, and a Religious Tradition," *Reviews in American History* 14 (March 1986): 25.

2. Melvin T. Smith, "Faithful History: Hazards and Limitations," *Journal of Mormon History* 9 (1982): 61.

3. Mario S. De Pillis, "Bearding Leone and Others in the Heartland of Mormon Historiography," *Journal of Mormon History* 8 (1981): 93.

4. Hubert Howe Bancroft, *The Book of the Fair: An Historical and Descriptive Presentation of the World's Science, Art, and Industry, as Viewed through the Columbian Exposition at Chicago in 1893* (Chicago: Bancroft Company, 1893), 2:831–32.

5. Ray Allen Billington, *Frederick Jackson Turner: Historian, Scholar, Teacher* (New York: Oxford University Press, 1973).

6. Martin Ridge, "The Life of an Idea: The Significance of Frederick Jackson Turner's Frontier Thesis," *Montana: The Magazine of Western History* 41 (Winter 1991): 2–13.

7. Frederick Jackson Turner, *The Frontier in American History* (New York: Henry Holt, 1920), 1.

8. Neal E. Lambert and Richard H. Cracroft, "Literary Form and Historical Understanding: Joseph Smith's First Vision," *Journal of Mormon History* 7 (1980): 31.

9. Marvin S. Hill, "The Rise of Mormonism in the Burned-over District: Another View," *New York History* 61 (October 1980): 417.

10. Gordon S. Wood, "Evangelical America and Early Mormonism," *New York History* 61 (October 1980): 361.

11. Thomas G. Alexander, "The Place of Joseph Smith in the Development of American Religion: A Historiographical Inquiry," *Journal of Mormon History* 5 (1978): 11.

12. Thomas F. O' Dea, *The Mormons* (Chicago: University of Chicago Press, 1957), 19–20; and Jan Shipps, "The Prophet Puzzle: Suggestions Leading toward a More Comprehensive Interpretation of Joseph Smith," *Journal of Mormon History* 1 (1974): 17.

13. Danel W. Bachman, "New Light on an Old Hypothesis: The Ohio Origins of the Revelation on Eternal Marriage," *Journal of Mormon History* 5 (1978): 19.

14. Lawrence Foster, "From Frontier Activism to Neo-Victorian Domesticity: Mormon Women in the Nineteenth and Twentieth Centuries," *Journal of Mormon History* 6 (1979): 7.

15. Gustive O. Larson, *The "Americanization" of Utah for Statehood* (San Marino, Calif.: Huntington Library, 1971), 1.

16. Foster, "From Frontier Activism to Neo-Victorian Domesticity," 6; and Marvin S. Hill, "Quest for Refuge: An Hypothesis as to the Social Origins and Nature of the Mormon Political Kingdom," *Journal of Mormon History* 2 (1975): 14.

17. Timothy L. Smith, "The Book of Mormon in a Biblical Culture," *Journal of Mormon History* 7 (1980): 12.

18. Marvin S. Hill, "Comments," *Journal of Mormon History* 3 (1976): 103–4.

19. Dean May, "The Mormons," in *Harvard Encyclopedia of American Ethnic Groups*, ed. Stephan Thernstrom (Cambridge: Harvard University Press, 1980), 720.

20. Richard L. Jensen, "Steaming Through: Arrangements for Mormon Emigration from Europe, 1869–1887," *Journal of Mormon History* 9 (1982): 22.

21. Ronald K. Esplin, "'A Place Prepared': Joseph, Brigham and the Quest for Promised Refuge in the West," *Journal of Mormon History* 9 (1982): 85–111.

22. Ibid., 88–92.

23. Charles S. Peterson, "Jacob Hamblin, Apostle to the Lamanites, and the Indian Mission," *Journal of Mormon History* 2 (1975): 29.

24. Charles S. Peterson, "A Mormon Village: One Man's West," *Journal of Mormon History* 3 (1976): 9.

25. De Pillis, "Bearding Leone and Others," 82.

26. Peterson, "Jacob Hamblin," 24–25.

27. Jan Shipps, *Mormonism: The Story of a New Religious Tradition* (Urbana: University of Illinois Press, 1985), 109–29.

28. Levi S. Peterson, "Juanita Brooks: Historian as Tragedian," *Journal of Mormon History* 3 (1976): 51–52; and Maureen Ursenbach Beecher, "Comment," ibid., 105–6.

29. Brian Q. Cannon, "Change Engulfs a Frontier Settlement: Ogden and Its Residents Respond to the Railroad," *Journal of Mormon History* 12 (1985): 23.

30. Charles S. Peterson, "The Limits of Learning in Pioneer Utah," *Journal of Mormon History* 10 (1983): 66.

31. Jensen, "Steaming Through," 21.

32. William Mulder, "Mormon Angles of Historical Vision: Some Maverick Reflections," *Journal of Mormon History* 3 (1976): 19–20.

33. May, "The Mormons," 723.

34. Richard Sherlock, "Mormon Migration and Settlement after 1875," *Journal of Mormon History* 2 (1975): 65–66; Jensen, "Steaming Through," 23.

35. Richard H. Jackson, ed., *The Mormon Role in the Settlement of the West* (Provo, Utah: Brigham Young University Press, 1978), xii.

36. Grant Underwood, "The New England Origins of Mormonism Revisited," *Journal of Mormon History* 15 (1989): 20.

37. Charles S. Peterson, "Mormon Village," 10.

38. Douglas D. Alder, "The Mormon Ward: Congregation or Community," *Journal of Mormon History* 5 (1978): 67.

39. Leonard J. Arrington, *Great Basin Kingdom: An Economic History of Latter-day Saints, 1830–1900* (Lincoln: University of Nebraska Press, 1966), 234.

40. Ibid.

41. William Mulder, "The Mormon Gathering," in *Mormonism and American Culture*, ed. Marvin S. Hill and James B. Allen (New York: Harper & Row, 1972), 99; Underwood, "New England Origins," 50.

42. Mulder, "The Mormon Gathering," 100.

43. Ibid.

44. Klaus Hansen, "The Political Kingdom as a Source of Conflict," in *Mormonism and American Culture*, 126.

45. Edward Leo Lyman, *Political Deliverance: The Mormon Quest for Statehood* (Urbana: University of Illinois Press, 1986).

CHAPTER 11

Peace Initiative: Using the Mormons to Rethink Culture and Ethnicity in American History

Patricia Nelson Limerick

In the summer of 1994, a group called the Flight Safety Foundation issued a report on the relationship between pilots and flight attendants. This relationship is often troubled; in some cases, it has been dangerous. In one instance, the foundation said, "the captain reported over the public address system that he had a problem with the *right* engine. Although the attendants . . . could see that [the] fire [was in] the *left* engine, they did nothing as the pilot shut down the wrong engine." "If the Engine's Burning," the *Washington Post* intelligently head-lined this article, "Tell the Pilot." But why on earth would someone *not* tell the pilot? Even though "cabin and flight deck crews share the same goals," the report offered its explanation, "the two crews have evolved into distinct cultures." Here is the most important thing to note in this parable from aviational ethnicity: The writers of the report took it for granted that living in a state of separate cultures meant living in a state of friction and hostility or, at the least, misunder-standing. Describing how these two cultures interact, the report said that pilots and flight attendants "sometimes show animosity toward one another, are often confused as to when to communicate problems, have little awareness of the other's duties in an emergency and sometimes don't even introduce themselves prior to a flight."[1]

The pilot says that the right engine is on fire. The flight attendants know that it is the left engine that is on fire, but because of cultural differences, the flight attendants do not speak—even though everybody is on the *same airplane*. What-ever this story tells us about the risks we take when we fasten our seatbelts, it tells us something considerably more important about the urgent need for people in this nation to think about the operations of culture and ethnicity in our times.

The words "culture" and "ethnicity" appear everywhere in the United States today, and they appear in tones ranging from despair and anger to pride and celebration. Perhaps the cheeriest usages appear in the marketplace, where, for instance, the word "ethnic" in front of the word "restaurant" has a happy effect on both the appetite and the wallet. Mail-order catalogs of women's clothing are also frequent and comfortable deployers of the word "ethnic." One catalog describes a flowing gauze outfit as "inspired by ethnic influences"; a striped vest, another catalog says, offers "ethnic dash for any outfit." "Ethnic" in the mail-order catalogs means embroidered, or brightly colored, or made of abundant, flowing material. "Ethnic," contrary to the shading given the word in newspaper stories about Rwanda and Bosnia, does not necessarily refer to clothing that one would wear to battle. An "ethnic dash" is not necessarily a flight for life.

American undergraduates are similarly inclined to the breezy and colorful school of ethnicity and culture. Twenty years ago, a curious habit of mind seemed to take over the students. Repeatedly, in midterm and final exams, they would refer to various "lifestyles"—to the "lifestyle" of the Pequot Indians or the "lifestyle" of the Puritans. It did not help me, in my adjustment to the students' fondness for this word, to hear a repeated radio advertisement for a furniture store. The store claimed to offer every kind of furniture you might want, whether, as the ad said, "your lifestyle is colonial or contemporary." It is a wonderful and wild notion to think of someone in the late twentieth century choosing to have a "colonial" lifestyle, with a few stools, no chairs, a milk churn, a fireplace to cook on, a few pots and, if privileged, a spoon or two, with life punctuated by an occasional raid or war of conquest and with a general sense of subordination to a distant empire.

When the word "lifestyle" appeared frequently in history exams, it seemed that we were not doing all we could to help the students see the past as the people of that time saw it themselves. Then, over the years, "lifestyle" seems to have dropped away and "culture" has taken its place, with "culture" functioning as a synonym for "lifestyle." The Plains Indians, for instance, many students writing exams will tell you, fought in the last half of the nineteenth century to "defend their culture" or to "preserve their culture." There stand the Lakota at Little Big Horn, rallying to defend a concept that white anthropologists were barely starting to create, circulate, and popularize. With the word "culture" as their incantation, students ride through history on a kind of magic carpet of time travel, visiting far-off places made familiar and comfortable by the fact that every group has a culture and every culture is, in turn, rich and complex, separate and intact, and equally well defined and well defended.

One of the most significant events in the intellectual and social history of the last century was this: academics invented the concept of culture and then completely lost control of it. On other occasions we may complain about the gap between the university and the world at large, but this is not one of those occasions. Every group these days has borrowed academic terminology and taken to talking self-consciously, and sometimes self-importantly, about their "culture."

In the last thirty years, sociologists, anthropologists, historians, and cultural critics have written a great many articles and books trying to define the concepts of ethnicity and culture. To some degree this is a matter of scholars struggling with other scholars over the meaning of key terms of inquiry. But it certainly seems that there is another message to be heard in all these publications, a message of academics saying to the general public, "The word 'culture' is our word, not yours. You should have asked our permission (which we probably would not have given) before you took it; and if you're not careful, you're going to hurt yourselves with it."

And, in truth, people have hurt themselves and hurt their neighbors with these words. "Culture" and "ethnicity" turn out to make very satisfactory verbal weapons. In 1969, the anthropologist Fredrik Barth wrote a very influential and instructive article arguing that the meaning of ethnicity lies more in its boundaries than in its core. Ethnicity, Barth said, is not a set of defined, consistent characteristics at the center of a group's being; it is much more a matter of negotiations at the group's edges, arrangements made when and where the group borders upon other groups.[2] Matters here have taken a remarkably ironic twist: the very word "ethnicity" can now function in public exchange as a boundary, the kind of boundary usually constructed of barbed wire and glass fragments. In many situations in the United States, statements about one's culture or one's ethnicity prove to be statements that carry an additional message, and that additional message says to outsiders, KEEP OUT.

In theory, historians should have a particular advantage in providing a kind of escort service across and over these discouraging boundaries. We should be able to provide perspective; we should be able to take the long view, the calm view, the "let's not fly off the handle" view. Historians should be able to provide a genuine social service in calm and reflective analysis of ethnicity and its workings.

But this is a service we have not yet performed. Sometimes we actually do engage in calm and reflective analysis, but we have a way of writing up the results in a literary style that shuts out laypeople and nonspecialists. We have also bogged ourselves down in charges of political correctness on one side and charges of racism and insensitivity on the other. Most importantly, we have backed away from any vision of human common ground. We have, instead, divided the world into a set of experiences—Catholic, Protestant, Jew, Mormon, Muslim; male and female, heterosexual and homosexual; Indian, Anglo American, African American, Mexican American, Asian American. Of course these are consequential categories, but they are also categories that overlap, and categories that are themselves internally full of variation and conflict. Nonetheless, we set these categories off by themselves and sometimes draw the conclusion that no doors or openings connect them: men will never understand women's experiences, Anglo Americans will never understand Mexican American experiences, African Americans will never understand Korean American experiences, and so it goes.

For the best reasons, this prospect panics me. Of course, we will never understand each other fully; of course, parts of our experiences will always remain
hidden from each other. But empathy and understanding still have the power to
cross many of these borders. I take considerable inspiration from the words of
Cornel West: "We simply cannot enter the twenty-first century," he writes, "at
each other's throats." Whatever our ethnicity or religion, "We are at a crucial
crossroad in the history of this nation—and we either hang together by com-
bating [the] forces that divide and degrade us or we hang separately."[3]

To avoid the prospect of separate hangings, we will have to show considerable courage. And when we look for examples of courage, contemporary Mormon intellectuals should be high on that list. I believe I know something, from
firsthand experience, about how it feels to be a historian in the midst of controversy, but there are a number of Mormon historians who know a lot more
about this than I do. Reappraising and rethinking the history of the American
West can sometimes make me feel that I have wandered into the midst of a bat-
tlefield, but I do not think there is any topic that can beat Mormon history for
its power to prove the proposition that how we write and interpret history matters—and matters to people who may never set foot in a college or university
history department.

Controversial changes in the writing of Mormon history, controversial changes
in the writing of Western American history, controversial changes in the writing
of national history: these changes are in many ways parallel and related. Reckoning with human diversity, with the economic underpinnings of social relationships, with gender, with the moral complexity of many actions that, in earlier
versions of history, once seemed simple: that has been the pattern of change
across the whole discipline of history. Mormon history and Western American
history have thus undergone very similar processes of transformation. Indeed,
when I was writing *The Legacy of Conquest,* I saw considerable common ground
in the cause of Mormon history and Western American history. Mormon history
is one of the most compelling, distinctive, and instructive components of regional
history; yet under the terms of the old frontier school of Western American history, Mormon history had to be dismissed and marginalized.

In his frontier thesis, Frederick Jackson Turner had argued that the frontier
had created a uniquely self-reliant, individualistic American pioneer. The Mormons, with their tightly knit social bonds and communitarian behavior, did not
do much to support Turner's argument. Turner thus reserved four words for
Mormons in his 1893 essay "The Significance of the Frontier," and it should tell
you something about the relevance of the Turner thesis to Mormonism that two
of those four words were "the" and "in." I refer to his brief reference to the location of the frontier in 1850, which makes a momentary mention of "the settlements in Utah."[4] In the same spirit, Turner's follower Ray Allen Billington told
the *story* of Utah in his narrative books, but when it came time to write about

the *meaning* of the frontier and the lessons of history, in *America's Frontier Heritage*, Billington followed Turner's lead and left out the Mormons.[5] The Mormons would not fit the frontier thesis, so Turner and Billington stuck by the frontier thesis and dismissed the Mormons. It seemed to me ten years ago, and still seems to me now, a much wiser choice to stick by the Mormons and dismiss the frontier thesis.

I had and have a personal stake in seeing that the history of Utah and the Latter-day Saints gets proper attention. My father was born and raised in Brigham City as part of the Danish LDS community there. My mother was raised in Salt Lake City, and though she was a Congregationalist, her life in Utah seems similar to Wallace Stegner's experience—never a member but still very much involved in LDS youth activities, with many close friendships uninterrupted and undiminished by religious differences. My father left the Church and my parents moved to California before I was born, but the story—and anecdotal—part of my heritage has a heavy Utah flavor to it.

In some ways, this background was the root of my conviction that the establishment of the Church of Jesus Christ of Latter-day Saints had produced a kind of ethnicity. Over the years, Catholic friends would say, "Only a Catholic can really feel guilt," or others would make reference to the drivenness and workaholicness that come with immersion in the Protestant work ethic. I certainly thought that I knew something about guilt and also about a devotion to work. Until I was in my twenties, I had never been in a Catholic Church, and I had only rarely been in Protestant churches. Where and how could I have picked up a Catholic sense of guilt or a Protestant work ethic? And if I hadn't picked those items up from the conventional sources, then whose sense of guilt and whose work ethic *do* I have?

I think you can guess my answer.

While I think that there is a phenomenon one can call Mormon ethnicity, I know these things are not simple. If I ever thought they were simple, I have had many fine opportunities to get over that presumption. Consider, for instance, the occasion fifteen years ago when I had in my Western American history course a Mexican American student from El Paso, a great supporter of Chicano rights. We were two-thirds of the way through the semester when this student came in to talk about his paper topic. I knew that he would want to write something about Spanish colonization of the Southwest or about discrimination against Mexican Americans in the twentieth century.

Instead, he said he would like to write about Mormonism. Mormonism?

This student was, in fact, a fourth-generation LDS. His family had been converted by Utah families who fled to Mexico during the polygamy persecutions. My first impressions had been right: he was very much a Chicano activist and proud of his Mexican heritage, but he was also a devoted Latter-day Saint, persuaded that he and his family had found their rightful place as redeemed Lamanites.[6]

This young man's complex heritage and identity, as well as his justified anger at the treatment of Mexican American people in El Paso, remind us of how complicated matters of ethnicity can be and also how controversial they are. This helps to explain the curious title of this essay, "Peace Initiative." Ethnic conflict is a very troubling element in the world today, and Bosnia and Rwanda are only the two most visible manifestations of that problem. Even though the United States is an enormous distance away from those two examples, ethnic friction is no small element of our current national experience.

In the project of addressing that friction, the use of the idea of ethnicity will be a key factor in our success or failure. Ethnicity has become our central concept for categorizing the qualities or traits or actions that identify a group of people as a unit, the features that distinguish one group of people from another. "Distinguish" is, of course, by no means a synonym for "divide"; ethnic groups can be distinguished from each other and still be quite compatible, even collaborative and mutually respectful. Ethnicity also provides us with a vital area of overlap between the interests and concerns of historians and the interests and concerns of laypeople. The idea of ethnicity makes everyone, at least momentarily, into a practicing historian. When you ask people what their ethnicity is, they engage themselves with history; they ask themselves questions about origin and causality; they place themselves in the context of the passage of time; they tie their personal identities into currents of change and continuity. Moreover, people asked to identify their ethnicity do not just report historical facts; they also clearly show themselves to be selectors, shapers, and interpreters of those facts.

Consider these examples from interviews by the sociologist Mary Waters speaking to Americans of European descent. Waters asked a nineteen-year-old college student named Bill Kerrigan how he would identify himself on a census form:

A: I would have put Irish.
Q: Why would you have answered that?
A: Well, my dad's name is Kerrigan and my mom's name is O'Leary, and I do have some German in me, but if you figure it out, I am about 75 percent Irish, so I say I am Irish.
Q: You usually don't say German when people ask?
A: No, no, I never say I am German. My dad just likes being Irish . . . I don't know, I guess I just never think of myself as being German.
Q: So your dad's father is the one who immigrated?
A: Yes. On this side it is Irish for generations. And then my grandmother's name is Dubois, which is French, partly German, partly French, and then the rest of the family is all Irish.[7]

As Mary Waters sums up, "In the course of a few questions, Bill labeled himself Irish, admitted to being part German but not identifying with it, and then as an afterthought added that he was also part French."[8]

Or consider a forty-six-year-old Irish and Italian woman interviewed by Waters, who gives an even better demonstration of the way in which ethnicity makes regular people into interpretative historians.

Q: When you were growing up did you consider yourself ethnic?
A: Yes, I was very strongly Italian, because . . . whenever I was in a bad mood, that was the Irish in me. So I always related the Irish with the bad things and the Italian with all of the good things. . . . I thought all the Irish were hotheads and all the Italians had clean houses and good food.[9]

The facts of this woman's origins say Irish and Italian, but her conditioning casts the Italian side as superior to the Irish. Thus, the inheritor of this legacy, showing a certain measure of self-esteem, settles on the characterization of Italian.

Here we have very literal case studies in the idea of the construction of ethnic identity, of Everywoman Her Own Historian, of Everyman His Own Historian. We have, as well, case studies in what is now established thinking about the idea of ethnicity: that ethnicity is much more a matter of construction, choice, consent, and interpretation, and much less a matter of literal inheritance, descent, and lineage. The people interviewed by Mary Waters had particularly open turf for choice. As what Waters calls "white ethnics," they could, if they wanted, choose to claim no ethnicity at all: whenever they wanted, they could drop the whole package—Irish, Italian, French, German, Polish—and simply say "American." You can choose nearly anything in America, the famed cultural pluralist Horace Kallen had said, but you cannot choose your grandfather. Now, as historian David Hollinger has observed, even that apparent knockout punch of an aphorism needs some rethinking. If you cannot choose a grandfather entirely from scratch, you can certainly choose which of your various grandfather-options you will accent. To the people interviewed by Mary Waters, the construction of ethnicity bordered on play: they could add or subtract, accent and de-emphasize, the pieces and parts of their ethnic identity without significant social cost, and with such flexibility and freedom that they looked as if they had agreed to team up with recent cultural theorists and put on a demonstration of the fact that ethnicity is a matter of consent, far more than descent.[10]

Other Americans would have a harder time putting on such a demonstration. We reach now the arena of ethnicity in which choice and consent seem to be much reduced, the arena in which the construction of ethnic identity could hardly be called "play." We come to the matter perhaps best summarized by the sociologist Robert Blauner in 1972. "Many of the ambiguities of American race relations," Blauner said, "stem from the fact that two principles of social division, race and ethnicity, were compressed into one." Or, as David Hollinger put it recently, "Exactly where ethnicity ends and race begins has been much contested in our time."[11] We understand race to be a socially constructed concept itself, of no particular validity as a category of nature and biology. We understand that there are hundreds of possible ways to define, for instance, African American culture and identity. In a fair and just world, African American ethnicity would be just as much a matter of individual free choice as is Irish American ethnicity or Italian American ethnicity.

In the last few years, a veritable cascade of books has testified to exactly the opposite proposition: that, on the contrary, African Americans continue to have the category "black" imposed upon them, whether or not that is their preference. Cornel West's *Race Matters* and Derrick Bell's *Faces at the Bottom of the Well: The Permanence of Racism* are probably the most widely recognized of these books. Jonathan Kozol's *Savage Inequalities: Children in America's Schools* and Alex Kotlowitz's *There Are No Children Here: The Story of Two Boys Growing Up in the Other America* take unflinching looks at the intersection of race and poverty. If one prefers to take one's doses of despair in autobiographical form, Brent Staples's *Parallel Time: Growing Up in Black and White* and Nathan McCall's *Makes Me Wanna Holler: A Young Black Man in America* make it clear how far away we are from a society that does not make blackness a penalty. You can read some of these books and try to tell yourself that our dilemma is a matter of class lines, poverty, and the inherited injuries of slavery and segregation. With widened economic opportunity and with the passage of decades since the end of slavery and the end of legal segregation, you can begin to hope that the historically inherited categories of black and white have surrendered much of their rigidity. But then you read Ellis Cose's *The Rage of a Privileged Class,* full of stories of the injuries and insults encountered by black professionals, managers, and executives, and differences of social class cease to be a sufficient explanation for white privilege and prejudice.[12]

Even though it is the most impersonal of all these books, *Two Nations: Black and White, Separate, Hostile, Unequal,* by the white political scientist Andrew Hacker, may be the most disheartening. Hacker offers, for instance, a haunting statistical fact: white Americans will stay in a neighborhood as long as the percentage of black residents remains at 8 percent or under.[13] The percentage of blacks in the American population is a little more than 12 percent, and so white Americans, even white Americans who say that they want to live in an integrated neighborhood, will begin moving out before the percentage of blacks in the neighborhood even reaches the percentage of blacks in the general population.

In an often quoted observation, the novelist Ishmael Reed has remarked that if the black novelist Alex Haley had followed his father's line of genealogy in the search for his own origins, then Haley's book *Roots* would have been set in Ireland, not Africa. But Americans continue with their traditional, and very arbitrary, categorizations of African American descent. Any black heritage at all will identify a person as black. As the historian Barbara J. Fields put it, we hold on to a convention "that considers a white woman capable of giving birth to a black child but denies that a black woman can give birth to a white child."[14]

Repeatedly finding themselves picked up and placed into ethnic categories that might or might not fit them, people of color have had considerable reason to resent the privilege of choice that white Americans have over the matter of their ethnicity. And yet, in recent times, white Americans have had their moments of resentment as well, moments in which our present constructions of ethnicity work equally well at denying the humanity and individuality of that group wearing the label "white American." A few years ago, I was in Oakland, California, talking with a group of schoolteachers of every ethnic background. One white teacher reported this discouraging event: She was attending a panel discussion where the phrases "people of color" and "person of color" were used repeatedly. Thus, when an African American panelist wanted to refer to a white person, the phrase "person of color" was still hanging in the air, leading the speaker to refer to the white individual as a "non–person of color." This newly coined phrase did not raise the spirits of the white people in the room.

Much of our language and many of our characterizations on this matter do seem to have come straight from the mind of Lewis Carroll. For researchers at Berkeley's Diversity Project, "white" has become "a residual category meaning either not Black, not Asian, not Chicano/Latino, etc. . . . meaning 'without color.'" Even the guiltiest white liberals would hesitate before identifying themselves, when asked for their ethnicity, as "without color." And this sad definition of whites as colorless nonpersons comes with notable variations. In his 1981 book on Mexican Americans in El Paso, historian Mario Garcia offered this definitional footnote: "In this study the term *Mexican* refers to all persons of Mexican descent but in particular [to] immigrants from Mexico. The term *Mexican American* refers to Mexicans born in the United States. . . . Finally, *American* or *Anglo* refers to all non-Mexicans, especially white citizens of the United States." As the adverb "especially" points out, by this definition, since they are non-Mexicans, African Americans get to be momentary honorary "Anglos." To Mormons in Utah, everyone who is not Mormon is Gentile; thus, Jews are Gentiles. And now in El Paso, blacks are Anglos.[15]

Mormons and Gentiles; Mexicans and Anglos; persons of color and non–persons of color; white Americans who think that enough, even too much, has been done to help black Americans recover from the injuries of the past, and black Americans who can provide everyday evidence that racial injuries only changed form and did not stop with *Brown v. Board of Education;* representatives of the culture of flight attendants who will not tell representatives of the culture of pilots which engine is on fire: Americans appear to have landed in the soup. *Not* in the melting pot. Just in a mess of disunited, fragmented, and clashing ethnicities and cultures.

One could go on and on with examples drawn from all sides and participating groups of the discouraging, divisive quality of many of our current public discussions of ethnicity in American history and life. Thus, I turn now to a hopeful paradox: as contested and controversial as the writing of Mormon history can be, we can talk about the idea of Mormon ethnicity in a comparatively calm and peaceful way. Then we can take the idea of ethnicity we develop in a discussion of Mormonism and apply it to other examples of ethnicity in a way that may actually reduce the friction and polarization of the usual discussions in that turf.

Some readers may be puzzling over that remark: Could she really think that a discussion of the terms of Mormon history will be calmer and less controversial than a discussion of, say, Mexican American history? I know the story of Leonard Arrington's too-brief term of duty as Church historian; I have read Lavina Fielding Anderson's essay in *Dialogue*, "The LDS Intellectual Community and Church Leadership: A Contemporary Chronology"; I have read Paul Toscano's impassioned *The Sanctity of Dissent*; I have followed, and admired, the career of D. Michael Quinn. I have kept track of press coverage of the disagreements between the General Authorities and Mormon intellectuals, and of the disciplinary action taken against historians and feminists. And yet I still think that a consideration of Mormon ethnicity provides a more tranquil and tractable way to approach the topic of ethnicity in the United States.[16]

Why? In part, because Mormon ethnicity allows scholars an arena for thinking about ethnicity as it applies to a group who, for most of their history, have had the white skin and European background of the American majority and whose distinctive consciousness was generated by events that occurred in the United States, not in the "old country." In accenting the whiteness of Mormons, I may seem to be forgetting the Mexican American Mormons of El Paso and Juarez, the African American Mormons whose lives were much changed by the 1978 revelation admitting black men to the priesthood, and all the Mormon converts in Polynesia, Asia, Latin America, and Africa. But still the majority of Mormons, through the majority of the Church's history, have been of European ancestry.

When ethnicity is associated with a skin color other than white, ethnicity can become a category so much imposed from the outside that it becomes harder to distinguish the workings of the individual's choice and consciousness. The history of discrimination on the basis of race can heat discussions of ethnicity to the point where it is, in truth, painful to touch them. While we will return to that arena, the fact that the majority of Mormons have been white allows us, at least temporarily, to cool down the terms of discussion of ethnic identity. And the case study of Mormonism provides us with a crucial reminder that we must examine the category "white" carefully and critically: whiteness or Anglo Americanness cannot remain the taken-for-granted definition of normality by which the peculiarity of the "other" cultures are measured. In their habits, beliefs, and customs, white people, heaven knows, can match any other group in the categories of peculiarity, eccentricity, and interest.

Moreover, Mormon ethnicity is not at the center of the disagreements between General Authorities and Mormon historians. It is also a topic on which we already have models of tranquil, uninjurious, reasoned, clarifying disagreement. In the fine collection of essays *The Mormon Presence in Canada,* two scholars, Armand Mauss and Keith Parry, take opposite sides on this question. Parry argues for the existence of a Mormon ethnicity, Mauss argues against it, and both writers preserve perfect equanimity and fairness of judgment.[17] In fact, following very closely in Jan Shipps's footsteps, I will soon argue that the issue of Mormon ethnicity provides a kind of intellectual refuge from present contention between the leadership and some of its members. Rather than taking us back into controversy, ethnicity provides a framework for thinking, calmly and reflectively, about the current dilemmas in the Church.

Let us try, now, to bring this theoretical framework into practice in a discussion of the origins and the shape of Mormon ethnicity in the last 165 years of history. I ask the forbearance of readers here because, for the next few pages, I will be restating some of the most familiar facts about LDS history and echoing a number of statements made better by other writers and analysts.[18]

The building blocks of a Mormon ethnicity are not difficult to locate. From the very beginning of the Church, faith in a particular theology was accompanied by a striking willingness to follow Joseph Smith's revelations and advice in day-to-day behavior. Membership in this church was also membership in a community with its own economic, social, and familial patterns. People who joined the Church were often cut off from family members who disapproved of their conversion and geographically separated from their places of origin as well. Even before the murder of Joseph Smith and the Mormons' departure from the Mississippi Valley, the conditions were close to ideal for the creation of a community in which religious belief laid the foundations for a new worldview, a new pattern of family organization, a new set of ambitions, a new combination of common bonds and obligations, a new definition of a separate peoplehood—all the components, in other words, of what we now call "ethnicity."

To this situation, already rich in possibilities for the creation of a culture or subculture, persecution and the migration to Utah provided the capstone. Framed in a forceful and compelling analogy to the persecution and exodus of the Israelites, the Mormon move to the Great Basin catalyzed the sense of a separate peoplehood. As a shared memory, full of the literal and direct testing of the spirit, this exodus was exactly the kind of event that would stay with a people forever, the kind of experience that would bind even those born too late to participate in it to a vision of the special identity that comes with a special history. Richard Bennett's book *Mormons at the Missouri* offers a particularly telling case study of the impact of migration in the formation of identity, as Winter Quarters provided the site for a crucial refining and testing of Mormon group purpose.[19]

Analogies to Israel went further than the exodus. As Jan Shipps has explained, by a "rhetorical construction of blood descent," Mormons became Abraham's descendants, even more explicitly defined as a chosen people. And a sense of kinship—a key component of ethnicity—came from other sources besides the vision of the Saints as the "seed of Abraham." Kinship came as well from the custom of adoption, in which adult Mormon men were sealed as sons to Church leaders, and from the proliferating ties created by plural marriage. Plural marriage thus added to the conditions of ethnicity in two ways: as another form of cultural distinctiveness, perhaps the best for dramatizing the Saints' separate status, and as a very effective way of making people into relatives, creating a wonderfully interwoven network of in-laws and kin.[20]

The idea—really the imperative—of the gathering of the Saints gave great force to the sense of peoplehood, while arrival in Deseret added place and geography to the forces supporting and sustaining ethnicity. As Promised Land, as Zion, the land just beyond the Rockies provided another foundation for identity, and the Saints invested enormous labor in making that land meet their standards for habitability, building towns and villages, homes and farms, that would add up to what many have called a characteristic Mormon landscape.[21]

The years of comparative isolation, with Mormons firmly the majority in most of Utah, southern Idaho, and northern Arizona, allowed group identity to become even more clearly defined. For instance, characteristic patterns of Mormon entertainment such as dancing and theater developed. In a time when Protestant Christians feared the danger and temptations of leisure and recreation, Joseph Smith and Brigham Young, as R. Laurence Moore has pointed out, had a "clear advantage. . . . They had much less to fear in the matter of leisure because they retained effective control over what happened when Mormons socialized with other Mormons."[22] English, German, Danish, Swedish, and Norwegian converts moved very quickly into this common culture. Scandinavian converts, William Mulder told us in *Homeward to Zion,* attended regular, English-speaking ward meetings but also had auxiliary Scandinavian meetings to ease their transition into both the language and the society.[23]

Some elements of imported European ethnicity might linger. I have heard from my father that his parents' old horse in Brigham City would stop plowing precisely at 3:30 P.M. and head for the house, demonstrating my Danish grandparents' continued affection for the cultural concept of the coffee break. Thus, it was particularly interesting for me to learn from Mulder that something a bit short of reverence for the Word of Wisdom was quite characteristic of Danish converts. And yet, with a few persistent variations in behavior, the blending of new immigrants into this new Mormon ethnicity seems to have proceeded with remarkable speed. Meanwhile, the practice of plural marriage and the federal government's mounting hostility to polygamy deepened the Mormon sense of distinctiveness and separateness, also providing an unusual historical legacy awaiting the reckoning of future generations of Saints.

The end of polygamy was a major and consequential moment in Mormon history, but Mormons soon found other ways to mark their boundaries and to define their separate identity. The distinctive elements of Mormon theology, endowments received in the temples, marriages sealed for time and eternity, the growing emphasis on the Word of Wisdom, the meetings and activities of the priesthood, the Relief Society, the Mutual, the Primary, the round of socials and games at ward meetinghouses, the quarterly stake conferences, the semiannual general conferences, the missionary experience of young men (and, after a while, of young women as well), the proxy baptisms and sealings performed on behalf of one's dead kindred, tithing, the creation of the Church welfare system, fast offering funds dedicated to the care of the poor, family home evenings, large families taking part in those evenings, and, perhaps more than anything, the told and retold stories of Mormon history made it very unlikely that Mormons would lose their distinctive ethnicity and disappear into a homogeneous, mainstream, American whole.

With considerably greater efficiency than I have shown, Leonard Arrington has summed up the case for regarding Mormons as both an ethnic group and a religious group. "Mormons," Arrington writes, "have (or at least used to have) a distinctive vocabulary, shared history, unique theological beliefs, definite in-group boundaries (prohibitions on the use of alcohol, tobacco, tea, and coffee), emphasis on in-group marriage, and a strong sense of peoplehood, which includes the 'brother' and 'sister' terminology."[24] If one thinks back to the "white ethnics" interviewed by Mary Waters, it is clear that people who chose to identify themselves as Mormon in more than religion could bring more clarity and concreteness to the project of identifying their ethnicity than the people in Waters's examples. It is, however, important to note Arrington's phrasing: "Mormons," the quotation begins, "have (or at least used to have)" these qualities of ethnicity. That "used to have" is the core of the problem. In the last thirty years, the Church has grown enormously and grown internationally. The Mormon diaspora of the twentieth century has weakened the ties between peoplehood and place considerably. The idea of a Zion or a promised land has to play a much diminished role in Mormon consciousness, when so many Mormons live so far from Utah. Moreover, many Mormons in the last few decades have ended up living in places where they are by no means a majority and where most of their working life is spent in the company of people who cannot—except, perhaps, by their indifference—reinforce any notion of Mormon identity. The Mormon story cannot any longer be the story of ethnicity by immersion that characterized the life of converts in the nineteenth century. Moreover, the spread of Mormonism into many nations and many cultures stretches the persuasive powers and influences of any one cultural system. Simply adjusting styles of greeting and personal friendship, ways of contracting marriages, or forms of expressing deference to accommodate all the world's cultures is a puzzle of the greatest magnitude.[25]

It does not take much in the way of predictive powers to guess that this situation would become fraught with considerable anxiety and tension. Thus it seems more than possible that, twenty or thirty years from now, historians of Mormonism might well adopt exactly the interpretative framework of ethnicity to explain the pattern of events in the Church in the last half of the twentieth century. I can, in other words, imagine scholarly articles or books that would put what are, to us, puzzling and unsettling recent events into an explanatory framework in which ethnicity was central. Historians of the future might write statements like the ones that I imagine in these next two paragraphs:

* * *

For 125 years, Mormon religious belief was securely supported by Mormon cultural practice: to be a Mormon was as much a matter of ethnic self-definition as it was a matter of membership in a religious denomination, and those two dimensions of Mormonism reliably reinforced each other. Mormon ethnicity drew its strength from sources that did not require much in the way of official supervision or control in the Saints' ties to the places of Utah, Idaho, and Arizona; in their well-rehearsed understanding of their common history and in their complicated network of kinship and descent, the Mormons did not need Church strictures to find plenty of reminders of their peoplehood.

In the last four decades of the twentieth century, however, these well-settled conditions began to change. Membership in the Church expanded enormously: with the idea of a geographical gathering no longer tenable, there was simply no quick way to match conversion to the LDS Church with a parallel conversion to Mormon ethnicity. Feeling understandable concern about this course of events, the General Authorities undertook to standardize Mormon thought and practice; the Correlation Committee was only one part of a larger process of response to the overstretching and decline of Mormon ethnic identity. In the nineteenth century, as Stanley Kimball remarked in his biography of Heber C. Kimball, "speculative theology was practiced in the Church."[26] Standardization of that theology came considerably later. Moreover, nineteenth-century Mormonism, as a group of women scholars argued in the collection of essays *Sisters in Spirit,* gave a considerably wider range of options to Mormon women; many activities, particularly in rituals of healing, which would later be confined to the practice of a male priesthood, were once open to women.[27] Thus, in the 1980s and 1990s, when the Church tried to address the loss of Mormon ethnicity with a greater centralization of control over Mormon thought, this was neither a restoration of early Mormonism nor a return to tradition. It was, in fact, a campaign of standardization that, ironically, in the effort to hold Mormons more tightly together, retreated from the distinctive elements of Mormonism, accenting instead the Church's similarity to conventional Christianity. Profoundly disturbing to Mormon intellectuals, and perhaps especially to Mormon historians, this campaign for standardization was in fact an understandable response to unsettling change in the Church's position in the world at large.

* * *

What I cannot write is a third paragraph that says what happened next. But as to the existence of a Mormon cultural identity—something that looked like, functioned like, and was experienced like ethnicity—of that proposition I feel quite certain.

Indeed, on some counts, this idea of Mormon ethnicity as a fading force, as a vestige and relic of a different time, is a puzzling one. If Mormon ethnicity is fading, why is the late twentieth century seeing such a remarkable and impressive flowering of Mormon literature? Anyone troubled by the prospect of a disappearing ethnic identity should read the Mormon creative writers—Mormon novelists, Mormon short-story writers, Mormon poets, and Mormon essayists.[28] In their work, a clear cultural identity thrives, and thrives in a way identifiable to any reader. When, in other words, you pick up a collection with the subtitle "Contemporary Mormon Short Stories," you do not become puzzled about why it would carry that subtitle. The common cultural elements, along with a familiar and distinctive vocabulary of wards, temples, stake presidents, bishops, missions, testimonies, Nephites, priesthood, Relief Society, and holidays on 6 April and 24 July, tell you that you are reading literature rooted in a particular ethnicity, although, of course, that literature also speaks to a broad set of human concerns. The groundedness of the short stories, the novels, and the essays persuade the reader that obituaries for Mormon ethnicity are decidedly premature.

Reading this literature causes one's imagination to play with the prospect of what might happen if the Church spent less time enforcing intellectual conformity and more time distributing and discussing this rich Mormon literature and (if we truly are living in a postliterate, postprint age) translating it into plays, movies, and music videos. This technique would allow stories to do what stories have always done best: convey the real meaning and appeal of life within a particular cultural tradition.

There may be some who would argue that when an ethnicity becomes the basis of a thriving literary tradition, it is already on the ropes, already on its way to status as the property of a small group of self-conscious intellectuals and no longer just the lived reality of regular folk. And that takes us back to the lessons of Mormon ethnicity for all of American history.

We are living, in the late twentieth century, in very self-conscious times. When we use any of these terms—"lifestyle," "culture," or "ethnicity"—for people of the past, we impose concepts that would have seemed peculiar and alien to them. Those terms are not, therefore, off limits, but there is a huge question of consciousness and choice raised here. I do not think that Latter-day Saints of the nineteenth century thought of themselves as having an ethnicity, but I think we are still entitled to look at the sum of their thinking and behavior and to use the word "ethnicity" to describe the common patterns of their lives. Nineteenth-century Latter-day Saints, one could say, had an ethnicity precisely because they did not have to think in those terms. They thought in terms of being a chosen people, the seed of Abraham, but mostly they behaved in ways that demonstrated their common habits and their shared worldview. In the immediacy of that behavior, they never had to draw back to inquire whether they were or were not being certifiably "ethnic."

In truth, one can find something to envy in the un-self-consciousness of the past. The current theoretical literature on ethnicity so strongly stresses the role of choice, of consent, and of construction that the idea of authenticity, of immediacy, of simply being who you are, without having to endure repeated bouts of strained and awkward self-definition, has moved out of our reach. It is a rare group today that can escape the curious and oddly nerve-racking experience of researching, describing, defining, asserting, clarifying, re-creating, and over-hauling their identity. Not only does every group and every subgroup have to have these discussions, they also have to go forward with the results, standing before the public, before federal agencies, before academic audiences, explaining the process, method, and assumptions by which they arrived at their ethnic identity. It is a peculiar state of affairs, but it is a state of affairs made even more trying by the enormous emotional and psychological freight that the idea of ethnicity now has to carry.

Explaining what I mean by that reference to the "enormous emotional and psychological freight" permits me to respond, at long last, to a conversation Jan Shipps and I have had many times. This is the essence of the conversation: Jan says that one of the greatest weaknesses of the New Western History is its failure to reckon with religious history. I think about that and then agree that she is absolutely right. Western historians do pay attention to Spanish missionaries in the Southwest or to Protestant and Jesuit missionaries in the Northwest. But you virtually have to be a missionary to catch our attention in explicitly religious terms; if you are just a regular old Westerner, we are a hundred times more likely to examine your economic and social behavior than your internal religious life. So Jan Shipps points out the failure of the New Western History to reckon with the wider meanings of faith: I agree completely with her, and then I rush on to the next task and do nothing to show that I have heard her.

This essay, however, provides the best opportunity I have ever had or am likely to have to show that I am paying attention to Jan. Even without the stimulus of conversation with her, the preparation of this essay would have left me mystified and bewildered by the assumption of secularity shared by many Western American historians, New or Old. In the spring of 1994, my colleague at the University of Colorado, Steven Epstein, gave a presentation with me at the National Endowment for the Humanities. I spoke on "New Directions in Western American History," and he spoke on "New Directions in Medieval History."

And to the astonishment of the audience, he persuaded them and me that there really are new directions in his well-established field. But one direction of inquiry, he suggested, remained both old and new. Medieval history was one field where no historian could ever neglect religious history. At every moment of medieval history, the historian is in the presence of faith, as well as the practical and material consequences of faith. I have thought frequently about that remark in reading Mormon history, because everything that Epstein said about medieval history is equally true of Mormon history.[29]

If one is not a Mormon historian but takes an excursion into this field, then one returns to one's own territory asking oneself a big question. If religious faith is an unavoidable and a central factor in Mormon history, then where did it go in Western American history in general? The notion of non-Mormon Westerners living in a fully secularized world, a world in which human consciousness inhabits a thoroughly and complacently material universe and never asks questions about the origins of life, the inescapability of death, and the purpose of existence, never asks those questions and never even stumbles over any answers —after a visit to Mormon history, this idea of a fully secularized modern American consciousness seems deeply improbable.

Religious belief is a well-established current in most phases of human history. It is hard to believe that for many twentieth-century Americans, it was a current that just stopped. If one holds this mystery in one's mind and then turns back to the public discussion of ethnicity in our times, a curious but inescapable idea comes to mind. In the fervor, defensiveness, and ardor of contemporary assertions of ethnic identity, something more than a popularized social science seems to be at work. I am not saying that assertions of ethnic identity are the exact equivalent of assertions of religious belief. But I am saying that assertions of ethnic identity partake of much of the same mental, even spiritual, energy of assertions of religious belief. By defining and claiming an ethnic identity, individuals try to place themselves in larger currents of life, try to find a sense of destiny and purpose, and try to get out from under, at least momentarily, the burden of being isolated individuals responsible for their own self-definition and direction at every moment.

The effort to locate and to rest on an identity, grounded in a context bigger than the individual, structures the search for religious belief. The same effort structures the modern search for ethnicity. We have been in the habit of writing about definitions of ethnicity as if we were exploring the mental equivalent of a clubhouse or a political headquarters. And yet, when we explore modern ethnicity, we are in terrain quite a bit closer to a church. The Latter-day Saint movement, Dean May reminds us, "began with a clear purpose—to build an enclave of order, a refuge from the increasingly diverse and individualistic world that modern liberalism had spawned." If the world created by liberalism was disorienting in the 1830s, the disorientation has by no means diminished over time,

and the search for ethnic roots is surely a response to that persistent disorientation. May continues: "The words that Joseph Smith used to express concern
over the distressing world he encountered—'no small stir and division,' 'great
confusion and bad feeling,' 'strife of words . . . and contest about opinions'—
have not lost their resonance or relevance today."[30] Our daily opportunities for
disorientation explain the common response many of us have when we hear of
an ethnicity that might be threatened, an identity that might be about to yield
to geographical dispersal or to the homogenizing forces of the mass media and
market. Even though we know how fruitful in friction and division ethnicity can
be, when we hear of a fading ethnic identity, many of us respond with an
instinctive, "Too bad!" and instantly hope that something can be done to stop
this loss of distinctiveness. Our world remains unsettling and unmoored, and
one cannot cheer when one familiar form of anchorage ceases to hold.

"Ethnicity is, above all, a form of commitment," Orlando Patterson wrote in
his eccentric but thought-provoking *Ethnic Chauvinism*. "It is an ideology, or
more properly, a faith; one that is often secular, but is also frequently a secular
faith layered on a more profound religious faith."[31] The advantage of studying
Mormon history is that ethnicity and religion were never separable. The reminder thus offered to scholars in all fields of ethnicity is that they are required
to proceed with care, respect, and an awareness of the dignity of the people they
study. When they write about ethnicity, scholars are exploring turf close to the
human soul. When Jan Shipps writes about Mormon people, we get one model
of this combination of inquiry with respect. In Shipps, we see the model of the
inquiry from outside, in which the inquirer admits both her distance and her
difference from the people under study but still offers empathy and a recognition of universal human concerns.[32] When Leonard Arrington writes about his
own people, we get another model: the inquiry from inside that recognizes that
one does one's own people no favor if one fudges on their behalf or offers them
something less than a full reckoning with their past.[33] Instead, writers such as
these offer some of the best examples we have of critical inquiry that never com-
promises the dignity of the people they are writing about but instead does them,
or their descendants, the honor of believing that they are prepared to take their
history seriously.

Mormonism, Susan Hendricks Swetnam concluded in her study of Mormon
pioneer life-story writing in Idaho, "is a *live* culture, a culture facing difficult
and integral challenges, rather than a homogenized set of unthinking conform-
ists."[34] Mormon poet Marden J. Clark made a similar point in his memorable
and moving poem, "Wasatch." Clark traced the geological origins of the Wasatch
Range in the movements of faults, tectonic plates, ancient seas, and rising mountains. "What refuge here," Clark asked, "For us as we look up in awe / And love
to these high peaks?" "Whose fault," he asked at the end, "If now these plates
again should stir?"[35]

In human history, there is no "if" about it. The mountains remain, but the conditions change. The context alters. The refuge shifts. The plates stir. The changing patterns of Mormon ethnicity and the current struggles over Mormon identity simultaneously set Latter-day Saints apart and bind them to the rest of humanity. In our understanding of ethnicity, in our distinctive and parallel searches for refuge, we claim our common ground.

Notes

1. Don Phillips, "If the Engine's Burning, Tell the Pilot: A Report Faults a Sometimes Fatal Failure to Communicate," *Washington Post Weekly Edition*, 6–12 June 1994, 32; emphasis mine.

2. Fredrik Barth, "Introduction," in *Ethnic Groups and Boundaries: The Social Organization of Cultural Difference*, ed. Fredrik Barth (Boston: Little, Brown, 1969).

3. Cornel West, *Race Matters* (New York: Random House, 1994), 159.

4. Frederick Jackson Turner, "The Significance of the Frontier in American History," in *The Frontier in American History* (1947; reprint, Tucson: University of Arizona Press, 1986), 8.

5. Ray Allen Billington, *America's Frontier Heritage* (New York: Holt, Rinehart and Winston, 1966). The index contains neither "Utah" nor "Mormonism."

6. F. LaMond Tullis, *Mormons in Mexico: The Dynamics of Faith and Culture* (Logan: Utah State University Press, 1987).

7. Mary C. Waters, *Ethnic Options: Choosing Identities in America* (Berkeley: University of California Press, 1990), 24.

8. Ibid.

9. Ibid., 25.

10. David A. Hollinger, "Postethnic America," *Contention* 2(1) (Fall 1992): 84. See particularly Herbert J. Gans, "Symbolic Ethnicity: The Future of Ethnic Groups and Cultures in America," *Ethnic and Racial Studies* 2(1) (January 1979): 1–20, and Werner Sollors, *Beyond Ethnicity: Consent and Descent in American Culture* (New York: Oxford University Press, 1986).

11. Robert Blauner, *Racial Oppression in America* (New York: Harper & Row, 1972), 117; Hollinger, "Postethnic America," 86.

12. Derrick A. Bell, *Faces at the Bottom of the Well: The Permanence of Racism* (New York: Basic Books, 1992); Jonathan Kozol, *Savage Inequalities: Children in America's Schools* (New York: Crown, 1991); Alex Kotlowitz, *There Are No Children Here: The Story of Two Boys Growing Up in the Other America* (New York: Doubleday, 1991); Brent A. Staples, *Parallel Time: Growing Up in Black and White* (New York: Pantheon, 1994); Nathan McCall, *Makes Me Wanna Holler: A Young Black Man in America* (New York: Random House, 1994); Ellis Cose, *The Rage of a Privileged Class* (New York: Harper Collins, 1993).

13. Andrew Hacker, *Two Nations: Black and White, Separate, Hostile, Unequal* (New York: Charles Scribner's Sons, 1992), 36.

14. Ishmael Reed, "Is Ethnicity Obsolete?", a panel discussion in *The Invention of Ethnicity*, ed. Werner Sollors (New York: Oxford University Press, 1989), 227; Barbara J. Fields, "Ideology and Race in American History," in *Region, Race, and Reconstruction*, ed. J. Morgan Kousser and James M. McPherson (New York: Oxford University Press, 1982), 149.

15. Peter Skerry, *Mexican American: The Ambivalent Minority* (New York: Free Press, 1993), 11; Mario T. Garcia, *Desert Immigrants: The Mexicans of El Paso, 1880–1920* (New Haven, Conn.: Yale University Press, 1981), 2.

16. Leonard J. Arrington, "The Founding of the LDS Church Historical Department, 1972," *Journal of Mormon History* 18(2) (Fall 1992): 41–56; Lavina Fielding Anderson, "The LDS Intellectual Community and Church Leadership: A Contemporary Chronology," *Dialogue: A Journal of Mormon Thought* 26(1) (Spring 1993): 7–64; Paul James Toscano, *The Sanctity of Dissent* (Salt Lake City: Signature Books, 1994); D. Michael Quinn, "On Being a Mormon Historian (and Its Aftermath)," in *Faithful History: Essays on Writing Mormon History,* ed. George D. Smith (Salt Lake City: Signature Books, 1992), 69–111; D. Michael Quinn, "Dilemmas of Feminists and Intellectuals in the Contemporary LDS Church," *Sunstone* 17(1) (June 1994): 67–73. See also D. Michael Quinn, ed., *The New Mormon History: Revisionist Essays on the Past* (Salt Lake City: Signature Books, 1992).

17. Armand L. Mauss, "Mormons as Ethnics: Variable Historical and International Implications of an Appealing Concept," and Keith Parry, "Mormons as Ethnics: A Canadian Perspective," in *The Mormon Presence in Canada,* ed. Brigham Y. Card, Herbert C. Northcutt, John E. Foster, Howard Palmer, and George K. Jarvis (Logan: Utah State University Press, 1990), 329–65.

18. The next few pages are drawn from Thomas G. Alexander, *Mormonism in Transition: A History of the Latter-day Saints, 1890–1930* (Urbana: University of Illinois Press, 1986); Leonard J. Arrington and Davis Bitton, *The Mormon Experience: A History of the Latter-day Saints* (New York: Knopf, 1979); Lawrence Foster, *Religion and Sexuality: The Shakers, the Mormons, and the Oneida Community* (New York: Oxford University Press, 1981); Klaus J. Hansen, *Mormonism and the American Experience* (Chicago: University of Chicago Press, 1981); Marvin S. Hill, *Quest for Refuge: The Mormon Flight from American Pluralism* (Salt Lake City: Signature Books, 1989); Mark P. Leone, *Roots of Modern Mormonism* (Cambridge: Harvard University Press, 1979); Armand L. Mauss, *The Angel and the Beehive: The Mormon Struggle with Assimilation* (Urbana: University of Illinois Press, 1994); Dean L. May, "Mormons," *Harvard Encyclopedia of American Ethnic Groups* (Cambridge: Belknap Press of Harvard University, 1980), 720–31; Thomas F. O'Dea, *The Mormons* (Chicago: University of Chicago Press, 1957); Jan Shipps, *Mormonism: The Story of a New Religious Tradition* (Urbana: University of Illinois Press, 1985); Jan Shipps, "Making Saints: In the Early Days and the Latter Days," in *Contemporary Mormonism,* ed. Marie Cornwall, Tim B. Heaton, and Lawrence A. Young (Urbana: University of Illinois Press, 1994), 64–83; and Jan Shipps, "Change, Change, and More Change: The Latter-day Saints since World War II," copy of paper in my possession.

19. Richard E. Bennett, *Mormons at the Missouri, 1846–1852, "And Should We Die"* (Norman: University of Oklahoma Press, 1987).

20. Shipps, "Making Saints," 69–70.

21. Richard V. Francaviglia, *The Mormon Landscape: Existence, Creation, and Perception of a Unique Image in the American West* (New York: AMS Press, 1978).

22. R. Laurence Moore, "Learning to Play: The Mormon Way and the Way of Other Americans," *Journal of Mormon History* 16 (1990): 89–106.

23. William Mulder, *Homeward to Zion: The Mormon Migration from Scandinavia* (Minneapolis: University of Minnesota Press, 1957). For another illuminating case study

of the relation between European ethnicity and Mormonism, see Frederick Stewart Buchanan, *"A Good Time Coming": Mormon Letters to Scotland* (Salt Lake City: University of Utah Press, 1988).

24. Leonard J. Arrington, *History of Idaho,* 2 vols. (Moscow: University of Idaho Press, 1994), 2:268.

25. See F. LaMond Tullis, ed., *Mormonism: A Faith for All Cultures* (Provo, Utah: Brigham Young University Press, 1978).

26. Stanley B. Kimball, *Heber C. Kimball: Mormon Patriarch and Pioneer* (Urbana: University of Illinois Press, 1981), 268.

27. Maureen Ursenbach Beecher and Lavina Fielding Anderson, eds., *Sisters in Spirit: Mormon Women in Historical and Cultural Perspective* (Urbana: University of Illinois Press, 1987). See also Maxine Hanks, ed., *Women and Authority: Re-emerging Mormon Feminism* (Salt Lake City: Signature Books, 1992).

28. Phyllis Barber, *And the Desert Shall Blossom* (Salt Lake City: Signature Books, 1993); Eugene England, ed., *Bright Angels and Familiars: Contemporary Mormon Stories* (Salt Lake City: Signature Books, 1992); Eugene England and Dennis Clark, *Harvest: Contemporary Mormon Poems* (Salt Lake City: Signature Books, 1989); Lewis Horne, *What Do Ducks Do in Winter? and Other Western Stories* (Salt Lake City: Signature Books, 1993); Levi S. Peterson, *The Canyons of Grace* (Chicago: University of Illinois Press, 1982); Levi S. Peterson, *The Backslider* (Salt Lake City: Signature Books, 1990); Levi S. Peterson, *Night Soil: New Stories* (Salt Lake City: Signature Books, 1990); Levi S. Peterson, ed., *Greening Wheat: Fifteen Mormon Short Stories* (Midvale, Utah: Orion Books, 1983); Douglas H. Thayer, *Under the Cottonwoods and Other Mormon Stories* (ca. 1977; reprint, Midvale, Utah: Orion Books, 1983); Terry Tempest Williams, *Refuge: An Unnatural History of Family and Place* (New York: Pantheon, 1991); and Terry Tempest Williams, *An Unspoken Hunger: Stories from the Field* (New York: Pantheon, 1994). See also studies of Mormon folklore: Hector Lee, *The Three Nephites: The Substance and Significance of the Legend in Folklore* (Albuquerque: University of New Mexico Press, 1949); Austin E. Fife and Alta Stephens Fife, *Saints of Sage and Saddle: Folklore among the Mormons* (1956; reprint, Salt Lake City: University of Utah Press, 1980); Susan Hendricks Swetnam, *Lives of the Saints in Southeast Idaho: An Introduction to Mormon Pioneer Life Story Writing* (Moscow: University of Idaho Press, 1991); and Barre Toelken, "Folklore in the American West," in *A Literary History of the American West* (Fort Worth: Texas Christian University Press, 1987), 29–67.

29. Steven Epstein, "New Directions in Medieval History," paper presented at the National Endowment for the Humanities, Chairman's Forum, Washington, D.C., April 1994. For contemporary applications of this theme, see Stephen L. Carter, *The Culture of Disbelief: How American Law and Politics Trivialize Religious Devotion* (New York: Basic Books, 1993).

30. Dean L. May, "Writing from Within as a Mormon," 4, paper presented at the American Historical Association, January 1994, San Francisco.

31. Orlando Patterson, *Ethnic Chauvinism: The Reactionary Impulse* (New York: Stein and Day, 1977), 10.

32. Lawrence Foster and Mario De Pillis also fit in this category. Lawrence Foster, "A Personal Odyssey: My Encounter with Mormon History," *Dialogue: A Journal of Mormon Thought* 16(3) (Autumn 1983): 87–98, is a particularly telling reflection on this topic.

33. Others who have joined Arrington in this approach are too numerous to mention. See the already cited Quinn, *The New Mormon History,* and Beecher and Anderson, *Sisters in Spirit.*

34. Swetnam, *Lives of the Saints,* 120.

35. Marden J. Clark, "Wasatch," in England and Clark, *Harvest,* 19.

CHAPTER 12

Mormon Women, Other Women: Paradoxes and Challenges

Anne Firor Scott

My title allows so many possibilities, all interesting, that I should begin by defining my terms. The "Mormon women" of this particular discussion are those Maureen Ursenbach Beecher has called the "leading sisters" of the nineteenth century, those who established and led the various Relief Societies and their associated organizations, beginning in Nauvoo in 1842. As daughters, sisters, and wives of the leading men of the Church, they constituted a small, visible elite, recognized and looked up to by Mormon women generally. Most of them were plural wives.[1]

The "other women" of my title also represent an elite, but not a small one. They were the women in the United States at large who organized and ran the thousands of women's voluntary associations through which nineteenth-century women shaped a public role for themselves.

These two groups of women shared roots. The first generation of both grew up, broadly speaking, in the same culture. At the time the Church of Jesus Christ of Latter-day Saints was organized, the prevailing ideology of gender in the United States was built on the doctrine of separate spheres. The male sphere was public and encompassed wage labor, the professions, government, business, and higher education. Woman's sphere was the private world of the home, child raising, and moral authority. Women were thought to be pious, compassionate, and intuitive by nature; men were said to have stronger minds. Wives were expected to obey their husbands—or, in the absence of a husband, a father or brother.

This division of function was supported with evidence from the Bible and was reinforced from the pulpit, the lecture platform, the popular novel, and scores of advice books. It was built into the law that women could not vote, hold office, sit on juries, or, if married, own property, unless by special dispensation. The division was also embodied in social custom. Women were not expected to hold high positions in any church, to go to college, to practice law, or to speak in public.

Women's status and experience in any society is always shaped by at least three things: the prevailing ideology of sex roles, the actual conditions of life, and the presence or absence of a demand for equality on the part of women themselves. In the United States in 1830, despite the uniformity of ideology, the conditions of women's lives varied widely, depending on region, class, race, ethnicity, and degree of affluence. A demand for "women's rights" was barely beginning to be articulated. The degree to which the ideology matched actual practice varied widely.

When the followers of Joseph Smith broke away from the dominant American culture and began to form their own unique subculture, they took with them the ideology of separate spheres and male superiority. Mormon theology was avowedly patriarchal and invested the custom of male domination with divine sanction. While Protestants everywhere relied on biblical sanction for female subordination, Mormon theology went a step further: men were defined as members of a priesthood whose authority over women was not to be questioned.

Because Mormon women and other American women started out, so to speak, together and then took different roads, the two groups present an unusual opportunity for comparison. If one asks what difference the different roads made, the fact that both groups of women organized and developed all-woman associations for a variety of purposes provides a well-defined focus for analysis. Was the experience of Mormon women in their voluntary associations markedly different from that of other women in the thousands of associations that, by the end of the nineteenth century, had come to dominate community life in every part of the country? Even a tentative effort to answer this question takes us into interesting speculations about the importance of ideology in shaping women's experience and in their progress toward emancipation and equality.

Let us look first at the broader picture, at women's associations in American society generally. Thirty years before Joseph Smith's first revelations, women had already begun to organize. In the 1790s, following patterns long since established by American men, they began to develop their own groups, first for the care of poor widows and orphans. Before long their concerns broadened to include the poor of either sex. Groups calling themselves by various names, but known generically as benevolent societies, began to spring up in the cities, towns, and villages. Then came women's missionary societies and, in quick succession, temperance, education, and moral reform associations. By the 1830s, when Mormonism appeared on the scene, women were forming the first all-female anti-slavery societies.

As the westward movement accelerated in the 1840s, women replicated their eastern experience in new communities. While men organized business and government, women took responsibility for establishing churches, schools, and welfare institutions.[2]

In the beginning, women's societies seemed so clearly to reflect the values attributed to women—compassionate care for the poor, concern for the morals of the family and the community—that hardly anybody realized just how subversive of the conventional scheme of male-female relations they might become.

The Civil War brought a vast increase in opportunity for women on both sides of the conflict to take public responsibility, especially in the North in the context of the United States Sanitary Commission. By the time the war ended, many women had had experience handling large budgets, organizing and transporting a massive volume of supplies, going themselves into highly dangerous situations—in short, exercising the kinds of public power that the ideology reserved for men.

It was a heady experience, and when the war ended, many women hoped to continue in what they modestly called a "wider sphere of usefulness." The rapid increase in population and the extreme mobility of the last half of the century, the growth in industry and cities, and the influx of immigrants all created new social challenges that ambitious women seized as opportunities. At the same time, more women were going to college, and the number of self-confident women, accustomed to thinking for themselves, began to increase.

In the midst of all this social change, a new wave of women's organizations took shape. They appeared in large towns and small, even in country villages: literary clubs for self-education, educational societies for founding women's colleges, working-women's societies to help wage earners, the vast Women's Christian Temperance Union with its "do everything" reform program, two national suffrage associations, settlement houses, educational and industrial unions, and so on and on. Each of these groups had a social agenda. Many of them undertook to create various other social institutions: schools, kindergartens, juvenile courts, school lunch programs, parks and playgrounds, public health programs, immigrants' protective associations, libraries, homes for orphans and for aged women, symphony orchestras, trade unions, museums—to name a few.

When the great Columbian Exposition opened in Chicago in 1893, women from all over the country came to demonstrate their varied public activities and to share enthusiasm and ideas, and they went home reinvigorated. The General Federation of Women's Clubs had almost a million members, and astute observers were characterizing the nineteenth century as the "woman's century." By this they probably referred to two things. First, women had visibly and in important ways begun to change community and social life all over the United States. In ten more years, a member of Congress would announce to his colleagues that "This is fast becoming a government of the women, for the women's views, and by the women's clubs."[3] Second, they meant the extraordinary change in women's status and in the prevailing ideology, brought about largely by their own efforts. One great driving force behind this remarkable change in the status and experience of women had been the voluntary associations, organized by and for women.

In the early twentieth century, the momentum of women organizing on their own behalf continued to grow and, by 1920, had modified the Constitution to make women full voting citizens, had opened wider the doors to education and the professions, and had provided a tool with which newly enfranchised women were able to exercise far-reaching political influence.[4]

Meanwhile, as this dramatic story was being played out from Boston to San Francisco, from Seattle to St. Augustine, and almost everywhere in between, what had been happening among the Mormons?

When Joseph Smith organized the Church of Jesus Christ of Latter-day Saints, he did more than offer a new theology. He laid the groundwork for what would rapidly become an unusual subculture, one that was destined to be quite different in some essential ways from the dominant American culture. Contrary to American custom, church and state were one. The authority of the men who ran this theocracy was seen to be of divine origin. Like other Americans, Mormons believed in separate spheres for men and women, but in their case the separation was at once more stringent in ideology and less stringent in everyday life than elsewhere. In theory and in theology, men were responsible for all public life, and in private life they were expected to rule their families. At the same time, the exigencies of the Mormon situation required women to be in charge when men were away, as they so frequently were, on Church business. Plural wives were often expected to earn their own keep and take full responsibility for their own children. The makings of a paradox are already evident. More was expected of Mormon women than of almost any other women in the country, but at the same time their responsibility to obey members of the priesthood was unquestioned. The practical demands on Mormon women grew during the first half century of the Church's existence. Theirs was the typical frontier experience made more rigorous by persecution, financial stringency, and the extraordinary challenge of settling in a most inhospitable environment.

In spite of all these pressures, Mormon women of the first generation, which included many converts from New England and upstate New York where women's associations had long flourished, moved rather quickly to establish a Female Relief Society. The first meeting, initiated by a woman, took place in Nauvoo in 1842. Joseph Smith made it a point to be there and advised the women as to how they should proceed. He encouraged the formation of a society "under the priesthood and after the pattern of the priesthood." He recognized ways in which such a group might be quite useful but was careful from the start to keep it under control. The choice of Emma Smith for president and other women close to Joseph Smith as counselors established a pattern that would continue for many years. From the fragmentary evidence about that first effort at organization, we may tentatively infer, first, that Joseph Smith saw a women's organization as a useful conduit through which Church policy would be carried to the members; second, that with the revelation about plural marriage in mind he particularly saw the need of female support; and, third, that he wanted to be sure that the women in charge were those he could trust. He told the sisters that they should seek to improve the morals of the community and thereby "save the elders the trouble of rebuking; that they may give their time to other duties."[5] The most important part of this early encounter between the women and the Prophet was that some of those who were there (and some present-day scholars agree) believed that Joseph Smith saw the organization as a parallel to the priesthood, or even as conferring priesthood status upon women.[6] Though this interpretation was never widely accepted, the leading women referred to it often in years to come.

The Relief Society not only undertook to care for the poor in the familiar pattern of the benevolent society but also contributed in various practical ways to the building of the Nauvoo Temple. The membership grew rapidly, from twenty-six to more than a thousand members, and in a short time the society took its first public stand when it petitioned the governor of Illinois to protect Joseph Smith from certain lawsuits then pending against him.[7] The society continued to be active during 1843, "forwarding the temple and relieving the wants of the poor." In a slight portent of things to come, one member resigned because she felt that the women were "taking the bishops' place in looking after the poor and soliciting donations."[8] In March 1844, what turned out to be the last recorded meeting of this first Relief Society was held. It has been suggested that Emma Smith's opposition to the practice of plural marriage had something to do with putting an abrupt end to the women's meetings, but in any case, by June of that year, Joseph Smith was dead and every hand in the community had to be turned to the problem of survival.

There were a few women's meetings in Winter Quarters, some for sewing and quilting, some for prayer, and some for various spiritual exercises. The revelation about polygamy, though not yet public, was already being followed by a few people, and plural wives began tentatively to discuss the matter with each other.[9] In later years, one important function of women's meetings would be that of supporting each other as they tried to learn how to live in polygamy.

Once the Saints were settled in the Great Basin, women's meetings began again. As early as 1851, a Female Council of Health heard lectures by physicians about health care and dress reform. Representatives of this group worked in all but two of the nineteen wards in Salt Lake City, caring for the health needs of poor people. As time went by, concern for the needs of Indians was added to their general responsibility for the poor. By 1854 there were twenty-two Indian Relief Societies, and during the Utah War (1857–58), women's groups were called upon to help clothe the army. In 1857, Sarah Melissa Granger Kimball was elected president of a Relief Society in the Fifteenth Ward of Salt Lake City. It is some indication of the strength of the women's desire to work together that so many groups were formed in the midst of the struggles of the 1850s.[10]

By the 1860s it was clear that Mormon society would survive and that its numbers were increasing rapidly. Each new outlying settlement meant more work to be done. At the same time, the completion of the transcontinental railroad brought with it a whole new set of challenges. One was the danger that money needed for capital accumulation and the creation of a viable economy would be spent importing goods from the east. Another was the threat of vastly increased non-Mormon settlement in Utah.

Contemplating this situation, Brigham Young decided that it was time to again make the women's Relief Societies a formal part of the Church structure. The bishops were told to set up units in every ward, and the redoubtable Eliza R. Snow, a widow of Joseph Smith and a plural wife of Brigham Young himself, was put in charge of the whole project.[11] Here as in so many aspects of early Mormon history, Brigham Young was a key figure. On the one hand, his views about the women were clear: they should obey their husbands and do as they were told. His advice to a young man was quite in character: "fit you up a little log cabin, if it is not more than ten feet square, and then get you a bird to put in your little cage. You can then work all day with satisfaction to yourself, considering that you have a home to go to, and a loving heart to welcome you."[12] But so too was his statement that "We believe that women are useful, not only to sweep houses, wash dishes, make beds, and raise babies, but that they should stand behind the counter, study law or physics [medicine], or become good bookkeepers and be able to do the business in any counting house, and all this to enlarge their sphere of usefulness for the benefit of society at large. In following these things they but answer the design of their creation."[13]

Believing firmly that men should make major decisions and that wives should always obey their husbands, he nevertheless saw clearly that the great utopian experiment could not succeed unless he used every scrap of talent available, so he praised and encouraged women and gave Eliza R. Snow a great deal of responsibility for bringing the women's energy to bear on some of his major projects.[14] As a Mormon scholar noted in 1942, Mormon thinking about women has been determined by two major forces: the Scriptures of the Church and the interpretation of those Scriptures by Church leaders, on the one hand, and the actual historical situation at various points in the Church's history.[15] This was one of the times when the needs of the historical situation and the interpretation of Brigham Young clearly overrode the formal tenets of theology.

It is not clear that Young's views were altogether shared by every bishop. For example, the minutes of the Fifteenth Ward Relief Society for January 1868 note that "Brother Bywater . . . [made] some lengthy remarks upon the good and evil that would result from Female gatherings and [he] believed that the good that will result from the Female Relief Society would overbalance the evil." Unfortunately, the secretary did not spell out just what evil the good brother feared, but she did note that he closed with "good exhortations to the sisters." From the record, it is clear that Mormon women had considerable tolerance for male exhortation; whether they were guided by it all is another matter.

In the early meetings of this particular Relief Society, Sarah Kimball, who had been chosen president, made it quite clear (though in diplomatic language) that she wanted the sisters to be as independent as possible. She had thought, she said, of asking the brothers for assistance but concluded that they had enough to do and that the women should learn to raise their own money. Women are inventive, she argued, and what they understood they could carry out.[16]

In St. George at about the same time, another bishop made his anxiety even more explicit: when it came to helping the poor, he said, the sisters could provide clothing but the dispensing of flour, meat, and so forth "is the responsibility of the Bishops. . . . Anytime you need help ask my brethren here to help you out." He was evidently fearful of allowing any male prerogative to be exercised by the women, for fear, I suppose, that one thing might lead to another.[17]

As local Relief Societies were formed, the bishops designated which women were to be officers—often members of their own families—and while the men fretted about giving women too much freedom, Brigham Young gave them big jobs to do. When the women proposed to found their own journal, with his great-niece Lula Greene as editor, he approved. The *Woman's Exponent* began publishing in 1870 and was soon bringing women all over the Great Basin in touch with each other.

The women were called upon to undertake vital tasks—building and managing cooperative stores, raising money for the Perpetual Emigration Fund, initiating silk culture, organizing the Deseret Silk Association, saving grain, developing home industries, promoting the United Order, organizing the younger women as well as themselves into "retrenchment societies" (as part of the effort to preserve capital), teaching children, and helping young women to go to medical school. By 1888 the Relief Society General Board owned land and buildings worth $95,000. They did all these things and more and, in the process, came to insist upon controlling the institutions they were creating.[18]

The grain storage program is a good example. Taking on the demanding task of collecting grain all over the territory and arranging for its storage against a day of famine, once a program was in place, the sisters assumed it was theirs to control. When local bishops assumed otherwise, the women stood on their rights and appealed to the General Authorities, who instructed the bishops to mind their manners and ask the women for grain when they needed it.[19]

The Relief Society did not confine itself to projects suggested by the priesthood. On its own initiative, the society built, staffed, and ran a hospital and a school for midwives, as well as a nursing school. Money was raised to help women secure training. Local societies undertook many forms of public service as need arose, including building libraries and kindergartens. In the process, members learned, as did their counterparts in other parts of the country, to run organizations, manage money, and speak on their feet. Their confidence improved accordingly.[20] Eliza R. Snow told the sisters in 1877 that their work in home industries "was doing just as much as an Elder who went forth to preach the Gospel."[21] For a time, power followed function, and the Relief Society grew in autonomy.

The right to vote, which Utah women were second in the nation to secure, was to some extent a gift from the male hierarchy. This did not mean, however, that Mormon women were indifferent about suffrage. In February 1870 the Fifteenth Ward Relief Society met to consider retrenchment and other matters, and several members spoke about the recent achievement. Eliza Snow suggested that a committee be set up to thank the governor for signing the bill (as the society had urged him to do). Then Sarah Kimball said that she had waited patiently for a long time for this event and, now that it had occurred, she was ready to, as the minutes put it, "openly declare herself a woman's rights woman, and called for those who would to back her up. Whereupon many manifested their approval." She went on to talk about the prejudice that women would have to overcome now that they were to be in public life.[22] Relief Society women were soon taking an active part in territorial politics, educating themselves as they went along.

Both suffrage and Relief Society work had results that Brigham Young, for all his foresight, had not envisioned. Having gotten the right to vote themselves, Relief Society women became strong supporters of the national suffrage movement, and Sarah Kimball became a vice president of one of the suffrage associations. If the pages of the *Woman's Exponent* may be taken as valid evidence, by the late 1870s the leading sisters were strong feminists who were thoroughly in touch with the women's movement in the rest of the country.

The *Exponent* itself developed in a direction perhaps not foreseen. Its masthead carried the slogan: "The Rights of the Women of Zion and the Rights of Women of all Nations." Emmeline B. Wells, its second editor, described the journal as "power in the hands of women."[23] From the very beginning the editors offered their readers a great deal of information about the women's rights movement as it was developing in the larger society. Nearly every question that agitated women's rights advocates elsewhere was discussed: dress reform, health, women's right to speak in public, equal pay, and opportunities for higher education. Women's accomplishments, large and small, were enthusiastically reported. The radical wing of the suffrage movement came in for repeated praise: Stanton and Anthony were viewed as heroines. In 1883, Emmeline Wells spoke of their influence: "[The] seed was planted in my soul by reading *The Revolution*

[Stanton and Anthony's radical journal]. . . . I could never have done the work I have done in this territory had it not been for the work Miss Anthony did before me."[24]

The *Exponent,* while recognizing the demands that plural marriage made on women, usually treated polygamy as a feminist cause. Over and over, a spirited defense of the institution was based on its capacity to liberate women and help them develop independence. Emmeline Wells's statement was typical: "[It] gives women the highest opportunities for self development, exercise of judgment, and arouses latent faculties, making them more truly cultivated in the actual realities of life, more independent in thought and mind, noble and unselfish."[25] Edward Tullidge commented in 1881 that the men at first had looked on the *Exponent* as a mere women's whim, harmless to be sure. But now, he said, it "wields more real power in our politics than all of the newspapers in Utah put together."[26]

Viewing all this activity and strong-minded behavior, it is not surprising to find the Mormon women at the Columbian Exposition taking a full part in that great whirl of woman-centered activity, sharing ideas and enthusiasm with women from all parts of the country. Back home in Utah after this encounter with other women leaders, activist women were almost immediately drawn into a battle to restore woman suffrage (which the Edmunds-Tucker Act had abolished in 1887). In 1895 the two political parties were engaged in electing delegates to a constitutional convention; both wooed potential women voters. The women, who demanded pledges of support for suffrage, made sure those pledges were remembered when the convention met. Orson F. Whitney, a leading Mormon, lived up to his pledge, arguing that "it is woman's destiny to have a voice in the affairs of government. . . . This great social upheaval, this woman's movement is making itself felt and heard." The result, he said, would justify "woman's participation in the great cause of reform." Brigham H. Roberts, another leading Mormon, argued with equal vigor on the other side, calling up all the familiar antifeminist arguments and telling women that they would unsex themselves and lose control of the "domestic empire" if they were able to vote.[27] (He did not explain why this dire result had not followed during the twenty-seven years that Mormon women voters had taken an active part in territorial affairs.)

The suffragists won and immediately afterward elected three women to the new state legislature, the best known of whom was a Democrat, Martha Hughes Cannon, the first woman in the United States to be elected to a state senate. A medical doctor and a longtime suffragist, she was a plural wife whose husband had also run in the same open primary and had been defeated. She had spoken at the Columbian Exposition and had strong ties with the national women's rights movement. Cannon's career in the legislature was a forecast of things to come. Her legislative work centered on public health, children's needs, education, and the problems of working women, subjects that would form the agenda of hundreds of women legislators after national suffrage was adopted in 1920.[28]

Looking back from 1900 over the fifty preceding years, we would have to agree with Maureen Beecher that during that time "women were their own acknowledged and unquestioned leaders. With operational power thus vested in a cohesive group of faithful, conscientious women, it is not surprising that they and their sisters contributed so remarkably to the political, educational, economic and social well being of the Mormon community and of the Intermountain West."[29]

If this analysis stopped in 1900, the conclusion would have to be that neither ideology nor formal male domination does much to alter the fundamental thrust of women's voluntary associations or the consequences of their existence for the society and for the women who take part. Leaders among Mormon women, while always giving lip service to the notion of woman's sphere, contributed to Mormon society in ways that they and others thought were as essential as the contributions of the priesthood. Working in their own groups, they developed self-confidence and exercised initiative, as did women in similar groups elsewhere. To be sure, the bishops came around and gave advice, but the women looked to their own officers for guidance. Woman's work was central to the success of the Mormon enterprise, and Church leaders told them so. In 1892, Joseph F. Smith praised the women in a speech full of strong statements about the inherent equality of male and female. "[W]hy shall one [sex] enjoy civil rights and the other be denied them?" he asked rhetorically.[30] Orson Whitney's speech to the constitutional convention was in the same vein. But even as he spoke, things were beginning to change. Brigham H. Roberts's speech provided a better forecast of the future than that of Whitney, as he called upon "Christian wives and mothers" to "retain that [domestic] empire, shun the political arena, avoid the rostrum, beware of unsexing yourselves. If you become embroiled in political agitation the queenly aureola that encircles your brow will fade away and the reverence that is paid you will disappear."[31] It was a far cry from Brigham Young.

In 1906 the same Joseph F. Smith who in 1892 had spoken so firmly about women's equality, now Church president, began to talk about the need for strengthening the priesthood as the governing body of the Church. He launched a reform movement for that purpose. Though the centralization that followed was general and applied to all the auxiliaries, it had the effect of restricting women and giving greater power to men.[32] Since 1896, women of the Relief Society General Board had been working to raise money for a building of their own. By the time the money was in hand, however, they were told that the bishops and several other groups would occupy the building with them. Whatever the intent (perhaps it was simply an economy move), to the women it was bound to seem like a renewed effort to keep tabs on their activities.

The question of women's precise spiritual role in the Church was also an issue. For many years women had practiced the spiritual functions of washing and anointing and of blessing and healing the sick. As we saw earlier, some women had obliquely argued that certain priestly functions belonged to women, acquired either through marriage or through Joseph Smith's words to the first Relief Society in Nauvoo, or both. For years some sisters had worried about these matters: just what could they and could they not do as good Mormons? In the mid-1890s, according to Ruth May Fox, later general president of the Young Women's Mutual Improvement Association, Zina Diantha Jacobs Smith Young, a plural wife of both Joseph Smith and Brigham Young and also Relief Society General President (1888–1901), had been asked whether women did indeed hold the priesthood in connection with their husbands. Her response was that "we should be thankful for the many blessings we enjoyed and say nothing about it. If you planted a grain of wheat and keep poking and looking at it to see if it was growing you would spoil the root."[33] Nevertheless, some women persisted in asking for guidance, and of course what they heard was that they could not consider themselves part of the priesthood.[34] Zina Young had been quite right: it would have been better not to ask.

Mormon women had never failed to take motherhood seriously. Yet in 1902, in what appears to have been an effort to reemphasize the doctrine of separate spheres, "mothers' classes" were initiated by the Relief Society, and by 1914 a plan of study on this subject was prepared that all the individual stakes were required to use. Progressive era women outside the Mormon community talked a great deal about motherhood at about this time—but for the purpose of arguing that their responsibility as mothers demanded that they undertake public efforts to improve the communities in which their children were growing up. The Relief Society materials concentrated instead on what mothers should do within their homes. In 1915 the independently owned *Exponent* closed down, and the *Relief Society Magazine*, owned by the society and therefore under the control of the Church, took its place. In 1916 the Relief Society visiting teachers, who for many years had been free to decide for themselves what they would talk about as they visited neighboring families, began to be instructed as to what they should say. Where were all these decisions being made? Surely not by the women alone.

In the early 1920s, in what must have seemed to some old-timers like a return to the good old days, the Relief Society joined other women's associations across the country, first in lobbying for the passage of the Sheppard-Towner Act for Maternal and Infant Health, and then in carrying out the statewide program that was required by the law.[35] In spite of this piece of contrary evidence, however, it seems clear that from the turn of the century, the independence and initiative of Relief Society women—the key women leaders in Mormon life—were under siege.[36] The society continued to do important work, but more and more it was drawn under the umbrella of Church policy. The women were no longer setting their own agenda.

This, then, is the puzzle: during the middle and late nineteenth century when powerful American public men had, for the most part, been adamantly antifeminist, Mormon leaders, beginning with Brigham Young, had been, at a minimum, ambivalent about and, at a maximum, supportive of strong, independent women. Through the years from 1850 to the turn of the century, the leading sisters in the Great Basin had been in step with or slightly in advance of the most advanced feminists in the country and had generally been accepted as such by those feminists. Emmeline Wells and Sarah Kimball deserve a place in the feminist pantheon along with Susan B. Anthony and Elizabeth Cady Stanton.

Then, just as American feminism generally was getting into high gear for its extraordinary push during the years 1900–1920, just as the new generation of college-educated women was moving to the fore in the suffrage associations, just as one state after another was moving into the suffrage column—in short, just as legal and social emancipation came to be a real possibility for many American women—Mormon women fell back. The male leaders of the Church changed their stance, and apparently, despite private bitterness, there was no public outcry from the women.

If this description is accurate, the central question is, Why did it happen that way? It is a question that has been raised by laypersons and historians alike, and the motivation for finding an answer is high among non-Mormons as well as Mormons.

The materials for seeking an answer are numerous. The Church is, of course, known for its concern for historical records, and primary sources abound. A large and growing body of writing on the history of Mormon women provides the beginning point. The answer is likely to be found, I think, not in one cause but in multiple causes, perhaps reinforcing each other. Let me suggest some of the places we might begin to look.

One obvious subject for examination is the Church's general ideological development after polygamy was outlawed and statehood achieved, and how that development affected women. Several historians have seen these two events as marking a dramatic change in Mormon life, including a turn away from the dreams of a utopian community and toward much more traditional economic goals. If that was the case, what were the precise implications for women?

Another subject for study might be called the generation question. The characters of the first generation of leading sisters were forged in a demanding frontier society. The Darwinian selection that always accompanied frontier settlement was perhaps more stringent among the Mormons than among most other settlers—and those who survived were likely to be the strongest and most independent, female as well as male.

Part of the generation question also has to do with converts. I understand that a large demographic study is under way among Church historians. Perhaps when it is finished, patterns of conversion will emerge. Were there marked differences in the kinds of people who joined the Church in its early, utopian days compared to those who joined when it had become a going concern? Did the people attracted to the Church after 1900 have belief systems that were likely to include a conservative view of women's roles?

Still another quite fascinating part of the generation question has to do with Mormon men. Brigham Young was a vital factor in the early development of women's leading part in Mormon society. Has anyone, I wonder, looked carefully at the presidents who followed him to analyze the evolution of their views on the woman question? Certainly it seems clear that by the time of the grain storage controversy during the First World War, when Emmeline Wells's name was signed to a document without her knowledge and the women's grain was given away without their consent, the General Authorities were no longer following the pattern laid down by Brigham Young.[37]

Then there was polygamy. In certain ways plural wives had, as they often argued, unusual opportunities for developing independence. I think—to choose one example—of Ellis Reynolds Shipp going off to study medicine in Philadelphia, encouraged by Brigham Young, financed by the Relief Society and her sister wives, leaving her children for those same sister wives to raise. Her career as a medical doctor, builder of medical institutions, trainer of midwives, and pioneer in so many ways would have been difficult, perhaps impossible, had she been her husband's only wife. The Relief Society president of the Salt Lake Stake wrote that the plural wife "became freer and can do herself individually things she never could have attempted before; and work out her individual character separate from her husband." Martha Hughes Cannon was quoted in the *San Francisco Examiner* as saying that "if her husband has four wives she had three weeks of freedom every single month." Many other similar quotations could be cited. It is significant that nearly all of the leading sisters of the first two generations were plural wives.

Perhaps polygamy figures in another way. As long as it was the received doctrine of the Church, it was absolutely essential to the survival of the community that women not become disaffected. During most of the late nineteenth century, the Mormon community was under attack by the federal government as well as by American public opinion on this issue. Had women apostatized in great numbers, the whole enterprise would have been doomed. From the point of view of the General Authorities, then, it was vital to have strong-minded women leaders who would speak up for the institution—and one way to do that was to give such leaders a chance to develop, to make them an integral part of the enterprise. Was this the explanation for the fact that the *Exponent* was permitted to take such radical stands? Once polygamy was ended, the women's support was no longer so vital. Coincidentally, perhaps, the *Exponent* soon disappeared, to be replaced by a journal controlled by the Church.

The most difficult part of the question I have posed is this: why did the very kinds of activity and experience that had prepared other American women to move rapidly toward emancipation apparently cease to work that way for Mormon women? Why did a group of leaders who had enjoyed a considerable measure of informal power and of independence, who had made themselves into significant characters, accept the restrictions that were gradually placed upon them? Why did they disengage from the national networks of women and go off in a different direction from those with whom they had once been so much in step—or, indeed, whom they had once led?

Some of the points I have raised about the change itself bear upon this issue as well. Perhaps the new generation was made up of different kinds of people, either because their experience had been less rigorous or because patterns of recruitment had changed—or both.

One hypothesis worth investigating would take us again to the comparative approach. American women in general have always faced a great deal of opposition when they have tried to change the structure of male-female relations. There is nothing Mormon leaders have said or done in this regard that could not be replicated in some record of non-Mormon men. We have only to recall the solemn words of the Supreme Court telling Myra Bradwell that she could not be admitted to the bar because God had designated men to apply and execute the laws, or the numerous heated debates in Congress with their dire prophecies of ruin if women voted.

The difference was that feminists who were not Mormons were free to fight back, and they had a variety of precepts available with which to counter antifeminist arguments. They could put the Declaration of Independence up against Saint Paul. The logic of the phrase "all men are created equal and endowed by their creator with certain inalienable rights," though it applied in 1776 to a minority of Americans, was in the end bound to work itself out. The very pluralism of American society gave women many grounds upon which to stand and fight.

Mormon women, by contrast, had no alternative doctrine. Mormon theology was the ideology of the government and of the community. That theology was wholly controlled by men. Since women are not admitted to the priesthood, there have been no women prophets. When the General Authorities began to practice overt antifeminism, devout Mormon women had no choice but to obey or to apostatize, which few wanted to do.[38]

Mormon women could, of course, have simply asserted their right to be part of the priesthood, to have general revelations. If any did so, I have not seen the record. So far as I know, there was no Mormon counterpart of Elizabeth Cady Stanton's *Woman's Bible* or of the secular *Declaration of Sentiments* adopted at Seneca Falls.

My task as I have defined it here is historical. I have not looked beyond 1920. But the questions are not of merely antiquarian interest, for our whole society is now in the midst of one of the periodic waves of antifeminism that seem to follow anytime women make great strides. This so-called backlash is most apparent in the defeat and seeming death of the Equal Rights Amendment, but it comes to the fore in many ways in small communities and large. Analysis of the past that will help us understand under what conditions women move toward equality and when they are pushed back from it is potentially of great significance to all of us who believe, with those women of 1848, that "all men and women are created equal and endowed by their creator with certain inalienable rights."

Notes

1. Maureen Ursenbach Beecher, "The 'Leading Sisters': A Female Hierarchy in Nineteenth Century Mormon Society," *Journal of Mormon History* 9 (1982): 26–39. D. Michael Quinn, "The Mormon Hierarchy 1832–1932: An American Elite" (PhD diss., Yale University, 1976), provides information about the group from which these women came.

2. See Nancy A. Hewitt, *Women's Activism and Social Change: Rochester, New York, 1822–1872* (Ithaca, N.Y.: Cornell University Press, 1984), for a fine description of this phenomenon in one community. Anne Firor Scott, *Making the Invisible Woman Visible*, Part II, "Voluntary Associations" (Champaign: University of Illinois Press, 1984), 259–94, provides a broad overview of the movement. See also Mary P. Ryan, *Cradle of the Middle Class: The Family in Oneida County, New York, 1790–1865* (New York: Cambridge University Press, 1981); Carroll Smith Rosenberg, *Religion and the Rise of the City: The New York City Mission Movement, 1812–1870* (Ithaca, N.Y.: Cornell University Press, 1971); and Barbara J. Berg, *The Remembered Gate: Origins of American Feminism—The Woman and the City, 1800–1860* (New York: Oxford University Press, 1978).

3. Mary I. Wood, *The History of the General Federation of Women's Clubs* (New York: General Federation of Women's Clubs, 1912), 206.

4. See Anne F. Scott and Andrew M. Scott, *One-Half the People: The Fight for Woman Suffrage*, 2nd ed. (Urbana: University of Illinois Press, 1982). J. Stanley Lemons, *The Woman Citizen: Social Feminism in the 1920s* (Champaign: University of Illinois Press, 1973), documents the political effectiveness of women in the 1920s, but much research on this subject remains to be done.

5. Relief Society Minutes, 17 March 1842, quoted in *A Centenary of Relief Society, 1842–1942* (Salt Lake City: General Board of Relief Society, 1942), 15.

6. Carol Cornwall Madsen, "Mormon Women and the Struggle for Definition," *Dialogue: A Journal of Mormon Thought* 14(4) (Winter 1981): 40–47.

7. *A Centenary of Relief Society, 1842–1942*, 16–17.

8. Ibid., 17.

9. Maureen Ursenbach Beecher, "Women at Winter Quarters," *Sunstone* 8(3) (July–August 1983): 11–29.

10. Richard L. Jensen, "Forgotten Relief Societies, 1844–67," *Dialogue: A Journal of Mormon Thought* 16(1) (Spring 1983): 105–25; Jill C. Mulvay, "The Liberal Shall Be Blessed: Sarah M. Kimball," *Utah Historical Quarterly* 44(3) (Summer 1976): 205–21.

11. Leonard J. Arrington, *Great Basin Kingdom: An Economic History of the Latter-day Saints, 1830–1900* (Cambridge: Harvard University Press, 1952), 251–52; and his *Brigham Young: American Moses* (New York: Knopf, 1985), 351.

12. Quoted in Arrington, *Brigham Young,* 302.

13. Ibid., 339.

14. Snow's own independence and self-image may be inferred from the fact that she still called herself Snow, not Smith or Young. Her talents were formidable and, had she been male, might well have led her into the First Presidency.

15. Ileen Ann Waspe LeCheminant, "The Status of Women in the Philosophy of Mormonism from 1830 to 1845" (Master's thesis, Brigham Young University, 1942).

16. Fifteenth Ward, Relief Society, Minutes, 18 September 1873, Church Archives, Church of Jesus Christ of Latter-day Saints, Salt Lake City (hereafter LDS Church Archives).

17. St. George Ward, Relief Society, LDS Church Archives.

18. All these projects and many others are recorded in successive issues of *Woman's Exponent,* 1873–90. See also Mulvay, "The Liberal Shall Be Blessed," 214–15.

19. Jessie L. Embry, "Grain Storage: The Balance of Power between Priesthood Authority and Relief Society Autonomy," *Dialogue: A Journal of Mormon Thought* 15(4) (Winter 1982): 59–66. Embry's article traces the gradual decline in women's control over their own institutions, but in the 1870s and 1980s, they managed well.

20. "Woman Against Woman," *Woman's Exponent* 7 (1 May 1879): 234.

21. "R. S. Reports," *Woman's Exponent* 6 (15 November 1877): 94.

22. Ladies Cooperative Retrenchment Society, Minutes, Saturday, 19 February 1870, LDS Church Archives. See also Mulvay, "The Liberal Shall Be Blessed," 218–19.

23. Sherilyn Cox Bennion, "The *Woman's Exponent*: Forty-Two Years of Speaking for Women," *Utah Historical Quarterly* 44(3) (Summer 1976): 222–39.

24. Emmeline B. Wells, *Woman's Exponent* (15 September 1883).

25. "Woman Against Woman," 234.

26. Bennion, "The *Woman's Exponent,*" 231.

27. Jean Bickmore White, "Woman's Place Is in the Constitution: The Struggle for Equal Rights in Utah in 1895," *Utah Historical Quarterly* 42 (Fall 1974): 344–69, and her "Gentle Persuaders: Utah's First Women Legislators," *Utah Historical Quarterly* 38(1) (Winter 1970): 31–49.

28. White, "Gentle Persuaders," 43–49.

29. Beecher, "Leading Sisters," 39.

30. Maureen Ursenbach Beecher, Carol Cornwall Madsen, and Jill Mulvay Derr, "The Latter-day Saints and Women's Rights, 1870–1920: A Brief Survey," *Task Papers in LDS History,* no. 29 (Salt Lake City: Historical Department, Church of Jesus Christ of Latter-day Saints, 1979), 13.

31. White, "Gentle Persuaders," 36.

32. Embry, "Grain Storage," 59–60.

33. Linda King Newell, "A Gift Given, A Gift Taken: Washing, Anointing, and Blessing the Sick among Mormon Women," *Sunstone* 6(6) (September–October 1981): 16–25.

34. Joseph F. Smith (1907), quoted in Madsen, "Mormon Women and the Struggle for Definition," 46.

35. Loretta L. Hefner, "The National Women's Relief Society and the U.S. Sheppard-Towner Act," *Utah Historical Quarterly* 50(3) (Summer 1982): 255–67.

36. Marilyn Warenski, *Patriarchs and Politics: The Plight of the Mormon Woman* (New York: McGraw-Hill, 1978).

37. Embry, "Grain Storage."

38. This is, of course, a very complex subject. See Claudia L. Bushman, "Mystics and Healers," in *Mormon Sisters: Women in Early Utah*, ed. Claudia L. Bushman (Cambridge, Mass.: Emmeline Press, 1976), 1–23, and Madsen, "Mormon Women and the Struggle for Definition," 41. In 1906, Orson F. Whitney said that Joseph Smith had taught that "the sisters . . . were to enjoy the benefit and blessings of the priesthood . . . the delegated authority of God." Did "enjoy" mean they could practice? It seems unlikely. Madsen's article is the strongest statement I have seen of women's rights to practice certain priesthood functions, but she stops short of arguing that they have an independent right to function as the priesthood does.

CHAPTER 13

The Mormon Message in the Context of Maori Culture

Peter Lineham

The issue of culture is always significant in religious history. It has been very important in the churches of New Zealand. The coexistence of a Christianized migrant population with an indigenous population which is the subject of Christian missionary outreach inevitably creates some real tensions. In New Zealand at the present time, the issue of culture and cultural relationships between the indigenous Maori population and Pakeha (European settlers) is at a very sensitive stage. Exactly 150 years ago, the British annexed New Zealand by way of formal agreement with the traditional rangatira (native leaders) of the country. This agreement, known as the Treaty of Waitangi, included clauses recognizing the continued authority of the rangatira and their lands. The promises of this document were subsequently ignored by the British and particularly by the settler population when they were given responsibility for the government of the colony.

The long history of grievances has now become politically explosive, for recent governments have recognized that the treaty has continued validity and that to "protect" the lands and customs of the tribes means that every institution in our country is having to weigh up how far it handicaps Maori from expressing themselves in their own cultural forms. The churches, whose early missionaries urged the Maori rangatira to sign the treaty, are now struggling to correct their treatment of the Maori section of their denominations. They have had to go back through their history in the delicate task of establishing where they went wrong.

The establishment of the Church of Jesus Christ of Latter-day Saints in New Zealand provides a curious variant to this theme. Mormons have prided themselves over the years for their success, where the orthodox churches failed, in making converts among several of the Maori tribes of New Zealand. Latter-day Saints often claim that their success was because the Church offered a different approach to the cultural issue than the other churches—that it effected a close identification with Maori culture.

The purpose of this essay is to examine with some care the Mormon impact among the Maori, with the intention of analyzing this claim. How and to what extent did this quintessentially American religion accommodate itself to Maori society and become a Maori religion? What was involved on both sides of the cultural exchange? For there is a form of cultural translation involved in people understanding a new religion, and it is, in effect, a kind of transaction in which the value of a new religion is assessed in terms of its demands and its offers. And to what extent did Mormon approaches differ from those of the orthodox churches? For the new religion must have been weighed up alongside its competitors. These are the questions this essay seeks to explore, although restrictions on time force me to focus principally on interpreting only the earliest years of the Mormon mission.[1]

How Major an Impact?

It seems surprising that the Maori community, known for its inclusiveness, anti-institutionalism, tea drinking, alcohol consumption, and smoking, would have adopted to any extent a faith that pointed in an opposite direction. Yet the Mormon message made a very significant impact among the Maori. Mormon missionaries attempted to preach to the Pakeha from as early as 1854, but they were almost completely unsuccessful. The limited impact is shown in the rather random location of the major Mormon branches in the period before 1880: Auckland, Karori near Wellington, and Kaiapoi near Christchurch. Most of their early Pakeha followers had, in fact, become Mormons before they came to New Zealand, and the missionaries who began to visit in 1854 spent their time regathering them. There was fairly intense opposition to the Mormons, much as there was in most other Anglo Saxon countries at this stage, except that the smaller scale of the community made more painful the unreceptive atmosphere. Questions about Mormon activity in Wellington were asked in the House of Representatives in 1871.[2] This situation did not change until after the First World War, although the missionaries made periodic attempts to break into a world that seemed uniquely closed to them. Because of polygamy, the Mormons were often seen as the most extreme of all the heterodox sects. In Christchurch (well known as a center of sectarian activities and a place where Mormons felt very much at home in the 1870s), Mormon preaching in Cathedral Square occasioned riots in 1881 and in 1901.[3]

The Latter-day Saints were committed to a worldwide mission, and their major means was the voluntary labor of men who held the Melchizedek Priesthood. Initially, this mission focused on summoning European New Zealanders to believe the gospel and return to Zion. It is a moot point why they began to reach out to Maori in the late 1870s. There is some evidence of a command to do so by the Quorum of Twelve and the First Presidency in the mid-1870s.[4] Doubtless the Church authorities were aware of the impact of the mission among the Hawaiian people. So, too, were the missionaries, for their ships always called at Honolulu on the way to New Zealand, and William John Bromley, for one, a New Zealand mission president whose influence was so important in commencing the ministry to the Maori, was most impressed by what he saw there.[5] To the missionaries, facing open hostility from the Pakeha community and a resultant sense of alienation, this mission obviously added a certain satisfaction to their work. A rather insecure missionary in the 1870s, Fred Hurst, finding himself alone in Wellington in 1876, lamented, "To tell the truth, I feel aweful lonely and now I don't really know what course to pursue for the best."[6] In later years the European community changed its attitude to steady and disdainful disinterest. In 1922, a departing Whangarei missionary commented, "We leave their district with practically nothing to show for our labors"—and asked to go back to laboring among the Maori.[7]

Yet commencing a mission to the Maori posed certain practical difficulties, which deterred progress for several years. Language was the most obvious difficulty, and missionaries staying only a short period could not readily overcome this obstacle. The earliest breakthrough into Maori society depended on local European members, until, in a critical decision, a future mission president, W. T. Stewart, was sent to live in a native village and learn the language. His success led to the development of a new pattern.[8] Despite attempts to confer the gift of language by miraculous endowment, no easy way to learn the language was found.[9] Hurst in the late 1870s planned to commission the translation of a tract into Maori, though he did not succeed; Bromley surmounted the serious difficulties of finding a willing translator in the early 1880s but then faced the puzzle of how to distribute it to the Maori, few of whom lived in towns.[10] There were other inherent problems in developing a mission to the Maori. Tracts were impossible to proofread and expensive to print when there was no income provided for the mission, and travel to remote regions in search of Maori posed physical difficulties.

The missionaries of the 1870s had marked deficiencies,[11] and Bromley, who served as presiding elder in the New Zealand Mission District from 1881, obviously represented a new type of enthusiasm. Hearing of the first Maori baptism, he declared, "This is news, and no doubt, it is the beginning of many baptisms among the natives"; six months later, hearing of another putative breakthrough, he remarked, "The seeds of truth is sown among the Maories and I believe when it takes root will produce much fruit, so might it be."[12] He soon learned that enthusiasm cannot solve all problems. Early in his mission, after fasting and prayer, he visited the Ngati Whatua marae (tribal gathering place) at Orakei, and the local rangatira agreed to read a statement of Mormon doctrines.[13]

Unfortunately, this rangatira was drunk upon Bromley's return. Bromley then urged the small team of missionaries to seek their own opportunities to witness to Maori, and several unsuccessful and perhaps ill-advised initiatives resulted. Missionaries testified to Maori visiting Auckland; one elder, J. P. Sorenson, made an unfortunate visit to the Prophet Te Whiti; and others attempted to gain access to the Maori king through his followers in Opotiki.[14]

Then, late in 1882, after Bromley had given up hope of a Maori mission, Thomas L. Cox and Hannah Cox, European converts who had previously lived in Auckland and had removed to Cambridge, in the Waikato region south of Auckland, made contact with a number of pa (Maori villages) along the Waikato River, particularly Waotu. At Christmas, Bromley visited the couple, and sensing a spiritual impulse, William J. McDonnell, an Auckland Mormon who knew the Maori language, also arrived. The three men were given an enthusiastic welcome by local Maori and were urged to stay and preach. Nine Maori were baptized in two days. "They apparently are calm, deliberate and in earnest in receiving the Gospel," wrote Alma Greenwood, one of the missionaries.[15] Soon there were sixty-five converts, and it was hastily agreed that a Maori branch should be organized at Waotu. Two missionaries were assigned there.[16] However, by 1884, missionary work in this area had collapsed. As exacerbating factors, Cox had declared bankruptcy, McDonnell had been suspended from the Church for slandering Bromley, and the Maori proved unwilling to refrain from drinking alcohol and were bitter over the removal of the one missionary who spoke Maori, W. T. Stewart.[17]

The major breakthrough came in the Wairarapa in 1883. A small European branch had been formed in the settlement of Carterton in 1881, and at the end of 1882, Elder Lucien C. Farr, while visiting this branch, discovered interest from a local rangatira. With the departure of Farr, Alma Greenwood was appointed president of Wellington District on 20 March, and when he cultivated the Maori contacts in the district, his work bore dramatic fruit. At the village of Papawai, speaking through a translator, Farr and Greenwood received a rapturous reception on 4–6 April, and after three days, a Maori was baptized. Within six months, a number of Maori were converted. All available missionaries were rushed in, with significant results. Then the missionaries received a telegram inviting them to the village of Taonoke in Hawke's Bay.[18] In the atmosphere of a mass revival, many Hawke's Bay Maori were baptized in several villages near Hastings. The new mission president, W. T. Stewart, went farther north to Nuhaka, near Wairoa, in mid-August 1884 and preached his way around Te Mahia peninsula. In the course of two months, some three hundred converts were made. Hirini Te Whaanga, one of the most significant Maori in the whole history of the mission, was baptized on 30 November 1884, became the first Maori to immigrate to Utah, and, when he returned on his own mission to New Zealand in 1898–99, was a very popular preacher.

Following their success in Nuhaka and the Te Mahia area, the missionary team continued north, accompanied by Ihaia Hopu Te Whakamairu, an influential convert baptized in 1883. They baptized sixty-four converts in the Waiapu area north of Gisborne and proceeded as far as the East Cape. Half of the members of the major hapu (subtribe) on this northern part of the coast became members of the Church.[19]

This was the impressive inauguration of a mission, which two years later swept some of the hapu of Ngapuhi in Northland with similar force and also built up a stronghold in the western Bay of Plenty. On 16 January 1885, the mission president, W. T. Stewart, divided his mission into five districts—Wellington (including the Wairarapa), Hawke's Bay, Mahia, Poverty Bay, and Auckland— and withdrew the missionaries from the South Island, the largest land mass in New Zealand.[20] While the Mormons made no significant impression among the Ngai Tahu, Ngati Porou, Tuhoe, or Te Ati Awa tribes and faced massive struggles before Tainui showed any interest, they could claim about three thousand members (about 8 percent of the Maori population) by 1890 and have since then been a significant force in the Maori community. The most recent census figures give them a little under 6 percent of the Maori population.[21]

Missionaries and Their Impact

When this progress was reported, a larger team of missionaries was sent to New Zealand, increasing the numbers from twelve in the mid-1880s to some sixty missionaries in the late 1930s. These missionaries, who were supposed to stay three years, were under the direction of the mission president, who assigned them in pairs in each district; the more experienced missionary was named district president. Their ages varied in the earlier periods from about seventeen to about forty. A few were married, but very few brought their wives. Their income was what they had saved or what their families sent them, often about ten dollars (about three pounds) a month. When they arrived, they were immediately assigned to a district and instructed to learn the language. It was a case of total immersion in the culture. Ezra T. Stevenson describes his experience in this typical account: "I, not knowing a word of greeting, was set down alone to find my way into a Maori village. . . . How when those simple natives gathered round me [I] understand their questions put in broken English, sat there and thought of what was before me! Yet I was not unhappy or lonesome, but knew that I had come to do God's work, and in my faithfulness He would continue as He had begun to raise up friends for me."[22]

The missionaries did not find it easy to adjust to this new environment. They usually lived with the local Maori branch president, sleeping on the floor and eating the local food. They struggled to find some way to avoid attacks by fleas at night, but massive slaughter wreaked upon them one night did not lessen the risk twenty-four hours later. They felt isolated. Often only when they walked to town to post their mail or met up with another missionary could they converse in English, since few Maori spoke English competently and other Europeans were not very friendly. They quickly learned to hongi (rub noses in the traditional Maori greeting), although they found it uncomfortable. They learned to be grateful for their kai (food), recognizing that "in fact our acceptance here as Maori missionaries depends somewhat on our ability to eat the food provided."[23] It was all too much for some. President Ezra Richards had to rebuke an elder who complained that he didn't like Maori people, didn't want to learn a new language, and was driven to distraction by fleas.[24] One Maori leader was "somewhat offended because Brother [John Burton?] would not rub noses with him. Wanted to know if his nose was holy."[25] Some elders could not develop the necessary adaptability and were sent home; others gritted their teeth and survived for a year or two.[26]

Yet many of them succeeded, too. Piripi Te Maori-o-te-rangi, the great Wairarapa rangatira, describing why he became a Latter-day Saint, emphasized that there was something very appealing about this style of mission:

Two strange men came to our home. They were unheralded by any pomp or display. They were not so much as dressed in the ordinary gown and tall hat worn by our preachers. . . . There was something very different about them from our ministers. We have been in the habit of building homes for our preachers, and fed them a little better than the ordinary folks; but when these things were offered to these two preachers from a strange land . . . they said: "No, we are your fellow servants, we are here to do you service, your equals, not your superiors. Let us eat with you, and of what you eat."[27]

This is an idealized account, of course, and the missionary journals convey a strong sense of culture shock. Furthermore, identification with the Maori was as much a matter of survival as a matter of policy. Nelson Spicer Bishop, from Fillmore, Utah, who served a mission during 1886–89, commented in his journal: "If you don't sit with them you won't learn their language, and [you] lose their goodwill, and without that, what influence? When in Rome, do as the Romans do. In Maoridom take things as you can get them and try to make yourself agreeable, and when an opportunity affords itself to teach them the better way, improve it, and do it kindly, for they despise a grumbler."[28] Thus, this cultural identification was to an extent forced onto the missionaries, for they had no resources to find another way to live.

Matthew Cowley, who served as a missionary from 1914 to 1919 and as mission president from 1938 to 1945, believed so totally in the philosophy of identification that he urged against hasty attempts to make converts. He told his Maori friend, Wi Duncan of Dannevirke: "We have the salvation of the Maori on our hands, and it is therefore imperative that our kaumatua (missionary) study the

Maori, his mind, characteristics, likes, and dislikes. Of course missionaries do not remain long enough to do the greatest amount of good and to study the natives as they should. . . . The most important factor of missionary work is not so much the making of converts as the making of friends."[29]

This policy only slowly evolved from a basis of necessity, and from observing how John W. Kaueleinamoku, a Hawaiian elder who served a mission from 1888 to 1890, had a much greater influence over fellow Polynesians than did Americans.[30] Although it is not clear how early a policy of identification was adopted, learning the Maori language was recognized as crucial to the mission strategy. By the 1880s, few Pakeha bothered to learn the native tongue, yet not many Maori knew more than a smattering of English and did not want to discuss spiritual issues in that tongue. Mormon elders would buy a Maori grammar written by William Leonard Williams, the Anglican bishop of Waiapu, and spend up to forty hours a week struggling to learn sentence forms and vocabulary, but their results were helped by their immersion in the culture. Although many remained incompetent at expressing more than greetings, others within six months were preaching in Maori, even if their congregations initially found the sermons rather amusing. The best-loved missionaries were always the best linguists.[31]

The Factor of Genealogy

The tradition in Maori society of hospitality to manihera (strangers) who come in peace no doubt also assisted the process of initial contact. The elders were normally welcomed when they came to new marae and were, like any minister, invited to lead the daily karakia (prayers). Maori were often fascinated to hear new things, and this made them want to hear an explanation for the restored gospel.[32] Hospitality sometimes went to extraordinary lengths. Catering for Mormon hui (conferences) was often provided by those of different religious backgrounds so that members could attend the meetings, and in 1897, a non-Mormon rangatira, Tamahau, built a huge house for the Wairarapa conference.[33]

Yet hospitality does not mean persuasion. What was it that the rangatira and other members saw in the message? What about the Mormon message was appealing in competition with the other religious traditions at that time? Historians in search of a simple general explanation have pointed to the correspondence between the Maori emphasis on whakapapa (family tree) and whanau (enlarged family unit) and the Mormon emphasis on genealogy and family and church community. These reasons are, however, in my opinion, quite unsatisfactory. It is true that the Mormon faith encourages the baptism by proxy of ancestors, but this approach required precise genealogical records quite unlike the Maori use of recited whakapapa to preserve family mythology and mana (spiritual power). The elders tried regularly to encourage interest in genealogy, but few Maori made the pilgrimage to the Hawaiian Temple when it was built, and the building of the temple in Hamilton has been described as part of a strategy to make Maori more consistent Mormons.[34] Nor did the elders in the early periods particularly emphasize the importance of families—that has been a more recent development—and nor was the family structure threatened in Maori society at the time.

Responses by Tribes and Chiefs

A far more obvious factor is that the restored gospel found sponsors within the Maori community. No nineteenth-century Maori movement, religious or cultural, ever overrode the tribal structure. Individual responses were possible outside the tribal framework, but converts such as those baptized in 1881 cut themselves off from their tribal communities. If we want to know why the Waikato community failed, one factor is surely that after the first Waikato baptisms, the missionaries received inquiries for information from the local rangatira, yet they followed up that interest with just one letter. In a tribal society, new religions need to be tribal movements if they are to achieve long-term success, as even the early Evangelical missionaries to New Zealand eventually realized.

The Mormon revival in 1883–84 was dependent on the conversion of a number of influential rangatira. In the Wairarapa, the first Maori converts were Ihaia Hopu Te Whakamairu and Manihera Te Whenuanui Rangitakaiwaho, who were baptized on 21 July 1883. Ihaia was a notable Ngati Kahungunu rangatira who had possibly served in the ministry of the Church of England.[35] He served as president of a branch at Te Ore Ore until his death three years later. Manihera was the rangatira of Papawal and the first patron of the preachers, but he waited until they had proved their loyalty to him and until Ihaia had responded before he agreed to baptism. In August 1883, Manihera became president of the first Wairarapa branch, at Papawai.[36] Ihaia also influenced Piripi Te Maori, the great Ngati Kahungunu rangatira from Waiotapu, who was famous for his efforts to preserve the lands of the Wairarapa hapu. Piripi delayed his baptism until 2 June 1887 but was a patron of the message from late 1883.[37] His advocacy of Mormon doctrines and his constant preaching influenced many others until his death in 1895, after which Mormon support in Wairarapa declined.

Tribal links and the sponsorship of rangatira explain much of the impact farther up the east coast of the North Island. Hohepa Otene Meihana, the rangatira of Taonoke who had invited the missionaries to Hawke's Bay, probably had tribal links with Ngati Kahungunu, and Piripi Te Maari had been raised on Mahia peninsula and had returned to Wairarapa only in the 1850s, so the missionaries had an excellent introduction to the rangatira of the hapu of Ngati Kahungunu in this peninsula. Hirini Te Rito Whaanga was the son of the famous rangatira Ihaka Whaanga, whose death in 1875 ended his domination of the peninsula.[38]

Ihaia Te Whakamairu accompanied the preachers as they journeyed farther north, and his presence probably explains the conversion of Henry Potae, son-in-law to Manihera and an important rangatira in his own right.[39] Overall the message made little impact among the Ngati Porou people of the east coast but flourished among their neighbors, Ngati Kahungunu. In many cases, minor rangatira or younger and disaffected sons of strong rangatira embraced the movement. As examples, one may cite Pukeroa Te AweAwe of Hawke's Bay (a relation of the great Te Peeti Te AweAwe) and Taramana Mita of Northland (president of the Kirikiri Branch).[40] In the Waikato, the domination of the Maori "king movement" was such that the king's lack of sympathy meant that access to the Waikato tribes was virtually prohibited in the early years.[41]

A church that attracted its membership through its rangatira members faced delicate problems in dealing with them. Such leaders were not beyond seeing themselves as having a privileged position in the Church's development. Otene Meihana of Hawke's Bay was, from the first, convinced that the elders and he had a reciprocal relationship. Shortly after he was baptized, he seized control of a priesthood meeting and, when the elders withdrew, sent them a deputation, threatening to withdraw from the Church if his demands were not met.[42] Otene did not carry out this threat, because he needed the elders for a basis of his authority as much as they needed him, but his pugnaciousness remained. Two years later, N. S. Bishop found that "President Otene here, studies the Bible nearly all the time. . . . When he learns something then he questions the Elders to catch them to show his smartness, and very often he is considerable off. He is touched with the big head and if one does not know the language real well there is no use to try to tell him he is [w]rong."[43] Four years later, William Douglass and John Burton had serious problems with Otene and required him to repent, but Otene chose instead to blame Burton.[44]

Correcting prominent men who had brought followers into the movement was a delicate responsibility. Pukeroa Te AweAwe's excommunication for horse racing was a painful experience for all concerned. President Ezra Richards eventually ruled that only the mission president could excommunicate a chief.[45]

Opposition to the Restored Gospel

This picture of chiefly support and its consequences must be balanced by an analysis of the ferocious opposition with which other chiefs confronted the Saints. Often these episodes can best be interpreted as a tribal response to an unwelcome intrusion from outside. In 1886 a number of prominent rangatira of Ngati Porou condemned the Mormons in a public meeting with the native minister, John Ballance, although two other rangatira, Anera Te Kahaki and John A. Jury, leapt to their defenses.[46] The most dramatic attack on the missionaries came at Te Kawakawa, near East Cape, that same year. While the missionaries were absent, the Maori Saints were bound, their Bibles confiscated, and two houses destroyed; they were forbidden to hold meetings. When two of the missionaries returned to help, they were tied to a fence for three days.[47] Two contributing causes of this incident may be identified. First, the Mormons lacked permission from the local rangatira, Te Hati Hokamau, to make converts in the area. Even where rangatira had no intention of becoming converts, they were often willing to tolerate the movement; without at least this minimal consent, successful proselyting was not possible. Second, the local Maori Anglican minister, Mohi Turei, was angered by the growth of the Mormons and their threat to his own status. The result was a court case in which Maori Mormons received rough justice.[48]

The combination of the two forces, chief and minister, is significant. In the Waikato, such a combination of opponents effectively stopped the growth of the Church.[49] Of the two, the more bitter opponent was the local Anglican clergy. Mihinare (Anglican) ministers did not confine themselves to warnings but complained to the Native Ministry of the government.[50]

Mormon and Anglican Conflict

Why was the Mihinare church so resolute an opponent of the Saints? The answer may seem obvious, but we must also realize that in the years after 1880, the European missionaries had been forced to leave their Maori flocks. The Maori ministers who remained received little financial support from the European community and little spiritual leadership from the diocesan bishops. The native ministers thus faced a period of intense hardship. Many of the former members who converted to Mormonism seem to have enjoyed criticizing and mocking the native ministers. "It was as good as a theater," wrote William Douglass with unchristian relish after one fierce encounter between the Anglican ministers and Mormon Maori converts.[51] In a lively discussion at the beginning of the Hawke's Bay revival in 1884, Maori investigators told elders that the native ministers had not explained the meaning of the Bible, had pandered to the rich, and were lazy. "When the white man came here first he brought the gun to shoot the Maori. Next he brought the gospel to shoot the Maori and his land. But the gospel which you bring shoots the kings, governors, ministers, churches and all."[52] The Mihinare church was very vulnerable to criticism—and criticize it the Mormon elders did. They began to attend Anglican services and collect evidence of their own of how its Maori ministers stumbled through written prayers, expected to be paid and given land, and often lacked moral standards and direction. In strident sermons, they labeled the ministers "hireling priests" and contrasted themselves as "unpaid servants of the people."[53]

Mormons and the Issue of Maori Land

The enthusiastic response of Maori audiences to the Mormon elders' accounts of "corrupt" Christianity deserves careful consideration. The elders noted the unusual fluidity of belief among some Maori Anglicans. A Maori leader told Alma Greenwood at Papawai in April 1883 that "the people . . . were in confusion in matters of religion, some believing one way and some another. . . . People were wavering in their belief and did not know what to do."[54] There is evidence that this wavering was provoked by problems more serious than their ministers' style. The key issue was land grievances.

Land was a highly sensitive issue in the years after the New Zealand wars of the 1860s and 1870s, and the Maori tended to blame the Mihinare church for the loss of their lands, since its ministers had advocated the Treaty of Waitangi and then backed the British army. Missionaries were often told: "You taught us to look up to heaven and stole the land from under our feet." The Mormon elders noted this attitude but did not realize how deeply it affected religious attitudes.[55] In fact a protest against the Mihinare church was almost always a political statement about the loss of land. The Parihaka incident of 1881, when the government evicted followers of the "prophet" Te Whiti who resisted the sale of land in his village in South Taranaki, further heightened this concern, and twenty years later, a Methodist minister noted "the influence of Parihaka still keeps many of the best men in opposition to the Gospel, and I much fear these, in many ways fine fellows, will die in opposition to the race that 'took their land.'"[56]

The Maori tribes who responded to the Mormon message felt strongly on this issue. It is significant that the Kotahitanga "native parliament" was based for part of the 1890s in Papawai and that its premier, Hamiora Mangai Kahia, a native lawyer, was a Mormon.[57] Manihera on occasion voiced his hostility to the queen and the government in front of the missionaries.[58]

There is no evidence that the Mormon elders ever spoke out against the settlers' seizure of the lands. Missionaries occasionally attended gatherings of Maori who were discussing land grievances, and once, while Alma Greenwood waited for a lunchtime adjournment of a land meeting in Papawai to get an opportunity to preach, the Maori delegate to Britain, Sydney D. Tawhango, showed him a copy of the treaty and Maori correspondence with the British monarch during the 1830s. Benjamin Goddard gave a lantern lecture in the Maori parliament whare (house) at Papawai,[59] and meetings of the land court often provided an opportunity for Mormon preachers; yet almost all the elders seem to have been unaware of the issues at stake.[60] They seem not to have realized that land grievances had a direct impact on Church membership.

It was not that the land issue turned Maori toward the Latter-day Saints but rather that it dented the credibility of the Mihinare church. While the LDS elders' records are silent on the subject, Maori oral tradition indicates that specific grievances with the Anglican church encouraged the secession of some of its members to the Latter-day Saints. In Porirua, lands had been given to the Anglican church for a Maori college. In a historic court case over these lands (*Wi Parata v. the Bishop of Wellington*, 1877) Judge Prendegast ruled that the Treaty of Waitangi was null and void and that therefore the uses of the land could be changed. The wholesale secession of the Porirua Maori community to the Latter-day Saints was no doubt in large part a result of this ruling. Similar factors probably explain the original breakthrough in the Wairarapa.[61] Consequently, almost all of the converts to the Mormon Church in its early years had previously been Anglican, even Anglican clergy.[62]

Why did they turn from the Church of England to the Latter-day Saints? Maori rangatira may have taken the view that adopting an American religion was a way to snub the British, but the preachers did not emphasize this response, and the only early LDS missionary who published remarks on this subject was Benjamin Goddard.[63] As Americans, most Mormons were proud of their republic (except when it attacked Mormon polygamists), and in one classic case, elders in the Manawatu district celebrated Utah's pioneer days by raising the Stars and Stripes over a marae and describing it as a sign of "advancing Maoridom."[64] There is no record of Mormons talking about the dispossession of American Indians from their lands when they identified Native Americans as descendants of Book of Mormon peoples.[65]

The Saints and Independent Maori Religions

The positive movement toward the restored gospel needs more explaining. Among Maori, the religious options were of course by no means restricted to the Mihinare church and the Mormons. In different locations, a great variety of religious leaders had a following. While the Anglican church remained dominant, the fastest-growing groups were adherents of the various Maori prophets. Pai Marire did not survive the war period of the 1860s and 1870s, but Te Kooti's religion, Ringatu, had an extensive following throughout the east coast where the Mormon preachers were also active. It is sometimes claimed that the Mormons "took over" from Te Kooti, but in fact many other prophets emerged after him.[66] These prophets were much more attractive to the majority of Maori than the Mormon elders. The two ways were so different that, in the early years, few followers switched between the two forms of religion. On the west coast, the principal leader viewed as a prophet was Te Whiti. A visit to his home at Parihaka by the excitable J. P. Sorenson was such a disaster that he shook the dust off his feet as he left. It was because Te Whiti was so strong an influence in Taranaki that the Mormon missionaries gained no following there.[67]

Other prophets were rarely interested in the Saints. While one Maori prophet, Matiu, was converted at Whakaoutu, this was an unusual event.[68] At Waipawa a prophet was able to inhibit Mormon access to the marae. In a great debate on religion at Papawai in 1888, the Anglican and Catholic debaters eventually withdrew, leaving only the Hau Hau (Ringatu followers of Te Kooti) and the Mormons, and a crucial argument of the Hau Hau speaker was that when God was ready to give the Maori a religion, he would do so directly and not through Pakeha people. The LDS elders eventually gave up the debate too. They subsequently found that villages, which sympathized with Te Kooti, would not receive them.[69] Ihaka Whaanga had gained a reputation as a strong opponent of the prophets before he became a Mormon, and it may be argued that his attraction to Mormonism lay in the fact that to follow them meant accepting some ties with Western society while making one's own choice about the form of Christianity espoused.

The Appeal of the "House of Israel" Doctrine

This analysis does not imply that the Mormons had nothing in common with other new religious traditions among the Maori. On the contrary, Mormon doctrines overlapped extensively with those of other religions. This is evident, for example, in the Mormon view that the Maori—like other Polynesian (but not Melanesian people)—were Lamanites, members of the House of Israel and cousins to the native North Americans.[70] Therefore, the elders of Zion offered to the Maori people an identity in their new scripture—the Book of Mormon.

Most Maori had, in fact, identified themselves with Israel for many years. This identification lay at the heart of many of the Maori independent religions, but it had originally been introduced by some of the Protestant missionaries, including Thomas Kendall, the first Anglican missionary teacher. The Reverend Richard Taylor had developed the thesis in his book *Te Ika a Maui*.[71] Although the view had lost ground in the European world, theories about Maori racial origins continued to be a subject of speculation. However, these theories more often posited an Aryan ancestry for Polynesians. Mormons were interested in the theories of Edward Tregear and Percy Smith and continued to cite them long after they had lost academic respectability.[72] The restored gospel provided a scriptural justification for racial theories. It associated the Mormon message with the popular Maori desire to "locate" themselves in the Bible. It was the manner in which the argument was developed, rather than the doctrine itself, that marked the Mormons out as distinctive.

The idea that Maori were of the House of Israel inspired some missionaries who hoped to be responsible for the conversion of God's covenant people.[73] It also heightened Maori interest in the Mormon message. At Papawai, Alma Greenwood gathered information from Manihera about Maori traditions and, in his sermons, interpreted them as indications that Maori ancestors came from Jerusalem, tracing their origins back through Fiji and Hawaii to America and thence to the Holy Land.[74] President W. T. Stewart, speaking in Maori at the 1885 conference, declared on the basis of Jeremiah 16 that the Lord who had scattered

Israel was now proposing to gather them.[75] When missionaries wanted to get support for translating the Book of Mormon, they emphasized that "it was a history of God's dealings with their [the Maori's] forefathers."[76]

The Maori obviously appreciated the interest the elders showed in their traditions. When the elders arrived in Hawke's Bay, local Maori interrogated them on the subject of the Maori relationship with Israel.[77] This emphasis was quickly noted by outside observers.[78] The subject also appealed to Maori Mormon preachers. Piripi Te Maori waxed eloquent on it,[79] and an 1892 address by Ngawawaea Poipoi tracing the ancestors of the Maori back to Abraham was noted as the most popular talk of the Te Rahu conference.[80] On another occasion, a congregation of Maori at Te Mahia "listened to [Poipoi, a native elder] with breathless interest" as he reviewed the history of the American Israelites and how Maori inherited their dark skin because of the disobedience of their ancestors. Maori Mormons seem to have accepted the prophecy in the Book of Mormon that they would receive white skins in a future dispensation.[81]

In some ways, the most curious aspect of the Israel doctrine was the limited impact it had on the elders' practice. Jewish ancestry made the Maori appealing converts, but the repeated attempts by various mission presidents to attract a European audience indicates that Israel was seen as having no more right to hear the gospel than the Europeans. Indeed, the LDS elders took a fairly unflattering view of the Maori people and, in certain respects, placed them on a lower rather than a higher plane than Europeans. "You are needed far worse among the Maoris than among the Europeans," said President Ezra Richards to a complaining missionary.[82] Kate Paxman, the wife of mission president William Paxman, commented on her arrival at Muriwai in 1886: "It is simply wonderful how these poor ignorant Natives love the elders who come to teach them. They fully appreciate their labors, but oh how degraded they are and what a vast amount of teaching and training they do need; it is indeed a labor of love and charity to come among them and try to elevate them from their fallen condition."[83] This attitude is little different from that of the orthodox missionaries. Whenever they were conscious of Maori responsiveness to their preaching, the LDS elders emphasized the Maori heritage in Israel, but whenever they were annoyed with Maori, they emphasized that, for their sins, they had been tainted with the Lamanite curse of a dark skin. Hurst in the 1870s felt that the Maori people in Wellington were "such a drunken, low, corrupt set around here [that] I have been ashamed to go near" them.[84] "If ever I thought of home it was here among such exceedingly dirty people," said William Douglass at Takapau.[85] Alma Greenwood, commenting on one of the early baptisms at Papawai, remarked that light had dawned on

> these aborigines, who have wandered in gross darkness, sin, indolence and loathsomeness. [The light was] even that same sweet influence which prompted their forefathers to leave the land of Jerusalem. One's mind instantaneously

reverts back to the annals of the History of Ancient America, in which is por-
traited [sic] the wanderings, troubles and wars, prophecies and heavenly principles which existed among the Aborigines of America. Also the wickedness
and disobedience to the commandments of God, which affected and brought
about their present state of degradation and savage condition.[86]

Maori Mormons were discouraged from immigrating to Zion in Utah, except
for wealthy tribal leaders such as Hirini Te Whaanga, a very prominent Maori
chief who emigrated in 1894. Ezra Richards, who was mission president in 1898,
instructed his elders "to be careful as to how they spoke on emigration, and not
to encourage it at present, but to strive earnestly to thoroughly ground the saints
in the Faith."[87] While there were specific reasons for this ruling, social factors
also intervened. Neither the United States government, the New Zealand government, nor the Church was prepared to encourage a major Maori emigration
for racial reasons.

A similar mix of faith and prudence is evident in ordinations to the priesthood. One week after their baptism, Ihaia and Manihera were offered ordination
to the Aaronic priesthood, and others followed when they agreed to accept the
Word of Wisdom and abstain from tobacco, alcohol, coffee, and tea.[88] As early as
1885, native missionaries were appointed, Otene Pomare being the first.[89] This
may seem rather daring, and given the lax standards of the first Maori ordained
to the Aaronic priesthood, perhaps it was, for it impressed Maori followers who
remembered that the Mihinare church waited twenty-five years before it ordained any Maori converts to the Anglican priesthood. The Aaronic priesthood
did not carry anything like the status of the Anglican ministry, but many Maori
assumed that it did and were reluctant to be ordained before knowing the commitment involved. They also showed a marked lack of ambition to rise to the
higher levels of the Melchizedek priesthood. For their part, the elders zealously
guarded their right to choose those to be ordained and were cautious in offering
ordination to the higher offices of the Aaronic priesthood and particularly to the
Melchizedek priesthood. In the first sixty years of the Maori mission, only a tiny
number of Maori received ordination to the Melchizedek priesthood. Only in the
1930s, due to the decline in missionary numbers in the period of the Great
Depression and World War II, was there an increase in the number of ordinations and a campaign to recruit Maori missionaries.[90] In this respect, too, the
Latter-day Saints were not altogether dissimilar to the other churches, allowing
for their different racial balance and different structure of ministry.

A New Authority

The central message preached by the LDS elders was that Christianity, which
had been corrupted for hundreds of years, was now being restored. The gospel

focused on the restoration of the unique order of the church. Elders frequently gave a potted religious history illustrating that all churches sprang from the same polluted Catholic stem.[91] The Church of Jesus Christ of Latter-day Saints is justly noted for the central place that it gives to organization and authority in religion, and this uniqueness was repeatedly emphasized in proselyting approaches.[92] Ironically, this emphasis was very similar to that of the Pikopiko (Catholic) church, and the description of the divinely instituted order of the Latter-day Saints must have reminded hearers of Catholic preaching. The implication of the doctrine was that the Zion elders had very considerable authority. Thus, the otherwise humble and young American preachers were men of great significance, for Maori gave to their kaumatua (elders) special veneration.[93] When religious debates occurred, including that at Papawai marae in March 1888, the authority vested in the Church was apparently much admired.[94]

Such an approach undoubtedly did not appeal to all Maori, for while the Maori community respected authority, it thought of it as based on mana, not position. Some of the rangatira were willing to respect the authority of the Church so long as it respected theirs, but there were uneasy boundaries between the two. Otene Meihana once put Edward Newby in his place, insisting, as Newby recorded in his journal, that "he (Otene) was timuaki [i.e., authority, the same title that was used to designate the mission president] in this district, and he didn't do certain things I said he he'd [*sic*] done—called me a liar. I said if he didn't retract I'd report him to President Stewart and cut him off. He said he'd cut me off."[95] William Douglass was horrified to find that one chief had the audacity to make the presidents of two branches who were sick confess their sins to him so that he could pray for their healing and restoration.[96] No Maori was appointed district president until the 1930s, when the supply of Utah elders dried up. In the view of the elders, Americans alone seemed to be adequate guardians of the pure gospel.

The Restoration of Prophecy

In some respects, the Latter-day Saints were quite like the independent prophetic movements. A key feature of the restored Church and the restored apostolate was the renewal of the prophetic gift. Evidence of prophecy led people to the Church. Many individual followers reported divine guidance by means of prophecies and dreams authenticating the restored gospel. The breakthrough at Waikato in 1882 was assisted when a Maori recollected a dream of the Apostle Peter accompanied by helpers. Bromley noted: "After telling the dream the Maori said when I saw you . . . the dream came fresh to my mind, and a firm impression was made upon my understanding that you were the men that the Apostle Peter was working with."[97] Piripi Te Maari told Greenwood of a strange dream the next year: "I saw a big meeting and lots of people in it. I was in the meeting and preached how bad things come to New Zealand to destroy the land and people he said. Three times a man was standing close to [me] who [was] very mild and sorry. When I looked at him he came to me and shook hands with me." Piripi saw a timely visit to him by Manihera and the two elders as the fulfillment of this dream.[98]

Many descendants of the early members of the Church recount similar visions received by their ancestors. The grandfather of one of the best known of Maori Mormons in later years, Stuart Meha, was sick in the attic while his daughter, Mere Te Hau, was talking to the missionaries below. He asked, "Where is this great light lighting up the room?" And this experience confirmed the missionaries' words to her. Other stories tell of the fulfillment of dreams about a new book of truth or about religious leaders who raised their hands to pray.

On a larger scale, the Mormon elders laid claim to certain of the widely known prophecies about the future of Maoridom. Many rangatira claimed a gift of insight, and in the course of the nineteenth century, the troubled history of the tribes had led to many visions of the future. The mana of a great leader such as Te Whiti or Te Kooti was related to his prophetic insights. Consider the case of Paora Te Potangaroa of the Wairarapa, a native prophet, whose words are often claimed by Latter-day Saints. He had gained a great reputation in his area as a leader and had begun to reinterpret Christianity in Maori terms. His prophecies over a number of years in the late 1870s predicted the future of the land and the people in traditional and Christian language. Then at the opening of the Nga-Tau-e-Waru whare at Te Ore Ore on 16 March 1881, he showed the vast crowd a symbolical flag and pronounced a prophecy about the future of the Maori people. He made various prophetic utterances in the next two months before he died. One of his prophecies, uttered on 9 April 1881, said: "There is a religious denomination coming for us; perhaps it will come from the sea, perhaps it will emerge here. Secondly, let the churches into the house—there will be a time when a religion will emerge for you and I and the Maori people."[99]

This prophecy is capable of several interpretations, and in the 1920s, the Ratana church seized control of the whare and the symbols of the prophecy. But in December 1883, Te Ore Ore became the setting for the second Maori branch organized in the Wairarapa after Papawai, and many Maori at that time obviously saw the Mormon preaching as the fulfillment of prophecy. The American elders, on the other hand, appreciated the importance of the prophecy only some years later.[100] Mormons have also claimed their church as the fulfillment of Te Toira of Mahia's prophecy given around 1830 of the uncertain fate awaiting the Ngati Maru people and of the birth of its future heirs, but non-Mormon accounts of the text of this prophecy are not so reminiscent of the words of Te Potangaroa, and the prophecy was interpreted by most Maori as a prediction of the emergence of Te Kooti, so it cannot have helped to establish the Mormon Church.[101]

The Mormon citation of prophecy satisfied many Maori. The lack of recognition of spiritual sight and the voice of God was a serious deficiency in the Mihinare church, although one should note that somewhat similar prophecies drew people to orthodox Christianity in the 1820s and 1830s. Mormons also offered an interpretation of the Bible (particularly the Old Testament and the book of Revelation) which probably appealed to the Maori interest in symbolical textual readings.[102] Passionate and fanciful exegesis of the Bible by Maori Saints (for example, rejecting Mihinare baptism because making the sign of the cross over a person was to consign the person to the evil power of the cross) reflected the way in which Maori interpreted stories of their own past.[103]

In 1889 the huge task of translating the Book of Mormon was undertaken in circumstances regarded as miraculous. While its accounts of Israel in America fascinated many Maori, it is difficult to judge the extent to which it became part of Maori literature. Probably the poor quality of the translation inhibited its acceptance. It is curious that there was quite strong opposition to the publication by some Maori Mormons, partly because they were expected to meet much of the expense just as they had for projects in the traditional churches, but also because at least one critic "did not believe the book to be true[;] that it was the work of white men."[104] Not all Maori wanted their prophecy to come from abroad. Hoani A. Jury (Te Whatahoro) lent some assistance in the early stages of the translation, and this was potentially significant since he had in the 1850s served as a scribe to the noted Wairarapa prophet Te Matorohanga, but the inadequacy of his English meant that the task of translating the Book of Mormon was taken over by a team of missionaries.[105]

Having admitted the validity of present prophecy, the Latter-day Saints soon found that few Maori were willing to assess either the principle or the content of their personal prophecies in the light of the revelations of the Church. The same tohunga (spiritual healers) who identified the divine status of the Church continued to find other sources of authority. Warnings against the local prophets became very common in the Church conferences of the 1890s.[106] Hone Paerata, a rangatira and branch president, was disciplined for recognizing non-LDS prophecies in 1898, and Haimona Potiti was excommunicated at Waikato District Conference in 1899 for apostasy "in that the man claimed to be a prophet, at this time it was upon the South Island."[107]

The Evidence of Healing

The same complex factors of reaction were evident in the Church's emphasis that the restored gospel restored the power to heal. The early missionaries were extremely active in administrations (anointing the sick with oil). Cox's healing of Miriama Rotorama, who was thought to be dead, was obviously important in encouraging Maori to respond to the preaching in Waotu. Many, many other stories could be told; for example, the Hawaiian elder John Kauleinamoku sent a note to the father of a sick girl assuring him in the name of the Lord that his daughter would recover. President Ezra Richards in a Maori community deeply affected by illness touched the sick without fear—although he sometimes changed his clothes afterwards. A few but not all of these healings were instantaneous, but in other cases, the frequency of the administrations showed the caring concern of the missionaries. Exorcisms of demons were also not uncommon, since many sicknesses had a component of witchcraft, causing "mate Maori" (sickness leading to death without physical causes).[108]

Religion and healing have always been associated in the Maori mind because of the traditional role of the tohunga, and the early Protestant missionaries took great interest in the sick although they did not seek miraculous cures.[109] In a community where the death rate was so high that most people expected the Maori race to die out, the elders' administrations were virtually a trial of their doctrine and a power encounter with the tohunga of the Maori community to ascertain who had divine authority. Initially, the elders won great respect for their successes. However, in the 1890s, there was concern among the elders about the new rise of the tohunga. Some Mormons complained that the elders had lost their former power. In the Wairarapa, Bishop reported a bitter comment from a Maori member who "did not think the people now of our church had the power that they anchiently had. I says was not your wife cured by the priesthood. Yes, says he, but you elders lay hands on the sick and they are not cured."[110] Evidence that members were resorting to the tohunga for cures caused deep concern, and the tohunga were repeatedly attacked by Utah elders. Five members were excommunicated at Takapau in 1894 for consulting the tohunga, and all other branches were warned at the same time.[111] In Maori history, this period was notable for a rising influence of the tohunga, and in 1909, to the pleasure of the elders, Parliament enacted the Suppression of Tohungas Act to reduce the influence of Rua Kenana, the head of a Maori prophetic movement.[112]

Conclusion

The Church of Jesus Christ of Latter-day Saints undertook a very complex cultural experiment in New Zealand. Unlike many local Europeans, Mormons experienced Maori culture firsthand and thus, to some extent, created an aura of a continuity of Maori and Mormon customs. Missionaries tended to be fascinated and puzzled by Maori culture. The annual conference gradually developed into a great social event, the hui tau, that attracted vast crowds, not all of them Mormon, who enjoyed the formal powhiri (welcome), haka (male dance of challenge), and hongi and the increasing emphasis on sport. Hui tau have been seen as the Latter-day Saints' symbolical embrace with Maori culture,[113] but the embrace was rather hesitant. President William Paxman prayed before an early hui tau that "influences foreign to the gospel should be bound, so that peace, unity and harmony might prevail."[114]

For although there was an identification with the Maori to some extent, the restored gospel was expected to change people and their culture. High standards were set for the new converts, and the transforming power of the new gospel was emphasized. Missionaries gave glowing accounts of the change. Herbert J. Sears, after a year's experience on his mission, comments, "As soon as they receive the Gospel, they turn from their intemperate and licentious habits, and a marked change is noticeable. The white inhabitants observe the change and stand amazed, unable to account for it, as other ministers have labored among the people for over 70 years, and have been unsuccessful in lifting the convert out of the mire. It requires a more perfect system of theology than they have taught, and more moral examples than they have set."[115] Such statements reveal the depths of the Mormon desire to see change on the part of the Maori convert. Naturally, such change validated the worth of the missionary effort. But deeper and more troubling, this desire also spelled out how problematic Maori culture was for Mormons. As time passed, the Church developed specific verdicts on a range of Maori customs, avoiding some and embracing others. Tangihangi (protracted traditional funerals), traditional karakia (prayers), and tattoos were discouraged, even reproved.[116] Maori culture was accepted only on conditions.

Only when we have appreciated this complex relationship between the Maori and the Mormons may we accurately compare the achievement of the Latter-day Saints among Maori with that of the orthodox churches. Their relative success looks different in different periods. There is no doubt that the moral edge lay with the Latter-day Saints in the 1880s, but by the 1890s the picture had changed somewhat, and the Mormons looked much like any struggling European church. All churches faced sharper tensions over cultural issues after World War I when T. W. Ratana of Wanganui began a distinctively Maori movement of healing, prophecy, and political justice. All the existing churches, Mihinare, Ringatu, and Mormon, lost many members to it. It was not until the 1930s, and particularly in the period of Matthew Cowley's presidency (1939–46) that Mormons decided they needed to be identified with Maori culture, and by holding a hui tau (Easter conference) at the Ngaruawahia marae of the "King Movement," they made a rapprochement with the most significant tribal leaders. Since at the same time most of the American elders had left New Zealand, this policy move was timely.

Thus, the Mormons benefited from their lack of converts among European New Zealanders. The Mihinare church, which before 1840 had gained massive support from the Maori was, after 1840 dominated by its huge European membership, which imposed its secular suspicions of the Maori on spiritual areas. Biculturalism was an open problem for them. The Mormon elders, in contrast, were able to focus on one cultural group to position the Church in the cultural world of the Maori and to avoid the entanglements of New Zealand politics, where cultural issues were often a source of tension. Curiously, the benefit was not as great as might have been expected. Partly this was due to the constant rotation of elders arriving and departing. The effort of learning the language and understanding Maori society required time, and there was always a sense of frustration about the difficulties of the missionary task. These problems might have been overcome if the missionaries had trusted their Maori members more, but for a variety of reasons—including American prejudices, the rigid structure of the Church, and the overwhelming sense that Maori were a depressed community—they did not do this until the 1930s. Thus, the so-called unique relationship between the Latter-day Saints and the Maori people proves to have little substance to it. Certainly, aspects of the Mormon message greatly appealed to the Maori people, but by the 1930s even these features had faded somewhat. After World War II, the relationship was replaced by a deliberately more European-style mission, which enabled Americanisms to be used without discomfort.

In 1990, when New Zealanders commemorate 150 years since the Treaty of Waitangi, high hopes are being expressed that the country may become a bicultural society. It is not sufficient for our many cultures to learn to coexist and tolerate one another; rather, our country is seeking to affirm simultaneously two cultural traditions. Unfortunately, this aspiration minimizes the degree to which culture is problematic, for no two cultures ever do match one another exactly, and no religious message can simply be stripped of one set of cultural associations and reclothed with others. The Latter-day Saints struggled to express themselves in New Zealand terms because American culture was dominant in their experience, and they had only one culture to adjust to in New Zealand. That struggle spells out how difficult it is for outsiders to identify with Maori culture. The experience of other churches suggests that European and indigenous cultures can never quite become equivalents. How complex, then, is religious conversion, and how difficult it is for us to understand how it occurs within cultures other than our own.

Notes

1. Existing accounts of the Church vary in quality. The most useful include Brian Hunt's Brigham Young University thesis subsequently published as *Zion in New Zealand: A History of the Church of Jesus Christ of Latter-day Saints in New Zealand, 1854–1977* (Templeview, Hamilton: Church College of New Zealand, 1977), and R. Lanier Britsch, *Unto the Islands of the Sea: A History of the Latter-day Saints in the Pacific* (Salt Lake City: Deseret Book, 1986), 253–345. Secular accounts of the Church include an excellent master's thesis in history by Ian Rewi Barker, "The Connexion: The Mormon Church and the Maori People" (Master's thesis, Victoria University of Wellington, 1967), although this did not draw upon the first (Australasian) volume of the mission history, and a brilliant master's thesis in anthropology and sociology by Erik G. Schwimmer, "Mormonism in a Maori Village: A Study in Social Change" (Master's thesis, University of British Columbia, 1965), although this study

was not historical in character and focused on one small Northland village. An interesting interpretative essay is Laurie H. Barber, "Another Look at the History of the Church of Latter-day Saints in New Zealand," in *Under the Southern Cross,* ed. John Hinchliff and Norman Simms (Auckland, NZ: Outrigger Publishers, 1980), 30–36. The author draws attention to the following new works on Mormons in New Zealand that have appeared since this article: Ian Barber, "Between Biculturalism and Assimilation: The Changing Place of Maori Culture in the Twentieth-Century New Zealand Mormon Church," *New Zealand Journal of History* 29(2) (1995): 142–69; Ian G. Barber and David Gilgen, "Between Covenant and Treaty: The LDS Future in New Zealand," *Dialogue: A Journal of Mormon Thought* 29(1) (1996): 207–22; Marjorie Newton, "Mormonism in New Zealand: A Historical Appraisal" (PhD thesis, University of Sydney, 1998); and Grant Underwood, "Mormonism, the Maori and Cultural Authenticity," *Journal of Pacific History* 35(2) (2000): 133–46.

2. *New Zealand Parliamentary Debates,* 18 October 1871, 11:390–91.

3. *New Zealand Herald* (Auckland), 7 March 1881, 5; *Canterbury Times* (Christchurch), 1 May 1901, 30; ibid., 2 October 1901, 29–30; *Press* (Christchurch), 29 April 1901, 5; ibid., 6 May 1901, 4; ibid., 1 October 1901, 3.

4. Frederick William Hurst, "Diary, 1833 to 14 March 1894," compiled by Samuel Harris Hurst and Ida Frederickson Hurst, typescript (Provo, Utah: Brigham Young University, 1961), 112.

5. William John Bromley, Journals and Notebook, 18 December 1880, Mss. 1913, LDS Church Archives.

6. Hurst, Diary, 23 January 1876, 135.

7. Membership Records of Kakanui, Waiomio, Nhawah, Waikare and Maungakahia branches, Family History Center microfilm #0128889, item 6, entry for October 1922; marked LDS film area, Historian's Office no. 7849; read at Palmerston North LDS Family History Center.

8. Alma Greenwood, Journal, 12 February 1883, Mss. 336, Perry Special Collections; Bromley, Journal, 13 and 17 March 1883; Bromley, "Presenting the Gospel to Maories," paper included in Bromley's journal, 3 March 1883.

9. Bromley, Journal, 5 April 1881.

10. Hurst, Diary, 20 February 1876; Australasian Mission History (CRMH 6048), 18 October 1881, LDS Church Archives. The mission history, compiled about 1900, collates Utah newspaper clippings and other sources, inserting them at the date of the event or writing, rather than at the date of publication, and giving a brief indication, often incomplete, of the source. Bromley, Journal, 11 March and 27–28 April 1881.

11. See Bromley, Journal, 3 and 9 September 1881.

12. Ibid., 20 October 1881, 30 March 1882.

13. Australasian Mission History, 18 October 1881; Bromley, Journal, 6 March and 20 March 1881.

14. Bromley, Journal, 13, 16, 18 June and 14 July 1881; J. P. Sorenson, "Biography, Diary, Genealogy and Family Records, 1885–1908," 12 and 17 June 1881, microfilm #436, Perry Special Collections.

15. Greenwood, Journal, 2 and 31 January 1883.

16. Bromley, Journal, 14 February 1883.

17. Greenwood, Journal, 28 February–6 March 1883; Bromley, Journal, 13, 17 March and 14 April 1881; Australasian Mission History, 30 December 1883. Curiously, Bromley never mentions the McDonnell case in his journal.

18. Australasian Mission History, 21 July 1883, 11 April 1884; Greenwood, Journal, 4–6 April 1883.

19. Australasian Mission History, November–December 1884; 15 June 1894.

20. Ibid., 18 January 1885; Edward Newby, Journals and Letters, 16 January 1884, Mss. 8513, LDS Church Archives.

21. New Zealand Government, Department of Statistics, *1986 Census of Population and Dwellings*, "Population Resident in New Zealand, Religious Profession and Sex by Ethnic Origin and Persons on New Zealand Maori and Pacific Island Polynesian Descent: One, Ethnic Origin." Data provided by the Department of Statistics, Christchurch.

22. Quoted in Australasian Mission History, 25 February 1890, from letter to *Deseret News*, vol. 40, p. 634.

23. Herber Cutler, Whangaroa, Bay of Islands, 11 November 1890, Letter to *Deseret Weekly News*, 42:153, in Australasian Mission History, 11 November 1890.

24. Clara Richards, *They Conquered by Faith: A Biography of Ezra and Amanda Richards* (Bountiful, Utah: Horizon Publishers, 1978), 55–60.

25. William Douglass, Journal Notes, 28 July 1891, Pacific Manuscripts Bureau microfilm #118, Research School of Pacific Studies, Australian National University, Canberra, Australia.

26. For example, W. S. Reid, mentioned in Australasian Mission History, 29 December 1889.

27. Quoted in Hunt, *Zion in New Zealand*, 18.

28. Nelson Spicer Bishop, Diary, 17 June 1887, typescript, 1948, Perry Special Collections.

29. Henry A. Smith, *Matthew Cowley: Man of Faith* (Salt Lake City: Bookcraft, 1954), 60.

30. Australasian Mission History, 27 May 1888.

31. J. S. Nye, Missionary Journal, 25 June and 14 October 1888, Mss. 8500, LDS Church Archives. See also Smith, *Matthew Cowley*, 47, 51.

32. For example, Douglass, Journal Notes, 27 May 1891.

33. Australasian Mission History, 23 March 1892 and 31 March 1897.

34. For efforts to develop interest in genealogy, see, for example, Richards, *They Conquered by Faith*, 54; New Zealand Mission History, 14 February 1898, LDS Church Archives; *Te Karere*, 30 (August 1936): 329–32; and ibid., 35 (October 1941), 804. This periodical was published fortnightly by the New Zealand Mission in Auckland beginning in 1907; copies at Parliamentary Library in Wellington. Schwimmer uses the argument of genealogical interest (Hunt, *Zion in New Zealand*, 20), but Barker, "The Connexion," 77, 123, notes the lack of interest.

35. Ihaia, Obituary by Edwin C. Davis, *Deseret News*, 1886, 603, in Australasian Mission History, April 1886. D. T. Barry's list of Maori clergy, prepared for the Church Missionary Society in 1905 and made available to me by R. M. Meha of the *Dictionary of New Zealand Biography* Unit, Wellington, does not list him. The first Maori clergy were ordained in 1855, so the tradition of Ihaia's forty years of ministry in the Church of England, reported in Davis's obituary, is unlikely.

36. Australasian Mission History, 26 August 1883; Greenwood, Journal, 21 July and 26 August 1883.

37. *Dictionary of New Zealand Biography*, ed. W. H. Oliver (Wellington, NZ: Allen & Unwin, 1990), 1:467–48; Greenwood, Journal, 30 August 1883.

38. Edward H. Anderson, "Events and Comments," *Improvement Era* 9 (January 1906): 260; *Dictionary of New Zealand Biography*, 1:584 (on Ihaka Whaanga) and 1:467–68 (on Piripi Te Maari).

39. Australasian Mission History, 9 September and 11 December 1884.

40. Australasian Mission History, 4 October 1895; *Dictionary of New Zealand Biography*, 1:442–43.

41. Charles Anderson, Waotu, Waikato, 13 December 1884, Letter to the *Deseret News* (1885), 140, in Australasian Mission History, 19 January 1885.

42. Newby, Journal, 19 January 1885.

43. Bishop, Diary, 15 June 1887.

44. Douglass, Journal Notes, 16 and 19 June, 22 July, and 4 November 1891; Australasian Mission History, 4 and 8 November 1891.

45. Australasian Mission History, 3 August 1894 and 8 April 1897.

46. Ibid., 7 April 1886.

47. Ibid., 14 February 1886. See also a confused account of this incident in Richards, *They Conquered by Faith*, 18–23.

48. *Deseret News*, 24 October 1888, 1122, in Australasian Mission History, 20 August 1888, and Mission Record A [Appendix], 61, 73.

49. *Deseret News* (1885), 140, in Australasian Mission History, 19 January 1885; *Church Gazette* (Auckland Diocese, Church of England), February 1901, 37, and May 1903, 92–93.

50. Heber Sears, Muriwai, New Zealand, 11 March 1887, Letter to *Deseret News*, n.d., in Australasian Mission History, 11 March 1887.

51. Douglass, Journal Notes, 20 May 1894.

52. Alma Greenwood, 11 April 1884, Letter to *Deseret News* (1884), 578, in Australasian Mission History, 11 April 1884. See also Douglass, Journal Notes, 10 September 1891.

53. George Batt, Letter to *Deseret Weekly News* 29 (1880): 679, in Australasian Mission History, 6 December 1880; Sears, Letter to *Deseret News;* see also Australasian Mission History, 9 January 1882.

54. Greenwood, Journal, 5 April 1883.

55. Elias Johnson, Letter to *Deseret News,* 23 May 1888, 294, in Australasian Mission History, 23 May 1888.

56. Wesleyan Methodist Church, *Home Mission and Church Extension Fund Report, 1903* (Auckland, NZ: Wesleyan Methodist Church, 1903), 12; copy in Methodist Archives, Christchurch, New Zealand.

57. Benjamin Goddard, Letter to *Deseret News,* 45:494, in Australasian Mission History, 6 September 1892.

58. Greenwood, Journal, 10 October 1883.

59. New Zealand Mission History, 20 March 1900.

60. Australasian Mission History, 30 December 1883 (Waikato), 25 March 1888 (Wairoa Land Court), 27 May 1888 and 17 August 1890 (Hawke's Bay).

61. Barker, "The Connexion," 45.

62. Australasian Mission History, 18 January 1885; G. V. Butterworth, "The Establishment of the Maori Bishopric," ca. 1980, not paginated, photocopy in my possession.

63. Benjamin Goddard, Letter to *Deseret News,* 48:172, in Australasian Mission History, 26 November 1892.

64. Benjamin Goddard, Letter to *Deseret News,* 49:396, in Australasian Mission History, 6 August 1894.

65. Newby, Journal, 20 April 1885.

66. B. Elsmore, *Mana from Heaven: A Century of Maori Prophets in New Zealand* (Tauranga, NZ: Moana Press, 1989). See also Barber, "Another Look."

67. Australasian Mission History, 30 August 1885; New Zealand Mission History, 12 January 1899; Bishop, Diary, 244–45; Douglass, Journal Notes, 7 October 1893.

68. Bromley, Journal, 6 and 20 March, 18 and 20 June 1881; Sorenson, Journal, 12–17 June 1881; Australasian Mission History, 3 November 1884 (Matiu).

69. Ezra T. Stevenson, Letter to *Deseret News*, 20 April 1888, 408, in Australasian Mission History, 20 March 1888, also 23 February 1890 and 9 April 1892; Bishop, Diary, 3–6 March 1888.

70. Norman Douglas, "The Sons of Lehi and the Seed of Cain: Racial Myths in Mormon Scripture and Their Relevance to the Pacific Islands," *Journal of Religious History* 8(1) (June 1974): 100.

71. J. Binney, *The Legacy of Guilt: A Life of Thomas Kendall* (Auckland, NZ: Oxford University Press, 1968), 131–33; Elsmore, *Mana from Heaven*, 63–66; K. Sorrenson, "How to Civilize Savages," *New Zealand Journal of History* 9(2) (October 1975): 98, 108.

72. William A. Cole and Elwin W. Jensen, *Israel in the Pacific* (Salt Lake City: Genealogical Society of Utah, 1961), 20.

73. Richards, *They Conquered by Faith*, 59.

74. Greenwood, Journal, 15 May and 13 October 1883; Australasian Mission History, 15 September 1883.

75. Australasian Mission History, 18 January 1885.

76. Ibid., 6 April 1888.

77. Alma Greenwood, Letter to *Deseret News*, 1884, 578, in Australasian Mission History, 11 April 1884. See also Otene Meihana, quoted in Newby, Journal, 16 March 1885.

78. *Church Gazette*, March 1888, 26.

79. Australasian Mission History, 29 January 1893; Bishop, Diary, 3 March 1888.

80. Australasian Mission History, 8–10 April 1892. Ngawawaea Poipoi's name is given here as Nga wa ca.

81. Report on the Easter Conference, New Zealand Mission, *Deseret News*, 48:680, in Australasian Mission History, 6 April 1894; Schwimmer, "Mormonism in a Maori Village," 7–8.

82. Richards, *They Conquered by Faith*, 59.

83. Kate Paxman, Missionary Journal, 3 July 1886, Mss/d/6714, LDS Church Archives.

84. Hurst, Journal, 26 March 1876.

85. Douglass, Journal Notes, 30 December 1891.

86. Greenwood, Journal, 1 February 1883.

87. New Zealand Mission History, 14 February 1898.

88. Greenwood, Journal, 28–29 July 1883.

89. Australasian Mission History, 30 August 1885.

90. Australasian Mission History, 17 and 18 February 1883; Schwimmer, "Mormonism in a Maori Village," 8–22; Barker, "The Connexion," 83; Newby, Journal, 25 May and 5 July 1885; *Te Karere*, May 1934, 236; "Native Maoris as Missionaries," *Improvement Era* 20 (December 1916): 178.

91. For example, see Bishop, Diary, 12 August 1887.

92. See, for example, Ngawawaea Poipoi of Nuhaka at Mahia Conference, Australasian Mission History, 7 September 1895.

93. J. S. Abbott, Diary, 22 December 1892, Pacific Manuscripts Bureau MF #119.

94. Bishop, Diary, 3–5 March 1888; *Deseret News*, 20 April 1888, 408, in Australasian Mission History, 20 March 1888.

95. Newby, Journal, 6 July 1885.

96. Douglass, Journal Notes, 9 February 1892.

97. Bromley, Journal, 25 December 1882.

98. Greenwood, Journal, 1 September 1883.

99. See Elsmore, *Mana from Heaven*, 284; *Dictionary of New Zealand Biography*, 1:480–81.

100. For accounts of this prophecy recorded by missionaries, see Greenwood, Journal, 5 April and 16 August 1883; Newby, Journal, 2 February 1885; *Deseret News*, 40:733, in Australasian Mission History, 6 April 1890. See also Barker, "The Connexion," 6, 33, 46; Matthew Cowley, "Maori Chief Predicts Coming of L.D.S.," *Improvement Era* (September 1950): 696–97; Britsch, *Unto the Islands of the Sea*, 274–76; Hunt, *Zion in New Zealand*, 9–11.

101. Barker, "The Connexion," 46; "Hirini Whaanga, A Maori Prophet," *Juvenile Instructor* 37 (1902): 152–53, as quoted in Britsch, *Unto the Islands of the Sea*, 272–73. Whaanga was from Mahia, and Te Toira's grandson, Teira Marutu, became a Mormon, a fact not mentioned in his entry in the *Dictionary of New Zealand Biography*, 1:463.

102. Douglass, Journal Notes, April 1891.

103. Morori Piripi, "The History of Ngati Wait," *Te Ao Hou* 57 (1966): 46–47; Richards, *They Conquered by Faith*, 23–25.

104. Nye, Journal, 18 November 1888; Australasian Mission History, 6 April 1888; Bishop, Diary, 9 April 1888.

105. *Dictionary of New Zealand Biography*, 1:214–15 (on Hoani Te Whataroa Jury); Australasian Mission History, 23 February 1886.

106. For example, Australasian Mission History, 11 June 1893; Douglass, Journal Notes, 23 July 1891.

107. New Zealand Mission History, 26 July 1898 and 21–22 January 1899. See also ibid., 25 November 1902, 30 March 1903; Barker, "The Connexion," 59.

108. Australasian Mission History, 17 March 1883, 6 February 1888; *Deseret News*, 23 March 1889, in ibid., 25 February 1889; Richards, *They Conquered by Faith*, 24–25; Kate Paxman, Journal, 30 July 1886; Douglass, Journal Notes, 28 September 1893.

109. J. M. R. Owens, "Missionary Medicine and Maori Health: The Record of the Wesleyan Mission to New Zealand before 1840," *Journal of the Polynesian Society* 81 (December 1972): 418–36.

110. Bishop, Diary, 2 December 1887. For a comment that the elders had lost their power to heal, see James C. Allan, Letter to *Deseret News*, 52:465, in Australasian Mission History, 7 September 1892.

111. Australasian Mission History, 8 August 1894 and 7 September 1895; New Zealand Mission History, 1–13 February 1898 and 7 March 1900.

112. See the report of the Mormon conference in *Auckland Weekly News*, 24 April 1902, 40. See also J. Binney, G. Chaplin and C. Wallace, *Mihaia: The Prophet Rua and His Community at Maungaupobatu* (Wellington, NZ: Oxford University Press, 1979).

113. Barker, "The Connexion," 52.

114. Australasian Mission History, 6 April 1889.

115. Heber J. Sears, Letter to the *Deseret News* (1887), 292, in Australasian Mission History, 30 January 1887.

116. Douglass, Journal Notes, 17 September and 16 December 1891, 1 February 1892; Bishop, Diary, 23 October 1888.

CHAPTER 14

National Perceptions of Utah's Statehood

Howard R. Lamar

The long and frustrating but dramatic history of Utah's struggle to gain statehood—or more accurately of the Mormon Church's efforts to gain statehood—has been told often, thoroughly, and well by both Utah and Western writers. It could be called a tragic tale that somehow ended on a most happy and successful note. The fantastic celebration of statehood in January 1896 in Salt Lake City with unforgettable parades and ceremonies and the powerful emotional drama of the transfer of the reins of government from federal territorial officials to the new state government brings one close to tears even after a century's passage.[1] With good reason, the statehood story has been the subject of articles, television shows, and conferences throughout 1996, for statehood symbolized both Mormon liberation and political maturation.

I note that your welcoming roadside signs say: "This is still the right place." Certainly it seemed the right place on Monday, 6 January 1896, as thousands gathered in Salt Lake City, creating crowds that, as the Associated Press reported to the entire nation, "made locomotion well-nigh impossible through the public thoroughfares."[2] (The word "gridlock" was not yet in fashion.) The Associated Press described how Grand Marshal Robert Taylor Burton and his aides guided the procession, which included "the Sixteenth Infantry, U.S.A. commanded by Gen. Penrose of Fort Douglas, the Utah National Guard, the State and city officers, the organized pioneers of the Grand Army of the Republic, Indian war veterans, and all the civil societies of this and surrounding cities."[3]

Patrick H. Lannan, owner of the *Salt Lake Tribune* and scarcely a friend of the Mormons, was so caught up in the spirit of celebration that he boasted to a reporter for the *Chicago Tribune,* "In almost every town of over 500 inhabitants . . . there were parades, speeches, fireworks, thanksgiving services and balls. Ogden and Provo led in this respect, the demonstrations there being on a large scale."[4]

Even so, those ceremonies could not match the visual spectacle, poignant speeches, and beautiful songs and music that greeted everyone who crowded into the Tabernacle that day. They were overwhelmed by a huge flag in the ceiling, its forty-fifth star made incandescent with red, white, and blue electric bulbs, with red, white, and blue streamers running from the flag down the walls to bunting and a huge American eagle set among the towering organ pipes. In addition an electric sign spelled out "UTAH."[5]

Once the ceremonies began, the transfer of political authority from Acting Governor Caleb Walton West to incoming Governor Heber M. Wells was probably the most moving and symbolic event of the day, but Governor Wells's inaugural address was equally extraordinary for its remarkable combination of a realistic factual approach and gracious prose.[6]

Although it is clear that the Associated Press carried a standard account of the statehood ceremonies to major newspapers across the nation, there has been less coverage of how other parts of the United States responded to the news that Utah was at last a state in the Union. In this address, I wish to focus my remarks on these national perceptions by looking at the comments about statehood, Utah's constitution, and its choice of its first two senators as found in a dozen major newspapers and magazines between July 1894, when President Grover Cleveland signed the Utah Enabling Act, and July 1896, when Utah's senators and its representative at large were part of the Washington scene. Incidentally, the regional newspapers reveal a surprising perspective on the older issues of polygamy and Church domination of Utah politics. In addition, their responses were generally so positive that it suggests that Utah leaders had carried out one of the most successful public relations campaigns ever mounted in the nineteenth century.

Before discussing newspaper coverage, however, let us start with a scene in the U.S. House of Representatives on 12 December 1893 when that body was considering House Bill No. 352, titled "To enable the people of Utah to form a constitution and a State government and be admitted into the Union on an equal footing with the original states." On that day, Congressman Joseph Wheeler of Alabama, an ex-Confederate general whose mastery of military strategy was reputedly second only to that of Stonewall Jackson and Jeb Stuart, moved consideration of Bill No. 352.[7] Wheeler was supported by Congressman Constantine Kilgore of Texas, another former Confederate general, although he disagreed on certain provisions.

Totally opposed, however, was Elijah Adams Morse, congressman from Massachusetts, who objected, saying the bill needed an amendment forbidding polygamy. Kilgore responded that it was not needed, then quoted President Benjamin Harrison's speech in Salt Lake City in which he told a Mormon audience that he believed in "one and only one uncrowned queen in every American home." Kilgore implied that all was well because the Mormons had taken Harrison's advice.

Congressman Morse then proceeded to dredge up all the old stereotypes about the mistreatment of Gentiles and how the territory was full of recently arrived immigrants who knew nothing about America. Nor could Morse resist referring to polygamy as the remaining of the twin "barbarisms" that the Republican Party had sworn to eradicate. But William Cogswell, also of Massachusetts, objected to Morse's remarks, saying, "All the evidence is against you."

When Morse retorted by citing the names of old Mormon leaders and their crimes, Congressman Case Broderick of Kansas, formerly a private in the Union army, responded by saying: "They are all dead, that crowd." At that point John Alfred Pickler of South Dakota asked if Morse's real objection was not polygamy but "the fact that it allows another Western State in the Union a representative upon the floor of Congress." Morse then tried the small population argument— namely, that it was unfair to have two senators for only 250,000 people when New York State had only two for its millions. The response was that Delaware and Rhode Island likewise had few people. Morse's rebuttal to that argument was that those two states had fought in the Revolution and that made it all right.

When pressed for the sources of his negative information, Morse said that he had a brother in a Utah coal company and that he had also read Ann Eliza Webb Young's story of her marriage to Brigham Young. (He mistakenly gave the title as *The Fifteenth Wife of Brigham Young*.) Congressman Wilson from Washington State was unimpressed, saying, "The non-Mormon people out there are a pretty robust set of people, and can take care of themselves." Unfazed, Morse retorted that there was a "very large population south of here that cannot take care of itself."[8]

At this point Utah's delegate, Joseph L. Rawlins, rose to say that statehood was a political and not a moral issue and, in a swipe at Morse, noted that the leaders who brought in polygamy were all born and educated in New England. That brought applause from the House members. Knowing that he had the sympathy of a majority of the Congressmen, Rawlins felt free not only to indulge in humorous hyperbole but to make jocular misstatements. For example, when asked if there were still Mormon and gentile newspapers in Utah, Rawlins said that was no longer the case.[9]

Mr. Wilson of Washington then asked if Utah becoming a state would "dispose of the Ute question and their removal from Colorado," to which Rawlins jocosely replied: "I think we will take the whites and leave Colorado to the Indians if we can get into the Union." To which the house responded with more laughter. Addressing Morse's charges more specifically, Rawlins said that Utah now had the population and a good educational system and that the outrages of the past, like the Mountain Meadows Massacre, were now history. One congressman then observed to Rawlins, "Why you were not even born when that happened." Rawlins corrected him: "I was only seven years (old) at the time but I did not participate in it." That produced even more laughter from the members. In a more serious vein, Rawlins observed that there had been a recent massacre of Chinese at Rock Springs and much violence in the recent Carnegie Steel strike. He then responded to Morse's citation of Ann Eliza Young's book by observing that Brigham Young was now dead; turning to Morse, he inquired facetiously, "Did you know that?" Here the *Congressional Record* reported "laughter and confusion in the Hall." Finally, Rawlins reminded his hearers, "Both the national parties in their platforms have declared in favor of the admission to the Territory," as had both parties in Utah.

After adopting certain amendments, the House passed Bill No. 352 the next day; the following summer, after more amendments, the Senate passed the bill on 10 July 1894. Three days later the House accepted the amendments—which were mostly about election dates and procedures—and voted overwhelmingly to admit Utah. On 24 July, a date already significant in Utah history, the House received a written message from the president's office that he had signed H.R. 352.[10] And, as is well known, during the next sixteen months, there followed a constitutional convention in March 1895 and an election of state officers, along with approval of the constitution in November 1895, so that by December 1895 everything had been done in preparation for statehood. Thus it was that on Saturday morning, 4 January 1896, Cleveland signed the declaration admitting Utah to statehood. When the news reached Salt Lake City by telegraph, shots were fired and the celebrating began.[11]

If we go back to the 1893 House proceedings for a moment, it is remarkable how quickly hostility had been changed to friendly support. That was not just happening in Congress, the national press, and in Utah but in neighboring Arizona as well. In his excellent study *Take Up Your Mission: Mormon Colonizing along the Little Colorado River, 1870–1900,* Charles S. Peterson recounts how, after experiencing years of hostility in Apache County, the Mormon settlers, with support from Governor John Zulick and the Cleveland administration, became active in Democratic politics. Although initially strongly anti-Mormon, after 1886 the Apache County Republicans also soon found that they needed Mormon votes to win elections. Peterson concludes that simultaneous development of party politics in the territory and division of church members between the two major parties created cross-currents of interests and political need which overrode the Mormon-Gentile cleavage, thus permitting an effective association of the two groups.[12]

Meanwhile to the north, the long and bitter anti-Mormon crusade in Idaho, epitomized in the careers of its first Republican delegate, Theodore F. Singiser, and U.S. Marshal Fred T. Dubois, was winding down. As Leonard Arrington has observed in his superb recent *History of Idaho*, Dubois had helped get the "harshest anti-Mormon legislation ever enacted" passed by the Idaho legislature. Mormons could not hold county offices or vote in general elections. At one point the legislature even carved out of Oneida a new anti-Mormon county, called Bingham.[13]

Two years after Idaho became a state in 1890, however, the Republican State Committee, led by William E. Borah, "dropped criticism of the Saints and welcomed them into the party." The Democratic State Committee soon followed "with a statement that they were willing to let the Saints vote." Arrington writes that in 1894, when the Mormon right to vote was finally cleared of legislative and judicial hurdles, in that year's elections "competition by both parties for the Mormon vote was intense." And when the new Idaho legislature met in February 1895, a combination of Republicans, Democrats, and Populists voted to repeal the anti-Mormon Test Oath of 1885. With that gesture of goodwill, concludes Arrington, "The Idaho anti-Mormon movement was over."[14]

Statehood Commentary from Leading Newspapers

Let us now look eastward and westward to see what some leading newspapers were saying about the prospect for statehood for Utah—the *New York Times*, the *Washington Post*, the *New Orleans Times-Picayune*, the *Chicago Tribune*, the *San Francisco Chronicle*, and the *Los Angeles Times*. In 1895 and 1896, the newspapers were preoccupied with the effects of the Panic of 1893, bitter debates over free silver, the rise of Populism, and a crisis with Great Britain over Venezuela leading to long discussions over the meaning of the Monroe Doctrine. Nevertheless, both the Mormons and Utah statehood got excellent coverage in the *New York Times* and in other papers across the nation.[15]

On 3 January 1896, the *Times* printed an article titled "Mormons Heading East: More Missionaries about to Enter Field Hereabouts." The story was based on an interview with Samuel W. Richards, president of the Eastern States Mission, and Arthur F. Barnes, a businessman from Utah. Richards commented that nine missionaries were already in the New York area with twenty additional elders about to come. The *Times* obligingly printed the "Articles of Faith" of the Church as well. Barnes described the five U.S. mission fields and then noted that the headquarters of the Eastern States Mission was in Brooklyn "just over the bridge."[16]

Barnes responded to the reporter's inevitable questions about polygamy by saying that missionaries never discuss polygamy since it is no longer practiced. Actually, both Richards and Barnes seemed to have their minds more on Utah politics, for they confided to the reporter that they were Democrats, then commented that the missionary forces had been used as a weapon against the Utah Democrats by such powerful Republican leaders as George Q. Cannon, first counselor in the First Presidency, who sent Mormon Democrats on missions so they could not strengthen their party at home.

This partisan lament was forgotten when, on the following day, the *Times* carried an upbeat article titled "Utah's Riches Untold: Statehood Will Be Followed by Great Developments." This time the Utah spokesman was businessman Spencer Clawson, who predicted that "Within a Few Years the New State Will Take a Prominent Place in the Mining World."[17] Clawson's optimistic prophecy neatly coincided with Cleveland's 4 January proclamation approving the Utah Constitution and declaring the territory a state.

The article noted the presence of a large body of Mormons in New York City—the St. Denis Hotel was "practically the headquarters of Utah representatives." The reporter observed that among those who will be in the city today are "A. H. Woodruff, son of Wilford Woodruff, the venerable President," Junius P. Wells, brother of the recently elected governor of Utah, and Spencer Clawson, who was not only a prominent Republican but "one of the largest wholesale dealers in Salt Lake City[,] . . . well known among the dry goods men in New York, as he has visited them annually for the last twenty-five years."[18]

In a subsequent interview held at the Waldorf, Clawson dwelled at length on the arrival of statehood. "Saturday will be a great day for Utah," for after six constitutions had been rejected, Utah now had one. When the new state constitution took effect on Monday and the new state officers were inaugurated, "All the people of the State will take part in the general rejoicing." Indeed, Clawson thought it would be the greatest political gathering in Utah's history but added, "Politics will cut no figure in the general rejoicing."[19]

Continuing in his role as economic prophet, Clawson asserted that statehood would bring rapid development, especially of a large mining industry. Further, Salt Lake City will become the chief "distribution point for Utah, Eastern Nevada, Western Colorado, Western Wyoming and Southern Idaho." Clawson listed Utah's resources as silver, iron, salt, water power, copper, coal, and just then gold because the cyanide process made it cheaper to extract. Finally, Clawson recalled that previously Utah did not know how to advertise as Colorado and Montana did, "but New York men are beginning to go there."[20]

On Sunday, 5 January, the *Times* reported that Cleveland had signed the Utah proclamation. After reassuring its readers that the new state legislature would not revoke the constitutional clause forbidding polygamy, the paper asserted, probably incorrectly, that the majority of incoming state officials were non-Mormon. Governor Heber M. Wells was a prominent businessman and a fine actor in the local fine arts.[21] (One assumes that when you have a new state it is best to start off with a governor who is a good rather than a bad actor.) The *Times* then speculated about whom the legislature would name as Utah's first two senators. And this question might well be called Act II of the Utah statehood drama.

When Frank J. Cannon, newspaperman and son of George Q. Cannon of the LDS First Presidency, and Arthur Brown, a non-Mormon lawyer and politician, were named Utah's senators later in January, the *Times*'s upbeat pro-Mormon stance suddenly cooled, obviously because "Both Are Strong Advocates of the Free Coinage of Silver." "The tone of the Senate will not be elevated by the Utah Senators," opined the *Times* sententiously, saying that Brown was so pugnacious he will be another Tillman.[22] On the other hand, Cannon "rather delights in his ability to play politics," makes flowery speeches, and uses stage techniques. In a contemptuous comparison, the newspaper predicted that Cannon "will almost be a counterpart of Senator Dubois of Idaho, who is noted for his manipulations in the Senate and his own State," and added further insult by declaring that Cannon's political prominence has not been due to his native ability but to his name and the power of his father, George Q. Cannon.[23]

If the *Times*'s preoccupation was with Utah's business potential and its senators' views on the silver issue, the *Washington Post* was concerned with politics, ceremony, and the constitution. It noted that on 4 January, "the signature of the proclamation was awaited with great interest by Gov. West and Delegate Cannon, just outside the President's room." West and Cannon were called in after the signing, and West was given the pen, which was later exhibited in Utah.[24]

The *Post* also carried a special article, datelined Salt Lake City, which noted that the committee on the inauguration consisted of George Q. Cannon, chairman of the Republican State Convention; Judge O. W. Powers, the Democratic chairman; and Dr. R. A. Hasbrouck, the Populist chairman.[25]

In addition to recounting details about the actual celebrations, the *Post* commented approvingly on the conservative nature of the Utah constitution with its emphasis on a small debt, a tax of no more than eight mills, a ban on the use of the credit power of the state for railroads, no appropriations for a capitol building for five years, and low salaries for state officials. Naturally, the paper also approved the clause forbidding polygamy and a promise of full provisions for public schools.

Although the *New York Times* and the *Washington Post* stressed different aspects, most of the content for both was provided by the Associated Press, as one realizes when looking at the Utah statehood coverage in the *New Orleans Times-Picayune*. Even so, the *Picayune*'s coverage was extensive and favorable. For this Southern paper, the theme of reconciliation in Governor Wells's inaugural address must have had very special meaning for readers with vivid memories of Radical Republican Reconstruction in Louisiana. One can imagine their thoughts as Wells rhetorically asked, what more in the way of proof is needed for sincerity than the fact that Judge Zane, who "sentenced hundreds of Mormons to the penitentiary, now sits upon this platform as the honored choice of the electors of Utah for the highest judicial office in the state" and "that a Mormon born and reared should be delivering from the same platform this address as the governor of Utah.[26]

Given the troubled and tragic past experiences of the Mormons at Nauvoo, it is perhaps not surprising that the *Chicago Tribune* gave what may have been the fullest coverage of statehood events outside of Utah itself. Certainly a major factor in such extensive coverage was a "Special Message to the *Tribune*," datelined 4 January from incoming Governor Wells.[27] Wells's *Tribune* message was certainly one of the most effective "soft sells" in behalf of statehood on record. Obviously, it was an arranged printing, and although it is clear that much of what he had to say was to be a part of his inaugural address, this text is more assertive. Wells began by noting correctly that Utah had a greater population than the states of Delaware, Nevada, Montana, Idaho, or North Dakota, then asserted: "Its industrial wealth is greater than any of its surrounding sisters"—a statement that Coloradans would probably have violently disputed. After *Tribune* readers were assured that there would always be separation of church and state and that polygamous marriages would continue to be prohibited, Wells declared, "Our youth have been taught that patriotic love for country perpetuates liberty." In a moving peroration Wells said, "Utah today stretches forth its arms and beckons to the densely-peopled districts of the East to come out and share its glories."[28]

The *Chicago Tribune* also interviewed Patrick H. Lannan, owner of the *Salt Lake Tribune*, who declared that "I think Statehood is for the best" but could not resist observing: "Nevertheless, it was the business houses and homes of the Mormons that bore the heaviest weight of bunting today, and it was the Mormon Temple that was brilliantly illuminated from ground to dome, and not the other Christian churches."[29]

The *Chicago Tribune* even printed congratulatory telegrams to Governor Wells. From Washington, D.C., Frank Cannon urged Wells "to lift your eyes to the mountains and kiss the valleys of our dear Mother Utah and thank God for freedom." From New York City, Spencer Clawson wired what I would call an economic potential message symbolically addressed to H. M. Wells, at the State Bank. The message was: "While on the summit how looketh the promised land?"[30]

The paper devoted an entire section to the "Story of the Efforts of Utah to Become a State," again possibly a planted article that featured interviews with both Church President Wilford Woodruff and C. C. Goodwin, politician and long-time editor of the anti-Mormon *Salt Lake Tribune*. Both men exhibited unbridled optimism. Woodruff thought that Utah had a fabulous mineral future: "Wait until the time when all these [minerals] begin to be put into commercial form!" Utah's climate was so healthy, he added, that it "is a natural sanitarium." Moreover, the diversified scenery will inspire children. "In Utah, twenty-five years hence, people may look for artists, poets, painters and sculptors."[31] One wonders if the parents of Solon and Gutzon Borglum were still living in Ogden and read Woodruff's words.

In turn, Goodwin explained how the national Democratic Party had failed to get statehood during Cleveland's first term and how that failure had lured John T. Caine and other leaders into the Republican Party. In sum, anyone reading the *Chicago Tribune* could come away with a history of Utah, some knowledge of its leaders, and a very positive image of the new state.

A sampling of two leading California newspapers reveals very different perspectives about the meaning of Utah statehood. The *San Francisco Chronicle*, for example, was obsessed with the national debate over whether to keep the gold standard or remonetize silver. One of its lead articles on 4 January 1896 was not about Utah but "The Plan to Make Arizona a State." The *Chronicle* lamented that Arizona's statehood would be opposed by the gold men in the House of Representatives where they had the majority, while it would be supported by the prosilver senators, who were a majority in the U.S. Senate. The prognosis was that the House would never admit a state that would send two more silver senators to Washington. Arizona being in effect an economic satellite of California, it is easy to see why events there were followed so closely. Indeed, the next day the *Chronicle* showed its true colors by declaring for Arizona statehood regardless of the silver crusade. To keep Arizona out, opined the *Chronicle*, "is a gross and unpardonable outrage upon the people of the Territory, who are citizens of the United States, and who are entitled to come to full stature of civic mankind."[32] One can only guess that Utah statehood had set the *Chronicle* to thinking about Arizona statehood, as, of course, Arizonians already were.

The *Chronicle's* associative reasoning appeared in another form after it had reprinted the standard Associated Press accounts of Cleveland's proclamation, statehood ceremonies in Salt Lake City, and the great rejoicing throughout Utah. However, in the same issue, it reported that South Carolina's new constitution disfranchised Negro voters, prohibited divorce, and outlawed the Pinkerton detectives, who had gained an unenviable reputation as strikebreakers who promoted violence to give labor a bad name. Exhibiting open contempt for South Carolina, the *Chronicle* wrote: "Taking the instrument altogether it is very typical of South Carolina."[33]

The *Chronicle* gave full and totally favorable coverage of the statehood ceremonies in Salt Lake, saying it promised to be "the biggest demonstration ever seen in the intermountain country."[34] In an editorial on Utah's admission, the paper asserted that the old fears of renewal of polygamy and Church domination were groundless. Reasonable people all now understand that these two issues are "outworn." Again revealing its own prosilver stand, the *Chronicle* declared Utah to be "sound as a dollar on the financial question." All Utahns "regardless of party believe silver is a true, genuine, historical, and necessary metal."[35]

Unlike many other newspapers, the *Chronicle* closely followed the contest for the first Utah Senate seats, noting in great detail why George Q. Cannon lost out to his son Frank, who, incidentally, had once been a reporter for the *Chronicle*. The paper also provided biographies of both Cannon and his fellow senator, Arthur Brown, who was described as a protectionist and a radical free silver advocate.[36] However, after praising Brown as a faithful Republican and "lawyer of marked ability," the *Chronicle* had second thoughts. On 16 January, the paper quoted the *Salt Lake Tribune* as saying that the choice of Arthur Brown for senator "will mean nothing good for the Republicans locally; it will signify nothing for Utah before the Nation."[37]

On the other hand, the paper saw Cannon as a good choice, whose voice in the Senate in favor of silver "will be heard along with those of Teller and Jones and Morgan." In praising Cannon, the *Chronicle* took its cue from an editorial in the *Rocky Mountain News* of Denver that called Cannon "thoroughly and heartily a Western man, full of Western ideas and energy and enterprise and at all times will be found defending the rights and interests of the great trans-Missouri region." Newspapermen especially should be pleased at Cannon's choice, added the Denver paper, for he "has long been one of Utah's brightest journalists, second in rank only to Judge Goodwin of the Salt Lake Tribune."[38] Goodwin, incidentally, had been the *Rocky Mountain News*'s choice for the second Utah Senate seat.

To the credit of the *Chronicle,* it followed the story of the Utah senators through the swearing-in ceremonies on 27 January. Ironically, it was Senator Fred Dubois of Idaho who presented Frank Cannon's credentials, while Senator Burrows of Michigan, which was Brown's home state, presented those of Brown.[39]

I would like to close my summary of how a number of newspapers from all over the nation covered Utah statehood with a brief look at the comments of the *Los Angeles Sunday Times.* Here one finds the first hint of editorial negativism when, on 29 December 1895, the *Times* printed an interview with Mormon Bishop Richard W. Hart, who was visiting relatives in Kansas during the Christmas holidays. Contrary to what everyone else was saying, Hart stated that the Church "will rule in the matter of choosing state officials" and, once free from federal influence, would again adopt polygamy. One begins to realize that Hart was not without personal reasons for his comments when he told the reporter that he already had three wives and was being urged to take a fourth on his return from missionary work in Georgia.[40] Only a day later, however, the *Los Angeles Times* had rejoined the chorus of praise in an article commending the Mormon settlers at Mesa, Arizona, and extolling what they had done throughout the Gila Valley.[41]

In addition to printing the usual Associated Press story about the inauguration, the *Times* described the inaugural ball as "by far the most notable social event that has ever taken place in the city," with "society, in gorgeous costume," trying "to eclipse the brilliancy of the 10,000 electric lights that shone from above."[42] (The more one reads, the more it seems that the largest cost of the Utah statehood celebrations was the electric bill.)

Later in January, the *Los Angeles Times* also wrote approvingly of Utah's constitution, focusing particularly on the clause that "guarantees to every citizen the right to accept employment whenever he can obtain it, and makes interference with this right a felony." Reading between the lines, it looks as if the paper was in favor of strikebreaking. Indeed, the paper supported this clause so strongly it urged that the provision should be embedded in the constitution of every state in the Union. And finally, the *Times* predicted that given Utah's wonderful resources, it "seems destined to become in due time, one of the greatest and richest states in the Union."[43]

All in all, both the Mormons and Utah statehood had about the most favorable national press from key newspapers that one could hope for. The reasons are both obvious and obscure. The strongest and by far the most significant was the Church's decision to cooperate with the federal government rather than resist. Second, the Church's political leadership was not only wide-ranging but often brilliant. Third, the favorable image conveyed to the national press by Salt Lake City editors and reporters was articulate and persuasive, especially after the *Salt Lake Tribune* joined in the effort. Fourth, both Mormon and non-Mormon businessmen had established major contacts with Eastern and California investors and businessmen. As is well known, Colonel Isaac Trumbo came to Utah representing Havemeyer sugar interests and hoping to be a senator. Frank Cannon was in the beet sugar business. Others wanted to build a railroad connecting Salt Lake and Los Angeles. Still others were excited by the gold discoveries at Mercur. Allusions to Utah with its mineral resources becoming a second South Africa were not uncommon. And of course, the ferocious debate over whether to remonetize silver or continue on the gold standard seemed destined to benefit Utah no matter how that debate was resolved, for Utah had both metals. Fifth, after years of resistance, Congress had admitted the four omnibus states in 1889 and Idaho and Wyoming in 1890. Of the six admitted, only one, Washington, had a population comparable to Utah's. Moreover, both American politicians and the public were disgusted by the contrast between relatively unpopulated and unprosperous Nevada and the booming, well-populated territory of Utah. Utah deserved a fair shake. As *The Nation* observed in 1894 when Congress passed the Enabling Act, "The only cause for regret about the admission of Utah is the fact that it was not annexed to Nevada and the two made one state. This were practicable now, but it will be next to impossible hereafter. As it is, the sage-brush State, with its petty population constantly dwindling, remains insoluble."[44]

In short, no state coming into the Union after the Civil War, with the exception of golden Colorado in 1876 and fertile, forested Washington in 1889, had as much in its favor as Utah. All agreed that the Mormons had indeed made the desert blossom as the rose, a phrase that was quoted ad nauseam.

Dissenting Views: Home Missionary Literature

But had all been forgiven? We recall C. C. Goodwin's observation that the Christian churches in Salt Lake City were not celebrating statehood. While it is well known that Protestant denominations, and especially the Methodists and Presbyterians, had crusaded against Mormonism and polygamy for more than thirty years, it was unclear whether their views had shifted after the Manifesto of 1890.

A sampling of Methodist, Presbyterian, and interdenominational home missionary journals provides revealing clues that the hostility was unabated. In the monthly publication of the General Assembly of the Presbyterian Church, *The Church at Home and Abroad,* phrases such as "a priest-ridden people" were still being used in 1894.[45] A Presbyterian minister, Reverend N. E. Clemenson, while reporting what seemed to be a successful Presbyterian revival and set of conversions in Mount Pleasant and Spanish Fork, still warned: "Utah's hope and future glory and prosperity lie in the Christianization of her people, in God's redeeming power and not in the intrigue, selfishness and folly of the politician. Give us first the territory for Christ and then we shall be ready thankfully, because safely, to receive Statehood."[46] A year later the journal sounded an alarm: "Mormon missions in almost every state in the Union have received a quickening impulse ever since the passage by congress of the enabling act by which Utah is coming out from under the national administration into the power of a sovereign state."[47] The one bright spot that the Presbyterians noted in their generally sober, even gloomy, reports was that their schools had helped foster a belief in and support for public schools in Utah.[48]

A far more realistic account of local Protestant missionary efforts appeared in the September 1896 issue of the *Methodist Review* by the Reverend F. S. Begge, who wrote: "Mormonism is the dominant religious, social, mercantile and political force in Utah, which has lately become one of the States of the Union. Beyond this, it is getting large control among the people of three outer States, Nevada, Idaho, and Wyoming, and is extending into Arizona and New Mexico. . . . It is in the West to stay." Begge added that most businessmen "do not care how many wives a man has if he can secure his trade." Moreover, although the Christian churches of the East had spent more than two million dollars in Utah over the last twenty-five years—more than was spent in any other western state or territory, the effort had been largely wasted. He lamented, "If two hundred real Mormons have been changed and made into earnest evangelical Christians during that time we have not been able to discover them." He then listed very cogent reasons for the gentile missionary failure, which I will not detail here.[49]

Needless to say, Begge's remarks sent his fellow missionaries into a state of shock, and at their annual meeting in Ogden during September 1896, they promised a rebuttal. Yet the Reverend T. C. Iliff, when asked to pen a response, declined to do so. So far as I have been able to ascertain, nothing but a brief and weak rejoinder ever came forth. Instead, the Methodists asserted, as had the Presbyterians and the Congregationalists, that "the Christian schools have wrought a marvelous reformation throughout the length and breadth of Utah."[50] As late as 1903, Joseph Bourne Clark, secretary of the Congregational Home Missionary Society, wrote a revealing book, *Leavening the Nation: The Story of American Home Missions.* Here, too, Clark admitted that missionary zeal in Utah was "inclined strongly towards educational effort. The hope of the people was felt to be in the children almost alone." But Clark ended his essay with an admonition to fight "Mormonism and Romanism."[51]

While Protestant missionary publications continued to show concern about Mormonism, a brief review of national journals and magazines suggests a striking lack of interest. During 1896, no coverage on Utah's statehood appeared in four major publications, the *Atlantic Monthly*, *Harper's Monthly*, the *North American Review*, and *The Review of Reviews*.

The Nation, on the other hand, was fascinated with the fact that the Utah Constitution allowed women to vote "on equal terms with men and establishes the novelty in judicial terms of a jury of eight men instead of the traditional twelve. . . . The newer States of the West are naturally far more ready to break with the traditions and try experiments than the older commonwealths of the East."[52] *The Nation* was much less enthusiastic about Utah's two Republican senators, however, arguing that they will be "'red hot' for free coinage. . . . The sound-money cause will thus be put at a further disadvantage in the Senate, where its representatives are already in a minority. The next thing to be expected is a strong movement for the admission of Arizona, New Mexico, and Oklahoma, and the consequent strengthening of the free-coinage element in the upper branch by six more votes."[53]

Sounding an uncannily contemporary note, *The Nation* concluded that the swearing in of two new senators from Utah brings the Senate to ninety members—"almost twice as many as sixty years ago. . . . The Senate was never so large a body as now, and it never stood lower in public esteem. . . . The Senate to-day is a less conservative body than the House, and it is more easily carried for any wild scheme. Not only has it lost its old hold upon the public, but it is regarded with a growing contempt."[54] This was written exactly one hundred years ago. So what else is news, ladies and gentlemen?

Evaluation and Analysis

One comes away from this admittedly selective survey of the national media's perceptions of Utah statehood with a sense of awe about how Utah's leaders carried it off. From 1890 onward, it was not only an extensive and coordinated campaign but often a brilliant one. Not every statehood campaign had a set of able lobbyists in Washington that included not just religious representatives but politicians from both parties. Few states had as able and vocal a set of business spokesmen in New York City—a group that incidentally had close connections with Mayor Abraham Hewitt. Not every potential state had such good connections to the news media or had an incoming governor who could send an eloquent special message to the *Chicago Tribune*. Not every statehood campaign could have avoided the silver and gold debate by seeming to embrace both sides.

Perhaps most remarkable of all, statehood was shepherded through the House and Senate not by delegate Rawlins alone but by a curious mixture of two former Confederate generals—Kilgore of Texas and Wheeler of Alabama, both Democrats—and three Union veterans: William Cogswell of Massachusetts; John Alfred Pickler, a Republican Congressman from South Dakota; and Case Broderick of Kansas. The latter had served on the Supreme Court of Idaho between 1884 and 1888 but had returned to his native Kansas, where he was elected to Congress.[55]

But that is only part of the story of coordinations. Though initially cool to Utah, President Benjamin Harrison not only promoted statehood for all western territories but had a western network that often had ties to his home state of Indiana. Indianians held territorial offices all over the West. Statehood supporter Senator John L. Wilson of Washington state hailed from Indiana, where his father had been a Congressman, and delegate Joseph Rawlins had attended Indiana University.[56]

Historians tend to isolate Utah's history not only from that of the nation but from that of the other western states. Yet the whole statehood saga suggests that this is an incorrect approach. Utah's troubles and fortunes were tied to issues that troubled other western states just as the territory had been bound to the national North/South fight over slavery, the attitudes of Radical Republicans, and the national silver crusade. The message one gets from recounting the Utah statehood story is that it was a symbolic event of great importance to the entire nation, whether the focus was constitutional, political, economic, or ideological.[57]

In conclusion, three general comments seem in order. The first is that Wilford Woodruff's Manifesto of 1890 not only liberated Utah Territory but much of the West and some of the nation itself. It looked as if Utah, Arizona, and Idaho were marching toward democracy, whereas South Carolina and the American South were not. Second, the late Richard Hofstadter has suggested that the West espoused free silver for cynical economic and political reasons only.[58] Hofstadter was tragically wrong. He did not understand that the Westerners saw silver as the key to a better way of life for the West and that Frank Cannon, Senator Henry Moore Teller of Colorado, and Congressman William Jennings Bryan of Nebraska were their trusted leaders in the cause. The dreams of what silver would do for the West, while not necessarily rational, were totally misunderstood by the East. As Leonard Schlup has noted, so committed was Senator Frank Cannon to free silver in its larger context that he walked out of the Republican National Convention of 1896 and joined the Teller rebels. Later in his career, he joined the Democrats to support William Jennings Bryan for the presidency not once but twice.[59] Certainly Cannon's commitment was more ideological than cynical.

And finally, it is said that the Spanish-American War of 1897–98 marks the true reconciliation of the North and South; symbolically, an ex-Confederate,

Congressman General Joe Wheeler, volunteered for service in that conflict and commanded black troops.[60] To me, however, that reconciliation began politically—and with great significance for the West—when Northern and Southern congressmen gave up pairing a Democratic or pro-Southern state with a Republican or pro-Northern one by deciding to admit the four omnibus states in 1889 and Idaho and Wyoming in 1890.[61] Utah's admission story is another, and by far the most dramatic, example of reconciliation, not just in Utah but in Congress and elsewhere—for example, in Arizona where Governor Zulick, backed by Cleveland, began to include Mormon settlers in the regular political process.[62]

Utah's statehood is a story with such a positive outcome that we certainly should still be celebrating it a century later, for it is evidence of a further step in the slow realization of a more complete American democracy. Most remarkable of all, Utah statehood occurred in 1896, with everyone approving, although the nation itself was in violent turmoil over economic, labor, financial, and third party issues. The way that political and public relations near-miracle was achieved is cause alone for prolonged celebration.

Notes

1. A convenient account of Utah's long struggle for statehood is Ken Verdoia and Richard Firmage, *Utah: The Struggle for Statehood* (Salt Lake City: University of Utah Press, 1996). See also Gustive O. Larson, *The "Americanization" of Utah for Statehood* (San Marino, Calif.: Huntington Library, 1971), and Howard R. Lamar, "Statehood for Utah: A Different Path," *Utah Historical Quarterly* 39 (Fall 1971): 307–27. A more contextual account is to be found in Lamar, *The Far Southwest, 1846–1912: A Territorial History* (New Haven, Conn.: Yale University Press, 1966), 378–414. Edward Leo Lyman, *Political Deliverance: The Mormon Quest for Utah Statehood* (Urbana: University of Illinois Press, 1986), traces the efforts of Mormon leaders working with the Republican Party to achieve statehood. No equivalent study of Democratic Party efforts to achieve statehood in the 1880s yet exists.

2. "The New State," *New Orleans Times-Picayune*, 7 January 1896, 9.

3. "New Star Cheered," *Chicago Tribune*, 5 January 1896, 1, 3. The *Tribune*'s description was a forecast of the parade printed a day before the actual parade.

4. Ibid., 3.

5. "The New State," *New Orleans Times-Picayune*, 7 January 1896, 9, describes the huge flag in some detail. For a slightly different description, see "Ready to Enter upon Their Duties," *San Francisco Chronicle*, 6 January 1896, 3. Excellent photographs of the highly decorated interior of the Mormon Tabernacle are in Verdoia and Firmage, *Utah*, 177–88.

6. "Utah's Officers Are Installed," *San Francisco Chronicle*, 7 January 1896, 4, quotes parts of Wells's inaugural address.

7. *Congressional Record*, 53rd Cong., 2nd sess., 1894, 26, pt. 1:118, 174–82. Unless otherwise noted, the account of the bill's passage comes from this source.

8. Morse was referring to the black population of the American South whose voting rights at that very moment were being denied by conservative white legislators.

9. Despite Rawlins's denial, the *Deseret News* still espoused Mormon views, while the *Salt Lake Tribune* espoused Gentile ones; naturally, they were hostile to each other.

10. These events may be followed in the *Congressional Record*, 26, pt. 7 (9 June–12 July 1894) 7251; pt. 8 (12 July–28 August 1894) 7384, 7425, 7514, 7836.

11. President Grover Cleveland signed the 4 January 1896 Utah Statehood Proclamation with no public fanfare. Indeed, Utah officials were kept waiting in an anteroom until he had signed the document with an ordinary wooden pen. Cleveland's disinterested attitude has been attributed to the press of financial crises, but one may surmise that he was also disappointed that Utah had gone Republican despite the efforts he and the Democratic Party had made to secure Utah's admission during his first term. See "The Forty-Fifth State," *New York Times*, 5 January 1896, 16, and "Inaugural of a State," *Washington Post*, 5 January 1896, 5.

12. Charles S. Peterson, *Take Up Your Mission: Mormon Colonizing along the Little Colorado River, 1870–1900* (Tucson: University of Arizona Press, 1973), 237–40, 241.

13. Leonard J. Arrington, *History of Idaho*, 2 vols. (Moscow: University of Idaho Press/Boise: Idaho State Historical Society, 1994), 1:370–77.

14. Ibid., 1:430–32.

15. Richard E. Welch Jr., *The Presidencies of Grover Cleveland* (Lawrence: University of Kansas Press, 1988); Samuel T. McSeveney, *The Politics of Depression: Political Behavior in the Northeast, 1893–1896* (New York: Oxford University Press, 1972).

16. "Mormons Working East: More Missionaries about to Enter the Field Hereabouts," *New York Times*, 3 January 1896, 5.

17. *New York Times*, 4 January 1896, 6. Clawson's remarks were used in a headline, hence the capitals.

18. Ibid. The paper also listed the following Utahns as being in New York: A. W. McCune, president of the Salt Lake City Railroad Company and a major stockholder in the *Salt Lake Herald;* Robert Patrick, Jr., M. A. Romney, A. W. Pullen, Selden I. Clawson, Walter Dinwoody, John Derm, a prominent training operator, Samuel W. Richards, Arthur F. Barnes, T. G. Odell, Fred Myer, William Ballentine, and Albert Scowcraft. The men named were described as businessmen in Salt Lake City and Ogden.

19. Ibid.

20. Ibid.

21. "The Forty-Fifth State," *New York Times*, 5 January 1896, 16.

22. Benjamin R. Tillman, then a senator from South Carolina, was not only outspoken in his speeches but also threatened to attack his enemies with a pitchfork.

23. "Utah's Senators Named," *New York Times*, 16 January 1896.

24. "Inaugural of a State," *Washington Post*, 5 January 1896, 5.

25. "Great Rejoicing at Salt Lake," *Washington Post*, 5 January 1896.

26. "The New State," *New Orleans Times-Picayune*, 7 January 1896, 9. An earlier North-South reconciliation impulse actually played a role in the congressional debates leading to the omnibus bill by which North and South Dakota, Montana, and Washington were admitted to the Union in 1889. See Howard R. Lamar, "Statehood for Washington: Symbol of a New Era," in *Washington Comes of Age: The State in the National Experience*, ed. David H. Stratton (Pullman: Washington State University Press, 1992), 113–29. The *Times-Picayune* seems to have lost interest in Utah after its rather impressive initial coverage and returned to its preoccupation with Populism, Southern issues, and sugar.

27. The favorable captions about Utah statehood in the *Chicago Tribune*, 5 January 1896, are intriguing: "New State Cheered"; "Utah Becomes a State Amid General Rejoicing";

"Flags to the Breeze"; "Move Is for the Best"; "Gov. Wells Sends a Special Message to 'The Tribune'"; "Five Years of Trial to Come."

28. *Chicago Tribune*, 5 January 1896, 1, 3.

29. Ibid., 3.

30. Ibid.

31. Ibid.

32. "The Plan to Make Arizona a State," *San Francisco Chronicle*, 4 January 1896, 6.

33. "Arizona Statehood," *San Francisco Chronicle*, 5 January 1896, 18.

34. *San Francisco Chronicle*, 6 January 1896, 3, 4.

35. "Utah's Admission," *San Francisco Chronicle*, 7 January 1896, 4.

36. The *Chronicle* followed Utah's senatorial fight from 9 January, when it speculated about Colonel Isaac Trumbo's chances to be a senator, to the choice of Cannon and Brown in mid-January. For an exceptionally detailed account of the complex maneuvering and final votes, see "Utah Republicans Select Senators," *San Francisco Chronicle*, 15 January 1896, 4.

37. "Congratulation and Regret," *San Francisco Chronicle*, 16 January 1896, 4.

38. *Rocky Mountain News*, 15 January 1896, as quoted in "Cannon a Popular Selection," *San Francisco Chronicle*, 16 January 1896, 4.

39. *San Francisco Chronicle*, 28 January 1896.

40. "Utah Still Mormon: Another Interview with Bishop Hart," *Los Angeles Sunday Times*, 29 December 1895, 3. The *Times* further identified Hart as a member of the last Territorial Legislature.

41. "A Mormon Colony to Start Near Phoenix," *Los Angeles Times*, 30 December 1895, 10.

42. "The State of Utah: An Imposing Installation of the New Administration," *Los Angeles Times*, 7 January 1896.

43. "Utah's Constitution," *Los Angeles Times*, 11 January 1896, 2.

44. *The Nation: A Weekly Journal* 59 (19 July 1894): 37–38.

45. "Report on Home Missions," *The Church at Home and Abroad* 15 (January 1894): 38. This periodical is subtitled *Published Monthly by Order of the General Assembly of the Presbyterian Church in the United States of America*. The actual publisher is its Board of Publications and Sabbath School Work, headquartered in Philadelphia.

46. "Report on Home Missions," *The Church at Home and Abroad* 15 (May 1894): 403.

47. "Report on Home Missions," *The Church at Home and Abroad* 17 (June 1895): 473.

48. "Public schools are steadily winning their way in Utah, and are among the forces upon which we most depend to make of that wonderful territory a glorious American state. Salt Lake City has already some of the finest and most modern public school buildings in the United States." "Report on Home Missions," *The Church at Home and Abroad* 17 (June 1895): 472.

49. *Methodist Review* 78 (September 1896): 754–57.

50. *Methodist Review* 78 (November 1896): 962–63.

51. Joseph B. Clark, *Leavening the Nation: The Story of American Home Missions* (New York: Baker and Taylor, 1903), 236–37. Clark also provides a useful list of the Protestant ministers who served as missionaries in Utah (234–36).

52. "The Week," *The Nation* 60 (23 May 1895): 392; and "The Week," *The Nation* 61 (14 November 1895): 338.

53. "The Week," *The Nation* 62 (9 January 1896): 23.

54. "The Week," *The Nation* 62 (30 January 1896): 88.

55. Convenient biographies of the above-named congressmen may be found in the *Biographical Directory of the American Congress, 1774–1971* (Washington, D.C.: U.S. Government Printing Office, 1971). For a more complete account of Joseph L. Rawlins's role, see Joseph L. Rawlins, *The Unfavored Son: The Autobiography of Joseph L. Rawlins* (n.p., 1956), and Joan Ray Harrow, "Joseph L. Rawlins, Father of Utah Statehood," *Utah Historical Quarterly* 44 (Winter 1976): 59–75.

56. As both senator and U.S. president, Benjamin Harrison was active in territorial affairs throughout the West, particularly in Dakota Territory. He was instrumental in creating Oklahoma Territory and in advancing the cause of civil government in Alaska. Harrison's role in Dakota Territory politics is detailed in Howard R. Lamar, *Dakota Territory, 1861–1889: A Study of Frontier Politics* (New Haven, Conn.: Yale University Press, 1956), 256–59, 264, 272.

57. Lamar, *Far Southwest*, 401–11.

58. Richard Hofstadter, *The Age of Reform: From Bryan to F.D.R.* (New York: Oxford University Press, 1955).

59. Leonard Schlup, "Utah Maverick: Frank J. Cannon and the Politics of Conscience in 1896," *Utah Historical Quarterly* 62 (Fall 1994): 335–48. Although no special collections on Utah statehood are mentioned in David J. Whittaker, *Mormon Americana: A Guide to the Sources and Collections in the United States* (Provo, Utah: BYU Studies, 1995), part II of this volume is invaluable for anyone seeking to trace the papers of Mormon political leaders during both the earlier and final statehood crusades. See especially "Biography," 70–74, and part II, 93–139. An obvious older source is Andrew Jenson, *Latter-day Saint Biographical Encyclopedia*, 4 vols. (Salt Lake City: Andrew Jenson History Co., 1901–36).

60. John Percy, *"Fightin' Joe" Wheeler* (University: Louisiana State University Press, 1941), and Willie Ruff, *A Call to Assembly: The Autobiography of a Musical Storyteller* (New York: Viking, 1991), 413–20, which provide moving accounts of Wheeler's relations with black troops in the Spanish-American War.

61. Lamar, "Statehood for Washington," 123–25.

62. Peterson, *Take Up Your Mission*, 237–38. See also Jean Bickmore White, "Prelude to Statehood: Coming Together in the 1890s," *Utah Historical Quarterly* 62 (Fall 1994): 300–315.

PART 3

Mormonism Considered
from Different Perspectives

Jan Shipps

By 1980, Mormonism was a mature religious movement. In the face of hostility and violence, it had passed through its beginning epoch successfully and had then moved on to become a significant if sometimes controversial religious tradition.[1] After its adherents (who called themselves Latter-day Saints) created short-lived kingdoms in Ohio, Missouri, and Illinois, the first Mormon prophet, Joseph Smith, was murdered. Although an often ignored splintering of the movement followed that tragedy, two of the most substantial Saintly bodies established permanent Zions, one in the intermountain region of the American West and the other in the Midwest. In both, stable institutions became centers around which two separate Mormon cultures developed.

For several reasons, but most especially because almost all of the huge convert harvest from Europe joined the Saints in the Great Basin, the body of mountain Saints grew so much larger than the body of prairie Saints that—if it was noticed at all—the latter was frequently mistakenly regarded as a schismatic offshoot of the former. In fact, both trace their genealogy to the Mormonism that existed during the lifetime of Joseph Smith; neither is an offshoot of the other. While the Church of Jesus Christ of Latter-day Saints was ten times as large as the Reorganized Church of Jesus Christ of Latter Day Saints in Mormonism's sesquicentennial year, both forms of Mormonism were looking forward and outward.[2]

Yet, as if they were taking stock, Saints from both Mormon traditions were engaged in a thorough examination of their histories during the celebration of their tradition's third jubilee, histories that were unitary until 1844 but diverged dramatically thereafter. As a professional society that brought historians from the two traditions together, the Mormon History Association (MHA) became the venue for reports and discussion of this close latter-day examination of Mormon beginnings on the part of both prairie Saint and mountain Saint historians, as well as a few non-Mormons who also studied Mormonism. The size disparity of the two institutional forms of the Mormon movement meant, however, that the lion's share of the attention that historians paid to establishing Zion was directed to the experience of the Utah church and the mountain Saints. Thus, it is not surprising that while the Tanner Lectures in part one of this collection deal with issues and address questions that are of great consequence to those who would understand Mormonism in all its fullness, the Tanner Lectures in part two are more or less entirely concerned with the experiences of the mountain Saints and their ecclesiastical institution.

With the exception of Laurie F. Maffly-Kipp's study "Looking West: Mormonism and the Pacific World," the lectures in this final section of the Tanner Lectures collection depart from this emphasis on Utah Mormonism. Their authors consider Mormonism from perspectives that reflect developments in the academy as the increasing application of social scientific and religious studies methodologies and attention to historiography turned the discipline of history, to employ Clifford Geertz's felicitous and helpful term, into a "blurred genre." Consequently, they nearly all regard Mormonism whole, as it were. Moreover, as their authors ponder the questions of how Mormonism is—or is not—like other religious traditions and what can be learned when Mormonism is treated as a case study, nearly all these lectures, even the ones on historiography, have a strong comparative component in which Mormonism is measured against and contrasted with other forms of religion.

While they do not address—and were not intended to address—the imbalance that virtually left the prairie Saints out of the MHA's handling of the post-1844 Mormon past, these lectures are a welcome and important reminder that narratives and analysis of the story of the Latter-day Saints who traveled west to establish a kingdom in the tops of the mountains are only a part of the history of the Saints. The primary reason this is true is that when the lectures in this section are read thoughtfully, they tell us as much about religion as they tell us about Mormonism, whether of the mountain or the prairie variety.

To the cognoscenti, to those who have followed Mormon history across the past half century, they also reveal something more. In virtually every case, in preparing their lectures, these Tanner scholars, as they might be called, worked their way through then-recent historical writing about the tradition. As a result, read in seriatim as they were presented, rather than gathered into subject-matter groupings, these lectures hold up a mirror that reflects the history of the doing of Mormon history across twenty years.

Although written by historian John G. Gager, sociologist Rodney Stark, and theologian Langdon Gilkey, the first three lectures in this section all address Mormonism from the perspective of religion and culture, a central issue in the discipline of religious studies (a discipline that was just coming into its own as these Tanner Lectures were inaugurated). Laurie F. Maffly-Kipp approaches her topics from a more traditional church history perspective, missiology, while the three concluding lectures by Henry Warner Bowden, Martin Marty, and Edwin S. Gaustad deal with the historiography of Mormonism, all of them doing so by placing the history of Mormon history in comparative perspective.

To a considerable extent, John G. Gager's 1982 lecture on the consequences of parallels between early Mormonism and early Christianity for the study of new religions set the stage for future Tanner lectures that used something other than a methodology that, however broad-ranging, asked questions that were more or less strictly historical—what happened, when, under what conditions, and with what consequences. Gager's use of the interpretive and explanatory models of social science in his signal study, *Kingdom and Community: The Social World of Early Christianity,* were brought to bear as he set the development of Mormonism alongside the development of Christianity. Moving beyond historical narrative, his main concern was discerning the forces that gave rise to both religions and accounted for their rapid and spectacular growth. These same issues would be addressed by Rodney Stark almost twenty years later with the significant difference that Stark extended the comparison from early Christianity to Judaism and the beginnings of Islam.

Gager and Stark both use the history of Mormonism to call into question the once almost universally accepted notion that mass conversions account for the success of early Christianity. Gager does so by showing that when Mormonism found a way to escape its radically millennialist character, it was able to grow into a successful religious movement. Its initial emphasis on the end time was replaced, first, by the construction of a literal kingdom and afterward by institution-building and culture-creation. Stark would hardly disagree, but he is more pragmatic and data-driven than theoretical, arguing that interpersonal ties are the primary factor in conversion. Consequently, he points to the extraordinary importance of kinship in the formation of the core group that generated the development of the Mormon movement. In addition, as would be expected from the coauthor with Roger Finke of *The Churching of America, 1776–1990: Winners and Losers in Our Religious Economy,* Stark describes rational choice as one of the prime movers in conversion and outlines his notion that whether they recognize it or not, many potential converts to Mormonism go through a rudimentary cost-benefit analysis before deciding to become Mormon.

Langdon Gilkey's learned ruminations on how the relationship between religion and culture is a persistent problem for all religions, not just Mormonism, is both thoughtful and helpful—as pertinent (in different ways) to the issues faced today both by the Church of Jesus Christ of Latter-day Saints and the Community of Christ as it was when the lecture was delivered in 1985. Gilkey began his lecture by describing two extremes, contrasting religions that dominate cultures by being in union with cultural power as that power is manifested politically, economically, socially, and sometimes even militarily with religions that withdraw from the larger culture, becoming separate and refusing (as far as possible) to participate in it in any way. But this Tanner lecturer devoted the great bulk of his remarks to religions that interpenetrate their host cultures by establishing a continuum along which religion at one end is dominant over culture (as it was in the Great Basin before Utah attained statehood) and at the other is so fully integrated into the culture that culture dominates. In describing the stations along this continuum, he noted that surrounding cultures are able to interpenetrate religious cultures and their central ecclesiastical institutions to varying degrees and that the greater that interpenetration, the more likely that the surrounding culture will itself take on religious dimensions—as has been demonstrated by the development of American civil religion.

When Gilkey presented his lecture to the MHA, he simply set forth his ideas about the persistently problematic relationship between religion and culture without using demonstrative examples from the history of the Latter-day Saints. In preparing the lecture for publication, he added a number of references to the RLDS and LDS experience. Overall, however, this lecture more than any other in this collection is addressed to how religion works in the world rather than how the relationship between religion and culture has been, from the very beginning, a persistent problem for the Latter-day Saints.

Despite his minimal attention to the Mormon case, Gilkey's observations about how the interweaving of a religious tradition with its cultural setting can cause sometimes "baffling" problems when religious communities undertake foreign missions draw attention to the usefulness of Laurie F. Maffly-Kipp's depiction of early LDS missions to the Society Islands as something more than a standard historical account of an early Mormon effort to make converts outside the United States. Maffly-Kipp's fine account of how Mormon missionaries often benefited from their outsider—in Gilkey's terms separationist—status tells the reader almost as much about where Mormonism fit into the American religious scene as about the Mormon mission in Tahiti.

Necessity occasioned by a lack of financial and other resources caused LDS missionaries to live in closer proximity to potential native converts than did missionaries of the Catholics and the various Protestant denominations. But what cemented the connections of the Mormon missionaries to the people of the South Seas was not this physical nearness so much as the fact that other Christians regarded the Saints (somewhat like the natives) as *other*. When the Saints challenged the cultural patterns and religious practices of the established denominations with their cultivation of the gifts of the Spirit, including visions and healings, it brought the natives closer to them, perhaps precisely because they were also *other*. As a result, the Saints were surprisingly successful in spreading the Mormon gospel in this foreign land.

But that was then and this is now, so much so that Gilkey's 1985 warning is fully echoed in the final paragraphs of the lecture Maffly-Kipp gave fifteen years later: a key difference in today's LDS foreign missionary, she says, is that "Mormon missionaries do not occupy the same oppositional stance to American political power as that of their forebears. They have become thoroughly associated with the United States as an imperial force in the eyes of other peoples, a fact that complicates the task of evangelization inasmuch as the Mormon message is now equated with assimilation to American civilization."[3] Those of us who watch the Mormon scene closely know that the church is aware of this situation and that at least some of the Saints regard it as a problem. Perusing Gilkey and Maffly-Kipp back-to-back will allow readers to see that the problem may be one that is not exclusive to the foreign mission field.

The three final lectures printed in this volume are all about the writing of Mormon history. Henry Warner Bowden's "From the Age of Science to an Age of Uncertainty: History and Mormon Studies in the Twentieth Century" is a virtual tour de force in Mormon intellectual history. Although the scholars who produced *Studies in Mormon History, 1830–97* know far more Mormon bibliography than any outsider could ever know, Bowden does not pretend that he is working in the same league. Yet his decision to set forth a broad framework in which to place the writing of church history generally and to fit the writing of Mormon history within that frame led to the construction of a lecture that will be of special use to professors and graduate students who need to develop an appreciation of the literature of Mormon history as a part of a larger project of teaching and writing about American church history and American religion.

Readers of Bowden's lecture will take away from it a manageable bibliography of Mormon history (up to 1988). But that is not all. Because his survey characterizes the schools of thought generated in the writing of religious history in the twentieth century in an effective manner, Bowden's lecture informs readers about the way the academic and history-writing culture changed from what it was in an era when theology was the standard interpretive tool for understanding church history to what it became in "the age of science," an era when a historian's objectivity was the route to fulfilling that "noble dream," to what it became at around 1960, a point in time when historians of all stripes, not just historians who studied religion, realized that complete objectivity was an impossible goal. Placing the work of Mormon historians alongside the work of church historians—the notion of B. H. Roberts being the Philip Schaff of Mormon history is particularly fascinating—Bowden found examples from church history as well as Mormon history to illuminate the categories he set forth. The result is remarkable in how it illustrates that Mormon history and American church history moved along parallel paths.

Martin E. Marty and Edwin S. Gaustad both deserve to be called deans of American religious history, for both have earned enormous respect within the academy. Interestingly enough, both are respected churchmen as well as historians. Their lectures, presented sequentially in 1983 and 1984 at a time when the community of Mormon historians was undergoing considerable stress, seem designed to reassure the community of historians who were writing about the Mormon past that professional history that was also faithful history was not a chimera.

As the memoirs of LDS Church Historian Leonard J. Arrington reveal, such reassurance was much needed, especially for those who were in the employ of one or the other of the principal Mormon churches.[4] Following a decade-long period when the archives of both churches had been open to any serious and legitimate researcher, a period that Davis Bitton dubbed "Camelot,"[5] the staff of the LDS Church Historical Department had been transferred to a newly organized Joseph Fielding Smith Institute of Church History at Brigham Young University. Copies of a spate of apparently important documents undercutting generally accepted versions of church history were circulating in the community, and while these documents were later identified as forgeries, before that they surely set the historical community on edge.[6] To make matters more problematical for Clio's Mormon practitioners, some orthodox church leaders in both churches and a few scholars (not many of them historians) were insistently calling the published work of certain LDS professional historians into question. This last group appeared to be particularly concerned about the published work of several historians who were non-Mormon—principally Lawrence Foster and Jan Shipps.

Perhaps more than any of the Tanner lecturers, Martin Marty was fully informed about the situation within the Mormon historical community at the time he prepared his lecture, for his lecture seemed to speak directly to the situation that members of the MHA were facing.[7] In "Two Integrities: An Address to the Crisis in Mormon Historiography," Marty made the argument that Mormon thought was undergoing a profound crisis not unlike the crisis in Roman Catholic thought before World War II. He described the crisis as one in which the LDS intellectual community was starting to treat Mormon history as history, in the sense of Mormon history fitting into the ongoingness of human social experience rather than being so abstracted from that experience that it took on a dogmatic character. This he identified as the rise of historical consciousness, something that had happened in most of Protestant Christianity at the time of the Enlightenment.

When historical consciousness surfaces, the role of the historian shifts from being a storyteller and defender of the faith to being a data collector, reporter, and analyst, an empirical task that almost necessarily introduces the hermeneutics of suspicion into writing about the past, even about past revelatory experiences. In order to preserve the integrity of both roles, Marty introduced Paul Ricoeur's concept of first (or primitive) and second naivete as ways of accepting spiritual truths.

After reviewing its implications for the non-Mormon Christian world, much of Marty's lecture was devoted to the way in which the rise of historical consciousness was playing out within Mormonism generally and, most especially, within the community of Mormon historians. Correctly identifying the critical Mormon issues as *generative*, as having to do with the reality of Joseph Smith's prophetic calling and the related issue of the coming forth of the Book of Mormon, Marty moved forward to categorize the various players in the Mormon arena (insiders, outsiders, church authorities, historians) and to argue forcefully that integrity is not the sole possession of any one of these players. He avers, instead, that there are multiple integrities that must be discerned and respected.

If Marty's lecture supplied a surprisingly accurate picture of what was then happening within Mormondom and within the Mormon historical community, Edwin S. Gaustad's lecture took the situation and "dramatis personae" for granted. Recognizing, as did Marty, that the rise of historical consciousness changes everything, Gaustad provided a useful set of distinctions to help both historians and their readers comprehend what had happened to Mormon history. After briefly describing the difference in historical theology and theological history in their classic forms, he made a valuable distinction between the consumers and producers of history. Then, speaking to the historians in the MHA, he mentioned the developments in the historical profession in the years after World War II, recognizing that the canons of the profession are as important to those who study religious history as anything else.

Religious historians, Sydney Ahlstrom wrote, are "allowed no immunity from the demands for evidence that historians generally make."[8] Yet Gaustad encouraged those who engage in writing about the Saints not to neglect theological history. Without transgressing historical canons, in their interpretations of the evidence, they may—quite as much as those who do historical theology—see the hand of God as time passes and the Saints go marching on.

To reiterate, all in all, the lectures in this section say as much about religion in a generic sense as they say about Mormon history. At the same time, they reflect contemporary developments in the fields of study that we call religious studies and church history. For all that, they are valuable resources in the study of Mormonism and can be read for profit by those anxious to learn more about this particular tradition and about how new religions develop.

Notes

1. Scholars debate the matter of whether Mormonism is a new religious tradition or whether, as the restored Church of Christ over which a prophet and the restored

priesthoods of Aaron and Melchizedek preside, it is simply an idiosyncratic form of Christianity. This is a debate about form and structure. When the debate takes a theological turn, as it often does, the question is legitimacy—that is, whether the Church of Jesus Christ of Latter-day Saints is, in fact, the restored Church of Christ that existed during the Apostolic era with the only restored priesthoods and, as such, the only true church currently on the face of the earth.

2. Jan Shipps, "The Mormons: Looking Forward and Outward" (contribution to a series on "The Churches: Where From Here"), *Christian Century*, 16–23 August 1978, 761–66. Due to the rapid rate of conversion to the Church of Jesus Christ of Latter-day Saints and a schism within the Reorganized Church (now known as the Community of Christ), the disparity in size has increased exponentially in the past quarter century.

3. Laurie F. Maffly-Kipp, "Looking West: Mormonism and the Pacific World," *Journal of Mormon History* 26(1) (Spring 2000): 62.

4. Leonard J. Arrington, *Adventures of a Church Historian* (Urbana and Chicago: University of Illinois Press, 1998), chap. 14.

5. Davis Bitton, "Ten Years in Camelot: A Personal Memoir," *Dialogue: A Journal of Mormon Thought* 16 (Autumn 1983): 9–33.

6. These were the notorious Hofmann documents, the most significant of which were probably an LDS Church blessing on the head of Joseph Smith III conferring his right to succeed his father as the president and prophet of the church, a letter from Joseph Smith to Josiah Stowell in which the prophet was portrayed as an experienced treasure hunter, and the famed Salamander Letter, containing an account written by one of the prophet's followers of the coming forth of the Book of Mormon that featured a white salamander rather than the Angel Moroni as the agent delivering the golden plates to Joseph Smith.

7. To some extent this was due to his having directed the dissertations of Marvin Hill and Lawrence Foster and to his having recently published Klaus Hansen's *Mormonism and the American Experience* (Chicago: University of Chicago Press, 1981) in the Chicago History of American Religion Series that he edited. But it was likewise due to the way Marty (who edits a newsletter, *Context: Martin E. Marty on Religion and Culture*) always seems to be clued in to everything going on in American religion.

8. Sydney E. Ahlstrom, "The Problem of the History of Religion in America," *Church History* 39 (June 1970): 233.

CHAPTER 15

Early Mormonism and Early Christianity: Some Parallels and Their Consequences for the Study of New Religions

John G. Gager

I am delighted and honored by the invitation from your program committee to deliver the third annual Tanner Lecture on the occasion of this seventeenth annual meeting of the Mormon History Association. I am particularly thankful for the opportunity this occasion has provided for reflecting about the foundations of my own academic discipline—the study of early Christianity—in a manner that is all too uncommon among academicians, whose ordinary behavior takes them ever more deeply into their own special areas and rarely forces them to examine their discipline in the light of other fields—or to view themselves, as Robert Burns once put it, as other people see us.

I must admit, however, that my enthusiasm about being here is somewhat tempered by a doubled-edged sense of anxiety: anxiety first of all because I stand before you, an audience of experts on Mormonism, as one whose knowledge and understanding of Mormon history has been acquired exclusively in the very recent past, and anxiety also because I suspect that there are very good reasons for the molelike quality of academics that I described just a moment ago. For whatever we may say about the ultimately therapeutic nature of examining our foundations and seeing ourselves as others see us, there can be no doubt that the experience itself is always uncomfortable, frequently disconcerting, and sometimes painful. I have dealt with my first anxiety by reassuring myself that your interest in my remarks today springs not from what I know about Mormonism but from what I know about early Christianity. As for my second source of anxiety, I have not yet discovered a solution. If my observations about early Mormonism and early Christianity should cause any discomfort or pain, I can only remind you that many learned outside observers of the early Christian movement lie silent and forgotten in their Mediterranean graves, while Christianity itself—no doubt strengthened by what it learned from these observers—survived to live and laugh another day.

But before I begin to speak about my topic proper, it may be useful for me to say a word or two about my own work as a historian of early Christianity. If you were to ask me what I saw as the most distinctive aspects of my approach to early Christianity, I would single out two items for special emphasis.

E. R. Dodds—a transcendentally great historian of ancient religion to whose work I will return in a bit—commented in one of his writings that he was interested less in the issues that separated the early Christians from their pagan contemporaries than in the attitudes and experiences that bound them together.[1] Like Dodds, I too am especially interested in those questions and problems that lead to what we might call our common humanity. Concretely, this means that I have rejected the view of one of my former teachers who argued that the primary task of the historian lies in describing the distinctiveness and particularity of historical movements and figures. Put positively, this means that I am no longer inclined to view the relationship between early Christianity and its cultural environment, whether Jewish or pagan, in terms of influences back and forth. It is not enough just to say that Christianity was influenced by apocalyptic Judaism or Platonic philosophy, for the truth of the matter is that there is no unchanging core that accepts or rejects input from the environment. The core itself is part of that environment, changes with it, and is inconceivable apart from it.[2]

The second distinctive focus of my own work has been in the use of interpretive and explanatory models from the social sciences—primarily social anthropology and social psychology. By applying these models to specific problem areas in the study of early Christianity, I have tried to demonstrate both that early Christianity shares certain basic characteristics with other new religions and that what we are able to learn of religious movements closer to our own time, about which we often have an abundance of information, can be put to use in explaining obscure or intractable problems in religions such as early Christianity, where the amount of available information is relatively sparse. Critics of this kind of comparative historical sociology—or, better, sociological historiography—have argued the line that sociologists are concerned with general laws of human behavior, whereas the task of historians is to describe specific or even unique events and movements. Other critics contend that such an approach is somehow reductionist, that it reduces religious issues to social forces, or, even worse, that it renders religious beliefs and practices themselves untenable and irrational. My response to these critics is that there is a kind of atheism implicit not only in social scientific approaches but in every other academic discipline as well. But the atheism I have in mind here is what Peter Berger calls "methodological atheism"—by which he simply means that the sociologist as sociologist or the historian as historian can never appeal to factors or forces that are beyond public inspection and scrutiny.[3] But by the same token, the sociologist as sociologist has nothing whatever to say about religious explanations of the sociological or historical accounts themselves. In Berger's own words,

Sociological theory must, by its own logic, view religion as a human projection, and by the same logic can have nothing to say about the possibility that this projection may refer to something other than the being of its projector. In other words, to say that religion is a human projection [by which he means that it can be fully analyzed and understood according to information available to every observer] does not logically preclude the possibility that the projected meanings may have an ultimate status independent of man.[4]

On this question, historians and sociologists have nothing further to say.

The relevance of Berger's observations to the study of early Mormonism and early Christianity I take to be far-reaching. Most historians—and especially those who lay great emphasis on the objective, value-free character of their work—are thinly veiled debunkers. In the study of early Christianity, this attitude has long been reflected in studies designed to deflate Christian claims about the nature and deeds of Jesus Christ. And in the study of early Mormonism, I have found very much the same sort of attitude among non-Mormon historians who have sought to discredit Mormonism in general by poking holes, for instance, in the story of Joseph Smith's production of the Book of Mormon and the Book of Abraham.[5] Of course, this generates the opposite and equally uncritical response among sympathetic historians of trying to defend the authenticity and accuracy of historical documents and figures, whereas their proper task ought to be the fullest possible explanation of those forces that gave rise to these new religions in the first place and that accounted for their startling growth in a relatively short period of time. In fact, it is precisely to these two fundamental and properly historical issues that I would like to direct our attention in the time remaining.

Let me begin by suggesting that some of the most interesting and fruitful recent developments in the study of early Christianity have resulted from the discovery that this particular new religion shares certain basic characteristics with millenarian movements in general. By recognizing these similarities and by drawing on studies of early modern and contemporary millenarian movements —here I think of works such as Peter Worsley's *The Trumpet Shall Sound;* K. O. L. Burridge's *New Heaven, New Earth;* Norman R. Cohn's *Pursuit of the Millennium;* and Sylvia Thrupp's *Millennial Dreams in Action*[6]—it has been possible to open entirely new vistas on the underlying dynamics that gave rise to the early Christian movement as a powerful new religion. I would argue that much the same potential for new insights could be discovered by a thoroughgoing analysis of early Mormonism as a millenarian movement—that is, as a religion whose basic source of energy and momentum derived from its sense of being

the chosen people of God living in the final days of history. This self-understanding
—which lies at the heart of all millenarian movements and distinguishes them
from all other forms of religious expression—must be seen as the source of that
explosive and transformative power that is characteristic of both early Christianity and early Mormonism.

Of course, I recognize that the work of Klaus J. Hansen in his *Quest for Empire*
and John F. Wilson in his Tanner Lecture of last year have made important steps
in this direction, not just in pointing to the millenarian enthusiasm of the early
movement but also in arguing that its millenarian character requires an altogether different kind of historiography.[7] To their observations, I would simply
add a footnote or two.

First, we need to recognize why it is that the millenarian origins of Mormonism are just now coming into focus as a central characteristic of the early years. I
begin with the assertion that the inevitable fate of all millenarian movements is
failure and collapse. By this I mean that they either (and the majority would
certainly fall into this class) disintegrate and disappear when their millennial
expectations remain unfulfilled or (and here I think of both Christianity and
Mormonism) they cease to be millenarian in the strict sense. Those movements
that survive the trauma of nonfulfillment usually do so in rather predictable
ways, some of which I have tried to elucidate in the case of early Christianity.[8] I
would argue that many of them apply equally to early Mormonism:

- They generate a series of rational explanations for the nonarrival of the millennium.[9]
- They reach out and seek to persuade others of the truth of their religion.
- They redirect their energies away from preparing for the End and toward the
  development of institutional structures.
- Finally, as an essential part of this reorientation, they either forget or suppress
  the memory of their millenarian origins, for it is precisely in the transformation of millennial energies into other forms of action that we can locate the
  key to survival and success, on the one hand, or disintegration and collapse,
  on the other.

My second footnote concerns a cluster of issues surrounding the question of
the social makeup of millenarian movements. My starting point here is an
observation of Peter Worsley in *The Trumpet Shall Sound:* "I am quite unre-
pentant, therefore, about cleaving to my basic assumption that *the millenarian
movements that have been historically important . . . are movements of the disinherited.*"[10] Hansen has spelled out the truth of this observation for the earliest
followers of Joseph Smith, while my own work has tried to do as much for the
early followers of Jesus.[11]

But having made this basic observation, we are forced to move a step further
in recognizing that millenarian movements will not arise wherever we find dis-

inherited persons or communities. Studies such as those of Worsley and Burridge have shown that the disinherited become mobilized only under certain kinds of premillenarian conditions.[12] Early Christianity, we know, arose at a time of intense messianic activity—with Jesus being but one of several messianic claimants in first-century Palestine. The nineteenth-century analog, I take it, would be found in what historians have called the "Burned-Over District" of New York State where Smith's work first began.[13] Rodney Stark's recent work, which seeks to demonstrate that cultic movements are most likely to form and flourish precisely at times of cultural uncertainty, when traditional religious institutions are in decline and at their weakest, would seem to add significant theoretical weight to those who have argued that the religious revivalism in Smith's time and region must be seen against the backdrop of a general decline in traditional religious beliefs and institutions.[14]

The third and final step in treating the social makeup of millenarian movements concerns the emergence of what I would call a distinctively millenarian lifestyle. Invariably, millenarian cults define themselves in opposition to prevailing values and codes. They do so precisely because—as the disinherited—they expect the coming kingdom to bring with it a dramatic reversal of present values and status. Early Christianity's promise that the "first will be last and the last first" is utterly typical of millenarian movements in their early stages. The notorious antinomian behavior of such movements is thus not an accidental trait but a perfectly consistent manifestation of their underlying logic and structure. Unrestrained prophecy, visions, revelations, and new patterns of sexual activity—including polygamy—are precisely what we would expect of a millenarian lifestyle in nineteenth-century America, and precisely what we would expect to disappear in those millenarian movements that survive the initial rush of enthusiasm, that cease to be properly millenarian and become important religious traditions.

In my concluding remarks I would like to address the issue of the success of Mormonism—and to do so by returning to E. R. Dodds, this time to his analysis of the success of early Christianity. Here we begin with a curious paradox that has plagued historians of both movements. One part of the task of doing history itself—but also, I would argue, part of the debunking instinct of most historians—is the task of stressing similarities between early Mormonism or Christianity and their respective environments. Perhaps as a reaction to claims from within the movements that their ideologies are utterly distinctive and without historical precedent, historians have tended to present a counterimage, according to which little if anything about the movements can be seen as unique or innovative. Here is where the paradox arises. For if early Mormonism or early Christianity are merely warmed-over versions of mid-nineteenth- or mid-third-century culture, then we are at a loss to explain why these particular movements, and not their many contemporary competitors, not only survived but also flourished in such a remarkable fashion. In other words, the more we are able to demonstrate fundamental similarities between these movements and their surrounding cultures, and the more we must dismiss their own self-understanding in relation to their cultural environment, the more we find ourselves unable to explain their success.

At this point, I would like to propose that a solution to this paradox may lie in Dodds's comments about the role of ideological exclusiveness in attracting new converts to the early Christian movement. Without in any way discounting the many and important resemblances between the Christian movement and the Greco-Roman culture of the Roman empire, Dodds makes Christianity's self-understanding as a religiously and ideologically exclusive faith—exclusive at the conscious level, no matter what we as historians may see happening at an unconscious level—into an essential factor in its eventual success:

> I will end this essay by mentioning briefly some of the psychological conditions which favoured its growth and contributed to its victory.
>
> In the first place, its *very exclusiveness*, its refusal to concede any value to alternative forms of worship, which nowadays is often felt to be a weakness, was in the circumstances of the time a source of strength. The religious tolerance which was the normal Greek and Roman practice had resulted by accumulation in a bewildering mass of alternatives. There were too many cults, too many mysteries, too many philosophies of life to choose from: you could pile one religious insurance on another, yet not feel safe. Christianity made a clean sweep. It lifted the burden of freedom from the shoulders of the individual: one choice, one irrevocable choice, and the road to salvation was clear. Pagan critics might mock at Christian intolerance, but in an age of anxiety any "totalist" creed exerts a powerful attraction.[15]

With these comments in mind we may return briefly to the Burned-Over District, to the religious confusion of the mid-nineteenth century, and to the survival and success of Mormonism.

My first observation is that these words of Dodds point us directly to Joseph Smith's vision of 1820, when he had prayed to God for guidance in deciding which of the competing religious movements were true.[16] The answer, of course, was that Smith should "join none of them for they were all wrong . . . all their creeds were an abomination in God's sight; all professors were corrupt." I take this foundational vision to be more than just a conversion story and more than the basis for Smith's own religious authority. At its heart, this account proclaims the radical discontinuity of Mormonism with the Christianity of its own time. Therein, according to Dodds's view, lay much of its appeal.

This sense of discontinuity, however, goes well beyond Christianity in the nineteenth century, for it expresses—again at the conscious level of ideological self-understanding—a far deeper sense of discontinuity with historical Christianity itself. In the case of early Christianity, as Dodds analyzes it, ideological exclusiveness took the form of a "NO!" to all forms of Greco-Roman religious solutions. The analogy in the case of Mormonism, in order to be complete, would have to take the form of a "NO!" to all forms of Christian religious solutions.

The evidence for this "NO!" lies not just in Smith's vision of 1820, not just in his demotion of the Christian Bible by virtue of his claim that it had been improperly translated, but equally in the foundational myth of the prophet Lehi. By having Lehi and his sons depart from Jerusalem before the destruction of the city in 587 B.C.—a destruction traditionally understood as brought about by Israel's iniquities—the line of descent to Joseph Smith and the Book of Mormon is safeguarded not only against any implication in those iniquities but also against any participation in the troubled history of later Judaism and Christianity. This symbolic meaning of Lehi's departure from Jerusalem around 600 B.C. is reduplicated, I would argue, in the account of Christ's preaching of his true gospel to the descendants of Lehi in the New World. The true Christian message is thus transmitted to the New World not by any human agents, not by any representatives of historical Christianity—who are, after all, an abomination in the sight of God—but by the risen Christ himself.

What this symbolic discontinuity means in terms of Mormon historiography is that it is not really adequate to speak of early Mormonism as a return to early Christianity. For if I am not mistaken, early Mormonism sought to short-circuit all historical continuity with Christianity and Judaism and thereby to eliminate both as competitors for the claim to represent the true people of God. Thus I would have serious doubts concerning Hansen's approving reference to the words of Fawn Brodie, that Mormonism was "intended to be to Christianity as Christianity was to Judaism: that is a reform and a consummation."[17]

Finally, just as early Christianity gradually modified its exclusivist stance as it moved into the mainstream of Roman society and culture, the same has been true of Mormonism. But concurrent with this movement we must take note, in the case of both religions, of three accompanying reactions that may be seen as virtually inevitable.

The first I would define as a countermovement directed precisely at tendencies toward accommodation and assimilation; this countermovement, typified in early Christianity by the figure of Tertullian, insists—in the end unsuccessfully—on preserving the full measure of cultural distinctiveness for the developing religion.

The second reaction, ironically, takes the form of defining heresy, or at least one form of heresy, in terms of those groups within the religion that adhere most closely to the original practices and beliefs of the early movement; by the late second century, those groups that still insisted on circumcision and Sabbath observance for all converts had come to be seen as heretical.

The third reaction, closely related to the second, arises in response to the crisis prompted by the disappearance of the first generation of charismatic leaders—that is, Jesus and the original disciples. There is evidence from the second century that points to a dispute between two groups concerning the nature of legitimate authority within the developing church. On the one side stood those who defined legitimate authority in terms of spiritual "descent" from the apostles, while on the other side stood those who looked to James, the brother of Jesus, and other members of Jesus's family, as fountainheads of legitimate religious authority.[18]

Notes

1. E. R. Dodds, *Pagan and Christian in an Age of Anxiety: Some Aspects of Religious Experience from Marcus Aurelius to Constantine* (Cambridge: Cambridge University Press, 1965), 5.

2. Such a view underlies Dodds's *Pagan and Christian* in terms of Christianity's early development outside Palestine. A similar view of early Palestinian Christianity may be found in Gerd Theissen, *Sociology of Early Palestinian Christianity* (Philadelphia: Fortress Press, 1978).

3. Peter L. Berger, *The Sacred Canopy: Elements of a Sociological Theory of Religion* (Garden City, N.Y.: Anchor Books, 1969), 180.

4. Ibid.

5. See the discussion in Mario S. De Pillis's review essay, "Klaus Hansen's True View of Mormonism," *Reviews in American History* 10 (March 1982): 65–71. I remain puzzled by an apparent contradiction between two assertions in the essay. On the one hand, De Pillis chides Hansen for allowing his account to be shaped by the old questions of partisanship with regard to Mormonism itself. On the other hand, he adds that it is disingenuous for Hansen "to assert that the historian is interested not in whether Mormonism is true or false" (66).

6. Peter Worsley, *The Trumpet Shall Sound: A Study of "Cargo" Cults in Melanesia,* 2nd rev. ed. (New York: Schocken, 1968); Kenelm Burridge, *New Heaven, New Earth: A Study of Millenarian Activities* (New York: Schocken, 1969); Norman R. Cohn, *The Pursuit of the Millennium: Revolutionary Millenarians and Mystical Anarchists of the Middle Ages,* rev. ed. (New York: Oxford University Press, 1970); Sylvia L. Thrupp, *Millennial Dreams in Action: Studies in Revolutionary Religious Movements* (New York: Schocken, 1970).

7. John F. Wilson, "Some Comparative Perspectives on the Early Mormon Movement and the Church-State Question, 1830–1845," *Journal of Mormon History* 8 (1981): 63–77; Klaus J. Hansen, *Quest for Empire: The Political Kingdom of God and the Council of Fifty in Mormon History* (1967; reprint, East Lansing: Michigan State University Press, 1970); and Klaus J. Hansen, *Mormonism and the American Experience* (Chicago: University of Chicago Press, 1981). In his review, De Pillis holds that Hansen has understated the millenarian character of early Mormonism. The issue, I think, is not that Hansen underestimates Mormonism as a millenarian movement but that his focus was directed toward other issues in this particular volume.

8. See my *Kingdom and Community: The Social World of Early Christianity* (Englewood Cliffs, N.J.: Prentice-Hall, 1975), 37–49, for a discussion of cognitive dissonance

theory in relation to the nonfulfillment of millennial expectations. The pioneering work in this area remains Leon Festinger, Henry W. Riecken, and Stanley Schachter, *When Prophecy Fails* (Minneapolis: University of Minnesota Press, 1956).

9. Hansen, *Quest for Empire*, 18–20.

10. Worsley, *The Trumpet Shall Sound*, xlii; emphasis his.

11. Hansen, *Mormonism and the American Experience*, 2, 41. Gager, *Kingdom and Community*, 22–28, uses relative deprivation theory.

12. Perhaps the most important of these conditions, though it will not be discussed here, is the emergence of the prophet. See Burridge, *New Heaven, New Earth*, 11–14, 153–64, and Hansen, *Mormonism and the American Experience*, 10–22.

13. See especially Whitney R. Cross, *The Burned-Over District: The Social and Intellectual History of Enthusiastic Religion in Western New York, 1800–1850* (Ithaca, N.Y.: Cornell University Press, 1950).

14. See Rodney Stark and William Sims Bainbridge, "Secularization and Cult Formation in the Jazz Age," *Journal for the Scientific Study of Religion* 20 (1981): 360–73. Stark's recent work in this area represents a fundamental challenge to all previous views of secularization as the inevitable concomitant or result of modernization. In this connection, we may note Klaus Hansen's observation: "Mormonism appeared on the American religious scene at precisely that moment when external religious authority, both intellectually and institutionally, was in headlong retreat" (*Mormonism and the American Experience*, 20).

15. Dodds, *Pagan and Christian*, 133–34; emphasis mine.

16. For discussion of the several versions of this first vision, see Hansen, *Mormonism and the American Experience*, 22–24, 221 n. 30. The only more radical statement of discontinuity that I know of in Christian history is to be found in the Gnostic documents from Nag Hammadi in Egypt, where different Gnostic communities trace their spiritual origins back to the time before creation itself, thereby avoiding any involvement in the story of Eden and the origins of evil in human history.

17. Quoted in Hansen, *Mormonism and the American Experience*, 18. Similar views are expressed throughout the literature on early Mormonism.

18. For a discussion of this much-disputed issue, see Hans von Campenhausen, "The Authority of Jesus' Relatives in the Early Church," in *Jerusalem and Rome: The Problem of Authority in the Early Church*, ed. Hans von Campenhausen and Henry Chadwick (Philadelphia: Fortress Press, 1966), 3–19.

CHAPTER 16

Extracting Social Scientific Models from Mormon History

Rodney Stark

Historians have become accustomed to exhortations that they ought to be applying social scientific models to their work. Thus, when the committee invited me to give this distinguished lecture, their underlying assumption must have been that any religious movement, including the Mormons, not only is unique but also is constrained by general social scientific principles. And I imagine that it was assumed that I would devote my time to explaining how some of these principles apply to Mormon history.

However, I think it will be far more useful if I do the opposite. Through the years, by close study of the Mormons I have tried to discover the general within the particular, to extract general social scientific models from Mormon historical materials. So I will devote my Tanner Lecture to summarizing several of these models in hopes that you will see some of the general implications of things you know so very well in particular.

Nearly fifteen years ago I published my first Mormon study with the flamboyant title "The Rise of a New World Faith."[1] In it I explained why the Mormons offered a "unique opportunity" to social scientists. I began by noting that it may be futile to try to understand the rise of new religions by studying the numerous small groups that constantly spring up, since none of these movements ever actually rises. Instead, each is doomed to obscurity from the start. Hence, even if we should discover the underlying principles governing these new religious movements, chances are that what we will have discovered are the laws of religious failure. To understand how new religions rise, we must study successful cases. I continued:

> It is, of course, too late to study how Islam arose in the 7th century, as it is too late to study the rise of the other great world faiths. Their formative periods are shrouded in the fog of unrecorded history. Despite the many admirable efforts to deduce "histories" of these great movements by sociologizing upon shreds

of texts, there are severe limits to what can be learned by these means. Sociologists of religion must await new developments to provide them with critical evidence.[2]

And then came the punch line: "I suggest that we need wait no longer, that the time of deliverance is now at hand. I shall give my reasons for believing that it is possible today to study that incredibly rare event: the rise of a new world religion."[3]

In that paper I presented two projections of Mormon membership for the next century (1980–2080). The low estimate was based on a growth rate of 30 percent per decade, which is far below the actual average rate of growth of 61 percent maintained by the Mormon Church during the three decades up to 1980. This low estimate would produce about 64 million Mormons in 2080. The high estimate was based on a growth rate of 50 percent per decade, still below the rate maintained during the preceding thirty years. Were it to be met, there would be about 267 million Mormons in 2080. Either total would qualify the Church of Jesus Christ of Latter-day Saints as a world religion.

These projections have attracted much attention and have sent any number of my colleagues and various journalists into extreme denial. But as I stand here, it is possible to compare the projections for the first seventeen years with actual membership figures. So far, membership is substantially higher than my most optimistic projection, the one that would result in 267 million Mormons worldwide in 2080 (table 1). For example, the actual membership total reached in 1997 exceeds the high projected total for 1999.

This little exercise in the arithmetic of the possible became of considerably more general interest when I began a book on the rise of Christianity.[4] One of the things that I felt it was urgent to establish was whether the ordinary process of conversion explained how Christianity had grown as large as it must have been by the start of the fourth century, or whether it was necessary to accept claims of mass conversions. That is, what rate of growth must we assume for Christianity to have grown from about one thousand members in the year 40 to about 6 million in the year 300? Historians, from Eusebius to Ramsay MacMullen, have unanimously asserted that such large numbers necessitate extraordinary bursts of mass conversions. Indeed, the great Adolf von Harnack wrote of the "inconceivable rapidity" of Christianity's "astonishing expansion" and repeated Augustine's claim that "Christianity must have reproduced itself by means of miracles, for the greatest miracle of all would have been the extraordinary extension of the religion apart from any miracles."[5]

Here I had an immense advantage over earlier historians because I knew from my Mormon statistics that the early growth of Christianity was in no way astonishing. All that was required for Christians to number 6 million within the time that history allows was a growth rate of 40 percent per decade, which is significantly lower than the current Mormon rate. I must admit that I have enjoyed all

Table 1. A comparison of projected and actual rates of Mormon
growth, 1980–97

	Estimate[*]	Low Estimate[**]	Actual Membership
1980	4,638,000		
1981	4,830,000	4,761,000	4,920,000
1982	5,030,000	4,888,000	5,161,000
1983	5,238,000	5,018,000	5,385,000
1984	5,455,000	5,151,000	5,641,000
1985	5,680,000	5,288,000	5,911,000
1986	5,915,000	5,429,000	6,167,000
1987	6,160,000	5,573,000	6,400,000
1988	6,415,000	5,721,000	6,721,000
1989	6,681,000	5,973,000	7,308,000
1990	6,957,000	6,029,000	7,761,000
1991	7,245,000	6,190,000	8,090,000
1992	7,545,000	6,354,000	8,404,000
1993	7,857,000	6,523,000	8,689,000
1994	8,182,000	6,697,000	9,024,569
1995	8,521,000	6,875,000	9,439,000
1996	8,834,000	7,058,000	9,694,000
1997	9,241,000	7,245,000	10,070,000
1998	9,623,000	7,438,000	
1999	10,021,000	7,636,000	
2000	10,436,000	7,838,000	
2005	12,782,000	8,937,000	
2010	15,654,000	10,190,000	
2015	19,172,000	11,618,000	
2020	23,480,000	13,246,000	
2040	52,830,000	22,387,000	
2060	118,867,000	37,833,000	
2080	267,452,000	63,939,000	

[*] 50 percent per decade (4.138 percent per year)
[**] 30 percent per decade (2.658 percent per year)

of the praise I have been given for generating this growth curve for early Christianity, but I also must admit that it was a very small achievement. I have made rather more important discoveries from close study of the Mormons.

In my first essay on the rise of Mormonism, I promised that I would soon publish a theoretical model of how new religions succeed, generalized from the Mormon example. I made good on that promise in 1987 and produced a more sophisticated version in 1996.[6] I will not summarize the model here but will emphasize several key elements that may be of particular interest to you.

Networks and Conversion

One of my earliest theoretical contributions to the social scientific study of religion concerned the central role of social relations in conversion to religious groups. This work did not begin with study of the Mormons but with the first dozen American members of the Unification Church, often referred to in the media as the Moonies. John Lofland, a fellow graduate student, and I wanted to understand how people became converts. Our interest was not in reaffiliation—such as when a Methodist becomes a Baptist—but in shifts across major religious traditions such as when a Baptist becomes a Hindu. At that time, the literature on conversion stressed the link between doctrine and deprivation. The approach used was to examine a group's doctrine to discover to whom it would have special appeal and to then assert that this appeal was the basis of conversion. Thus, one noted that Christian Science offered a cure for all ailments and reasoned that it mainly drew its converts from the ranks of the afflicted. Of course, one could as easily have argued that only persons with a history of unusually good health could be convinced that illness was all in the mind, which would, of course, lead to an entirely contrary conclusion about Christian Science converts. Lofland and I decided that no real progress could be made in explaining conversion barricaded behind the library stacks, so we went out to see it happen.

Our observations reduced doctrinal appeals to a very minor initial role. Yes, after people have joined a new religious movement and have fully learned its doctrines and forms of worship, they emphasize the centrality of belief in their conversion. But having observed these same people before and during their conversions, Lofland and I knew better. More typically, when people encountered the Unificationists they found their religious concerns rather odd. If they continued to associate with the group, it was only because they liked some of the members. Sometimes they were relatives or old friends of members. And it was this social connection that led to their conversions. As Lofland and I put it, "conversion was coming to accept the opinions of one's friends [or relatives]."[7]

Subsequent studies have shown that, in fact, interpersonal ties are the primary factor in conversion, and my more recent work on this phenomenon is based on the proposition that when an individual's attachments to a member or members of another religion outweigh his or her attachments to nonmembers, conversion will occur. The most common instance of this sort of conversion is, of course, through marriage. But less serious attachments often suffice.

In the case of most new religious movements, conversion is based on the formation of attachments to outsiders, and the typical convert is a person deficient in ties to others because of situational or psychological factors. Thus the Unificationists became very skilled at forming friendships with newcomers to the city, most of them young, whose close ties (if any) were all to persons too far away to observe their ongoing conversion. The same finding turns up in study after study of similar groups.[8] However, when movements depend on befriending isolates, their growth will be very slow. Why? Because when new members are selected for lack of ties to nonmembers, they rarely connect the group to other potential converts. Thus, growth requires that these religious movements constantly form new ties to nonmembers despite being increasingly composed of members deficient in the social skills needed to play the active role in forming such relationships.[9] Any movement growing as rapidly as the Mormons or as fast as the early Christians must have done cannot be based on recruiting isolates. Rather, most new converts must open the way to new social networks—to the conversion of their friends and relatives.

It was in seeking to document this proposition that I first benefited from a close look at things Mormon. Armand Mauss provided me with data on the outcomes of a large number of contacts between Mormon missionaries and nonmembers. When the contact occurred through a door-to-door cold call, only one in a thousand eventually resulted in a conversion. But when the contact was arranged and hosted by a Mormon friend or relative of the potential recruit, conversion took place half of the time.[10] It thus became obvious that Mormon conversion is not primarily the result of efforts by missionaries but is produced by rank-and-file Mormons who spread their faith to relatives and friends. Indeed, I summarized an article from the *Ensign* that offers a thirteen-step set of tactics for doing precisely that, repeatedly advising that all discussion of religion be delayed and minimized.[11]

My interests in conversion and the growth of religious movements have taken me back to Mormon data again and again. Recently I have devoted a good deal of effort to reconstructing the earliest Mormon social networks, starting with the Smith family. I know you all are aware that in the beginning, Mormon conversion was very much a kinship affair. Indeed, I have read discussions of this fact in books written by many members of this audience. Nevertheless, I doubt that any of you fully appreciates the extent to which the Latter-day Saints began as one big family or how long this remained true, and at what extraordinary distances.

I will be able to identify and analyze the early Mormon networks far more accurately and efficiently than has been possible as soon as my student Christopher Bader and I finish reconstructing the superb data file entitled *Membership of the Church of Jesus Christ of Latter-day Saints: 1830–1848*, compiled by Susan Easton Black and included in the LDS Family History Suite CD-ROM, available in your nearest Beehive Bookstore.[12] Dr. Black did a wonderful job of gathering material, but it is difficult to use her data for sociological research because it is in a single, huge text file. What we are doing is converting it into a file consisting of individual cases with the capacity to link cases on the basis of marriage or kinship. I anticipate that this reconstructed file will make it possible to instantly identify and list all members of Sidney Rigdon's church who were baptized in Kirtland, Ohio, late in 1830, for example. The search engine in the available CD turns up only about a dozen such people, but trustworthy histories report that there must have been at least 130. Most of these cases fail to turn up because the coding is inconsistent, but these are problems easily solved when cases can be examined on an entirely comparable basis. For example, although we have transformed only 1,337 of the more than 28,000 individuals included in the text file, we have already found several people whose place of baptism is missing but who were baptized a day or two before they received a patriarchal blessing in Kirtland at the time in question. So there they are, and it is already clear that most everyone was related to most everyone else.

In fact, even without this database, I already have learned enough to see that literally thousands of these early converts formed a huge interlocking kinship network existing long before Joseph Smith Jr. had any revelations. Today, I will restrict myself to several brief examples.

In April 1830, Samuel Smith met Phinehas Young in Mendon, New York, a town fifteen miles from Palmyra. Phinehas was a Methodist circuit rider whose home was in Mendon. When Samuel Smith attempted to interest him in a copy of the Book of Mormon, he accepted because he had already heard about its contents from his sister Rhoda and her husband John Greene, who was also a Methodist circuit rider. Rhoda had received a copy from Samuel Smith during a previous visit to Mendon. Phinehas wanted a copy so that he could prepare himself to refute it among his fellow Methodists, especially since the Greenes thought it had merit. Phinehas studied it for a week and could not find the errors he had anticipated. So he lent it to his father Joseph Young, who thought it "the greatest work . . . he had ever seen" and then he gave it to his sister Fanny, who called it "a revelation."[13]

However, as I have stressed, by themselves *scriptures do not make converts*. Despite their very positive reactions to the Book of Mormon, nothing happened. It required two more years of interacting with committed Mormons before the Youngs were ready. Then, in April 1832, John Young and his wife Hannah, four sons, three daughters-in-law, two daughters, and two sons-in-law were baptized as Mormons. A month later two more of Joseph Young's daughters and their husbands were baptized. The next year another Young son, daughter, and son-in-law were baptized. By building strong friendship ties to several members of one family, the Mormons gained twenty converts including Brigham Young!

But there's more. Vilate, the sister of Fanny Young's husband Roswell Murray, was married to Heber C. Kimball, who also was Brigham Young's closest friend; indeed, the Youngs and the Kimballs were cousins. The day after the first baptism of Youngs, all the Kimballs were baptized, too. Not only were Brigham Young and Heber Kimball cousins to each other, but both were distant cousins of Joseph Smith, kinship ties of which they all were well aware.[14]

Now, for another instance. In 1837, Joseph Smith directed that missionaries be sent to Great Britain. The British Mission was so successful that for a period beginning in the late 1840s, there were more Mormons in the British Isles than in the United States, despite large-scale Mormon emigration from Britain. In fact, the combination of Mormons in Britain and first-generation British

Mormon immigrants made up the majority of all Mormons from 1845 until 1895.[15] Many have suggested how economic and social conditions in Great Britain at this time created a receptive audience for the Mormon message,[16] but my interest here is limited to the network aspects. How did the missionaries get started? Who would listen? Who had reason to trust them?

After landing in Liverpool, the Mormon missionary party went directly to the textile manufacturing city of Preston. There they were given access to the pulpits of three Nonconformist churches, and for several weeks, they freely preached the Mormon doctrine, to great effect. Joseph Fielding was the missionary who had made these arrangements well in advance of their departure from the United States. The three English pastors who opened their pulpits to them were Fielding's brother and his two brothers-in-law.[17]

Having stressed the network character of conversion, it now is time to admit that doctrine does matter. Even if people do not pursue a new faith because they find its doctrines irresistible, doctrine does tend to impede or facilitate religious choices. It does this in two primary ways. One way involves the principle of the conservation of religious capital. The other is as doctrine shapes the social norms within religious groups.

Religious Capital and Conversion

As I became more familiar with Mormon statistics, I noticed that they were much more successful in some places than others. Eventually, I recognized a pattern: Mormon growth usually is more rapid in Christian than in non-Christian societies. This encouraged me to examine other recent religious movements and to notice that groups retaining substantial Christian cultural elements (such as Christian Science or, more recently, the Children of God) have done far better in the United States than have various non-Christian faiths based in Hinduism or other Eastern religions (such as Theosophy or the Hare Krishnas). I formulated an explanation of this pattern.

The starting point of all worthwhile social theories is the recognition that people attempt to make rational choices, to pay attention to the potential costs and benefits when selecting a course of action. Put another way, people attempt to maximize. As used in economics, attempts at maximization usually involve capital and the attempt to acquire the most while expending the least. In my recent work, I use far more general forms of capital: social and religious.

We have already examined the role of social capital in conversion. Our relationships with others represent very substantial investments of time, energy, emotion, and even material. Moreover, we can draw upon this capital in times of need; our friends will rally to our support. Put another way, most people, most of the time, have accumulated a network of relationships that they regard as valuable. When people base their religious choices on the preferences of those to whom they are attached, they conserve (maximize) their social capital—they do not risk their attachments by failure to conform, and therefore they do not face the potential need to replace their attachments.

For a long time, I minimized the importance of religious factors in religious choices in order to emphasize the importance of social capital. But it bothered me to do so because I knew full well that selecting a religion is not exactly like joining a secular club. Belief is the central aspect of religion, and therefore one's beliefs do matter but in a more subtle fashion than has been assumed by those who attribute religious choices to doctrinal appeal. To understand this point, it will be necessary to conceptualize religion as a form of cultural capital, a term coined by French sociologist Pierre Bourdieu to identify the investments or "sunk costs" that culture represents to each individual.[18]

Culture refers to the complex pattern of living that directs human social life, the things each new generation must learn and to which eventually they may add. That is, culture consists of the sum total of human creations—intellectual, technical, and moral. To become normal humans, all newborns must master the cultural package deemed essential in their society, including the religion of their parents. The process of acquiring culture is known as socialization. And when we are being socialized into our culture, we also are investing in it— expending time and effort in learning, understanding, and remembering cultural material. For example, persons raised to be Christians accumulate a substantial store of Christian culture: not only doctrines but prayers, hymns, rituals, history, and personal memories. People tend to stay put and to not migrate or emigrate, not only to protect social capital but also to protect their cultural capital. For example, someone who is already proficient in French maximizes that possession by remaining within a French-speaking community rather than moving and having to invest in learning a new language and all of the other essential parts of a new culture. By the same token, being already proficient in Roman Catholicism, one maximizes by remaining within the bosom of the church.[19]

As I define it, religious capital consists of the degree of mastery of any particular religious culture. And I reason thus: in making religious choices, people will attempt to conserve their religious capital.

What this means is that, generally speaking, the greater their store of religious capital (the more they have invested in a faith), the more costly it is for people to change faiths. This fact helps us recognize why converts overwhelmingly are recruited from the ranks of those lacking a prior religious commitment or having only a nominal connection to a religious group. This pattern not only has turned up repeatedly in studies of new religious movements but can also be seen in the fact that in the United States, the single most unstable "religion" of origin is "no religious preference." While the great majority of those raised with a religious affiliation retain that affiliation, the great majority of those who say that their family had no religion join a religion as adults. Or as another example, one might well suppose that converts to a thriving Mexican millenarian colony of "Traditional Catholics" (who reject the Vatican II reforms) would come from the ranks of the very pious. But Miguel C. Leatham found that those who joined had been "quite marginal Catholics at the time of recruitment," having "extremely low mass attendance"; some had not even been baptized.[20] Thus, at least one basis for these conversions is that a lack of prior religious commitment makes it inexpensive (in terms of religious capital) to take up a new faith.

The empirical literature is entirely supportive of the proposition that when people change religions, they tend to select the option that maximizes their conservation of religious capital by switching to a religious body very similar to the one in which they were raised. Thus, people raised in one Jewish Hasidic body are more apt to shift to another than to join a Conservative synagogue, are more likely to join a Conservative than a Reform synagogue, and are far more apt to become Reform Jews than Unitarians. Similarly, people raised in an evangelical Protestant denomination tend to switch to another, a process that Reginald Bibby and Merlin Brinkerhoff describe as "the circulation of saints."[21] Many subsequent studies have found that the tendency to select a new church that very closely resembles one's previous affiliation holds across the theological spectrum.

The principle also holds even when we examine more dramatic shifts in affiliation. Consider the situation of a young person from a traditional Christian background and living in a Christian society who is deciding whether to join the Mormons or the Hare Kishnas. By becoming a Mormon, this person retains his or her entire Christian culture and simply adds to it. The Mormon missionaries, noting that the person has copies of the Old Testament and the New Testament, suggest that an additional Scripture, the Book of Mormon, will complete the set. In contrast, the Hare Krishna missionaries note that the person has the "wrong" scriptures and must discard the Bible in exchange for the Bhagavad Gita. The principle of the conservation of religious capital predicts (and explains) why the overwhelming majority of converts within a Christian context select the Mormon rather than the Hare Krishna option. It also helps us understand why the Hare Krishnas have outdone the Mormons in India and among American immigrants from India. It sheds light, too, on why the Jehovah's Witnesses are growing far more rapidly than the Mormons in Europe but why the two are doing about equally well in Asia, where neither has any advantage in terms of religious capital.

The Word as Flesh

Doctrine also plays a substantial role in shaping the social life of religious groups, aspects of which are of special importance to any outsider thinking of becoming a member. I was able to overcome my sociological training and to recognize that the Word can indeed become flesh mainly because of the Mormon example.

Anyone who lives around Mormons and pays attention must be struck by the worldly rewards of membership. Mormons not only benefit from the promise of immense rewards to come in the next world, but they shower one another with rewards in this one. By asking much of their members, the Mormon Church gains the resources to give them much. Far more than members of most other American faiths, Mormons can feel secure against misfortune and hard times. This is not an accident, nor is it a holdover from frontier customs. Again and again when I have discussed these practices with Mormons, they quickly offer Scripture as their justification. Mormons maintain their own system of social services because they believe that God commands them to do so. And here, too, my work on early Christianity profited greatly from my Mormon experiences.

It is not fashionable to argue that the early Christians took seriously such ideas as being their brothers' keepers. Nor would most sociologists have suggested that Christians really would have acted on such notions to nurse the sick in times of plague, to sustain widows and orphans, to purchase the freedom of slaves, or to provide decent burial for the dead—this *despite* the fact that both early Christian and pagan sources agree that it was all true! Most sociologists know better than to believe such stuff. We have been taught that ideas are but epiphenomena flowing upward from underlying material conditions. But anyone who has watched their Mormon friends make substantial sacrifices on behalf of others—open their home to an abandoned wife and children or regularly take a former neighbor now suffering from Alzheimer's disease out for a picnic—knows enough to look for such forms of religious behavior elsewhere. I was able to understand the very attractive social and material rewards of early Christianity because I had seen people who became Mormons after having initially formed a favorable impression of the group on these grounds alone.

Revelations

As my final topic, I would like to discuss how immersion in Mormon history led me to formulate and then to extend a theory of revelations. The most basic question confronting the social scientific study of religion concerns the sources of religious culture. Given that the major Western religions are all based on revelations, the question becomes, How do "revelations" occur? To the extent that we cannot answer this question, we remain ignorant of the origins of our entire subject matter.

Despite being the question, it has seldom been raised because the answer has seemed obvious to most social scientists: those who claim to have received revelations—to have communicated with the supernatural—are either crazy or crooked, and sometimes both. Indeed, even many social scientists who will permit the rational choice axiom in explanations of more mundane religious phenomena find it quite impossible to accept that normal people can sincerely believe they have communicated with the divine. Although scholars seldom express such views openly, it long has been the orthodox position that the world's major religious figures, including Moses, Jesus, and Muhammad, as well as thousands of more recent revelators such as Anne Hutchinson, Joseph Smith, Bernadette Soubirous, and the Reverend Sun M. Moon, were psychotics, frauds, or both. When Bainbridge and I surveyed the literature on revelation a few years ago, we found that although the topic had been little covered, the psychopathological interpretation was the overwhelming favorite, with conscious fraud treated as the only plausible alternative.[22]

In that essay, Bainbridge and I reworked this literature and systematized our own field observations to state three models of revelation. The first gives systematic statement to the psychopathology model. Here revelations are traced not simply to mental illness but also to abnormal mental states induced by drugs or fasting. The second model substitutes chicanery for psychopathology and characterizes some religious founders as entrepreneurs. Finally, we codified a subcultural-evolution model of revelation wherein a small group, interacting intensely over a period of time, assembles a revelation bit by bit, without anyone being aware of the social processes taking place. Here, at least, we made room for revelations involving neither craziness nor corruption.

Since the publication of that article, it has become increasingly clear that these three models fail to account for very many cases of revelations—including the most significant ones. There have been precious few cases in which there is any persuasive evidence that the founder of a new religious movement had any symptoms of mental problems.[23] Of course, lack of visible signs is no impediment for Freudians and others who are entirely willing to infer psychopathology from religious behavior per se, but for those of us lacking conviction in Freud's revelations, the apparent normalcy of scores of well-documented cases requires that we dismiss this approach. Moreover, it seems equally clear that few of the apparently sane recipients of revelations were crooks. Too many of them made personal sacrifices utterly incompatible with such an assessment. Finally, the subcultural-evolution model will not take up the slack, for the majority of cases seem not to fit it either. Hence, the need for a new approach was patent.

Eventually, I found the basis for such an approach in a close examination of how Spencer W. Kimball received the revelation that blacks should be admitted to the Mormon priesthood. Kimball reported no voices from beyond, no burning bushes, and no apparitions. He spoke only of the many hours he spent in the "upper room of the temple supplicating the Lord for divine guidance."[24] The actual process by which he received his revelation would seem to involve nothing more (or less) than achieving a state of complete certainty about what God wanted him to do.

Couldn't any sincere believer have revelations that way? Clearly, this episode demonstrated the possibility that many revelations can be understood in rational terms, and I soon realized that this assumption could be extended even to the more dramatic episodes of revelations, including those that do involve visions and voices. So I proceeded to construct a model of revelations based on the starting assumption that normal people can, through entirely normal means, have revelations, including revelations sufficiently profound to serve as the basis of new religions.

In that essay I was careful to acknowledge the possibility that revelations actually occur. It is beyond the capacity of science to demonstrate that the divine does not communicate directly with certain individuals; there is no possibility of constructing an appropriate detector. We must, therefore, admit the possibility of an active supernatural realm closed to scientific exploration. To confess these limits to scientific epistemology is not to suggest that we cease efforts to account for religious phenomena within a scientific framework. Indeed, as I shall take up in my conclusion, there is no necessary incompatibility between these efforts and faith.

My initial model of how revelations occur is available in several versions.[25] In constructing it, I ended up giving considerable attention to famous religious founders, and I was very struck by some amazing similarities between Joseph Smith and Muhammad. Both the Book of Mormon and the Qur'an were produced mostly in public situations, having been dictated as others took down the words. In both cases, the witnesses report that both Joseph Smith and Muhammad appeared to be reading or hearing the text, not composing it; there were not a lot of false starts and long pauses as would be expected had the revelator been making it up as he went. These descriptions led me to comparisons with Mozart and Gershwin, since music simply "came" to them and they claimed that they played or wrote down things they heard rather than things they created. Had they heard or glimpsed new scriptures rather than music, one easily can suppose that they would have concluded that these were being revealed to them.

I also noted the extent to which both Joseph Smith and Muhammad received very strong and unwavering support from their immediate families, confirming that their visions were truly of divine origin and should be pursued. In time, these and other aspects led me to the notion of "Holy Families," and in a new essay I spell out the importance of networks, not only for producing converts but also for sustaining prophets.[26] Let me sketch this approach.

Imagine yourself living a life of solitary contemplation. Then one day new truths are revealed to you by a divine being. By new truths, I mean a revelation that does not simply ratify current religious conceptions but one that adds to or departs from these conceptions to a significant degree. Having imparted a heterodox revelation, the divine being directs you to communicate it to the world, which means that you must found a heretical religious movement. Having no close friends to reassure you or to help spread the word, somehow you now must find someone who will believe you, and then another, and another. It is a daunting prospect.

But what if, instead of living a solitary life, you are a respected member of an intense primary group? It would seem far less difficult to share your revelation with people who love and trust you than to convince strangers. Moreover, if members of your immediate social network can be converted, they constitute a ready-made religious movement. Furthermore, it will be much easier to convince others that your revelation is authentic if they already believe that humans sometimes do receive revelations. Finally and ironically, while it is far easier for religions to begin within a tight primary group, to achieve substantial growth a new religion must burst the confines of these intense relationships to become an open and expanding network. Let me state these points more formally.

For heretical religious movements based on revelations to succeed:

1. There must exist a general cultural tradition of communications with the divine, and the recipient of the revelation(s) must have direct contact with someone who has had such communications. Not only must it be plausible to the recipient and potential followers that revelations occur, but there also must be a role model so that a given individual may anticipate divine contact and comprehend such an episode as a revelation. Implicit here is a reinforcement model of religious experiences and revelations.

2. The recipient of the revelation must be a respected member of an intense primary group. Revelations cannot be sustained and transformed into successful new religions by lonely prophets but are invariably rooted in preexisting networks having a high level of social solidarity. Indeed, new religious movements based on revelations typically are family affairs. But whether a religious founder's primary group is based on kinship, what is important is that it is a durable, face-to-face network with very high levels of trust and affection.

3. The founding network must be, or must become, an open network, able to build ties to outsiders, especially to outside networks. A major cause of the failure of new religious movements is that they are, or become, so intensely inward that it is impossible for them to form the bonds to outsiders necessary for recruitment.

It should be obvious how these three propositions fit the origins of the Latter-day Saints. The Smith family took the reality of revelations for granted, as did most of their neighbors. Many local people reported having vivid religious experiences, including Joseph Smith Sr. Hence, when the eighteen-year-old Joseph Jr. had his initial vision of the Angel Moroni, the first person he told was his father, who, according to Richard L. Bushman, "expressed no skepticism. Having learned himself to trust in visions, he accepted his son's story and counseled him to do exactly as the angel said."[27] Subsequently, Joseph Smith Jr.'s entire nuclear family was supportive and, eventually, so were numerous uncles, aunts, and cousins at various removes.

Muhammad's story is very similar. Revelation was taken for granted in Arabic culture in Muhammad's time. In part this was a result of the constant and close contact with Christians and Jews. Communities of both faiths existed all over the Arabian peninsula in these days, some of them within Muhammad's Mecca. In fact, at the start of his prophetic career, Muhammad assumed that Christians and Jews would embrace his revelations, since he believed himself to be the last in a line of prophets beginning with Abraham and including Jesus. Moreover, there was an indigenous Arabic tradition of revelation that was especially well developed among the *hanif,* apparently a monotheistic sect in Arabia including elements of both Christianity and Judaism and possibly being a refuge for heretics from both. Scholars now generally accept that the *hanif* reflected the existence of "a national Arabian monotheism which was a preparatory stage to Islam."[28]

Muhammad was directly influenced by two of the four founders of the *hanif* movement. One was his cousin Ubaydallah ibn Jahsh, who also was among Muhammad's early converts, and the other was his wife's cousin Waraqa ibn Naufal, a famous ascetic and visionary who not only authenticated Muhammad's earliest visions but also spurred him on in pursuit of revelations.[29]

Muhammad was about forty when he first began to have visions. They occurred in the month of Ramadan,[30] during which he had for several years begun to seclude himself in a cave on Mount Hiraa. Here "Muhammad spent his days and nights in contemplation and worship. He addressed his worship to the Creator of the universe."[31] This practice may have been prompted by "the old visionary Waraqa," who had converted to Christianity, is thought to have known Hebrew, and had long been predicting the coming of an Arabian prophet.[32] Eventually Muhammad began to have vivid dreams involving angels and to experience mysterious phenomena such as lights and sounds without sources. These upset him; he feared that he was losing his sanity or had been possessed by an evil spirit. When he confided in his wife Kahdijah, she immediately reassured him and quickly consulted her cousin Waraqa, who accepted these phenomena as signs that greater revelations would be forthcoming.[33] Subsequently, when Kahdijah brought Muhammad to consult him, Waraqa cried out, "If you have spoken the truth to me, O Kahdijah, there has come to him the greatest *namus* who came to Moses aforetime, and lo, he is the prophet of his people." Later, when he encountered Muhammad in the marketplace, Waraqa kissed him on the forehead as a mark of his mission as the "new prophet of the one God."[34] Indeed, Waraqa "serves as a kind of John the Baptist in the accounts of Muhammad's early revelations."[35]

Thus reassured, Muhammad accepted his mission, expected to receive major new revelations, and soon did. Through all that was to come, the support of Kahdijah and Waraqa remained constant. Muhammad, an orphan, seems to have had little contact with his siblings, and his two sons died in infancy; otherwise, those family members probably would have been part of the founding core of Islam, just as Joseph Smith's parents and siblings were prominent early Mormons. Kahdijah's and Muhammad's two adopted sons were Muhammad's cousin Ali and Zayd ibn-Harithah, whom they had originally purchased as a slave. These adopted sons became Muhammad's third and fourth converts (after Kahdijah and Waraqa). The couple's four daughters—Fatimah, Zaynab, Ruqayya, and Umm Kulthum—all converted and so did three of Muhammad's cousins (including the famous *hanif* Ubaydallah), Asmar, wife of his cousin Ja'far, Muhammad's aunt, and his freed slave, Umm Ayman, a woman who had cared for him in infancy.

The first convert from outside Muhammad's family, and the fifth to accept the new faith, was Abu-Bakr, Muhammad's oldest and closest friend. Occupying a bridge position[36] in the network, Abu-Bakr brought the new faith to "a group of five men who became the mainstay of the young [movement]."[37] These five were close friends and business associates. One was Abu-Bakr's cousin, and another was yet another of Kahdijah's cousins. Like Muhammad, Abu-Bakr had great sympathy for slaves and, throughout his life, spent much of his income to purchase and free people from bondage. Two of the earliest converts to Islam were slaves whom he freed, including Bilal, who gained lasting fame as the first muezzin (or crier) to call the faithful to prayer.

These examples do not begin to exhaust the similarities between Muhammad and Joseph Smith. But they suffice. Having noted them, I found it both encouraging and fascinating to see how a model of revelations, rooted in observations of the Mormons, fit another famous case. Then, somewhat to my surprise, I discovered that the model fully fits Jesus and probably Moses as well.

There has emerged a new consensus among historians of early Christianity that Jesus had four brothers and at least two sisters, all of whom were among his earliest and strongest supporters, and the significance of John the Baptist as a role model is well known. This is not an appropriate place to deal with the statement attributed to Jesus that "a prophet is not without honour, save in his own country, and in his own house" (Matt. 13:57; see also Mark 6:4). I merely note that early church fathers such as Origen and Tertullian dismissed this claim as entirely figurative since it was not historically true. In fact, the Apostle Paul claimed that the "brothers of the Lord" and their wives traveled with Jesus during his ministry (1 Cor. 9). Fortunately, I need not fight this battle, as it appears to be over.

Finally, to the extent that we can glimpse actual history through the mists of oral traditions and the Pentateuch, the Moses story also is one of close family support—indeed, his siblings Aaron and Miriam had revelations too, and his wife and father-in-law may have done so as well.

The similarities across these four major cases are many and significant. There seems compelling evidence that cultural and social supports are needed to make people receptive to revelations. Joseph Smith, Muhammad, Jesus, and Moses were on close terms with others who had visions and revelations. Their holy families played a central role in sustaining their missions, and all four movements grew on the basis of network linkages. While these similarities sustain my theoretical propositions, unfortunately they can also be twisted to support the view that religions are nothing more than human inventions and that all of the faithful are misled or myopic. This fallacy has gone unchallenged in social science journals for far too long. Therefore, in closing, let me briefly explain why the social scientific study of religion is as compatible with faith as it is with skepticism.

Conclusion

The basis of the fallacy is the notion that, to be true, religions must be immune to social scientific analysis, being inexplicable enigmas. For example, it is assumed that if believers, and especially founders, can be shown to behave in predictable ways, subject to normal human desires and motivations, then their religion must be a wholly naturalistic phenomenon, having no supernatural aspects. From this view, the fact that these four major religions conform to a social scientific model is proof of their purely human origins. Why else, skeptics ask, would the recipients of revelations have role models? Why would they require social support to proceed with their missions? Why would movements spread through networks on the basis of interpersonal relations rather than on the basis of scriptural merit?

This typical form of attack on the credibility of religion ignores what all believers readily acknowledge: that there is always a human side to religious phenomena. Mormons, Muslims, Christians, and Jews believe that the divine could convert the whole world in an instant, that the option to sin could be removed, and that other such miracles easily could be accomplished. But followers of these faiths also assume that this is not the divine intention. Rather, they believe that the divine acts through history, employing imperfect human agents. It therefore involves no inherently irreligious assumptions to seek to understand the human side of religious phenomena, including revelations, in human terms. Thus, for example, there is nothing discreditable in discovering that those who train and supervise missionaries are concerned with developing effective tactics, with sustaining morale, and with all the other common issues arising from organized human action. Moreover, all four faiths depict the humanity of their founders, and from the point of view of believers, there is nothing blasphemous about examining their human sides and observing that they behaved in recognizably human ways. The social scientific study of religion attempts to do nothing more.

Notes

1. Rodney Stark, "The Rise of a New World Faith," *Review of Religious Research* 26 (September 1984): 18–27.

2. Ibid., 18.

3. Ibid.

4. Rodney Stark, *The Rise of Christianity: A Sociologist Reconsiders History* (Princeton, N.J.: Princeton University Press, 1996).

5. Adolf von Harnack, *The Mission and Expansion of Christianity in the First Three Centuries*, 2 vols. (New York: Putnam, 1908), 2:335–36.

6. Rodney Stark, "How New Religions Succeed: A Theoretical Model," in *The Future of Religious Movements*, ed. David Bromley and Phillip E. Hammond (Macon, Ga.: Mercer University Press, 1987), 11–29; and Stark, "Why Religious Movements Succeed or Fail: A Revised General Model," *Journal of Contemporary Religion* 12 (May 1996): 133–46.

7. John Lofland and Rodney Stark, "Becoming a World-Saver: A Theory of Conversion to a Deviant Perspective," *American Sociological Review* 30 (1965): 871.

8. William Sims Bainbridge, *The Sociology of Religious Movements* (New York: Routledge, 1997).

9. Rodney Stark and Lynne Roberts, "The Arithmetic of Social Movements: Theoretical Implications," *Sociological Analysis* 43 (Spring 1982): 53–67.

10. Rodney Stark and William Sims Bainbridge, "Networks of Faith: Interpersonal Bonds and Recruitment to Cults and Sects," *American Journal of Sociology* 85 (1980): 1376–95.

11. Ibid.

12. Susan Easton Black, *Membership of The Church of Jesus Christ of Latter-day Saints: 1830–1848*, LDS Family History Suite, CD-ROM (Orem, Utah: Infobases, 1996).

13. Leonard J. Arrington, *Brigham Young: American Moses* (New York: Knopf, 1985), 19–20.

14. D. Michael Quinn, *The Mormon Hierarchy: Extensions of Power* (Salt Lake City: Signature Books, 1997), 165.

15. Rodney Stark, "The Basis of Mormon Success: A Theoretical Application," in *Latter-day Saint Social Life: Social Research on the LDS Church and Its Members*, ed. James T. Duke (Provo, Utah: Religious Studies Center, Brigham Young University, 1998), 29–70.

16. Arrington, *Brigham Young;* James B. Allen, Ronald K. Esplin, and David J. Whittaker, *Men with a Mission, 1837–1841: The Quorum of the Twelve Apostles in the British Isles* (Salt Lake City: Deseret Book, 1992).

17. Allen, Esplin, and Whittaker, *Men with a Mission*, chap. 2.

18. Pierre Bourdieu, *Distinction: A Social Critique of the Judgement of Taste* (Cambridge: Harvard University Press, 1984).

19. Laurence R. Iannaccone, "Religious Participation: A Human Capital Approach," *Journal for the Scientific Study of Religion* 29 (September 1990): 297–314.

20. Miguel C. Leatham, "Rethinking Religious Decision-Making in Peasant Millenarianism: The Case of Nueva Jeruslén," *Journal of Contemporary Religion* 12 (October 1997): 295–309.

21. Reginald W. Bibby and Merlin B. Brinkerhoff, "The Circulation of the Saints: A Study of People Who Join Conservative Churches," *Journal for the Scientific Study of Religion* 12 (September 1973): 273–83.

22. William Sims Bainbridge and Rodney Stark, "Cult Formation: Three Compatible Models," *Sociological Analysis* 40 (Winter 1979): 283–95.

23. Mental patients who claim to talk to God or to be Muhammad are of no interest. At issue is the mental health of people who succeed in convincing others to accept the authenticity of their revelations, not the incidence of religious imagery in the delusions of the mentally ill.

24. Quoted in Armand L. Mauss, "The Fading of the Pharaohs' Curse: The Decline and Fall of the Priesthood Ban against Blacks in the Mormon Church," *Dialogue: A Journal of Mormon Thought* 14(3) (Autumn 1981): 27.

25. Rodney Stark, "How Sane People Talk to the Gods: A Rational Theory of Revelations," in *Innovations in Religious Traditions: Essays in the Interpretation of Religious Change,* ed. Michael W. Williams, Collet Cox, and Martin S. Jaffe (Berlin: Mouton de Gruyter, 1992), 19–34; and Stark, "Normal Revelations: A Rational Model of 'Mystical' Experiences," in *Religion and the Social Order,* Vol. 1, ed. David G. Bromley (Greenwich, Conn.: JAI Press, 1991), 239–51.

26. Rodney Stark, "A Theory of Revelations," *Journal for the Scientific Study of Religion* 38 (June 1999): 287–308.

27. Richard L. Bushman, *Joseph Smith and the Beginnings of Mormonism* (Urbana: University of Illinois Press, 1984), 63.

28. J. Fueck, "The Originality of the Arabian Prophet," *Studies on Islam,* trans. and ed. Merlin L. Swartz (1936; reprint, New York: Oxford University Press, 1981), 91.

29. Karen Armstrong, *Muhammad: A Biography of the Prophet* (San Francisco: HarperSanFrancisco, 1992); Caesar E. Farah, *Islam: Beliefs and Observances,* 5th ed. (Hauppauge, N.Y.: Barron's, 1994); Robert Payne, *The History of Islam* (New York: Barnes and Noble, 1959); F. E. Peters, *Muhammad and the Origins of Islam* (Albany: State University of New York Press, 1994); Maxime Rodinson, *Muhammad* (New York: Pantheon, 1980); M. A. Salahi, *Muhammad: Man and Prophet* (Shaftesbury, UK: Element, 1995); David Waines, *An Introduction to Islam* (Cambridge: Cambridge University Press, 1995); W. Montgomery Watt, *Muhammad: Prophet and Statesman* (London: Oxford University Press, 1961).

30. This holy period and the custom of making a pilgrimage to Mecca preceded Islam, having been well established in Arab paganism.

31. Salahi, *Muhammad,* 62.

32. Payne, *The History of Islam.*

33. Ibid., 16.

34. Salahi, *Muhammad,* 85.

35. Peters, *Muhammad and the Origins of Islam,* 123.

36. A bridge position person links two or more networks. Oliver Cowdery bridged the Smith family with the Whitmer family.

37. Watt, *Muhammad: Prophet and Statesman,* 35.

CHAPTER 17

Religion and Culture: A Persistent Problem

Langdon Gilkey

Let me begin with a few prefatory remarks. First, it is a distinct and signal honor for me to be invited to address this association. This is the first time I have been among you, and it is exciting. In another sense, however, I am coming home. My mother spent her childhood from four to about fourteen years of age among Mormons, in Salt Lake City. Her father, a kindly, liberal-spirited clergyman, was the pastor of the Congregational Church in Salt Lake City during the decade from 1892 to about 1902, at which point the family moved to San Diego. Thus I grew up two decades later surrounded by my grandfather's stories and my mother's memories of her girlhood in the very center of your world.

Second, I know that I do not need to remind you that I represent a slightly different tradition from your own. Any theologian, but also any reflective thinker, who addresses an important theme does so with what has been called a pre-understanding, a set of assumptions and norms that guide his or her thought. Thus, when I speak to you on the crucial theme of the relation of religion to culture, of church to its surrounding world, I do so with, I hope, a generous common ground between us, but also on the basis of the deep convictions, standards, and hopes that come to me from my own Christian tradition. You will, I am sure, notice this. I trust that, despite this, my remarks will seem relevant and helpful to your own deliberations.

Finally, in what follows I am making a number of additions to the address as given. That address omitted all references to either the RLDS Church or the LDS Church in its analysis of the relation of religious communities to their wider cultural environment. Rather, I referred explicitly only to Christian communities, to the Southern Baptists, the Roman Catholics, and so on. It did not seem appropriate for me, as a guest of the Mormon History Association and as an outsider, to comment upon issues in your common life and certainly not to lecture you on your obligations to your Lord. As any attentive listener will have guessed, however, as I wrote I did have in mind issues within the Mormon community; otherwise, I would hardly have chosen the topic or developed it as I did. Now I have been urged by those in charge of publication to make explicit those implicit references and to add them to the text. At first I hesitated for the reason stated to do even this. But my desire to fulfill the terms of the initial invitation to me has prevailed, and so, with no little trepidation, I add these references to my original text.

* * *

It is, perhaps, a bit brazen of me to speak to the Mormon History Association on the theme of religion and culture. Church historians thrive on this relation; as historians, what they do is to help us understand religious groups in relation to their historical context, that is, as deeply related to their culture. Traditionally, theologians have tended to ignore this relation. Theology is, they say, eternal; culture is historical. Theological truth is, so to speak, lowered down from on high into a historical context, but it is not of that context. Hence, the relation is not instructive for theology, only for the external life of the churches.

I do not agree with this view. Theologies, along with the community's ethical rules and standards, are as much related to that community's cultural setting as are the designs of the churches, the size of their bricks, and their modes of keeping their financial accounts. What is more, theological analysis, in union with historical analysis, can help us to understand this relation, to see what its constitutive elements are and thus to deal creatively with the important issues involved in the relation of church to culture. As a consequence, I wish to share with you a theological analysis of the relation of religious community to world. Whether such an analysis is relevant to your concerns, I leave to you; I believe it is relevant to mine and to the Christian churches with which I am associated.

In stressing the intimate relation of religion to its cultural setting, it is important at the outset that I maintain the differences or distinctions between them. Many academic students of religion do not recognize these distinctions, seeing religion as a human projection, even if a valuable and interesting one. Thus, they view religion in general as merely a function of culture, and usually a dependent, uncreative—in fact, a frequently destructive—epiphenomenon. Again I do not agree. Religion is a response, not a projection; it is a response to the ultimate and the sacred in reality, that is, to God. Thus, as each religion understands itself, each religious community is established on revelation, on the manifestation of sacred reality to or through a person and to a community, and it is maintained by the witness and obedience of that community to that manifestation. A believing theologian (and I consider myself to be one) can hardly say less than this, for the task of the theologian is to reflect on that manifestation to his or her community and to seek to understand all of existence in its light. I shall use the word *religion*, then, or religious community, to refer to a community of believing, worshiping, and obedient (at least in intention) people who have responded to the manifestation to them of God's nature and God's will and who undertake to live out the implications of that manifestation. Our question, then, is this, What is the relation of such a community—a church, as we call it in Christian language—to its surrounding culture?

Two different sorts of relation have characterized most of religion's history. On the one hand, there has been domination. In union with the power of the state and also with economic power, the church or its equivalent has shared in political rule; has supervised the spiritual, moral, and aesthetic life of the community; and in most cases (though not all) has prevented rival religious and ethical systems from appearing and flourishing. This was true in archaic cultures such as Egypt, China, and Japan; in Christendom until the Enlightenment; and in most Islamic countries. It has also been true of selected groups within our American history, such as the Puritan establishment in the Massachusetts Bay colony and later in Connecticut, and Anglicanism in the colony of Virginia. It was also, I gather, characteristic of the early rule of the LDS Church in the territory of Utah.

In such a relation there can be little freedom either of religion or of intellectual, moral, or social expression. The wider social community represents a solid, monolithic, and often repressive spiritual substance dominated, supervised, and controlled by one church. My own Baptist ancestors in Rhode Island and in Maine objected to this, as did the Quakers in Pennsylvania; in effective union with the Enlightenment critics of established religion in Virginia, as well as the practical proponents of pluralism in New York and New Jersey, they managed to separate church and state in the constitutional founding of our country. Religion in this role, said the Baptists and the Quakers, destroys itself: the spirit cannot be forced from the outside and live, and a church that takes up the sword and uses the state to enlarge itself and its own rule dies by the sword it wields. It may gain the world, but it loses its own soul, and it endangers the souls of those who inhabit its territory. I hope those Baptists who now call for a "Christian America," a country run by Christians and for Christians, will hearken to these words of their Baptist forefathers. For as the history of Christian empires, Christian nations, and Christian parties shows so clearly, by that route lies the death of the spirit and the slow extinction of true religion.

The other traditional answer to the problem of culture has been separation. Sensing deeply that society as a whole is shot through with evil ways as well as with religious indifference and even blasphemy, serious religious communities have withdrawn in whole or in part. Some have followed monastic rules of chastity and poverty; others have refused property, use of the sword, social privileges and rank, the jurisdiction of courts, and so on; still others, such as the Amish, have abjured the tools and automobiles as well as the social customs of modern consumer culture. To these, participation in government, in the judiciary or law enforcement, in the military, and certainly in banking or business—even enjoying academic tenure!—is inconceivable for a real church member.

This has been—and is—an impressive response, characteristic of some of my own Baptist tradition and some of your own, if I understand it correctly. However, we should be clear that insofar as members of such a community participate in the day-to-day life of the wider world, they have ceased to be in separation from the world. They then are "called out of the world" only in name and in nostalgia, no longer in reality. If their jobs are in the world's businesses, banks, and institutions, if their paychecks and rewards come thereby, if their universities are part of the common academic life and intercollegiate athletic life, if their houses are in the world's streets and their leaders in the world's government, not to mention their leisure time in the world's country clubs, they are no longer "in separation" at all; rather, they are as much a part of the world as is a Catholic businessman in a European Catholic country. The Baptists often forget this fact, although they largely rule Texas. Nevertheless, it is true. Such social, political, and economic power prevents their being in any meaningful sense a withdrawn community. The problem of culture and of its relation to their religion is an issue for their common religious life just as it is for their personal life. Once the members of a religious community are in the world, the religious community itself is in it, and thus its best move is to recognize and deal with that social fact.

I need hardly add that all of this now applies to both of the communities of the Mormon tradition, the RLDS in Missouri and the LDS in Utah. The membership of each is present in power in the business, governmental, agricultural, and military life of the country, as well as its academic life, and this presence is increasingly evident to the entire society. In fact, not unlike the Southern Baptists, the LDS Church in Utah and in surrounding states dominates the economic, political, and social life of that region. Despite, therefore, its early history of confrontation with and withdrawal from American society, the Mormon community now represents an active, influential, and effective portion of that society. In the past century it has become deeply intertwined with American cultural life, and it now faces all the issues that arise when a withdrawn community becomes associated with and consequently shaped by its wider social environment.

Actually, once their members join a cultural world and participate fully in its life, some of these "withdrawn" groups—and the Baptists are a good example—tend to yearn to take that world over, to dominate it, and to shape it into their own image. Having ruled their separated community in its isolation, now they seek to rule the world they have joined. Thus, like the medieval Catholic Church before them, they are in danger of losing their own soul in the process. Sects, beginning as rebels against dominant churches, themselves dream of becoming "church types," of becoming the spiritual rulers of the wider community from which they once withdrew. The Moonies are another example of this strange reversal.

Most of us, and thus most of our religious communities, are thoroughly in the world, in corporations, colleges, universities, hospitals, and government. The problem of the relation of our religious communities to culture is a problem for us. It is, moreover, an extremely complex problem, one that bears both a sociological-historical and a theological analysis if we are to think of it aright.

Santayana once remarked, "Those who are ignorant of history are condemned to repeat it." We might paraphrase this to read: those religious communities who do not seek to understand sociologically and historically their role in society and the dangers and possibilities of that role in the light of their theological and ethical traditions are condemned to repeat the worst errors of church history and so to endanger their religious task within the world. To be sure, sophistication at the intellectual level—in historical study, in the sociology of religion, in scriptural scholarship, in ethical and theological reflection—will not save the church. But without some real awareness of its role, its tradition, and its possibilities, the church can hardly direct itself intelligibly or creatively. Life for members of the very sophisticated, talented, and powerful LDS and RLDS churches, as an effective part of a complex society, is itself exceedingly complex. Only if that complexity is itself understood in part in its relation to its tradition and its requirements can the community be true to itself. As in anything in a technical and complex society, that takes education and professional expertise: in history, sociology of religion, scriptural studies, ethics, and theology, esoteric as all of these may at first glance seem to be. Let us therefore begin—and begin with the positive side, the close alliance or union of a religious community with its surrounding culture.

In what ways do religious communities and their culture *interpenetrate* when the members of a religious community are in the world? First of all, as Paul Tillich pointed out, a surrounding culture provides the *forms* for any religious community within it: forms of speech and of dress, of course; forms of social relations in and out of church; manners and customs; notions of good and bad. But on a deeper level, it provides ways of thinking and believing, even ways of worshiping; goals and standards; what is expected of us; many of the rules by which we judge one another and ourselves.[1] A religion expresses its culture, its world, religiously; American Catholics and the Southern Baptists express their churches in an *American* way, as any foreign visitor will note at once. Thus, all of our American religious groups think, believe, and judge in American ways—though they may not be at all aware of that fact. This is natural. Our wider society provides us with our "plausibility structure," as Peter Berger puts it—all that we take for granted. So, quite naturally, the way we function religiously (in our religious communities) reflects and is patterned on that whole set of assumptions, standards, and goals that we call our culture and that shapes us.[2]

This seems harmless enough, and in many cases it is. There are, however, two sorts of rather baffling and serious problems that arise out of this situation. First of all, this interweaving of a religious tradition with its cultural setting has bizarre results when that religious community embarks upon the missionary enterprise in cultures outside of the original or shaping culture. Partly consciously and partly unconsciously, Christian missions, both Catholic and Protestant, took with them Western technology, social structures and beliefs, moral standards and customs, even Western dress and manners wherever they sought also to take the gospel. To many of them, the adoption of Western clothes and daily habits appeared to be as significant morally and even spiritually as was conversion to the Christian faith. Only recently, as the antipathy of other cultures to the dominance of Western culture has reached conscious articulation, have mission groups become painfully conscious of this and, chagrined at being ambassadors of the "middle-Western way of life," sought to reinterpret their missionary calling. How, they have asked themselves, can we speak to others of our faith without urging on them every other aspect of our cultural life that we take for granted? As a powerful missionary faith, one that is now expressed in and through American ways and so reflects American civilization, Mormonism presently faces this same problem. Again, naivete can here, as it did for nineteenth-century missionaries, only lead to an uncomprehending American imperialism; at this time of day this is hardly innocent. Only deep sociological, historical, ethical, and theological study and reflection can preserve us from exporting more of ourselves than the Lord might wish!

The second problem is that religious communities reflect and copy the errors and the sins of their cultural milieu as well as its virtues. And in reflecting these baleful habits of the wider community, the religious community blesses them, gives them the sanctity of religion, and thus solidifies and perpetuates them. We can see this very plainly in other cultures. For example, Hinduism in India is a caste-dominated religion, and the religious consequently sanctifies caste; most of the churches in Germany of the 1930s were Nazi churches, supporting the imperial aggression and the anti-Semitic bent of Nazi Germany; and the present churches in South Africa, with some notable exceptions, practice apartheid and attempt to justify it. Our own churches were segregated in a segregated culture, and they remain predominantly materialistic in a material, consumer culture. Unless the church works at it, the sins of its world quickly contaminate the church; if it is in the world, a heedless church is ruled by the world it is in. If the churches fail to deal with these moral issues of public policy and public practice, they will sink because of them and will rightly be blamed for them.

The church, then, reflects in its life and its goals the social world around it. Even more, culture instigates, encourages, and "breeds" religion and the religious, though it probably has no intention of doing so. When a culture is growing, expanding, and clearly resolving its problems, as America has done and felt it has done in the last century and a half, the forms of its cultural life tend themselves to become sacred, to be revered, to rise beyond critique, to embody an aura of supreme value and even of holiness. Think of what "the American way of life" has come to mean and of how our developments in science, technology, and industrial organization, not to mention democracy and capitalism, have been and still are identified for all of us with "civilization," with almost the final end or goal of human history's progress! A successful culture produces a religious myth about itself; in turn, that myth joins with the religious communities of its society and becomes central to, if not the center of, *their* religious message. Thus have churches all through history, as well as traditional religions, been intensely nationalistic, representing the city-state, the empire, and the nation as central to what they are. They have also represented the class and the race to which their powerful members belong and are loyal. A strong culture takes over and directs the religious communities that live within it.

Quite frankly, I am not familiar enough with the preaching, teaching, and general ethos of the Mormon community to comment with any assurance on this point. How much the messages of the RLDS and the LDS and the goals and promises of their faith include or incarnate American goals and promises, how much the triumph of the Saints incorporates within itself the triumph of America—these things I simply do not know. Any sensitive Mormon will know about these matters. However, the way the churches function politically, through their representatives in Congress, in government, and in public life generally, leads an observer to guess that this may well be a problem—that, in other words, the sense of the identity of Mormon life with American cultural values is a good deal stronger than is a sense of a prophetic calling within that community to criticize these values and, insofar as it may be morally necessary, to separate itself from them. Such distance from its surrounding culture was the early tradition of the Saints; whether it is at present, only one of them might say.

But not every time is a time of growth for a society's life; not every culture's story ends up a success story. Cultures and society have "times of trouble," as Arnold Toynbee put it;[3] Rome did, medieval culture did, Europe's empires did; and many feel, if they do not yet know, that this now may be true of Western culture as a whole. At such times of trouble, problems seem to multiply faster than do resolutions. The creative sources of the culture's life now seem to become oppressive and destructive, as the feudal structure ultimately did. And as a consequence, the sense of certainty, of confidence, of "at homeness in the universe" vanishes. Right now the three bases of Western and American confidence—science, technology, and expanding industrialism—appear to be doing this, that is, creating our most serious dilemmas rather than resolving our most feared problems. One thinks of the development of destructive weapons, the dehumanization of much of life in a technological age, and the impending crisis of the environment caused by expanding industrialism to see how the very bases of our civilization have become or can become the causes of our new vulnerability and the harbingers of our mortality. In such times, anxiety mounts, uncertainty grows, and values seem weakened—and no wonder, for the cultural grounds for well-being and confidence, the foundations for hope in the future, are now shaken. In such times, religion grows. New religious cults, including Christianity, poured into the weakened Hellenistic Roman world, and religious fears and fanaticism spread through the crumbling society of the late Middle Ages. In our own time, conservative forms of traditional religion, both Protestant and Catholic, have grown in all parts of the country, and now new religious cults proliferate in our cities.

Most significant of all, such times of upheaval and anxiety produce pseudo-religions—secular forms of the religious, social ideologies that take on the forms and characteristics of religion. These are familiar to us in the twentieth century, though the Enlightenment and the nineteenth century would never have believed them possible in modern life. The prime examples are, of course, Nazism, fascism, and communism, both Stalinist and Maoist. In these cases, social theories that are embodied at the center of a community's life become almost religions, with all the traits of traditional established religions. Some of these team up with traditional religions in the ordinary sense of that word, as Japanese nationalism and militarism did with indigenous Japanese Shinto, as Iranian nationalism has done with the Shi'ite religion, and as American nationalism might at some future date do with Protestant fundamentalism.

The "religious" role of these ideologies has been instigated by the anxieties and the emptiness of culture in trouble, and such ideologies represent clearly the interweaving of national, possibly racist, and certainly cultural elements with religious impulses, beliefs, and fanaticism. In this sense, religion in its broadest sense has been the troublemaker as well as the creative healer in our twentieth-century experience.

One new element—an unexpected element—has appeared in these last remarks. This is the religious dimension of culture itself, a dimension that complicates exceedingly the relations of special religious communities to their wider cultural matrix. This is unexpected (though it should not have been) because since the Enlightenment, and certainly in America, it has been assumed that religion exists only in churches and that, as a consequence, culture is secular, run according to natural laws (for example, those of the free market) and governed by natural goals: the goals of life, liberty, and the pursuit of happiness. We have known, of course, that in traditional, premodern cultures this separation of religion and the wider culture was not the case. Religion and culture were there united; religious authority governed all of cultural life. In turn, each aspect of culture, each profession and vocation, the family, and all other important social institutions and relations had religious foundations. Thus, all of culture had a religious dimension, a "religious substance," as Tillich called it.[4] Since the

Enlightenment, reflective thought about society and religion has generally assumed that this age-old union of culture and religion was now quite over with and that modern cultures could and would become genuinely secular.

This is the point, I think, that twentieth-century experience has radically questioned. The religious substance characteristic of traditional cultures, such as those of Egypt, China, India, and Japan, has not vanished with the appearance of secular societies. Not only have orthodox forms of traditional religions and cults been on the rise but also, what is really interesting, what one can only call "the religious," the religious dimension of society itself, has appeared in a new form in the public sphere. This is the new role that ideologies have performed in modern social experience.

Interestingly, the concept and the word *ideology* appeared just after the French Revolution, when organized religion had at last been officially banished from its role as spiritually dominant. In this original usage, ideologies were systems of ideas about the social world that claimed to be science and that sought to direct society. This dual claim still remains, as in Marxism and in the social theories of democracy-capitalism. Nevertheless, when embodied socially, as the system of symbols that structure, guide, and direct a living social community, each of these tends to become something else. They take on the aura, the authority, the immense creativity, and the danger of a religion.

In Marxism, this transformation from a social science to an analog with religion is particularly clear. The set of symbols constituting the ideology now interprets all of experience; like classical religions, they give that experience moral and religious meaning by describing the development of good and evil in history, by thus explaining our sufferings, and by promising a radical consummation at the end. They tell us what is real, how we and all around us fit in, and where we are going and why. Thus they tell us what we should do, what is creative, and what is destructive, and therefore how the community must be governed, how its institutions should be formed and should function, and what its priorities of education are. Like religions, they provide the foundations for relevant social institutions, for common law, for personal habits, and for school curricula. Also—and most surprising—the distinction between orthodoxy and heresy begins to appear; unconditional assent is required of all who participate in the community; and theologians, important and learned interpreters of doctrines and of laws, become important to the ruling authorities. The dominant role of Marxist theoreticians and the importance of new sacramental rites, as at weddings, at vocational beginnings, and at death, characterize life in Moscow as they do Catholic existence in Rome.

While they have been more evident in Marxist countries and in fascist Germany, these characteristics appear in milder form among us in America. The American way of life, with its amalgam of democratic, capitalistic, and scientific/technological elements, has much this same role with us, and to many it has the same ultimate claim on our assent and obedience as does a religion, as the demands "America, love it or leave it" or "My country right or wrong" clearly show. Secular societies, like traditional religious societies, are held together by commitment to a common religious substance (as Augustine put it, a common or shared love): that is, by a sacred set of social and historical symbols (the American Story and the American Dream), by an elusive but significant set of rites and practices, by an unspoken "law" of belief and obedience that everyone tacitly knows and that all real believers must follow. The religious did not disappear when the churches were separated from the state; it is apt to reappear, not only in the form of the private associations of religion, but also, as before, at the very center of public life. The ultimate convictions that bind a community together provide the foundation, the structure, and the norms of that community's common life, and these convictions represent an ultimate, religious concern for its people.

This religious dimension of cultural life, its "civil religion," complicates gravely the relation of special religious communities to their culture. Its presence means that each religious community, in uniting itself to its culture, not only takes on the *secular* characteristics of that culture's life, such as automobiles and bathrooms, social customs and ideas, vocations, habits of business life, modes of speech, and fashions of entertainment, but it also unites with the society's *religious* substance, with a set of ultimate and volatile convictions, standards, and goals—and that union may well lead to trouble.

These unions may be infinitely destructive whenever the culture's religious dimension is ultranationalist, racist, and imperialist as in Shinto Japan and fascist Germany, or utopian and nationalistic imperialist as in Soviet Marxism, or segregated and nationalist as in South Africa. In each case, the religious communities of the society were faced and are faced with a brutal alternative: worship either the alien deity of the wider community or your own true god. You cannot, as the Barmen Declaration in prewar Germany declared, worship both. And we note, incidentally, that the protest against fascist, communist, or segregated tyrannies has come more from those religious communities than from others in the community, even from professors and academics.

These are, of course, extreme cases. But they dominate the landscape of our century, and no one who heeds the cultural atmosphere of our land can fail to see incipient signs of this tendency among us. Whenever anxiety about the community's welfare and its future, about the meaning and possibilities of individual life, and about the social structures that give life security and worth, whenever anxiety about these things becomes deep and sharp enough, then the community is ripe for this sort of reaction. And under these conditions, no peoples are completely immune to fanaticism.

Thus, the relation of a religious community to its culture, once it thoroughly joins the culture, is a complex and deep one. A religious community takes on the forms of its culture's life. Its religious content and fervor are instigated and fueled by both the success and the vulnerabilities of the culture's life, and often, to its satisfaction but frequently to its disquiet, it finds itself making union with or having to resist the culture's own inherent and constitutive religious substance. To most people in a religious community in a wider culture—for example, to most American Methodists, Baptists, Catholics, and, in all probability, Mormons as well—the union of their religious faith with the ultimate convictions and loyalties of American cultural life is as natural as are air, water, and sky themselves. Of course, Christianity and Americanism go together. Who could question that?

Yet history shows how questionable such an assumption can occasionally become; not infrequently such union with a culture's "gods" has represented a betrayal of fidelity to one's own. The identity of Christianity with the Roman Empire, with the assumptions and customs of medieval life, with the class structure and empires of modern Europe, and with the slave society of early America was immeasurably dubious and compromising to Christianity. More recently, the identity with Nazi Germany and segregated South Africa has been a disaster for church and society alike. The natural relation of a religious community to its culture may well be creative, but it can also be infinitely destructive, an example of idolatry and of blasphemy.

Our question is, therefore, what kind of guidance can there be for thinking out more responsibly rather than reacting merely viscerally to the question of the proper relation of a religious community to its cultural matrix? It would be wrong to imply that however risky union with a culture always is, it is against the biblical or the Christian perspective. We cannot say that separation from all cultures is the command of the Scriptures. This perspective, as I see it, says both yes and no to culture; it adopts both a priestly and a prophetic role toward culture.

The Old Testament is, I believe, clear in its affirmation of the value and legitimacy of culture. God established a society there, the people of Israel, and gave to it its forms and social structures: its forms of government, its laws, its daily customs, and its modes of relation. This is, moreover, on a biblical perspective very intelligible: God created men and women as cocreators with himself; as intelligent, purposive, and free; and thus as able to fashion culture and refashion their world into innumerable new forms. Culture is basically the creative result of the image of God in man and woman. It is also the basis for the worldly well-being of human life; we live in and from society, and our values are largely those springing from and preserved by a creative society. Thus is the social symbol of the Kingdom, the apex and goal of the biblical promises: a community governed by God's will and therefore creative of human worth. The values of the world's life—peace, order, justice, equality, and fairness—are also the values of God's kingdom. In the biblical perspective, a fulfilled world and a realized religious community, a realized church, ultimately come together. Each of us experiences this union in fragmentary form whenever we ponder public policy and weigh our own decisions as Christian citizens. We find that as loyal members of our religious communities, we must needs support the values of our democratic and humanitarian tradition.

With regard to the Mormon community, especially in Utah, this may mean a slight shift of perspective. To an outsider, it seems clear that that original community identified its own "natural" society and its values with the religious beliefs, rules, and customs of the growing community of Saints as they moved west. This identification, which is characteristic of "withdrawn" or "separated" communities, continued in Utah through many decades into the end of the nineteenth century. But then, with the granting of statehood to Utah and the resulting official union of that community with the wider culture of America, an important shift occurred. The community environment became American society as a whole. By now, the cultural environment for almost all Mormons is unquestionably America, their common ways "the American way of life," and their common social values the values of that way of life. Hence arise both the opportunity and the problem. Mormons are now characterized as never before with not only a new set of customs but also a new set of beliefs and standards, and even more of values. The religious substance of American culture has made union with that of the community of the Saints—and this is something new for both. It is absolutely vital that, as a consequence, the Saints be aware of this change and consider carefully what sort of rethinking it may require in their theological, ethical, and social judgments, if their convictions are to keep in touch with their own new reality.

These democratic and humanitarian values have their ultimate roots in biblical tradition, to be sure, as also in the Greek. In modern life, especially in the eighteenth century, they were borne more by the intellectual and the bourgeois classes, the secular and anticlerical revolutionary forces, than by the churches. Thus, in supporting these values, as I feel a Christian should, we in the churches are making union with the religious substance of our democratic tradition. We are "priests," conservers, defenders, and teachers of a national and cultural tradition allied to our religious tradition but by no means identical with it. When our society deviates from this natural or secular founding covenant, when it betrays justice, freedom, equality, or peace, then as faithful priests we must call it back to itself, and we must seek to lure it into finer embodiments of those things that it, and we, value and profess.

In the Scriptures, the priestly is balanced by the prophetic, and this is also true of the relation of the religious community to the wider culture. As our faith teaches, the world is fallen away from God as well as created and redeemed by God. Thus does it regularly betray its covenant. It shows indifference rather than responsibility for the ills of others; it manifests pride in making its own life and that of its group central to and dominant over the life of others; and it is suffused with concupiscence or greed for more than it can consume or even discard. These are the marks of sin, and in the end, sin results in suffering for those who are weak, and in destruction, even self-destruction, for those who oppress the weak. Today this is by no means pious rhetoric. Our very virtues and capacities, scientific intelligence, and technical know-how have given us immense power, and our industrial genius can cover and reshape the earth. Yet used in bad faith—heedlessly, selfishly, and obsessively—these creative powers can destroy us. This danger stems from sin and not ignorance. It is not lack of knowledge or lack of technology that threatens us; it is lack of wisdom, self-understanding, and self-control, the absence of the humility, serenity, and grace that come out of deep religious faith.

Clearly, as full members of the American community, the Mormon community has gained—as have other communities—from the wealth and power given to all of us. Correspondingly, however, we all share in the responsibility that they be used wisely and with self-control, not with heedless and selfish national or class self-interest. This responsibility requires, as it always has done, a sense of prophetic criticism as well as of priestly support, criticism of both the culture that supports and nourishes us and our "church" that is so supported and nourished. Again, it is incumbent on the LDS and RLDS churches to ponder carefully how to shoulder and effectively embody this new responsibility.

The ills of culture, like its ultimate faiths, represent a religious dimension and call for a prophetic word of judgment, of reconciliation, and of renewal. The church must here distance itself from its cultural home in order to redeem that home and to redeem itself as inhabiting that home. It must criticize its culture in order to bring it back to itself, to bring to it, as the Lutherans say, both the law that judges and the gospel that heals.

Thus we return to our starting point. The religious community, if true to itself, is not identical with its cultural environment, however deeply entwined with America it may feel and be. It arises from beyond history, even from beyond our American history, in response to the revelation of God. And it represents in its many relations with culture a point of transcendence, a point where the judgment and the love of God transcend the successes and the failures of the wider society, as they transcend all our personal efforts and failings. It represents this transcendent point to the world, for without that point, there is no victory over the sin and the death that conquer us all.

Finally, as the highest level of spiritual discernment, the religious community knows that this transcendent judgment stands over the church itself as well as over the church's world. For as at Calvary, the church, like the world, betrays its Lord, and it needs continual judgment, forgiveness, and renewed grace if it is to do its task in the world. A church that knows not its own waywardness can, as has been shown so often in church history, unite with the world's power to dominate the world rather than to serve it. Only if it knows itself forgiven can the church be a servant to the world, and as our Lord himself showed, only a servant can help to redeem. Thus does the church, like its Lord, move from priest to prophet to servant, and thus can it be the hope of the world.

* * *

If there be any "word" that these remarks contains for the two communities, the LDS and the RLDS, it is that they both—perhaps in slightly varying ways—now embody a new relation to their cultural matrix, a much closer and more essential relation than heretofore in their history. They are now fully *of* and not just *in* the American world. This relationship raises all sorts of new problems as well as manifesting opportunities for their common life.

For example, they are deeply involved in both scientific and secular academic disciplines. How are these disciplines, with their rules, requirements, and standards, related to the beliefs and traditions of the Mormons? These questions represent the beginning, and only the beginning, of inescapable theological problems for the community. This raises both religious and ethical questions— questions of the religious stance of this community amidst the "gods" of American life, and questions of the obedient and faithful action of the religious community with regard to public policies. These are questions of vast import to our social world and to our own souls: questions of peace and war, selfishness and generosity, intolerance of others and charity and caring for them. There is no avoiding these issues while we live between the oceans. Not to avoid them is to have to deal with them. If we are to serve God, we must face them responsibly, intelligibly, and with caring, else we do not serve God at all.

Such responsible response requires wisdom and understanding as well as virtue. Correspondingly, it necessitates knowledge of our tradition, coherent consciousness of our common beliefs, and clear articulation of our common standards—the study of history, theology, and theological ethics. Otherwise, reacting with our viscera instead of our minds, we are condemned to repeat all the errors that every community is prone to. Somewhere within the vast energy, wealth, and intellectual power of the LDS and RLDS communities must be lodged, in special groups whose responsibility is for these very matters, professional and scholarly study and discussion of historical, theological, and ethical issues. The community must take responsibility for the graduate and professional education of its interested members in these important advanced subject matters. No such study replaces "grace," let us be sure. But knowledge and understanding do help us to do our best to be true to our own traditions and to the needs of our common world.

Notes

1. See Paul Tillich, *Systematic Theology* (Chicago: University of Chicago Press, 1951), and *Dynamics of Faith* (New York: Harper and Row, 1957).

2. See Peter Berger, *The Social Construction of Reality: A Treatise in the Sociology of Knowledge* (New York: Irvington, 1980).

3. See Arnold Toynbee, *A Study of History: Abridgement of Volumes I–VI*, ed. D. C. Somervell, reprint ed. (New York: Oxford University Press, 1987).

4. See Paul Tillich, *The Courage to Be*, 2nd ed. (New Haven, Conn.: Yale University Press, 2000).

CHAPTER 18

Looking West: Mormonism and the Pacific World

Laurie F. Maffly-Kipp

On 24 July 1851, Louisa Barnes Pratt spent the day fulfilling her customary duties. As the wife of Addison Pratt, one of the first Mormon missionaries in the Society Islands (of which Tahiti is a part), she oversaw the teaching of the natives and children alongside the other missionary wives. Her older daughters helped out with these responsibilities; they were assigned students of their own to school in the ways of civilization. Louisa's obligations were even more demanding on the many occasions when her husband was called away to responsibilities on another island, as he had been nearly three weeks earlier. And he was still gone. On that particular day, she spent the entire afternoon in the meetinghouse that doubled as a school. Only when she returned home late in the day did she notice the date, which prompted her to write in her journal: "It never once occurred to our minds that the day was passing away unheeded; we had intended in some way to celebrate it, but the ship left on the 4th and the most of the white men being gone away on her there were not enough of us to make it any object to get up a feast or party."[1]

We can all sympathize with Louisa's plight. How many times have we, caught up in the round of daily tasks, forgotten an important birthday or anniversary that we had fully intended to commemorate? But there was more involved for Louisa than the human propensity to let something slip. Circumstances rendered celebration of this most important of days very difficult. She had students to attend to. All the white men of the settlement were away, which added to her workload and may have made a party with both native women and men imprudent. Most telling, though, was her statement that there were not enough people who would consider the occasion worth marking. Unlike Utah, where Louisa may well have witnessed the elaborate 1849 procession led by dozens of bishops, women in white, and marching bands, Pioneer Day held little meaning for the growing number of native converts in the South Seas.[2] Although there is no doubt that even in Utah the holiday grew only gradually to become the extravaganza that it is today, Louisa's other comments about native practices indicate that the locals would have relished a good party if a reasonable motive had been offered. But instead, living in a place with novel rhythms and patterns of living, she had temporarily forgotten.

Now let us move forward to 1896. Andrew Jenson, the historian who oversaw the compilation of nineteenth-century missionary manuscript histories, visited many of the sites about which he wrote to assess the current status of the LDS Church in these far-flung locations. When he reached Tahiti, he encountered an elderly resident and early Mormon convert who remembered the formative years of missionary work there nearly a half century earlier. The resident commented to Jenson that when Benjamin Grouard, an early missionary, arrived there in 1847, "he changed the Sabbath to correct time." His comments indicated the LDS elders set his people on a new historical course, radically changing their sense of the world.[3]

Time, space, memory, and history. All of these concepts seem encapsulated by these two anecdotes, one a tale of *displacement* through travel, the other of *replacement* through conversion. We cannot be entirely sure what the elderly Tahitian intended by the evocative phrase "he changed the Sabbath to correct time," but surely it suggests that his awareness of time and space had been radically altered through his embrace of Mormonism. Similarly, the fact that Louisa Pratt could forget one of the founding events in the experience of the young LDS Church implies that her own awareness of time had shifted in this new place; she was now learning what it meant, experientially, to be Mormon in a new location.

This, of course, is what religion does. It reorients the believer, it reorders one's sense of time and place and redraws the sacred map of one's life and one's surroundings.[4] The normative story of early Mormonism itself follows this pattern: it has often been portrayed as a religious movement inextricably bound to a particular time and space, anchored there by a sacred story and a community of memory. It was, we have often been told, "quintessentially American," a westward migrating band of settlers who proclaimed the ultimate sanctity of the American landscape, a people who achieved a particular fusion of sacred and profane in the material construction of an earthly Zion. Some came from other places, of course—from England, from Scandinavia, from other parts of Europe. But all were pulled into a new sense of religious geography and history defined by a westward trek. Many scholars, following Brigham Young, have linked the spatial movement across the American continent to the process of "making Saints," so that today, through collective and ritualized memorialization, this movement has become integral to religious identity.[5]

Yet there are other voices, faint but insistent, from the nineteenth-century missionary texts that speak of a distinctive ordering process. We know little about them: only scattered words and anecdotes noted by others, or the very occasional letter written by a convert literate in English. They tell a somewhat different story, one no less Mormon but with a particular sense of what it meant to "become a people." Theirs is not the traditional story of migration and settlement in Zion. They were not necessarily led to the Church by the promise of a gathering, or by the sanctity of the temple rituals (since most knew they would not enter a temple in this life), or even by the many elements of a Mormon lifestyle that came to be so associated with the Church in the Great Basin. They did not become Saints, in the majority sense. Yet they came into the fold, sometimes in surprisingly large numbers, and thereafter the "Sabbath was changed to correct time." In 1847, less than four years after the initiation of missions to the Pacific Islands, the Church could claim two thousand members in the Society Islands, roughly twice the number of Scottish Saints at the same moment.[6]

This lecture reconsiders, in broad brush strokes, those early Pacific Saints who converted in the first waves of missionary activity prior to about 1890. I argue that their understanding of Mormon identity was quite distinct from the Saint-making that was occurring simultaneously on the American continent. Because of the many constraints of isolation and what one historian has aptly called the "tyranny of distance,"[7] as well as the unsettled state of the Church back home, many of the first converts to Mormonism encountered a religious system that was, in certain respects, relatively unformed and adaptable. But more than this, they brought to their embrace of the faith particular ways of seeing the world based on indigenous customs, beliefs, and political needs in the face of an increasingly bewildering colonial situation. Theirs was a faith shaped not only by a context of Protestant persecution and intolerance, although this was surely part of it, but also by the complexities of imperialism and missionary competition in the emerging global arena of the Pacific world. To understand the emergence of Pacific Mormonism necessitates, therefore, consideration not only of the development of relations between LDS missionaries and indigenous peoples but also attention to the diverse and competitive religious world in which their new identity was forged.

Missionary Migration to the Pacific Basin

Long before colonial governments moved in to occupy the islands of Polynesia, European and American missionaries had discovered the inherent possibilities of proselytism there. Protestant missionaries began to arrive in the islands in 1797, when the London Missionary Society (LMS), a Calvinist organization, sent thirty emissaries to Tahiti, led by four ordained ministers. Almost immediately, they reported astounding success in converting the local populations: by 1815, King Pomare II had reconquered Tahiti and proclaimed Christianity the national religion. In 1820, an American association, the American Board of

Commissioners for Foreign Missions (ABCFM), arrived in the Sandwich Islands. In short order, they baptized several important members of the royal family. Similarly, in the ensuing decades, the Methodists moved into Tonga and Fiji, and several French Roman Catholic orders established stations in Tahiti and the Marquesas, although their numbers never rivaled those of the Protestants. By the 1840s, when the first Mormon elders arrived in the Society Islands, much of the eastern Pacific, peopled primarily by Polynesians, had a considerable degree of exposure to, if not full acceptance of, Protestant religion.[8]

Mormon missionaries arrived relatively late in this era of religious migration, and they entered immediately into arenas of conflict. Between 1843, when the first three elders departed for the Society Islands, and the 1890s, when the Church experienced tremendous success among the Maori of New Zealand, LDS missionaries had visited every major Polynesian island group. These fields were part of a larger sphere of Pacific enterprise for the nineteenth-century Church that included California, the west coast of South America, Samoa, Tonga, and Australia. Many of these achievements are well known to Mormon scholars and have been thoroughly recounted in the work of R. Lanier Britsch. By 1852, when local political events abruptly ended the missionary venture, the Church had baptized several thousand natives scattered over dozens of islands. In Hawaii by 1889, the Honolulu branch of the Church probably was larger than any other outside of Utah, with 891 members. By 1913, nearly a quarter of the native Hawaiian population claimed membership in the LDS Church. And in New Zealand, in the closing two decades of the last century, nearly 10 percent of the Maori population professed the faith.[9]

But throughout these decades, LDS missionaries never failed to lament the persecution and competition provoked by the presence of other Christians, who were equally intent on converting the local populations. Early in his sojourn in the Sandwich Islands, future apostle George Q. Cannon recorded his dismay at the intensity of religious conflict. Speaking of the native peoples, he surmised that

> Had there been no priestcraft among them, misleading them and poisoning their minds against the truth, and tempting them with worldly advantages and popularity, the entire nation, I am convinced, could have been readily brought to receive and believe in the principles of the gospel. But everything was done to have them shun us, to inspire them with suspicion, to make us unpopular. These influences, with those vicious and destructive practices which are fast hurrying the nation to extinction, were against us. But for all this, we had wonderful success among them.[10]

Cannon concluded that "the Sandwich Islander is being destroyed and blotted from the face of the earth, by too much of what is called in Babylon, civilization."[11] Early missionaries filled their journals and diaries with discussions of mutual antagonisms and missed opportunities, as Saints saw their paths to progress blocked at every turn by the false teachings of their rivals.

Paradoxically, Cannon may have been exactly wrong in this regard. I would suggest that it was in large measure the attention brought to LDS missionaries through the constant ridicule of religious rivals that attracted the initial interest of indigenous peoples. Mormons, a persecuted minority on the American continent, felt the myriad effects of this status and its social consequences in the mission field. Yet even though the missionaries regarded this situation negatively, their marginality had unintended and even positive consequences for their ability to communicate with native peoples.

Further, the element of choice afforded to potential converts by the diversity of religious groups in many instances highlighted the distinctive ways of the Mormons. From the native perspective, then, the arrival of LDS missionaries opened up the possibility of a spiritual marketplace in which Protestants were forced to vie more persuasively for their attention and in which their newfound power of choice gave them additional political leverage in the face of Euro-American political domination. Like their brothers and sisters in Utah, then, Mormons in the Pacific felt the effects of religious and political persecution. But the differing political and cultural context in which this encounter took place lent a distinctive quality to the development of the faith in the South Seas.

Going Native

From the start, educational, social, and political differences distinguished Mormon missionaries from their Christian competitors. Mormons prior to 1890 were American but not American, of the same culture, in many respects, but a people set apart. They were a self-designated "peculiar people." This cultural ambiguity, which rendered them the objects of European and American scorn, also distinguished them in the eyes of local populations. Although some natives clearly saw Mormons as just another set of whites intent on "reforming" them,[12] more often islanders differentiated them from their Protestant counterparts in ways that proved advantageous from a religious perspective.

At the most basic level, Mormon male missionaries, often young, poor, and sometimes uneducated, frequently were forced to live among the natives in ways that Protestant ministers did not. By the time Mormons arrived on the Pacific scene, missionaries of the LMS and other evangelical groups had moved beyond their more charismatic, first-generation roots and were quickly establishing themselves economically and educationally within island societies. The second-generation clergy often exacted a tax from local peoples to pay for their missionary expenses. Generally, these clergy were well-educated men who saw their sacred calling as something that set them apart from the objects of their labor. For both social and ideological reasons, they favored a separation of the cultures.

Socially, British missionaries in particular tended to style themselves as "English gentlemen" after their years of theological schooling. They lived apart, engaged their missionary pupils as servants, and maintained a lifestyle marked by as much British-derived refinement as they could manage. And ideologically, they favored limiting their encounters with natives to discrete moments of preaching and teaching because it reinforced what clergy saw as the appropriate line of demarcation between the sacred and the mundane elements of life. At least one missionary had a policy of never letting natives enter his house because of the "corrosive influence" they might have on his children.[13]

Contrast this position to the first weeks of George Q. Cannon's stay in Hawaii. Along with a group of young, relatively inexperienced missionaries, Cannon arrived on Maui with barely enough money to afford a roof over his head. Not being able to pay for a rooming house, he and his companion rented a "native house," the term for the most primitive of dwellings that had neither a floor nor a solid roof. It was, in other words, a thatched hut, much like that occupied by most islanders. The native owner, taking pity upon the group because they were white, managed to secure a table and three chairs, at which they ate local fare cooked by their landlord.[14] If poverty enforced a particular proximity to native peoples, so too did the challenge of language acquisition. Addison Pratt lived among the natives in the Society Islands as a teacher, but because he was simultaneously trying to learn the local language, he was forced into a role reversal, attending school himself and going to services conducted by natives.[15]

The material circumstances of the LDS missionaries typically brought them into closer proximity to indigenous peoples than the cautious distance cultivated by Protestant clergy. But this familiarity and less-studied approach to proselytization was not attributable to a greater cultural enlightenment on the part of the Saints. Like other Euro-Americans, white Mormons experienced an awkward divide between themselves and their native charges. As several historians have noted, the call to preach to the Lamanites encoded a double message: On the one hand, missionaries carried an announcement of salvation and future hope; on the other, they reminded converts that they were degraded, uncivilized creatures who had fallen from the virtues of their ancestors.[16] Throughout the history of outreach in the Pacific, LDS missionaries voiced tremendous unease with indigenous practices and vacillated between emphasizing the importance of assimilating natives into Western civilization and guardedly incorporating local practices into the Church.[17] George Q. Cannon reiterated that he admired the islanders yet consistently asserted the need for an unclouded line of influence from the missionary to the missionized: "the Lord sends His Elders out to teach and not to be taught," he insisted. "The man who goes out expecting the people to whom he is sent, to teach, enlighten and benefit him commits a great blunder. He does not understand the nature of his priesthood and calling."[18]

But if American Saints criticized the natives, their theology more often suggested another target for condemnation. Like Cannon, who asserted that the Sandwich Islanders would have easily accepted the gospel had they not been seduced by the vicious ways of the Gentiles, Saints frequently blamed indigenous degradation on the influence of Europeans and Americans. Although Mormons simultaneously appreciated that Protestants had "laid the groundwork" for the reception of the restored gospel in the islands, they blamed all defects on prolonged exposure to corrupt whites. Unlike Protestant missionaries, who could censure only the natives for their own "uncivilized" behavior, the Mormon critique of Euro-American civilization left a way out—a means by which they could condemn practices but still see the local peoples as relatively blameless. These assumptions made their close contact with the natives less problematic, in certain respects.

We can only wonder, however, how local peoples perceived the distinctions that LDS missionaries made between the Euro-American theological tradition, which was to be rejected as false, and many other trappings of American culture—clothing, sexual mores, manners, and a particular approach to education—which were to be embraced. It fostered a spiritual and cultural chemistry at odds with the Protestant approach to Christian culture that some of them already had accepted. If the Protestants asked for a strict division between the sacred and the profane, they also wanted to reform many of the less spiritual elements of native life. The Mormons, on the other hand, sought a particular amalgam of the divine and the mundane but, at the same time, urged the natives to distill the admixture of Euro-American ways, keeping some desirable elements and shedding others. Polynesian peoples, often accused by whites of living in "undisciplined" ways that defied logic, must surely have puzzled over the competing patterns of right living communicated by their missionary visitors.[19]

Songs, Signs, and Wonders

Despite LDS intentions, then, material resources dictated a higher degree of intimacy than that experienced in the Protestant missionary setting. In like manner, Mormon strategies of spreading the gospel also unintentionally induced a style of intercultural communication more familiar to indigenous peoples. Missionary work among the Protestants and Catholics most often consisted of preaching (proclaiming and interpreting the Bible), teaching language skills (to facilitate individual comprehension of the Scriptures), and catechesis (a study of lessons and precepts derived from biblical truths). Theirs was, by any measure, a text-based religious movement, albeit one that relied on the most progressive British and American educational techniques.[20] By the mid-nineteenth century, Protestants had translated the gospel widely and circulated copies of the Bible in the vernacular throughout their fields of labor. To be sure, for many natives the association of Protestant missionaries with European and American culture was a strong asset, particularly among those peoples who looked upon the acquisition of new technologies (literacy being chief among them) proffered by their missionary neighbors as a valuable resource.[21]

Mormons, cognizant of the potent skills they could offer alongside the gospel message, were anxious to communicate through print, a concern attested to by early publishing efforts in Great Britain, Australia, and Hawaii. Missionaries reported handing out tracts wherever they went, and many spent the better part of their days disseminating the few copies of the Book of Mormon or the works of Orson Pratt and his brother, Parley P. Pratt, that were available to them. As David Whittaker has noted, the real problem was not simply the accessibility of literature but the fact that it was obtainable only in English and thus was quite useless in the native context. In Tahiti the few books furnished to the missionaries were given out to Americans and British on passing ships. Even in the first years of involvement in Australia, although language was not an issue, the mission was so poorly supplied that the two local copies of the Book of Mormon were read aloud in meetings at the Sydney Branch.[22]

Although the American Saints lamented this state of affairs, the dearth of texts encouraged a different quality of relationship with their native charges. Forced immediately out of their books, missionaries paraphrased, told stories, testified, prayed, and sang—in short, used precisely the kind of communicative techniques familiar to members of an oral culture. Louisa Pratt lamented the lack of privacy that the work entailed but marveled at the apparent enthusiasm of the Tahitians for this approach: "the house for the first two months was nearly always thronged at night with the people talking reading and singing." Her husband, Addison, noted: "All the Pacific Islanders have a great desire for learning psalms and hymn tunes . . . [;] when they once learn a tune, they never tire of singing it. They will collect at a neighbor's house at dark and sing a new tune over and over till midnight."[23] The Pratts also used local feasts as a way to mark and celebrate the reorganization of time, something apparently motivated by native desires. Louisa reflected that "Every little turn in their affairs must be celebrated by a feast, even to changing the Sabbath."[24]

Other aspects of Mormon spiritual practice also resonated with traditional native ways. Most of the Protestant evangelists in the region, it must be remembered, were Calvinist and therefore harbored a deep suspicion of religious enthusiasms, eschewing the manifestation of spiritual gifts in the present age as heretical. Latter-day Saints, in contrast, cultivated the gifts of the Spirit, and their necessary lack of emphasis on written materials only highlighted this distinguishing characteristic. Pacific Mission president Parley P. Pratt pointed out in an 1854 circular that "this Christianity of the New Testament is a system of visions, angels, revelations, prophesyings, gifts, healing, etc. Such a system you can never oppose—it speaks and acts for itself; its votaries know what they experience, see, hear and feel."[25]

Throughout early missionary accounts, perhaps the most often reported scene was that of a healing by a missionary. James Brown, serving in Tahiti between 1850 and 1852, recounted extensive experiences of anointing and healing the sick and preaching "on the signs, gifts of healings, etc."[26] Healing was also an important means by which missionary wives could interact with native women. Having brought along her consecrated oil, Louisa Pratt was in constant demand: "The females had great faith in the oil," she observed. They repaid her for her ministrations with food and other gifts, cementing the bonds of reciprocity.[27]

Mormon missionaries, because of their commitment to continuous revelation, also put more stock in prophecy and visions than their Protestant counterparts; this feature of the LDS faith also had structural parallels in traditional native beliefs and practices. Peter Turner, a Methodist missionary in Tonga, expressed frustration that the natives wanted more "mystical" and "visionary" accounts of religious experience than he felt comfortable providing. His charges said that they had visions of heaven and Christ, and they wanted an opportunity to speak with him about such spiritual manifestations. Turner, however, could only instruct them to be suspicious of these experiences.[28]

Mormons, in contrast, not only brought a faith that encompassed and legitimated the expression of spiritual power by the individual but also brought information about a particular prophet. Louisa Pratt hung pictures of Joseph and Hyrum Smith on the wall in her bedroom and was startled that "all the people on the Island came to look at [them]." One evening, she described how a visiting man left the gathered group to look at the picture: "he kneeled before it in order that the painting might come in range with his eyes, . . . For a quarter of an hour he looked steadfastly upon it, I believe without turning his eyes." Louisa did not assume that the man was engaged in worship, concluding rather that "he wished undoubtedly to imprint the lineaments of the features upon his mind."[29]

While we cannot always presume to understand how native peoples interpreted particular religious behaviors and incorporated them into their shifting understandings of the world, by all accounts Mormon spiritual practices helped bring islanders into the community by meshing well with previously existent customs. Cannon remarked that the local people already believed in the laying on of hands for the sick. "It was not contrary to their traditions for them to believe in this ordinance, for their old native priests before the missionaries came, had considerable power which they exercised, and in which the people had confidence."[30]

Yet the easier "fit" between Mormon religious practices and indigenous customs also raised the specter of the potential confusion, or even the purposeful mixing, of the two modes of religion. If Mormonism offered a way to build

upon certain aspects of the native past, it also had powers that rivaled or competed with traditional spirits in ways that the missionaries found more disconcerting. In Tahiti, Brown baptized a couple, then healed their infant of an illness.
A short time later, he watched as an older couple entered the room, walked over
and kissed the baby, "then went through some ancient heathen ceremony that I
could not understand." When the baby died within the hour, Brown asked the
parents to explain what had happened. They told him that the couple "had
power with evil spirits, and had afflicted [the baby] in the first place." Brown's
priesthood had apparently broken their power, and "they could not reunite it
with the babe until they could come and touch it; and when they had done that,
the parents and all concerned lost faith, and could not resist the influence that
came with the old pair of witches."[31] While Brown was uncomfortable with this
admixture of religious powers, it is clear that the natives were not; pragmatic in
their beliefs, they chose to accept the work of whichever healer seemed most
powerful.

Brown's incident also underscores the point that Mormon missionaries, often
traveling alone without much of an institutional life to show the local peoples,
also looked more traditionally powerful than did other Christians. The distance
of Mormon missionaries from the bureaucratic apparatus of the church, while
clearly a source of sorrow for them, ironically often elevated them in the eyes of
the islanders. Protestant missionaries, because of their greater structural organization and ties to local Euro-American officials, were more likely to be perceived as colonial government agents.[32] Mormons, by comparison, looked more
like the traditional spiritual entrepreneurs or healers with whom the natives
were familiar, and thus their techniques may have been more easily accepted.

The potential correspondence between indigenous and Mormon healing and
prophetic traditions also provided a point of leverage for natives against Protestant missionaries; it is clear that natives rapidly gained sophistication in playing
the politics of the missionaries to their advantage. Brown recorded another incident in which a young woman who had been healed of an illness became the
focal point of conflict between rival religious groups over who would take credit
for her recovery. Her family disagreed among themselves about who had been
responsible, finally telling the Protestant delegation that it had been their doing.
But Brown later reported with some satisfaction on his final visit with her: "she
ran out to meet me, and told me that she had not been sick one day since she
had been baptized."[33] One can only imagine the family meeting during which
the natives debated whose side they should take.

In sum, then, Mormon religious practices—some improvised, others quite
deliberately charismatic and experiential—also distinguished them from their
Christian missionary colleagues, providing a mode of experience that was filled
with the spirit. Clearly, it offered natives a religious option quite distinct from
that proffered by evangelicals, one that was, in significant respects, less demand-

ing that they totally renounce their previous way of life. But the very resonance with their traditional beliefs that made Mormon ways attractive also raised the possibility of inventive mixing with older traditions. One could be fairly certain that a native Congregationalist would not confuse catechism lessons with ancient Hawaiian rituals, but Mormon healings, anointings, and claims of prophetic experiences had such close cultural analogs with older religions that the two could be—and were—sometimes creatively fused instead of the latter being superseded by the gospel. Once again, both the promise and peril of Mormon missionary intimacy were evident.

A Storied People

Now to turn to the stories, for stories lay at the heart of the Mormon message. Several scholars have pointed out recently that the Book of Mormon provided a story for indigenous peoples of the New World, that it gave them ways to place themselves religiously in a sacred narrative, and that this acquisition of a story was a chief attraction of the church for Polynesian peoples. This is undoubtedly true. LDS missionaries approached potential converts by holding up the Book of Mormon (if they had a copy to spare) and declaring that they had brought with them a history of their own people, a message of hope and ultimate salvation. In New Zealand, missionaries claimed to see remnants of the divinely revealed religion in the practices of the Maori. As backhanded a compliment as this message might be, it does seem clear, as Grant Underwood has pointed out, that the Maori, along with other Polynesians, found in the Book of Mormon a "culturally compatible resource for defining their identity."[34]

But the concept of defining an identity in the first place is something that bears further analysis in light of the colonial context. Scholars know very little about the collective self-understanding of Polynesian peoples in the era before contact with Europeans and Americans. After the arrival of whites beginning in the late eighteenth century, native peoples almost immediately began adapting and integrating new beliefs and practices into their ways of life. Most importantly for our purposes here is that unlike in our own society, where our notion of peoplehood is based on a sense of common heritage rooted in genetic attributes, customs, and language, the peoples of Oceania may have had little if any conception of ethnicity or peoplehood, at least in the modern sense, prior to the arrival of missionaries and entrepreneurs.[35] What this meant, scholars have suggested, is that natives had little attachment to the idea that traditional practices and beliefs ought to be preserved as part of a cultural legacy; in other words, the idea that who one was fundamentally was not necessarily related intimately to observing the ways of one's genetic forebears to of having a story to tell about the endurance of familial characteristics at all. The notion of having a past in common with others of like genetic makeup was not necessarily an aspect of this Pacific self-understanding.[36]

This observation, I think, makes the acquisition of a religious identity through the Book of Mormon an even more consequential act, one intimately connected to the colonial context. What was crucial was not just the type of identity it provided but also the process through which genetically based identity became a salient mode of self-understanding. Polynesians did not necessarily need to name themselves as a people before the arrival of Europeans, and with the colonial invasion, a negative identity (*who we are not*) became just as important as a positive one (*who we are*). Thus, it was not important solely that they were part of the House of Israel but also that they were not Gentiles, those increasingly oppressive officials who had made necessary their adaptation to a new self-awareness in the first place. In 1851, Louisa Pratt reported speaking at a women's meeting about the origins of the Book of Mormon. Significantly, one of the natives asked "if the ancient Nephites were Europeans. I told them they were the ancient fathers of the Tahitians. At this they appeared greatly interested, and wished to learn more about the book."[37]

I am admittedly speculating on this point, but I suspect that what was communicated most immediately to native peoples was the identity structure framed by the Book of Mormon accounts, not the details of the players involved. Although the narrative itself is certainly unique, what was also distinctive in the non-Euro-American context was the assembly of religious geography and the placement of particular peoples joined by family groupings within a sacred mapping of the world. It should also be noted that native peoples began to make these connections even in the face of missionary ambivalence about the placement of Pacific Islanders in the sacred story. Recent scholarship has argued persuasively that the first several generations of Mormons were ambivalent, if not categorically conflicted, about the ultimate importance of racial and ethnic distinctions in the plan of salvation. Were these differences eternal ones, ordained in the premortal existence? And what role would they play in the unfolding of history? The Polynesian peoples, in particular, were tenuously located in early Mormon descriptions (Louisa Pratt was well ahead of both her time and Church authorities); only later generations would agree definitively that Pacific Islanders were, in keeping with the Book of Mormon portrayal, the descendants of Hagoth and his fellow migrants from the Old World, and thus members of the House of Israel in their own right.[38]

Despite the ambiguity of these mental maps, the LDS commitment to the literal unfolding of the destiny of the House of Israel meant that early Mormons had a remarkably intricate awareness of human diversity and its religious import. They had a deeply racialized—one might even say tribalized—view of sacred history, inasmuch as their commitment to the Old Testament narrative and its New World counterpart also brought them back to a tale of race and place. Whether those human differences would be important in the hereafter or exactly where particular peoples, including the Pacific Islanders, fit into the equation was in some respects less important than the overall predisposition to locate and understand new people and new experiences in light of a sacred story embedded in a sacred landscape.[39] This feature of Mormon religious identity proved particularly compelling to natives in an emerging colonial context.

Aside from reading themselves directly into the story, natives in a colonized situation could also interpret the story of more recent Mormon persecution on another level that we should not overlook. Even if islanders had yet to make the connection between their own community and the journey of Hagoth to the New World, some were still captivated, and their hearts turned, by the ongoing persecution of American Mormons in their own homeland and throughout the Pacific and by the critique of Euro-American culture that lay at the heart of Mormon claims to legitimacy. When Parley P. Pratt described the Mormons in his first Pacific Mission pamphlet as a people "disfranchised, robbed, plundered, dispersed, slandered in every possible way, and driven to the mountains and deserts of the American interior," one might have thought this a strange way to attract followers.[40]

But the description held potential resonance for almost every indigenous group in the nineteenth-century Pacific, and for some it still does. As late as the 1960s, Ian Barber concluded that many urban Maori still viewed their church as non-European. In other words, they identify strongly with the LDS Church as symbolic of an ongoing oppositional stance toward a colonizing power. Like the African American adaptation of the Old Testament theme of chosenness, the ongoing history of the Mormon people exhibited an internal logic and message of hope that stood on its own.[41]

It takes nothing away from the spiritual power of the Mormon message to suggest that native converts also saw in their new fellowship a solution to some of the political complications forced upon them by European and American political occupation. God may still work in history through natural, as well as more dramatically supernatural, means. Moreover, conversion entails a turning of the soul, a change of heart, and one cannot change hearts without first achieving a degree of intimacy. This is exactly what LDS missionaries, sometimes intentionally and often in spite of themselves, did so well in the Pacific. They lived among the native peoples, they used familiar techniques of communication and encouraged immediate religious experience and expression, they offered a means of molding identity, and they told a story of persecution and triumph. Many islanders could see that the Mormons were a "peculiar people" because they were ridiculed and rejected before native eyes, cast out by the very people who were systematically overturning native ways of life. While we still have more silences than voices to tell us exactly how Pacific Islanders understood what they saw, heard, and felt, the moments of human intimacy are apparent.

Conclusions

The Pacific Basin was an international crossroads in the nineteenth century. Today, I have discussed two particular types of encounters that took place there. First, it was a religious meeting point for Protestants, Catholics, Mormons, and indigenous peoples throughout the region. But it was also a cultural meeting point for islanders and the Europeans and Americans who came seeking profit, power, and the truth of the gospel. I have tried to sketch out some of the points of contact and conflict that comprised the early mission fields and to describe the ways in which American Mormons presented distinctive practical and theological alternatives to native peoples by placing themselves over against European and American colonial powers.

However, these were alternatives that Pacific peoples had to make sense of, to integrate into a larger framework in which the world as they once knew it was falling away. Just as American missionaries, coming to the South Seas, packed away in their bags their own cultural luggage and communal memories, experiencing a sense of displacement, so too did natives bring to the encounter a context of engagement with whites that colored their views and shaped their decisions, forcing them into a replacement within their own land. While it must always be remembered that, in most situations, many more natives remained indifferent or hostile to Mormonism than converted to it, the reasons for its appeal lay in both its religious and its political distinctiveness.

Moreover, as far away from Utah as the South Seas is, some of this story must certainly resonate with the normative Mormon westering saga. It is not a tale of spatial movement, to be sure, but it is a narrative of changed spaces and times. Like the Utah pioneers, Pacific Mormons were a people dominated by, and persecuted by, ruling powers in their midst.[42] For both groups, faith provided a point of resistance in a politically oppressive situation. In both contexts, belief in the restored gospel mixed with native cultural traditions and even catalyzed splinter movements that accepted parts of the original faith but not others. In both settings, time and space were transformed, and the past became new again. What the early Polynesian Saints lacked, however, that the Utah Saints achieved very early on were the technological skills and material resources to record and begin to assess their own history.

As the LDS Church reaches another cultural crossing, as it becomes ever more cognizant of its increasingly multicultural membership, these stories of origin, of replacement and displacement, will multiply. As much of a nineteenth-century saga as this is, it has many contemporary resonances in discussions over unity and diversity in the Church at the close of the twentieth century. A key difference today is that Mormon missionaries do not occupy the same oppositional stance to American political power as that inhabited by their forebears. They have become thoroughly associated with the United States as an imperial force in the eyes of other peoples, a fact that complicates the task of evangelization inasmuch as the Mormon message is now equated with assimilation to American civilization.

Yet in a global context, the question of the religious mapping of a sacred story is still a salient issue. Mormons living "on the margins" of the sacred tent, glimpsing the tradition as it has been constructed and memorialized from a different vantage point, will certainly be more suspicious of readily equating American values with restored gospel truths. Like the early Pacific missionaries, they may choose to draw distinctions between the precepts that unify the faith and the cultural presumptions that diversify it. And they will bring to the community other sacred stories. It remains to be seen how the Church as an institution will respond and whether these new voices will be interpreted as a threat or a welcoming call.

Notes

1. S. George Ellsworth, ed., *The History of Louisa Barnes Pratt: The Autobiography of a Mormon Missionary Widow and Pioneer* (Logan: Utah State University Press, 1998), 137.

2. Davis Bitton, "The Ritualization of Mormon History," in *The Ritualization of Mormon History and Other Essays*, ed. Davis Bitton (Urbana: University of Illinois Press, 1994), 173.

3. Andrew Jenson, French Polynesia Mission Manuscript History, n.p., Church Archives, Church of Jesus Christ of Latter-day Saints (hereafter LDS Church Archives), Salt Lake City.

4. Jonathan Z. Smith, *To Take Place: Toward Theory in Ritual* (Chicago: University of Chicago Press, 1987). On religious geography, see Belden C. Lane, *Landscapes of the Sacred: Geography and Narrative in American Spirituality* (New York: Paulist Press, 1988).

5. On the religious geography of Mormonism, see David E. Sopher, *Geography of Religions* (Englewood Cliffs, N.J.: Prentice-Hall, 1967), 57; and Richard L. Bushman, *Making Space for the Mormons: Ideas of Sacred Geography in Joseph Smith's America*, Leonard J. Arrington Mormon History Lecture Series, Vol. 2 (Logan: Utah State University Press, 1997).

6. David J. Whittaker, "Early Mormon Pamphleteering" (PhD diss., Brigham Young University, 1982), 284n9.

7. This evocative phrase is borrowed from Geoffrey Blainey, *The Tyranny of Distance: How Distance Shaped Australia's History* (Melbourne: Macmillan, 1975).

8. Charles W. Forman, *The Island Churches of the South Pacific: Emergence in the Twentieth Century* (Maryknoll, N.Y.: Orbis Books, 1982), 3–10; and Niel Gunson, *Messengers of Grace: Evangelical Missionaries in the South Seas, 1797–1860* (Melbourne: Oxford University Press, 1978), 12–27. Although Roman Catholics gained many converts in the Marquesas, which became almost completely Catholic, they were much less successful in areas where the Protestants had entered the field first. See Ralph M. Wiltgen, *The Founding of the Roman Catholic Church in Oceania, 1825 to 1850* (Canberra: Australian National University Press, 1979).

9. The rich literature on Mormonism in the Pacific Basin is growing rapidly. Among the most salient for this study were Ian Barber, "Between Biculturalism and Assimilation:

The Changing Place of Maori Culture in the Twentieth-Century New Zealand Mormon Church," *New Zealand Journal of History* 29(2) (October 1995): 142–69; R. Lanier Britsch, *Unto the Islands of the Sea: A History of the Latter-day Saints in the Pacific* (Salt Lake City: Deseret Book, 1986); S. George Ellsworth, *Zion in Paradise: Early Mormons in the South Seas* (Logan: Faculty Association, Utah State University, 1959); Grant Underwood, "Mormonism, the Maori, and Cultural Authenticity," *Journal of Pacific History* 35(2) (September 2000): 133–46; David J. Whittaker, "Mormon Missiology: An Introduction and Guide to the Sources," 1998, photocopy of typescript courtesy of Whittaker; and David J. Whittaker, with the assistance of Chris McClellan, "Mormon Missions and Missionaries: A Bibliographic Guide to Published and Manuscript Sources," 1993, photocopy of typescript courtesy of Whittaker.

10. George Q. Cannon, *My First Mission*, Faith-Promoting Series, No. 1 (Salt Lake City: Juvenile Instructor Office, 1879), 44–45.

11. Ibid., 45.

12. American Mormon James Brown, whether because of temperament or timing, seemed to attract the wrath of local officials and natives alike, who associated him with American aggression. He was driven off one of the Society Islands by the colonial governor and exiled from another by islanders who threatened to kill him. He recalled that the natives held councils to see "what could be done to get rid of the 'plant Mormonism,' from America,' before it spread over the island and became master." James Brown, *Giant of the Lord: Life of a Pioneer* (1902; reprint, Salt Lake City: Bookcraft, 1960), 255.

13. Gunson, *Messengers of Grace*, 133–35, 204. See also Andrew Thornley, "Religious Interaction," in *Culture Contact in the Pacific: Essays on Contact, Encounter, and Response*, ed. Max Quanchi and Ron Adams (Cambridge: Cambridge University Press, 1993), 73–82.

14. Cannon, *My First Mission*, 12–13.

15. Ellsworth, *Zion in Paradise*, 11.

16. Norman Douglas, "The Sons of Lehi and the Seed of Cain: Racial Myths in Mormon Scripture and Their Relevance to the Pacific Islands," *Journal of Religious History* 8(1) (June 1974): 94; David J. Whittaker, "Mormons and Native Americans: A Historical and Bibliographical Introduction," *Dialogue: A Journal of Mormon Thought* 18 (Winter 1985): 33–64.

17. See Barber, "Between Biculturalism."

18. Cannon, *My First Mission*, 56.

19. On cultural change and islander responses, see Thornley, "Religious Interaction," 74–77. On the particular problems faced by native women, see Patricia Grimshaw, *Paths of Duty: American Missionary Wives in Nineteenth-Century Hawaii* (Honolulu: University of Hawaii Press, 1989); Margaret Jolly and Martha Macintyre, eds., *Family and Gender in the Pacific: Domestic Contradictions and the Colonial Impact* (Cambridge: Cambridge University Press, 1989); and Carol Cornwall Madsen, "Mormon Missionary Wives in Nineteenth Century Polynesia," *Journal of Mormon History* 13 (1986–87): 61–85.

20. Gunson, *Messengers of Grace*, 237–38.

21. Thornley, "Religious Interaction," 78.

22. Whittaker, "Early Mormon Pamphleteering," 282; Marjorie Newton, *Southern Cross Saints: The Mormons in Australia* (Laie, Hawaii: Institute for Polynesian Studies, 1991), 56; Ellsworth, *Zion in Paradise*, 20.

23. Ellsworth, *History of Louisa Barnes Pratt,* 128; Jenson, French Polynesia Mission Manuscript History, n.p.

24. Ellsworth, *History of Louisa Barnes Pratt,* 161.

25. *Autobiography of Parley Parker Pratt,* ed. Parley P. Pratt Jr. (1938; reprint, Salt Lake City: Deseret Book, 1985), 378.

26. Brown, *Giant of the Lord,* 228.

27. Ellsworth, *History of Louisa Barnes Pratt,* 128, 154.

28. Gunson, *Messengers of Grace,* 229.

29. Ellsworth, *History of Louisa Barnes Pratt,* 128. Underwood, "Cultural Authenticity," discusses similar resonances among the Maori.

30. Cannon, *My First Mission,* 56.

31. Brown, *Giant of the Lord,* 229–30.

32. Gunson, *Messengers of Grace,* 143.

33. Brown, *Giant of the Lord,* 208.

34. Douglas, "Sons of Lehi," 100; Underwood, "Cultural Authenticity," 133. See also Barber, "Between Biculturalism."

35. Alan Howard, "Cultural Paradigms, History, and the Search for Identity in Oceania," in *Cultural Identity and Ethnicity in the Pacific,* ed. Jocelyn Linnekin and Lin Poyer (Honolulu: University of Hawaii Press, 1990), 260.

36. The subject of ethnic identity is too complex to enter into fully here. These conclusions should not be taken to suggest that Polynesian peoples had no self-conception, or group conceptions, whatsoever. What is in question is the genetic basis of that self-understanding. In a social world in which, prior to colonial contact, people lived among others who were quite similar physically, linguistically, and culturally, it is likely that these markers did not form the basis for any understanding of difference. For more discussion of this point, see Geoffrey M. White and John Kirkpatrick, eds., *Person, Self and Experience: Exploring Pacific Ethnopsychologies* (Berkeley: University of California Press, 1985).

37. Ellsworth, *History of Louisa Barnes Pratt,* 149.

38. For recent explorations of the historical development of Mormonism as an ethnic marker, see Arnold H. Green, "Gathering and Election: Israelite Descent and Universalism in Mormon Discourse," *Journal of Mormon History* 25(1) (Spring 1999): 195–228; and Armand Mauss, "In Search of Ephraim: Traditional Mormon Conceptions of Lineage and Race," ibid., 131–73. See also Douglas, "Sons of Lehi."

39. I find it significant, in this respect, that William Mulder, "The Mormon Gathering," in *Mormonism and American Culture,* ed. Marvin S. Hill and James B. Allen (New York: Harper & Row, 1972), 94, notes that the concept of the new settlement, articulated as early as 1830, described the gathering not by relation to a specific geographical location but by proximity to particular peoples: the settlement would take place "on the borders of the Lamanites." On the same theme and its relation to Native Americans, see Ronald W. Walker, "Seeking the 'Remnant': The Native American during the Joseph Smith Period," *Journal of Mormon History* 19(1) (Spring 1993): 1–33. Both studies suggest that Mormon sacred geography was inextricably bound to the locations of particular peoples, not to the natural landscape alone.

40. Pratt, "Proclamation . . . ," in *The Essential Parley P. Pratt* (Salt Lake City: Signature Books, 1990), 155.

41. Barber, "Between Biculturalism and Assimilation," 167. On resonances with the African American theme of chosenness, see Albert J. Raboteau, "African Americans, Exodus, and the American Israel," in *A Fire in the Bones: Reflections on African-American Religious History,* ed. Albert J. Raboteau (Boston: Beacon Press, 1995), 17–36.

42. For a sustained discussion of American imperialism in Utah, see D. W. Meinig, "The Mormon Nation and the American Empire," *Journal of Mormon History* 22(1) (Spring 1996): 33–51.

CHAPTER 19

From the Age of Science to an Age of Uncertainty: History and Mormon Studies in the Twentieth Century

Henry Warner Bowden

Those of us who analyze historical writings use questions that few other historians incorporate in their work. Instead of focusing on the prima facie aspects of a finished volume, we ask why someone thought such a topic was important in the first place, why the subject matter was defined one way rather than another, which methods of inquiry were employed, and what interpretation was placed on the evidence. Students of historiography also take a longer view to chart trends among historians as one set of paradigms succeeds another. We are able to discern which ideas about investigative procedure and interpretive theory are in vogue at particular times and how they give place to others. Using written histories as primary documents, we add a chapter to intellectual history that chronicles varying perceptions of the past. Each school of thought teaches us something about the cultural nexus that fostered it. No history is definitive, because changing conditions create a need to revise knowledge about the past. Studying histories in successive ages gives us valuable information about the climates of opinion that affected scholars living under their influence.

This point of view is already well established among those who belong to the Mormon History Association. James B. Allen, for example, pointed out that history written by contemporaries is a key to understanding any particular present and that "as conditions change the questions society and its historians ask of the present also change. . . . History thus becomes an ever-changing thing as the historians of every generation interpret and reinterpret for the time in which they write."[1] It strikes me that this is a natural and inevitable consequence of human affairs and that one need not be saddened, as is Richard L. Bushman, who finds it "disconcerting to observe the oscillations in historical fashion and to recognize how one's own times affect the view of the past."[2] A calmer and wiser voice is that of Thomas G. Alexander, who observed that "As conditions change, new questions will undoubtedly arise crying for satisfactory answers, and many old questions will have to be asked again since the answers satisfactory to one group of people may be found incomplete by another."[3]

Without belaboring this obvious point, I propose to demarcate the historiographical parameters that have emerged through twentieth-century scholarly experience. One justification for doing so is premised on the thought that the unexamined life is not worth living. All of us as historians can benefit from understanding what our intellectual milieu is like and how it developed to its present state. So the following overview describes the origins and fundamental characteristics of the context in which most historians work today. I hope that providing this general framework will stimulate members of the Mormon History Association to reflect on their own historical efforts and to identify themselves in reference to it, either agreeing with or dissenting from predominant canons. I do not suggest that these attitudes and procedures used by most historians are normative. All they do is delineate the limits observed by those in the mainstream of American scholarship. Mormon historians, as is the case with all others, may then affirm those general standards, reject them in favor of some other approach, or develop combinations of both shared rubrics and their own scholarly preferences that they consider appropriate to a specific field of study.

In the early decades of this century there were two competing views about history, two versions of what constituted proper approach and acceptable content. Church historians were particularly strong on one side, holding that "Church and History [were] . . . so closely united, that respect and love towards the first, may be said to be essentially the same [as] a proper sense of what is comprised in the other." People in this frame of reference were convinced that a "proper point of observation" was necessary in order to understand how the Church and other historical experience fit together. So it was axiomatic that "A right conception of the Church [was] . . . the conducting genius of the Church historian."[4] Those who sought an adequate understanding of the past had to begin by accepting a priori conceptions based on theological definitions of the subject matter. They affirmed contemporary standards of accuracy and honesty, but their confessional orientation committed them to the fundamental objective of depicting God's activity in human settings. Historians of this sort said that sympathetic union with one's subject was crucial to true understanding; "an unbeliever could produce only a repulsive caricature or at best a lifeless statue." As one representative spokesman insisted, "The recognition of God in history is the first principle of all sound philosophy of history. . . . He who denies the hand of Providence in the affairs of the world and the church is intellectually or spiritually blind."[5]

Alongside this conception, other scholars supported notions of history derived from science instead of theology. This alternative view sought to eliminate prior assumptions and unsupported speculation, to clear the air of all biases in order to get at the bare facts of each case. The keys to accurate and undistorted history were empirical observation and explanations limited to natural causation. By staying with tangible, observable facts, by describing events "as they actually happened," this school of thought purported to make history as much a science in the humanities as other studies were sciences of physical data. Scientific historians favored inductive reasoning from secular evidence and scorned metaphysical speculation, especially any interpolation of providential activity in mundane settings. Speaking about God in history required the historian to act as a prophet, but scientific historians believed that "What seems to be providential in history is but the reflex of the mind that contemplates it."[6] The differences between secular and sacred history, between empirical naturalism and theological preconceptions, were clear as this century began. As time elapsed, more and more historians chose the scientific model, while history associated with faith received less and less support.

By 1920 scientific ideology dominated American historical scholarship, and an index of that triumph is the way church historians adjusted to empirical procedures and humanistic explanations. Advocates of less ambitious ideas about the craft held that it could no longer serve theological predilections. Strict attention to the limits of human investigation precluded any concern about religious consequences. This modified view declared that proper church history did not "rest upon emotional or dogmic or propagandist bases, but, so far as possible, upon purely historical considerations." The study of religious persons or groups was "nothing more nor less than one chapter in that continuous record of human affairs to which we give the name of history in general." Historical narratives that invoked supernatural agents exceeded proper procedures; anything constructed to serve higher ends violated the rules and was guilty of "trimming the plain human record to suit [its] own fancy." Churches were seen as earthly institutions whose evidence was open to the same methods of critical inquiry as used with other topics. By not relying on supernatural factors, church historians shared the constricted but solid means of understanding the past where "No glamor of antiquity, no weight of tradition, no presumption as to good intention can cover violation of those rules laid down by modern science as the unshakable foundations of historical certainty."[7]

But how could this kind of church history read evidence with secular eyes when documents themselves referred to supernatural occurrences? One could not accept them at face value, because science precluded such reality. One could not deny them and write history after ruling out part of the record. This form of church history mediated between the two extremes, distinguishing between human belief in providential events and divine activity itself. Bearing in mind the limits of method and perception, the argument ran thus:

[H]istorical evidence concerns only such things as are perceptible to human powers and can be recorded by human means. Miracles—*all* miracles—are excluded from the historian's function, because no human evidence can establish the fact of miracle. Yet the fact of *belief* in miracle is as obvious a human phenomenon within Christianity as in every other religion. As such the historian is bound to deal with it, never for a moment with the object of proving or disproving the alleged miracle, but only to set the effects of this belief in their right place in the record he is trying to interpret.[8]

Thus, where beliefs in the superhuman were authenticated facts in historical records, they could be used as human factors that affected cultural surroundings. The supernatural itself was a subject for metaphysics, not history, because its intangible quality placed it beyond any hope of documentation or verification through commonly accepted means of observation.

This modified view of church history illustrates how thoroughly scientific ideals replaced theological ones in historical scholarship. In the vast majority of cases of those who studied religious phenomena, by the 1920s they had adopted the secular standards of humanistic inquiry. Strict attention to observable evidence, explanations and interpretations restricted to natural possibilities, procedures, and results differing in no way from other historical endeavors—these characteristics indicated how completely science had come to define truth on the basis of a single standard.

Then that standard collapsed under devastating criticism. Some people had expressed some misgivings about scientific ideals in earlier years, but the attack did not reach crisis proportions until the 1930s. Carl Becker was probably the most trenchant critic of the way historical investigation had been equated with scientific procedure. Most professional historians assumed that data existed objectively and that historians could read evidence without distorting biases. But Becker maintained that actual practice belied the ideal. Everyone, he said, brought preconceptions to the evidence they studied, and these biases were shaped by contemporary culture. Historical narratives did not put forth self-evident truths because each account was "an imaginative creation, a personal possession which each of us . . . fashions out of his individual experience." Historians could not observe events with neutral eyes; patterns were not inherent in the facts themselves; their significance did not manifest itself to a disinterested chronicler. In Becker's estimation, no historian "stuck to the facts"; rather, "the facts stuck to him, if he has any ideas to attract them." In opposition to the model of detached observation, he argued that "complete detachment would produce few histories, and none worthwhile; for the really detached mind is a dead mind." Rejecting the scientific ideal, he noted that "all historical writing, even the most honest, is unconsciously subjective, since every age is bound, in spite of itself, to make the dead perform whatever tricks it finds necessary for its own peace of mind."[9]

Charles A. Beard voiced similar reservations about "that noble dream" wherein facts contained inherent meaning and dispassionate observers could perceive truth without intervening predispositions. In addition to the impact Becker had already made, Beard's influence effectively terminated the ideal of scientific objectivity and inaugurated the modern period of historiography that we still occupy. Enumerated in succinct propositions, Beard's dissection of moribund science exposed five false assumptions: (1) that the past exists independently outside human minds; (2) that historians can know this past and describe it "with strict impartiality, somewhat as a mirror reflects any object to which it is held up";[10] (3) that historians can divest themselves of all religious, political, social, economic, and moral interests; (4) that events possess inherent meaning that impartial historians can accurately portray; and (5) that observers are able to perceive causal relationships and historical significance through purely rational effort.

After burying this debris, Beard suggested that there are three levels of historical reality. As past actuality, history comprises everything that has occurred. Much on that level has been lost, but recorded history embraces all traceable affirmations of those occurrences. When historians reconstruct the past, their tertiary form of history constitutes a select portion of what the fragmentary record discloses. Every investigator arranges and interprets material according to ideas absorbed from an acculturated perspective. The historian's effort is thus "an act of faith," and "His faith is at bottom a conviction that something true can be known about the movement of history and his conviction is a subjective decision, not a purely objective discovery."[11]

Many responses to this barrage of criticism filled the pages of professional journals in the 1930s. The residual consensus was that historical investigation did in fact harbor elements of subjectivity, relativity, and indeterminism. Historians thereafter strove to be as honest as possible about their preconceptions and still to be as accurate as possible while treating materials in their chosen field. So the age of science ended around 1935 when historiographical ideals based on Baconian empiricism collapsed. This was a boon in that intellectual tyranny based on a single standard ceased and historians could work with personally constructed methods that made sense to them. It was a bane in that nothing replaced the old orthodoxy with another overarching perspective to which practitioners might conform. The modern period enjoys freedom of choice, but its options entail feelings of uncertainty. Historians now approach a variety of subjects in different ways, and they no longer think there is a single mode of operation for everyone to follow. Relativity allows any history to claim legitimacy, but this fact raises the question of complete relativism where hopes for general historical validity are sacrificed to special interest groups who sponsor competing studies. The modern period has no canon, and professional historians in general are not certain as to which method or interpretive perspective is the proper one to follow—or whether there ought to be one at all.

The modern period of historiography is an age of uncertainty wherein scholars acknowledge that every investigation contains some subjective elements. Candor about one's own approach begets tolerance toward others, and in this more self-consciously open context, church historians have pursued their work without having to justify it according to an arbitrary, external rubric. They use their own frames of reference when probing for causal explanations, and they employ priorities of their own choosing when piecing together an intelligible sequence of events. Modern students of both secular and religious topics have reassessed the nature of historical understanding. Recognizing their relative insights, they now affirm what the old historiographical model had deplored: "Historical facts . . . gain their meaning when by order, selection and interpretation they are related to a frame of reference. . . . Without relation to some theory the fact is an isolated entity with dubious value and little meaning."[12] The rest of contemporary scholarship is best understood in light of how historians select, order, and give meaning to data by relating them to frames of reference that for various reasons they find compelling.

In light of these major developments, one can postulate that the modern historiographical period began around 1935, and we are still in it. For church historians, students of religious phenomena, or historians of a people identified by religious affirmations, our current intellectual atmosphere has two negative characteristics: any history derived from a priori theological assumptions is still suspect, and the ideal of history based on scientific models of detached objectivity is dead. Modern historians use mundane procedures of humanistic inquiry, and they know that the results of their work are relative to subjective proclivities and different angles of vision. A third, more positive characteristic of the new era is that in the absence of one standard for all historical studies, scholars are free to investigate topics from a variety of deliberately chosen, finite perspectives. Each line of historical inquiry is considered useful and productive when the questions asked and answers formulated resonate with people who share the same frame of reference, with those who have the same concerns about a segment of the past. Modern historians thus work in a context of natural explanation, subjective insights relative to differing perspectives, and professional modesty that no longer dreams of absolute truth or definitive treatment of a topic.

In trying to place Mormon historical efforts in this larger framework, one notion worth considering is that they comprise in 150 years a microcosm of Christian historiography spread through two millennia. Accepting the helpful guidelines laid out by James Allen and Thomas Alexander, we can isolate four types of writing. The first phase was polemic, full of exposés and apologetics, attacks and defense. Vigorous tractates published by Mormons and anti-Mormons in the nineteenth century correspond to a long list of earlier writings that stretched from Origen's *Contra Celsum* to the Protestant *Magdeburg Centuries* and on to Cotton Mather's *Magnalia Christi Americana*. Succeeding this period of special pleading came venerative scholars who combined pious attitudes about their subject with careful attempts to describe it accurately. B. H. Roberts embodied this frame of mind among Mormons, and his volumes resemble those produced by other church historians such as J. L. Mosheim, T. Mommsen, and P. Schaff. Then progressive scholars appeared who interpreted materials from secular cultural standards and argued for adaption to social change. Samuel Woolley Taylor, Marilyn Warenski, and Laurel B. Andrew have treated Mormonism in this way, producing studies that parallel others in the larger field authored by A. C. McGiffert and S. J. Case. Fourth, in the explosion of historical scholarship of the past thirty-five years, Mormon historians have conducted their investigations in much the same way as fellow historians of other religious phenomena. We can place the names of Juanita Brooks, Leonard J. Arrington, Klaus Hansen, and Davis Bitton alongside those of Robert T. Handy, Henry F. May, Martin E. Marty, and Sydney E. Ahlstrom because all of them belong to, and operate within, the setting of modern historical scholarship.

It is not my purpose to dwell on this telescoping of Christian historiography and the evolution of Mormon writings that repeated similar contours in less than a tenth of the time. I think it will be more helpful to look at broad schools of thought generated in the twentieth century to see what interests church historians have pursued and to suggest where significant Mormon studies fit these patterns.

Once scientific ideology relaxed its grip, some church historians once again raised the old argument that their subject contained spiritual qualities that set it apart from other phenomena. These advocates valued past ecclesiastical experience for its religious importance, not its cultural function. Churches had a sacred core where researchers were enjoined to identify "the Holy Community entrusted with the means of salvation." Anyone who wished to understand religious events in their deepest sense had to get beneath surface realities and "tell the story against the background of ultimate meanings." One supporter said that the proper historian "stands on the boundary between symbol and fact, between myth and history, because the events with which he deals are transfigured by the Holy." Knowing that interpretations of meaning in historical evidence always included preconceptions, he or she found it legitimate to "clothe a concrete, historical event in a vesture woven by the religious imagination." Of course, it was important to investigate exactly what happened in situations. "But we have, too, to recognize how these incidents themselves reveal something to us of God, and in consequence are more than events, because they are the medium of revelation."[13] This school of thought saw church history as a solemn task of describing events with scrupulous care in order to see in them the hand of God at work.

Another church historian called for a return to theological priorities by pointing out deficiencies in what he called "positivistic" interpretations. Instead of those empty views, nothing less than "the Christian vision of history" could supply insight into the direction and meaning of human experience. A proper orientation in investigators made their writings superior to mere secularists because ultimately they sought to answer the question, "How much of this [evidence] belongs to the story of God's redemption of mankind?" Concrete data blended with a renewed appreciation of churches as representatives of transcendent reality, and church historians were again enabled to "trace the actualization of the Gospel in human history."[14]

It is important to note that very few modern scholars responded favorably to such pleas for reinstating "high" church history. The argument for a history that enhanced theology made sense to those concerned with building neo-orthodox systems, but practicing historians paid it little heed. Interestingly enough, one can find a similar call to exalted history in recent Mormon thought, with the same general response.

William Mulder has afforded us some useful descriptions of people in the modern period who want to put "their secular learning in the service of sacred history." This type of Mormon historian stands within a long Christian tradition of those who perceived "within the grand design of world history . . . a series of gospel dispensations in which God's purposes unfold as events in time." This mythic dimension, derived from theological commitment, directs the angle of vision with which investigators read evidence and report findings. Historians who acknowledge the guiding influence of a priori assumptions about revealed religion can produce writings faithful to some thesis and design already furnished. "The Mormon historian, as any religiously motivated historian must, chooses his conception of history as a divine script acted out on this planetary stage."[15]

In addition to the eclectic portrait Mulder sketched, other Mormon historians have alluded to their work with a concern to integrate theology with their more mundane pursuits. Richard Bushman pointed to belief in God as a guide, though not a simple one, to relevant history. He held that God enters history in various ways and that "our faith certainly compels us to search for Him as best we can." Bushman recommended various interpretive structures that put God to the forefront. Of these, he noted, "The most obvious subject for Mormon historians is the history of the Church, the story of God's revelation to his people and the implementation of His will in the earth."[16] Others have struck this note almost as an afterthought. Leonard J. Arrington discussed the feasibility of different viewpoints in Mormon history and then tacked on this benediction: "May the images conveyed by our historians help us to continue the restoration of the Gospel of the Master, and may they assist us in the building the Kingdom of God on earth."[17] Thomas Alexander steered between the Scylla of secular reductionism and the Charybdis of theologically dominated history, but he too included the notion that historians should "interpret God and his actions," even while doing so in indirect ways.[18]

These few "high" church invocations aside, most acute Mormon scholars today have echoed attitudes about our craft as a humanistic field. They have thought through for themselves the collective wisdom that accrues to the modern histori-ographical period. To begin with, they have noted how misleading the scientific model is. One of the best practitioners concluded that "objectivity was impossi-ble since all historians must continue to look with their eyes, interpret with their brains, and understand from the context of their own experience." He asserted that absolute detachment was both impossible and undesirable: "It is impossible because all individuals carry a set of cultural baggage which inevitably colors their perspective. It is undesirable since, if historians are to understand the expe-riences and motivations of actors in times past, they must exercise creative imag-ination and intuition." The study of human experience has no parallel with positivistic natural sciences; it focuses rather on products of the human mind, and this requires "creative imagination and intuition for their interpretation."[19]

Given our present situation where choices have to be made, Mormon schol-ars are aware of this need. As one outstanding historian noted, making self-conscious decisions about one's perspective is important because "given the multitude of facts, historians by picking and choosing can make quite different and plausible stories" about the same material. Indeed, "more important than how you answer a question is what question you ask in the first place. Not until you decide [what] you want to know ... do you even bother to look at all the facts on those subjects stored away in the archives."[20] Another agrees, adding that "the criteria for including evidence are, by their very nature, subjective." Historians will perceive their materials and fashion their hypotheses on the basis of what they consider relevant to various topics. And they will "naturally seek to answer those questions most important to them and those who share their world view." Modern Mormon scholars have also recognized that even though subjectivity is inevitable, it does not mean that one historical narrative is as good as another. Professionals and laymen alike recognize that the best histories "include evidence that we perceive as relevant and that try to answer questions important to us." Such works are the product of balanced perspective, "a judicious and intuitive weighing of the products of the minds of people in times past," a viewpoint that allows one "to come to reasonable interpretations of their thought."[21]

In their musings about the opportunities and limits of historical inquiry, many Mormon scholars have begun to put some distance between theological interests and their professional responsibilities. As one observer noted, this opens the field to serious studies based on different viewpoints. "Not only do Latter-day Saints have the framework within which to understand their past as an existentialist history rather than as a branch of dogmatics and polemics, but interested people who are not Latter-day Saints and who do not share Mormon faith assumptions also have the opportunity to discover Mormon history as a legitimate rather than an aberrant phenomenon in American culture." This achievement within Mormon circles is similar to that of other religious scholars in the modern period because it has moved away from the need "to struggle with the *a priori* issue of the legitimacy of . . . faith assumptions." The mutual interests of students of a human past "replaces mutual anxiety over dogma."[22]

One of the reasons for finessing the question of dogma and for desensitizing the issue of "faithful history" is that Mormon historians acknowledge with their gentile colleagues that research methods yield modest results. As Melvin T. Smith reminded us, "History as a discipline is a finite study of human beings." This does not mean that humans are confined to finite realms but that the ways we have of investigating them are limited to finite procedures. Leonard J. Arrington and Davis Bitton concur: "The tools of secular scholarship are crude and inadequate instruments for measuring mystical theophanies."[23] Marvin Hill also knows that the historian's vantage point and methods of inquiry have restricted applicability. One might want to use tangible historical evidence to verify whether or not Joseph Smith was really a prophet of God. But Hill does not think "that question can be finally answered by historians who deal with human artifacts. . . . The historian has no sources written with the finger of God to prove that Joseph Smith was called to his divine mission, nor does he have any human sources to prove conclusively that he was not." That is all the historian can do, given the limits of his mundane approach. One's answer to the ultimate or cosmic question will "depend entirely upon the [religious] assumptions he brings to it . . . upon personal predilection, not historical evidence."[24]

Mormon historians recognize that our commonly accepted tools and methods cannot answer all questions put to them about the past. But they do not despair, any more than do church historians in other circles, that religion is irrelevant in history. Whatever the ultimate truth of religious affirmations, people made them. Though historians cannot verify intangibles, they can determine that human beings did orient their lives around such ideas and values. Beliefs existed in persons, and whether true or false, historians can observe their effect on human activity. One close student of Mormon history described the middle ground by means of a concrete example: "I am not much disposed to believe that Joseph actually spoke through Brigham. However, there is no question that at an early date the belief was disseminated among the Mormon people that this thing actually had happened, and this was the reason the belief merited inclusion in the essay on history. I am sure you will grant me the commonplace . . . that it is not things themselves but what people believe about things and how they react to things that shape the development of society."[25]

Perhaps William Mulder put it best in his plea that Mormon historiography allow for writings from several angles of vision. There is a legitimacy, he said, in history written without religious assumptions. This genre could hold faith temporarily in abeyance and still "remain well-tempered, creative rather than corrosive." His summation was that "a creative skepticism is not disbelief but the tension between multiple and equally magnetic possibilities of interpretation."[26]

This seems much the same kind of observation as that made by Leonard Arrington, who declared that critical history is "a private and not a Church venture. Although this history is intended to imbue the written record with meaning and significance, the Church cannot afford to place its official stamp of approval on any 'private' interpretation of its past. Interpretations are influenced by styles and ideas of the times, not to say the personalities and experiences of historians. . . . [And the forthright investigator] ought to be free to suggest interpretations without placing his faith and loyalty on the line."[27]

Or the same scholar again, this time in 1965, the year when *Dialogue* began publication and the Mormon History Association was founded: "The Mormon religion and its history are subject to discussion, if not to argument, and . . . any particular feature of Mormon life is fair game for detached examination and clarification. . . . The details of Mormon history and culture can be studied in human or naturalistic terms—indeed, must be so studied—and without thus rejecting the divinity of the Church's origin and work."[28]

Focusing on these ideas about historical scholarship has brought us to the point of seeing how much "the New Mormon History" fits the larger intellectual context of which it forms a part. Mormon historians resemble most of their colleagues when they emphasize humanistic interests instead of evangelical ones, treating LDS experience as part of human life instead of vindicating faith assumptions about God in history.[29] They fit the general framework of modern historiography when they relax with a "warts and all" attitude about reporting, a comfortable acceptance of human complexity that "includes the failures as well as the achievements, the weaknesses as well as the strengths, the individual derelictions as well as the heroism and self-sacrifice" of those germane to the story.[30] This healthy outlook welcomes findings from a number of perspectives: "studies in which the social, cultural, political, and economic history are woven together to prove the lives of the LDS people." The New Mormon History is very much like other facets of church history in affirming that "secular and spiritual motivation coexist in human affairs and that a sympathetic but critical evaluation of the Mormon past, using techniques derived from historical, humanistic, social-scientific, and religious perspectives could help in understanding what [is] at base a religious movement."[31]

Over the course of this century, historians have hammered out standard procedures for accomplishing their work. Most of them have stopped trying to locate God in mundane evidence, but this does not represent the complete triumph of secularism over theology, of this-worldly concerns over transcendental ones. Several scholars continue to integrate religious sensitivity with what they study. But now, instead of using faith to direct the means of research and reporting, they apply religious insights as reflective comments on the work after it is produced. This latter-day blending of theology and history does not use documentary materials to verify providential action. It uses the results of secular investigation as a solid basis on which to discuss further meaning that might be seen in the record. It does not manage evidence or impose unnatural causation on human events. With this self-imposed rigor, however, it keeps alive a legitimate dimension of the historian's task that is worth taking seriously. The end result is not ideologically dominated history. For historians of this sort, whose subjective perceptions are every bit as complex as the topics they study, their work rests on critical scholarship and offers comments about meaning and direction in human life. Some historians employ this additional dimension; others decline the option. But whether we do or not, I suggest that we can now recognize where the option fits in the minds of our colleagues and how it is congruent with modern rubrics in our profession.[32]

In addition to "high" church history, the modern period has seen three other distinctive emphases. One popular school of thought underlined the importance of churches by highlighting their impact on the culture around them. As a subtle form of apologetics, its great strength lay in using massive accumulations of data to show that churches influenced social values. Instead of agreeing that environments imposed characteristics on people, this viewpoint held that organized groups, especially religious ones, influenced behavior and modified the environment in which people lived. Churches worth studying were "those which came to power and influence as a consequence of their successful coping with" challenges around them. The best way to understand Christianity was not to focus on revelation or parochial details but to "include every phase of the impact of that faith upon mankind." Historians of this sort demonstrated how individual lives had been transformed, political systems reformed, public health improved, and standards of living upgraded. All of them subsumed a genre that wrote appreciatively of Christianity as a beneficial force in advancing human endeavors.[33]

In my own reading of Mormon studies, I see a great many publications that fit within this broad framework. As with other works that initially led me to propose this category, they fit imperfectly and overlap with other frames of reference. I do not mean to imply that they belong here and nowhere else. But of all the many pertinent titles, I believe that Leonard Arrington's *Great Basin Kingdom* is relevant here because his study of economic institutions and church policies demonstrated the impact that LDS people had on a particular region of the country. Robert Flanders's *Nauvoo* also concentrated on the influence that religion had on a geographical and chronological segment of society. And in their sociological interpretation of adaptation processes, Gordon and Gary Shepherd's *Kingdom Transformed* shed light on historical settings. Their concepts of group identity, social solidarity, and organizational commitment help historians understand more fully what took place in the subject matter they investigate.[34]

Another type of church history appeared at midcentury when many historians began emphasizing consensus rather than conflict in their interpretive viewpoint. Perhaps dismayed by competing ideologies and global violence, they con-structed a past where institutions were stable and basic values persisted across the generations. Some church historians did this by highlighting perennial themes such as pacifism, freedom of speech, and religious toleration, urging their worth as antidotes to "secular paganism." Others spoke to present-day needs by isolat-ing what needed to be done instead of extolling timeless virtues. One scholar of this sort thought that American society suffered from a split personality: part of its tradition drew on cosmopolitan attitudes that viewed all religions as equal; the other part still discriminated among confessions and indulged in sectarian particularism. The result was a malaise of "bifurcated minds" with which peo-ple tried to be good citizens and good church members for different reasons. So this historian hoped that he would contribute to consensus by helping contem-porary thinkers face up to an inherited inconsistency and resolve it to society's current benefit.[35]

A great many Mormon histories fit this framework where shared values are emphasized. The interesting variable here is that some publications stress tradi-tions held inside the group, showing how they have sustained corporate survival in the face of external threats. Other publications seek out a consensus between Mormon values and characteristics in the larger context of American culture. The "insider" kind of emphasis on common bonds can be seen in the textbook over-view by James Allen and Glen Leonard. Another inclusive treatment by Leonard J. Arrington and Davis Bitton contains elements of singing the Lord's song in a strange land, while at the same time it touches on adjustments to the broader cul-tural environment. Before either of these eclectic tomes appeared, Marvin Hill and James Allen edited a small volume of interpretive essays along this line. Regarding the larger American setting, one should never forget William Mulder's little gem on Mormonism and the western historical tradition. It is also worth pointing out that studies of Mormons in transition continue to appear. A recent one in this category is Thomas Alexander's account of persistent LDS cohesion as its people became more fully integrated with the mainstream culture.[36]

A fourth and final emphasis in modern church historiography comes from a preference that many scholars have for focusing on ideas. A great many church historians fit this category, possibly because they have always regarded doctrine as central to religious affairs. Some of them pursue "intellectual history," which treats ideas as a major cause behind human activity. Others incline to "history of ideas," which discusses systems of thought with only secondary interest in their pragmatic value. Intellectual historians point out how ideas have "notably affected the course of history, molding the beliefs and behavior of generations of mankind." For them, truly effective Christian intellectuals were those con-cerned about practical matters, not those who embroidered the theological sleeves of ritual and polity. And because of that practical concern, Western civi-lization has made notable improvements in political theory, natural science, and liberty of conscience. Historians of ideas maintain that "the speculations of serious and competent . . . thinkers have an intrinsic worth that has nothing to do with their direct impact upon politics or programs." For them, the primary objective is to define and classify the fundamental concepts of a historical group. Their findings do apply to ecclesiastical organization and social relationships, but this comes only after the whole system of metaphysics and natural order has been worked out. The basic focus is not on "chronology so much as structure, nor [on] the morphology so much as the anatomy."[37]

Mormon studies include many publications that feature the importance of ideas, but I shall mention only two authors as exemplars of the separable approaches mentioned above. Klaus Hansen's *Quest for Empire* can be seen as a long disquisition on how the idea of a political Kingdom of God was an important key to understanding the Mormon past. Similarly, his later study of *Mormonism and the American Experience* concentrates on interaction with cultural influences and the ideas that are relevant to such a crucial exchange. His observations about intellectual development regarding race, death, economics and politics, and sexuality and marriage open the way to further investigation of these elemental topics. As far as a historian of ideas is concerned, I suggest that Jan Shipps fills that niche.[38] Her patient research in Mormon primary sources prompts me to liken her to Perry Miller, who labored similarly among Puritan materials. Her profound and empathetic volume *Mormonism: The Story of a New Religious Tradition* can be said to have done for Mormon studies what Miller's *The New England Mind: The Seventeenth Century* did for Puritans. Another parallel worth mentioning is that each of them was an "outsider" who shed much appreciated light on a subject at some remove from their personal convictions. One cannot help observing, too, that Miller wrote a sequel to his first volume of *The New England Mind,* and so we may entertain the hope that Shipps will do the same.

There is one more facet of Mormon studies that I must not omit, though it fits none of my prefabricated categories. In 1972, Hill and Allen remarked that there were "very few adequate biographies of Mormon leaders in Utah."[39] Since then a score of tremendously informative biographies have appeared. These include books about men and women in both centuries, about those on center stage as well as those less centrally placed, disclosing the trials of discipleship as well as Mormon enigmas.[40] This energetic outpouring evinces the same rigor and sophistication that we have seen at work in all other phases of modern historiography.

So now I hope we have a better grasp of trends that have shaped our present scholarly setting. Most of us use one or a combination of perspectives that feature the theological rectitude of religious groups, their social effectiveness, their retention of consensus, and their intellectual vigor. These four categories did not emerge in any logical order or progressive sequence during the twentieth century. They have overlapped in appearance and can be blended according to each scholar's preference. Having moved from a single standard regnant in the Age of Science, our guild now enjoys a rich variety of procedures and possible interpretations. We are stimulated to further inquiry without having to worry about allegiance to either religious or secular orthodoxy. But now we are in an Age of Uncertainty where historians are reconciled to never achieving absolute truth or appealing to more than a limited number of readers. Freedom carries with it the perplexing clamor of diverse historical interpretations. Still, we are bold to pursue our task, which now self-consciously recognizes the importance of critical judgment alongside painstaking method as we search the past for contemporary relevance.

Notes

1. James B. Allen, "Since 1950: Creators and Creations of Mormon History," in *New Views of Mormon History: A Collection of Essays in Honor of Leonard J. Arrington*, ed. Davis Bitton and Maureen Ursenbach Beecher (Salt Lake City: University of Utah Press, 1987), 407.

2. Richard L. Bushman, "Faithful History," *Dialogue: A Journal of Mormon Thought* 4 (Winter 1969): 13.

3. Thomas G. Alexander, "Toward the New Mormon History: An Examination of the Literature on the Latter-day Saints in the Far West," in *Historians and the American West*, ed. Michael P. Malone (Lincoln: University of Nebraska Press, 1983), 361.

4. Philip Schaff, *What Is Church History? A Vindication of the Idea of Historical Development* (Philadelphia: J. B. Lippincott, 1846), 9, 37.

5. Philip Schaff, *Theological Propaedeutic* (New York: Charles Scribner's Sons, 1892), 236, 257–58.

6. Justin Winsor, "The Perils of Historical Narrative," *Atlantic Monthly* 66 (September 1890): 294.

7. Ephraim Emerton, "A Definition of Church History," *Papers of the American Society of Church History*, 2nd ser., 7 (New York: G. P. Putnam's Sons, 1923), 56, 58–60.

8. Ibid., 63.

9. Carl L. Becker, "Some Aspects of the Influence of Social Problems and Ideas upon the Study and Writing of History," *American Journal of Sociology* 18 (March 1913): 641; "Everyman His Own Historian," *American Historical Review* 37 (January 1932): 221–36; "Detachment and the Writing of History," *Atlantic Monthly* 106 (October 1910): 524; *The Heavenly City of the Eighteenth Century Philosophers* (New Haven, Conn.: Yale University Press, 1932), 44.

10. Charles A. Beard, "That Noble Dream," *American Historical Review* 41 (October 1935): 76.

11. Charles A. Beard, "Written History as an Act of Faith," *American Historical Review* 39 (January 1934): 219–21, 226.

12. Charles Woolsey Cole, "The Relativity of History," *Political Science Quarterly* 48 (June 1933): 165.

13. Cyril C. Richardson, "Church History Past and Present," *Union Seminary Quarterly Review* 5 (November 1949): 12–14.

14. James Hastings Nichols, "The History of Christianity," in *Religion,* ed. Paul Ramsey (Englewood Cliffs, N.J.: Prentice-Hall, 1965), 157, 171–72, 201; Nichols, "The Art of Church History," *Church History* 20 (March 1951): 8–9.

15. William Mulder, "Mormon Angles of Vision: Some Maverick Reflections," *Journal of Mormon History* 3 (1976): 13, 15–16.

16. Bushman, "Faithful History," 17–18.

17. Leonard J. Arrington, "The Search for Truth and Meaning in Mormon History," *Dialogue: A Journal of Mormon Thought* 3 (Summer 1968): 65.

18. Thomas G. Alexander, "Historiography and the New Mormon History: A Historian's Perspective," *Dialogue: A Journal of Mormon Thought* 19 (Fall 1986): 46.

19. Ibid., 32, 38, 42.

20. Bushman, "Faithful History," 14.

21. Alexander, "Historiography and the New Mormon History," 36, 39.

22. Robert B. Flanders, "Some Reflections on the New Mormon History," *Dialogue: A Journal of Mormon Thought* 9 (Spring 1974): 40.

23. Quoted in Alexander, "Historiography and the New Mormon History," 39.

24. Marvin S. Hill, "Brodie Revisited: A Reappraisal," *Dialogue: A Journal of Mormon Thought* 7 (Winter 1972): 72. See also his dated but valuable "Survey: The Historiography of Mormonism," *Church History* 28 (December 1959): 418–26.

25. Letter to S. A. Burgess, 1942, quoted in *Dale Morgan on Early Mormonism: Correspondence and a New History,* ed. John Phillip Walker (Salt Lake City: Signature Books, 1986), 39.

26. Mulder, "Mormon Angles of Vision," 21.

27. Arrington, "The Search for Truth and Meaning," 60.

28. As cited in Moses Rischin, "The New Mormon History," *American West* 6 (March 1969): 49. An arresting spatial metaphor expressing the same idea can be found in Nels Anderson, *Desert Saints: The Mormon Frontier in Utah* (Chicago: University of Chicago Press, 1942), xix. Here Anderson symbolized the point by saying that as a historian, he worked in the basement of the St. George Temple where records were kept in a vault; he did not venture to the upper floors where sacred ordinances were performed.

29. See Flanders, "Some Reflections on the New Mormon History," 34, 37.

30. Arrington, "The Search for Truth and Meaning," 65.

31. Alexander, "Toward the New Mormon History," 344.

32. See Henry Warner Bowden, "Ends and Means in Church History," *Church History* 54 (March 1985): 74–88, for a more detailed consideration of where theology continues to apply in modern historical studies.

33. William Warren Sweet, *The American Churches: An Interpretation* (New York: Abingdon-Cokesbury, 1948), 7–8, and his "The American Churches," *Annals of the American Academy of Political and Social Science* 256 (March 1948): 46; Kenneth Scott Latourette, "New Perspectives in Church History," *Journal of Religion* 21 (October 1941): 432–33; Latourette, *Anno Domini: Jesus, History, and God* (New York: Harper and Brothers, 1940), 46.

34. Leonard J. Arrington, *Great Basin Kingdom: An Economic History of the Latter-day Saints, 1830–1900* (Cambridge: Harvard University Press, 1958); Robert B. Flanders, *Nauvoo: Kingdom on the Mississippi* (Urbana: University of Illinois Press, 1965); Gary Shepherd and Gordon Shepherd, *A Kingdom Transformed: Themes in the Development of Mormonism* (Salt Lake City: University of Utah Press, 1984). Another title that might

belong here is Mark P. Leone, *Roots of Modern Mormonism* (Cambridge: Harvard University Press, 1979).

35. Roland H. Bainton, *The Travail of Religious Liberty: Nine Biographical Studies* (Philadelphia: Westminster Press, 1951), 14, 253, and his *Christendom: A Short History of Christianity and Its Impact on Western Civilization* (New York: Harper & Row, 1966), vol. 2:197; Sidney E. Mead, *The Nation with the Soul of a Church* (New York: Harper & Row, 1975), vi–vii, 4–5, 21–22, 59–61, 117–18, and his *The Lively Experiment: The Shaping of Christianity in America* (New York: Harper & Row, 1963), 15, 52–56.

36. James B. Allen and Glen M. Leonard, *The Story of the Latter-day Saints* (Salt Lake City: Deseret Book, 1976); Leonard J. Arrington and Davis Bitton, *The Mormon Experience: A History of the Latter-day Saints* (New York: Knopf, 1979); Marvin S. Hill and James B. Allen, eds., *Mormonism and American Culture* (New York: Harper & Row, 1972); William Mulder, *Mormonism in American History* (Salt Lake City: University of Utah Press, 1981); Thomas G. Alexander, *Mormonism in Transition: The Latter-day Saints and Their Church, 1890–1930* (Urbana: University of Illinois Press, 1986).

37. John T. McNeill, *Christian Hope for World Society* (New York: Willett, Clark, 1937), 436–37; and McNeill, ed., *Calvin: Institutes of the Christian Religion* (Philadelphia: Westminster Press, 1960), vol. 1, xxix, li; Perry Miller, *Orthodoxy in Massachusetts, 1630–1650: A Generic Study* (Cambridge: Harvard University Press, 1933), xxv–xxvi; Terry Miller, *The New England Mind: The Seventeenth Century* (New York: Macmillan, 1939), vii.

38. Klaus Hansen, *Quest for Empire: The Political Kingdom of God and the Council of Fifty in Mormon History* (East Lansing: Michigan State University Press, 1967), and his *Mormonism and the American Experience* (Chicago: University of Chicago Press, 1981); Jan Shipps, *Mormonism: The Story of a New Religious Tradition* (Urbana: University of Illinois Press, 1985). See also Alexander, "Toward the New Mormon History," 366 n. 25, for additional listings of intellectual history studies.

39. Hill and Allen, *Mormonism and American Culture*, 187.

40. Printed earlier but reissued and still to be reckoned with is Fawn Brodie's *No Man Knows My History: The Life of Joseph Smith, the Mormon Prophet* (New York: Knopf, 1945, 1971); Donna Hill, *Joseph Smith: The First Mormon* (Garden City, N.Y.: Doubleday, 1974, 1977); Vicky Burgess-Olson, ed., *Sister Saints* (Provo, Utah: Brigham Young University Press, 1978); Stanley B. Kimball, *Heber C. Kimball: Mormon Patriarch and Pioneer* (Urbana: University of Illinois Press, 1981); Linda King Newell and Valeen Tippets Avery, *Mormon Enigma: Emma Hale Smith, Prophet's Wife, Elect Lady, Polygamy's Foe* (Garden City, N.Y.: Doubleday, 1984); Richard L. Bushman, *Joseph Smith and the Beginnings of Mormonism* (Urbana: University of Illinois Press, 1984); Leonard J. Arrington, *Brigham Young: American Moses* (New York: Knopf, 1985); Breck England, *The Life and Thought of Orson Pratt* (Salt Lake City: University of Utah Press, 1985); James B. Allen, *Trials of Discipleship: The Story of William Clayton, a Mormon* (Urbana: University of Illinois Press, 1987); Sheri L. Dew, *Ezra Taft Benson: A Biography* (Salt Lake City: Deseret Book, 1987).

CHAPTER 20

Two Integrities: An Address to the Crisis in Mormon Historiography

Martin Marty

Mormon thought is experiencing a crisis comparable to but more profound than that which Roman Catholicism recognized around the time of the Second Vatican Council (1962–63). Whatever other changes were occurring in the Catholic Church, there was a dramatic, sometimes traumatic shift in ways of regarding the tradition. One of the conventional ways of speaking of this shift comes from the observation of philosopher Bernard Lonergan. He and others in his train argued that Catholicism was moving from a "classic" view of dogma to a thoroughly "historical" view of faith.

In the classic view, Catholic teaching had come intact, as it were, protected from contingency, from a revealing God. Deposited in Scripture, church tradition, and especially dogma, it was protected from anything but ordinary or trivial historical accidents. In the new vision, this classic understanding gave place to an approach that saw Catholic events, thought, and experience as being at all points and in every way colored by the contingencies and accidents of history. God was revealed in the midst of this history.

Mormonism never was constituted around anything so formal and, as was believed by Catholics, uncontingent as dogma. From the beginning, this faith was always characterized by its thoroughly historical mode and mold. Yet almost inevitably, this understanding after a century took on what we might call a "historically classical" form. Today, in what some might regard as a dramatic and traumatic shift among Mormon intellectuals, there is a move so expansive and sudden that it hardly needs chronicling.[1] While tautology might sound cute, one could say that this shift is from a "historically classic" to a "historically historical" understanding. A focus on this issue can serve as a reexamination of the historian's vocation—whether this be of the believing "insider" or the non- or other-believing and "outsider" version. At the same time, the inquiry can point to some of the limits of historical contributions to issues of faith and certitude.

History and the Historian

Whatever else historians do, there are at least two components in their work. They deal with the past, and they tell stories. As G. J. Renier[2] reminds us, their subject is the human social past (in contrast to, say, "natural history"). And while today various structuralism and "cliometric" statistical approaches may obscure the story character, overall the historical mode is one of narrative, of story. Stories have subjects. Here things begin to get interesting.

We may not know exactly why anyone else follows the vocation of the historian. When one is a historian, it is also hard to account for the choice of subject. Some people who are Mormon will choose to write on other than Mormon history: roofing technology in Virginia, dairy farming in Wisconsin, or the middle years of Michael the Drunkard may be compelling subjects to some. Others will inquire about the past of their own people. Meanwhile, some people who are not Mormon will abandon other subjects and find themselves drawn to the history of the Saints. Historians cannot all avoid the story of the social past of a movement of up to 5 million people. It would be inconceivable that they escape the notice of non-Mormons, Gentiles. At once, two sets of people set out on similar topics. This often has produced clashes.

The ethics of the profession call historians to do careful research, not to hide evidence; to be suspicious when handling sources; and then to be fair. People used to say that they should be "objective," but objectivity seems to be a dream denied. This means that historians have to be reasonably aware of their assumptions, the viewpoints they bring, the thought worlds of the people they are representing at second hand. What results, all thoughtful historians agree, is not a reproduction of reality, which cannot even be grasped by people on the scene during events, but "a social construction of reality." The historian invents. Historical construction or invention is more delicate when the subject is the experience of the sacred in the life of people, of a people. The sacred, Rudolf Otto's *mysterium tremendum et fascinans,* appears in the midst of the mundane and ordinary world with an Otherness that sometimes threatens, often eludes, and forever beguiles the historian who comes in range of it. Because people who respond to the sacred stake their arrangement of life and their eternal hopes on this experience, they bring to it a passion that often leads them to want to be protected from historians and other social scientists. "Our" sacred, "our" Otherness, we think, is different—pure, uncontingent, protected from accident, beyond the scope of inquiring historians, be they insiders or outsiders.

Most of the time both those internal to the history of a people and a faith as well as those external to it can go about their business without creating suspicion or arousing a defensive spirit. So long as the life of the people proceeds routinely, they may not pay much attention to what historians discover and publish. It is when people are in a period of crisis that they notice the historians.

Renier has a charming passage on how historians, used to obscurity, become suddenly relevant when people "stop to think." They are especially on the spot when what they discover and publish *causes* the people to "stop to think." They have successfully done so, from within and without, in the case of Mormons in recent times.

Stopping to Think about Historicity and Religion

The Mormon ferment of today, like the Catholic analog during and after Vatican II, is a species of a genus that we might call "the crisis of historical consciousness." This crisis cut to the marrow in the Protestant body of thoughtful scholars in western Europe in the nineteenth century and continues, though it has been lived with in various ways and thus seems more domesticated, in the late twentieth century. Before the Enlightenment and the rise of a critical history focused on Christianity, professional historians were ordinarily cast as storytellers who were defenders of the faith. A few learned to direct their suspicions against forgeries and frauds such as the Donation of Constantine. Most were called, if they were Catholic, to summon events from the past to certify the truth of Catholicism over against Protestantism. Needless to say, vice versa.

This meant that the ordinary historian was much like other believers in respect to the people's past. It is useful here to introduce Paul Ricoeur's concept of "primitive naivete,"[3] by which he means nothing pejorative or condescending, merely something that designates. Children have such a naivete: they receive and accept more or less without question a world, a worldview, and views from parents and nurses and teachers. Tribal people can sustain a similar naivete: they know other tribes with other ways only from a distance, at best. Or they find no threat in these because they see no lure: other ways belong to the enemy. Isolated people, whether in a valley or an urban ghetto in a pluralist society, even in the age of mass media, can sustain the naivete. So can people in massive isolations of the sort that bind together every fifth human, religions such as Islam. In most places where it is strong, it has a monopoly, and the Muslim never knows and need never consider alternative ways of being or believing.

The primitive naivete of Catholic Europe, protected by space from the Muslim and contrived space in the form of ghetto walls from the Jews, was challenged with the introduction of variety by the Protestant Reformation on Western soil. Yet it waited for the Enlightenment to introduce the full-fledged assault on this naivete. The Enlightenment brought other religions close to home: one thinks of Lessing's *Nathan der Weise* as a typical attempt to see rough parity between Christianity, Judaism, and Islam. The Enlightenment went further: while beginning to relativize Christian distinctives in the face of other ways, it also used critical tools on Christian texts and traces from the past.

In the nineteenth century, the age of modern critical history, the crisis of historical consciousness became intense and drastic. Now no events, experiences, traces, or texts were exempt from scrutiny by historians who believed that they could be value-free, dispassionate. Today, of course, no one sees them as being successful in their search. They were tainted by radical Hegelian dialectics, neo-Kantian rigorisms, or the biases of a positivism that thought it could be unbiased. We may see these critical historians as naive in this respect. Otherwise, they were highly successful at destroying the primitive naivete among those who read them seriously. The responses could vary among these readers. Some lost faith, while others shored it up with defensive fundamentalism that focused on papal infallibility or biblical inerrancy. Most adapted their way of looking at faith and lived with it in transformed ways. Whatever else happened, however, the believer who made the passage beyond primitive naivete was very busy picking and choosing responsive attitudes.

The Christian Crisis of Historical Consciousness

Protestantism, like Catholicism, had a "classical" aspect through its own dogmatic structure. All Christians then, like the Saints now, had much at stake because their faith was so thoroughly historical in character. It lived by reference to events such as the creation, the call of Israel through its exodus and exile, the happening of Jesus Christ and especially his death and resurrection within calendrical history, and the calling into being of a historical people, the Church. To see these events as shaped by historical forces, their traces and texts unexempt from critical examination, altered responses of faith and practice.

The clash between classic and historical views was stated classically by Lessing (1729–81), the Lutheran minister's son who became an Enlightenment philosopher. He argued what has since become a commonplace: a historical truth was not capable of logical demonstration. Reported miracles, from creation through the signs and wonders that accompany biblical accounts of Israel and Jesus and through the visions that led to the vocations of prophets and apostles down to the resurrection of Christ, could never thus demonstrate the truth of Christianity. "Accidental truths of history can never become the necessary truths of reason." Lessing called the gulf between the truths of history and the truths of reason "the ugly broad ditch which I cannot get across, however often and however earnestly I have tried to make the leap."[4]

Henceforth, whoever believed in God and the integrity of God's people while aware of what Lessing and his successors posed clearly had to believe in a different way—Ricoeur would say through a "second naivete." After criticism, people believe not in spite of but through interpretation. Much of educated catholic (Catholic and Protestant) Christianity is made up of people who thus believe.

They would not call themselves "literalists" about history and would even question whether self-styled literalists are really literal or whether these do not select which events to protect from scrutiny under the leaky canopy of historical contingency.

The transit to the second mode of being and believing was not easy; a little garland of testimonies should suffice to recall it. John Viscount Lord Morley spoke of the subsequently developed "triumph of the principle of relativity in historic judgment," the "substitution of *becoming for being*, the relative for the absolute, dynamic movement for dogmatic immobility." The result was what historian Friedrich Meinecke called "one of the greatest spiritual revolutions which western thought has experienced." Ernst Troeltsch, a great Christian scholar, personalized it in a way that speaks to and for many. He had come with a solid belief in the events and the demonstrability of events that made up the Christian story, protected from and within the rest of history. Like others, he personally had felt "the demand of the religious consciousness for certainty, for unity, and for peace." But, "I soon discovered that the historical studies which had so largely formed me, and the theology and philosophy in which I was now immersed, stood in sharp opposition, indeed even in conflict, with one another. I was confronted, upon the one hand, with the perpetual flux of the historian's data, and the distrustful attitude of the historical critic towards conventional traditions." So Christianity was henceforth "a purely historical, individual, relative phenomenon." Further, the inference from all this was "that a religion, in the several forms assumed by it, always depends upon the intellectual, social, and national conditions among which it exists." Gone for him was "the absolute validity of Christianity."[5]

Not all scholars took Troeltsch's course. Critical historians who are Christian believers abound in most Catholic and Protestant communions. Yet the testimony of a profound and empathic figure such as Troeltsch has led them not to be disdainful of people who take "literalistic" or "fundamentalistic" ways of responding to the crisis—just as they have to hope for sympathy and understanding from those who resist and, in resisting, show the depth of the crisis of historical consciousness.

Where "primitive naivete" is simply no longer possible but the desire for faith is matched by the presence of faith and participation in the life of a people, it is clear that people who live with and pass through the crisis of historical consciousness may have the same "object" of faith but believe in different ways. We must at least entertain the possibility that there can be integrity in the response of believers who believe after criticism, through interpretation.

The Saints' Crisis of Historical Consciousness

From the earliest years there have been Mormons who left the faith because their view of the historical events that gave shape to it no longer permitted them to sustain it. Others remained with the Mormon people but were uneasy and made their own adjustment. We may safely assume that all thoughtful people must have some struggles with elements of a complex history. Faith attached to or mediated through historical events has always had some dimensions of an "offense" or "scandal" to the insider, just as it has been *only* that to the outsider who despises. Awareness of pettinesses and peccadillos among leaders or injustices in the record of a people—one thinks of the Christian crusades and Inquisition or papal corruption in many ages—has to be some sort of threat to the clarity of faith's vision, though it clearly has not meant the loss of faith or abandonment of peoplehood on the part of so many who are aware. Those more familiar than I with Mormon history can point and have pointed to questioners within the historical profession through the years.

As far as the profession as a whole and the intellectual community at large are concerned, however, the crisis has been noticeable only in the past two decades and urgent only in very recent years. This delay can be attributed to the hostility of the gentile world, geographical remoteness from alien forces, and the necessarily defensive agenda of the Mormon churches and people long protected by the Saints. Serene in their grasp of Mormon faith, the historians could busy themselves marshaling evidence to defend the integrity of the people. More often, they simply chronicled the story of the amazing formation, trek, colonization, and expansion of a people—subjects that have to stir the hearts of either insiders or outsiders who have a musical ear for human drama.

Someday the crisis had to come. Few others of the 20,870 separate denominations listed in the most recent encyclopedia of Christianity have as much at stake so far as "historicness" is concerned as do Mormons. The character of their shaping events takes on a different nature in that these occurred so recently, on familiar soil, in check-outable times and places, *after* historical "science" had become developed. The shaping events of classic Christianity, whose story Mormons share, are accessible almost entirely through insider Christian sources alone. The Romans ignored them. Mormon events, meanwhile, occur inside a history chronicled by small town newspaper editors, diarists, hostile letter writers, contemporary historians. The beginnings are not so shrouded in obscurity as are Christian beginnings that were recorded especially in the New Testament. People now alive in their nineties who talked as little children to people then in their eighties have "memories" that link them to the years of Mormon beginnings. There is no place to hide. What can be sequestered in Mormon archives and put beyond the range of historians can often be approached by sources outside them. While Mormon iconography developed impressively early in its history, the images of Mormon beginnings are not yet haloed or sanctioned the way Christian beginnings are by their reflection in stained glass, their inspiration in centuries of classical music. There is little protection for Mormon sacredness.

Whoever knows how Christian faith survives and can survive knowledge of all the evidence of fallibility and scandal that occurred through history will understand why the outsider historian finds trivial the question of whether the faith is threatened by the revelation of human shortcomings in the later administration of the Mormon churches. Of course, for public relations reasons, one likes to portray one's heroes and Saints as saints. Lives of quality and character and policies of justice and fairness enhance one's identification with them and the people at large. Yet intellectually, these are not of much interest. One can cut through all the peripheral issues and see that most of the writing on Mormon history that poses the issue of the crisis of historical consciousness focuses finally on Joseph Smith's First Vision, often capitalized to set it apart, and then, many agree, most importantly on the later vision that led to a second capitalization, the Book of Mormon.

Let me clear the air with a stark, almost crude, but still lighthearted and well-intended analogy.

* * *

When Cardinal de Polignac told Madame du Deffand that the martyr St. Denis, the first Bishop of Paris, had walked a hundred miles carrying his head in his hand, Madame du Deffand correctly observed, "In such a promenade it is the first step that is difficult."[6]

By analogy, if the beginning of the promenade of Mormon history, the First Vision and the Book of Mormon, can survive the crisis, then the rest of the promenade follows, and nothing that happens in it can really detract from the miracle of the whole. If the first steps do not survive, there can be only antiquarian—not fateful or faith-full—interest in the rest of the story.

When the historical crisis comes it can, of course, be addressed by fiat. Authority can invoke authority and silence the questioning, suppress curiosity, rule inquiry out of bounds, close off the sources, purge the questioners. Now and then rumors and reports of policies somewhere in this range of "heteronomy," to use Paul Tillich's term, reach the ears of Gentiles. If these occur, ecclesiastically, they are "none of our business." Intellectually, professionally, and personally, of course, one cares and feels sympathy for Mormon historians, who are believers and belongers through "secondary naivete" or "after criticism" or "through interpretation." At the very least, one will also hear the whisper of those driven away or silenced: *eppur si muove.* Galileo kept integrity by murmuring such a truth after authority forced him to recant, to say that against all evidence the world did *not* move. "And yet it moves!"

Suppressed historians may busy themselves trying to comprehend the integrity of those who guard the tradition, eager as these are to protect the faith of Mormons who live in "primitive naivete." Yet historians can be understandably frustrated if they feel that their gift, which would help people pass to another, secondary, mode of being and believing, is a priori denied. Still, this is a matter of internal ecclesiastical concern, and it would come with bad grace for a guest to intervene or pursue the matter much beyond the point of observation.

It *does* belong to the historian's vocation, however, to say that alongside the unreflective faith of Christian believers who have not come to the crisis of historical consciousness there are reflective, historically conscious people who do believe. There may be something of worth in their history, a history of great complexity, that might serve Mormons through analogy and precedent. There can be more than one kind of integrity in faith and peoplehood.

Focusing the Mormon Crisis Issues

Having dismissed as secondary, late stages in the promenade, both what we might call "political embarrassments" and "borderline religious issues" (such as the role of Masonry, the development and demise of polygamy), we can concentrate on what I will call the *generative* issues. They come down to what historians of religion call "theophany," the appearance of gods or godlike figures, and "revelation," the disclosure from one order of being and reality to another. The First Vision belongs to the category of theophany, the Book of Mormon to revelation.

The four accounts of the First Vision do not quite match, a fact no less and no more interesting than that details in the four Christian Gospels do not always match. What matters is the event, which is accessible only through these traces. It is hard to read Mormon history as I have for twenty years without coming to agree with Neal E. Lambert and Richard H. Cracroft that this First Vision is "that pivotal event which is so central to the message of Mormonism that belief therein has become a touchstone of faith for the orthodox Mormon and Mormon convert." James B. Allen says that it is "second only to belief in the divinity of Jesus of Nazareth," because "Next to the resurrection of Christ, nothing holds a more central place in modern Mormon thought than that sacred event of 1820."[7] Reflective Mormons have to cross Lessing's "ugly ditch" as they face up to such events.

Second, and more urgently, the vision of 1823, the story of golden plates and seer stones and the text translated and published as the Book of Mormon, is both theophany and revelation. While the book may go unread by many Mormons—it always surprises Gentiles to see how little awareness of much of its content there is among their Mormon neighbors—it is the event itself, the whole generative shape of the discovery, translation, and publication, that has made up a single base for Mormon history. When historians call into question both the process and the product, they come to or stand on holy ground. Not all Mormon historians devote their energies to these generative events, just as I as a historian of twentieth-century Christianity do not have to do research on the resurrection of Jesus: "It's not my period." Yet the basis for faith and concerns for events that follow are at stake when professional colleagues converge on these focal issues.

Understanding the Mormon Issues

After 150 years, when historians inside or outside the Mormon community focus on the generative events, it has become conventional to see them as concentrating on a direct, simple question. It is all supposed to come down to "Was Joseph Smith a prophet or a fraud?" To say "prophet" made one a Saint, for how could one then stay away from the history and people that issue from these events? To say "fraud" is precisely what made one leave Mormonism or never convert in the first place. That was that.

Then, two things happened. Many non-Mormon historians bracketed that question. Seeing 4 million and more people shaped by Smith's theophany and revelational vision, people who, in many cases, were as intelligent and "modern" as they, the historians asked a new range of questions. If they would get hung up on the prophet/fraud dialectic, however much it may have nagged or tantalized them, they could not get to another range of questions. What sort of people are these people? What sort of faith is this faith? What sort of prophet with what sort of theophany and revelation was Joseph Smith? His consciousness, his "myth," and his effect could be pursued if one refused to be tyrannized by the literal stark prophet/fraud polarity in the question.

Meanwhile, Saints' historians asked more radical questions than before. They had to move through history and interpretation toward a "second naivete" that made possible transformed belief and persistent identification with the people. They brought new instruments to their inquiry into Mormon origins; shortly I shall detail what strike me as the three main approaches used by outsiders and insiders alike.

For now, a very obvious and important point needs to be made. According to the norms and approaches of the historical profession, the "ground rules" accepted by historians, it would be impossible to prove that Smith was a prophet. As Renier reminds us, past events are, as events, wholly lost to us. We have only traces, testimonies, texts. As historians, we cannot get behind those testimonies to the New York hills where the visions occurred, and we cannot regress in time. There is no way in which empirical evidence can produce for our verification the "two personages" or the later angel of the visions. If by some now-inconceivable time machine device we could be there, we might be duly impressed that *something* was happening beyond the ordinary. But in 1820 and 1823, as in 1983, we would be suspicious of visions—and Smith called them that—because they can be contrived, can elude ordinary analysis without themselves being extraordinary. We can see some things more remarkable on television or on stage any day of a week, yet these do not inspire the response of faith.

Conversely, of course, historians may find it possible to prove to their own satisfaction that Smith was a fraud. This is hard to do with the First Vision, if we grant that somewhat different accountings of detail on four occasions are no more challenges to its integrity than are the four Gospel accounts to the Gospel event. It could be easier to do, and many have done so to their own and others' satisfaction, with respect to the Book of Mormon, so far as both its external circumstances and internal character are concerned. Yet this proving of fraudulence has not been compelling—not "proof"—to millions of Saints, who do not really lie abed in suspense lest the next discovery or assault achieve what the first eight-score years of attack could not achieve. For our purposes it is more important to note that the issue of fraud, hoax, or charlatanry simply need not, does not, preoccupy the historical profession most of the time.

It is not necessary here to detail fully two of the three approaches to questions beyond the prophet/fraud issue addressed to generative Mormon events. I need only cite them and point to major statements of the issue. The first family has been familiarly summarized in Klaus Hansen's *Mormonism and the American Experience*. We might call the studies summarized and enlarged upon there "consciousness" studies, contributions to the question of the consciousness of a modern prophet. After reference to social and environmental contexts and explanations, Hansen moves to the consciousness sphere.

Quoting Jan Shipps, Hansen develops first "the analogy of musical genius," and then, more speculatively, Julian Jaynes's hypotheses about consciousness as it relates to hemispheres of the brain. Other "possible explanatory frameworks for getting a handle on Smith's revelations" include non-Mormon T. L. Brink's summaries of four alternatives derived from "depth psychology." On their basis, Brink can assume that Joseph Smith "was a man who was of sound mind and sincere religious convictions." Sigmund Freud, more plausibly C. G. Jung, and then Alfred Adler and Erik Erikson are called as witnesses to make plausible the prophethood and throw light on prophetic character.[8]

Emphatically, in my understanding of the historical approach, none of these produce proof that Smith was a prophet or fraud. Instead, they make possible a different level of urgent inquiry, make plausible the concepts of Smith's "soundness" and "sincerity." I should add that Larry Foster has developed his own approaches to prophetic consciousness, approaches that have made it possible for him sometimes to speak up more emphatically for Smith than many Mormons can or do.[9] These scholars show that one can use psychological instruments to illumine without falling into a reductionism that would insist that Smith was "nothing but" an exemplar of this or that stage of adolescent psychology, or whatever.

The second address to the crisis of Mormon historical consciousness comes from a cluster of scholars whose work is focused in and summarized by another non-Mormon, Jan Shipps. Aware as is Hansen from within that the issue of prophet/fraud is in many ways a question of faith that can be illumined by but not proven by historical inquiry, Shipps employs still another discipline for her work, *Religionsgeschichte,* which in America is usually translated as "History of Religion." ("History" here is not the same as ordinary "history of religions" but implies a somewhat different set of methods and has far less interest in narrative. It may be more taken with synchrony than diachrony, with structure than with happening.)

For Shipps's purposes, to begin with the First Vision casts the questions in an inappropriate light; the Book of Mormon here (as in Foster's work) is determinative. With the Book of Mormon the public career of the prophet began, and here it becomes accessible to the historian. Shipps is interested explicitly in shifting the focus from prophet/fraud questions to the notion that Smith's story is "best understood in the context of his sequential assumption of positions/roles that allowed the Saints to recover a usable past." That was his *religious* function and achievement. She can go on to say that when one sees how this endeavor legitimated the prophetic task, "the question of whether Smith was prophet or fraud is not particularly important."[10]

The sixth chapter, "In and Out of Time," of Shipps's book will suggest the promise of the History of Religion approaches for ordinary historians.[11] The sacred and non-sacred, wrote Mircea Eliade, are "different modes of being in the world." Historians using their ordinary canons have to be aware of this difference. They must be aware that the original Mormons saw their prophet and themselves stepping outside ordinary time and space, beyond the reach of conventional critical criteria. Temporally, they wanted to live "once again at the beginning, *in illo tempore,*" the kind of time that lies beyond empirical evidence.

Guilford Dudley has written that "the mystic time of beginnings is sacred by definition." The experience on the hill in New York or, for Shipps more important, the Mormon entry into the Promised Land was "entry into sacred space" *and* sacred time. This did not mean that the Mormons ever were anything but practical people; they were not insubstantial or otherworldly. Yet their special kind of millennialism removed many of their claims beyond the realm of the mundane and practical and has served to provide extraordinary interpretations for the life of the people. Mundane Mormons even today "possess the means of reentering sacred time and space" in their temples and special times. These help endow their peoplehood with value and guarantee that the mythic dimensions of their history, which remain beyond the range of historians' destruction, also become a part of their historical constructions. Shipps shows how creative it is to ask other than the prophet/fraud question of Smith and the Book.

A third approach, not yet fully developed but rich in promise, is the hermeneutical. This version of "interpretation theory" helps Mormon intellectuals make the passage from primitive to secondary naivete, or from belief before criticism to belief through criticism and interpretation. It also helps both Mormons and non-Mormons in the historical profession understand each other and do some justice to the generative events without being mired in the prophet/fraud polarity or posing. I will close with some references to it.

The Interpretive Enterprise and Its Promise

I propose a hermeneutical approach to the problem of Mormon texts. By texts I mean both those that impart Joseph Smith's visions and the Book of Mormon itself. Contemporary hermeneutics, the focus of so much philosophical passion today, can be treated extremely technically, in ways that would seem alien to most historians. Yet the subject has on occasion been rather simply introduced, and I shall depend upon a summary by a noted literary critic, E. D. Hirsch, to outline it.[12]

Hermeneutics, he points out, is associated with Hermes, the divine messenger between the gods and men. (The parallel name is *Interpres,* from which we get "interpretation.") God's hidden message needs such a conveyor to ordinary people. In 1927, Martin Heidegger, in *Sein und Zeit,* borrowed a term from hermeneutics, *Vorverständnis,* or "preunderstanding," to launch the modern debate. He showed that unprejudiced, objective knowledge was not possible. All knowledge is bound in part by "preknowing" that is determined by our historical, social, and personal backgrounds. Such preknowing, for example, determines in large measure what attitudes we have toward and what we derive from Islamic, Marxist, Christian, or Mormon texts.

"Pre-understanding," to step back further, derives from Wilhelm Dilthey (1833–1911), who showed how understanding of a text is a circular process. As a non-Mormon, I can discuss the Book of Mormon in such terms.

> First, we encounter words and clauses which have no distinct meaning until we know how they function in the text as a whole. But since we can only know the whole meaning through the various parts of the text, and since we cannot know before what the parts mean or how they work together before we know the whole text, we find ourselves in a logical puzzle, a circularity. This is the famous "hermeneutical circle." It can be broken only by resolving the question of which came first, the chicken or the egg, the whole or the part. By general agreement, from which there has been virtually no dissent, the question of priority is decided in favor of the whole. The whole must be known in some fashion before we know the part. For how can I know that I am seeing a nose unless I first know that I am seeing a face? And from the doctrine of the priority of the whole came the doctrine of pre-understanding. Since we must know the whole before the part, we must assume some kind of pre-understanding in all interpretation.[13]

Muslim children come to Muslim texts and Mormon children come to Mormon texts with preunderstandings that allow them to grasp the whole before they take apart the parts. These preunderstandings, no doubt often creatively, bias their understandings of the whole and the parts. Those who stand outside the circle have great difficulty sharing the understandings that come from the preunderstandings, though, of course, there can be and are conversions that bring illuminations of texts "from within," as it were.

Fortunately, for our purposes, philosophers Jean Nabert and Paul Ricoeur have developed the theme of a "hermeneutics . . . of testimony."[14] The philosophy of testimony evokes an enormous paradox. Nabert in *L'Essai sur le mal* asks, in the spirit of Lessing, "Does one have the right to invest with an absolute character a moment of history?" This must be addressed. Now, testimony begins with a "quasi-empirical meaning"; it "designates the action of testifying, that is, of relating what one has seen or heard." Then comes the sort of transfer on which all Mormon faith depends: "there is the one who testifies and the one who hears the testimony. The witness has seen, but the one who receives his testimony has not seen but hears," and it is in this hearing that faith or unfaith is decided. The statement and the story constitute "information on the basis of which one forms an opinion about a sequence of events, the connection of an action, the motives for the act, the character of the person, in short on the meaning of what has happened."

When, asks Ricoeur, do we give testimony and listen to it? It occurs in a form of discourse called "the trial," which, whether they have noticed it or not, defenders and attackers of Joseph Smith so regularly establish. "Hence the question: what is a true witness, a faithful witness?" Ricoeur connects witness with the Greek word *martus;* the witness is linked with the martyr. "A man becomes a martyr because he is first a witness. . . . It is necessary, then, that the just die." And "the witness is the man who is identified with the just cause which the crowd and the great hate and who, for this just cause, risks his life." Thus "Testimony is the action . . . as it attests outside of himself, to the interior man, to his conviction, to his faith."

This is the point at which the religious meaning of testimony is most clear. Historical faith connects what one "testifies *for*"—a meaning—with the notion that he is testifying *that* something has happened—which signifies this meaning. There is tension between confession of faith and narration of things seen, but it is this tension that means that faith is dependent upon testimony, not sight, not "proof."

Mormons are people who, though aware of many historical ambiguities in the record and fallibilities in the Prophet Joseph Smith, also see in his character, vocation, career, and witnessing—finally, martyrdom—a credentialing that leads them to connect confession of faith with "something that has happened."

We have connected Jean Nabert and Paul Ricoeur with the hermeneutics of being the testifier, the witness. When one deals with the text of the Book of Mormon, the issue now becomes the hermeneutics of testimony. Ricoeur asks, "do we have the right to invest a moment of history with an absolute character? One needs a hermeneutics, a philosophy of interpretation." Here Nabert remarks that "consciousness makes itself judge of the divine and consequently chooses its God or its gods." Testimony gives something to interpretation, but it also demands to be interpreted. There is the story of an event and a demand for decision, a choice that the testimony functions to awaken faith in the truth. "The judge in a court makes up his mind about things seen only by hearing [them] said."

It is interesting to this Gentile to notice that the Book of Mormon is not widely read in the Church. People come to faith because living witnesses base their speaking and way of life on what they have read and "heard" there—and a new generation of children or converts comes to faith by "hearing." None of them sees golden plates to authenticate this faith. There is "no manifestation of the absolute without the crisis of false testimony, with the decision which distinguished between sign and idol." The Mormon believer and the non-Mormon rejecter are on the same terms, so far as material traces of actual past events are concerned.

Nabert speaks of this norm for judging the divine as "the expression of the greatest effort that consciousness can make in order to take away the conditions which prevent it from attaining complete satisfaction." Faith is not absolute knowledge of an event that is forever lost except through testimony. Here is the break between "reason and faith, . . . philosophy and religion." And "this is what signifies the 'trial,' the 'crisis' of testimony." We must "choose between philosophy of absolute knowledge and the hermeneutics of testimony." The enforcer of orthodoxy who limits the inquiry of the historian wants history to do what a "philosophy of absolute knowledge" would do. The historian, to whom past events are lost and for whom only traces in testimony remain, lives with "the hermeneutics of testimony" which is, in the end, at the basis of all faith.

I must add a word on how a text such as the Book of Mormon ministers in the tension and authenticates itself as testimony. To summarize almost to the point of cliché a very complicated set of developments in "interpretation theory," let us say that one moves through and beyond both historical and literary criticism to the interpretive level. That is, one wants to understand "the world behind the text," the world of Joseph Smith and the events described in the Book of Mormon. Yet having learned all that can be learned is not what either brings about or destroys faith. Second, one can use literary tools to understand the world "of the text." What is its genre or form? Yet here, too, is not the birth or death of faith. Instead one deals with "the world in front of the text," for here testimony forces its challenge.

Not was Joseph Smith a prophet or a fraud, but does the Book of Mormon connect confession and event in such a way that it discloses possible modes of being or thinking or behaving that the reader or, better, the listener (to a contemporary witness based on it) must entertain the risk of acceptance or rejection of the testimony? That is where faith or unfaith is born. David Tracy, employing an insight from Hans-Georg Gadamer, says that here is "the fusion of horizons": "the reader overcomes the strangeness of another horizon not by empathizing with the psychic state or cultural situation of the author but rather by understanding the basic vision of the author implied by the text and the mode-of-being-in-the-world referred to by the text."[15] One is henceforth freed from the burdens of "psychologizing" and is less burdened by concern over the exact reference to literal historical events.

Are there analogies in "ordinary Christians'" approaches to the issues of trace or testimony and event in respect to the resurrection of Jesus? How far do historical inquiry and doubt go, and where must one make that leap "from trace to event" that is at the basis of narrative and, in some respects, of faith itself?

In a conservative Protestant survey, evangelical biblical scholar Daniel Fuller set forth a typology that began with "attempts to sustain knowledge of the Resurrection apart from historical reasoning," and then "partially from historical reasoning." Of greatest interest to Fuller is a third category, German theologian Wolfhart Pannenberg's "attempt to sustain knowledge of the resurrection wholly by historical reason."[16]

Fuller's choice of Pannenberg was fortunate, because Pannenberg is an extremely formidable and sophisticated theologian, not someone to whom the term "fundamentalist" could be applied in any pejorative sense. "[T]rue faith is first awakened through an impartial observation of these events." Revelation is mediated only by history because "the events of history speak their own language, the language of the events, [and] this language can only be heard in the world of ideas of the people in which these events occurred."[17]

Pannenberg moves, then, from universal history to the testimony of the first witnesses and then and thus jumps to the events that presumably lie behind it. Fuller paraphrases this leap on the basis of a lecture by Pannenberg:

[W]hile there is much in the resurrection reports that is mythical, yet it is impossible to explain them wholly as the work of the apostles' imagination. The apostles were too discouraged after the death of Jesus to have talked themselves into believing that Jesus was risen. The only satisfactory explanation for their sudden faith was that Jesus appeared to them. Furthermore, the early Christian community could not have survived if the tomb of Jesus had not been empty. An occupied tomb would not only have destroyed their faith, but it would have given the Jewish polemic against the church an invincible weapon. Hence it is impossible to charge off the Biblical reports of the resurrection wholly to the imagination, and, consequently, [we may arrive at] an historical verification of the resurrection.[18]

Many critics have pointed out that Pannenberg as philosopher of history makes claims that no ordinary detective-historian would be content with. One body snatcher could have emptied the tomb. So Pannenberg does not have "material" evidence but only oral-and-then-written "testimony."

Fuller judges that "Pannenberg has provided some insights into how it is possible for historical reason to bridge Lessing's ugly ditch and therefore find a complete basis for faith in history."[19] However, there are at least two difficulties. Pannenberg's mode of reasoning to get to a basis for faith in history is extremely complex and abstruse. It is grounded in philosophies that many believers would find alien. Therefore, "only those can have an immediate knowledge of revelation who are trained historians." Or, only those can have faith who tend to be dependent upon sophisticated historians. For him, "there should be no talk of supernaturalism, which is unacceptable for the critically oriented reason of the historian, because it arbitrarily cuts off historical investigation of immanental causes and analogies through the assertion of a transcendental intervention."[20]

Fuller chooses to see the basis of faith better outlined by an earlier historian—the author of Luke and Acts. He contrasts how faith is born in the light of Luke's testimony or that of the early Christians about whom he writes:

> Pannenberg, it will be remembered, wants to make faith the possibility for all men by having what is, virtually, a priesthood of historians. Theology's task, as he sees it, is to assert the credibility of the Christian proclamation, so that laymen can believe it because of the authority that the theologian, with special historical skills, can provide. It does not seem, however, that Luke, who finds the basis for revelational knowledge in history, makes historical reasoning the exclusive way to such knowledge. Acts 11:24 is a passage of particular interest in this connection because it tells how a number of people came to believe on the basis of the moral impact of the minister, rather than by accepting his authority or by employing historical reasoning to get back to the truth of the resurrection. "[Barnabas] was a good man, full of the Holy Spirit and of faith. And [as a result] a large company was added to the Lord."[21]

So with Paul. The argument for the resurrection is made as a result of Paul's change in conduct:

> Thus it is understandable how Luke could have stressed that the faith of the apostles and of a Theophilus must come through a reasoning based on infallible proofs, and yet declare that many believed as Barnabas preached, for Barnabas was himself an infallible proof of his message. . . . faith is possible for every man who is confronted with a Barnabas, for everyone who is rational is capable of seeing the infallible proof represented by such a man. Such a system of thought does keep Christianity as an historical religion, rather than one whose knowledge is immediately accessible to all. . . . But such a system does not make all men dependent upon a priesthood of theologians who can follow historical reasoning to know that Jesus rose from the dead.[22]

The claim, then, is simple, bold, and emphatic: the historical craft never allows us to revisit *any events* except in and through and insofar as traces are satisfying. The empty tomb is not convincingly recoverable today to provide a basis for faith in the resurrection. The texts repeating the testimony of Paul, Barnabas, and other early witnesses and those dependent upon witness are all that Christians have—and that is enough. These texts disclose meanings and offer possible modes of thinking and being for those to whom faith in the resurrection and its fruits would otherwise not occur. So with Mormon texts, the testimony of Smith and witnesses.

Conclusion

How frustrating all this must be to someone who wants to prove Smith a prophet or a fraud, or to make the issue the only one to interest insider or outsider historians! We have argued that it is impossible for historians as historians to prove that Smith was a prophet and improbable that they will prove him a fraud. Instead, they seek to understand. That is a modest but still important task in the communities of both faith and inquiry. Similarly, historians cannot prove that the Book of Mormon was translated from golden plates and have not proven that it was simply a fiction of Joseph Smith. Instead, they seek to understand its revelatory appeal, the claims it makes, and why it discloses modes of being and of believing that millions of Saints would otherwise not entertain.

If what I have outlined makes any sense at all, it might be a contribution to a lowering of suspicions of historians by Mormon guardians. At the same time it does not try to pretend away the depth of the crisis of historical consciousness for history-based Mormondom. The motive for this all is not to commend Mormon history to the secular academy, as if the Mormon historians had to be driven by a push for relevance and respectability. The secular academy that despises Mormonism also has to despise Islam, Catholicism, and Protestantism—all of which make theophanic and revelational claims similar to those of Mormonism. Yet Islamic, Catholic, and Protestant historians have found means of pursuing their work and displaying their integrity.

There are many kinds of integrity. Some of these are appropriate to insiders and others to outsiders, some to church authorities and some to historians, some to those with "primitive naivete" and others to those who live in "second naivete." Confusing these integrities is almost as destructive to them as is dismissing those sorts that are appropriate to other people in other callings. Discernment of them and empathy across the lines of the vocations of people who display them seem to be the most promising forms of address to the present crisis of historical consciousness.

Notes

1. I have kept footnoting to a minimum. It seems unnecessary, perhaps futile, and certainly imperial for me to take up more journal space than I already am doing by cit-

ing the scores if not hundreds of articles in the *Journal of Mormon History, Dialogue, Sunstone,* and elsewhere, devoted to the historical debate. I assume the present readership's familiarity with its main features or can by mentioning these journals direct new readers to the scene. Some of the debate is of a polemical character directed at people such as Klaus Hansen, Marvin Hill, Jan Shipps, Larry Foster, and other historians from whom I have gained so much of my understanding of Mormon history. I myself have been the subject of some criticism. To cite it would be a temptation to turn or give the appearance of turning this lecture into a response to criticism or, worse, an ad hominem counterattack. Were that to happen, the whole effort would be misread.

2. For the dependencies upon Renier, see G. J. Renier, *History: Its Purpose and Method* (Boston: Beacon Press, 1950), chap. 1 (for the social or collective character of history and its story character), and chap. 2 (for "events and traces"). See also p. 14 on "stopping to think."

3. On "primitive" and "second" naivete, see Paul Ricoeur, *The Symbolism of Evil* (New York: Harper & Row, 1967), 351–52: "For the second immediacy that we seek and the second naivete that we await are no longer accessible to us anywhere else than in a hermeneutics; we can believe only by interpreting. It is the 'modern' mode of belief in symbols, an expression of the distress of modernity and a remedy for that distress. . . . This second naivete aims to be the postcritical equivalent of the precritical hierophany." Again: "If we can no longer live the great symbolisms of the sacred in accordance with the original belief in them, we can, we modern men, aim at a second naivete in and through criticism. In short, it is by interpreting that we can *hear* again" (351–52).

4. Quoted in Daniel P. Fuller, *Easter Faith and History* (Grand Rapids, Mich.: William B. Eerdmans, 1965), 33–35.

5. Morley, Meinecke, and Troeltsch are quoted in Franklin L. Baumer, *Religion and the Rise of Scepticism* (New York: Harcourt, Brace, 1960), 156–58.

6. Paul Elmen, *The Restoration of Meaning to Contemporary Life* (Garden City, N.Y.: Doubleday, 1958), 189.

7. Neal E. Lambert and Richard H. Cracroft, "Literary Form and Historical Understanding: Joseph Smith's First Vision in Mormon Religious Thought," *Journal of Mormon History* 7 (1980): 31; and James B. Allen, "Emergence of a Fundamental: The Expanding Role of Joseph Smith's First Vision in Mormon Religious Thought," *Journal of Mormon History* 7 (1980): 43.

8. Klaus J. Hansen, *Mormonism and the American Experience* (Chicago: University of Chicago Press, 1981), 15–27.

9. Lawrence Foster, *Religion and Sexuality: Three American Communal Experiments of the Nineteenth Century* (New York: Oxford University Press, 1981), 128–30, and elsewhere in Foster's writings.

10. Jan Shipps, *Mormonism: The Story of a New Religious Tradition* (Urbana: University of Illinois Press, 1984), 38–39.

11. Shipps, *Mormonism,* 109–29.

12. E. D. Hirsch Jr., "Carnal Knowledge," *New York Review of Books,* 14 June 1979, 18–20.

13. Ibid., 18.

14. Paul Ricoeur, "The Hermeneutics of Testimony," in *Essays on Biblical Interpretation* (Philadelphia: Fortress Press, 1980), 119–54 passim.

15. David Tracy, *Blessed Rage for Order: The New Pluralism in Theology* (New York: Seabury, 1975), 72–79, esp. 78.

16. Fuller, *Easter Faith and History*, 177.
17. Ibid., 182–83.
18. Ibid., 181–82.
19. Ibid., 187.
20. Ibid., 186.
21. Ibid., 237–38.
22. Ibid., 240–41.

CHAPTER 21

Historical Theology and Theological History: Mormon Possibilities

Edwin Gaustad

Some years ago when I was invited to address a Mormon theological confer-ence, I spent a good deal of time talking about history. Today, having been invited to address the Mormon History Association (MHA), it perhaps will not surprise you that I choose to give some attention to theology. This perversity on my part I am able to attribute to original sin. Since you may not find that doc-trine fully persuasive, I leave you wholly free to find other excuses for the bizarre behavior of academics.

Allow me also a preliminary word of appreciation, and perhaps of wonder as well, for your charity and your daring in inviting the Outsider to come Inside, not merely to observe and learn, but even to speak and to declare with assurance in areas where you have spent your lives.[1] I do not believe that in behaving so generously you run the risk of having your faith undermined. I do fear, however, the real risk of having your intelligence insulted. For the Outsider is in danger of announcing some startling new insight that will only remind you of a dozen or so articles delicately nuancing that theme, of the three conferences given over to that very subject, of the brilliant doctoral dissertation that settled the issue en-tirely and definitively—ten years ago! It is a fearful thing to fall into the hands of the *informed* and angry Saint. This audience knows the Mormon past extra-ordinarily well; indeed, you set an example to most other religious groups in America who, by and large, can only come up with the name of an eponymous hero or two, a few facts concerning him or her, and but little sense of how today's church arrived at where and what it is now from where and what it was then. I cannot offhand suggest the name of any other religious group in Amer-ica where so large a segment of the membership knows so much about so few: that first generation of larger-than-life believers.

So instead of adding to that storehouse (if indeed I could), I choose rather to invite reflections about the LDS past, about the encounters between faith and history that can turn out to be either destructive or creative. I wish to talk with you about *meaning*, with the clear implication that only then are we really talking about *history*. Together, we can explore some possibilities, always acknowledging that possibilities are inevitably haunted by the risk of failure, by the loss resulting from options not seized, by the tragedy arising from cheaper or even tawdry alternatives chosen.

Historical Theology

Many a divinity school curriculum draws distinctions between biblical theology, systematic theology, and historical theology—along with such recent variations as black or feminist or liberation theology. Historical theology is that mode of thinking about God that reflects the changing understandings over time. In this discipline, history is taken seriously; the development in religious ideas and institutions is faced openly; the richness that comes from varied perspectives is acknowledged gladly. Most Christian theologians, however arranged denominationally, resist a study of theology that refuses to budge beyond the first century of the Christian era. No Justin Martyrs or Cyprians, no Clement of Alexandria or Origen, no Athanasius or Nicene Creed, no Augustine or *City of God*—the very notion is absurd. Historical theology, in some traditions more self-consciously than in others, is built in.

In the Church of Jesus Christ of Latter-day Saints, it may be a bit more difficult to see how it is or should be built in. The LDS history, the extracanonical history at any rate, seems so brief, so recent, a mere century and a half. How can one expect to build a discipline of historical theology in only a dozen or so decades? Such an effort might even seem pretentious, overly ambitious. On the other hand, there are those who expect great things of the very young, often impossible things. One can destroy a child's confidence by keeping expectations unrealistically high; hope is shattered; resentment and withdrawal may result. The young American nation, intimidated by the longer, richer histories of European nations, endured the insults of those who demanded too much too soon. In 1820 in the pages of the *Edinburgh Review*, the Reverend Sydney Smith maliciously inquired: "In the four quarters of the globe, who reads an American book? or goes to an American play? or looks at an American picture or statue? What does the world yet owe to American physicians or surgeons? . . . What new substances have their chemists discovered? What new constellations have been discovered by [their] telescopes?"[2] Smith didn't really expect answers to his questions: to ask was enough. To ask the question was to make the charge: a nation uncivilized, barbaric, unlearned, unpromising, God-forsaken.

A similar series of ill-tempered questions could be put to institutional Mormonism: in the four quarters of the globe, who reads a Mormon book? or goes to a Mormon play? or looks at a Mormon picture or statue? Now I know that those questions do have answers—as they did for America in 1820—but that is beside the point. Such questions do not seek answers any more than did those of Sydney Smith. A nation still hacking its way across a wilderness was not yet in position to produce its Mozart or Rembrandt; a church still overcoming geographical separation and cultural insulation may not quite be in a position to assume its pathbreaking role in intellectual and artistic leadership. Quite beyond that, however, Smith's questions and those similar to it are grossly unfair, for they assume that every nation in every generation produces a great flowering of geniuses, that every church at any moment is peopled with a multitude of cultural giants. Such we know is simply not the case.

So with respect to historical theology and the LDS Church, one easy choice (although it is really a nonchoice) is merely to wait: to wait for that Augustine or Calvin or Tillich or whoever can move theological understanding from its nineteenth-century provenance into a later and larger world of thought and culture. But that nonchoice rates passivity higher than activity, elevates the law of inertia way above the power of men and women to shape their lives and enlarge their vision.

Beside the alternative marked "Wait" is another marked "Don't Wait." Two options here with respect to historical theology present themselves. The first is to seize that 150 years of the Mormon past with all its historical vibrancy and movement, seeing it as an amply stocked storehouse for much vibrancy and movement in theology. Mormon history from 1830 to 1980 is about as unstatic as one can find anywhere in the modern world. Mormon theology from 1830 to 1980 has every reason, every opportunity to be equally unstatic: lively, responsive, adaptive, creative—always in continuity, to be sure, with that which has gone before. If one asks whether the church of the 1980s is the same as the church of the 1830s, the answer must be a profound and thoughtful "yes"— immediately followed by a profound and thoughtful "no." No one assumes this church or any other church to be frozen in time and space, nor does anyone assume that this church or any other church begins each day anew. Similarly, in historical theology no one assumes that Augustine, for example, failed to absorb, reflect upon, respond to the tumult and the anti-Christian slander of his own time. Neither does one assume, however, that the Bishop of Hippo turned away from the preceding 400 years, or that he did not struggle with utmost sincerity, with passionate ferocity, to be wholly true to the "faith once delivered unto the saints."

The early Christian church, part of an empire far larger and far unfriendlier than that confronting the followers of Joseph Smith, could easily have been seduced into a retreat from all history, into a paralysis of all theology. Jesus was misunderstood, then killed; many of that generation of leadership were also silenced, exiled, exterminated; schism and separation and recrimination began early and continued late; from Nero's madness to Diocletian's deadly efficiency, hundreds, then thousands, lost property, title, life. Hardly a time for theological exploration, one would conclude, but more a time for hunkering down, for digging in deeper, building the walls higher, for closing one's mind to Greek ideas or Roman philosophers or the latest cultural currents. And yet, as we know, that is hardly the story of those first 150 years of Christian history. Churchmen labored to show how Christian theology had broad areas of compatibility with Greek philosophy, how Jewish history and literature prepared for and contributed to Christian insights and understandings, how Roman law and order made possible a missionary expansion inconceivable a couple of centuries earlier, or a few centuries later.

Within those intellectual currents swirling about the early Christian church, one option concerned the proper stance of this young institution with respect to history. Some argued that this newest Jewish sect should renounce its Jewishness, cut itself off from its Hebraic origins and its ethnic coloration and its outmoded, maybe even embarrassing Sinaitic deity. If only the Christian cult would forget history, then Christ could, like Isis and Osiris, like Dionysius or Mithra, stand at the head of a truly universal, "academically respectable," "fully accredited" world religion. But this early church rejected this Gnostic temptation; it would not sell its birthright, it would not deny or dismiss its rude heritage. On the other hand, many others argued that this newest Jewish sect could survive only by holding to the shelter that Judaism provided; instead of forsaking the Torah, Christianity should intensify loyalty to it, allowing the very best Jews to enroll in a graduate seminar where a special loyalty to a particular rabbi could be discussed. "Survive through the security and familiarity of the safe harbor" was the advice; "avoid the dangers and temptations of uncharted seas" was the counsel. But the early church rejected this easy option as well. On the one hand, it would not forsake history; on the other hand, it would not be hobbled or hemmed in by history. One must embrace both particularity and universality. History gave the primitive church firm root in rich soil, but history's power to emancipate also gave it newness of life.

One can therefore do much with 150 years of ecclesiastical life, as one can with 150 years of national life. Consider the movement in American history from the presidency of George Washington to World War II, a span of a mere 150 years. In denominational growth, one can do far worse than follow the example of the early Church in (1) choosing to remember the past and (2) refusing to be circumscribed by that past. Of course, it must be granted that the early church also spent much time in ferreting out heresies and the heretics (it seemed determined to leave few for future generations to locate or define), in discouraging dissent and too much spiritual equality, in gradually substituting the soberness of authority for the enthusiasm of the spirit. So this history, like all others, offers us some rare gems to preserve and polish but also many rough rocks to be avoided or discarded. The central point of this swift and superficial review remains, however: the clear evidence that the early church was not impervious to history, that it was created in time and not out of time, that it was neither fixed nor frozen in changeless form. Rather, even this brief period of 150 years represents a significant unfolding, enlarging, evolving, enriching, historically conditioned understanding of God's wondrous ways being worked out in the complex affairs of men and of nations.

There is a second option under the category of "Don't Wait": to engage in some historical theology now. This is to move beyond the 150 years that Mormonism has chalked up so far into that larger realm heralded by the official title of this latter-day Church of Jesus Christ. This option involves taking great gulps of Christian history and Christian thought over twenty centuries in order to better appropriate, illuminate, elaborate (perhaps even to translate) the central doctrines of the Utah or the Missouri church. Just as we often place American history in the larger context of Western civilization or world history to gain perspective and a sense of proportion, so we, camping on our separate denominational sites, need some sense of the lay of all that land. We can locate ourselves better on a map or chart in this way, of course, but the gain is far more than that. We can now begin to walk with and think with the giants who have walked this way before, enlarging our sympathies, deepening our concerns, escaping our parochial limits.

A few years ago I was invited to a Seventh-day Adventist institution as outside examiner of a doctoral dissertation concerned with the doctrine of "sanctuary." This is a central doctrine in Adventist history, pertinent to the Second Coming of Christ, but more broadly pertinent to human hopes and human disappointments regarding God's hand in history. Adventism was fascinated with "sanctuary," while most of the rest of Christendom was seemingly oblivious or indifferent to that acute doctrinal issue. Yet a comprehensive historical theology would, I believe, help us to identify common concerns, concerns gathered under the term "sanctuary" for Adventists but gathered under such terms as "Incarnation" or "Kingdom of God" for many others. One discovers that a whole world of fellow-seekers, fellow-thinkers awaits.

Outsiders may regard LDS theology as so distinctive, exotic, or indigenous that finding theological pen pals across the centuries will turn out to be a futile, fruitless task. True, much is distinctive, much is unique. But a great many issues with which early and modern Mormons wrestle have been on the theological mat many, many times before: atonement, Christian perfection, election, progress, revelation, the purity of the church, eschatology—to name just a few. Mormons, like most other religious groups, often speak of theological "distinctives." And critics of Mormonism, like those of other religious groups, also tend to concentrate on "distinctives," though in a sharply contrasting tone of voice.

Baptists speak of their commitment to religious liberty and to the voluntary church, Methodists of their Wesleyan concern for perfection and therefore for social reform, Episcopalians of their moderate middle way and their liturgical attention to beauty and order, Churches of Christ of their fidelity to the New Testament in all matters of faith and order. And the list could easily go on. Now there is clearly nothing wrong with all this, just so long as the rhetoric of "distinctives" does not short-circuit every other intellectual wire, just so long as historical theology does not become only another excuse for narcissistic introspection. As we all know, a pardonable pride in uniqueness tends to collapse into an unpardonable surrender to self-righteous satisfaction. Then we come to the larger world and its "inferior" religions only through the reading of pamphlets and tracts entitled "The Errors of _____" or "Twenty Easy Arguments Against _____." In contrast, we know our own religious position chiefly through such titles as "The Truths of _____" or "Thirty Sure Evidences for _____." When I stand before a book rack filled with such material, I suddenly understand how Carrie Nation felt when she walked into a saloon.

The trick that we as religious historians are called upon to perform is to take the "distinctives," the particularity, the uniqueness, and demonstrate how it relates to or sheds light upon the universality, the commonality, the human condition. Your life "shall be bound in the bundle of the living," wrote the author of one of the most particularistic, historically conditioned books of the Bible (1 Sam. 25:29). And the reason that it remains something of a neat trick to carry believers from the particular to the universal is that some artistry is required, some skill, some professionalism. Most of us can get from a discussion of our particular mothers to a consideration of the nature of motherhood in general without feeling threatened and without feeling any disloyalty to the one who brought us into this world. In a discussion of our own religious heritage, however, it is harder to move to a reflection on the religious quest in general without some anxiety, some queasiness regarding our loyalty. Yet historical theology should assist us in this regard, enlarging our sympathetic understanding so that we can multiply the number of those whom we are prepared to call "brother" and "sister."

Such thoughts as these may seem slightly mistargeted when aimed at historians. But as you all well know, historians in the LDS Church (and in the MHA) are in a position to play a unique role. You are *the* scholarly profession within the church; this alone is enough to guarantee you a vulnerable position on the firing line (being fired at, more than firing). In no other denomination in American religious life do the *historians* occupy so central, so sensitive, so potentially significant a place. You do not have to compete with an array of systematic theologians or canonized philosophers; you do not have to sit at the feet of countless biblical scholars and literary critics; you, most of all, do not have to pay respects to (or at least steer clear of) hundreds of anti-intellectual, power-grabbing, pulpit-pounding preachers. What advantages you enjoy!

On the other hand, what burdens you bear! For the ancient, unending battle between faith and reason becomes in this fellowship largely a struggle between faith and history: that is, the canons of revelation and authority versus the canons of scholarship and public truth. By "public truth," I mean only a truth that is accessible to all, not esoteric, not hidden or privileged. The pressure point within Mormonism is more history than, say, biology or astronomy or philosophy, for at least two fairly obvious reasons: (1) Mormon history is recent and therefore more sensitive—it still has some flavor of "let it all remain within the family where it belongs"—and (2) that history is dramatic, distinct, and endlessly controversial from Joseph Smith's First Vision to next year's farthest mission. LDS youthfulness is a feature shared with such other made-in-America denominations as Seventh-day Adventism, Christian Science, Disciples of Christ, and an enormous number of Pentecostal and Holiness bodies. Some of the groups guard original manuscripts jealously, some decline to take history (any history, including their own) seriously, while still others quarrel at length about whether they really are "new" or only a revival of or return to that which is original and "old." Mormons have no monopoly on the anxieties of history.

Mormon historians, on the other hand, do have—if not a monopoly—at least a heavy responsibility as both custodial and interpretive figures. Historians, for example, are presumably more practiced in rising above the egocentric captivity of the here and now. They can take the long view. Indeed, Spinoza centuries ago advised us to look at all things under the aspect of eternity, and the Psalmist encouraged us to think in a time frame that was "from everlasting to everlasting" (Ps. 90:2). For mere mortals, these are tough demands. But history can take us some steps along that road, enabling us to escape the passion of the moment, the cliché of the campaign, the slogans of this or of any single generation. If we cannot look at events and ideas under the aspect of eternity, we historians should at the very least be able ourselves, and help others, to look at these things under the aspect of history: to weigh, evaluate, and judge over a broad span of time and in the long run.

In the first and most significant of the Jehovah's Witnesses cases to be heard by the U.S. Supreme Court (*Cantwell v. Connecticut*, 1940), Justice Owen J. Roberts speaking for the entire Court defended the right of the Witnesses to propagate their views in these words:

> In the realm of religious faith, and in that of political belief, sharp differences arise. In both fields the tenets of one man may seem rankest error to his neighbor. To persuade others to his own point of view, the pleader, as we know, at times, resorts to exaggeration, to vilification . . . and even to false statement. But the people of this nation have ordained in the light of history, that, in spite of the probability of excesses and abuses, these liberties are, in the long view, essential to enlightened opinion and right conduct on the part of the citizens of a democracy.[3]

"The light of history" and "the long view"—on these our dearest freedoms no less than our deepest understandings depend. Much of the tension between faith and history results from the differences between those who look for the "short-term consequences for orthodoxy" and those more concerned about the "long-term accumulations of wisdom."[4] We should not demand of free speech, or freedom of the press, or of religious history that it balance its books every Friday night. Long-term investments pay dividends too.

Whatever else may be argued about in Mormon history, one facet cannot be debated: namely, that this history is taken seriously. Mormons are not tempted to behave like the Transcendentalists, of whom Andrews Norton once wrote: "the solid earth is not stable enough for them to rest on. They have firm footing on the clouds."[5] For Mormons, on the contrary, history is recognized for its power, its accessibility, its rewards. The Reverend James Maury of Fredericksville Parish in colonial Virginia and an early teacher of Thomas Jefferson asked: "what Exercise, . . . is more happily adapted to further . . . [the] great purposes of Education; such as entertaining the Fancy, strengthening the Judgement, forming the Taste, fixing the Morals, & mending the Heart, than the Study of History?" In addition to all this, history exercises one's memory and enriches one's understanding, and finally, it proves "eminently serviceable" through all stages of life, from that of the young scholars to those "most advanced."[6]

If that language sounds too quaint or dated, we can shift to a more contemporary patois. Sterling McMurrin writes of the "liberalizing power of the study of history. . . . There is no intellectual pursuit more calculated to make a free person . . . to free him from his own cultural bondage, and no history is more liberating than the history of religion."[7] McMurrin recognizes that it is precisely in the area of religion that some have greatest difficulty allowing history to do its "liberating thing." As in personal, infantile, sexual relationships, we repress, suppress, forget, deny, protest until—at exorbitant rates—we are forced by psychoanalysis to face history, our own private history. Then the historical truth makes us free. So in religion, we often fear the freedom that history can bring. We are reluctant to enter the Holy of Holies, fearing to find it empty (which it is) when with our imaginations it has been so richly and wrongly filled. We are prepared to affirm that everything has development, except that in which we firmly believe. Everyone went through the absurdity of birth, and the even greater absurdity of puberty, except those whom we choose to exempt from all history and therefore from all humanity. (The earliest heresy concerning Jesus was not a denial of his divinity, but of his humanity.) The temptation is powerful: to take that which we revere and wrench it away from its nurturing soil, thinking thereby that we preserve it pure and unsullied; what we do, of course, is cut it off from all that gives life; we destroy that which we would save.

Yet why does it seem, some will ask, that history comes to us so often as faith-threatening rather than as faith-enforcing? Jan Shipps has written of the folly of trying to divide all history into the "faithful" on the one hand and the "unfaithful" on the other,[8] to which I would add that the opposite of history that is "debunk" may be history that is only "bunk." Our categories are far too simple, our expectations in the short run far too high, our Friday night balance sheets far too obtrusive. Of course, in religious history, as in music history, art history, or any other kind of history, there must be sensitivity, appreciation, awareness. An unfeeling clod, though a historian, is still (I regret to say) an unfeeling clod. David Levin of Stanford in a long review of Peter Gay's book on Puritan historians observed of the author: "What he fails to see is that in studying Puritan history he is shackled by his own skepticism."[9] Devotion must not be blind, but analysis must not be indifferent.

Religious history may present special difficulties as well as special opportunities, but so much of what we discuss and debate is endemic to the discipline of history itself. I can well imagine Xenophon or Thucydides dropping in at the American Historical Association, listening for a time to one of our heated historiographical wrangles, then rising to say, "Yes, well, the fellows were all talking about that just the other day!" Sometimes our progress in historical understanding seems to take great strides ahead; at other points, however, we are apparently condemned to go over the same ground again and again. We do have fine lines to walk: between cynicism on the one hand and credulity on the other, between grand theory unrelated to hard facts and an obsession with petty detail unrelated to significance or structure. We will always have much to argue about, much to revise, even much to apologize for. However great our skill, honest our intent, prodigious our effort, it will remain true that we see through a glass darkly. We believe that there is meaning in history—this makes the quest worthwhile. We know that our perceptions are partial—this makes the quest fallible. *Seeing* through a glass darkly is better than not seeing at all, but seeing through a glass darkly is a persisting lesson in humility, finitude, and impermanence. Even as we revise the work of an earlier generation, so verily, verily, shall we be revised!

Historical theology, therefore, cannot escape the built-in limits of history. Nor can it escape the built-in limits of theology. Theology, after all, is not God thinking about God, but it is men and women—finite, limited, self-interested, astigmatic, biased—thinking about God. While historical theology can and does multiply the options presented to us, it makes the impermanent and mutable even more apparent to us. This is not all loss. For humankind has suffered far more from a theology that was absolutely certain and unfailingly dogmatic than it ever has from a theology that acknowledges its limits and never quite finishes its task.

Theological History

The phrase "theological history" all by itself is quite enough to send shudders up and down the spine of most historians. For theological history bristles with problems and generally conceals its possibilities. If history begins with a fixed and finished theology, then to what extent can the historical enterprise be an honest exploration? a genuine adventure? a perceptive probing of half-hidden causes and mysterious motivations? Or does history become a mere matter of filling in the detail, of providing a splash of color here and a delicate embroidery there? Is the historian like the small child who "draws a picture" by the mechanical method of connecting the numbers of a predetermined sketch? History "by the numbers," if history it be, would have very little appeal to any of us—little appeal to heart or mind or soul. The pursuit of truth is reduced to attaching labels, identifying enemies, confirming convictions.

"Theological" as a modifier for "history," we may well fear, threatens to take us back to an earlier prescientific, precritical, prerational age: faith and reason at war all over again! For "faith," one may read church or creed or sacred canon or living authority; for "reason," one may read philosophy or science or common sense—or history. In the last two thousand years or so of Western civilization, the sharp points of conflict in history have been many: Hellenic thought against Hebraic canon, mystery religions against monotheism, Aristotle against the church fathers, a new science against a familiar astronomy and comforting biology, and natural reason against biblical revelation. In each conflict, the *initial* reaction was a gauntlet hurled down, a clear and coercive alternative thrust forward: either the faith of our fathers or excommunication, either loyalty to that handed down from above or an exit visa to warmer regions below.

That has been the initial reaction. But in virtually every instance of such confrontations, the *ultimate* reaction has been to reject the simpleminded "either/or" in favor of a more reflective, more comprehensive "both/and." Greek against Hebrew? Athens against Jerusalem? Not really, as Christianity embraced both and helped bring into being a whole civilization fed by these two powerful streams. Monotheism against the savior gods of the mystery cults? Not really, as Christianity drew from both, making in the doctrine of the Trinity, said Whitehead, the only real improvement on Plato. Aristotle or Augustine? Both, said Thomas Aquinas in a theological synthesis that has endured for hundreds of years. Either Genesis or geology? Either Christ or culture? Either history or orthodoxy? The false alternatives continue to be pressed upon us; the comprehensive embrace of both continues to challenge us.

In religious history we feel the challenge even more forcefully these days because the discipline itself is changing. As Sydney Ahlstrom pointed out several years ago, "religious history has become a field of study within the larger frame of world history. It no longer enjoys any rights of sanctuary. It is allowed no immunity from the demands for evidence that historians generally make."[10] The rules have changed. Denominational history was once only in-house history; the wider world was left behind, as one followed a closed circuit, a private path. One might even speak knowingly (if unhelpfully) of *Heilsgeschichte* in opposition to *Weltgeschichte,* and all the people might say "Amen." Of course, as Ahlstrom also made clear, religious history like any other "benefits from learned and insightful historians who are sympathetic, deeply versed, and sensitively attuned to their subject matter."[11] But to be either read or believed, these historians must play by the same rules, provide the same sorts of evidence, speak to the same large audience. And however sensitive and attuned, they must remember that they are historians first, resisting the temptation to start out as theologians and then become mere manipulators of history. They cannot be historians if they deny that anything ever changes, if on the contrary they assert "that nothing genuinely important for religion or morals has really happened in time."[12] This latter position is not so much theological history as it is theology against history, but it remains one of the reasons that the very phrase "theological history" can turn the blood cold. The dangers are real.

They are most real when insecurities abound, when history and culture seem to threaten more than confirm, when enemies appear all around—or even within—the camp. I wish to maintain that the LDS Church at this point in its own history and at this space in American culture has far more reason to feel secure than otherwise. This church is secure sociologically. It has a sense of community that is the envy of most other religious bodies in America. (The new social history, now not really so "new," announces the discovery of community and brings forth a rash of community studies; LDS historians are way ahead of this game, so much so that one might well give them credit for having virtually invented "community.") The LDS Church also has an unusually strong sense of family and an earnest commitment thereto. It has an ability to make the church —even in urban, crowded, distracted, splintered America—a true center of life: for worship, for study, for recreation, for shepherding one through life's crises, pains, joys. The LDS Church is also, I believe, secure psychologically. Here is a faith that has already moved mountains and made deserts bloom, not one that merely promises to do so. It continues to ride the waves of success, moving counter to those strong tides today of declining membership, declining confidence, declining financial and personal commitment. No spiritual malaise here! On the contrary, positive reinforcement (to use today's cliché) surrounds the Saint on every side: support, assurance, aid, comfort, all steadied and balanced by an internal gyroscope of impressive power. And I would even argue that the Church of Jesus Christ of Latter-day Saints is secure historically. At least this is true in the sense that so much of that history is already an open book, so much of it has already provided that liberation, that emancipation that all genuine encounter with history affords. If the Church really is this secure, then why a struggle over who owns the Mormon past?

In part, the struggle is endemic to denominational history, to company history. One always confronts this question, along with the widely varied answers: How triumphalist and celebrationist should our history be? Other questions, all

versions of this one, abound: How much is history a sanctification of our heritage and a canonization of our progenitors? How much should it ring with partisan self-righteousness and the rhetoric of "death to all my (and the Lord's)
enemies"? To what degree is our approach to the past one that sees history
mainly as a collection of proof-texts? Again and again, religious history as company history arrays along two opposing sides the guardians of the past who
would keep the religion pure and the explorers of the past who would keep the
religion alive. In the pursuit of historical understanding, the ceaseless pursuit,
the present always speaks to the past, as well as the past speaking to the present.
Dialogue, not monologue, is history's proper mode of communication. "History," Herbert Butterfield wrote, "is not the study of origins; rather it is the
analysis of all the mediations by which the past was turned into our present."[13]
The mediations may be quite complex, quite unforeseen. It may turn out that
we have come to where we now are more by historical accident than by our
intentional design.

In all of this, is there any sense to, any place for "theological history"? Of
course, it has dangers; the question now is whether it also has possibilities. Those
who might see it as a welcome rescue from hard analysis and long research would
surely destroy all promising possibility. The simple question "What happened in
history?" is of course never simple, and the easy resort to Providence or self-
interest or class struggle as the glib and overarching explanation of every event,
the nub of every cause, does not constitute a model for Rodin's *Man Thinking*. It
is a better model for *Man Copping Out*, and so far as denominational history is
concerned, it will surely result in giving Providence a bad name.

There comes a point, however, after all the hard analysis and long research,
when one is ready to ask what it all means. At that juncture, theology may legit-
imately contribute to a pattern or sense of purpose. Extended historical investigations do not yield their own philosophy of history any more than repeated
scientific experimentations inexorably lead to their own philosophy of science.
Faith may interact with history not to explain what happened in the past but to
illumine what it means. In Christian history, as Albert Outler has pointed out,
"God's providence does not amount to his predetermination of historical
events. It is, rather, his real presence in every crisis of human decision—where
history's *meanings* are born or aborted." This understanding gives new power
and new freedom—a new freedom "toward our past and future [that] is at least
part of what Christians have meant by 'salvation.'"[14]

Or to utilize the words and thoughts of yet another church historian, Sidney E.
Mead, "the study of the history-that-happens is always somehow the study of the
works of God in history. . . . The perceptive historian sees what Whitehead called
'the eternal greatness incarnate in the passage of temporal fact.' And in this sense
[Mead concludes] church history is a continuous meditation on the meaning of
the incarnation."[15]

That kind of religious history is, I suggest, too fine and rare a gem to be passed over in favor of expeditions up the side of Mount Ararat or even, for that matter, to Palmyra. No mediation (Butterfield) there by which the past is turned into the present; no meditation (Mead) there on how God's works may speak even more powerfully than God's words to modern mankind. One word spoken in understanding outweighs a hundred recited in an imposed repetition.

Mormon historians, as we have noted above, are not obliged to sit for hours at the feet of other scholars, to listen endlessly to the exegete or nod sleepily before the official philosopher. Their territory is open and largely unfenced. Their challenge is not unlike that of Joshua, who said to the Israelites that they should be prepared "when your children ask in time to come, 'What do these stones mean to you?'" (Josh. 4:6). It is in answering that question that one becomes a historian—good or bad, of course. But it is the question that we cannot hand over to anyone else, to other authorities, other societies, other learned folk. When examining the stones, the bones, the words, the deeds, our task is to discover and then expound what it all means.

Notes

1. See R. Laurence Moore, "Insiders and Outsiders in American Historical Narrative and American History," *American Historical Review* 87 (April 1982): 390–412.

2. *Edinburgh Review* 65 (January 1820), quoted by William R. Hutchison in his presidential address to the American Society of Church History, "Innocence Abroad: The 'American Religion' in Europe," *Church History* 51 (March 1982): 71.

3. Quoted in Robert T. Miller and Ronald B. Flowers, *Toward Benevolent Neutrality: Church, State, and the Supreme Court* (Waco, Tex.: Baylor University Press, 1977), 81.

4. James L. Clayton, "Does History Undermine Faith?" *Sunstone* 7 (March–April 1982), 34. Clayton, in my view, overstates his case, arguing at one point that "Subservience to a particular religion is therefore incompatible with honest inquiry, whether by historians or by anyone else" (34). "Subservience" is of course a loaded word, but if he means that identification or affiliation with a particular religion is incompatible with the task of the historian, he goes well beyond any proposition that I would be willing to defend.

5. Quoted in Perry Miller, ed., *The Transcendentalists: An Anthology* (Cambridge: Harvard University Press, 1950), 211.

6. James Maury, Letter to Robert Jackson, 17 July 1762, quoted in *Papers of the Albemarle County Historical Society* (Charlottesville, Va.: Albermarle County Historical Society, 1942), 2:49–50.

7. Sterling M. McMurrin, "Religion and the Denial of History," *Sunstone* 7 (March–April 1982): 47.

8. Jan Shipps, "The Mormon Past: Revealed or Revisited?" *Sunstone* 6 (November–December 1981): 56.

9. David Levin, "Review Essay of Peter Gay, *A Loss of Mastery: Puritan Historians in Colonial America*," *History and Theory* 7 (1968): 385–93; the quotation is from p. 385.

10. Sydney E. Ahlstrom, "The Problem of the History of Religion in America," *Church History* 39 (June 1970): 233.

11. Ibid.

12. McMurrin, "Religion and the Denial of History," 48. He adds: "In religion, the prophets make history and the theologians destroy it."

13. H. Butterfield, *The Whig Interpretation of History* (1931; reprint, London: G. Bell and Sons, 1951), 47.

14. Albert C. Outler, "Theodosius' Horse: Reflections on the Predicament of the Church Historian," *Church History* 34 (September 1965): 260; italics his.

15. Sidney E. Mead, "Church History Explained," *Church History* 32 (March 1963): 29.

DEAN L. MAY (1938–2003) was a professor of history at the University of Utah and a past president of the Mormon History Association. His books include *Three Frontiers: Family, Land, and Society in the American West, 1850–1900; Utah: A People's History;* and *From New Deal to New Economics: The American Liberal Response to the Recession of 1937.*

* * *

REID L. NEILSON is a PhD candidate in religious studies at the University of North Carolina at Chapel Hill. In addition to authoring two family biographies, he is the editor of *The Rise of Mormonism* and the coeditor of *Believing History: Latter-day Saint Essays* and *Taking the Gospel to the Japanese, 1901–2001.*

Notes on Contributors

THOMAS G. ALEXANDER, Lemuel Harrison Redd Jr. Professor of Western American History Emeritus at Brigham Young University, is one of the leaders of the New Mormon History and a past president of the Mormon History Association. His books include *Mormonism in Transition: A History of the Latter-day Saints, 1890–1930; Things in Heaven and Earth: The Life and Times of Wilford Woodruff, a Mormon Prophet;* and *Utah, The Right Place: The Official Centennial History.*

HENRY WARNER BOWDEN, Professor of Religion at Rutgers University, is a former president of the American Society of Church History. He has published a number of works including *Church History in the Age of Science: Historiographical Patterns in the United States, 1876–1918; American Indians and Christian Missions: Studies in Cultural Conflict;* and *Church History in an Age of Uncertainty: Historiographical Patterns in the United States, 1906–1990.* Dr. Bowden presented "From the Age of Science to an Age of Uncertainty: History and Mormon Studies in the Twentieth Century" at the twenty-third annual conference of the Mormon History Association at Utah State University, Logan, Utah, in 1988. It was first published in the *Journal of Mormon History* 15 (1989): 105–20.

RICHARD LYMAN BUSHMAN, Gouverneur Morris Professor of History Emeritus at Columbia University, has taught and written about early American culture for more than forty years. He is a past president of the Mormon History Association and the author of several books, including *From Puritan to Yankee: Character and the Social Order in Connecticut, 1690–1765; Joseph Smith and the Beginnings of Mormonism; The Refinement of America: Persons, Houses, Cities;* and *Joseph Smith: Rough Stone Rolling.*

JOHN G. GAGER, Professor of Religion at Princeton University, is a specialist in religions of the Roman Empire, especially early Christianity and its relations to ancient Judaism. His works include *Kingdom and Community: The Social World of Early Christianity; The Origins of Anti-Semitism: Attitudes toward Judaism in Pagan and Christian Antiquity;* and *Reinventing Paul.* Dr. Gager presented "Early Mormonism and Early Christianity: Some Parallels and Their Consequences for the Study of New Religions" at the seventeenth annual conference of the Mormon History Association at Weber State College, Ogden, Utah, in 1982. It was first published in the *Journal of Mormon History* 9 (1982): 53–60.

EDWIN GAUSTAD, Professor of History and Religious Studies Emeritus at the University of California, Riverside, is one of the most honored names in the pantheon of American church historians. His works include *A Religious History of America; The Rise of Adventism: Religion and Society in Mid-Nineteenth-Century America; A Documentary History of Religion in America;* and *New Historical Atlas of Religion in America.* Dr. Gaustad presented "Historical Theology and Theological History: Mormon Possibilities" at the nineteenth annual conference of the Mormon History Association at Brigham Young University, Provo, Utah, in 1984. It was first published in the *Journal of Mormon History* 11 (1984): 99–111.

LANGDON GILKEY, Shailer Mathews Professor of Theology Emeritus at the University of Chicago Divinity School, is one of the premier Protestant theologians in the United States. His books include *Naming the Whirlwind: The Renewal of God-Language; Religion and the Scientific Future: Reflections on Myth, Science, and Theology;* and *Creationism on Trial: Evolution and God at Little Rock.* Dr. Gilkey presented "Religion and Culture: A Persistent Problem" at the twentieth annual conference of the Mormon History Association at Independence, Missouri, in 1985. It was first published in the *Journal of Mormon History* 12 (1985): 29–41.

JOHN F. C. HARRISON, Professor of History Emeritus at the University of Sussex, England, is a British social historian who has published widely on Victorian England and nineteenth-century social movements. His books include *Society and Politics in England, 1780–1960: A Selection of Readings and Comments; Quest for the New Moral World: Robert Owen and the Owenites in Britain and America;*

and *The English Common People: A Social History from the Norman Conquest to the Present*. Dr. Harrison presented "The Popular History of Early Victorian Britain: A Mormon Contribution" at the twenty-second annual conference of the Mormon History Association at Oxford and Liverpool, England, in 1987. It was first published in the *Journal of Mormon History* 14 (1988): 3–15.

NATHAN O. HATCH, President of Wake Forest University, is one of the key figures in neoconservative Protestant scholarship. He has published *The Sacred Cause of Liberty: Republican Thought and the Millennium in Revolutionary New England; The Professions in American History;* and *The Democratization of American Christianity*. Dr. Hatch presented "Mormon and Methodist: Popular Religion in the Crucible of the Free Market" at the twenty-seventh annual conference of the Mormon History Association at Graceland College in Lamoni, Iowa, in 1993. It was first published in the *Journal of Mormon History* 20(1) (Spring 1994): 24–45.

RICHARD T. HUGHES, Distinguished Professor of Religion and Director of the Center for Faith and Learning at Pepperdine University, has published many books on the history of American Christianity, including *Illusions of Innocence: Protestant Primitivism in America, 1630–1875; Reviving the Ancient Faith: The Story of Churches of Christ in America;* and *Myths America Lives By*. Dr. Hughes presented "Two Restoration Traditions: Mormons and Churches of Christ in the Nineteenth Century" at the twenty-seventh annual conference of the Mormon History Association at Dixie College, St. George, Utah, in 1992. It was first published in the *Journal of Mormon History* 19(1) (Spring 1993): 34–52.

HOWARD R. LAMAR, Sterling Professor of History Emeritus at Yale University, is known as the Dean of Western American History. His books include *Dakota Territory, 1861–1889: A Study of Frontier Politics; The Far Southwest, 1846–1912: A Territorial History;* and *The New Encyclopedia of the American West*. Dr. Lamar presented "National Perceptions of Utah's Statehood" at the thirtieth annual conference of the Mormon History Association at Snowbird, Utah, in 1996. It was first published in the *Journal of Mormon History* 23(1) (Spring 1997): 42–65.

PATRICIA NELSON LIMERICK, Professor of History at the University of Colorado, Boulder, is one of the leading figures in the "New Western History" and a former president of the Western History Association. Her works include *The Legacy of Conquest: The Unbroken Past of the American West; Sweet Medicine: Sites of Indian Massacres, Battlefields, and Treaties;* and *Something in the Soil: Legacies and Reckonings in the New West*. Dr. Limerick presented "Peace Initiative: Using the Mormons to Rethink Culture and Ethnicity in American History" at the twenty-eighth annual conference of the Mormon History Association at Park

City, Utah, in 1994. It was first published in the *Journal of Mormon History* 21(2) (Fall 1996): 1–31.

PETER LINEHAM, Associate Professor of History at Massey University, New Zealand, has published a number of works on eighteenth- and nineteenth-century English and New Zealand religious history, including *There We Found Brethren: A History of Assemblies of Brethren in New Zealand; No Ordinary Union: The Story of the Scripture Union, Children's Special Service Mission, and Crusader Movement of New Zealand, 1880–1980;* and *Bible & Society: A Sesquicentennial History of the Bible Society in New Zealand.* Dr. Lineham presented "The Mormon Message in the Context of Maori Culture" at the twenty-fifth annual conference of the Mormon History Association at BYU-Hawaii, Laie, Hawaii, in June 1990. It was first published in the *Journal of Mormon History* 17 (1991): 62–93.

LAURIE F. MAFFLY-KIPP, Associate Professor of Religious Studies and director of graduate studies at the University of North Carolina at Chapel Hill, has written extensively on religion on the Pacific borderlands of the Americas and African American religions. Her works include *Religion and Society in Frontier California* and the forthcoming study of African American communal narratives. Dr. Maffly-Kipp presented "Looking West: Mormonism and the Pacific World" at the thirty-third annual conference of the Mormon History Association at Ogden, Utah, in 1999. It was first published in the *Journal of Mormon History* 26(1) (Spring 2000): 40–64.

MARTIN MARTY, Fairfax M. Cone Distinguished Service Professor Emeritus at the University of Chicago Divinity School, may well be the most highly regarded historian of American Christianity today. His voluminous corpus of scholarly works include *Righteous Empire: The Protestant Experience in America; Pilgrims in Their Own Land: 500 Years of Religion in America;* and *Fundamentalisms Observed.* Dr. Marty presented "Two Integrities: An Address to the Crisis in Mormon Historiography" at the eighteenth annual conference of the Mormon History Association at Omaha, Nebraska, in 1983. It was first published in the *Journal of Mormon History* 10 (1983): 3–19.

D. W. MEINIG, Maxwell Research Professor of Geography at Syracuse University, at Syracuse, New York, is an influential geographer whose published works include *Southwest: Three Peoples in Geographical Change, 1600–1700; The Interpretation of Ordinary Landscapes: Geographical Essays;* and *The Shaping of America: A Geographical Perspective on 500 years of History.* Dr. Meinig presented "The Mormon Nation and the American Empire" at the twenty-ninth annual conference of the Mormon History Association at Kingston, Ontario, Canada, in 1995. It was first published in the *Journal of Mormon History* 22(1) (Spring 1996): 33–52.

R. LAURENCE MOORE, Howard A. Newman Professor of American Studies at Cornell University, Ithaca, New York, is a historian whose work, although carefully executed, often includes interpretations that are controversial enough to keep his name in the public eye. In particular, his *Religious Outsiders and the Making of Americans* caused a great stir in the scholarly community. Among his many other works are *In Search of White Crows: Spiritualism, Parapsychology, and American Culture,* and *The Godless Constitution: The Case against Religious Correctness.* Dr. Moore presented "Learning to Play: The Mormon Way and the Way of Other Americans" at the twenty-fourth annual conference of the Mormon History Association at Quincy, Iowa, and Nauvoo, Illinois, in 1989. It was first published in the *Journal of Mormon History* 16 (1990): 89–106.

MARTIN RIDGE, the late Senior Research Associate at the Huntington Library in San Marino and Professor of History Emeritus at the California Institute of Technology, served as editor of the *Mississippi Valley Historical Review.* A distinguished scholar of the American West, he published a number of works including *America's Frontier Story: A Documentary History of Westward Expansion; Westward Expansion: A History of the American Frontier;* and *History, Frontier, and Section: Three Essays.* Dr. Ridge presented "Mormon Deliverance and the Closing of the Frontier" at the twenty-sixth annual conference of the Mormon History Association at Claremont Colleges, San Bernardino, California, in 1991. It was first published in the *Journal of Mormon History* 22(1) (Spring 1992): 137–53.

GLENDA RILEY, Alexander M. Bracken Professor of History Emeritus at Ball State University, is a specialist on women in the American West. Her authored books include *Frontierswomen; The Iowa Experience; Women and Indians on the Frontier, 1825–1915;* and *The Life and Legacy of Annie Oakley.* Dr. Riley presented "Sesquicentennial Reflections: A Comparative View of Mormon and Gentile Women on the Westward Trail" at the thirty-first annual conference of the Mormon History Association at Omaha, Nebraska, in 1997. It was first published in the *Journal of Mormon History* 24(1) (Spring 1998): 28–54.

ANNE FIROR SCOTT, W. K. Boyd Professor of History Emeritus at Duke University, is one of the pioneers in Women's Studies. She has published *Natural Allies: Women's Associations in American History; The Southern Lady: From Pedestal to Politics, 1830–1930;* and *Making the Invisible Woman Visible.* Dr. Scott presented "Mormon Women, Other Women: Paradoxes and Challenges" at the twenty-first annual conference of the Mormon History Association at Salt Lake City in 1986. It was first published in the *Journal of Mormon History* 13 (1986–87): 3–19.

JAN SHIPPS, Professor of History and Religious Studies Emeritus at Indiana University-Purdue University Indianapolis, is one of the foremost scholars of

Mormonism and a past president of the Mormon History Association. She is the author of *Mormonism: The Story of a New Religious Tradition* and *Sojourner in the Promised Land: Forty Years among the Mormons* and the coeditor of *The Journals of William E. McLellin.*

TIMOTHY L. SMITH, the late Professor of History Emeritus at Johns Hopkins University and former director of the Program in American Religious History, made his name in the profession with *Revivalism and Social Reform: American Protestantism on the Eve of the Civil War.* An ordained Nazarene minister, he published a number of works about his own tradition, including *Called Unto Holiness: The Story of the Nazarenes* and *Whitefield & Wesley on the New Birth.* Dr. Smith presented "The Book of Mormon in a Biblical Culture" at the fifteenth annual conference of the Mormon History Association at Canandaigua, New York, in 1980. It was first published in the *Journal of Mormon History* 7 (1980): 3–21.

RODNEY STARK, Professor of the Social Sciences at Baylor University, is one of the leading thinkers in the scientific study of religion. He has published more than two dozen books, including *The Future of Religion: Secularization, Revival, and Cult Formation; The Churching of America, 1776–1990: Winners and Losers in Our Religious Economy;* and *The Rise of Christianity: A Sociologist Reconsiders History.* Dr. Stark presented "Extracting Social Scientific Models from Mormon History" at the thirty-second annual conference of the Mormon History Association at Washington, D.C., in 1998. It was first published in the *Journal of Mormon History* 25(1) (Spring 1999): 174–94.

JOHN F. WILSON, Agate Brown and George L. Collord Professor of Religion Emeritus at Princeton University, also served as the dean of the graduate school for many years. Among his publications are *Pulpit in Parliament: Puritanism during the English Civil Wars, 1640–1648; Public Religion in American Culture;* and *Church and State in American History: Key Documents, Decisions, and Commentary from the Past Three Centuries.* Dr. Wilson presented "Some Comparative Perspectives on the Early Mormon Movement and the Church-State Question, 1830–1845" at the sixteenth annual conference of the Mormon History Association at Ricks College, Rexburg, Idaho, in 1981. It was first published in the *Journal of Mormon History* 8 (1981): 63–77.

GORDON S. WOOD, Alva O. Way University Professor and Professor of History at Brown University, has written extensively on early American history. He is the author of a number of landmark books including *The Creation of the American Republic, 1776–1787; The Rising Glory of America, 1760–1820; The Radicalism of* *the American Revolution;* and *The Americanization of Benjamin Franklin.* Dr. Wood presented "Evangelical America and Early Mormonism" at the fifteenth annual conference of the Mormon History Association at Canandaigua, New York, in 1980. It was first published in *New York History* 61 (October 1980): 359–86.

INDEX

Zion, 82–83, 87, 88, 176, 197, 320–21;
America as, 136; as the concept of
homeland, 130; as a style of life, 180–81
Zion's Camp, 89; expedition to Missouri, 86

Zions Cooperative Mercantile Institution
(ZCMI), 131
Zulick, John, 253, 264

The University of Illinois Press
is a founding member of the
Association of American University Presses.

Typeset in 10.5/13 Adobe Minion
Composed by BookComp, Inc.
Manufactured by Thomson-Shore, Inc.

University of Illinois Press
1325 South Oak Street
Champaign, IL 61820-6903
www.press.uillinois.edu